Psychosocial Dynamics of Effective Behavior

edited by

HAROLD W. BERNARD

Oregon State System
of Higher Education
Portland, Oregon

and

WESLEY C. HUCKINS

Wright State University
Dayton, Ohio

Holbrook Press, Boston

Library of Congress Catalog Card Number: 70-148948

Table of Contents

Preface

This book provides a cross-section of typical issues and concerns of courses in the psychology of adjustment. It places emphasis upon personal effectiveness. It is intended to supplement and complement classroom presentations and basic texts.

This collection of readings offers certain advantages to students and to professors. First, it provides for an expansion of reading experience and furnishes emphases in certain areas. Second, its use will acquaint students with recognized leaders in the psychology of adjustment area. Also, the increasing number of articles being published makes discriminating reading both necessary and difficult. In this book of readings at least part of the process of selection already has been done. Another advantage is simply that a book of readings makes assigned selections maximally available to students. The completion of required reading is not dependent, for example, upon the number of copies of a certain periodical available in the college library.

We have included articles which raise issues pertinent to college students and whet their reading appetites. Selections were made purposely to reinforce the point of view that adjustment is no more a matter of adapting and conforming to the social milieu than it is of actively making a difference and influencing one's interpersonal environments. Adjustment should be of as much concern to the average person who wants to use his potential to advantage as it is to the abnormal or atypical person who is striving for social acceptance and hoping to become more like others. Each needs to manage himself and to influence his environment in the process of becoming more than he is—to actualize himself and to realize his possibilities.

The belief that becoming more personally effective is a process which may be learned is a corollary to this point of view. Articles were chosen which recognize the inevitability and responsibility of personal choice and the use of one's own behavior as a means of influencing relationships.

There is too much in the field of psychology that relates to problems of adjustment to include in one volume. For the purpose of narrowing the field, we have chosen the reading selections in terms of our experience in counselor education and in counseling centers. The problems which most frequently lead counselees to seek psychological help have defined the areas in which we sought the views and experiences of authors.

Our experiences have also demonstrated that outsiders—parents, professors, counselors, psychologists, psychiatrists—can do little to further another's adjustment. The final responsibility lies with the individual. Articles which highlight such responsibility are the ones to which we gave preference.

We are pleased that so many outstanding authors permitted use of their materials. Authors were not solicited because of their prominence, but because of the value of their ideas and the clarity with which they present their views. There is good reason why authorities such as Bonner, Burchinal, Eiseley, Frankel, Gardner, Halleck, Harlow, Hayakawa, Lipset, Maslow, Murphy, Rogers, and certainly many others, are so well known— and good reasons why the student of adjustment should become acquainted with their ideas.

Selections were made on an interdisciplinary basis. Authors include politicians, anthropologists, psychologists, and psychiatrists—but all are humanists. All project a concern for people and for their growth and effectiveness. We, the editors, are indebted to these contributors.

We believe that in an area as complex and inclusive as adjustment, basic texts by one author or author team should be supplemented by a variety of orientations, values, and convictions. This book provides such a supplement. In addition, it is specifically designed to supplement our text, *Dynamics of Personal Adjustment*.

Harold W. Bernard
Wesley C. Huckins

Section 1
Conceptions of Humanity

At the very heart of the psychology of adjustment is what a person thinks of himself, and of his—and humanity's—potential for becoming. A person must have developed some point of view before his surroundings and their use in developing his potentials have much meaning for him. His concept of humanity and mankind in general is basic to understanding himself and his fellows. The selections in this section are intended to modify the reader's own outlook. Perhaps, at least, he will re-think and re-affirm his position. This is as it should be. An unexamined and inflexible frame of reference serves more to maintain what already is than it does to promote development. Ideas imposed from external sources (e.g., authors and instructors) provide less impetus for action than those which are contemplated, discussed and then personally selected by the individual.

It is with the idea of providing intellectual variety from which the reader may choose and develop ideas that the selections for this and subsequent sections are presented. Eiseley's essay provides an out-of-the-ordinary introduction. He denies that man is tough. In fact, it has been tenderness which has allowed him to become what he is. Also, he indicates that a person is more than the product of his past. He is a creature of vision and of dreams. He is the molder of his own future and the futures of others.

Eiseley recognizes major paradox in the behavior of men. "Man," he says, "is the molder of things rather than their victim." Then he goes on to suggest that modern man is as much a slave to the machine and to pyramiding technology as he is its master. That which man has created to help in subjugating his environment has now become an environment that he is unable to control.

Although modern man can project physical and impersonal power by pushing buttons, he has no machines or regimes which help him to increase his capacity for affection and tenderness. Human affiliation, the author says, is fundamental to his survival. Perhaps part of the problem of interpersonal discord is the tendency to discuss it in terms of such generalities as man, society, and the culture. The problem and the challenge must be specific to the individual. To get results the question must be: "What am I doing about the specifics of my caring, my tenderness, and my humanness?"

Taking such a personal inventory is essential for "involvement" and meaning. Concerns which are relevant to one's self command his attention and his action. Discussions which are directed to mankind, society, the culture, or the universe in general tend to affect no one individual very much. Each person has continually to ask, "How about me?" The question posed by Murphy—"Where is the human race going?"—requires such an approach. The answer—if any—as furnished by the selection, appears more pertinent to the individual than to the group. More than any specific answer, however, the feeling of continuing acceleration toward an undetermined future comes through. The author points out that although human beings may be able to change profoundly in a relatively short time, we do not use our knowledge very well in directing this change. It is also true that the person who must be assured of a favorable outcome is likely not to act at all. Somehow or another, some idea of purpose and assurance that our behavior is effective is necessary. Here the editors would emphasize, as Murphy does, that the concept of feedback may have much value. He says: ". . . it is only when you can get feedback, when you can get information from the people around you about the consequences of what you yourself are doing, that you can make a responsible decision."

The relationship of feedback and identity is so close that it seems that the words need to be used concomitantly. One explanation of the generation gap is that youth has insufficient time with adults to establish a role through feedback. The consequence is that among young people today there exists a primacy of role *versus* goal. It has been said that youth is role-oriented before it is goal-oriented; whereas the older generation was goal-oriented and then role-oriented. Whether or not this is an accurate generalization, there are many who believe that identity (role) is an insistent need of youth. One must be somebody, be a cause, be needed. The editors (of the older generation) believe that identity calls for effort, struggle, and sometimes discomfort. In Krill's article he performs three services that we think the reader will appreciate. For one thing he provides a concept of what existential philosophy might mean. (Have you heard the word without being sure of its referents and then, on questioning, found the user of the word "existential" equally unsure?) In the second place he offers some suggestions as to how anomie—the other side of the role-and-identity coin—might be avoided or counteracted. In the third place he makes the use of outside help in the resolution of personal dilemmas seem to be a normal and wise thing to do. This last point of view will be reiterated in Section 12, "Using Psychological Help."

Paul Ehrlich, speaking through David Rorvik, stresses a point that makes it seem that we had better "get with" a goal—the goal of saving our environment (and ourselves) from total destruction. Perhaps talking to young people about ecological havoc is in about the same category as discussing with them the depression of the '30's. The young people have no idea of joblessness, bank failure, and mortgage foreclosure, nor of clear rivers, forests to reconvert carbon dioxide back to carbon and oxygen, clean air, bountiful wild life. But those who have seen man's self-defeating actions offset his gains in one lifetime share Ehrlich's alarm. His message and warning have very much to say about what man shall be. In evaluating the condition of man, it does not seem necessary to conclude that man must be his own worst enemy. A few people say "No" but it does seem that wise choices may yet alter the collision course of mankind. We are intrigued with the idea that a person must be an active agent in those decisions which affect him directly if he is to say something about where that part of the human race which he represents is going.

An Evolutionist Looks at Modern Man

LOREN EISELEY
Chairman, Department of Anthropology
University of Pennsylvania

In the age of technology which now surrounds us, and which boasts of its triumphs over nature, one thing is ever more apparent to the anthropologist—the student of man. We have not really conquered nature because we have not conquered ourselves. It is modern man, *Homo sapiens*, "the wise" as he styles himself, who is now the secret nightmare of man. It is his own long shadow that falls across his restless nights and that follows soundlessly after the pacing feet of statesmen.

Not long ago I chanced to walk through the Hall of Man in one of the country's large museums. Persons of great learning had been instrumental in erecting those exhibits, and I hoped to find there some clue as to human destiny, some key that might unlock in a few succinct sentences the nature of man. The exhibit ended in a question mark before an atomic machine and a graph showing the almost incredible energy that now lay open to the hand of man. Needless to say, I agreed with the question mark which ended the history of humanity within that hall.

But as I turned and went in the other direction, step by step, eon by eon, back into the past, I came to a scarcely human thing crouched over a little fire of sticks and peering up at me under shaggy brows. The caption read: "Man begins his technological climb up the energy ladder. He discovers fire." I walked a short way backward and forward. I read the captions. I looked again at the creatures huddled over a fire of sticks—at the woman clutching a child to her breast. Again I searched the hall. This was the sum total of all that science had here seen fit to emphasize graphically as important to the human story. The hunters' tools were there, the economic revolution effected by agriculture was ably presented. Summarized before my eyes, populations grew, cities and empires rose and fell, and still man's energy accumulated.

One saw another thing. One saw the armored legions grow and

Loren Eiseley, "An Evolutionist Looks at Modern Man," in Richard Thruelson and John Kobler (eds.), *Adventures of the Mind,* published by Alfred A. Knopf, 1961, pp. 3–16, and copyright by Curtis Publishing Company. Reprinted with permission of *The Saturday Evening Post* © 1962.

grow until at last continent confronted continent and the powers of death to a world lay in the hands of the descendants of that maned woman and her consort by the fire of sticks.

I hesitated again before those forgotten engines of the past, for it seemed to me that there was lacking here some clue, some vital essence of the creature man, and that I was looking upon stone and polished sword and catapult from some place just a little remote and distorted. "This is the history of man," the caption ran through my head, and at that moment, finally, I knew I was looking at the past through the eyes of a modern twentieth-century American, or for that matter, a Russian. There was no basic difference.

In that whole exhibit were ranged the energies of wheat and fire and oil, but of what man had dreamed in his relations with other men, there was little trace. Yet it is only on paper, or, in human heads, we might say in paraphrase of Shaw, that man has sought successfully to transcend himself, his appetites and his desires. In that great room was scarcely a hint of the most remarkable story of all, the rise of a value-creating animal and the way in which his intangible dreams had been modified and transformed to bring him to the world he faces today.

The educated public has come to accept the verdict of science that man, along with the plant and animal world about us, is the product of endless evolutionary divergence and change. In accepting this verdict of science, however, men have frequently failed to inquire in what way human evolution may differ from that of other animals, or by what extra dangers and responsibilities the human brain may be haunted. In the revolt from the fanatical religiosity of past centuries we have too often welcomed with open arms a dogmatic scientific naturalism which, like the devil with Faust, seemed to offer unlimited material power over nature while, at the same time, assuring us that our moral responsibilities were limited and excusable since we were, after all, only the natural evolutionary culmination of a line of apes that chanced to descend upon the ground.

Darwin and his compatriots, struggling to establish for their day a new and quite amazing interpretation of human history, placed great emphasis upon man's relationship to the animal world about him. Indeed, at times they overemphasized man's kinship with the existing apes, partly because of their anxiety to prove the reality of man's descent from lower forms of life, partly because in their lifetime the course of human evolution was very imperfectly known from fossils. The result was that Darwin's own interpretation of the early stages of human evolution wavered between a theory involving an early and Edenlike seclusion on some oceanic island, to a later more ferocious and competitive existence on one of the major continents.

These extremes of interpretation need not concern us now except to illustrate the hesitancy with which Darwin attempted to account for some of the peculiar qualities of man. Today we are well convinced of the general course of man's rise from some ancient anthropoid line. Each year new fossil evidence of this fact is brought to our attention. Each year the public grows more accustomed to this history, feels more at home in the natural world which it casually assumes to be dominated by struggle, by a dog-eat-dog interpretation of existence which descends to us from the Darwinian period.

Some time ago I had a letter from a professional friend of mine commenting upon the education his daughter was receiving at a polite finishing school. "She has been taught," he wrote to me a little sadly, "that there are two kinds of people, the tough- and the tender-minded. Her professor, whose science I will not name, informed her that the tough-minded would survive."

This archaic remark shook me. I knew it was not the product of the great selfless masters of the field, but it betrayed an attitude which demanded an answer. In that answer is contained the whole uniqueness of man. Man has not really survived by toughness in a major sense—even the great evolutionists Darwin and Wallace had had trouble with that aspect of man—instead, he has survived through tenderness. Man in his arrogance may boast that the battle is to the strong, that pity and affection are signs of weakness. Nevertheless, in spite of the widespread popularity of such ideas, the truth is that if man at heart were not a tender creature toward his kind, a loving creature in a peculiarly special way, he would long since have left his bones to the wild dogs that roved the African grasslands where he first essayed the great adventure of becoming human.

The professor who growled to his class of future mothers about being tough-minded spent a childhood which is among the most helpless and prolonged of any living creature. If our parents had actually practiced certain of the philosophies that now flourish among us, or if our remote ancestors had achieved that degree of sophistication which would have enabled them to discount their social responsibilities for the day's pleasure, we—you and I and all of us—would never have enjoyed the experience of living.

Man, in the achievement of a unique gift—a thinking brain capable of weighing stars or atoms—cannot grow that brain in the nine months before birth. It is, moreover, a peculiarly plastic brain, intended to receive impressions from the social world around it. Instinct, unlike the case in the world of animals, is here reduced to a minimum. This brain must grow and learn, be able to profit by experience. In man much of that growth and learning comes after birth. The result is that the human infant enters the world in a peculiarly helpless and undeveloped condition. His childhood is lengthy because his developing brain must receive a large store of information and ways of behavior from the social group into which it is born. It must acquire the complicated tool of speech.

The demands of learning thus placed upon the human off-spring are greater than in any other animal. They have made necessary the existence of a continued family, rather than the casual sex life of many of the lower animals. Although the family differs in many of its minor features in distinct societies, it is always and everywhere marked by its tender and continuing care of the human offspring through the lengthened period of childhood.

The social regulations of all human groups promote the welfare of the young. Man's first normal experience of life involves maternal and paternal care and affection. It continues over the years of childhood. Thus the creature who strives at times to deny the love within himself, to reject the responsibilities to which he owes his own existence, who grows vocal about "tough-mindedness" and "the struggle for existence," is striving to reject his own human heritage. For without the mysteriously increased growth rate of the brain and the correlated willingness of fallible, loving adults to spend years in nursing the helpless offspring they have produced, man would long since have vanished from the earth.

We take the simple facts of human life too much for granted. To the student of human evolution this remarkable and unique adjustment of our peculiar infancy to a lengthened family relationship between adults is one of the more mysterious episodes in the history of life. It is so strange, in fact, that only in one group of creatures—that giving rise to man—has it been successfully developed in the three billion years or so that life has existed on the planet. Family life is a fact that underlies everything else about man—his capacity for absorbing culture, his ability to learn—

everything, in short, that enables us to call him human. He is born of love and he exists by reason of a love more continuous than in any other form of life. Yet this, in all irony, is the creature who professes to pierce the shams of life and to live by tough-mindedness!

Let us see how this nascent and once-aspiring creature now lives in great danger of re-entering the specialized trap that his ancestors escaped from ages ago when they evolved a brain capable of abstract thought. "Man is the dwarf of himself," Emerson once wrote, and never, perhaps, has he been more of a dwarf than in this age where he appears to wield so much power. The only sign of health remaining to him is the fact that he is still capable of creeping out of the interior of his thickening crust of technological accomplishment to gaze around him with a sense of dissatisfaction and unease.

He has every reason to feel this way. For man has never lived before in so great an age of exterior accomplishment, so tremendous a projection of himself into his machines, nor yet so disheartening a period in all that stands for the nobler aspects of the human dream. His spiritual yearnings to transcend his own evil qualities are dimming as he is constantly reminded of his animal past. His desire to fly away to Mars, still warring, still haunted by his own black shadow, is the adolescent escape mechanism of a creature who would prefer to infect the outer planets with his problems than to master them at home.

Even now in the enthusiasm for new discoveries, reported public interviews with scientists tend to run increasingly toward a future replete with more inventions, stores of energy, babies in bottles, deadlier weapons. Relatively few have spoken of values, ethics, art, religion—all those intangible aspects of life which set the tone of a civilization and determine, in the end, whether it will be cruel or humane; whether, in other words, the modern world, so far as its interior spiritual life is concerned, will be stainless steel like its exterior, or display the rich fabric of genuine human experience. The very indifference of many scientists to such matters reveals how far man has already gone toward the world of the "outside," of no memory, of contempt toward all that makes up the human tradition.

"Wars will be fought in space," prophesied a high military authority recently. "Teach children the hard things first." "Ah, but what hard things?" the teacher asks, because youth is shaped in the teaching and becomes what he is taught. Without spiritual insight and generosity, without the ability to rise beyond power and mechanical extensions, man will encounter in place of the nature which gave him birth only that vast, expanding genie rising from his own brain—himself. Nothing more terrible threatens to confront him in his final hour.

It is increasingly plain that if we read the past as a justification for a kind of moral complacency, an animal limit which justifies military remarks such as "man will always fight," we have not read it well. Until man came, it is true, the evolution of life had been an evolution of parts. It had been hook and clutching bur and fang, struggling upward in an agelong effort. Life had been shaped by the blind forces of the inanimate world. All it had that was different was the will to crawl, the will to find the crevice, the niche, the foothold on this mountain of inanimate matter, and to hold its place against the forces which ever seek to disperse and destroy the substance of life. In all that prehuman world there had been no animal capable of looking back or forward. No living creature had wept above another's grave. There had been nothing to comprehend the whole.

For three billion years that rule remained unbroken. At the end of that time there occurred a small soundless concussion. In a sense it was the most terrible explosion in the world, because it forecast and contained all the rest. The coruscating heat of atomic fission, the red depths of the hydrogen bomb—all were potentially contained in a little packet of gray matter that, somewhere between about a million and 600,000 years ago, quite suddenly appears to have begun to multiply itself in the thick-walled cranium of a ground-dwelling ape.

The event itself took place in silence, the silence of cells multiplying at an enormous pace under a small bone roof, the silence of some great fungus coming up at night in a forest glade. The eruption had about it the utter unpredictability of nature when she chooses to bypass her accepted laws and to hurtle headlong into some new and unguessed experiment. Even the solar system has now felt the impact of that tiny, soundless explosion. The fact that it was the product of evolutionary forces does not lessen its remarkable quality.

For three billion years, until an ageless watcher might have turned away in weariness, nothing had moved but the slime and its creations. Toward the end of that time a small, unprepossessing animal sat on his haunches by a rock pile on a waste of open ground. He clutched a stick and chewed the end of it meditatively. He was setting the fuse of the great explosion. In his head was the first twinkle of that tenuous rainbow bridge which stretches between earth and the city of the gods.

At that moment the ancestor of man had become the molder of things, rather than their victim, but he had, at the same time, suffered a major loss of instinctive adjustments to life. As the psychologist Jung very aptly remarks: "The forlornness of consciousness in our world is due primarily to the loss of instinct, and the reason for this lies in the development of the human mind over the past eon."

In a recent paper given before the Research Conference on Growth and Aging, my colleague, Dr. W. M. Krogman, remarked that "The mind of man, the learning potential of an evolved cerebral cortex, enabled him to focus upon the *quality* of things rather than mere quantity." Man has become, in other words, a value-creating animal. He sets his own goals and more and more exerts his own will upon recalcitrant matter and the natural forces of the universe. In this activity he has passed from the specialized evolution of the parts of the body to a projection of such "part" evolution upon his machines and implements. In this respect man is a unique being. Having achieved high intellectual ability, he may remain comparatively unchanged in structure while all around him other animals are still subjected to the old laws of specialized selection. His brain evolves parts and replaces them, but only upon man's mechanical inventions: his tools. This fact gives man a kind of freedom which none of the crawlers-up-the-mountain ever had. He is, as the philosopher Henri Bergson once remarked, a reservoir of indetermination; his power of choice for good or evil is enormous.

It is here that we come upon what I choose to call the "unnatural" aspect of man; unnatural, that is, in the sense that there is nothing else like it on the planet. Even Darwin confessed that his principle of limited perfection—that is, the conception that life would evolve only sufficiently to maintain itself in competition with other life or to adjust to changes in its environment—had been upset in the case of man. A part, such as a tooth or an eye, could reach perfection only for a given purpose in a particular environment. With man, however, Darwin professed to observe no foreseeable limit to the development of the mental faculties.

Psychology had once regarded human nature as something consisting of separate abilities given to man at the time of creation. Mind was a fixed, unchanging thing that molded history. Now it was to be seen as malleable and moving, subject like the body, though in a different and more mysterious way, to change. Perhaps, indeed, there was no such thing as human nature in the old fixed sense, except the human ability to become what it most desired in terms of the social world in which it existed. As we have seen, the mind's power of choice has opened to man a tremendous freedom, but it is a freedom whose moral implications only a few great spiritual leaders have fully grasped.

Increasingly, at the very height of the human achievement, there loom two obstacles which threaten to cast man back into the world of parts, tools and processes, in a way he has scarcely imagined. In fact there are times when it appears man is so occupied with the world he is now creating that he has already lost a sense for what may be missing in his society. He is deeply influenced by his knowledge of the past and the animal limitations which it seems to place upon his earlier spiritual aspirations. Equally, he confuses "progress" with his mechanical extensions which represent his triumph over the caprices of biological selection. Man, in a new way, shows formidable signs of taking the road of the dinosaurs, though by quite another track.

On a night during the period of the Korean War I sat with an old hunter at a campfire in the wilds of Wyoming. Around us in the mountain dark were geological strata that contained the remains of dinosaurs. My companion threw a log upon the fire. As the flames rose upward, I could see the bronzed old American face looking at me across the fire. It could have been a face from any period out of the frontier past. And it was the frontier that spoke to me from the man who had two sons in Korea.

"America," he said, "needs a strong enemy. It will keep her from getting fat and make her strong."

I nodded dubiously. It was a philosophy of the frontier, of the woods. But I saw in my mind's eye the fate of the colossi that lay about us in the stone. They had warred and thundered, shaken the earth with their tread, grown larger, armored themselves with great shields of bone, and teeth like bear traps. Spikes had glistened on their tails and foreheads. In the end they had vanished with their monstrous tumult, and some small, ratlike mammals and a few birds had come hesitantly into the arena they had vacated. It had been a war of parts, won, not by the participants, but by some small, relatively intelligent creatures that had hidden in the trees.

"We need a strong enemy," my friend repeated. I did not doubt it was being said also in the Siberian forests and on the Manchurian plains. Faster and faster labor the technicians, the scientists of parts. They labor so today. The pace grows ever swifter. Already, and I quote from one recent industrial report, "scientists and engineers can be utilized more effectively by confining their work almost entirely to the field of their specialization." This remark indicates the re-emergence of the war of parts, and if continued, it forecasts the death of all we claim as human. Such statements convey a failure to grasp that it is the creative thinker capable of using his brain out of the immediate context of his surroundings who is the innovator, the religious leader, the artist, the man who in all ages has been, in the words of Lancelot Whyte, "the very creator of humanity."

"Man," John Burroughs once remarked, "is like the trainer of wild beasts who, at his peril, for one instant relaxes his mastery over them. Gravity, electricity, fire, flood, hurricane, will crush or consume him if his hands are unsteady or his wits tardy." It is true that man has been badly knocked about by raw nature, but that nature has never organized her powers for the deliberate purpose of destroying man. He has even benefited and had his wits sharpened by her vagaries. Man has survived the long inexorable marchings of the glacial ice that pressed him back upon the Mediterranean and threatened his annihilation in Europe. He has left his bones under the boiling mud of volcanic upheavals. He has known drought and famine—the careless buffets of the storm that blows unceasingly through nature. He has seen cities go down, cities full of adept artisans and clever technicians, cities fallen to the sands when an old enemy cut off the water supply.

Who was that enemy? It was man. He is the other face of that nature man has feared. Now, in an age when man lays his hands upon the lightning, and heat in millions of degrees shudders in his confining mechanisms, an old shadow, a monstrous growing shadow, falls across the doorway of all the world's laboratories. It is merely man, merely the creature by the fire of sticks, merely the museum wielder of the sling and spear, but now grown large enough to shadow the sun. This creature thinks with all the malignant concentration that man has so far escaped in nature, and it thinks toward just one purpose—the creation of the ultimate weapon. Ultimate,

ultimate, and still more ultimate, as if there were a growing secret zero in its mind.

So terrible is the fascination of that zero, so much does it appeal to some ancient power-loving streak in our still primitive natures, that whether men plan aggression or defense from it, they are, in degree, corrupted. At heart they know the word "neutral" has lost its meaning; that the blow, if it falls, will mean what the ultimate weapon means—death to green grass and singing bird, death to a world.

Nevertheless, as I have said, no creature in the world demands more love than man; no creature is less adapted to survive without it. Man is a paradox. Individually most men hate and fear war in spite of much of the talk of professional militarists about instinct. Men have to be drummed to war, propagandized to war, assured their cause is righteous. Even dictators have to render lip service to humanitarian principles. None of this sounds particularly as though an "instinct" for war existed. There are, instead, things from the old dark midnight of the past that suffice as well for evil purposes. Fear of the stranger, when the stranger was two eyes in the dark beyond the fire at a cave mouth; aggressive hungers that were stoked to a high pitch by nature in the million years of man's wandering across the wastes of an open world. Man is not completed—that is the secret of his paradoxical behavior. He is not made. He is, perhaps, about to be. Once long ago in the Middle Ages he was called *Homo duplex*—a thing half of dust and half of spirit. The term well expresses his predicament.

Today we know a great deal about human evolution, but as scientists we have failed, I sometimes think, to convey successfully to the public the marvel of the human transformation. We have shown man the anthropoidal skulls of his ancestors. We have convinced him that the human brain is an instrument of ancient origin which has not sprung full blown into being, but rather partakes of both the old and the new; that it includes the imperfections which are written into the substance of all moving and growing life. The vestigal organs that are concealed here and there in our bodies and which tell tales of the long past—of trees and waters in our lost ancestral world—have their corollary in the mind of man. His flashes of unreasoning temper, his frustrations, his occasional irrationalities are, some of them, echoes out of an older, more primitive machine. Yet signs of affection and mutual co-operation, love of beauty, dreams of a future life, can be traced into forms of man physically more primitive than ourselves.

Now, however, it is the present which concerns us—the present that creates tomorrow. Who contends for it—the rocket century with its vast zero looming over the future? The now is *our* responsibility, not that of the hoarse-voiced animal that came from the wood in a dream and made our today. Nor can we call to those pleasant, wide-browed people whom we strive to conjure up as inhabiting the comfortable future of our novels and dreams. They are lost in the unfathomable, formless future which we are engaged in shaping. Do we want them deeply? Do we want them enough, in the heavy-handed violence of this day, to live toward them at all cost, to struggle once more against the destructive forces of nature? To stand up and face, as every man must face, that ancient lurking shadow of himself? Is the price of acquiring brains, brains to look before and after in the universe, only to mean subservience to man after escaping subservience to nature that has lasted for a million years? Is it to mean acquiescence in the plans of those clever intellects who talk glibly of psychological "break-throughs" and the subliminal control of nations? Is it for this that men have labored up the dark pathway behind us and died often and blindly for some vision they could scarcely see?

A society has an image of itself, its way of life. This image is a wavering, composite picture reflected from millions of minds. If the image is largely compounded of the events of the present; if tradition is weak, the past forgotten, that image can alter by subtle degrees. A "cold war" such as we are fighting demands great tenacity in democratic institutions. Secrecy grows, technicians multiply, two great societies shoulder each other down a road that may look increasingly alike to both. The humane tradition—arts, letters, philosophy, the social sciences—threatens to be ignored as unrealistic in what has become a technological race for survival.

Man was a social animal long before he was man. But when he created huge societies and elaborated the world of culture that surrounds him today, he was acting, in some degree, consciously. Man, unlike the animal, is aware of the nature of his society. His conscious image of it is tremendously important in shaping what it will become. It is this that helps to build the human future, and why the future must be fought for day by day in the lives of innumerable and humble men.

Man, whether he engages in war or not, is in a pyramiding technological society whose values are largely directed outward upon things. The important fact in such a material age is that we do not abandon or forget that man has always sought to transcend himself spiritually, and that this is part of his strange heritage. It is a heritage which must be preserved in our schools and churches, for in a society without deep historical memory, the future ceases to exist and the present becomes a meaningless cacophony. A future worth contemplating will not be achieved solely by flights to the far side of the moon. It will not be found in space. It will be achieved, if it is achieved at all, only in our individual hearts. This is the choice that has been presented man, as a free agent, as one who can look before and after in the cosmos.

And if indeed men do achieve that victory, they will know, with the greater insight they will then possess, that it is not a human victory, but nature's new and final triumph in the human heart— perhaps that nature which is also God. "The rationality of man," a great theologian once wrote, "is the little telltale rift in Nature which shows there is something beyond or behind her." It remains for man, in his moral freedom, to prove that statement true.

FURTHER READING

EISELEY, LOREN: *Darwin's Century*. New York: Doubleday and Company; 1958.

————: *The Immense Journey*. New York: Random House; 1957.

DE CHARDIN, PIERRE TEILHARD: *The Phenomenon of Man*. New York: Harper and Brothers; 1959.

CLARK, W. E. LE GROS: *The Fossil Evidence for Human Evolution*. Chicago: University of Chicago Press; 1955.

FRANKEL, CHARLES: *The Case for Modern Man*. New York: Harper and Brothers; 1956.

Where Is the Human Race Going?

GARDNER MURPHY
Director of Research
Menninger Foundation, Topeka, Kansas

I suppose the honest answer to the question, "Where is the human race going?" would be: *nobody knows.* However, if you look through the public prints, you see some very confident judgments which we must at least have the honesty to take seriously enough to allow ourselves a few minutes of analysis. Where is it going? We are told: to the dogs; to the moon; to the world of supermen; to an existence free of pain, and, perhaps, even free of desire; to a region of self-fulfillment; to the unity of the cosmos, or to the individuality of an interstellar hermit. Actually, there are quite grave reasons to believe that we will succeed either in rapid deterioration or in violent and completely successful international or other forms of human destructiveness.

We are learning so much about the physical world and getting control of such violent forces that a few people here and there could very well unleash the whirlwind; and, instead of being able to say candidly that our increasing knowledge of people offers a certain antidote, you will have to admit that in more and more perilous instances we find that we are using our knowledge of people to erode or wash away the sources of self-respect. Consider, for example, the kinds of things that any study of the brainwashing techniques makes clear to you, i.e., ways of depersonalizing human beings. We are finding all sorts of ways in which a science of psychology can be used to enable the few to control the many with more and more unanswerable force. Nietzsche's conception of the superman can be quoted today in terms of the issue of our transcending what has always been known as "human" through our becoming something uniquely and utterly defiantly different from humanity as it stands there in our historical record. You can take this, depending on your temperament, either as a sign of the ascent above the abyss or as the drop into the abyss.

There have been all sorts of very interesting importations re-

A chapter in Richard E. Farson (ed.), *Science and Human Affairs* (Palo Alto, Calif.: Science and Behavior Books, 1965), pp. 7–17. Reprinted by permission of the editor and publisher.

cently of devices offering solace and comfort which, I think, for a long time under pioneer conditions, we repudiated. There are a great many forms of comfort which can be had rather inexpensively, e.g., tranquilizing drugs and existentialism. There are all sorts of devices for achieving a sense of freedom from the harrying and harassing world of pain. Or we can reject these and say that it is only by full realization of pain that we are human, that it is only through the utter stoic acquiescence in the sorrows written in the book of life that we can become human; therefore, let us move in the direction of a self-fulfillment written in terms of suffering. Hand in hand with this, of course, is the recent importation of many fascinating ideas, from India particularly, and from those branches of Buddhism which moved northeast into Burma, China and Japan. Those doctrines established a very rich tradition in favor of escape from the meaninglessness and suffering in life—not so much by doctrines as by practices—which would involve freedom from sharply defined ego or individualized kinds of desire, thereby achieving some fulfillment paradoxically without the self.

Of course there are many of us who have felt that we must deal honestly with a possibility that Soviet Russia and Red China have begun to make clear, namely, that one can find many ways of achieving a certain integrity, e.g., a certain unity in national life, without the tremendous burden of perpetual struggle and competition. We have to ask ourselves whether, under the conditions of industrialization, there may be between these two evils, escapism and the totalitarian system, a certain unity that would be less destructive than these other alternatives.

Let me note here the so-called isolation researches. Such studies started with men drifting on rafts across the Pacific or stationed in the Arctic through dark and cold, listening for signals of the utmost importance which must be caught. It is interesting to see how far you can go in setting up special research rooms in which you can simulate or intensify these conditions, and in which you actually find certain new kinds of human nature: certain unsuspected forms, certain proneness to various ways of perceiving, or feeling, or thinking, produced quickly and easily in normal people, that you would have thought were extraordinarily hard to produce at all.

This has raised the question whether or not we really know the *limits* of human beings. Now this has, for a psychologist, so much challenge that he simply cannot seek safety in saying that these things are too fraught with terror to be faced. He must face them. He must look into the stress researches of today and say how far human beings can be pushed, not in terms of any vivisectionist's interest in just getting generalizations for abstract biological science, but rather in terms of what are the scientific and ethical margins which define how far you can properly press the individual. How much is the human nature as we know it simply an expression of certain kinds of flaccidity or gentleness or ease in an individualistic society? To what degree shall we still recognize humanity—and what kinds of new humanity will we find—when new drugs, new relaxation techniques, new forcing devices in the classroom, new ways of getting ten times as much out of a child, are brought into play? Fascinating questions. Do we know, under the amazing pressures of today, how richly we can increase a child's capacity to perceive, to think, to feel, with new techniques? To what extent is he still going to be human if these devices geometrically increase for the next twenty, thirty, forty years? What are the moral decisions that have to be made if these forcing techniques really achieve the amazing success that they seem likely to achieve?

So actually as a result of analyzing all of these questions, we consider the possibility of putting an end to pain through drugs, relaxation, and all the ways of moving human beings. Then we come to a point when we say, "But now, let's talk realistically." Are all of these things unrealistic, after all? And doesn't that mean, essentially, that we will pin you down to the few things that are realistic and keep your attention on those?

First, I would say they are all absolutely unrealistic. I would also say that the assumption that tomorrow will be like today is utterly unrealistic. If you say that you imagine a very different kind of human nature, either in 1984 or 2000; if you say this is an unrealistic kind of thinking, I would say "yes"; if you imagine the world of 1984 will be anything like the world of 1964, this is just unrealistic.

It has been shown by social scientists many times that the pace of change is positively accelerated. It is not a straight line increase; it rolls up on itself like a snowball. If you and I are going to make anything like the beginning of an intelligent choice, this is only going to be done by assuming not only that all of the present forces will continue, many of them at an accelerated pace, but also by assuming that there will be sudden jumps. There will be new discoveries which will bring in new dimensions of experience. Considering the rate at which scientific discovery and technological, engineering, medical and other skills are growing, there is every reason to believe that within twenty, thirty, or forty years the extrapolation technique will be the most unrealistic of all; i.e., the statement that there will be just so much more of what we already have will be the least realistic of all the possibilities that can be imagined.

In view of the perilous rate of today's change, it might be difficult to accept the idea of a so-called basic human nature that could still be recognized in the future. This idea, one of the hardest to establish, is that there is some hard core of inner, unchanging human nature. It is perfectly true that genetic changes, changes actually related to mutations—sudden and fundamental, usually irreversible, changes in the genetic materials at the amino acid level—this kind of thing only moves at a certain rate. I'm not saying that mankind is going to be, as the result of new mutations, utterly different in ten years. In terms of the slowness of human reproduction, typically three or even four generations per century, it is very hard to see how the recombination of genetic materials could give rise to a human nature utterly different within two or three hundred years. But even here we have to be extremely careful. The experimental production of mutations has been a standard device with mammals for quite a while, and more and more is being learned.

One of the most cautious of the prophets of today is Sir George P. Thomson. In this book, *The Foreseeable Future,* he said that we are already about at the point of being able to hit with an electron microscope a region in the chromosome involving two genes. Perhaps it won't be very long before we shall be in direct commerce, literally, with a single genetic unit. If it is considered that there are both experimental and random effects with animals which can be taken into account for control purposes and that mass trends can be studied, this means that every type of interbreeding that is going on—for example, in Southeast Asia the massive interpenetration and recombination of the various phases of the gene pool, i.e., the combination of all the genes of human beings in new relationships—will probably give us, certainly within this century, quite a lot of interesting, new typological aspects of human nature.

It is not as controversial but it is more obvious to point out that nutrition is already making big changes. I am not speaking of these changes as inherited, I am not assuming the inheritance of acquired characteristics at all, but I am saying that there were vast differences between the young men examined in the World War I draft and those in World War II. Many other studies have apparently indicated that rapid fundamental physical changes are going on. Together with this are the expected changes in the functioning of the central nervous system. The best controlled study that I know of dealing with this was one done in Scotland, which shows that in a period of a few years there apparently has been a very considerable rise in IQ levels as a result of general forces that are broadly called the process of industrialization.

It is often a question of taste whether you insist on the changes as being pure genetic changes or whether you insist on their being pure environmental or ecological changes. Nature does not work totally one way or the other in most cases; it is rather a combination, or potentiation, of one system of forces with or by the other. The genetic changes, relatively unimportant in themselves, may occur with reference to a certain strategy of nature in such a way as to be quite important, and vice versa. There are also many instances of biological change which are related to resistance to disease. We know a great deal about this in veterinary medicine. Within a hundred years, massive control of all sorts of common animal diseases, e.g., cattle diseases, has been achieved.

At last, after much delay in a struggle of various vested interests, we have come to accept as a matter of course—and this is an amazing thing in the Western democracies—the idea that a person has no longer the right to resist vaccination or inoculation or diphtheria protection. Now I think of what we heard in my childhood, and what was said very vigorously during the nineteenth century, about the person's right to protect his body against any type of interference—i.e., the fundamentally unethical character of the use of a needle to inject a substance into the body. This conception of human control could hardly be argued today. A man has no immunity from the basic biochemical, the basic metabolic and immunological processes. Consequently, we are again involved in a series of grave questions about how far we may go, because there is not the slightest doubt that we can change man at an accelerated pace through modern medicine.

Now all of these things taken together are child's play compared with the rate at which man is changing as a result of socioeconomic factors, a good many of which can be directly spelled out and some of which are more complicated. But suppose I remind you that at about the time of Shakespeare, very rapid changes were occurring with regard to the conception of the obligation of man to man, and particularly with regard to the inviolacy of the body against torture and against the death penalty. Just before Shakespeare, Sir Thomas More, the first great utopian, began his study of Utopia with the fact that men were being tried and condemned to hanging in batches of twenty because it had been demonstrated that a certain theft had occurred and it saved a lot of time and trouble to take care of the accused in batches of twenty instead of individually. This was the kind of common, standard ethic with which Sir Thomas More was dealing. Routine treatment of people for petty theft was to chop off arms or feet. These practices do indeed still exist in certain despotisms in the world.

But there has been a massive move with regard to certain fundamental ideological patterns which was accelerated to a great degree by the French Revolution. The word "torture" is now used anywhere in the western world with horror. The term "torture" under the Nazi regime, and to some limited degree under other regimes, has connoted, of course, the use of more than the usual police techniques of getting quick confessions. These techniques have been used in such ways as to break down self-respect or even self-awareness, to try to beat the individuality out of men. They have been used also in attempts to get whole families to implicate one another. From such a point of view it is interesting to see the screaming self-defense which has arisen. Even if in times of dire national threat it is discovered that devices involving duress are used on the individual, there must be elaborate "justification." There have, in other words, been quite deep changes of feeling within such a short span as three or four hundred years. I do not mean at all to deny that there are apt to be eddies, backwashes, reversals in historical processes. But I would remind you that the historian has given us very full documentation for more than mere changes in social techniques. The historian has documented changes in *basic attitude*. We have beautiful studies of the rising level of civilization in the American Colonies and since the Revolutionary War. We don't happen to combine them in the same breath with the way in which farmers would come from miles around to a crossroads to witness a hanging. This was a more interesting and available event than the circus type of phenomena. The conception then was that the death of a human being was something to be generally enjoyed by a group. I bring up unpleasant things of this sort because I think it is part of my obligation to try to force upon you the idea that I am not thinking of trifling amenities such as teaching children to be polite in different ways from those of our great-grandparents, but rather of the fact that some of the humanitarian tide of the last few centuries is real and at the level of deep personal feeling.

It is hard to convince you that you can change human beings by socioeconomic processes. Fortunately we know a good deal about how this happens. We don't know all, but we do know that the creation of a middle class by the process of building up capital for the so-called wool runs, i.e., capital to develop lands where the sheep could move back and forth, and the development of a banking system in the Netherlands and in Italy in the late medieval period and the fourteenth and fifteenth centuries, led very rapidly to the development of a middle class whose ideology was based upon individuality and not upon the traditional standard of laws and codes. These laws and codes differed for the military (the knights), for the landed gentry, for the yeoman, for the serf, for the thralls. These people differed and, as the prayer book says, they were people of different "conditions." You were born into a certain condition in life and your duty was to live according to that station or "condition in life to which God had called you." There was, as Nietzsche said later, a master ethic and a slave ethic. But the time came when the flotsam and jetsam met, and all kinds of people from all kinds of places managed to scrape together many types of capital and begin to claim that we all have something in common; we don't have ancestry in common, we don't have location in common, but we do have a sort of common faith, and that is to struggle against oppression and make our way.

To a considerable degree, this swelling middle group led to the establishment of an ideological system which, though it had its beginnings in the struggle to achieve a certain economic position, entailed by the time of the French Revolution quite deep, complex, and ever widening ideological consequences. Now I do not say that the ideological consequences followed in any simple causal relation. But I do say that you can tease out of this a massive system of changes, largely of a socioeconomic character, which came in such a way as to potentiate a series of moral and religious concepts that had been relatively ineffective until added to and given new strength by the tidal wave of the new economic trend. Consequently, I would say it is possible to demonstrate that human beings can change in a very profound sense in a relatively short time.

Nothing could be more stultifying and stifling than the idea that the basic core qualities—the things that people think and feel themselves—cannot be changed. I don't know any way to cope with arguments of this sort except to be empirical. One of the most beautiful of all scholarly studies that this problem suggests is presented in Gilbert Murray's book, *Five Stages of Greek Religion*. Murray poses a question about the swashbuckling, long-haired Achaean pirates—a primitive, violent group of spoiled children whose adventures at the time of the siege of Troy are told in the Iliad. Murray wonders how these people, within two or three centuries, could become the infinitely subtle and truly magnificent people who wrote the Athenian dramas. How could you get the plays of Aeschylus against the background of Homer, who had written only a few hundred years before? How could you get the subtlety and magnificence of the Greek philosophy from the incredible, ponderous, and uncouth primitive philosophy which preceded? The solution, Murray shows, is that there was at the same time both biological and cultural interaction of these long-haired Achaeans with the Minoan people who had established themselves on the island of Crete and the islands of the Aegean, and who had a very rich civilization but demonstrated none of the particular violence and fire which the Homeric heroes had. Murray's evidence documents the thesis that if you get both biological and cultural changes, you can get a biosocial interaction and produce incredibly different kinds of human beings within a very short time.

Other illustrations work just as well. People like to take the artistic expression in the Renaissance as a derivation from Byzantium, then trace it through the period of the proto-Renaissance, until they reach the High Renaissance exemplified by Raphael and Michaelangelo. Other people like to do this in regard to Indian history, and the process works just as well: Nehru's *Discovery of India* and some of the other studies show that you can establish evidence of the same kind of process from the time of the so-called Aryan invaders, the people of the *Rig Veda*, to the people who developed the Vedantist philosophies. A very short time and very profound changes!

The reason for stressing both our contemporary examples and our historical examples is that nothing has moved at anything like the whirlwind pace that we are going through today. If people can change in two or three centuries, what can they do when science is massively mobilized in such a way that instead of simply guessing, we discover relatively simple and generalized rules and formulae like $E=MC^2$, from which tremendous weal or woe may derive just because the complexities of nature have been stated in a very simple way. We are beginning to hope that education and politics may in the same way derive, and use, sources of a similar simplicity and power.

I want to stress particularly a kind of second-order result of these new powers. We ordinarily assume that you can get people to move faster, make fewer mistakes, and get to their goals sooner. With this additional skill, they can master the problems of a little higher order of complexity. We do not ordinarily notice how adding to the stature of a man's mind results in a short time in his seeing problems that he never had seen. And when he goes on to attack these problems he suddenly gets a perspective, a new outlook, and feels a thrill within himself at the possibility of looking out over these vast new vistas. This new outlook is not a purely geometric increase in the creative powers of the individual. James Harvey Robinson, one of the first of the modern prophets to understand this issue, wrote in *The Mind in the Making* that there can be "indefinitely *more* mind, now that we have the trick," that is, as we discover the ways in which the training of the mind can be used. This holds true in elementary school, high school, college, and at the doctoral level in professional school. An example of this is the sort of training in music or the arts in which you train the child to observe, to look, to use, and to listen. With this kind of learning you find that many individuals get loose from the teacher. They just go down the freeway in their own fashion. What you are doing is to touch depths of the human mind that have never been touched before. Now this idea that the human mind might cease to *be* the thing that we have known before as the human mind was vaguely grasped by Plato in *The Republic* and by some of the Encyclopedists and philosophers of the modern period in France and Britain.

I know some of you who are inwardly churning, thinking this is a little too easy, perhaps we are going too fast, will say that if this last point is really sound, then there would be types of minds coming commonly into existence that simply could not have existed in ancient Greece or even at the time of Leonardo da Vinci. Is this a little absurd? So I thought I would quote to you what Aristotle had to say on this point. In the *Politics*, Aristotle argues that there is no basic need for large areas of new knowledge. He uses the curious phrase: ". . . most things *are* known." The trouble is not scarcity of knowledge, but that we do not use what we know. Well, how much did he know? What was his conception of the human body? Let's look at it in comparison with what we know today. What was inside the skin from Aristotle's point of view, without a microscope, without a test tube, without a piece of litmus paper? You perhaps remember that, also, the brain was apparently helpful in the secretion of tears. A towering genius like Aristotle could not carry out the kind of intellectual operations that even a second-year experimental psychologist does today because the funded capital to do this kind of thing took centuries to achieve. The same is true in the arts. Suppose you have a tremendous composer like Palestrina. Can you get from Palestrina to Beethoven in one jump? You can't do this. You have to go *through* the Viennese tradition. You have to go through Haydn and Mozart to get to Beethoven. You find in every one of these instances that there is a sort of collective and ever-growing, geometrical, multidimensional enrichment in the human mind.

Then someone comes along and says that human nature is always the same. Well, I don't know, maybe he means some hypothetical human nature that we can't ever observe. Very likely he does; or he may mean something rather trivial, such as that people get their feelings hurt because of pride or vanity or power-needs. You can see things operating in your dog. You can see them operating in the zoo or in the most higher animals. They exhibit ease in taking offense, and so forth. If that is all they mean by human nature, let them have their little quip. But when the expression is typically and seriously used to confine man to the traditional conception that he has to be essentially as he has been, it is the most unrealistic of all the concepts that this view of human nature could give us.

We can expect, then, biological changes of several different sorts—certainly many involving changes in the body and in the brain. We can expect social changes which are even more important and are coming even more rapidly. We can expect biosocial changes, or the potentiation or interaction of both groups of changes at a whirlwind pace. Some of us have been inclined to scoff at science fiction as moving too fast in its portrayal of human possibilities. This so-called fiction has consistently moved much too slowly. When I was a boy we read Frank Baum's *The Master Key*. The prediction was that there would ultimately be a device by which concentrated foods could be carried and we wouldn't have to go around with bulky foods. This device would be quite meaningful for the military, an Antarctic expedition, or what not, and research moved fast in this field. Then there was the old business about taking hold of natural forces to float you where you wanted to go and of course one thought of the glider, using forces somewhat like those of the larger birds which soar aloft when they catch the right convection, the right wind current. We are beginning to think more and more of ways of latching onto other energies to find out what their potential is, to carry us with the stream of forces present within nature. Frank Baum's system of predictions now seems almost as tame as that of Bellamy's *Looking Backward*, in which, looking ahead 120 years, Bellamy got as far as predicting the existence of a primitive radio in about the year two thousand. Science fiction, then, has been a timid guide, and one of the main concerns is to breed a generation which is not afraid of giving us what we very much need, namely, a rich, dramatic, powerful, realistic picture of men and women living in a world just around the corner. These people would be just as basically, probably more basically human than we are because they would have less of the traditional brutality. They would be people with a somewhat rarefied and purified conception of the human as I've been trying to spell it out. They would be freer, more and more, of the vestiges of the jungle that are still very much with us.

I have been trying to insert here and there, into many of these paragraphs, the conception that you don't get very far by extrapolating. That is what an engineer does when he says we have gone up so many feet in each mile and then in the next hundred yards on the map we shall climb above sea level so many more feet. This won't work. It isn't the way the thing goes at all, because there are choice-points, in the strict sense of the term, all the way along. In a remarkable little book entitled *What is Life?* Erwin Schrodinger, one of the world's great physicists, wrote that the process by which life is coming into existence cannot possibly be continuous; it must be discontinuous. It must involve a series of steps, sudden dramatic quantum kinds of steps. Now these go on appearing, except that it is seven hundred leagues instead of seven, and in new media. We don't even move just under the sea like Jules Verne, or in the air like Leonardo da Vinci. We are thinking of getting so far off mother earth that we are not only free of oxygen, but even of weight. We are free of a great deal, but we are still human.

Considering the possibility that one might at any point along the way here say that vast new potentials occur, how shall we take this? Fewer and fewer people are qualified by knowledge to make the decisions, and fewer and fewer people have the sensitivities to make moral decisions of this larger kind. More and more important in a democracy is that one choose people who have the kind of fiber—not only knowledge, but also the character—that it takes to carry out this prophetic role and to take this kind of responsibility. More and more concern for the basic quality of human beings will inevitably play a large part in the choice. At the same time there is a need for encouraging training and for devices which will stimulate and set free the mind of the mass who must at least understand, to some degree, what kinds of choice-points the leaders are facing. In his little book on *The Human Use of Human Beings* Norbert Wiener gives us a fascinating conception: that it is only when you can get feedback, when you can get information from the people around you about the consequences of what you yourself are doing, that you can make a responsible decision.

Some interesting thoughts will occur if you speculate about what will happen if, in the interest of national defense or any other long-range goal, we decide we can't trust people with the basic philosophical decisions about where they and you want to go, as members of the human family; the kinds of things they want and don't want their children and great-grandchildren to live through, and the kinds of humanity they hope will come into existence. You can fall back on an easy fatalism. Yes, you can say, it is there in the interstellar charts. You can say there is something in the nature of the case that man can't know, although that would seem to be defied by the whole nature of this analysis. You can say, let it be battled out and see whose ideas will win. You can say, ultimately, that the competition is not a competition between individuals but between political systems.

Let us indeed give all of our energies to getting the strongest possible barricade against immediate danger, taking each step necessary in terms of preservation of our own right to think, and look off to some distant time when we might have a chance to sit down, relax, and think over the question of where we want to go as human beings. Yes, we can do all of these things. But the point I want to make clear is this: there is somebody who is going to make the decision. And if people like you and me—people concerned with the simpler and more direct obvious tasks of living, including helping in the education of children, helping in the planning and guiding of communities by taking a responsible place as citizens—if we don't take this responsibility, it does get taken by fewer, fewer, and fewer. Can you really seriously believe that the only issue is to prevent despotic or totalitarian systems from oppressing democracies? It is relatively easy to convert one's own society to such a thoughtless and uncontemplative system of sheep-like activity, and if you do, it doesn't really make much difference whether you call it a democracy or autocracy. You get to the point at which we are not actively participating in studying and choosing and determining the choice-points for the future. In other words, if we cringe and fall back from the question of exerting our maximal influences as human beings with reference to the decision of where we go, then we have nobody to blame but ourselves if the direction is easily taken over by the despots or by purely impersonal forces in which neither despot nor anything else counts, but only a blind, impersonal, sphinx-like inscrutable force in nature.

Human beings *have* the kind of capacity that I am arguing for. This is one of the moments, the eleventh hour, fifty-ninth minute kind of situation, in which the choice-point must be seized by ordinary people because they are the only kind of people who can offer any serious competition to fatalism. There is a great deal of warring and confusion about where humanity is going, but it seems to me as I read the public prints that we assume a certain constancy of direction. I have mentioned one illustration, namely, that a little old core inside of us is supposed to be constant, acting to maintain a certain direction. Or the environment is said to be constant. An ecological statement says that the wind will go on blowing at the same tempo from the same quarter, and therefore it will bend wheat fields in the same way. Or we say that the relation of the exceptional genius to the common man will remain as it has always been, thus actually taking out whatever vitality may be left in the ordinary, average, well-intentioned people striving to understand, striving to play some sort of role.

Finally, as destructive as anything is the conception that, along with automation and other devices for steam-rolling and making uniform and simple and flat all sorts of human processes, we can get rid completely of the factor of individuality which has been subtly present in regard to every choice we have tried to make. Actually it is a very exciting thing to realize that with the understanding of such processes, automation and a thousand other factors making for uniformity can be so used that at the choice-point there is *more* freedom rather than less. A very simple illustration is the use of so-called modern automatic teaching devices, which can save the teacher so much time that she can give time, energy, attention, affection and concern to individual problems. If one recognizes the general fact that all of us—scientists, artists, teachers, citizens, parents, or any combination of these—believe that there are real choices, then we don't have to fight science. We don't have to argue that inevitably a steam-rolling process will roll us completely flat if we follow its implications and apply it to our lives. On the contrary, it is largely through science that the more hopeful aspects of what I am trying to describe will come into existence. The kind of science that will be useful, really basically helpful to man in making these choices, will be one in which the scientific method is always used to bring out and make more clear and more precious the individuality of each person who is to gain from and exploit the use of science. If there is any practical reason for democracy, it lies not in abstract political considerations but in the hope that the application of these modern forces to human welfare will be largely at the level of increasing the riches of the individual personality.

Existential Psychotherapy and the Problem of Anomie

DONALD F. KRILL
Assistant Professor, Graduate School of Social Work
University of Denver

Anomie, the author believes, encourages a pattern that leads to emotional disturbance. When anomie is part of an emotional problem the issue of treatment becomes partly philosophical in nature. The author describes the state of anomie, cites advantages of existential psychotherapy, lists the five most important goals of treatment, and then discusses these goals in detail. The goals cited are aiding the process of disillusionment, confronting freedom, discovering meaning in suffering, realizing the necessity of dia-

Reprinted with permission of the National Association of Social Workers, from *Social Work,* Vol. 14, No. 2 (April, 1969), pp. 33–49.

logue, and accepting the way of commitment. Methods by which these goals may be achieved are presented.

A characteristic of the present age is the increasing freedom of people from traditional ties and associated systems of mores, folkways, and religious disciplines, coupled with the fact that instead of flowering in their newfound freedom a large share have become muddled, confused, highly anxious, and self-driving, and in general resort to ways of "escaping their freedom."[1] Such modern maladies as alcoholism, increased divorce rates, overuse and experimental use of drugs, and the general entertainment and recreation manias have been linked with this desperate flight or search (which one it is depending, perhaps, on the person).

In 1962 Pollak presented several ideas related to this issue:

Strangely enough, the clients who represent the greatest challenge to social work and a wider community at the present time do not suffer from the scars of submission to the reality principle. They suffer from the ineffectiveness of having retained the pleasure principle as a guide of living. They lead a life of normlessness conceptualized by Merton as anomie. . . . With people who are victims of anomie we have no theory of helping and tradition of success. The culture of social work here is faced with the challenge of becoming a rearing and binding, superego demanding profession rather than of being a liberating one. . . . Here social workers will have to come to terms with a phenomena of normlessness which makes liberating or improving efforts miss the mark.[2]

Many respond to this problem by talking all the more vehemently of the need for increased services in education, welfare, and mental health, but while there is truth in this they miss the central point that is being proclaimed by the existentialists: People have lost contact with many basic human realities that they must accept and understand if they are to have a sense of personal direction or meaning in their lives. One need only look at present-day common behavior patterns and voiced attitudes to see this. With regard to the concept of human love, closeness, and intimacy, it can be seen that marital disappointments are commonly dealt with by divorce,

[1] Erich Fromm, *Escape from Freedom* (New York: Holt, Rinehart & Winston, 1941).
[2] Otto Pollak, "Social Determinants of Family Behavior." Paper presented at the Mid-Continent Regional Institute, National Association of Social Workers, Kansas City, Mo., April 1962, p. 6.

adultery, alcoholism, increased work (the notion that more money or prestige will change the marriage), and individualized social circles that allow two near-strangers to remain together under the same roof "for the sake of the children." The concept of death is often dealt with by avoidance of it as a fact with implicit meaning for present conduct or weak hopes for some scientific "deep-freeze" solution, and of course by the whole ridiculous ritual of the funeral parlors.

EFFORTS OF THE CHURCH

The illusion behind such maneuvers is the widely held belief that one can manipulate and control life in such a way as to bring oneself happiness, security, and freedom from suffering. This idea has been nourished throughout this century by utopian hopes stemming from scientific rationalism. The effort has backfired insofar as men have become increasingly estranged from many realities of the human condition. These attitudes have at the same time considerably weakened the position of the church, which in the past had been the fount for people's sense of direction and meaning and the support for their capacity to endure hardship. Needless to say, the church, especially since the Reformation, has had its part in nurturing the very hopes in scientific rationalism that have weakened its influence. Now the church itself is struggling for a new language and new means with which to express its fundamental ideas, knowing that people have been alienated and disillusioned and have come to feel indifferent toward traditional presentations of beliefs and truths.[3]

The church, as mentioned, has always concerned itself with the conflicts, ideas, feelings, and behavior that make up the state of mind called anomie. Presumably, the church should have important contributions to make to the psychiatric and social work professions in their efforts to cope with this problem. An interesting development in society has been furthered by those serious students of or searchers after a religion that refuses to return to Sunday school

[3] This is the basic conflict in the "Honest to God" debate. *See* John A. T. Robinson, *Honest to God* (Philadelphia: Westminster Press, 1963); and David L. Edwards, *The Honest to God Debate* (Philadelphia: Westminster Press, 1963).

fantasies, hopes, rituals, and platitudes. The new religious vitality is one that seeks a sense of direction and unity in the intimacy of direct experience with this world of tasks, suffering, and possibilities. The forerunners of this surge were such religious existentialist thinkers as Dostoevsky, Kierkegaard, Berdyaev, Bergson, Jaspers, Marcel, Maritain, Tillich, Niebuhr, Barth, and Buber. This is the true religious revival and has nothing to do with increased church attendance, faith healing, and the renewed interest in Gospel singing. A profound movement toward unity among the world's religions is in progress and this includes a strong effort toward a unity between religion and science as well.

A similar movement has occurred apart from the church, yet seems related to the same precipitating conditions and personal needs. This has expressed itself in the arts and literature and theoretically in the avid interest of many in existential philosophy and Zen Buddhism—two areas of modern thought representing West and East that are remarkably similar in their concern for the discovery of meaning in the direct, immediate experience of life as one lives it.

The existentialist movement in the fields of psychiatry and psychology may well provide a body of knowledge that is highly valuable and useful in our quest for some answers to the problem of anomie. Existentialism is a philosophy derived from man's immediate experience of the world in which he lives—a confrontation with the realities of the human condition and the establishment of a personalized meaning from them. As a philosophy of daily experience it should be capable of speaking meaningfully about ideas that can be grasped by the unsophisticated, much as a novel does.

Pollak's words (". . . becoming a rearing and binding, super-ego demanding profession") are provocative to the ears of social workers who have identified their goals, along psychoanalytic lines, to be in marked contrast with his suggestion. There is the ring here of paternalism, authoritarianism, and a judgmental attitude. But let us look at what the church has attempted to accomplish over its many centuries of existence and what this may have to say to us through the modern views of existentialism.

The church has always attempted to deal with the sufferings of people by providing them with a sense of meaning that transcends their own self-derived, suffering-based feelings of futility about life. Religious people have found courage to endure through acceptance of what is considered to be divine revelation. The fundamental services of religion to an individual are the provision of guidance in his way of living and the experience of union with an ultimate reality that relates him to others and all that exists through the transcendant power in which he believes. Religious dogmas, orders, sects, rituals, sermons, discussion groups, sacraments, social action, study, prayer, and meditation are some of the varied efforts to accomplish these two basic services. This variety of approaches reflects the church's efforts to serve people of varying capacities and levels of motivation and understanding. The mental health movement faces a similar problem.

Psychiatry cannot be equated with religion, for the sphere of divine revelation and speculation on the mystery of transcendance is beyond the scope and capacity of scientific methods. But the human need for guidance in the management of one's life and the experience of unity through relatedness to others outside oneself are certainly within its realm. It is here that the existentalist movement has attempted to relate a philosophy of life to mankind's problems by focusing, as the church has done, on guidance and relatedness. This is why the existentialist movement is most commonly characterized as stressing meaning in life and authenticity in relationships.

EXISTENTIALISM VERSUS ANOMIE

Elsewhere the writer defined the concern of existentialism as "meaningful living through self-encounter in the situation at hand despite a world of apparent futility."[4] Essentially, this means that one derives or helps another derive an attitude and direction toward life by becoming increasingly aware of life as he lives it and what this living entails. It is for this reason that the problem of anomie—of aimless, futile, normless lives—can be constructively related to by existentialist thought.

The process of growth in existentialism emphasizes the following reality concepts: increasing awareness of self-deceptions that attempt to define the self as fixed and secure; confrontation with the knowledge of personal freedom and its accompanying responsibilities; discovery of meaning in one's sufferings that actually helps

---

[4] Donald F. Krill, "Existentialism: A Philosophy for Our Current Revolutions," *Social Service Review,* Vol. 40, No. 3 (September 1966), p. 291.

establish a direction in life; realization of the necessity of dialogue or intimacy that nurtures change, courage, and self-assertion; and finally a decision for continued commitment that prizes freedom above attachment to childhood strivings and self-deceptions. This commitment is characterized by responsive action in the world of tasks, duties, and possibilities, in contrast to narcissism and self-pity.[5]

Let us contrast this with patterns of thought and behavior implicit in the state of mind labeled anomie. The characteristic of normlessness mentioned by Pollak is a result of several attitudes about oneself and also oneself in relation to others and the world in general. These attitudes are antiexistential in content because of the nature of the implicit beliefs and assumptions about freedom, responsibility, suffering, authenticity, love, and commitment. The sources of these attitudes are many and have been ably described by such social critics as Erich Fromm, Allen Wheelis, Colin Wilson, David Riesman, and William Whyte.

Anomie is derived from a Greek word meaning "lack of law." As a sociological concept it describes the breakdown or failure of those forces (standards, sanctions, norms, rules, values) that ordinarily bind people together in some organized social whole. This social whole is characterized by a sense of duty and obligation of people toward one another that preserves organization. There are different degrees of anomie and it may take several forms, outlined by Cohen as "confrontation by a situation for which there are no relevant rules, vagueness or ambiguity of the relevant rules, or lack of consensus on which rules are relevant and in the interpretation of rules."[6]

Tiryakian states:

To liberate the individual from all social constraint, adds Durkheim, is to abandon him to his unlimited wants, to demoralize him and to lead him to despair. What the individual should feel, more acutely than ever before, is the need for moral rules.[7]

[5] *Ibid.* This entire article is a development of these ideas.
[6] Albert K. Cohen, "The Study of Social Disorganization and Deviant Behavior," in Robert K. Merton, Leonard Brown, and Leonard S. Cottrell, Jr., eds., *Sociology Today: Problems and Prospects* (New York: Basic Books, 1959), p. 481.
[7] Edward A. Tiryakian, *Sociologism and Existentialism* (Englewood Cliffs, N.J.: Prentice-Hall, 1962), p. 31.

He suggests that what is latent in the writings of Durkheim that differentiates the notions of solidarity and anomie are societal analogues of what the existentialist terms an individual's "authentic" and "unauthentic" existence.

ANOMIC MAN

The existentialists have enriched our understanding of "anomic man" in both fictional and philosophical descriptions of the "unauthentic man," the man of "bad faith," and "alienated man." These assessments demonstrate that the anomic state of mind and attitude are not to be limited to delinquent, sociopathic, multiply deprived individuals but apply to an ever increasing number of people at all levels of present-day society. Attitudes typical of anomic man will now be examined.

There is a sense of aimless drifting, or at times being helplessly driven, both of which relate to one's sense of impotence and personal insignificance. One considers oneself as being fixed in place either by tradition, heredity, social position, or psychological and social determinism. One has been formed, or perhaps victimized, by the powers that be or by those that were before.

Paradoxically, along with this sense of missing personal freedom and hence diminished responsibility there is an increased expectation that one's surrounding environment should change in such a way as to bring one increased comfort, protection, and happiness. The experience of suffering is therefore often felt to be unfair, and bitterness as well as envy arises toward others in more fortunate circumstances. Quick and easy solutions are sought to manipulate the environment in order to reduce any personal pain and bring about a state of pleasure or comfort. The variety of efforts is vast and extends from pills and television to infidelity and alcoholism.

A Mexican-American leader recently defended his people, who are accused of filling the jails and reformatories of the Southwest, with this interesting observation:

When a Mexican kid is brought before the judge he is usually honest in admitting he committed the crime and ready to accept whatever consequences come—leaving his future to God. When an Anglo is in the same situation, he'll do anything possible to avoid a charge of guilty to get out of being punished.[8]

One's sense of self as a feeling, thinking, changing person is replaced by a notion of self as dependent on support from outside. One plays roles or "markets oneself" in such a way as to manipulate others to view one in a specific way that meets one's needs. Relationships are characterized by superficiality, calculation, and "game-playing." Other props used are the identification of self with groups, such as religious, political, or professional, or with slogans and characteristics of models found in society and given acceptance or even acclaim, such as "the good Joe, the hustler, the smart operator, the playboy, the status seeker. . . ."[9] When such supports are challenged or threatened, one is prepared to fight righteously and defend his self-identity to the bitter end.

What is apparent in this entire description is that one hides one's inner self both from others and from one's own sensitive judgment. There is an ongoing effort to gratify needs by actions and manipulations and a fleeing from being alone with oneself. Such exercises as meditation and self-examination become foreign, or if adopted are used with magical, naïve expectations that usually end in disappointment. Intuition and spontaneity tend to be lost or warped.[10] The simple joys to be found in the beauty and mystery of life and responsive participation in the ongoing order of things are rare. One feels alienated from other people, the world, and oneself, yet hides this fundamental panic beneath desperate efforts to grasp, contain, and fortify a sense of identity, false as it is.

ADVANTAGES OF EXISTENTIAL PSYCHOTHERAPY

This description of attitudes and behavior is not a presentation of symptoms, but rather of a way of life—an anti-existentialist way of living—that has developed to significant proportions in our age.

[8] Rudolph Gonzales, lecture-discussion given to the Child Psychiatry Department of the University of Colorado Medical Center, Denver, November 1966.

[9] A comprehensive elaboration of these "models" is found in Henry Winthrop, "American National Character and the Existentialist Posture," *Journal of Existentialism*, Vol. 6, No. 24 (Summer 1966), pp. 405–419.

[10] This theme is fully developed in Franz E. Winkler, MD, *Man, The Bridge Between Two Worlds* (New York: Harper & Bros., 1960).

Because anomie can be considered to be an attitude toward life, existential psychotherapy has a unique advantage over many other forms of psychotherapy. The outstanding difference does not lie in techniques or methods, for the existential approach may occur with insight, crisis-oriented, family, group, or supportive therapies. It may be directive, nondirective, or analytical. The uniqueness of existential psychotherapy is that it attempts a philosophical re-orientation through the use of therapy content and behavior. There is a process of challenge, re-education, and reconstruction of the patient's basic way of viewing himself, his relation to others, and the world at large.

The mental health professional performing the therapy (here-after called the therapist) holds to a number of existential philo-sophical premises based on his perception and understanding of reality. The experiences that are lived through in therapy are util-ized to demonstrate and highlight the philosophical implications of those realities apparent in these experiences. Soon experiences take on new meanings for patients, who are helped to rethink and re-develop their own outlook on life in a fresh manner.

It is true that the patient takes on certain values and philo-sophical attitudes of the therapist. This occurs in any form of psychotherapy to a certain degree. What is important here is that the therapist knowingly permits this. He has in mind certain exis-tential realities within his philosophical frame of reference that he wants the patient to see, understand, and accept if he is to overcome his problems. The goal in this approach is not insight into early traumas, reassurance, catharsis, or enabling the patient to grow in a nondirective atmosphere. It may include any or all of these, but the goal itself is a philosophical re-education through direct experience.

The relation between anomie and emotional illness must also be understood. Each can exist without the presence of the other; how-ever, in our present society both occur simultaneously and are inter-related in a vast and growing number of cases. The attitudes of anomie actually predispose the person to emotional illness.

The general view among existentialists of the development of emotional disorders stresses the following factors. Two human needs are considered most fundamental: (1) to be loved and to experience a sense of unity with what is other than oneself and (2) to grow through ongoing creative and responsive change. These are interre-lated inasmuch as the mature person, at the moment he is authenti-cally creative by responding to the tasks and opportunities of the world about him, is also experiencing a sense of unity by feeling needed or being a vital and unique part of his own specific area of the world (life space).

A child needs the trust and confidence of his parents to develop as a loving and creative person. As he discovers certain creative or loving expressions to be unacceptable to his parents, he experiences the threat of loss of love. With this goes the fear of a disintegration of his sense of self, for one's early identity is dependent on approval and acceptance by one's parents. This fear of parental rejection is equal to the adult fear of death, for the meanings are precisely the same. To live, to preserve some sense of self, a person willingly gives up or hides those aspects of personality that would produce rejection and adapts himself to what he believes his parents want from him, thus making himself acceptable and of worth. This pattern of self-conformity to a necessitated image in childhood continues into adulthood; one relates to others as if it were still necessary to uphold the same image in order to be acceptable and loved.

What is apparent here are the elements of calculated choice of behavior initially and ongoing manipulative efforts to maintain for others a set image of oneself. Trouble results from the fact that manipulative behavior fosters distance rather than love and intimacy in relationships, and also the clinging effort to maintain and express only specific aspects of the self results in frustration of free and creative growth. The two fundamental needs become endangered and the result is symptoms that cry out distress and a need for help. Guilt and anxiety are often seen to be reality based. Anxiety may be experienced when a person realizes that he could act in a spontaneous and creative way that would express his true, responsive self in a situation, yet to do so would endanger the image he feels he must preserve to be acceptable to others and himself. Guilt may occur when he chooses behavior that preserves his own childhood-based image at the expense of a growth possibility. Genuine open communication and sincere efforts of self-examination actually threaten the image that one wishes to maintain and are thus avoided.

TREATMENT GOALS

Anomie encourages a pattern that leads to emotional disturbance insofar as it emphasizes a helpless, weak, predetermined notion of oneself as lacking freedom and responsibility; a manipulative view of human relationships that nourishes superficiality, deceit, and distance; and an avoidance of pain as one tries with various self-deceptions to resist the meaning of guilt and anxiety in order to hide from what is real within oneself. The causes of anomie are sociological and historical, but the existence of anomie is itself an important contribution to mental illness. When anomie is a part of the emotional problem, it should be dealt with and the issue of treatment then becomes partly philosophical in nature.

The specific treatment goals for existential psychotherapy are essentially philosophical achievements in terms of a patient's coming to grips with those aspects of reality that will produce a significant change in his view of life and his relation to it. The five goals that would appear most important are these:

1. Aiding the process of disillusionment.
2. Confronting freedom.
3. Discovering meaning in suffering.
4. Realizing the necessity of dialogue.
5. Accepting the way of commitment.

Therapeutic techniques familiarize the patient with these goals, or realities, both by educational guidance and direct experience, much as the church directed its people toward spiritual growth. The balance of this paper will present methods by which these goals may be achieved. Emphasis will not be on an analytical or long-term insight-oriented psychotherapy from the existential framework, but rather on techniques useful for casework, group work, and reality-oriented psychotherapy.[11]

The description of therapy may seem somewhat disjointed, since the author's intention is to develop an over-all sense of direction for therapy rather than a complete system applicable to all clients. There is, of course, the question of which people would most benefit from this approach.

This same question must now honestly be asked about psychoanalytic psychotherapy. Studies of its results with many clients who seemed appropriate middle-class candidates for therapy as well as

[11] Two recent books illustrating the existential-analytical view are Avery D. Weisman, MD, *The Existential. Core of Psychoanalysis* (Boston: Little, Brown & Co., 1965) ; and J. F. T. Bugental, *The Search for Authenticity* (New York: Holt, Rinehart & Winston, 1965).

of persons in low-income groups have clearly indicated its gross ineffectiveness. It has had its successes too, but such studies raise radical questions about whether it is the most useful approach for our age. The entire community psychiatry movement is a vivid response to doubts about traditional methods and efforts toward new, creative approaches.

To what group of clients does Pollak refer when he speaks of "victims of anomie"?[12] Is there a difference between this group and those people who manifest anomic symptoms as a result of depressive conflict? Existential psychotherapy is not being suggested here as a cure-all, nor is it possible to say with assurance exactly what sorts of persons will benefit from it, any more than psychoanalytic practitioners can comfortably state this. May and Frankl have both expressed the view that the existential approach is more attuned to the problems of our age.[13] Fromm, sharing many of the existential concerns about the plight of modern man, has challenged the psychoanalytic approach on this same basis.[14] The reality-oriented psychotherapists (including Glasser, Ellis, Mowrer, and O'Connell) utilize techniques that are closely aligned with the existential treatment goals mentioned, and have worked successfully with neurotics, psychotics, and sociopaths. As early as 1933 Jung made the following relevant comments:

A psycho-neurosis must be understood as the suffering of a human being who has not discovered what life means to him. . . . Among all my patients in the second half of life—that is to say, over thirty-five—there has not been one whose problem in the last resort was not that of finding a religious outlook on life. . . . This of course has nothing whatever to do with a particular creed or membership of a church. . . . Today this eruption of destructive forces has already taken place, and man suffers from it in spirit. . . . That is why we psychotherapists must occupy ourselves with problems which, strictly speaking, belong to the theologian. But we cannot leave these questions for theology to answer; the urgent, psychic needs of suffering people confront us with them day after day.[15]

[12] *Op. cit.*

[13] Rollo May, ed., *Existential Psychology* (New York: Random House, 1961), p. 21. Viktor Frankl, *The Doctor and the Soul* (New York: Alfred A. Knopf, 1955), pp. 3–26.

[14] Erich Fromm, D. T. Suzuki, and Richard Demartino, *Zen Buddhism and Psychoanalysis* (New York: Evergreen Publishing Co., 1963), pp. 135–136.

[15] C. G. Jung, *Modern Man in Search of a Soul* (New York: Harcourt, Brace & Co., 1933), pp. 225, 229, and 241.

AIDING THE PROCESS OF DISILLUSIONMENT

The major task with this goal is gradually to reveal to the patient the reality that the very way he goes about thinking of himself and relating to other people defeats his purpose. His efforts at self-assurance and manipulation of those to whom he wishes to be close are marked with inconsistencies and self-deceptions that result in alienation and the limited expression of his potentialities. Habit patterns are revealed to him that consistently distort reality in his daily living. This process is anxiety provoking, of course, and requires the accompanying nurture of the therapeutic relationship.

The therapist must be well trained and experienced in the knowledge and operation of self-deception. Perhaps his most direct acquaintance with this is to have undergone psychoanalysis or psychotherapy himself. A corresponding discipline occurs in those religious orders that require intense self-examination by priests, monks, and the like in a search for personal truth. It is perhaps unfortunate that modern Protestant seminaries have for the most part replaced such personal struggle and discipline with rational teaching of history and theory.

A therapist aims initially at understanding the specific, unique patterns his client uses in viewing and relating to his world of tasks and relationships and his sense of self-adequacy. It is often important to develop some historical picture of the client to identify the presence of early patterns that still carry over into his present life adjustment. The existence of these patterns is also identified in the way the patient relates to the therapist. Because of the therapist's ability to maintain himself as a free, authentic person in the therapeutic relationship, he fails to be manipulated by the client's habitual efforts, although his interest and understanding remain solid and intact. As a free person, the therapist has no egotistical investment in curing or failing to cure the client. He offers reality, with himself as a therapeutic agent, but the client must always realize that the choice between change and growth on the one hand and flight toward the security of habitual patterns on the other is his own.

This process of challenging a person's manner of viewing his problem (as well as his general life conduct) can be illustrated in part by the techniques used with an open-ended therapy group for alcoholics conducted by the author. An alcoholic who wishes to join the group is told quite directly at the beginning how his problem will be viewed. This is done in a brief individual orientation session with the therapist. The prospective group member is told that alcoholics usually drink for a specific reason and the reason has to do with feelings that are difficult to bear without the aid of alcohol. Such feelings result from the way he sees himself and also the manner in which he relates to those with whom he wishes to have a close relationship. To benefit from therapy he must abstain from alcohol so that he can experience the feelings behind his drinking and talk about them in the group. By being as open and honest as possible, the group can help him come to an understanding of his problems and change them, so that the suffering caused by inner feelings can be managed better or diminished. It is emphasized that alcoholics can be helped in different ways, but if the client wants group therapy he must accept this notion of the helping process.

In the course of therapy he will usually find opposition to his personal view of his problems. Such ideas as the alcoholic's being born this way, having an incurable disease, or being inherently weak or hopelessly dependent are simply not accepted by the group. What is stressed instead is that the alcoholic never learned appropriate and workable means of expressing and meeting his needs. The manipulative ritual with his spouse is a good example. The cycle of drinking, fighting, threatening separation, confessing failure and appealing for another chance during the hangover period, and the final acceptance by the martyred wife provide several elements of closeness. There is an exchange of feelings, including anger, hurt, despair, contrition, forgiveness, and refound hope. But the closeness is short lived and must be repeated because it fails to deal with the genuine daily relationship struggles between the marital partners.

During therapy it becomes increasingly apparent to the alcoholic that his efforts to control interactions with other group members are related to the specific view he has of himself as a person, which he feels obliged to maintain. Yet this image and his strivings to maintain it are the sources of both his failure at intimacy and his inability to satisfy his needs, as well as an infringement on his ability to think and express himself in new ways.

The following Zen story illustrates how a monk's view of others stemmed from his own self-image. A perceptive friend disillusions his self-complacency.

Following a heavy rain, two Zen monks were walking together along a muddy road. They came upon a dismayed young maiden in a quandary about how she might cross the road without soiling her low-hanging silk kimono. "Come on, girl," said one monk as he lifted her in his arms and carried her across. The two monks resumed their journey without a word to each other. Finally, at a temple at which they were lodging that evening the second monk could no longer restrain himself: "We monks don't go near females, especially not young and lovely ones. It is dangerous. Why did you do that?" The first monk whimsically replied, "I left the girl there. Are you still carrying her?"[16]

CONFRONTING FREEDOM

In therapy the process of disillusionment dwells on the negative side of personality wherein values, attitudes, judgments, and behavior are revealed to be colored by childhood assumptions. This view of self is counterbalanced by an increasing awareness of the adult part of oneself, which is characterized by the freedom and responsibility available to a person in his daily functioning. Some basic ideas about the nature of the self and its capacity for freedom are stressed.

The self is never a fixed, closed, totally predetermined form; it is only a person's own fears and self-deceptions that make him think this is the case. Everyone is considered to be responsible in accordance with his age. Each is also a completely unique person unlike anyone who ever was or ever will be. His adult self is in a constant process of change and growth. The process of growth requires the ongoing assertion of freedom—the capacity to transcend what one has been before. A person chooses his future direction and utilizes his past knowledge and experiences as he relates to the present, deciding what is to emerge in him. He alone is responsible for his aspirations and whether he strives to fulfill them.

The person comes to see that while he is possessed by childhood strivings that seem to inhibit and interfere with his desired growth, this need not be accepted fatalistically. He chose these patterns as a child because of circumstances that at that time seemed to necessi-

---

[16] Paul Reps, *Zen Flesh, Zen Bones* (Garden City, N.Y.: Anchor Books, Doubleday & Co., 1961), p. 18.

tate them. But as an adult he possesses the same freedom to choose differently and, because he is an adult, the circumstances are no longer the same. It is only his fear that seems to make them so. He can manage new reality-based judgments of situations and how he will respond to them. A certain detachment from identified childhood strivings will be required, and the resulting sense of uncertainty will be painful, yet as a human being he does possess the freedom to accomplish change. His sense of direction will arise entirely from his own unique assessment of the duties, responsibilities, and inner promptings in his daily life. A responsive relatedness to what is going on about him helps him respond to the adult needs and potential within him.

Therapy is partly the teaching of a basic skill: how one may choose a response that is different from the one prompted by identified childhood strivings and their accompanying feelings. It encourages a developing sensitivity to meaning and reality in the confronting therapeutic situation. The client is repeatedly faced with the fact that he does have some choice in the matter at hand, and many of his rationalizations to the contrary are based on his fear and need to maintain old props for security. Therapy, then, does not emphasize the nature of his early bondage that must be relived and changed through the handling of transference manifestations, nor is it viewed as a complete remaking of a person's basic character. Instead, it helps the client to identify actual reality-based choices in the present situation and find satisfaction by asserting himself as a free being.[17] Consistent with the emphasis on the client's capacity to choose freely and decide his own direction from what lies within himself is the therapist's willingness to allow him to accept or reject therapeutic interpretations or suggestions. The therapist is not an authority on the specific manner in which a client is to choose and live his life, although he is an authority on the basic elements of the human condition and what this means with regard to the development of emotional disorders and the way toward growth and change.

A client's direct experience of his freedom to rise above the powerful negative driving forces in his daily life is a crucial therapeutic happening. Helping him to recognize choices he had hidden from himself is one way of accomplishing this. There may be many

---

[17] A detailed description of this technique is found in Richard L. Sutherland, "Choosing—As Therapeutic Aim, Method and Philosophy," *Journal of Existential Psychiatry,* Vol. 2, No. 8 (Spring 1962), pp. 371–392.

other ways that to date have not been explored and attempted in a sufficiently significant fashion.[18]

The logotherapy of Frankl includes a number of such examples. He sometimes utilizes humor and exaggeration of notions based on a client's neurotic assumptions about his own helpless condition. His aim is always to enable the client to acquire a new perspective on his symptoms and his own nature so that he does not continue to identify his total self with his neurotic symptoms, compulsions, or feelings. He also may suggest that a patient imagine himself to be twenty years older and review his present situation from that vantage point. The patient is able to identify instances in which more desirable choices might have been made by him "back then," and by so doing grasps the importance of the unique opportunity facing him at the present moment.[19]

Kondo, writing on "Zen in Psychotherapy" suggests as an adjunct to therapy the use of sitting meditation, which provides the patient with an experience of "single-mindedness"—an intuitive sense of the unity of body and mind that can enable him to detach himself from old childhood strivings bidding for present control.[20] The exercises of Gestalt psychology are aimed at a similar accomplishment.[21]

Another unique approach is Japan's *Morita* therapy. This is a therapy for hospitalized patients that is related to the philosophy of Zen Buddhism, which itself has many similarities to existentialism. Upon being hospitalized, a patient is placed in solitary confinement for the first several days, with only himself and his thoughts for company. He is asked to maintain a diary from the day of admission. Gradually he is permitted simple work activities and limited contact with a therapist. His range of contacts and tasks is slowly broadened and he begins to experience a sense of satisfaction in performing minor functions and relating to something other than himself. The nature of his problem is interpreted to him by the therapist, who has studied his diary. This interpretation has nothing

[18] One method utilizing casework techniques was described in Gerald K. Rubin, "Helping a Clinic Patient Modify Self-destructive Thinking," *Social Work*, Vol. 7, No. 1 (January 1962), pp. 76–80.

[19] Viktor Frankl, *The Doctor and the Soul* (New York: Alfred A. Knopf, 1957).

[20] Akihisa Kondo, "Zen in Psychotherapy: The Virtue of Sitting," *Chicago Review*, Vol. 12, No. 2 (Summer 1958).

[21] *See* Frederick S. Perls, Ralph F. Hefferline, and Paul Goodman, *Gestalt Therapy* (New York: Julian Press, 1951).

to do with early trauma or deep insight into childhood relationships. Rather, it is aimed at emphasizing the foolishness and futility of the self-preoccupied existence the patient maintained until his hospitalization. It is further directed at arousing a sense of humility and genuine acceptance of his daily life circumstances as being not only bearable but an intrinsic vehicle for meaning and satisfaction, if he would only perform the tasks required of him instead of brooding over his unhappy lot in life. This treatment approach is continued until the patient is discharged from the hospital in anywhere from one to two months.

What is important in these approaches is the patient's developing awareness of a different aspect of himself—that part of him is beyond the control of childhood striving and compulsive feelings. This aspect of self can manage a perspective over his total self and situation and thereby direct his choices in new ways. This part of him is also adult, creative, and—most important—real. There are lessons to be learned here from the novelists and film-makers who depict men and women discovering new and critical perspectives of their lives. Dickens' *A Christmas Carol* is a classic example, as is Dostoevsky's *Crime and Punishment*. The same theme occurs in Bergman's film *Wild Strawberries* and Fellini's *8½*. In *La Strada* Fellini presents a delightful vignette in which the feeble-minded heroine of the film is confronted by the clown-high-wire artist in a moment of utter despair. He laughs at her troubled face and tells her how foolish it is to feel her life is completely meaningless. He picks up a pebble and tells her that even this serves some purpose— that if it did not, then there would be no purpose in the entire starstrewn heavens. This statement at this particular time resulted in a profound change in the young woman.

The root of one's hope and sense of dignity lies within the preservation of belief in one's freedom, as well as its assertion over and against the forces that seem determined to defeat one. This is quite apparent in the thinking of many alcoholics involved in the therapy group mentioned earlier. The commitment to abstinence from alcohol emphasized by Alcoholics Anonymous reflects the same idea. One alcoholic who has been "dry" for five years put it this way: "My choice is to drink again and face complete hopelessness or else to refuse alcohol and stand at least a fighting chance for happiness sometime." Here is commitment that accepts suffering and frustration without a guarantee of bliss. What is rewarding is the free and ongoing act of refusing to use alcohol as an escape.

As mentioned, in group therapy the notions about the alcoholic being some predetermined, unchangeable kind of being are challenged. It is important that group members sense the personal belief of the therapist in their capacity for freedom. The therapist must always go beyond the role of a sympathetic nursemaid to the "hopelessly sick and downtrodden."

A technique similar to some of Frankl's ideas was used effectively with this group. It had to do with handling the frustrations of one member as his assertive efforts at communication in the group continually failed. He could state his ideas openly until someone disagreed and requested that he clarify something. Then he experienced a blocking of thought that resulted in his having to back down. Next he would withdraw emotionally from the group and feel increasingly depressed at being overpowered by his own anxiety. It was pointed out that he had identified an important pattern within himself. While it was true that he could not control the rising feelings of anxiety and subsequent blocking, he did have control over how he reacted to this. On the one hand, he could give himself up to the notion that he was impotent and helpless and withdraw from any further efforts. On the other hand, he could strive to maintain attention to the continuing group discussion, so that when his anxiety subsided somewhat he could again assert any ideas he might have on some aspect of the discussion. When he was later able to do this, it was emphasized that he was not allowing the feelings to control him, but could find satisfaction in remaining the assertive kind of person he wanted to be in the group.

Repeated assertion that two parts of an individual can be identified—that which strives for new ways of thought, expression, and action and that which is fearful of this because of certain false assumptions about self and others based on childhood experiences—has been found to be quite meaningful to the group. The question that follows is: "Which of these two parts rules in you?"

DISCOVERING MEANING IN SUFFERING

The central theme in the writings of Dostoevsky and Kazantzakis is that suffering is an inherent part of life and one's growth as a person is dependent on acceptance of and being willing to grapple with the suffering. This same thesis must form a crucial part of psychotherapy. The therapeutic stance is that one can learn from one's suffering, but to do so one must bring it out into the open where it can be faced.

A client will seldom be thrown by the frightening and guilt-ridden aspect of himself if the therapist is not. The therapist must be willing to share the client's sufferings by simply being there, as Rogers emphasizes.[22] His acceptance and deep understanding of this suffering can be conveyed by avoidance of reassurance or easy solutions. He may occasionally reveal examples of his own or another's personal struggles, to emphasize that suffering is a shared human condition.[23] Therapeutic techniques are often used to help a person endure his suffering instead of becoming embittered by it or clinging to weak notions of how it may someday be replaced by pleasure and comfort.

In the group of alcoholics described, an important part of the discussion content is learning to read the underlying meanings in what a person presents. These may be expressions or descriptions of guilt, anxiety, anger, depression, somatic illnesses, or acting-out behavior. Essentially, it is some feeling or behavior that has troubled a person about himself. The group's effort, then, is to examine the factors surrounding the occurrence in order to discover its meaning. Perhaps the person's response was not only natural, but could be considered mature. On the other hand, it may reveal an important aspect of a person's problematic life pattern. Guilt may reveal the inhibition of growth potential in a situation or behavior that is seen as being in conflict with what the person feels he could or should be doing. Anxiety may indicate that he has the potential to behave in a significantly different way but fears the consequences of so doing. Anger is often seen to be a way of blaming others for what are really one's own shortcomings. These concepts of common meanings associated with varying kinds of feelings soon become useful tools for group members to apply to themselves as well as to one another in subsequent meetings.

For example, a relatively new member of the group, 37 years

[22] Carl Rogers, "Becoming a Person," in Simon Doniger, ed., *Healing: Human and Divine* (New York: Association Press, 1957), p. 61.

[23] This openness by the therapist is described in Sidney M. Jourard, *The Transparent Self* (Princeton, N.J.: D. Van Nostrand Co., 1964), pp. 39–65. O. Hobart Mowrer also emphasizes such openness in his integrity therapy. A critique of his over-all approach is made by Donald F. Krill in "Psychoanalysis, Mowrer and the Existentialist," *Pastoral Psychology*, Vol. 16 (October 1965), pp. 27–36.

old, commented that he was operating at "low gear" and could see no reason for this other than what he had once been told by a psychiatrist—that he must constantly punish himself because his parents had always been critical of him. Another group member inquired when the depression had become more apparent to him. The onset was pinned down to the previous Saturday night when he had wanted to go to a movie with his wife, who had encouraged him to go alone since she wanted to do her hair that evening. He had accepted this and gone alone. Further questioning by the group led him to see his disappointment and annoyance and his failure to let his wife know what he was feeling. Because he was afraid to show his own needs to her he had avoided any effort either toward changing her decision or attaining a closer understanding with her. The result was loneliness, resentment, and guilt over his own passivity. This incident revealed a pattern in their marital relationship related to his own fear of being hurt if he exposed a dependency need.

Then there is the type of suffering that either must be endured for a long time—perhaps for life—or else evaded by drinking: loneliness and a sense of emptiness, often accompanied by bitterness and envy. The person may have no friends or spouse, or a spouse who resists all efforts at a more intimate relationship. Perhaps the alcoholic, despite his efforts, finds himself unable to be more open and direct even within the therapy group. Here the only creative effort possible may be the continued endurance of suffering. It is natural to envy those whose upbringing, capacities, and circumstances have resulted in a far easier adaptation to life. Yet to endure suffering can still be meaningful. For some it will be a gesture of faith that relates them to a divine force or power. For others it will be a way of remaining true to the human condition—refusing false havens. For still others it will be a means of relating to the fraternity of alcoholics, who often find courage and hope in the continued sobriety of their brothers.

Suffering is a human reality not to be seen as a meaningless, chaotic disruption of a person's life. There is no pleasure principle norm that says to suffer is to be out of kilter with life. The opposite is the case—to live is to accept suffering. Its acceptance depends on some understanding of its hidden meaning—often seeing it as a guide toward potential growth. Suffering gives direction to one's freedom.

REALIZING THE NECESSITY OF DIALOGUE

All that has been said with regard to disillusionment, freedom, and suffering would be no more than empty thoughts without the nourishment of dialogue. Creative growth and change are seldom intellectual decisions activated by willpower alone. The supportive sense of intimacy and relatedness involved here does not apply only to the therapeutic relationship. As mentioned, it may be an experience of unity with a deity, with fellow alcoholics, or with the human condition.

What must take place in the dialogue of therapy is revelation by the client of what is unique within himself, to which the therapist responds with interest, concern, acceptance, and validation of the client's feelings about himself. This does not, of course, mean continuing approval, but the willingness of the therapist to grasp and understand what is being revealed, even in the throes of disagreement. Increasing directness and openness of communication are therefore necessary. Also required is the lessening of manipulative efforts to control the relationship. There is a risk in allowing another person to respond to one freely. When a person ceases his efforts to control another's image of him, he often experiences a feeling of extreme panic, for his sense of self seems to be at the mercy of another's unknown response. Yet true dialogue requires this, and one of the most significant accomplishments in therapy is for two persons to be authentic and free in relation to one another. This, of course, requires that the therapist reveal himself as a human being with feelings, thoughts, and spontaneity.[24] The client must come to see himself as co-equal with the therapist by virtue of his humanity, and the therapist, to encourage this, must be adept at avoiding the client's efforts to control him.

The capacities both to trust and verbalize are inseparable from such dialogue. Clients will therefore vary in their ability to relate in the way described, and the therapist must carefully assess the modifiability of the client. For some people an effort to change meaningful relationships will be the goal sought. For others a more

---

[24] The concept of therapeutic openness and authenticity is well developed in Helen E. Durkin, *The Group in Depth* (New York: International Universities Press, 1961), sect. 2, pp. 249–276.

open dialogue with the therapist alone will be the only effort to implement this necessary aspect of the human condition.[25]

Group and family therapy are excellent proving grounds for examining methods of communication and the reason for failures of dialogue. In the group of alcoholics again, from time to time the specific ingredients of dialogue are structured. There is the initiator and the listener. Courage is often required to initiate a problem, for the response of others is uncertain. Courage is again needed by the listener in his attempt to develop the picture the initiator has begun through sincere curiosity. Responses such as advice-giving, early intellectual interpretations, and silence are frequently identified as defenses against a closer involvement with the initiator's problem. Genuine interest and an effort to understand more deeply may lead the listener to disagree with or challenge the initiator, with the accompanying threat of conflict. It may also lead the initiator to expect to receive a satisfactory solution to his problem from the listener, which the listener is fearful he may not be able to produce. On the other hand, the initiator may feel obliged to accept a listener's advice—even though he is doubtful of its applicability—and be silent in an effort to avoid conflict and the risk of displeasing others in their efforts to be of help.

The fears mentioned in efforts at dialogue can often be clarified in such a way that an individual will see and experience the fact that his very maneuvers to preserve a specific self-image negate the possibility of closeness. To become aware of this is also to realize the self-destructive aspects of one's manipulation of others. One may be more secure through feeling one has control of another person, but for genuine love and closeness to occur, the other must be allowed freedom of response. A gesture of love from another whom one feels one has successfully manipulated can be little more than emotional masturbation. One's own growth and knowledge of oneself is also dependent on the free assessment of others whose view is naturally different in some respects from one's own. To resist another's free opinion is to close off an opportunity for personal growth.

[25] A differentiation of therapy goals in accord with categories of client modifiability is described in Donald F. Krill, "A Framework for Determining Client Modifiability," *Social Casework*, Vol. 49, No. 10 (December 1968), pp. 602–611.

ACCEPTING THE WAY OF COMMITMENT

The way of commitment refers to a loyalty to those realities of the human condition one has discovered to be true and meaningful for oneself. The basis for a new philosophy is found in the realization of the nature and pattern of certain childhood strivings and a disillusionment with some previous way of achieving self-security; recognition that there is a part of oneself that is adult, free, and spontaneous; the finding of ongoing direction and a sense of meaning in one's sufferings; and finally through experiencing some possibility of genuine, sincere intimacy with another. As members of the described group of alcoholics stay on in therapy, these reality factors often become part of their lives as is manifested in the framework within which they use therapy sessions and relate to one another's problems. Gradually they have integrated elements of a new life-style.

It is helpful to think in terms of a model of the committed and authentic person as representing the ideal result of an acceptance of the existential realities described in this paper. While such a model would not be an expectation for all patients, it does add clarity and direction to our thinking. The characteristics are the opposite of those describing the state of anomie. One's sense of self is not seen as fixed, determined, or able to be constructed and secured by some set of achievements that prove one adequate because others finally recognize and applaud one. Rather, one's sense of self, as a narcissistic ego, is laughed at for its foolish and self-defeating strivings. Humor—as the capacity to laugh at oneself—is a natural characteristic. The self is seen now as having an ongoing relation to the world, constantly changing as new situations arise, forever being tapped by new possibilities, suspicious of the self-satisfaction that can lead to rigidity. The self as the center of attention and fortification increasingly is lost and replaced by a more avid interest in others, the tasks of one's daily life, and the beauty and wonder of the world about us. As the young English friend of Zorba the Greek said of him, "Zorba sees everything every day as if for the first time."[26] As one disciplines oneself away from self-clinging and delu-

---

[26] Nikos Kazantzakis, *Zorba the Greek* (New York: Simon & Schuster, 1959) p. 51.

sional attachments to childhood strivings, a creative spontaneity unfolds that is invested in many aspects of one's life—not focused in one isolated area of achievement.

This new state of self is similar to the mindlessness and nothingness in Zen Buddhism, meaning that the mind operates freely without attachment. The inflow of intuitive response with this state of mindlessness is illustrated in a Zen tale of a young man who wanted to learn the art of swordsmanship and apprenticed himself to a master swordsman. He was, however, disappointed when he was refused permission even to hold a sword, but instead had to prepare his master's meals and perform various chores. As the student went about these chores he was periodically assaulted by his master, who would suddenly appear and hit him with a stick. The student was told to defend himself, but every time he prepared for an assault from one direction, it would come from another. Finally, in utter confusion and helplessness, he gave up his hyperalertness. It was only then that he could intuitively sense the direction of the next attack and defend himself adequately. This is a practice of discipline in certain forms of personal combat in Japan even today.

This turnabout way of viewing the self is also the essence of true religious conversion. In religious terms, the self becomes detached from the idols of past devotion and is related now to the will of God, viewing the tasks and relationships of daily life as calling forth a response from oneself that in turn accomplishes a sense of divine unity in the act of free, open, and giving relatedness.

Buber describes this turnabout experience as a change from a reacting "I-it" relation to the world to a responding "I-Thou" relation. Instead of using people in one's environment as objects to support and gratify a self-image, one "enters into relation with the other," whatever form this might take, and such a contact is characterized by awe, respect, care, and creative response.[27] Tillich speaks of this experience as discovering the "courage to be" as a result of experiencing oneself as "being grasped by the power of Being itself." As one feels that one's most ego-gratifying strivings are illusory and false, one also has a sense of being affirmed as worthy and acceptable in spite of the fact that such acceptance has not been earned by the energy expended in these false strivings. The acceptance of this affirmative experience allows one to carry out one's daily tasks with a lessened need for the old security striving. One's "acceptance of

[27] The best critique of Buber's thought is found in Maurice S. Friedman, *Martin Buber: The Life of Dialogue* (New York: Harper & Bros., 1959).

being accepted" is seen to be a reunion with the transcendent power of Being that gives meaning to life.[28]

A nonreligious discussion of this same theme is found in Frankl's logotherapy, which is designed to arouse an awareness of the "task character of life." This concept is developed by using the realities of the patient's everyday life. Considering such factors as family background, the nature of time, awareness of death, ever changing circumstances, and ever changing personality, the therapist emphasizes that every person is singular, is unique. Not only will there never be another like him but even the exact circumstances of a momentary situation will never again be precisely the same, so that each decision possesses uniqueness. He is free to respond to the moment at hand, and when he grasps the tremendous sense of responsibility that goes with his uniqueness (which he bears sole responsibility for shaping), then his daily tasks take on a special meaning never before experienced. When he has truly reached this stage, he loses his self-preoccupation in a new sense of responsible relatedness to daily happenings. This might be labeled a new form of self-concern, but the essential difference is that the direction is outward—giving, doing, creating, and enduring—rather than inwardly striving, securing, protecting, and possessing.

A significant portion of Frankl's logotherapeutic technique is designed to enlighten a patient about the kinds of values or possibilities that seem to await realization or actualization in his concrete life circumstance. Values are seen to be creative, experiential, and attitudinal in nature and vary, of course, with the patient. Creative values may refer to work tasks or even to those that may be artistic or athletic. Experiential values have to do with enjoyment of the world about one and this includes the closeness of an interaction in personal relationships. Attitudinal values are those that can be realized as one accepts and endures suffering that is unavoidable or unchangeable. From this perspective, it is apparent that some values can be identified as real and meaningful for any patient, regardless of the nature of his limits and circumstances.[29]

Mowrer and Glasser state that the key factor in therapy is helping a patient identify for himself clearly how he believes he ought to behave—what values seem important to him personally. He can then identify how his actual decisions and behavior are at

[28] Paul Tillich, *The Courage To Be* (New Haven: Yale University Press, 1952).

[29] Frankl, *op. cit.*

odds with the way he wants to be. The necessity of changed behavior is stressed, regardless of the feelings involved, in order to bring about the person's increased acceptance of himself as worthy and hence as acceptable to others. Self-pity and self-preoccupation are replaced by identification of one's value and by commitment.[30]

CONCLUSION

The problem of anomie should be seen as a way of life in itself that must be countered by philosophical efforts that become meaningful through the process of psychotherapy. Existentialism is an especially useful philosophical base because it draws its central themes from man's immediate experience of his life. Its emphases on disillusionment, freedom, suffering, authentic relationships, and commitment deal directly with their opposites, which are characteristics of anomie. Existentialism should not be considered a completed philosophical system, but rather a series of emphasized realities that can be adapted to other forms of philosophy and religious belief, depending on the background and thought of the individual therapist.

A danger in the misuse of psychoanalytic thought is the reduction of man to primitive animal drives. Notions of chaos and determinism prevail in this attitude about man's nature, and the resulting pleasure principle goal for people is simply insufficient for those experiencing anomie. The process, common among many psychoanalytically oriented therapists, of classifying and categorizing symptoms and behavioral expressions according to a system based on the primacy of animal drives accentuates this very problem. This process is viewed as "scientific" because it is wholly materialistic, but it is not scientific at all. The belief in the primacy of animal drives is as much a faith as the assumptions espoused in existentialism and other humanistic psychologies.

For the existentialists, man's biological drives are important and must be understood, but they do not fully explain man's nature. As a matter of fact, emphasis on the primacy of instinctual drives is a way of viewing human beings at their minimum level of function-

---

[30] O. Hobart Mowrer, *The Crisis in Psychiatry and Religion* (Princeton, N.J.: D. Van Nostrand Co., 1961); William Glasser, *Reality Therapy: A New Approach to Psychiatry* (New York: Harper & Row, 1965).

ing rather than their maximum level. At this maximum level man
has freedom, the power to transcend his egotistical strivings, courage to venture, and a capacity to endure. The spirit is available to
men, but they must sometimes seek it out to become aware of its
existence. Kazantzakis, in *The Last Temptation of Christ*, expressed
the nature of this spirit by proclaiming man as the being who gives
wings to matter.

Freud was reported to have said to Binswanger, the existentialist psychoanalyst: "Yes, the spirit is everything. . . . Mankind has
always known that it possesses spirit; I had to show it that there
are also instincts."[31] Freud's contribution has been immense and he
responded honestly and courageously to what he viewed as the
problems of his society. But the repression of sexuality, with its
resulting neuroses, is not the most common problem in our modern
society of *Playboy*, the Hollywood love goddesses, and birth control. To reestablish meaning and direction in people's lives there is a
need in the psychotherapeutic method for philosophical guidance
and value education. By leaving this up to the church a therapist is
being blind to the essential function of therapy for anomic man.
This presents an identity problem for many therapists who have
long been fond of criticizing and belittling the church, for now, as
therapists, they are called on to serve patients in the very way in
which for centuries the church has attempted to serve them.

Ecology's Angry Lobbyist

DAVID M. RORVIK, Journalist

"I'm scared. I have a 14-year-old daughter whom I love very much.
I know a lot of young people, and their world is being destroyed. *My*
world is being destroyed. I'm 37, and I'd kind of like to live to be 67
in a reasonably pleasant world, not die in some kind of holocaust in
the next decade."

[31] Ludwig Binswanger, *Sigmund Freud: Reminiscences of a Friendship*
(New York: Grune & Stratton, 1957), p. 81.

From *Look,* 34 (No. 8): 42–44, April 21, 1970 with permission of the
author.

Dr. Paul R. Ehrlich is running for his life. Lots of people are running after him. Magazines as diverse as *Ramparts*, *Playboy* and *McCall's* want his articles; television cameras are becoming a permanent fixture in his office at Stanford University, where the national networks and even the Voice of America seek his skull-splitting views on the state-of-the-environment ("going to hell, and Nixon is doing worse than nothing to stop it"); colleges are clamoring for his body ("I'm booked a year ahead on personal appearances and get around two dozen requests a day"); famous photographers want him to sit still for their cameras (Richard Avedon asked for a three-hour sitting, was offered ten minutes); Johnny Carson has featured him twice in six weeks.

And all the while, he keeps running—only faster, 18 hours a day, 80,000 miles a year, warning us that population has been increasing faster than the food supply since 1958, and 10 to 20 million people are already starving to death each year and that three-fourths of the world now goes to bed hungry each night, that the accumulation of DDT and similar poisons could bring the life-providing processes of photosynthesis to a halt and leave the oceans as dead as Lake Erie by 1979, that even Americans will probably be subjected to water rationing by 1974 and food rationing by the end of the decade, that hepatitis and epidemic dysentery rates could easily climb by 500 percent in this country between 1970 and 1974, on account of crowding and increasingly polluted water, that the prospects of worldwide plague and thermonuclear war grow more distinct each day as population pressures on a fragile environment and finite natural resources mount.

Paul Ehrlich an alarmist? "I certainly am," he said. "After all, I'm alarmed."

Professor of biology and former director of Graduate Studies for the Department of Biological Sciences at Stanford, author of 80 scientific papers and a number of books, including *The Population Bomb* (over 950,000 paperback copies in print), he strides to any platform and literally wraps his lanky 6′ 2″ frame around the podium. He exhibits short hair but long sideburns ("I get away with a lot this way") and a wrinkled suit that hangs on him like camel skin. When he speaks, it is an urgent, nonstop, rapid-fire rumble.

It took one million years, he says, to double the world population from 2.5 million people to 5 million in 6000 B.C. Now we're pressing 4 *billion*, and the doubling time is only 37 years. If we kept on at this rate, Ehrlich says, we'd have 60 million billion people in another 900 years—"or about 100 persons for each square foot of the earth's surface." But surely we can ultimately move to some other planet? Forget it. Ehrlich marshals figures showing that even if Americans were willing to reduce their standard of living to 18 percent of its present level, they could still only export to the stars *one day's* increase in the population *each year.* And even if we did manage to get to the other planets, he says, "in a few thousand years, at the current growth rate, all the material in the visible universe would have been converted into people, and the sphere of people would be expanding outward at the speed of light!" Similarly, the notion that wars help check population is laid to rest with the disclosure that "all battle deaths suffered by Americans in all wars [more than 600,000] have been more than made up for by births in the last three days."

He flays the men he calls environmental villains, ecological Uncle Toms, "dum-dums and Yo-Yos" of the Establishment:

Presidential Science Adviser Lee DuBridge—"His field, physics, is fading into the background; it deals with relatively simple systems and is no longer as relevant as it once was. Yet the politicians still think physics is the only real science and inevitably turn to physicists for advice. These are people who believe that scientists aren't supposed to take political, activist stances, hence not likely to give frank advice. The science adviser today should be a biologist or behavioral scientist, not a physicist."

The National Academy of Sciences—"Another part of the never-take-a-stand science establishment. It would be unable to give a unanimous decision if asked whether the sun will rise tomorrow."

The Atomic Energy Commission—"Its stand in regard to radiation levels is that if you can't prove they're going to kill you, they're all right. They're too busy promoting nuclear power to regulate it."

The Pope—"I have a great deal of compassion for serious Catholics who have been placed in a moral bind by the Pope's insistence on adherence to mindless policies against contraception. Why should anybody take sexual advice from the Pope? Thanks to the suppression of contraceptive devices, abortion is the commonest form of birth control in the world today, which is disgraceful. And abortion is most prevalent where the laws are most restrictive. In Italy, for example, the abortion rate is estimated to be nearly equal to the birthrate. Death is said to result in about four percent of these illegal Italian abortions; and in Santiago, Chile, bungled abortions are estimated to account for more than 40 percent of all hospital admissions."

The so-called "Green Revolution," which some economists claim will increase the yield of the soil and thus save us all—"The Green Revolution, which puts emphasis on vast and dense plantings of single types of grain, creating monocultures, is going to turn brown. Among other things, without genetic variability in crops, you can't stay ahead of the bugs and the pests. They've got miracle rats to go along with their miracle rice now in the Philippines. Look at the Green Revolution created by the potato in Ireland a couple of centuries ago. The impoverished two million people there rapidly bred up to about eight million, and along came the potato blight. Two million people died of starvation and another two million managed to emigrate. If you consider that today there's no place to migrate to, the cost of giving a new food to two million people *without* population control could be the ultimate death of four million people! The economists never take these complexities into consideration."

Family planning—"Even if we prevented all *unwanted* children, the goal of family planning, we would still have a severe population problem. People *want* too many children. Family planning is a disaster because it is giving people a false sense of security. No one should have more than two children; anything beyond that is irresponsible, suicidal."

The Gross National Product—"Gross is the word for it. We've got to shift from what economist Kenneth Boulding calls our 'Cowboy Economy,' in which both production and consumption are regarded with great favor and which is, in his words, 'associated with reckless, exploitative . . . behavior,' to a Spaceman Economy, in which we recognize that there are no unlimited reservoirs, either for extraction or pollution, and in which consumption must be minimized."

The Department of Agriculture—"A subsidiary of the petrochemical industry that produces DDT and the other insecticides. The Department has no ecological knowhow whatever and is strongly in league with the very elements it ought to be regulating. Letting Agriculture control registration of pesticides is like letting the fox guard the henhouse."

The petrochemical industry—"Pesticides, in general, are *designed* to fail. The industry profits by this because when they do fail, their recommendation is to use *more* pesticides. The industry also cleverly recommends spraying on a regular schedule whether the bugs are there or not—a sort of 'preventive' approach that actually has the opposite effect. By spraying, as they recommend, late in the winter and then every two weeks in the season, you guarantee that the pests you are after will develop resistance. Beyond this, pesticides don't work because they almost always kill off far more of the predators that eat the plant pests than the pests themselves. The reason for this is simple: the pests, over a period of millions of years, have evolved means of handling poisons that the plants themselves produce as defenses. The pests are adept at this, but the predators aren't. And when the spray kills off the predators, the pest population explodes. The scientific approach to pest control is to enhance the plants' natural defenses, not introduce substances that dangerously upset the ecological balance."

President Nixon—"His State of the Union message makes it abundantly clear that he can be counted on to do practically nothing. He addressed himself to one tiny part of the problem—sewage disposal—and the $4 billion he allocated in Federal funds for use over the next five years is totally inadequate. To make matters worse, the type of sewage plants this money is going into are the type that foul up the water with phosphates and nitrates. And if we ever should get our own country on the right road with the right leaders, we're still going to have to work doubly hard to see to it that their counterparts in the Soviet Union, China and so on are also removed from power and put out on the happy farm where they belong."

Though Ehrlich denies that he's any sort of hero, he happily acknowledges the emergence of a new youth movement based on the population-pollution issue. He insists that it must become more than just a youth movement. "If anything is going to bring us all together, poor, rich, black, white, young, old, this has got to be it," he says. "Some of the black militants now are saying that population control is a white plot to commit genocide against the blacks. Unfortunately, some of the whites talking up population control *do* mean population control for the blacks, or the poor or the Indians. Like most racist plots, however, this one is incompetent—because if the blacks actually listened and had smaller families, it would mean more black power. Fathers would be more likely to stay with their families, the kids would get better educations, better nutrition and so on.

But it's not for the whites to tell the blacks what to do. Their birthrate is a little higher than ours, but they've been so stomped on that they haven't had a chance to do the looting and polluting of the environment that the whites have. Affluence and effluence go hand in hand. We Americans, comprising only six percent of the world's people, consume 30 percent of the world's available resources each year. So you can see that each American child puts far more strain on the world environment than each Asian child. We've got to put our own house in order before we start telling Asians and Africans what to do."

He also encourages the old to join in. "We ought to have swinging old people," he says. "The two groups of people most mistrusted are the very old and the very young. And they could form a great force for change, if they could come together and put pressure on the middle group that is responsible for much of the destruction of the environment."

Ehrlich argues that the young "share a disdain for material things, a fascination for nature and an interest in what might be called an ecological way of life. These attitudes are the antithesis of those of the Old Left, of Socialism and Communism, which resemble Judeo-Christian attitudes in encouraging the exploitation of nature."

Ehrlich asks the young not to be misled by those who say the environment is a "safe" issue, that they are being co-opted, weaned away from the "real" issues of Vietnam, poverty, race and so on. "Your cause is a lost cause without population control," he says, "and race, war, poverty and environment are really part and parcel of the same big mess. The wars we're fighting in Vietnam and Laos, for example, are immensely destructive to the environment. We've defoliated an estimated 20 percent of Vietnam, and much of the ecological destruction there is going to be permanent. Students have got to inform themselves on problems in their areas and then become teachers—fast. I think the Environmental Teach-In, April 22, is going to have tremendous impact. I hope that the participants will zero in on the politicians, make it clear we aren't going to settle for their lies and do-nothing attitudes. . . ."

"The movement is going to generate a lot of civil disobedience, similar to what we saw in the early days of civil rights: demonstrations, picketing, sit-ins. I think we will soon begin to see boycotting of the automobile industry, the big oil companies, the utilities and so on. Among other things, people are just going to stop paying their bills. One clue that we're making real progress will come when politicians start telling it like it is and to hell with the consequences."

Ehrlich's forthcoming book, *Population Resources and Environment,* sums it up: "Spaceship Earth is now filled to capacity or beyond, and running out of food. And yet people traveling first class are, without thinking, demolishing the ship's already overstrained life-support systems. . . . Thermonuclear bombs, poison gases, and super-germs are being manufactured and stockpiled. . . . [But] many of the passengers still view the chaos with cheerful optimism. . . ."

If neither party produces a presidential nominee in 1972 pledged to a crash program to save the environment, Ehrlich predicts a new party will offer such a man. An activist organization he helped start last year, Zero Population Growth, may provide the base. ZPG now has a membership of over 8,000 and it is doubling every two months. It wants legalized abortion, a maximum of two children a family, Government support of birth control, tax incentives for smaller families and candidates dedicated to environmental reform.

Ehrlich rules himself unsuited for public office. Rather than become more involved in public life after 1972, he may withdraw altogether. "When you reach a point where you realize further efforts will be futile, you may as well look after yourself and your friends and enjoy what little time you have left. That point for me is 1972."

In the meantime, though, he keeps running, burning up time he would much rather spend with his pretty wife Anne or his daughter Lisa, flying his own plane or carrying on research projects in evolution, finishing studies on the effects of crowding on humans, getting back to his field projects. "I'm no hair-shirt hero," he says again. "This is just a survival reaction. I'm running for my life."

Culture and the Individual

Each of us can influence his own learning and become an active agent in structuring his own development as an effective human being. The nature of the personal relationships which pervade one's life is an important factor in what one learns about being human. Fraiberg's article gives considerable food for thought in this respect. If the ego defenses and behavior patterns of emotional insulation and isolation are learned and well set before age two, as she suggests, people can be irretrievably crippled by what happens very early in their lives. There can be "retardation in all areas of development . . . . impairment in memory and consequently in all the complex functions of human intelligence."

Being handicapped and disadvantaged, however, is a matter of degree as well as a matter of area. Our cultural emphasis upon the strong, stoical, unemotional role for the male is an example of such emotional poverty. It well may be just as true that human capacities and feelings which are denied and unused also become disfunctional. Hence, it is not enough that a person learns how to love and to be loved by age two, it also is essential that he continue to practice this behavior if he is to maintain the ability.

Psychologists and educators long have been aware that causal environments must be influenced in relation to the age of the subject. If one is to help babies, one must influence parents. If parents are to provide experiences and models which do not lead to "diseases of non-attachment," they must look to their own interpersonal behaviors. For one does not transmit what he cannot demonstrate. Children can be taught inadvertently, not to relate with depth and affection by parents who are not aware of their own problems of interacting with others. While it may be too late for many of us to become totally the warmly affectionate models we would like for our children, is not too late to move in that direction. Each reader may begin by using his personal contacts as sources for gaining feedback about his own behavior in this important area of human interaction.

Feedback, as Murphy suggests (Reading 2), is essential for effective decision making. And decision making, in turn, is essential for the whole process of becoming and being an individual. In a culture in which personal status depends upon being right and in which mistakes are demeaning, choosing and deciding are risky. This appears to be the premise for Frankel's assertion that being an individual is an "awful idea." We suspect, however, that this is said with tongue in cheek. At any rate, his selection carries more than its quota of pertinent and pithy statements. Reading in depth is necessary for he offers plenty to ponder upon. For example, why did he title his article as he did? We find more challenge than awfulness in what the author has to say and more reason to hope than to despair. Also, we see nothing so bad about "an intensification of experience." Actually this is living. It is better to feel the doubts which accompany decision than to be of no consequence and to be accountable for nothing. Further, we like the author's recognition that the proper use of machines and specialization can provide conditions for a larger realization of individuality. It well may be that the person who knows how to use the "amplification systems" provided by his culture has an important key to personal impact, identity, and actualization of self. We agree with Maslow (Reading 47) that this is the proper business of education.

Fraiberg shows that the individual is a product of his culture; Frankel indicates that individuals, through the exercise of choice, are responsible for what they become; and Mitchell illustrates how culture and choice may, and must, be combined. There is much we like about Mitchell's presentation besides the fact that he provides an integrating theme for this section. His use of the simile of a chronically ill patient and the sad state of race relations in this country is quite appropriate in the psychology of adjustment. His emphasis on the fact that racism is irrational rather than rational might well be expanded to consider the proposition that much of our struggle for better adjustment is irrational rather than rational. Recognizing this fact is a step toward integrating the rational and emotional phases of life into more effective adjustment patterns.

The problems of personal adjustment can never be separated from those of social adjustment. Many have said that white and black must get along. Somehow this idea seems to us to be limited and divisionary. The problem for each and all of us is that of achieving full humanity without regard for such superficialities as skin color, hair texture, facial features, and, yes, IQ (Reading 4). Mitchell seems to be emphasizing this point as he writes of the necessity of all of us—white and black—to be self-certain and the need we have for intergating all persons as Americans. To the extent that each of us can achieve such self- and social-acceptance, then the problems of urban crises, youth crises, racism, and personal adjustment will all be somewhat lessened. All of the articles in this section are telling us that we are the culture.

The Origins of Human Bonds
SELMA FRAIBERG

III

In the earliest years of psychoanalysis, Freud discovered that conflicts between the claims of love and the claims of aggression were
central to all personality development. As early as 1905 he demonstrated through the study of a five-year-old boy, "Little Hans,"
how the animal phobias of early childhood represent a displacement
of aggressive and libidinous impulses from the love objects, the
parents, to a symbol of dangerous impulses, the animal. The phobia
served the function of keeping the dangerous impulses in a state of
repression and of preserving the tender feelings toward the parents
in a state of relative harmony. This is not to say, of course, that
conflicts between drives must lead to neurotic solutions. There are
other solutions available in childhood, among them the redirection
of hostile impulses in play and in the imagination. But in all these
instances of normal development and even in the case of childhood
neuroses, the motive for redirection of hostile impulses is love. *It is
because the loved person is valued above all other things that the
child gradually modifies his aggressive impulses and finds alternative modes of expression that are sanctioned by love.*

In all this we can see an extraordinary correspondence between
the regulation of human drives and the phylogenetic origins of the
love bond as constructed from the data of comparative ethology.
Perhaps it might even strike us as a banal statement that human
aggression should be modified by love. We are accustomed to take
human bonds as a biological datum in human infancy. There would
be no point in writing this essay if it were not for another story that
is emerging from the study of a large body of data in psychoanalysis, psychiatry, and psychology on the diseases of non-attachment.

The group of disorders that I am here calling "the diseases of
non-attachment" are, strictly speaking, diseases of the ego, struc-

Parts III through VI of the article in *Commentary,* 44 (No. 6): 51–57,
December, 1967. Reprinted from *Commentary,* by permission; Copyright ©
1967 by the American Jewish Committee.

tural weaknesses or malformations which occur during the formative period of ego development, the first eighteen months of life.
These disorders are not classified as neuroses. A neurosis, properly
speaking, can only exist where there is ego organization, where there
is an agency that is capable of self-observation, self-criticism, and
the regulation of internal needs and of the conditions for their
expression. In a neurosis there may be disorders in love relationships, but there is no primary incapacity for human attachments.
Similarly, we need to discriminate between the diseases of non-
attachment and psychoses. In a psychosis there may be a breakdown or rupture of human bonds and disorders of thinking which
are related to the loss of boundaries between "self" and "not self"—
all of which may testify to structural weakness in ego organization—but this breakdown does not imply a primary incapacity for
human attachments.

The distinguishing chracteristic of the diseases of non-attachment is the incapacity of the person to form human bonds. In
personal encounter with such an individual there is an almost
perceptible feeling of intervening space, of remoteness, of "no connection." The life histories of people with such a disease reveal no
single significant human relationship. The narrative of their lives
reads like a vagrant journey with chance encounters and transient
partnerships. Since no partner is valued, any one partner can be
exchanged for any other; in the absence of love, there is no pain in
loss. Indeed, the other striking characteristic of such people is their
impoverished emotional range. There is no joy, no grief, no guilt,
and no remorse. In the absence of human ties, a conscience cannot
be formed; even the qualities of self-observation and self-criticism
fail to develop. Many of these people strike us as singularly humorless, which may appear to be a trifling addition to this long catalogue of human deficits, but I think it is significant. For smiling and
laughter, as Lorenz tells us, are among the tribal signs that unite the
members of the human fraternity, and somewhere in the lonely past
of these hollow men and women, the sign was not passed on.

Some of these men and women are to be found in institutions
for the mentally ill, a good many of them are part of the floating
populations of prisons. A very large number of them have settled
inconspicuously in the disordered landscape of a slum, or a carnie
show, or underworld enterprises where the absence of human connections can afford vocation and specialization. For the women
among them, prostitution affords professional scope for the condi-

tion of emotional deadness. Many of them marry and produce children, or produce children and do not marry. And because tenderness or even obligatory parental postures were never a part of their experience, they are indifferent to their young, or sometimes "inhumanly cruel," as we say, except that cruelty to the young appears to be a rare occurrence outside of the human race.

A good many of these hollow men remain anonymous in our society. But there are conditions under which they rise from anonymity and confront us with dead, unsmiling faces. The disease of emotional poverty creates its own appetite for powerful sensation. The deadness within becomes the source of an intolerable tension—quite simply, I think, the ultimate terror of not-being, the dissolution of self. The deadness within demands at times powerful psychic jolts in order to affirm existence. Some get their jolts from drugs. Others are driven to perform brutal acts. We can learn from Jean Genet of the sense of exalted existential awareness that climaxes such acts. Victims of such acts of brutality are chosen indiscriminately and anonymously. There is no motive, as such, because the man who has no human connections does not have specific objects for his hatred. When caught for his crimes, he often brings new horror to the case in his confession. There is no remorse, often no self-defense. The dead voice recounts the crime in precise detail. There was no grievance against the victim: ". . . he was a very nice gentleman. . . . I thought so right up to the minute I slit his throat," said one of the killers in Truman Capote's *In Cold Blood*.

Among those who are driven to brutal acts we can sometimes see how aggression and sexuality are fused in a terrible consummatory experience. It is as if the drives themselves are all that can be summoned from the void, and the violent discharge of these drives becomes an affirmation of being, like a scream from the tomb. Yet it would be a mistake to think that such criminals are endowed with stronger sexual urges than others. For the sober clinical truth is that these are men without potency and women without sexual desire, under any of the conditions that normally favor sexual response. These men and women who have never experienced human bonds have a diffuse and impoverished sexuality. When it takes the form of a violent sexual act it is not the sexual component that gives terrible urgency to the act, but the force of aggression; the two drives are fused in the act. When we consider the ways in which, in early childhood, the love bond normally serves the redirection of aggression from the love object, we obtain a clue: the absence of human bonds can promote a morbid alliance between sexual and aggressive drives and a mode of discharge in which a destructive form of aggression becomes the condition under which the sexual drive becomes manifest.

From these descriptions we can see that the diseases of non-attachment give rise to a broad range of disordered personalities. But if I have emphasized the potential for crime and violence in this group, I do not wish to distort the picture. A large number of these men and women distinguish themselves in no other way than in that they exhibit an attitude of indifference to life and an absence of human connections.

The hollow man can inform us considerably about the problem we are pursuing, the relations between the formation of human love bonds and the regulation of the aggressive drive. In those instances where we have been able to obtain histories of such patients, it appears that there were never any significant human ties, as far back as memory or earlier records could inform us. Often the early childhood histories told a dreary story of lost and broken connections. A child would be farmed out to relatives, or foster parents, or institutions: the blurred outlines of one family faded into those of another, as the child, already anonymous, shifted beds and families in monotonous succession. The change of address would be factually noted in an agency record. Or it might be a child who had been reared in his own family, a family of "no connections," unwanted, neglected, and sometimes brutally treated. In either case, by the time these children entered school, the teachers, attendance officers, or school social workers would be reporting for the record such problems as "impulsive, uncontrolled behavior," "easily frustrated," "can't get close to him," "doesn't seem to care about anything." Today we see many of these children in Head Start programs. These are the three- and four-year olds who seem unaware of other people or things, silent, unsmiling, poor ghosts of children who wander through a brightly painted nursery as if it were a cemetery. Count it a victory if, after six months of work with such a child, you can get him to smile in greeting or learn your name.

Once extensive study was begun on the problems of unattached children, some of the missing links in etiology appeared. We now know that if we fail in our work with these children, if we cannot bring them into a human relationship, their future is predictable. They become, of course, the permanently unattached men and women of the next generation. But beyond this we have made an extraordinary and sobering discovery. An unattached child, even at the age of three or four, cannot easily attach himself even when he is provided with the most favorable conditions for the formation of a human bond. The most expert clinical workers and foster parents can testify that to win such a child, to make him care, to become important to him, to be needed by him, and finally to be loved by him, is the work of months and years. Yet all of this, including the achievement of a binding love for a partner, normally takes place, without psychiatric consultation, in ordinary homes and with ordinary babies, during the first year of life.

This brings us to another part of the story, and to further links with the biological studies of Lorenz. Research into the problems of attachment and non-attachment has begun to move further and further back into early childhood, and finally to the period of infancy. Here too it is pathology that has led the way and informed us more fully of the normal course of attachment behavior in children.

IV

Since World War II, a very large number of studies have appeared which deal with the absence or rupture of human ties in infancy. There is strong evidence to indicate that either of these two conditions can produce certain disturbances in the later functioning of the child and can impair to varying degrees the capacity of the child to bind himself to human partners later in childhood. A number of these studies were carried out in infant institutions. Others followed children who had spent their infancy and early years in a succession of foster homes. In each of the studies that I shall refer to here, the constitutional adequacy of the baby at birth was established by objective tests. When control groups were employed, as they were in some of the studies, there was careful matching of the original family background. These investigations have been conducted by some of the most distinguished men and women working in child psychoanalysis, child psychiatry, and pediatrics—among them Anna Freud, Dorothy Burlingham, René Spitz, John Bowlby, William Goldfarb, Sally Provence, and Rose Lipton.

The institutional studies have enabled us to follow the development of babies who were reared without any possibility of establishing a human partnership. Typically, even in the best institutions, a baby is cared for by a corps of nurses and aides, and three such corps, working in shifts, have responsibility for large groups of babies in a ward.* The foster-home studies, on the other hand, together with studies of "separation effects," have enabled us to investigate a group of babies and young children who had known mothering and human partnerships at one or another period of early development and who suffered loss of the mother and often repeated separations from a succession of substitute mothers. In one set of studies, then, the groups of babies had in common the experience of no human partnerships; in the other, the babies had suffered ruptures of human ties in early development.

Within these two large groups the data from all studies confirm each other in these essential facts: children who have been deprived of mothering, and who have formed no personal human bonds during the first two years of life, show permanent impairment of the capacity to make human attachments in later childhood, even when substitute families are provided for them. The degree of impairment is roughly equivalent to the degree of deprivation. Thus, if one constructs a rating scale, with the institution studied by Spitz at the lowest end of the scale and the institution studied by Provence and Lipton at the other end of the scale, measurable differences may be discerned between the two groups of babies in their respective capacity to respond to human stimulation. But even in the "better" institution of the Provence and Lipton study, there is gross retardation in all areas of development when compared with a control group, and permanent effects in the kind and quality of human attachments demonstrated by these children in foster homes in later childhood. In the Spitz studies, the degree of deprivation in a hygienic and totally impersonal environment was so extreme that the babies deteriorated to the mental level of imbeciles at the end of the second year and showed no response to the appearance of a human figure. The motion picture made of these mute, solemn children, lying stuperous in their cribs, is one of the little-known horror films of our time.

As the number of studies has increased in recent years and

---

* We should carefully distinguish this kind of group care from that provided babies and young children in a *kibbutz*. The *kibbutz* baby has a mother and is usually breast-fed by her. Studies show that the *kibbutz* baby is attached to his mother and that the mother remains central in his early development. The group care of the *kibbutz* does not deprive the baby of mothering, whereas such deprivation is the crucial point of the studies I cite in this essay.

come to encompass more diverse populations and age groups, we have become able to see the "variables" at work here. (A "variable"—a monstrous term to use when one is speaking of human babies—signifies in this case the degree and kind of deprivation.) They can be tested in the following way. As we group the findings on all the follow-up studies it becomes clear that the *age* at which the child suffered deprivation of human ties is closely correlated to certain effects in later personality and the capacity to sustain human ties. For example, in some of the studies, children had suffered maternal deprivation or rupture of human connections at various stages in early childhood. As we sort out the data we see a convergence of signs showing that the period of greatest vulnerability with respect to later development is in the period under two years of life. When, for any reason, a child has spent the whole or a large part of his infancy in an environment that could not provide him with human partners or the conditions for sustained human attachments, the later development of this child demonstrates measurable effects in three areas: (1) Children thus deprived show varying degrees of impairment in the capacity to attach themselves to substitute parents or, in fact, to any persons. They seem to form their relationships on the basis of need and satisfaction of need (a characteristic of the infant's earliest relationship to the nurturing person). One "need-satisfying person" can substitute for another, quite independently of his personal qualities. (2) There is impairment of intellectual function during the first eighteen months of life which remains consistent in follow-up testing of these children. Specifically, it is conceptual thinking that remains depressed even when favorable environments are provided for such children in the second and third years of life. Language itself, which was grossly retarded in all the infant studies of these children, improves to some extent under more favorable environmental conditions but remains nevertheless an area of retardation. (3) Disorders of impulse control, particularly in the area of aggression, are reported in all follow-up studies of these children.

The significance of these findings goes far beyond the special case of infants reared in institutions or in a succession of foster homes. The institutional studies tell us how a baby develops in an environment that cannot provide a mother, or, in fact, any human partners. But there are many thousands of babies reared in pathological homes, who have, in effect, no mother and no significant human attachments during the first two years of life. A mother who is severely depressed, or a psychotic, or an addict, is also, for all practical purposes, a mother who is absent from her baby. A baby who is stored like a package with neighbors and relatives while his mother works may come to know as many indifferent caretakers as a baby in the lowest grade of institution and, at the age of one or two years, can resemble in all significant ways the emotionally deprived babies of such an institution.

V

The information available to us from all of these studies indicates that the period of human infancy is the critical period for the establishment of human bonds. From the evidence, it appears that a child who fails to make the vital human connections in infancy will have varying degrees of difficulty in making them in later childhood. In all of this there is an extraordinary correspondence with the findings of ethologists regarding the criticial period for attachments in animals.

If I now proceed to construct some parallels, I should also make some cautious discriminations between attachment behavior in human infancy and that in animals. The phenomenon of "imprinting," for example, which Lorenz describes, has no true equivalent in human infancy. When Lorenz hand-rears a gosling he elicits an attachment from the baby goose by producing the call notes of the mother goose. In effect he produces the code signal that releases an instinctual response. The unlocking of the instinctual code guarantees that the instinct will attach itself to *this* object, the producer of the signal. The registration of certain key characteristics of the object gives its own guarantees that this object and no other can elicit the specific instinctual response. From this point on, the baby gosling accepts Dr. Lorenz as its "mother"; the attachment of the baby animal to Lorenz is selective and permanent. The conditions favoring release of instinctual behavior are governed by a kind of biological timetable. In the case of attachment behavior, there is a critical period in the infancy of the animal that favors imprinting. Following this period the instinct wanes and the possibility of forming a new and permanent attachment ends.

It is not difficult to find analogies to this process in the attachment behavior of the human infant, but the process of forming human bonds is infinitely more complex. The development of attachment behavior in human infancy follows a biological pattern, but we have no true equivalents for "imprinting" because the function of memory in the first eighteen months of a human baby's life is far removed from the simple registrations of stimuli that take place in the baby animal. Yet even the marvelous and uniquely human achievements of cognitive development are dependent upon adequacy in instinctual gratification, for we can demonstrate through a large body of research that where need satisfaction is not adequate there will be impairment in memory and consequently in all the complex functions of human intelligence.

Similarly, there is no single moment in time in which the human infant—unlike the lower animals—makes his attachment to his mother. There is no single act or signal which elicits the permanent bond between infant and mother. Instead, we have an extended period in infancy for the development of attachment behavior and a sequential development that leads to the establishment of human bonds. By the time a baby is eight or nine months old he demonstrates his attachment by producing all of the characteristics that we identify as human love. He shows preference for his mother and wants repeated demonstrations of her love; he can only be conforted by his mother, he initiates games of affection with her, and he shows anxiety, distress, and even grief if a prolonged separation from her takes place.

I do not wish to give the impression that this process is so complex or hazardous that only extraordinary parents can produce a baby with strong human bonds. It is achieved regularly by ordinary parents with ordinary babies without benefit of psychiatric consultation. It requires no outstanding measures beyond satisfaction of a baby's biological needs in the early period of infancy through feeding, comfort in distress, and the provision of nutriments for sensory and motor experience—all of which are simply "givens" in a normal home. But above all it requires that there be human partners who become for the baby the embodiment of need satisfaction, comfort, and well-being. All of this, too, is normally given in ordinary families, without any reflection on the part of the parents that they are engaged in initiating a baby into the human fraternity.

Finally, where the attachment of a baby animal to its mother is guaranteed by interlocking messages and responses on an instinctual basis, we have no such instinctual code to guarantee the attachment of a human infant to his mother. This means, of course, that there are an infinite number of normal variations in patterns of mothering and great diversity in the mode of communication between baby and mother. Any of a vast number of variations in the pattern can be accommodated in the human baby's development and still ensure that a human bond will be achieved. The minimum guarantee for the evolution of the human bond is prolonged intimacy with a nurturing person, a condition that was once biologically insured through breast feeding. In the case of the bottle-fed baby, the insurance must be provided by the mother herself, who "builds in" the conditions for intimacy and continuity of the mothering experience. As bottle feeding has become common among all social groups in our society, continuity of the nurturing experience becomes more and more dependent upon the personality of the mother and environmental conditions that favor, or fail to favor, intimacy between the baby and his mother.

The bond which is ensured in a moment of time between a baby animal and its mother is, in the case of the human baby, the product of a complex sequential development, a process that evolves during the first eighteen months of life. The instinctual patterns are elicited through the human environment, but they do not take the form of instinctual release phenomena in terms of a code and its unlocking. What we see in the evolution of the human bond is a *language* between partners, a "dialogue," as Spitz puts it, in which messages from the infant are interpreted by his mother and messages from the mother are taken as signals by the baby. This early dialogue of "need" and "an answer to need," becomes a highly differentiated signal system in the early months of life; it is, properly speaking, the matrix of human language and of the human bond itself.

The dialogue begins with the cry that brings a human partner. Long before the human baby experiences the connection between his cry and the appearance of a human face, and long before he can use the cry as a signal, he must have had the experience in which the cry is "answered." Need and the expressive vocalization of need set up the dialogue between the baby and his human partners. Normally, too, there is a range of expressive signs in a baby's behavior which his mother interprets through her intimacy with him—the empty mouthing: "He's hungry"; fretful sounds: "He's cranky, he's ready for his nap"; a complaining sound: "He wants company"; arms extended: "He wants to be picked up." Sometimes the mother's interpretation may not be the correct one, but she has acted upon the baby's signal in some way, and this is the crucial point. The baby learns that his signals bring mother and bring need satisfaction in a specific or general way.

The institutional baby has no partner who is tuned in to his signals. As Provence and Lipton demonstrate in their institutional study, since there is no one to read the baby's signs there is finally no motive for producing signals. The expressive vocalizations drop out or appear undifferentiated in these babies. And long after they have been moved to homes with foster families, speech development remains impoverished.

The animal baby makes a selective response to his mother in the early hours of life, and distinguishes his mother from other members of the species. The human baby discovers the uniqueness of his mother in a succession of stages throughout the first year. How do we know this? Among other ways, through the study of the smiling response of the human infant. Our tribal greeting sign, the smile, undergoes a marvelous course of differentiation in the first year. Since the smile connotes "recognition," among other things, we may study differential smiling as one of the signs in the evolution of attachment behavior. In this way Peter Wolff of Harvard has found that the human baby in the third and fourth weeks of life will smile selectively in response to his mother's voice. Wolff can demonstrate experimentally that no other voice and no other sounds in the same frequency range will elicit the baby's smile. Wolff's finding should end the controversy over the "gas smile," and mothers who always disagreed with pediatricians on this score are thus vindicated in their wisdom.

At about eight weeks of age, the baby smiles in response to the human face. As René Spitz has demonstrated, the smile is elicited by the configuration of the upper half of the human face. A mask, representing eyes and forehead, will also elicit the baby's smile at this age. The baby of this age does not yet make a *visual* discrimination among his mother's face, other familiar faces, and strange faces. But between the age of six weeks and eight months the smile of the baby grows more and more selective, and at about eight months of age the baby demonstrates through his smile a clear discrimination of the mother's face from the faces of other familiar persons or the face of a stranger. Presented with a strange face at eight months, the baby will typically become solemn, quizzical, or unfriendly, and may even set up a howl. This means that a form of recognition memory for familiar faces has emerged in the infant. But in order that recognition memory appear, there must be thousands of repetitions in the presentation of certain faces, to produce the indelible tracing of *this* face with *these* characteristics, which can be later discriminated from all other faces with the general characteristic of the human face. This does not mean that a mother or other family members need to be constantly in the baby's perceptual field, it does not mean that, if someone else occasionally takes over the care of the baby, his memory capacity will be impaired. But it does mean that there must be one or more persons who remain central and stable in the early experience of the baby so that the conditions for early memory function be present. And it means, too, that such a central person must be associated with pleasure and need gratification because memory itself must be energized through the emotional import of experience. By the time a baby is eight months old, the mother is discriminated from all other persons, and the baby shows his need for her and his attachment to her by distress when she leaves him and by grief reactions when absence is prolonged beyond his tolerance. At this stage, when the mother has become the indispensable human partner, we can speak of love, and under all normal circumstances this love becomes a permanent bond, one that will embrace not only the mother but other human partners and, in a certain sense, the whole human fraternity.

The baby who is deprived of human partners can also be measured by his smile, or by the absence of a smile. If the human deprivation is extreme, no smile appears at any stage of infancy. In the institution studied by Provence and Lipton the babies smiled at the appearance of a human face, and while the smile was rarely joyful or rapturous, it was a smile. But whereas at a certain age babies normally discriminate among human faces by producing a *selective* smile, the institutional babies smiled indifferently at all comers. There was nothing in the last months of the first year or even in the second year to indicate that these babies discriminated among the various faces that presented themselves, nothing to indicate that one person was valued above other persons. There was no reaction to the disappearance or loss of any one person in this environment. In short, there was no attachment to any one person. And in this study, as in others, it was seen that even when families were found for these children in the second or third year of life there was a marked incapacity to bind themselves to any one person.

These were the same babies who showed a consistent type of

mental retardation in follow-up studies. In the areas of abstract thinking and generalization these children and, in fact, institutional babies in all studies, demonstrated marked impairment in later childhood. In ways that we still do not entirely understand, this disability in thinking is related to impoverishment in the structures that underlie memory in the first year of life. The diffusion and lack of focus in the early sense-experience of these infants, and the absence of significant human figures which normally register as the first mental traces, produce an unstable substratum for later and more complex mental acts.

The third generalization to be drawn from all these studies has to do with "impulse control," and specifically the control of aggression. From all reports, including those on the model institution directed and studied by Anna Freud and Dorothy Burlingham and the "good" institution investigated by Provence and Lipton, it emerges that such children show marked impulsivity, intolerance of frustration, and rages and tantrums far beyond the age in childhood where one would normally expect such behavior. Over twenty years ago Anna Freud drew the lesson from her institutional study that the problems of aggression in these children were due to the absence of intimate and stable love ties. Under the most favorable circumstances, the group care provided by the institution usually cannot produce durable love bonds in an infant. Everything we have learned since this sobering study by Anna Freud has confirmed her findings twice over.

And this brings us back full circle to Lorenz's study of aggression and the bond. The progressive modification of the aggressive drive takes place under the aegis of the love drives. Where there are no human bonds there is no motive for redirection, for the regulation and control of aggressive urges. The parallel with animal studies is exact.

VI

If we read our evidence correctly, the formation of the love bond takes place during human infancy. The later capacity of the ego to regulate the aggressive drive is very largely dependent upon the quality and the durability of these bonds. The absence of human bonds in infancy or the rupture of human bonds in early life can have permanent effects upon the later capacity for human attachments and for the regulation of aggression.

It would be a mistake, of course, to blame all human ills on failure in early nurture. There are other conditions in the course of human development which can affect the capacity to love and the regulation of drives. Yet, the implications of maternal deprivation studies are far-reaching and, if properly interpreted, carry their own prescription for the prevention of the diseases of non-attachment. As I see it, the full significance of the research on the diseases of non-attachment may be this: We have isolated a territory in which the diseases of non-attachment originate. These bondless men, women, and children constitute one of the largest aberrant populations in the world today, contributing far beyond their numbers to social disease and disorder. These are the people who are unable to fulfill the most ordinary human obligations in work, in friendship, in marriage, and in child-rearing. The condition of non-attachment leaves a void in their personality where conscience should be. Where there are no human attachments there can be no conscience. As a consequence, the hollow men and women contribute very largely to the criminal population. It is this group, too, that produces a particular kind of criminal, whose crimes, whether they be petty or atrocious, are always characterized by indifference. The potential for violence and destructive acts is far greater among these bondless men and women; the absence of human bonds leaves a free "unbound" aggression to pursue its erratic course.

The cure for such diseases is not simple. All of us in clinical work can testify to that. But, to a very large extent, the diseases of non-attachment can be eradicated at the source, by ensuring stable human partnerships for every baby. If we take the evidence seriously we must look upon a baby deprived of human partners as a baby in deadly peril. This is a baby who is being robbed of his humanity.

The Awful Idea of Being an Individual

CHARLES FRANKEL, Department of Philosophy
Columbia University, New York City

No doubt it is merely obstinacy on my part that leads me to ignore the standard approach to the theme that is about to occupy us. That theme is the nature, responsibilities, and prospects of the individual. The standard approach to this theme is to begin by announcing that the individual is in serious trouble. He has been uprooted by modern society, and debauched by modern culture; he has been softened by the modern State, and turned into an automaton by modern industry; he is loaded with responsibilities by modern democracy which he is incapable of bearing; and, as if all this were not enough, an international conspiracy is out to get him.

Having thus cheered everyone up, the standard approach goes on to place the blame for this state of affairs. Without fear or favor, it names the culprit. He is the individual. Conformist yet self-centered, alienated yet mindlessly absorbed in his materialistic pursuits, the individual sits by passively, so the story goes, refusing to accept his responsibility for the condition of the world. Then, having named the disease and identified the cause, the standard approach moves serenely to its conclusion. What is the purpose of all our blood, sweat, and tears? What is the *raison d'étre* for our economic system, our foreign policy, our hydrogen bombs? It is the preservation of the individual—this creature whose efficiency and intelligence, whose happy life and attractiveness and courage, the standard approach has been celebrating so persuasively.

I hope a kind interpretation will be placed on my decision not to employ this approach in discussing the individual and his prospects. It is not that I am unaware of its charms. The standard approach would allow me to demonstrate that I am not complacent, that I seek radical cures for radical disorders, and that, when the chips are down, I will not be stopped by respect for logic from stating on just which side of the fence I stand. Still, I am prepared to give up these advantages for the sake of discussing the much-mooted question of the individual in the modern world in what I think are more fruitful terms. Let us neither bury the individual nor praise him. Let us ask who he is, and why he should be alternately pitied as a victim of modern life, condemned as the source of our troubles, and glorified as the summit of creation.

It will help us to look at the question freshly, I think, if we start by noticing some of the ways in which we employ the concept of individuality.

Perhaps the first and simplest way is when we speak of "an individual" in the straightforward numerical sense of the term. This match and this match and this match are each individual matches, because each can be separately counted, and because, when counted, each adds the number 1 to the sum. And it is simply one of the characteristics of our ordinary experience that some things are identifiably separate from other things, and therefore separately countable, and that some things are not.

Thus, if you are asked to count the stars in the sky, you will know what is meant even though you may find that there are too many stars to count. But if you are asked to count the skies, you will merely be puzzled. You can count the drops of water falling from an eyedropper into a glass, but you cannot count the water in the glass. You can count the grains of sand in the desert, but you cannot count the heat you feel, though it is palpable and measurable. And most pertinent to our subject, you can count human beings. They come in physically separate bodies. No doubt, this is hardly arresting news. But if our world did not contain human individuals in this rudimentary sense of the term, we should certainly not be as concerned as we are about the moral and political ideal of individuality.

Still, this is, of course, only the barest beginning of what we mean when we speak of "an individual." Numerical individuality is not what we are talking about when we praise or condemn "the individual" or worry about the future of individualism. Slave traders no doubt counted their individual slaves; this did not mean that they recognized that their slaves were individuals. We also mean something else by "an individual." I shall call this the comparative meaning of the term.

Take two separate individuals, and one will be blond and the other red-haired, one will be thin, the other fat. It is a common fact of life that individuals, numerically speaking, are also different, qualitatively speaking. Compared to one another, each is singular not only because each counts for one but because each is odd. This is the second common way in which we use the term "individual." We use it when we wish to point to the fact that a man has special characteristics when compared to another man, or to other members of the group, or to a presumed average.

But now we come to those aspects of the idea of an individual which make it an idea that contains much more than meets the casual eye. For when we compare one thing to another, and decide, as a consequence, that we have an individual in front of us, we make this comparison only between things that seem to us to bear certain important resemblances to each other too. If we compared a man to a dog, for example, and called the man an individual because he refused to bark at the sight of a bone, this would call attention to our own singularity, not to his. On the other hand, when we compare two men and one barks at bones, he has shown a strikingly individual characteristic. In short, the idea of an individual is tacitly correlated, generally, to the idea of a type or a class.

Equally important, our recognition of individuals is also correlated to our notions of what is important—what makes a difference from the point of view of our practical, moral, or intellectual values. After all, if you take any two things, it is always possible to show that there is some respect in which they are alike and another respect in which they are different. Cabbages and kings both have circulatory systems; this blue-eyed, blond child is fifteen minutes younger than his blue-eyed, blond identical twin. The heart of the issue lies in what we consider a significant difference. This regular fellow, who perfectly echoes the opinions of all regular fellows and perfectly copies their dress and deportment, is no doubt at the same time one more little echo, one more perfect Xeroxed copy. He is, therefore, unquestionably an individual, numerically speaking. And since being an individual is highly regarded in all the best circles these days, he may put in a claim to be an individual in comparative terms as well, offering as evidence the fact that he has a wife named Isolde, a distinction that no other regular fellow shares. It is doubtful, however, that any of us would honor his claim to be an individual for this reason alone.

In speaking of individuals, in sum, a great deal normally depends on the particular system of classification and the particular scheme of values we choose to employ. And this brings us to the full-fledged use of the term "individual," to what is involved when we speak of "*the* individual" and of individualism. This might be called the systematic use of the term. If we want to know what we mean by an "individual" in other than a bare numerical sense, and in other than the simplest comparative sense, we must look not only to simple, observable physical facts but to something a little less innocent and a little more complex. We must look to a system of definitions and guiding principles. For what is individual, logically speaking, is opposed to what is general or universal. The specification of individuality, if it is more than mere numerical individuality, *is always relative to some particular system of general ideas.*

I do not make this point simply for its intrinsic interest. There is a moral to it. There is much talk these days, and much debate, about "creativity" and "conformity," about the respective merits of "self-expression" and "discipline," about the conflict between the demand for equality, on one side, and the rights of the individual, on the other. A good deal of this talk, on both sides of the fence, strikes me as vapid. For it makes very little sense, it conveys no information but only a conviction of piety, to speak of "the individual" *in vacuo*. To say that a man is an individual is to say that in some respects he does not fit the rules. But this tells us little about him unless we know what rules he does not fit; and it does not tell us what to think of his individuality, or whether to applaud or condemn it, unless we know what to think of these rules.

Thus, despite a good deal of sentimentality on the subject, "dissent" is not the name of an unqualified virtue. Dissent is a useful and necessary phase of inquiry, of social reform, and of the discovery of one's own individuality. Certainly, when there is nothing to be said for a belief except that it is generally believed, and nothing to be said for doing something except that the crowd is doing it, there are good reasons, judging from the experience of our species, to suspect that the belief is false and the practice discreditable. And yet there is no wholesale case for being a dissenter. Assent, not dissent, is the desirable action when the propositions before the mind are true, or the moral proposals under consideration good. Everything depends, in a word, on what the dissenter dissents from.

We come, then, to the heart of our question. Granted that we cannot understand what is meant by "an individual" in the systematic sense of the term unless we know the rules and values to which the idea is correlated, what, then, are the rules and values that give meaning to the special concept of "the individual" that has characterized Western society and the Western moral outlook—or has been said to characterize that society and outlook—in the modern world? For when we today speak of *"the* individual" we are not speaking of any old individual, but of a special type of man and a peculiar ideal of life; and not all individuals belong to this type, and fewer still exemplify the ideal.

The concept of the individual, as we have come to know and use it, is the product of a gigantic historical process of social disengagement. In this process, which has taken many centuries, and which is still going on—the process has only begun in many parts of the world—it came to be denied that the identity of any man could be fixed, or his rights and responsibilities assigned, simply in terms of his membership in any social group or any congeries of such groups. Family, village, craft, class, church, and sex, it came to be believed, told men something about who people were, and what their rights and opportunities should be; but these classifications did not tell everything. Men and women were no longer conceived as finding their *raison d'être* wholly as parts of the social procession, or merely as links in the great chain of mutual services and obligations. The doctrine of individualism came to insist, on the contrary, that their identities were more than could be fixed by any card of identity, more than could be caught by any system of classification. And the object of individualism as a social movement was to release men from irrevocable subservience to any group, and to give them some choice about their associations and obligations.

The concept of the individual, as it emerged in the modern world, thus denied principles for the governance of man that had long been accepted. It expressed a series of radical renunciations. The tests of pastoral approval or ancient authority were rejected in intellectual matters; established convention was declared irrelevant in the arts; birth and inherited privilege, it came to be thought, should no longer carry an immediate sanction in society; commands imposed from the outside came to be regarded as a very poor foundation for morality. And implicit in these rejections and denials, of course, there was a positive idea and ideal. It was the concept of the free, mobile individual, moving around from place to place, moving up or down in society as he had the chance, and retaining, as the one continuing thread of personal identity, through all these changes and choices, his judging mind, his feeling heart, his personal conscience—the judging mind of Descartes, the feeling heart of Rousseau, the personal conscience of Kant.

It is the ideal of an individual for whom the fundamental and continuing experience of life is the experience of choice, and of personal responsibility for one's choices. Individualism as an ideal, indeed, does not, when thoroughly understood, promise anything particularly comforting, like pleasure or happiness. It does not guarantee either pleasure or happiness as a reward for being an individual. It promises, for better and often for worse, only a heightened consciousness of one's own existence and character—only an intensification of experience, whatever the experience is.

The concept of *the* individual, then, is the concept not simply of numerical individuals but of individuals freed from any fore-ordained place or rank, and carrying with them fundamental guarantees of liberty and security, no matter where they are or with whom they deal. And the scheme of values on which this concept turns is a radically new one as the history of mankind goes. For the words that go with the concept of the individual are words like "doubt," "decision," and "choice." Above all, choice. Men discover their individual identities when they make a break with what they have been told, when they decide, despite the group, to go it alone. And if "doubt," "decision," and "choice" strike us as names for a miserable condition of life, then so much the worse for us. For there is no getting around the fact that the thought of being an individual, when its full force dawns on one, is a rather formidable and frightening thought.

What are the prospects of this ideal of the individual? What are the prospects for preserving and producing people who rather enjoy the awful idea of being an individual? I do not have a crystal ball. The future of the individual depends on many different things. I would say, however, that among these many things three seem to me peculiarly decisive. The first is a proper estimate of the meaning of contemporary tendencies of change in industry, government, science, and administration. The second is the development of a morality relevant to the special contexts that have been created in our society for individual behavior. And the third is the degree to which we can learn to make our peace with the idea of individuality, and properly to appraise the responsibilities that go with it.

As to the significance of contemporary changes, it is very commonly believed that the growth of our society, the organization of work around assembly lines and inside bureaucracies, the advent of the mass media, and the leveling effects, so called, of democratic institutions and the Welfare State, have all condemned the individual to a relatively quick, though not quite painless, death. With respect to these tendencies, I would not say, with the infant bug in *Pogo* who ran for President, that everything is just fine. But apocalyptic views concerning the inevitable consequences of these tendencies are not justified. Specialization, cities, the growth of skills, the higher levels of education needed in modern societies, the opening of opportunities and, lest it be forgotten, the replacement of routine work by machines provide conditions for the larger realization of individuality if we wish to use them in that way. There is no guarantee that we will; but those who mourn the inevitable death of the individual, it seems to me, are often merely complaining that the burdens that go with being an individual—the doubts, the choices, the work, the need for imagination—are very great. That is true enough, but individuals have never been made except by bearing these burdens.

A willingness to bear such burdens, however, is naturally dependent on a conception of what these burdens are. And it is true that the context for action by individuals today has largely changed. Increasingly, the man who would make a difference in the world has to work through large organizations, bureaucratically organized. In such organizations it is sometimes hard to recognize one's own contribution; and it is enormously difficult to move such organizations, to produce changes in them against the sheer force of their inertia. Most difficult and troublesome of all, when a man works in a large organization he is under dual directives. He has a responsibility to live by the bureaucratic discipline, to respect the organization's rules or the society's reasons for having him in the position he fills; but he also has a responsibility to look beyond his position, to take the measure of what he is doing, and to think and judge for himself. The proper balancing of these dual claims upon the individual is the recurrent, and perhaps most characteristic, moral problem of our day.

In facing this problem, however, it will help to recognize that there is almost certainly no formula that will solve it in a wholesale way. The recognition that it exists, the awareness on the part of the individual in a large organization that there are, after all, two sides to his obligations, is, indeed, a very large part of what is needed to deal with it. Moreover, in its essentials, the problem, it seems to me, is simply part of a difficult process of education in which the Western community has been engaged for some centuries. It is continuous with the problem of transforming the character of moral reflection and moral imagination that has been with us since the advent of the ideal of the free, mobile individual.

Individualism registers the fact that relations between people have become fluid and subject to change. It registers the fact that the loyalties and obligations of human beings, because the ties of kinship, neighborhood, and personal association are all looser, are likely to be more impersonal, more abstract. And in consequence, in place of the particular loyalties and the string of personal obligations that constitute morality in traditional societies, it substitutes a critical and reflective morality, appealing to abstract principles like conscience, to general standards like utility, to disinterested and universally oriented feelings like the sentiment of humanity. The problem of bureaucratic morality is a part and product of such developments, and has to be solved in such terms. And it is because, in general, the moral problems of an individualistic social order are problems of this abstract sort that so heavy a burden falls on our capacities to educate and to communicate. Men are not likely to recognize their responsibilities immediately or intuitively in a world like ours. These responsibilities need to be dramatized for the most conscientious of us, and they need to be analyzed and weighed if we can make any claim to conscientiousness at all.

But what are these responsibilities—the responsibilities that go with individuality? Obviously, there is no official, unchanging list. But certain responsibilities do appear to be basic and to provide a cue to the rest. One, a prerequisite to all the others, is the responsibility to respect the rights, the individuality, of others. A second is to recognize, as we have come increasingly to recognize over the past generation, that there is a great difference between an abstract right to be free and individual and the effective power to exercise that right. It is one thing to have a legal right to work, think, or live as one wishes. It is another thing to have the resources, the information, the associations and the education to do so. An active regard for the rights of others, a concern that these rights be used and enjoyed, entails a concern to create conditions in which these others have the opportunity to be themselves and to choose their way of life. Individualism, in a word, needs conscious social organization and support—the provision of education, the creation of diverse opportunities, and the provision of the elementary economic securities requisite for the fulfillment of the individual's design of life. It is a mistake to imagine, in fact, that classic individualism denied the dependence of the free individual on social groups; it merely opposed his being irrevocably bound down to any group. We lean on one another, we have always leaned on one another, whether we are individuals or not.

Individualism, indeed, has always been associated with the ideal of equality of opportunity. Opportunity to do what? In the end, there is only one fundamental opportunity that seems to me to matter; all other opportunities are merely conditions for it. It is the opportunity to live the kind of life one wants. But this opportunity is not something that is simply given to most men. It has to be created for them. Once they have it, they may misuse it or ignore it. That is their business. But doubts about the validity of individualism as a moral ideal, doubts that most men will know what to do with it or that they really want it, are, to say the least, premature. Most men have not yet had a chance to try individualism under circumstances that might constitute a fair test.

The Urban Crisis and the Search for Identity

HOWARD E. MITCHELL
Professor of Urbanism and Human Resources
University of Pennsylvania, Philadelphia

"Confronted by the 'New Negro,' the white man finds himself in a confused and ambiguous position. The 'New Negro' is already a relatively complicated human being. His mentality has adapted to the times and to city life. He is not afraid to compete freely with the white man, and, above all, he intends to succeed in life at all costs."[1]

The above description may well fit the young black of the urban ghetto in the United States in the late sixties. Instead, the author, Florestan Fernandes, is writing about the situation of the Negro or mulatto in the city of São Paulo, Brazil. His statement

From *Social Casework,* 50: 10–15, 1969.
[1] Florestan Fernandes, The Weight of the Past, *Daedalus,* 96:574 (Spring 1967).

calls attention to the fact that there are certain universals in black-white relationships that transcend national boundaries in western cultures. Indeed some scholars have traced the problem to its historical origins and suggest that Caucasians have always regarded those unlike themselves as exotic, different, and strange.[2] Fernandes' description of the Negro in São Paulo today also suggests that a reciprocal relationship exists between the "new" Negro and the white man's perception of him.

The thesis of this article is that one of the most striking manifestations of urban change and stress upon minorities is seen in the current impact on the Negro and his search for identity. The search for identity is not only intimately related to how the Negro is perceived by the white man but also implies that the white man must himself seek a new identity vis-à-vis the Negro. The weight of the years of slavery and subsequent history should require no further documentation to make the point that the white people needed to keep the poor Negroes in an inferior status to enhance their own image. L. D. Reddick, for example, points out that an early film showing the Negro Jack Johnson knocking out the white ex-champion Jim Jeffries was frequently banned because it was so disturbing to white audiences.[3] Moreover, Reddick states, it was also disturbing to many Negroes who had been saturated with Sambo and Rastus characterizations.

Drawing loosely upon a medical model, urban America in regard to race relations may be viewed as a chronically ill patient. During the late sixties the patient, suffering from a long-standing "urban condition," has been wheeled into the operating room. The surgical team has exposed the patient's dynamically diseased system. Onlookers in the surgical amphitheater are divided in opinion as to whether the interrelated diseased organs—one black and one white—should be treated or the patient should be sewed up and sent home, despite the fact that his initial symptoms have not abated and will not abate of their own accord. The members of the surgical team are neither spiritually nor morally ready for the task before them. The use of operating procedures is primarily dictated by the

[2] See Harry Hoetink, *The Two Variants in Caribbean Race Relations* (Oxford University Press, New York, 1967).

[3] L. D. Reddick, Educational Programs for the Improvement of Race Relations: Motion Pictures, Radio, the Press and Libraries, *The Journal of Negro Education,* 13:370 (Summer 1944).

availability of advanced technology and not by humane consideration or conscience.

Some observers on the fringe of the audience are vocal about
what needs to be done. Disturbing the cool rationality of the operating room, they advocate the simple separation of the larger, white
organ from the smaller, black organ and the strengthening of each
in its self-contained way. The majority thinks there is something
gestalt-like about the diseased system, but expresses its view in low
whispers. The entire system, according to the majority, is at a stage
of growth at which anything that affects one organ intimately
affects the other.

CRISIS AND OPPORTUNITY

Unquestionably our society faces a critical period in race relations.
At the same time, however, the crisis provides an opportunity to get
at the core problem of the urban condition, which is basically the
result of technological change. Not only in America but also
throughout the world man is more mobile and knows more about his
environment and the world of others than he did in earlier times.
Great numbers of the people of Asia, Africa, and the urban slum
have become aware of life beyond the boundaries of their current
living situation. Moreover, the new industrial technology and widespread urbanization compel the youth in all cultures to prepare
themselves with new skills to face novel situations. In an American
society that values achievement, an increasingly high priority is
placed on the educational passport to a recently automated job. The
school dropout who follows the Horatio Alger script to a successful
career in the American marketplace is becoming a rarity. The
dropout is not necessarily doomed to unemployment, however.
According to a recent report of the National Commission on Technology, Automation, and Economic Progress, minimal education is
not in itself a cause of unemployment; it determines *when* a man
will get a job. The commission views the labor market as "a gigantic
'shape up,' with members of the labor force queued in order of their
relative attractiveness. . . . The total number employed and unemployed depends primarily on the general state of economic activity."[4]

[4] *Technology and the American Economy*, Vol. 1, report of the National
Commission on Technology, Automation, and Economic Progress (U.S. Government Printing Office, Washington, D.C., February 1966), 23.

During an earlier crisis—the Great Depression of the thirties—the Negro made significant gains in his fight for first-class citizenship. He benefited from the efforts of the New Deal's collectivistic welfare state to replace outmoded individualism. In the post-World War II era legislative action, championed by civil rights groups and supported by the courts and government action, sought to intervene by means of politically inspired programs to create a Great Society as instantaneously as possible. The reality of the use of power in a less than perfect democracy was that most of the programs aimed at equalizing opportunities and curing the urban condition followed a strange logic. For example, after May 17, 1954, when the United States Supreme Court ruled on the desegregation of schools, a rational approach would have suggested that integration be attempted first in the most educationally advantaged and economically secure populations and regions of the country. Instead, initial emphasis was placed on the gradual desegregation of the schools attended by poor whites and Negroes in the Deep South. Logical thinking that would have dictated setting a successful precedent among the more highly educated whites and blacks in selected northern communities did not prevail. If such communities were not ready for black and white children to share an educational experience, it is unlikely that low-income southern communities and school systems were ready. In fact at that stage of needed urban educational change, most northern urban school districts were still blatantly denying prevalent conditions of *de facto* segregation. In both North and South, a vast difference was revealed between the legalization of desegregation and its actualization.

The young black person growing up in the impoverished urban ghetto of the post-World War II period experienced the impact of the desegregation struggle. He came to appreciate the fact that if he was to get a job, he had to leave the blighted area in which he had been forced to live and in which he had been undereducated in schools of poorer quality than those in middle-income, predominantly white residential communities.[5] Even more frequently than his elders, he had to leave the neighborhood to find work, because many traditional places of employment had moved to the suburbs. Often he sought employment or recreation by moving within the

[5] See James S. Coleman and others, *Equality of Educational Opportunity* (U.S. Department of Health, Education, and Welfare, Washington, D.C., 1966); and U.S. Commission on Civil Rights, *Racial Isolation in the Public Schools* (U.S. Government Printing Office, Washington, D.C., 1967).

collective strength of the neighborhood gang to strange "turf." The possession of an automobile became essential to the ghetto youth, partly because it was part of the American dream and partly because he had been taught little about the use of transportation in the urban system. Confronted by a situation very different from that faced by the immigrants from Europe during the first part of the twentieth century, these newest immigrants to the cities—Negroes and Puerto Ricans in the East and Mexican-Americans in the West —found that not only middle-income and wealthy people had fled to the suburbs for a variety of reasons but so also had many public and private institutions. When industry moved out along the urban expressways and federally subsidized freeways because of tax incentives, better access, greater parking facilities, and higher quality schools for the children of its work force, many churches and other public and private institutions moved as well.

Adding insult to injury, many upwardly mobile white citizens, commenting on the condition of the most recent urban immigrants, declare, "Those people must first pull themselves up by their bootstraps as we did." They overlook the fact that when hyphenated Americans flocked to our shores in the late nineteenth and early twentieth centuries institutions were created to assist the immigrants in their acculturation and development. The recent Black Power thrust in many Negro communities may be interpreted as the Negro's self-determined effort to create his own institutions because public and private institutions and services have largely been unresponsive to his needs.

QUEST FOR A NEW IMAGE

Perhaps more because of communication media than any other technological or social phenomena, the Negro has become aware of the other world and the unequal distribution of the rewards of power in American society. The Negro college youth who participated in the sit-ins at Greensboro, North Carolina, in the middle fifties and the masses of Negro youth in the ghettos of Watts, Hough, South Chicago, or Harlem today all recognize they live in a new world. The demands of that new world are different, and meeting the demands requires a new image of the self. The old image with which the Negro was confronted in textbook, mass media, employment, housing, and conversation is passing. Thus, in the midst of the rapid state of transition in our industrialized, urbanized society, the Negro American is in search of a new image.

The search is articulated in arguments for self-determination, Black Power, the importance of "soul," and identification with Afro-American culture and history. Just as the post-World War I period heightened the tempo of living for Negro Americans and brought about "The Negro Renaissance"—articulated in the poems of Langston Hughes and Countee Cullen, the philosophy of Alain Locke, and the blues and jazz creations of scores of Negro musicians—the fifties and sixties mark another stage in the Negro's search for his individual and collective identity.

Often the search for identity is awkwardly conducted. James Q. Wilson points out that Black Power—"like any movement among persons who are becoming politically self-conscious, whether here or in 'developing nations'—will produce its full measure of confusion, disorder, and demagoguery."[6] Moreover, some militant leaders put forward arguments of questionable scientific validity. There is question, for example, concerning the long-range advisability of using the mark of oppression, skin color, as the symbol of advancement and status. The astute student of the identity process Erik H. Erikson indicates the danger of "an inner regrouping of imagery, almost a *negative conversion*, by which erstwhile negative identity elements become totally dominant. . . ."[7] Erikson, interestingly, is referring to the similarity in this respect of the operation of the identity process in post-Versailles German youth and in the youth of today who are attracted to such militant groups as the Black Muslims. Erikson notes that the German youth—

once so sensitive to foreign critique, but then on the rebound from a love of *Kultur* which promised no realistic identity, fell for the Nazi transvaluation of civilized values. The transitory Nazi identity, however, based as it was on a *totalism* marked by the radical *exclusion* of foreignness and especially Jewishness, failed to integrate the rich identity elements of Germanness, reaching instead for a pseudologic pervasion of history. Obviously both radical segregationism, with its burning crosses, and Black Muslimism are the counterparts of such a phenomenon in this country.[8]

[6] James Q. Wilson, The Urban Unease: Community vs. City, *The Public Interest*, 12:38 (Summer 1968).

[7] Erik H. Erikson, *Identity: Youth and Crisis* (W. W. Norton and Co., New York, 1968), 313.

[8] Erikson, *Identity* . . . , 313.

America, Erikson writes, has never been hospitable to totalistic turns, and he suggests, as an alternative to an exclusive totalism—

the wholeness of a *more inclusive identity*. What *historical actuality* can the Negro American count on and what wider identity will permit him to be self-certain as a Negro (or a descendant of Negroes) *and* integrated as an American? For we must know that when all the *realities* are classified and investigated, and all the studies assessed, the question remains: what are the historical actualities that a developing identity can count on?[9]

I share Erikson's impatience with persons who equate the term identity with the question Who am I?

The pertinent question, if it can be put into the first person at all, would be, "What do I want to make of myself, and what do I have to work with?" But such awareness of inner motivations is at best useful in replacing infantile wishes and adolescent fancies with realistic goals. Beyond that, only a restored or better-trained sense of historical actuality can lead to a deployment of those energies which both activate and are activated by potential developments.[10]

Many "culturally deprived" Negro youths are currently demonstrating how their potentialities for development become historical fact in the brave and dignified way they meet sudden historical demands. Robert Coles, the psychiatrist, directs attention to the unexpected strength of Negro children undergoing the strains of integration into Southern all-white schools.[11]

RESOLUTION OF THE URBAN CONDITION

The philosopher William T. Fontaine recalls that W. E. B. DuBois concerned himself with the same problem in his early, well-received work *The Souls of Black Folk*. Fontaine states that DuBois especially concerned himself with the self in terms of the value standards used in its evaluation, its biological and cultural aspects, and the relation of these to the ambivalent life Negroes must lead in

[9] Erikson, *Identity* . . . , 314.
[10] Erikson, *Identity* . . . , 314.
[11] Robert Coles, *Children of Crisis: A Study of Courage and Fear* (Little, Brown and Co., Boston, 1964).

America.[12] The problem for the American Negro has been that he possesses a "double consciousness," one aspect of which is dominated by the value standards of the larger, white culture and the other dominated by the black subculture. DuBois anticipated Ralph Ellison and James Baldwin in demanding the liberation of an identity. He concludes that there is need to reexamine and make a comparative valuation of the two value standards. DuBois argued sharply that the Negro does not come empty-handed seeking equality; he possesses values that need to be added to the American culture. Might not our country "replace her brutal, arbitrary blundering with light-hearted but determined Negro humility? Is there not a need for 'simple faith' in this 'dusty desert of dollars and smartness'?"[13]

DuBois, in an early stage, wrote as if this might all come about as a rational process. It is now known, however, that the resolution of racism is not easy, since the basis of racism is largely irrational. In fact Fontaine muses that DuBois probably did his writing as he rode the Jim Crow car to Nashville. "And he must ride this way, if he is to ride at all because the white man has the power. It is not Truth, but power that makes things good, bad, right, wrong, beautiful, ugly. When a group attains a position of power, value, as an intrinsic property, attaches to its position. And as far as the comparative worth of the powerful and the weak is concerned, the powerful create the kind of social order they want, and the weak can but adjust and conform to the mold."[14]

Most of the gains made by the Negro in the labor movement of the New Deal, in the armed services, and from his own efforts have followed the same pattern. Deliberate action to benefit Negroes has been taken only when it was profitable for the policy-makers. Fontaine remarks that Franklin D. Roosevelt was spoken of as "the patrician as opportunist. . . . The record shows that, in every case, he recognized that the times were propitious for removing certain restrictions of segregation."[15]

The tactics and timing of the past are no longer adequate. Young black radicals incite the young to forget the American dream of equality for all, and the young are vulnerable to such appeals

[12] William T. Fontaine, *Reflections on Segregation, Desegregation, Power and Morals* (Charles C Thomas, Springfield, Illinois, 1967), 9.
[13] Fontaine, *Reflections* . . . , 12.
[14] Fontaine, *Reflections* . . . , 13.
[15] Fontaine, *Reflections* . . . , 103.

because they have become deeply cynical as a result of their cumulative deprivation. They are ready to risk the confrontation of Black Power and White Power extremists. Their readiness leads, however, to an escalation of hostilities between racists in both groups and threatens to transform our democratic society into a police state. But it must be remembered that all Americans are participants in this drama and not merely those directly involved in the contest. When white Americans withdraw support from the civil rights movement at the first cry of Black Power and self-defense by violent means, they are not taking a neutral position. Inaction in this regard is not a form of action, but it is often reactionary. To condemn Black Power and not oppose white supremacy is playing into the hands of both black and white radicals. That is not to say that the violence promoted by some Black Power militants is not to be repudiated. Clearly the white person is required to make fine discriminations in order to understand the Negro's struggle.[16]

The novelist Ralph Ellison remarks:

For one thing, the oversimplified and very often unfortunate slogans which are advanced in the civil rights movement act as slogans always do. Why do we demand that terrible, encyclopedic nuances be found in the slogans of the civil rights movement? No slogans have ever had that kind of complexity. They would not be slogans if they did. The other thing is that part of the struggle . . . has always been not to get away from the Negro community, but to have the right to discover what one wanted on the outside and what one could conveniently get rid of on the inside. That seems to me very American. I think it is one of the assumptions which is implicit in a pluralistic society, and I see no particular reason for people to be upset by the possibility that we are actually going to achieve it.[17]

CONCLUSION

If a pluralistic American community is to be achieved, it will be in the cities, where historically the great social changes take place. The resolution of the "urban condition" requires not only that the black American seeks a new identity but that the white American also seeks a new identity. Both affluent and nonaffluent youth, black and

[16] See Aaron Wildavsky, The Empty-head Blues: Black Rebellion and White Reaction, *The Public Interest*, 11:3–16 (Spring 1968).

[17] Transcript of the American Academy Conference on the Negro American, May 14–15, 1965, *Daedalus*, 95: 408–09 (Winter 1966).

white, are in the forefront of this quest. They seem to be saying that they want equal access to the privileges and the responsibilities of American society. They seem to be saying that they want the right to determine their destiny more fully. The affluent white youth and the impoverished black youth of the urban slum resent the constraints imposed on them in their separate communities. At the same time technology in the form of greater informational inputs and the more diverse cultural contacts that accompany increased mobility maximize the opportunities for choices and voluntary contacts. Our youths appear to be telling us that they have been handicapped during their socialization and that they want to lose their old identities as quickly as possible and develop new identities that will equip them to make better judgments in our visual, mobile urban society. They are ready to fight for equality and participation both on the university campus and in the ghetto streets. Negro youths have something special to demonstrate to white youths in this respect. As Talcott Parsons points out, the Negro group in this society, more than any other group, has been on a special mission—as a symbolic carrier of the value of equality.

Insofar as the mission is internally successful, it will be established as a collective entity which has made a contribution of the first order to what I think . . . is one of the crucial problems of American society. The problem is not a Negro problem, but a general problem: the sense of what the necessary and appropriate meaning of equality is in this society. I think that this is altogether adequate ground on which to establish a highly valued collective identity, in which others may participate, but which is especially the Negro identity.[18]

Such an achievement is critically needed for the recovery and survival of our urban "patient" and for our increasing involvement with and leadership in the nonwhite world.

[18] Transcript . . . , 411.

Ideals and Values in Adjustment

There is much to trigger thought processes in Broudy's treatment of "Art, Science, and New Values." This is not because one must agree or disagree with the positions which the author takes but because he raises a number of issues and because there is plenty of opportunity to accede or to question. The editors, for example, would agree that there is a "surfeit of freedom" and that there is more than we "know how or are willing to use." We would agree further that "the power and freedom we have lost is not always identical with the power and freedom we have gained." But we would question, at least to the point of clarification, that "the power we have lost" is the individual power to shape our own destiny. For power abounds in our world and there are more opportunities than ever for an individual to amplify his own personal impact. Technology and the explosion of knowledge furnish the means; and the unprecedented masses of one's fellows provide that his efforts will not go unnoticed, that his efforts will affect many.

We, too, see a shift of freedom, but it is from a previous freedom of physical movement to an exponential increase in the freedom of the intellect. Here there is nothing so restricting as ignorance; and we are doubling the fund of human knowledge about every ten years. The frontier of today lies in the realm of ideas and this well may present more challenge, more power, and more freedom to those who can move with it than any of the borders we have broken through in the past. Conformity in thinking can only recreate the conventional and maintain what already exists. This culture is committed to go beyond the bounds of the now possible. It has, it must, and it will permit individuality and freedom to an unprecedented degree.

Change constantly is increasing in momentum and magnitude. Those beliefs and values which once furnished a basis for psychological security and a guide for moral behavior no longer are invested with the permanence they once had. It is no longer possible to predict and to structure tomorrow on the basis of yesterday. According to psychiatrist Halleck, the generation gap is a product of this. For today's youth, an irrelevant past and an unpredictable future leave only the experience and the relationships of the present which can be depended upon.

According to Halleck the rapidity of change puts a premium on flexibility. He recognizes that it is not easy to be flexible and committed at the same time. Yet it appears this must be done if living is to combine progress and growth with reason and purpose. This is not an "either-or" situation. The attitudes of all generations are needed. Surely one cannot live in the past or for the future without missing much of what life now has to offer. Just as surely, he cannot allow immediate gratification to become his sole reason for living. For there will be a tomorrow. If we are not to repeat and add to today's mistakes, we had better look to tomorrow and our responsibility for shaping it.

Buhler lends emphasis to the concept that ideals and values, rather than technology and materialism, are what give meaning to life. She seem to us to be saying that the generation gap is perennial—not just a phenomenon of these times. The gap consists of the absence of relatedness to others. And this absence, paradoxically, is within us— a lack of something to give, a lack of sufficient worth to be able to share with others. Self-doubt, says Buhler, is not a function of age, i.e., adulthood or adolescence. Doubt can begin at any time—and may be overcome, endured, or intensified.

It was not our plan to find articles that emphasized

a theme but those which seemed to have most meaning kept emphasizing one: Freedom and responsibility are inseparable; pain and joy are inseparable aspects of learning and being. Buhler suggests that Europeans, more than Americans, know the phenomenon of polarity. In the United States, no matter how miserable we feel, we say, "Fine, just fine," when someone politely inquires. Fortunately, Buhler not only describes but she prescribes. The unhealthy predominance of loneliness, the devastating aspect of loneliness can be controverted by learning, at an early age, to describe one's feelings and to be honest about them. This may become, she hopes, a recognized adjunct to education. (See also the article by Carl R. Rogers on page 576.)

Previous articles have mentioned the necessity for and the difficulty of making decisions. Buhler says that decisions create loneliness—it means that one is becoming himself, is separating himself from the herd. And a final point of interest is that, in the conclusion, Buhler makes a brand new point that is only implied in the main article.

Elsewhere in these readings the editors have made the points that the solving of one problem almost inevitably raises other questions which clamor for solution. They emphasize that the process of gaining answers—because it can be reapplied—is more important in the long run than any specific solution. This is important because effective living is largely a problem solving process. People rarely are content for long with what they have and what they know. Because the process of gaining answers serves to expand knowledge, increase awareness and open new possibilities, it is never-ending. While solutions may be generated in an additive manner, new problems tend to increase exponentially. Pressing problems of the seventies will be replaced by other concerns in the eighties.

The editors are struck by the necessity for changes in human attitudes and the relative ineffectiveness of economics and technology without these. They do not expect readers to agree on the priorities but they do hope the necessity and power for action will be personalized beyond the "vested interests" and "technology" mentioned by Heilbronner. The answers concern each of us. It is futile to wave the responsibility aside by ascribing it to someone else or by falling back on the old cliche, "Whatever will be, will be." We can afford no longer to let the future happen by accident.

Art, Science, and New Values

HARRY S. BROUDY
Professor of Philosophy of Education
University of Illinois

There is a familiar saying to the effect that our troubles multiply as our statistics improve. Crime, insanity, and sin in general are blown up—to use a photographic term made notorious by a recent film— by our instant communication systems. We are forced to become conscious of evil and ugliness that our grandfathers were able to keep *sub rosa* and probably subconscious. In those days, it seems, sin and crime and evil could be confined to ghettos of one kind or another, and gentlewomen could be sequestered from them, at least until discreet accounts appeared in genteel novels appropriate to their age, station, and sensibility.

If we are consciously preoccupied with evil and violence, it is not because we choose to be; there simply is no escape from it, not under the mask of decorum, nor under the lid that suppresses the id. It is as if a huge chain of department stores operated by Lucifer flooded us with a stream of unwanted merchandise; as if *Walpurgis-nacht* were being staged nightly on our front lawn without so much as a by-your-leave.

I find it impossible to reassure myself that our troubles are caused by nothing more than our increased awareness of them. For one thing, the world is fuller of people than ever before; so absolutely, not merely relatively, there is more likelihood of suicide, divorce, and crimes of violence, including the apparently senseless ones. Furthermore, the closer people are packed together, the more delicately constructed and tuned the social machine must be if they are to live without abrading each other. There is little evidence that our social institutions or our individual dispositions have achieved the quality needed to cope with the increased density of men and events.

But all this and numerous other symbols and symptoms of social trouble are familiar to you. Also there is general agreement as to the cause of the trouble: a value breakdown variously described by sociologists, psychologists, the undertaker school of theologians,

From *Phi Delta Kappan*, 49: 115–119, 1967.

and artists. There is no need to add to these outpourings, but I shall venture a hypothesis—which there is no time to argue—as to why so much of the protest is so repetitive, so sincere, and so ineffectual. We seem to be in the grip of something like a muscular spasm in which antagonistic muscles keep a limb rigid and its owner in impotent agony. Most of our protest literature is seized by a spasm caused by trying to hold to two antagonistic doctrines at the same time. One is that our ills result from our inability or unwillingness to face reality. The other is that there is no way of distinguishing reality from illusion. How, then, is one to know what attitude to take toward black power, red-necks, purple hawks, and off-white doves? Are they reality or masks for reality?

The scapegoat of this spasm is the middle-class value syndrome, whatever that is construed to be. But is it the values that make the middle-class objectionable or is it the holding of them by the middle class that makes the values bad? How embarrassing this situation can be is illustrated by the predicament of the public schools. We are to redeem the disadvantaged, but not presumably by imposing middle-class values and demands upon them. But if one asks in what way the disadvantaged are disadvantaged, we are told they lack the means to achieve what seems suspiciously like middle-class values. Now I think that one can with some consistency hold that class is the criterion of value, as I believe the Marxists do. Or one can maintain that there is a criterion that transcends class and cultural peculiarities. Finally, one can hold to a denial of all value criteria. This is a kind of nihilism, and I take it that some of the protestors profess it. If so, they are chargeable not so much with logical inconsistency as with social ingratitude. For to live in society at all is to live off the common store of Nature's gifts and human labor, and to draw on this store while rejecting the means of maintaining it is a selfishness which issues from a kind of social stupidity. Nihilism, to succeed, must become a club from which most of mankind must be excluded.

So I take the view that the talk about the death of God—the real issue is not whether He is dead, but rather whether He was ever alive—and the more sensational rejection of all value norms is a kind of romantic shock treatment aimed at foolish complacency, mindless for courage in their time. Neither the young nor the old can reject the generic virtues, for this is not a matter of choice at all. We refuse cruelty, and muted humanity. This has been solemnized by Existentialists of varying degrees of seriousness and intellectual competence, and it has been exploited by publishers, film makers, and other suppliers of the adolescent market.

My own experience with students has included a number of informal inquiries in trying to ascertain what they really love and hate, and what they would do if the freedom they demand were really given to them. I can only report that only on the most rare occasions have they been willing to accept real liberty to shape their own studies or their lives—especially when the price of liberty was accountability for the wrong choices. I have found that young people—even the wildest protestors—do not reject honesty, decency, kindness, justice, dignity of the person, yes, even chastity. On the contrary, the protests are justified in the name of these virtues. The young do not say, "Down with courage"; rather, they are puzzled and angered by what passes to let anyone reject them, even if he says he does, because these are the rules of eligibility for membership in the human family. If creatures—on whatever planet we should happen to find them—are really insensitive to these virtues or values, we would simply classify them as nonhuman and treat them accordingly.

The young have the right to expect that the behavioral meanings of the generic invariant virtues be made clear by the elders of their epoch; they have a right to expect an education that will allow them to learn, explore, and appraise these behavioral forms; they have a right to expect from the learned men of their times enlightenment and guidance in the exploration of the new values.

SCIENCE A SOURCE FOR NEW VALUES

I shall suggest that if we shift the usual focus of our demands from science and the arts a bit we may get answers that will not make it necessary to seek our salvation in contrived happenings, exotic drugs, and dazed surrender to incoherent messages and subtle "massages." I shall argue that science and science-based technology are not merely the source of nonmoral, amoral, or immoral means. On the contrary, I shall invite your consideration of the notion that science is a source for new values, i.e., for the new behavioral forms of the old virtues. Conversely, I shall argue that the arts are not merely the celebrations of values to which we are already committed, and that even though art may need no other excuse for being, it nevertheless is a great instrument for the achievement of whatever values we do espouse. Indeed, without art we do not really perceive the value of anything, for art gives value a perceptible shape and makes it a candidate for imaginative appropriation. In short, I invite you to consider seriously the possibility that science is not our only source of means and the arts our only source of ends.

If the field of our moral obligation is constituted by the value possibilities that we cannot refuse to realize or try to realize, scientifically based technology is the most dynamic single factor in determining the scope of our possible duty. Every time new power is put into our hands, a shift in the moral economy occurs because it changes the domain of what we *can* do, out of which emerges the domain of what we *ought* to do.

It now looks as if the natural scientists with complicated assists from technologists have removed "impossibility" as a valid ground of exculpation in such matters as race discrimination, peace, and social justice. Delaying actions, counsels of moderation, linguistic evasions are, therefore, seen ever more clearly for what they are. The brighter the youth, the more clearly do they see, and the quicker their indignation. Indeed, we must resign ourselves to forfeiting moral credit even when we do move in the right direction, for it is difficult to distinguish, for example, which factors in our current war on poverty and inequality are altruistic and which are motivated by the shrewd realization that if our economy is to leap forever from strength to strength, it cannot afford pockets of poverty and ignorance. When humanitarian deeds are economically necessary and politically expedient, virtue runs rampant. As between a good society and no society the choice requires little moral heroism.

Since one is never obligated to do the impossible, and since all that is possible is not necessarily obligatory, the value quest is more than a search for means to given ends. Both ends and means are transformed by expansions and contractions in the spheres of possibility. For example, the fight against cancer and vaccination for smallpox were not objects of moral obligation for Socrates, but they are for us. The abolition of poverty, overpopulation, pollution of air and water, and the abatement of ignorance are all matters of our obligation, because the power is clearly available for their accomplishment. Once technology makes social justice possible, we cannot get by with good intentions.

So, oddly enough, in an age that complains of constraint by

vast bureaucratic concentrations of power snarled in red tape, there is really a surfeit of freedom, more by far than we know how or are willing to use. The paradox, however, is dissolved rather simply. The power and freedom we have lost is not always identical with the power and freedom we have gained. For the power we have gained is likely to take the form of collective, corporate power, entailing on our part not only a will to use it, but also a will to unite with others in using it. Much of the power we have lost is the individual power to shape our own destiny, whether it be in our economic, political, or social life.

The shift is traumatic in at least two ways. First, it renounces the image of the moral quest as the slaying of dragons by heroes. It means the devaluation of the moral agent in the traditional sense. The scenario of the good life as a series of donations to worthy causes, memberships in diverse uplifting organizations, and endless attendance at committee meetings is neither dramatic nor exciting. Second, it shakes rudely, rapidly, and repeatedly our convictions as to what we ought to do and want. Conventional morality ceases to be the reliable flywheel of daily life. To be and to remain moral requires moral intelligence, an almost daily reassessment of resources; in short, a nondramatic strenuousness. As we shall see later, the commitments men make are ruled as much, if not more, by aesthetic fitness than logical cogency or even practical efficiency. The Greeks' imagination outran possibility, so they conjured up a set of specialized gods to make up the difference. Our possibilities have outrun our imagination, and we look to the artists to conjure up images of life that would make these possibilities aesthetically interesting and some irresistible.

The responses to this situation are about what one might expect. Middle-aged citizens go through the motions of donating, belonging, and attending, but half-heartedly, for they long for the days when the moral life was an individual encounter between heroes and villains. They have learned that it is vain and naïve to try to fix the responsibility for misdeeds, whether committed on one's automobile or on the state treasury, but that there is no culprit they will not believe to their dying day. They try to understand it all, they endure much, but they forgive nothing.

The half-hearted virtue of the middle-aged is almost correctly diagnosed by the young as complacency, indifference, hypocrisy, and perhaps even cowardice. This, I believe, lies at the root of the more spectacular protests of Sartre, Genet, and the off-Broadway theatre. It lies at the root of the explosive resentment of some of our students—and some of our best students, at that. To them the undramatic mechanics of democratic action is equated with the conventional morality of the middle class, obfuscated by statistics and made corny by sentimentality. They cannot find their identity or reality in it. They feel that a more dramatic, a more dangerous gesture alone will prove their reality and presumably their honesty —to be thrown in jail for civil rights, to shock one's parents, to disgust the community. Even the avant-garde have not apparently gotten beyond the belief that without a hair shirt the claim to moral integrity is a fraud. To those who have found such a shirt, it often becomes a Linus blanket. Integrity without a hair shirt, or more correctly, one with the hair on the inside of our own skin, is a deeper and more serious moral assignment than either the old or the new guard realizes. The proper face of internal suffering may be quite different from what some of our contemporary critics think it is, but art has not yet come up with the new face.

THE MORAL MEANINGS OF SEX

I shall discuss sexual behavior as one example of the transvaluation of values made necessary by science-technology, because of all the acts in our physiological repertoire, none is so intense in its demands and rewards, and yet, for the individual if not the race, so postponable. It thus comes under the dominion of choice and morality. Further, because it is involved with life-giving and life-sustaining, church, state, and family are inordinately concerned with the most private of intimacies. And in modern times, at least, it has become inextricably woven with romance, glamour, status, and sanity.

But once science made it reliably possible to sever the bond between sex and life-giving, the moral meanings of sexual behavior had to be redefined, for it released the sexual act from a great part of its burden of social consequences. The moral dimension of sex now has to be sought more in personal relations and individual character rather than in social consequences. Sex morality is now personal rather than tribal.

The easy evasion of pregnancy has made it possible to reduce the domain of moral responsibility in the personal domain also. The James Bond or Playboy philosophy of sex is not so implausible, if the human context of sex is reduced to the hedonic and aesthetic properties of *love-making*. (Note that one *makes* it.) Can the human context be reduced so radically? The evidence of civilized society seems to be against it. We cannot refrain from humanizing even the most obviously physiological functions: eating becomes dining just as lust, before we know it, turns into love and romance. Birth and death have been ritualized no end; other physiological functions such as digestion and elimination have defied human sublimation, so we devote our efforts to keeping them out of sight and conversation. When these and other vegetative functions get out of kilter to the point where life or death depends solely on them, we are at the nadir of humanness. Surgeons and nurses, in doing what they must under these circumstances, make short shrift of personal dignity. Because civilization consists pretty largely of transforming physiological necessities into human possibilities, science, in making it possible to demoralize sex, does not make it more plausible that we shall use the new freedom to do so. On the contrary, the new sexual freedom can be used not to demoralize sex but to moralize it far more profoundly than was heretofore possible, once the human relationships that sex engenders become objects of choice rather than forced upon us by biological accidents or the fear of them. Sex relationships become a challenge to integration with all other values, and, above all, a challenge to be consonant with the type of personality one has chosen to become.

But how does one bring about this reflected choice unless the experience is there to be reflected upon? And how does one control the consequences of such experiences so that they remain developmental rather than destructive? What social institutions have we developed for this form of character development? Lacking appropriate institutions—for the ones we have are predicated on equating sex with reproduction—our adolescents have coped with the situation in a clumsy way. Sometimes they establish Bohemian regions within cities or on the unofficial spaces of the campus. Sometimes they leave home for the anonymity and freedom of the city. But by and large it is technology in the form of the automobile and contraceptive devices that furnish the means of escape from parental surveillance, albeit not from guilt feelings.

These solutions are satisfactory to nobody, and I suggest that art has yet to come up with a life style that satisfactorily embodies the new value possibilities in sexual relations. The James Bond and Playboy images are bids in that direction, but they exemplify the demoralization of sex rather than its new moralization. No new life style for the contemporaneous woman has yet emerged. The roles of wife, prostitute, and casual companion we are familiar with, but a variety of free-spirited heroines served up by current fiction and film must still be classified as the probings of art to find such a new form.

REINTERPRETING PATRIOTISM, COURAGE, HEROISM

We are in a similar state with respect to war and aggression. Technology has made war logically obsolete and cooperation a moral and practical imperative. Technology has depersonalized and thereby demoralized war, and this has created a need for the reinterpretation of such notions as patriotism, courage, and heroism. These virtues historically have been defined by the exigencies of wars fought by heroes against villains. If war is no longer justifiable, what becomes of these virtues?

Three wars in which the United States has participated in the last 50 years have failed to turn up a convincing heroic life style for the soldier. The glory of battle has been displaced by a dreary resignation to endure what could not be cured. The Vietnam affair is the last stage of disillusionment with military service even among those who do not seek to avoid it. That art has been unable to glorify the modern soldier is a better sign of the bankruptcy of war than any logical argument.

For we do not really lack moral equivalents of war—we have dozens of them, ranging from the conquest of disease to the conquest of injustice, but these all entail peaceful cooperation, which aesthetically is poor stuff, difficult to dramatize. Drama demands personified conflict and danger and publicity. The hero must be sung and glorified. He must overcome real villains. But as I have already mentioned, it is difficult to do poems or paintings about peace and democracy if one is to remain true to their pedestrian complexity. Yet until the new forms of heroism—heroism of an inner, humbler, and deeper sort—are made perceptible to the imagination by art, the moral equivalents of war will not displace war itself.

Science cannot of itself determine the shape of the concrete life styles that can embody the value potentials it creates. For one thing, any number of life patterns could serve as embodiments of the new values or value ideals. Furthermore, science cannot shape ideals out of the possibilities it describes. For an ideal is more than a possibility; it is also a command to take some possibility seriously enough to manifest it. This imperative germinates within the person when a sensuous model of the good seduces him into an irresistible desire to imitate it. But which image will so charm him we cannot even guess. Why the images of Greece and Rome inflamed the youth of the Renaissance to almost ridiculous forms of emulation is hard to say even after it happened; it was impossible to predict it before it happened.

RESPONSIBILITIES OF THE ARTIST

Where do these models come from? First, from the people around us, but when the rate of social change is high, we get a generational gap, and the young cease to look for life models in the population over 30. Yet at best real people are hard to idealize; they forever betray their reality. The inspirational values of biography (especially if truthful) are, I believe, overestimated. The really influential personalities—Socrates, Jesus, Gandhi—are outsize figures, and until their behavior transcends the limits of common sense they do not serve as effective models. But it is precisely their carrying out of an ideal literally and to extremes that gives their lives a dramatic quality, i.e., makes them suitable for the artistic imagination. Once the myth-making power of the artist fixes on the hero's life as a nucleus, it selects those features of his life that enhance the deviations, and so the hero becomes a legend, a remote but powerful object of imitation. Folk art or popular art, not to speak of Madison Avenue, is forever engaged in the same sort of model building; one wonders how many American men's lives were affected by the 150 or so variants of the Horatio Alger hero. The break in the perceptual habits of the common man demanded by contemporary serious art has, for a time at least, lowered the direct influence of the serious artist, and it is the James Bond, the hippie, the Playboy that tend to shape the aspirations of the adolescent—of whatever chronological age.

The advances in communication technology which have mushroomed the effect of commercial art create a moral responsibility for the educator to narrow the gap between the mass public and the serious contemporary artist. It is encouraging to note that the recent surge of courses variously called the humanities, aesthetic education, and the allied arts in the high school is not abating, and, with luck, aesthetic literacy for the vast majority of our people may be more than a hopeless wish. The fact that serious art is now in fashion, that paintings are being stolen from museums, and that the great mass media magazines feel safe in devoting space to the arts are other good signs. Finally, although government support of the arts creates problems, it recognizes officially the role of serious art in the culture.

Just as the history of science furnishes the great exemplars of our intellectual achievement, so the history of the arts furnish great exemplars of the value commitments of the great epochs of the past. Because adventitious, capricious, and local variations are sifted by history into oblivion, the surviving masterpieces represent the invariants of the human quest—the generic powers of man's intellect and imagination. But it is to contemporary art that we must look for early signs of what is wrong with reality, for the signs that old behavioral forms are no longer suitable, and it is to the artist that we look for the new bottles fit to hold the new wine that science is continually producing. How does art do this?

We touch here upon the great mystique of art. Somehow the early artistic instincts of the people have never lost their potency. The first clue that something is wrong with the world is a sense of aesthetic incongruity. For example, the account of the death of John F. Kennedy given by the Warren Report may have been factually correct, but aesthetically it was an outrage. So great an effect aesthetically demands an appropriate cause with plots and world-shaking personalities for dramatic plausibility. This inveterate susceptibility of man to the aesthetic categories gives art great power, and therefore great responsibility, a responsibility from which serious art understandably but vainly has tried to rid itself.

Yet neither the artist nor the scientist as artist and scientist can be true to himself if he tries to make his science or his art serve the moral quest. To saddle scientists and artists with the task of the educator and reformer is a mistake, and efforts to promote dialogue between them for this purpose or to turn them into political scientists are misguided. If they are any good in thinking about Vietnam or the racial problem, it is not by virtue of their scientific or artistic accomplishments, but by virtue of their general education and the happy circumstances that enabled them to cultivate their human capacities for thought and feeling.

No, the scientist as scientist must exploit science, and the artist as artist must exploit his imaginative impulses to create shapes of life and feeling. The exploration of these possibilities for life is the task of all of us insofar as we are cultivated human beings. Furnishing the contents and forms of thought that bring men to this state of cultivation is the first task of general education.

In closing, I can only reiterate that in these times of trouble not all shouts of alienation, lostness, and meaninglessness are equally significant. For the virtues that define humanity can give us direction and purpose and significance and identity, if we stop making believe that we no longer believe in them. Our moral sphere is enlarged not destroyed, for our power is far greater than our will to use it. This is neither a cheap nor easy optimism, for we have yet to find and define a life form that will make the new heroism, the new courage, the new temperance, the new justice both morally edifying and aesthetically seductive. Thousands of our fellow human beings see no hope of realizing these value potentials and the proper human stance for them is despair—quiet despair, shrieking despair, violent despair, tragic despair. But shouts of despair for mankind on the part of those who have not strained even half of their nerves to do what can be done, who claim to have lost identities they never toiled to establish, who are defiant without risk—this is a comic despair, for it is as if a drowning man roars for help and is rescued by a brigade of life guards—in two feet of water.

Why They'd Rather Do Their Own Thing
SEYMOUR L. HALLECK
Professor of Psychiatry
University of Wisconsin

On either side of today's generation gap, the young and the old often see each other as guided by opposite values. Each group insists that his own value system is the right one. Students insist that their parents' values are misguided and out of date. Their

Reprinted by permission from *Think* Magazine, 34: 3–7, September–October, 1968. Published by IBM, copyright 1968 by International Business Machines Corporation.

parents fear that youth either lack values or are adopting new ones that are unwholesome.

How much do student values differ from their parents'?

The most striking change in student value systems is in the direction of values which lead to immediate gratification. Students today have little reverence for the past and little hope for the future. They are trying to live in the present.

The most important reason for this is the ever-increasing rate of change which characterizes our society. When no one can predict what the world will be like in 20, 10 or even 5 years, man must alter his psychological perspectives. The lessons of the past become less relevant; planning for the future appears futile. One is driven to gear his value systems toward enjoyment of the present.

Financial success and competitive striving for success have a revered place in the American value system—the person who devotes himself to the long-term struggle for acquisition of status and goods will be rewarded in the future. Where the future is unpredictable, however, such values lose meaning. Youth who are in the process of preparing themselves for adult roles are more likely to appreciate the uncertainty of the future than their parents. Consider, for example, the different perspectives of a mother and son in discussing the boy's prospects as a physician. The mother sees a doctor as a scientist and helper, one who does good works within the community and is rewarded with prestige and money. The son, however, is aware that by the time he spends 12 years training to become a medical specialist the nature of medical practice will hardly resemble what it is today. If he has hopes of using medicine as a vehicle for satisfying his needs for personal interaction with people, he may become uncomfortable at the thought that medicine of the future may be highly scientific and impersonal. Medicine may not, of course, go in such directions, but no one can really tell him in which direction it will go. One can consider almost any profession in a similar manner.

"YOU GOT ME, DAD"

The differences in perspectives of the generations is beautifully illustrated in *The Graduate,* a film in which the main character is "a little worried about his future." When he is angrily asked by his father, "What did I send you to college for?" the graduate replies, "You got me, Dad." I am told when this scene is viewed by student audiences they break out into wild cheers. When I saw the movie with a much older audience, the reaction was one of dismay. The graduate's remarks poignantly reflect the differing perspectives of the generations. Youth are no lazier, no more hedonistic or passive than their parents. Rather, conditions do not favor future-oriented values, and youth are being forced into the role of the "now" generation.

This, perhaps, is one reason why college students tend to downgrade the acquisition of property, why they are unimpressed and sometimes even contemptuous of it. Recruiters for industrial firms on our campuses are learning that some of the best students are not interested in business careers. Few young people can view a life that is dedicated to trade and the acquisition of wealth as meaningful. Some conservative adults fear that this new devaluation of capitalistic enterprise represents a shift to communistic or socialistic philosophies. This fear seems exaggerated. Acquisition of capital is a rational enterprise only when there is some reason to believe that it will have the same usefulness in the future as it does in the present. When this is not true the amount of self-expenditure involved in obtaining capital seems wasted.

The rejection of material values may account for certain kinds of selective stealing on the part of college students. It is probably true that more students than ever engage in shoplifting. This behavior is usually rationalized by the argument that big companies are too impersonal to be affected by minor pilfering and that since property is not very important anyway, there is no harm done in taking some of it away from those who have too much. Surprisingly, no large organization, even those created by students themselves, is immune: at the University of Wisconsin a new student cooperative is in danger of going out of business because of shoplifting.

As reverence for property has diminished, youth have come to value the intrinsic worth of human relationships. There is an emphasis on being rather than doing. Youth are preoccupied with the need for being good people who can form good relationships. Whether they are more capable than their parents of finding such relationships is debatable, but their commitment to the search for intimacy is indisputable. A "beautiful" person, in the vernacular of today's youth, is not one who is physically attractive or one who has the personal qualities that guarantee success. He is an individual who has the capacity to relate openly and warmly with others.

In focusing upon one another's personal worth, youth have emphasized the development of their innate potentialities. Unwilling to evaluate themselves by the measure of what they can produce or sustain, they focus on the process of creativity and its appreciation. The attractiveness of psychedelic drugs may be related to this new emphasis. By altering the state of their own consciousness many students hope to find new truth and power—creativity—by looking inward. But in using such drugs they also demonstrate their lack of conviction that they can shape the world and are searching for a strength and constancy within an unreal inner world.

INCREASING SKEPTICISM

Not only creative activities but also intellectual pursuits are increasingly valued as ends rather than means. This change has important ramifications for our educational system. Adults are accustomed to thinking of education as a means to success and progress. Since these values do not have the same meaning to youth, they are skeptical of the practical benefits of learning. They tend to see education as an end in itself, something to be enjoyed, even worshiped as a noble activity of man. There is much emphasis on doing away with the competitive aspects of education, with the regimentation and emphasis on grading that has served to produce citizens who would easily fit into an industrial society. Nothing enrages students more than the feeling that they are being processed to take their place in a competitive society rather than being educated to become better people.

It can be argued that youth's rejection of some of the values of the Protestant ethic or of capitalism is a result of newfound affluence and leisure. It is probably true that those who have been raised in an affluent world do not find it easy to appreciate the value of sacrifice and hard work. Yet, while affluence seems to play some role in reinforcing an emphasis on "nowness" it is also true that all classes of youth, even those who have been raised in poverty, show similar characteristics. Poor and oppressed youth may still be committed to finding a place in this capitalistic system, but even among them the rumblings of discontent with our society seem to be related to more than their inability to share in our affluence. They, too, seem to be showing an increasing skepticism toward hope and planning.

The rate of change in our society also seems to make youth more aware of the problems of commitment and fidelity. Earlier generations resolved this ambivalence by institutionalizing their commitments. Only 20 years ago the young college man's obligations to his family, his career and his community were clearly defined. Today, young people talk about the need for fidelity and at the same time emphasize the philosophy of "doing your own thing and being responsible to no one but oneself." The problem here is that while an orientation toward life in the present is more likely to increase concern with human values, it also puts a premium on flexibility. It is not easy to be flexible and committed at the same time. When the future is uncertain, one must travel lightly, must be wary of how he invests his emotional energy and must be ready to move on when there is change. Where "coolness" and intimacy are valued concurrently there exists a situation of conflict which produces a variety of unpleasant emotional reactions.

Social change influences other values, including society's attitude toward change itself. Throughout history youth have always been more open to change than their elders. There are natural reasons for this. As one grows older, his commitments to others encourage him to hold onto his position in life by supporting the status quo.

Youth today, as in the past, seem to revere change but they are also peculiarly wary of it. They are highly indignant of injustices perpetrated by the status quo. Nevertheless, in their uncertainties as to the future they have difficulty in coming up with the long-term plans for change. The New Left can propose few alternatives to our present society and can only speak of tearing it down.

A second major shift in the value systems of today's youth is also related to changes in society, particularly to the impact of new communications media. The rearing of children requires a certain degree of protectivenss and even deception; if children were prematurely exposed to information about the harsh realities of life they simply could not tolerate it. But the new media deluge today's youth with information. Children learn the cynical truths of life at a very young age. They can sense when parents and other authority figures are mildly deceptive and know when those in authority are outright deceitful or hypocritical. No institution—family, church, the university or even the law—can any longer hide behind dogma or tradition.

One of the things that is happening in every society exposed to new technology and new media, is that young people are vigorously questioning whatever arbitrary structure is imposed upon them. When students begin to perceive what is so often a weak intellectual base for behavioral demands made upon them, they become angry and rebellious. Simple answers such as, "We should do it this way because it is right," or "because we have always done it this way," will no longer satisfy them. It is futile to demand that young people bring more order into their lives unless the merits of such order can be persuasively described.

EXCESSIVE FREEDOM, EMOTIONAL CHAOS

At the moment, youth's capacity to decipher the inconsistencies and hypocrisies of the older generation has led them to adopt some rather extreme value positions with regard to the issue of freedom. Young people place increasing emphasis on the virtues of a structureless world and many seem convinced that total freedom from the dictates of authority would be an ideal existence.

This new emphasis on freedom is not without emotional consequences. Even the most rebellious student is still dominated by certain dependency needs which create an almost automatic drive toward obedience. Furthermore, as I shall attempt to elaborate later, structure and the need to rely on the wisdom or strength of others seems to be an innate human need. There comes a point when too much freedom, particularly freedom to choose from an almost unlimited set of alternatives, becomes incapacitating and paralyzing. In the struggle for autonomy some youths seem to achieve a premature or pseudomature autonomy which does not satisfy their needs, and tends to breed emotional chaos.

Another aspect of value change related to the impact of media has to do with the issue of self-revelation. In a world where deception can be easily exposed and where youth have seen so many of their faithful beliefs ruthlessly destroyed, there is a tendency to value openness in interpersonal relationships. Many of today's youth are quite willing to reveal themselves. They will talk openly of things that would have shamed their elders.

TOLERANCE AND MORALITY

A final aspect of value change related to the impact of media has to do with the issue of power. Youth are keenly aware of the capacity of the establishment to oppress others. They are also sensitive to what is often an irrational basis by which established power justifies its tenure. Students are learning they can diminish certain oppressions in their own life by attacking what often turns out to be a highly vulnerable and surprisingly defenseless authority.

Sometimes value differences between generations cannot be phrased in terms of direct conflict. Both adults and students, for example, advocate racial and ethnic tolerance. Yet, youth are probably more capabe of adhering to this value than their parents. An adult would be more likely to limit his advocacy of tolerance when that value began to interfere with other values such as stability, status or wealth. In other situations, what appears to be a value conflict between generations is in reality an argument over which generation is more honest in its pursuit of values.

In emphasizing personal values and good relationships youth tend to maintain that they are more concerned with the needs of mankind and more compassionate than their parents. It is probably true that young people raised in a world which has been perceptually shrunk by the new media do have a great awareness of the plight of their oppressed fellows. Yet, it is rare to see this awareness translated into calls for action. The percentage of young people who are prepared to sacrifice comforts in order to help their fellowman is not overwhelming. I doubt that compassion either as a value or as an actuality is an exclusive possession of any generation. In this regard we must be aware of the existence of contradictory value systems among youth. While some are talking about the brotherhood of man, others are talking about the need for individual values and the importance of putting individual needs ahead of society's.

If we consider the values of adhering to principle versus willingness to compromise, we again find little change but much criticism between generations. Both parents and students at times accuse one another of being unwilling to adhere to principle. Both accuse one another of being unable to compromise. Students accuse parents of "selling out" for personal gain. Adults accuse students of being unwilling to compromise their idealism in the face of the realities of existence. Students accuse adults of blind adherence to irrational causes, an accusation particularly relevant to the war in Vietnam; most students see it as a conflict perpetuated by an adult generation unwilling to compromise ill-founded and destructive principles.

Is there a value crisis in American life today? In my opinion we are moving toward a crisis related to the manner in which values are generated and maintained in a changing world. As old values are attacked we are not creating new ones to replace them. There is a real danger that values of any kind may be losing their power, that young people in particular may find themselves existing in a value-less world. There may be an inherent rightness in doing away with traditional values that seem irrational and cannot be justified. Yet, if such values are indiscriminately destroyed before they are re-placed by more rational values, our society will experience an unprecedented degree of chaos.

Those who are entrusted with the teaching of values in our society—educators, theologians, law enforcement officers and parents—seem totally unprepared to move from dogmatic to rational presentation of value systems. As their authority is threatened, some resort to preaching and exhortation rather than to reflection. Our youth respond by despair and viodence.

Our society has an obvious need for a value system based on rational efforts to enhance the well-being of man. Such a system must recognize man's biological needs. It must be practical enough to provide answers as to how men can live together in peace and stability. Finally, it must recognize that certain values at times have to be institutionalized if for no other reason than to provide stability during periods of intensive change.

SOME VALUES TO LIVE BY

It is presumptuous for anyone, including a psychiatrist, to attempt to tell other people how they should live. Yet I am convinced if one is concerned with other people's health and happiness he can find only so many guidelines by emphasizing adjustment or adaptation to what is. I do not believe that man can go on adjusting to chang-ing conditions of our world and still be man. If there is to be a healthy society of the future we must search for positive values which transcend the nature of the immediate environment. No one can present a value system that is relevant to all men in all ages. I believe, however, that we know enough to at least try to describe certain basic guidelines.

• There is ample scientific evidence that without some capacity to share strong feelings of affection with another person it is not possible to lead a happy or useful life. Most varieties of mental illness and many physical ailments may be traced directly to feelings that one is not receiving enough affection. This condition arises when man lacks the capacity to relate himself intimately to others. Any society then must come to value intimacy or love. Closely related to this is the value of compassion. Man is a unique animal insofar as he is able to identify with the feelings of others. He needs to feel a sense of community, to identify himself as a member of a society in which he is not a bystander.

• A second value is openness to experience. I use this expression in a broad sense to include the ability to seek and evaluate without prejudice the wide variety of experience possible within the limits of one's commitment to others. Openness to experience means openness to change and personal growth. This includes the capacity to be aware of oneself. A person cannot be fully aware of the world unless he has some capacity to understand the manner in which he perceives that world. Self-understanding also implies being at ease with one's past. The healthy man cannot live wholly in the present nor can he base his existence on future rewards.

• A third value is the ability to find an optimum amount of freedom. Although man needs to love others and rely on others if he is to survive, he must also be able to experience his distinctiveness. When man sacrifices autonomy or freedom he finds a certain amount of comfort, but this is always at the expense of adopting the role of the lesser being, someone not quite as good as others.

• Because man is the only animal who is physically and psychologically helpless for a large part of his young life, he learns to rely on structure and authority as a prerequisite to comfort. Whatever tendency he might have to outgrow this need is thwarted by his appreciation of the imminence of his own death. Man is the only animal who comprehends his own mortality and he cannot live with this knowledge without belief in some power that transcends his own. For some individuals belief in a supreme being suffices. Others sustain themselves through belief in the perfectibility of man. In either case, man must have an ideology that he can value.

• Man also has an innate need to interact with his environment and alter it in a manner which provides him with a sense of mastery. It is not crucial how he gains mastery. He may find it in daily work, in organized play or in efforts to create new art, music or literature. What is important is that man must to some extent be active and must experience his activity as either having an impact on other people or as having the capacity to alter his physical surroundings.

• On a pragmatic basis it would seem obvious that we must come to value order. Man can tolerate only so much change without experiencing his existence as chaotic. I am not speaking of change which relieves oppression and injustice. Such change is obviously useful. Changes brought about by scientific and technological progress, however, need to be rigorously scrutinized and controlled. A reverence for progress (except for that progress which directly contributes toward making man a better human being as opposed to making him a more comfortable human being) must be replaced by a valuation of stability.

• Another value which is probably more correctly based on pragmatism than biology is the capacity to assume responsibility for one's own behavior. Adherence to this value provides dignity for the individual and stability for the group. It is the belief in this capacity to lead a responsible life which allows a man to experience himself as a unique animal who has some choice in his own destiny. He who denies responsibility for his actions or thoughts cannot be free since he must live as though he were governed by uncontrollable forces.

• Another pragmatic value is honesty, the willingness to avoid deceiving oneself or others and the willingness to search for truth. Men could lead dishonest lives and survive with comfort. Yet almost any philosophy concerned with the betterment of man advocates the honest life. While there is much disagreement as to the content of the truth, few individuals—young or old—would argue with the contention that he who deceives himself or others is leading an inadequate life.

• The events of the past months have convincingly demonstrated our society's urgent need to find a way of inculcating the value of nonviolence in our people. Because man is an aggressive animal it will no doubt be necessary to resort to institutionalized, even programmed methods of forcing real acceptance of this value. It seems to me we have no other choice.

• Finally, every society must find the means of revering their elderly members. When aging means being less respected, less powerful and less relevant to this society, there can never be any joyous anticipation of the future. The question of how we can find some means of evaluating older members of our community may ultimately be the most illuminating issue in our quest to understand student values in a changing world.

THE PRICE OF WISDOM

The calamity of modern existence is that the world changes so fast that there is little likelihood that the old will continue to remain very much wiser than the young. In this regard it is distressing to note how few young Americans can identify one older American whom they deeply admire.

As the old become relatively less wise, their influence is maintained primarily by the acquisition of political and economic power. The values which they pass onto the young are then more likely to be shaped by institution and custom than by their understanding of actual human needs. I have previously described how youth are increasingly capable of recognizing the arbitrary nature of power and values which are imposed upon them by their elders. It is likely that they will continue to use their new knowledge militantly to search for more rational values and for more pragmatic divisions of power. But even as they attack the adult world they become trapped in destroying themselves. For if they make their parents irrelevant they will surely make themselves irrelevant.

In drifting into a youth-oriented culture we have ignored the teachings of philosophers who have since the time of Plato emphasized the need to revere maturity. We are often told that our youth are our future. Yet, unless we can create a world which offers the possibility of aging with grace, honor and meaningfulness, no one can look forward to the future.

Loneliness in Maturity

CHARLOTTE BUHLER
Assistant Clinical Professor of Psychiatry
Medical School, University of Southern California

In *Camino Real,* a play by Tennesee Williams (1964), the character Don Quixote says: "Loneliness, loneliness—when so many are lonely as seem to be lonely, it would be inexcusably selfish to be lonely alone."

Of course, it is improbable that the real Don Quixote would have expressed this thought because it is only in this century that people have become so consciously aware of individual loneliness—man's existential loneliness. Clark Moustakas (1961), in his excellent little book, distinguishes *existential loneliness* as an inevitable part of human experience from another type of loneliness, namely that of *self-alienation* or *self-rejection.*

Moustakas, May (1953) and others emphasize strongly modern man's alienation. Moustakas says,

The separation of self from others and from nature constitutes the primary condition of loneliness anxiety in modern societies. The unhappiness, misery, fakery, pretense, the surface meetings, the failure to find genuine human contact often result in a fear and dread of loneliness.

But he also knows and says:

Strange as it may seem, the individual in being lonely, if let be, will realize himself in loneliness and create a bond or sense of fundamental relatedness with others. Loneliness expands the individual's wholeness, perceptiveness, sensitivity, and humanity. It enables the person to realize human ties and awarenesses hitherto unknown.

This means that modern man's awareness of his aloneness as an individual in this world makes him more aware and appreciative of human relationships.

It is this normal, i.e., non-neurotic, aspect of loneliness that I wish to discuss.

The word *loneliness,* as Melanie Allen pointed out in a

From *Journal of Humanistic Psychology,* 9: 167–181, 1969.

thoughtful historical study, does not appear in either the ancient literature or, strangely enough, in that of the Middle Ages (Allen, 1968). Instead, the word used is *aloneness*. Apart from the fact that semantics is probably a factor, especially in translations, I would not eliminate the possibility that in earlier times people may have felt longing—in addition to the feeling of loneliness and implied by the feeling of aloneness—a feeling that nobody else was with them and a feeling that then might have led to many other experiences like the feeling of being forsaken, of being bereaved, of being without help or of not belonging.

From the time of the Romanticism, the word *loneliness* is used often in literature. Although loneliness is usually expressed with respect to the social being of a person, Goethe in *The sorrows of Werther* (1774) relates loneliness to *existence*. "It is becoming certain to me," Werther says, "certain and ever more certain, that little importance attaches to the existence of any being, very little."

From then on, with the increasing mechanization of our lives and with the increasing awareness of the immensity of the Universe, as well as with the increasing awareness of the separateness and solitude of our individual existences—with all this the agony over our loneliness as human beings deepened.

Many of us are no longer convinced that there is somebody in this Universe to turn to who will hear our prayers, and no longer are we sure that as individuals we matter. There is a strange contradiction, I always think, between the immense importance we inwardly give to ourselves as individuals, and the complete insignificance seen from the outside we seem to have as individuals.

These considerations make it clear that our present feelings about loneliness belong to our present culture and its kind of existential awareness. While the earth is very much, as Hannah Arendt (1958) points out in her brilliant essay, "the quintessence of the human condition," our present feelings of solitude seem so much more desperate because of the possible objective meaninglessness of our existence.

THE DEVELOPMENT OF IDENTITY AND LONELINESS

This problem of the meaning of our existence begins to haunt the thoughtful adolescent, and though formerly appeased by churches and the community of believers, may now follow the thinking person all through his life. It may culminate in the terrifying realization of the aging widow or widower that the one they loved and belonged with may possibly have disappeared without having left a trace in the Universe.

These doubts accentuate cruelly the loneliness feelings of the people of our time. They throw us back to seeking closer community with other men, to finding help through mutual understanding, through closeness, through improving our common human lot. I think this is one of the explanations why in our time the issue of better communication and better mutual understanding has become so pronounced and so widely spread. Communication and mutual understanding with others seem to alleviate our lonely condition.

The longing for understanding and closeness may also be found in children, even though they may not as yet participate in our modern existential problems. But children can feel very lonely. Often this is realized when we explore memories of childhood feelings with an adult patient. Masters of child analysis may even get a young child to express those feelings directly. The child's urge to be close, to be understood is a preconscious reaction to the fact of his isolation as an individual.

Longing might be called a natural state of mind in an adolescent because his needs for love and for a partner of his own are maturing in him. The development of these needs accompanies the need for increasing detachment from parents and family; thus, the experience of aloneness becomes natural for this period. In modern times, it acquires the qualities of loneliness to the extent that the adolescent becomes painfully conscious of his isolation as an individual and of the need to find closeness and understanding. He looks for understanding friends and for the one partner to love and to be close to forever.

Yet modern youths are skeptical regarding the possibility of finding the closeness and belonging they yearn for. The main reason for this lies in their greater awareness of the *self*, and of the core of their own existence. Because, who are they, they ask, where are they going? How can they belong, how can they be understood, if they do not understand themselves and if they are torn in their innermost selves.

"Who am I? Where am I going?" is one of the most frequently asked questions of our time.

Self-doubt and uncertainty about goals is a characteristic of our time, not just an age-characteristic problem of the adolescent years. These questions pursue many people far into adulthood and, tragically, sometimes even into advanced years.

This is why, when we set out today to study loneliness in adulthood and old age, we begin with a problem which previously concerned adolescence only; a problem which, in many cases, is not resolved in adolescence—the problem of the *self*. This is the self that cannot find itself and therefore leaves the individual in uncertainty, about himself and about many other things.

Yet an adult is expected to "feel sure" about what to believe in, what values to pursue, what to expect from marital partnership, or what to tell one's children when they ask about God and the chaotic events in social and world affairs.

An uncertainty about beliefs and values and about oneself makes the modern adult feel like a lonely adolescent long beyond the time of adolescence. In psychology, this phenomenon is called *the lack of identity* or *loss of identity* of our time. It is more a lack than a loss, because loss would presuppose that something was once there and then was lost. But the actual problem is that many people have never established a feeling of personal identity in the first place.

Is this the neurosis of our time? This is a widely discussed question. Allen Wheelis, in his excellent book *The quest for identity* (1958), devotes a careful discussion to this problem. Wheelis says:

Identity is a coherent sense of self. It depends upon the awareness that one's endeavors and one's life make sense, that they are meaningful in the context in which life is lived. It depends also upon stable values, and upon the conviction that one's actions and values are harmoniously related. It is a sense of wholeness, of integration, of knowing what is right and what is wrong and of being able to choose.

During the past fifty years there has been a change in the experienced quality of life, with the result that identity is now harder to achieve and harder to maintain. The formerly dedicated Marxist who now is unsure of everything; the Christian who loses his faith; the workman who comes to feel that his work is piecemeal and meaningless; the scientist who decides that science is futile, that the fate of the world will be determined by power politics—such persons are of our time, and they suffer the loss or impairment of identity.

Identity can survive major conflict provided the supporting framework of life is stable, but not when that framework is lost. One cannot exert leverage except from a fixed point.

The inability to establish a clear and definite identity results from those uncertainties that Wheelis touches on in his examples. These uncertainties manifest themselves in complaints, one of which is loneliness. In his struggle to find beliefs and values, the individual feels lonely, even desperate; he feels he no longer belongs with those who feel a part of tradition and establishment. He longs for people with whom he can find understanding. Yet often he doubts that anybody can really help him. "I feel so full of doubts," said a 23-year-old patient to me, "that sometimes I cannot even move."

Wheelis sees in this the *neurosis* of our time which is quite different from previous forms of neurosis in which one or more definite symptoms prevailed. These symptoms still occur: we still find the older type of neurosis, if we want to label it such—obsessions, compulsions, phobias, or physical symptoms without physical causes.

These symptoms were understood as the eruption of a previously repressed impulse, as inadequate and unconscious substitute solutions for appropriate solutions of problems and conflicts.

Currently the complaints of middle-aged people are frequently that they are unhappy because they cannot find themselves, or life does not make any sense, or that they don't know what to live for—in all this they feel lonely.

"I really don't know what is right for me to do," a woman in her early thirties said to me. "Shall I stay in this marriage with this man whom I don't feel I love, and make it go the best I can, or shall I divorce and try to find somebody with whom I truly belong?"

Another unmarried woman in her late thirties said: "I am conscience stricken, but not because I live sort of promiscuously and have various affairs. But I feel guilty because in all this I don't develop myself as a person, I don't accomplish anything." What this woman says is that her disturbed conscience is not that which Freud called the *superego* and represents society's moral code, but she is disturbed by what we would call her *humanistic conscience*, the knowledge that she is not developing her innermost self or bringing her best potentials to self-realization.

The above case represents more nearly a character disorder as Wheelis calls these most frequent problems of our time, rather than a neurosis. Neurotic tendencies we find in the first case (let us call her Sheila); she develops nausea and various pains, instead of confronting her problem with the best of her ability.

The second woman (let us call her Lucy) does what is considered typical of character disorders; namely, she acts out, allowing her impulse to gratify her, unable to tackle her real problems.

The loneliness that these people experience results from the fact that they do not just naively call themselves sick, as the first woman could have when she had nausea and pains, or declare naively that she is rebelling against society (authorities), as in the second case; rather they *know* and are aware of the reality of their struggle to lead a meaningful existence. When seeking the help of a therapist they ask for help to find the way to an appropriate human existence.

Since this is a problem for so many today, it seems to me that psychotherapy, especially group therapy, has become a necessary adjunct to education because neither parents nor schools seem to help the growing youth find himself as a human being.

Many fall by the wayside in developing all sorts of new neurotic symptoms, such as drug-addiction, escape into Hippie lives, and into an alienation from which it is hard for them to find a way back. But many more, it seems to me, are looking for help; these are a challenge to the therapist because they require a new clarification of how an adequate human existence should be conceived.

THE IMAGE OF MAN AND LONELINESS

We need, it seems to me, a new image of man. The traditional ideals of our culture involve the very conscientious person in a hopeless struggle for a perfectionism which is unrealistic, particularly within the framework of our society. The less highly motivated person feels that when it comes to practical problems of living ideals must often be sacrificed.

Several of my colleagues and I feel that we should clarify for ourselves the attainable traits of appropriate living and that we can and should work on these with the people we want to help.

I have tried to do so by analyzing the main traits of some truly well functioning persons. The image I obtained was confirmed when some of my patients brought it out in their self-descriptions, after the painful process of reaching self-understanding and self-redirection.

In summarizing what I had found to be attained traits in these persons, I came to the following picture. There is love and feeling, awareness and honesty of self-appraisal. There is the ability to enjoy things, interests, the will to accomplish something with hopeful belief in the anticipation of the future, and flexibility enough to accept limitations. There is the good will to do right as best one can, while preserving one's inner freedom and self-respect.

In the love and feeling acquired particularly in group psychotherapy, there is a self-realization in the lonely individual who finds a fundamental sense of relatedness with others, as described by Moustakas. This mature person feels his loneliness less because he relates in caring for others.

It seems to me that central to this image of the adequate mature person is the acceptance of full *responsibility* for oneself, while trying to bring out one's best potentials in the terms described above. This seems to me to be the most difficult task of life, the loneliest experience of the grown-up person of today because it has to be so very much based on the individual's judgment of what is right for him. (Moustakas points to the loneliness of persons in very responsible positions in public life.)

In a time where we can no longer be sure of doing right by following a tradition, or a moral rule, or any institutional dogma or ordering principle, in a time where we have to decide for ourselves as individuals what values we want to pursue, the responsibility to make decisions even in everyday life problems is great.

I need not remind you of everybody's responsibility to find a position, or take a stand, in the matters of war, our public life, our social problems. But responsibility of individual decisions reaches far into our daily life. Some of these everyday personal problems have led to the most heated arguments, as e.g. problems in the areas of sex and of the raising and disciplining of children and teenagers.

A young woman (let us call her *Grace*) who had a seemingly happy marriage came in great despair to me regarding the continuous disagreement between her and her husband with respect to matters of sex. Their own sex life, felt Grace, was satisfying to both, which was confirmed by her husband Dick. In fact, they both felt they loved each other dearly. Grace was of the opinion that they should belong to each other exclusively, while Dick's point of view was that occasionally he wanted to feel free to step out, without having to hide it or to have a bad conscience about it. In fact, he wanted them both to become members of the Sexual Freedom League. He found sexual exclusiveness too possessive. She felt not only jealous, but left out, lonely and uncertain about what stand to take.

Unlike earlier times, there are today, as you know, quite a large number of advocates of sexual freedom. The decision about it has become a matter of individual responsibility while it used to be a matter ruled by institutional principles, dogmas, and social traditions.

The raising of *children* has become in our time a lonely responsibility not only in the very controversial matters of discipline, but even more so in the guidance of teenagers. As psychologists we become witnesses of the unspeakable shame and guilt of parents whose teenage children participate in excesses of the present youth revolt, in behavioral excesses that may be ruinous to their future lives.

Responsibility and the shame and guilt resulting from wrong decisions and failures seems to me the most decisively isolating factor of the middle-aged adult's existence. Adults are usually ashamed to talk about being lonely, which youths do much more easily. Thus we have to go to our poets and writers to get the full impact of what is going on in our time. Modern writers overflow with expressions of the contemporary person's feelings of loneliness and alienation.

But, as I said before, we have to try to distinguish between neurotic alienation and the feeling of loneliness that modern man experiences *existentially*. The line is not always easy to draw since everyone has a few neurotic trends. But I think there is a difference between Saul Bellow's "Dangling Man" (1944) who sits and waits, and who when thinking of going to work has to admit to himself he does not know how to use his freedom—and on the other hand the loneliness of the hero in Hemingway's *Farewell to Arms* (1929).

"What's the matter?" Catherine said.
"I don't know."
"I know. You haven't anything to do. All you have is me and I go away."
"That's true."
"I'm sorry, darling. I know it must be a dreadful feeling to have nothing at all suddenly."
"My life used to be full of everything," I said, "Now if you aren't with me I haven't a thing in the world."

What is different is that Hemingway's loneliness includes love and care, while Bellow's man is a nonrelating person who cannot really love.

Loneliness through the loss of the lover is felt by everyone as a normal loneliness, especially in our time where the union and mutual understanding in love remains as one of the few experiences that may alleviate an individual's loneliness partly or even completely.

Loneliness may come through the loss of a person who has been giving direction, support, a hold, a belonging without one knowing it. William Maxwell (1937) describes a mother's death in which the whole family is thrown into disorientation, into emptiness, with no recognition of their own souls to draw from. Of course, this is most difficult for aging persons who seem to be surrounded by the dying out of their generation, their husbands, wives, friends, and their contemporaries with whom they formed meaningful relationships. (This subject will occupy us a little later.)

MEANING, CONTEMPORARY VALUES AND LONELINESS

More than ever before we seem not only to be supported, but also to derive our very meaning of life from our relationships with certain people, individuals or groups, who confirm us in what we are and what we are doing, and who, if we lose them, leave us feeling lost, completely deprived and endangered in the very foundations of our existence. Many Europeans went through this experience when thrown out by the Nazis, they more or less completely lost their established identities, and had to try to find new roots in all sorts of other countries and cultures. Many had to establish themselves completely anew among strangers.

As I said before, adults are usually ashamed of giving in to feelings like loneliness. They feel they are expected to be in control. In America, they were even expected to feel "happy" at all times and to answer "fine" when anyone asked them how they were. We Europeans were usually struck by this more than by anything else when we came here. We, of course, knew *Weltschmerz;* we had Hermann Hesse's *Demian* (1919) and Thomas Mann's *Magic Mountain* (1924) half a century earlier, and in Vienna, when asked how you were, you could easily say "lousy."

On the other hand, existential loneliness hits America now perhaps particularly strong, just because of the previously prevailing optimism about life.

While the youth of our time can afford to and takes the right not to commit themselves and to demand rebelliously for answers to their questions regarding a meaningful existence—as if anybody could find answers for them but themselves—and while the aged, by and large, do not want to be bothered and often withdraw from the problems, the middle-aged adult is caught right in the center. He is the accused one. He knows his lot in life is to take responsibility, to live life appropriately, and to set an example.

But how few people are equipped for and capable of setting an example of meaningful living becomes clearer every day. Most adults of our time have gone or stumbled into adult life with traditional concepts about their responsibilities. The average man wants to lead what he thinks a "decent" life with a decent job and income, a decent family life, while "getting on" with people he encounters. With this attitude, he may become smug, convinced and principled so that he does not acknowledge any problems in his way of life.

I think an amazing example of triviality is the uncle in *Life* magazine's recent article on the generation gap, which was excerpted from *The gap* by Larber and Fladell (1968). This good man is shown wandering around with his nephew through various Hippie establishments in Manhattan, sure of himself and his way of life as against all this, and sure of knowing the answers to the youngster's questions and attacks. So when the nephew says, "All you want is to get rich," the uncle answers: "No, all I want is to *make a living.*"

And this then is supposed to be a meaningful concept of life? I must say, that I would not blame the nephew had he retorted: "To Hell with that as a life goal"; after all is this what we are living for? This uncle, in fact, did not even do justice to his own life because he could have said that he lived for beloved persons, his wife and family whom he wished to make feel secure and happy. Of course, this person was not equipped to look even slightly deeper into the anguish that all sorts of crises of life bring about that hit the existentially less anchored person harder than the one who has unshaken beliefs.

The loneliness of adult responsibilities in crises situations and the feelings of guilt and shame in failures seem to me the most characteristic forms of loneliness in the adult's life. Career, marriage and family are the major areas of problems and conflicts, of failures and crises calling for strength, for understanding of self and of others and for decisions in which the individual may find himself alone.

Divorces and career changes are also problems of our time that, except for callous persons, mean serious conflicts and guilt feelings. Responsible people feel the loneliness in the face of serious decisions they have to reach, or the loneliness in guilt after a wrong course of action.

It is often asked why we see today an increase in decisions to divorce. These frequent marital crises have to do with the fact of the great individuality of modern man who experiences the loneliness of his individuality and who has difficulties in finding the partner he can be close to and with whom he can share his innermost feelings. The following is from a 55-year-old client:

We lived side by side. I always liked my wife, she was a quiet, friendly person, she kept our household well in order, she always looked nice, in her free time she played Bridge with friends or golf. Our relationship seemed to be pleasant, but we never talked about anything important at all. I myself had an extremely strenuous job as a manager of a big plant, I worked very late hours and sometimes we did not see each other all day, and when I came home, often she had gone to bed and slept. Twice or three times in the earlier years of our 30 year long marriage, she said it was too bad we did not get children. But she did not want to adopt any. I regretted it too, but I was too busy to give it more than fleeting thoughts. Our sex relations were fair, I always thought she was satisfied. We never talked about it. For many years, I did not take any vacations. I suggested that she should take some time off and visit perhaps Eastern relatives which she did. We had a few friends with whom we visited. Mostly they were business acquaintances and the relationships were not close. Sometimes I thought it must be lonely for her in this house without children. She denied it when I asked her. We decided to get two big dogs to keep her company.

It hit me like a ton of brick, when suddenly one day, 2 years ago, Betty announced she wanted a divorce. She said she had never loved me, and she felt I did not really love her, I just was used to her. I had given her presents and she had kept house for us and that was all. We had nothing in common as persons.

First, I did not even understand what she was talking about. I was so hurt. I thought I had been good to her, as she was good to me. I thought we both were quiet and nontalkative people and each kept his thoughts to himself. Now I found out that for years, Betty had been angry and that in spite of my giving her many things, she had felt neglected as a person, whatever that was.

Then I found out there was another man and she wanted to marry him. She had met him by accident, he was gay and sociable, divorced, an employee, a man without any consequence.

So it is sex, I said and I was enraged that she preferred this nobody to me. But it was not sex, she said; it was that they understood each other as two persons, that they could talk and really share things and understand each other.

I tried to talk to her, to persuade her I would change. Suddenly I felt she was dear to me and that I had lost her. Suddenly I realized that I did not even know what it meant to be close to anybody. Suddenly it struck me that I had never thought about anything in life, except how to do my job, and that my relationships with people were all superficial and meaningless. Meaning, what was that, I asked myself. And suddenly, I realized I was lonely, I needed somebody to talk to, to understand, and that, Doctor, is why I am here.

Dan's, of course, is an extreme case of lack of communication, of human emptiness. He needed this loss to find out how lonely he really was. But there are many others, perhaps more vociferous and more sharing in interests and activities, yet live side by side in their loneliness because they do not know how to open up and how to reach each other; when they try they find they are too different and their understanding is incomplete.

COMPLETION OF THE LIFE CYCLE

If at the one end of life adolescence seems to be the age during which an individual becomes aware of his loneliness, hoping for the closeness of love, companionship and belonging, so at the other end of life, old age is again a time of even deeper loneliness. Now it is the loneliness of having been left alone, of having been left over by a life companion, by friends who died or friends who moved on to other places and who could not be replaced. The many widowed persons, especially women, represent in a way the essence of loneliness, and the more fulfilling the relationship with a marital partner was the more this is true. This shows where the one appeasement of human loneliness lies: it is the union with one other person, ideally speaking, one who responds to a person's physical and emotional yearning and helps the searching soul and mind of the partner through understanding and participation.

In this lies the main remedy human beings are seeking—to overcome their loneliness. A great many, if not discouraged early, look forever for the kind of union with another human being that saves them from their loneliness. In adolescence, they are looking hopefully toward it; in old age, they feel, if they found it and lost it again, forever lost, deprived and bereaved.

But then, how many people in our time of any age find this consolation, this answer to their loneliness? There are many who hope in vain and who in the end give up because they never found what they were hoping for. This fact seems to be due in great measure to the increasing singularity and isolation of the individual.

The difference of feelings of old age bereavement as compared with previous years seems to me to lie in the resultant experience of having had or never having had this essentially fulfilling union.

However even here, the reactions seem to be individually different. If we read the aging Simone de Beauvoir's statments (1965), she is nothing but desperate about her aging. We see that she does not derive satisfaction from the deeply uniting relationships she must have had. Is the reason that they did not last, or could the reason be that she had no children, the second type of potentially deeply integrating relationship in human life? Or are these explanations too simple for persons so existentially lonely as she and her friend Sartre were?

The loneliness of the aging person is enhanced by the dying away of the friends of their own generation, the people with whom they belonged. And of course, the lessening of their contacts, their participation, their importance, retirement from jobs, and from public offices cause perhaps the greatest loneliness of all for which there is no alleviation or remedy. Perhaps an exception lies in certain religious faiths and religious concepts of life and the Universe, and in conjunction with them certain decisions of which we will speak at the end. In addition to loss of importance and of close relationships, the retired aging person loses the feeling of being needed by anyone, if they ever were so before.

Unfortunately in our Western Civilization, the older person does not, as is the case in certain other societies, receive prestige and honors for presumably having acquired wisdom and experiences of value for younger members of family groups or communities.

These conditions become worse if illness is added to the other hardships. Serious illness isolates a person at all times. Clark Moustakas sensitively discusses the loneliness of some very sick individuals who were beyond help. Thomas Mann described years ago the not only isolating, but also corrupting influence of serious illness, tuberculosis in this case, in *The Magic Mountain*. The estrangement of sickness in old age is perhaps the most hopeless of all conditions of loneliness because of the finality of this fate. The complaint of the sick old person has a ring of reality as no other and his depression seems unmitigable. The feeling for these hard realities of life seems today to be much more general than ever before. It was a real surprise to me when I found the "Beatles" (1966), the most successful youngsters of our time, sing songs about the loneliness and terror of old age.

> When I am 64,
> When I get older, losing my hair,
>   many years from now,
> Will you still be sending me a Valentine,
> Birthday greetings, bottle of wine?
> If I've been out till quarter to three,
>   would you lock the door?
> Will you still need me, will you still
>   feed me—

In relation to this poem, Art Kane says, "Eleanor Rigby is very lonely, has no friends and no one gives a damn. No one cares for her and when she dies no one even comes to her funeral except the preacher who buries her, but really is there because he has to be."

Of course, today we do much to help old people remain integrated in society and life. We have courses for the development of old people's potentialities (Otto, 1968). We have enormously improved hygiene and medical services that help a large number of people remain active and busy until advanced age. But, in spite of all this, depression and loneliness seem to take hold of a very large number of old people, as one of my tests recently showed (Buhler, 1968).

The loneliness of old age and of oncoming death are experienced with less despair by those who believe in a better life hereafter as against those who are nonbelievers or skeptics. Hermann Feifel (1959) and others showed in their studies on attitudes to death what a great difference it makes whether a person has this belief or not.

Besides the believers, there is one other fortunate group of old people, namely those who to their last days are able to produce something that they and others enjoy, that they find worthwhile to do and that they find relates them to others. Think of the delightful figure of Grandma Moses who started on her career in her fifties and painted to her and everybody's pleasure still in her nineties and who declared toward the end that she did not feel old, that she was satisfied with her life and that life is what we make it. Some may think she was a naive and lucky person. However, in our time there are many who, while aging and facing death at any time, find their satisfaction in and closeness to others by devoting themselves to accomplishing things for and with people. They leave behind, hopefully, the memory of and the incentive to the continuation of their dedication. This seems to carry quite a number of active elderly people of our time, Albert Schweitzer for example.

Others do not find peace in this. Bertrand Russell (1967, 1968), one of the sharpest and deepest thinkers of our time, found happiness and peace for some years, as he says, in the sense of "responsibility, providing a purpose for daily activities, the hope that one's children may succeed where one has failed, that they may carry on one's work when death or senility puts an end to one's own efforts. . . ." These efforts also "supply a biological escape from death, making one's own life part of the whole stream. . . ." This was in his early fifties.

But when some years later Will Durant asked Russell in a moving as well as deeply thoughtful letter "what meaning life had" for him, Lord Russell answered: "I do not see how I can answer your question intelligently." At that moment he saw no meaning whatsoever in life.

Of course the skeptic of our time cannot usually escape that easily in the satisfaction even of creative activity because he is not sure that what he does will make one iota of difference in the course of time and of world events.

This then is the real source of his loneliness, that he has lost the certainty of the closeness to a god and the certainty of the meaningfulness of his individual existence. *This loneliness is metaphysical.* Because of his skepticism about his existence, even closeness to people secures only a relative consolation more than a solution; a consolation while he is with and among the people, but hardly any longer, when he approaches the ultimate loneliness of death.

CONCLUSION

As purely intellectual theoreticians, this is where we would have to end the discussion. Bertrand Russell (1959) concludes that while he "hoped to find religious satisfaction in philosophy," an honest investigation shows that philosophy and science give no answer. His only personal answer was ultimately that he found relief from his loneliness in the ecstasy of love. "Now, old and near my end," he says in a beautiful poem, "I have known you, and, knowing you, I have found both ecstasy and peace. I know rest, after so many lonely years. I know what life and love may be—now, if I sleep, I shall sleep fulfilled." But as we said before, this experience of lasting ecstasy in love is granted only to very few.

However, I will not end here. There is, as I found, one other approach to the problem of his existential loneliness, an approach which man has tried at all times and is also making now, and increasingly often. It is an experience lifting him in a way out of life, lifting him over the terror and despair of his human loneliness; it is the experience of *mystical oneness* with all men and with the Universe.

There are various descriptions of this. One is found in Hermann Hesse's *Siddhartha* (1951), who at the end of a long and desperate trip of life, leading him "to the greatest mental depths, to thoughts of suicide," hears something new in what he describes as "the river's voice full of longing, smarting woe, full of insatiable desire." When he listened intently, he could no longer distinguish the different happy and unhappy voices.

When Siddhartha listened attentively to this river, to this song of a thousand voices; when he did not listen to the sorrow of laughter; when he did not bind his soul to any one particular voice and absorb it in his Self, but heard them all, the whole, the *unity;* then the great song of a thousand voices consisted of one word: Om-perfection.

Another poet of our own time and culture gives perhaps a deeper expression to the tragic, even if accepted experience of our human fate, of our re-merging—so to speak, into the Universe in death, possibly without even leaving a trace.

Eugene Vale in his *Thirteenth apostle* (1959), depicts Donald Webb as discovering, when approaching the end of his hopeless mountain climb "that he was about to meet death—and in death, himself." He had accepted death and he also had found "the other man, the Padre, his guide in the eerie depths of solitude"—and, he decides, "together they would look at the mountain, and then they would eat and go toward death, because there was nothing else they could do—because they could not resist the mountain's unearthly lure."

REFERENCES

ALLEN, M. Loneliness: An historical, social and literary survey. Unpublished manuscript, Los Angeles, 1968.

ARENDT, H. *The human condition.* Chicago: University of Chicago Press, 1958.

BEATLES: (P. McCartney and J. Lennon), "Eleanor Rigby," (BMI), 1966. (Recorded music)

BELLOW, S. *Dangling man.* New York: Vanguard, 1944.

BULHER, C. Psychotherapy and the image of man. *Psychotherapy, theory, research and practice,* 1968, *5* (2), 89–94.

DE BEAUVOIR, S. *Force of circumstance.* New York: Putnam, 1965.

FEIFEL, H. *The meaning of death.* New York: McGraw-Hill, 1959.

GOETHE, W. VON. *Werther.* New York: New American Library, 1962.

HEMINGWAY, E. *A farewell to arms.* New York: Scribner's, 1929.

HESSE, H. *Demian.* (Tr. by M. ROLOFF & M. LEBECK.) New York: Harper, 1965.

HESSE, H. *Siddartha.* (Tr. by H. ROSNER.) New York: New Directions, 1951.

LORBER, R. & FLADELL, E. *The gap.* New York: McGraw-Hill, 1968.

MANN, T. *The magic mountain.* Middlesex, England: Penguin Foundation, 1960.

MAXWELL, W. *They came like swallows.* New York: Harper, 1937.

MAY, R. *Man's search for himself.* New York: Norton, 1953.

MOUSTAKAS, C. E. *Loneliness.* Englewood Cliffs, N.J.: Prentice-Hall, 1961.

OTTO, H. A. *Human potentialities: The challenge and the promise.* St. Louis: Warren H. Green, 1968.

RUSSELL, B. *The autobiography of Bertrand Russell (1872–1914).* Boston: Little, Brown and Company, 1967.

RUSSELL, B. *The autobiography of Bertrand Russell (1914–1944).* Boston: Little, Brown and Company, 1968.

RUSSELL, B. *My philosophical development.* New York: Simon and Schuster, 1959.

VALE, E. *The thirteenth apostle.* New York: Scribner's, 1959.

WHEELIS, A. *The quest for identity.* New York: Norton, 1958.

WILLIAMS, T. *Three plays: The rose tatoo, Camino Real, Sweet bird of youth.* New York: New Directions, 1964.

Priorities for the Seventies

ROBERT L. HEILBRONER
New School for Social Research, New York City

To talk about national priorities is to talk about precedence, the order in which things are ranked. It is not difficult to establish what that order is in America today. Military needs rank above civilian needs. Private interests rank above public interests. The claims of the affluent take precedence over those of the poor. This is all so familiar that it no longer even has the power to rouse us to indignation. There is no shock value left in saying that we are a militaristic nation, or a people uninterested in the elimination of poverty, or a citizenry whose only response to the decay of the cities is a decision to move to the suburbs. To get a rise out of people, these days, one has to say something really outrageous, such as that the main cultural effect of advertising on television is to teach our children that grown-ups tell lies for money.

But I do not want to expatiate on the present order of things. For I presume that to talk of priorities is to determine what they *should* be. What should come first? What ought to be on top of the agenda?

To ask such questions is to invite pious answers. I shall try to avoid the pieties by grouping my priorities into three categories. The first has to do with our immediate survival—not as a nation-state, but as a *decent* nation-state. The second has to do with our ultimate salvation. The third with our moving from survival to salvation.

The initial set of priorities is simple to specify. It consists of three courses of action necessary to restore American society to life. The first of these is the demilitarization of the national budget. That budget now calls for the expenditure of $80-billion a year for military purposes. Its rationale is that it will permit us to fight simultaneously two "major" (though, of course, non-nuclear) wars and one "minor" or "brushfire" war. This requires the maintenance of eighteen army divisions, as against eleven in 1961; of 11,000

From *Saturday Review*, 53 (No. 1): 17–19+, January 3, 1970. Copyright 1969, Saturday Review, Inc.

deliverable nuclear warheads, compared with 1,100 in 1961; of a naval force far larger than that of any other nation in the world.

Politically, economically—even militarily—this budget is a disaster for America. It has sucked into the service of fear and death the energies and resources desperately needed for hope and life. Until and unless that budget is significantly cut, there will be little chance of restoring vitality to American society.

By how much can it be cut? The Nixon administration proposes to reduce it by $4- to $6-billion by June 1971, and by an equivalent amount each year for another four years. *Fortune* magazine claims it can be cut faster—$17.6-billion less by June 1972. Seymour Melman, professor of industrial engineering at Columbia University, has stated that it can be slashed by over $50-billion—and his reduced budget would still leave 2,300,000 men under arms, an obliterative power aimed at 156 Soviet cities, and an air and naval armada of staggering dimensions.

This conflicting testimony suggests that the question of how much the budget can be cut depends not on expertise alone, but on outlook—on how much one wants to reassign into other channels the resources absorbed by the military. Here let us make a first approximation as to how much the military budget can be cut by determining how large are the life-giving aims to which we must now give priority. I see two of these as being essential for the attainment of decency in American society. One is the long overdue relief of poverty. In 1967, 10 per cent of all white families, 35 per cent of all black families, and 58 per cent of all black families over age sixty-five, lived in poverty—a condition that we define by the expenditure for food of $4.90 per person per week. *Per week.* To raise these families to levels of minimum adequacy will require annual transfer payments of approximately $10- to $15-billion. This is half the annual cost of the Vietnam war. I would make this conversion of death into life a first guide to the demilitarization of the budget.

A second guide is provided by the remaining essential priority for American decency. This is the need to rebuild the cities before they collapse on us. This means not only replacing the hideous tenements and junkyards and prison-like schools of the slums, but providing the services needed to make urban living tolerable—regular garbage collection, dependable police protection, and adequate recreational facilities.

It has been estimated that New York City alone would need $4.3-billion per year for ten years to replace its slums. To provide proper levels of health and educational services would add another billion. And then there are Chicago and Newark and Washington and Los Angeles. It would take at least $20- to $25-billion a year for at least a decade to begin to make the American city viable.

These objectives are minimal requirements for America. Fortunately, they are easy to accomplish—at least in a technical sense. There will be no problem in cutting the military budget by the necessary $30- to $40-billion once that task is entrusted to men who are not prisoners of the military-industrial superiority complex. There are no great problems in the alleviation of poverty that the direct disbursement of money to the poor will not tolerably remedy. And whereas I do not doubt that it will be hard to build new cities handsomely and well, I do not think it will be difficult to tear down the rotten hulks that now constitute the slums, and to replace them with something that is unmistakably better.

Thus the essential priorities have the virtue of being as simple as they are compelling. This does not mean, however, that we will therefore attend to them. On the contrary, the chances are good that we will not do what must be done, or at best will act halfheartedly, in token fashion. The power of the vested interests of business and politics and labor in the preservation of military spending is enormous. The unwillingness of the American upper and middle classes to assist the less fortunate is a clear matter of record. The resistance to the repair of the cities is too well documented to require exposition here. Hence, we may never rise to the simple challenge of making America viable. In that case it is easy to make a prognosis for this country. It will be even more than it is today a dangerous, dirty, and depressing place in which to live. There will be an America, but it will not be a civilized America.

There is, however, at least a fighting chance that we *will* cut the military budget, that we *will* declare poverty to be an anachronistic social disease, that we *will* begin to halt the process of urban deterioration. Let me therefore speak of another set of priorities—one that many people would place even higher on the list than my initial three. They are, first, the elimination of racism in the United States, and second, the enlistment of the enthusiasm—or at least the tolerance—of the younger generation.

I have said that these priorities have to do with our salvation rather than with our survival. This is because their achievement would lift the spirit of America as if a great shadow had been removed from its soul. But like all salvations, this one is not near at hand. For unlike the first set of priorities, which is well within our power to accomplish, this second set lies beyond our present capabilities. Even if we manage to cut the military budget, to end poverty, to rebuild the cities, the bitter fact remains that we do not know how to change the deep conviction within the hearts of millions of Americans that blackness spells inferiority. Neither do we know how to win the enthusiasm of young people—and I mean the best and soberest of them, not the drop-outs and the do-nothings—for a society that is technocratic, bureaucratic, and depersonalized.

Thus the second set of priorities is considerably different from the first. It constitutes a distant goal, not an immediate target. Any projection of what America should try to become that does not include the goals of racial equality and youthful enlistment is seriously deficient, but any projection that does not expect that we will be a racist and alienated society for a long while is simply unrealistic.

What then are we to do in the meantime? How are we to set for ourselves a course that is within the bounds of realism and that will yet move us toward the long-term goals we seek? This brings me to my third set of priorities—a set of tasks neither so simple as the first, nor so difficult as the second. I shall offer four such tasks—not in any particular order of urgency—as exemplifying the *kinds* of priorities we need in order to move from mere survival toward ultimate salvation.

I begin with a proposal that will seem small by comparison with the large-scale goals discussed so far. Yet, it is important for a society that seeks to lessen racial tensions and to win the approbation of the young. It consists of a full-scale effort to improve the treatment of criminality in the United States.

No one knows exactly how large is the criminal population of the United States, but certainly it is very large. Two million persons a year pass through the major prisons and "reformatories," some 300,000 residing in them at any given time. Another 800,000 are on probation or parole; a still larger number lurk on the fringes of serious misbehavior, but have so far escaped the law. Our response to this core of seriously disturbed and dangerous persons is to send a certain number, who are unfortunate enough to get caught, to prison. These prisons include among them the foulest places in America—charnel houses comparable to Nazi concentration camps. At Tucker State Farm in Arkansas, inmates have been reported to be forty to sixty pounds underweight, and have been subjected to acts of unspeakable cruelty, and even to murder. The sadistic practices in military stockades have become notorious. But even the more humane institutions largely fail in their purposes. In New York State the rate of recidivism for crimes of comparable importance is 50 per cent. A recent FBI study of 18,000 federal offenders released in 1963 showed that 63 per cent had been arrested again five years later.

Indeed, as every criminologist will testify, prisons mainly serve not to deter, but to confirm and train the inmate for a career in criminality. These institutions exist not for the humanization but for the brutalization of their charges.

What is to be done? One inkling of the course to be followed is provided by reflecting on the statistics of prison care. In federal adult institutions we average one custodial person per seven inmates; one educational person per 121 inmates; one treatment person per 179 inmates. In local institutions and jails the ratio of educational or treatment personnel to inmates broadens to one to 550. In some state correctional institutions the ratio is as high as one to 2,400.

Another clue is suggested by the fact that work-release camps, widely used abroad to bridge the gap between prison and normal life, are available here in only four states. Still another is the clear need for the early detection of asocial behavior among school children, and for the application of therapy before, not after, criminality has become a way of life.

It must be obvious that an all-out effort to lessen criminality is not nearly so simple to achieve as slicing the military budget or tearing down the slums. But neither is it so difficult to achieve as racial tolerance. I suggest it is an objective well worth being placed high on the list of those "middle" priorities for which we are now seeking examples.

Recently, the Administration has declared the reform of prisons to be a major objective. Let us now see if this rhetoric will be translated into action.

My second suggestion is not unrelated to the first. Only it concerns not criminals, but those who represent the other end of the spectrum—the symbols of law and order, the police forces of America. I propose that an important item on the agenda must be an effort to contain and control a police arm that is already a principal reason for black anger and youthful disgust.

First, a few words to spell out the problem. In New York City, the Patrolmen's Benevolent Association, itself a potent force for reaction (as witness its key role in the defeat of the Civilian Review Board), is now outflanked on the right by "law enforcement" groups of super-patriot vigilantes who on several occasions have taken the law into their own hands. The actions of the Chicago police force as seen on national television during the Democratic convention do not require further comment here. In Detroit the United Press reports "open hostility" between the city's mainly white police force and the city's 40 per cent black population. At Berkeley, Harvard, and Columbia we have witnessed the dreadful spectacle of policemen smashing indiscriminately at students and using tear gas and Mace.

There is no simple cure for this ugly situation. Police forces are recruited largely from the lower middle class; they bring with them deeply ingrained attitudes of racial contempt and envious hostility to privileged youth. But there are at least a few measures that can be taken to prevent what is already a dangerous rift from widening further. To begin with, one way to minimize police abuse of Negroes is to minimize occasions for contact with them. The obvious conclusion is that black ghettos must be given the funds and the authorization to form their own police forces. Another necessary step is to lessen the contact of police forces with college youth; the legalization of marijuana would help in this regard. So would the training of special, highly paid, *unarmed*, elite police forces who would be used to direct all police actions having to do with civil demonstrations.

I do not doubt that there are many other ways to attack the problem. What is essential is to take measures now that will prevent the police from driving a permanent wedge between white and black, between student and government. Mace, tear gas, and billy clubs are weapons of repression, not of order. Few steps would contribute more to the return of American self-respect than those that would assist the growth of law and order among the forces of law and order.

Here, too, the report of the Eisenhower Commission signals an overdue awakening of public consciousness. But here again we shall have to see whether this awareness will be translated into action.

My third suggestion seemingly departs markedly from the first two. It concerns a wider problem than criminality or police misbehavior, but not a less pressing problem. It is how to rescue the environment from the devastating impact of an unregulated technology.

I need mention only a few well-known results of this ferocious process of destruction. Lake Erie is dead. The beaches at Santa Barbara are deserted. The air in New York is dangerous to breathe. We are drowning in a sea of swill; in a normal year the United States "produces" 142 million tons of smoke and fumes, seven million junked cars, twenty million tons of waste paper, forty-eight billion used cans, and fifty trillion gallons of industrial sewage. And presiding over this rampant process of environmental overloading is the most fearsome reality of all—a population that is still increasing like an uncontrollable cancer on the surface of the globe. I know of no more sobering statistic in this regard than that between now and 1980 the number of women in the most fertile age brackets, eighteen to thirty-two, will double.

Aghast at this terrific imbalance between the power of technology and the capacity of society to control and order the effects of technology, some people are calling for a moratorium on technology, for a kind of national breathing space while we decide how to deal with such problems as the sonic boom and the new supertankers. But this approach ignores the fact that it is not new technology alone that breeds trouble, but the cumulative effect of our existing technology; perhaps no single cause is more responsible for air pollution than the familiar combustion engine.

Hence, I call for a different priority in dealing with this crucial question—not for less technology, but for more technology *of a different kind*. For clearly what we need are technological answers to technological problems. We need a reliable method of birth control suitable for application among illiterate and superstitious peoples. We need an exhaustless automobile, a noiseless and versatile airplane. We need new methods of reducing and coping with wastes—radioactive, sewage, gaseous, and liquid. We need new modes of transporting goods and people, within cities and between them.

The priority then is technological research—research aimed at devising the techniques needed to live in a place that we have just begun to recognize as (in Kenneth Boulding's phrase) our Spaceship Earth. There is a further consideration here, as well. Many people wonder where we can direct the energies of the engineers, draftsmen, scientists, and skilled workmen who are now employed in building weapons systems, once we cut our military budget. I suggest that the design of a technology for our planetary spaceship will provide challenge enough to occupy their attention for a long time. We have not hesitated to support private enterprise for years while it devoted its organizational talents to producing instruments of war. We must now begin to apply equally lavish support while private enterprise perfects the instruments of peace. There would be an important side effect to such a civilian-industrial complex. It is that young people who are bored or repelled by the prospect of joining an industrial establishment, one of whose most spectacular accomplishments has been the rape of the environment, will, I believe, feel differently if they are offered an opportunity to work in research and development that has as its aim the renewal and reconstitution of this planet as a human habitat.

The items I have suggested as middle priorities could be extended into a long list. But what I am suggesting, after all, are only the *kinds* of tasks that cry out for attention, not each and every one of them.

But to speak of priorities without mentioning education seems wrong, especially for someone in education. The question is, what is there to say? What is there left to declare about the process of schooling that has not been said again and again? Perhaps I can suggest just one thing, aimed specifically at the upper echelons of the educational apparatus. It is a proposal that the universities add a new orientation to their traditional goals and programs. I urge that they deliberately set out to become the laboratories of applied research into the future. I urge that they direct a major portion of their efforts toward research into, training for, and advocacy of programs for social change.

It may be said that there is no precedent for such an orientation of education toward action, and that the pursuit of such a course will endanger the traditional purity and aloofness of the academic community. The reply would be more convincing did not the precedent already exist and were not the purity already sullied. Scientists of all kinds, in the social as well as in the physical disciplines, have not hesitated to work on programs for social change—financed by the Department of Defense, the Office of Naval Research, NASA, etc.—programs designed to alter the world by high explosives in some cases, by cooptation or skillful propaganda in others.

Some members of the academic community, aware of the destruction they have helped to commit, have now begun to withdraw from contact with the war machine. That is to their credit. But what is needed now is for them to redirect their energies to the peace machine. We live in a time during which social experimentation—in the factory, in the office, in the city; in economic policy, in political institutions, in life-styles—is essential if a technologically dominated future is not simply to mold us willy-nilly to its requirements. The forces of change in our time render obsolete many of the institutions of managerial capitalism and centrally planned socialism alike; new institutions, new modes of social control and social cohesion now have to be invented and tried.

In part the university must continue its traditional role, studying this period of historic transformation with all the detachment and objectivity it can muster. But that is not enough. As Marx wrote: "The philosophers have only *interpreted* the world; the thing, however, is to change it." As the last item on my agenda, I would like to make the university the locus of action for the initiation of such change.

Motivation and Adjustive Responses

The articles included in this section are at almost opposite ends of a continuum. MacKinnon says that openness to experience, awareness of self, and the internal direction of behavior are basic attributes of the effective, self-expressive and creative person. Bartley tells us that fatigue occurs mostly in the absence of interest and involvement and that it reflects a person's general orientation toward life. Both indicate that people function as psychosomatic wholes. One is not likely to be physically tired without being psychologically and mentally fatigued as well. He probably will not function creatively unless he is absorbed and challenged by the task and unless he feels that there is some chance of dealing with it.

MacKinnon's article deals primarily with creativity and creative people. But there are varying degrees of creative potential in us all. And there appears to be a high similarity between those who are self-actualized and those who are creative. In these respects MacKinnon's description furnishes a model. Our aspirations now can be more specific in terms of personal behaviors and characteristics than in terms of the mere prescription, "Be self actualized and creative."

All of us cannot become highly creative but we can learn to be more effective and more active than we presently are. One learns many of the attitudes which cause him to feel either involved or uninterested. He can learn enthusiasm or he can learn apathy as an orientation toward living. That is, one can learn, and at a relatively early age probably has already done so, ways of looking at things, attitudes, or perceptual sets which will act as influences upon his behavior. These will function to motivate him to try or not to try something. Inasmuch as such learned predispositions are not organic or innate (not inherited), one should be able, in theory at least, to change or modify them. Because fatigue is less a result of energy depletion than of attitude, a change of attitude or learning of a different orientation should enable a person to use more of what he has and to do it more effectively. Questions which each person needs to answer and about which psychology should become more concerned are: "How much of personal limitations result from attitudes?" and "What can any one of us do to discover and to deal with those which restrict our own effectiveness?"

One description of the attitudes which motivate one either to coping or to defensive behaviors is provided by Toussieng. His article is particularly valuable in the study of adjustment and motivation because it is so close to what might be called the classical point of view: Youth's search is for identity; identity is hampered because of technology and rapid change, which destroys continuity; lack of continuity creates a generation gap; and generation gap causes one to be motivated by his unsophisticated peers. The fact that this chain of circumstances is operative might well be studied as a working hypothesis by adults who wish to understand the motives and adjustive patterns of youth. It is an especially pertinent thesis in relation to those young people who try to escape their identification with the establishment or with mankind.

The foregoing point of view has potential dangers for the young person. It could provide an excuse for behaviors which to date have proved to be ineffective, if not downright hazardous. In between stimulus (technological environment and rapid change) and response lies the opportunity for decision making—for the exercise of individuality and perhaps the motivation for creative endeavor.

Undergraduate students may need some assistance in interpreting the statistics in Schneider's article but the message is so important that it cannot be neglected. It is made clear that one becomes human, one becomes a worthwhile person, one uses his potential to best advantage when he receives feedback from others. It may be that the important message is that parents and teachers should provide plentiful and more positive feedback. But the implication of the article is no less important: What one does elicits or inhibits feedback. One has the opportunty and responsibility of seeking friends and acquaintances who will provide confirming feedback on integrative kinds of behaviors. Perpetuating contacts with those who confirm weaknesses may be a form of slow suicide.

Conditions for Effective Personality Change

DONALD W. MACKINNON
Director, Institute of Personality Assessment and Research
University of California, Berkeley

For the past six years, we of the Institute of Personality Assessment and Research on the Berkeley campus of the University of California have had a rare privilege. We have studied intensively nationwide samples of men and women who have been nominated by their peers for the unusual creativeness with which they have practiced their particular art, science or profession.

The fields of creative endeavor which we have had an opportunity to study have been creative writing (Barron, 1962), architecture (MacKinnon, 1962), mathematics, industrial research, physical science and engineering (Gough and Woodworth, 1960; MacKinnon, 1961). If one considers these activities in relation to the distinction often made between artistic and scientific creativity, it may be noted that we have sampled both of these domains as well as overlapping domains of creative striving which require that the practitioner be at one and the same time both artist and scientist.

Artistic creativity, represented in our studies by the work of the writers, results in products that are clearly expressions of the creator's inner states, his needs, perceptions, motivations and the like. In this type of creativity, the creator externalizes something of himself into the public field.

In scientific creativity, the creative product is unrelated to the creator as a person, who in his creative work acts largely as a mediator between externally defined needs and goals. In this kind of creativeness, the creator, represented in our studies by industrial researchers, physical scientists, and engineers, simply operates on some aspect of his environment in such a manner as to produce a novel and appropriate product, but he adds little of himself to the resultant.

Domains of creative striving in which the practitioner must be

Donald W. MacKinnon. "Conditions for Effective Personality Change." *Nurturing Individual Potential.* A. Harry Passow, editor. Washington, D.C.: Association for Supervision and Curriculum Development, 1964, pp. 12–27. Reprinted with permission of the Association for Supervision and Curriculum Development and Donald W. MacKinnon. Copyright ©, 1964, by the Association for Supervision and Curriculum Development.

both artist and scientist were represented in our researches by mathematicians and architects. Mathematicians contribute to science, yet in a very real sense their important creative efforts are as much as anything else personal cosmologies in which they express themselves as does the artist in his creations. So too in architecture, creative products are both an expression of the architect and thus a very personal product, and at the same time an impersonal meeting of the demands of an external problem.

It is primarily from having studied highly effective persons in each of these domains of creative endeavor that this paper is directed to the main theme, "Nurturing Individual Potential," and to the more specific topic, "Conditions for Effective Personality Change." Only by relating the more specific topic to the more general theme can one keep a sense of the direction in this field. If one were to focus his discussion solely on the "conditions for effective personality change," he might review what is known about the conditions created and utilized in prison and concentration camps and in programs of brainwashing for the bringing about of effective, in the sense of enduring, changes in personality. Such matters are not our concern here, however, but rather those conditions within the individual and in his life space, especially his educational environment, which we have reason to believe would most effectively facilitate and encourage the development of his potentialities to be a creative person.

The creative individual, as we have seen him, is an impressive person, and he is so because he has to such a large degree realized his potentialities. He has become in great measure the person he was capable of becoming. It is for that reason that a careful examination of his characteristics, his attitudes, interests, values, cognitive styles, abilities, and the like, and the life forces which have nurtured his creative potentialities, insofar as we can discover them, is our first order of business in attempting to gain insight into the conditions which make for effective change.

It is a good deal easier, however, to describe the creative person than to say with confidence how he became the person he is. It is one thing to discover the salient traits of mature, creative, productive individuals. It is quite another matter to conclude that the traits of creative persons observed several years after school and college characterized these same individuals when they were students. Nor can we be certain that finding these same traits in youngsters today will identify those with creative potential. Only empirical, longitudinal research, which we do not yet have, can settle such issues. Nevertheless, considering the nature of the traits which differentiate highly creative adults from their less creative peers, I would hazard the guess that most students with creative potential have personality structures congruent with, though possibly less sharply delineated than, those of mature creative persons.

The problem is further complicated by the fact that though our creative subjects have told us about their experiences at home, in school and in college, and the forces and persons and situations which, as they see it, nurtured their creativity, these are, after all, self-reports subject to the misperceptions and self-deceptions of all self-reports. Even if we were to assume that their reports are essentially accurate we would still have no assurance that the conditions in school and society, the qualities of interpersonal relations between instructor and student, and the aspects of the teaching-learning process which would appear to have contributed to creative development a generation ago would facilitate rather than inhibit creativity if these same factors were created in today's quite different world and far different educational climate.

Having noted this by way of caution, let us turn to the traits of highly creative persons and the implications, as the writer sees them, of their traits for those conditions most likely to nurture and encourage creative potential.

TRAITS OF CREATIVE PERSONS

Creative persons are, to an extraordinary degree, open to experience, to the experience of their inner life as well as of their outer environment and culture. This would seem to be almost the basic condition for change, namely that one be receptive to new elements of experience. One of the most important dimensions along which persons differ is that of the open or the closed mind. The open-minded person is keenly perceptive, the closed-minded individual is strongly judgmental. Though it is an oversimplification to state it so bluntly, it is nonetheless true that whenever a person uses his mind for any purpose he performs either an act of perception (he becomes aware of something) or an act of judgment (he comes to a conclusion about something). And most persons are inclined to show a rather consistent preference for and greater pleasure in one or the other of these; preferring either to perceive or to judge.

One who emphasizes and prefers an attitude of judging will lead a life that is controlled, carefully planned, and orderly, and when the preference for judging is habitual and strong he becomes judgmental and in the extreme prone to prejudging. He is then the prejudiced person.

On the other hand, a preference for the perceptive attitude results in a life that is more open to experience both from within and from outside, and characterized by flexibility and spontaneity.

Several of our tests, as one would expect, reveal the creative person to be perceptive and open to experience.

The *Minnesota Multiphasic Personality Inventory* (*MMPI*) (Hathaway and McKinley, 1945) is a test designed to measure tendencies toward the major psychiatric disturbances such as depression, hysteria, paranoia, schizophrenia and the like. On the eight scales which measure the strength of these dispositions in the person, our creative subjects earn mean or average scores which range from five to 10 points above the general population's standard score of 50. It must be noted, however, that elevated scores on these scales do not have the same meaning for the personality functioning of persons who, like our subjects, are getting along reasonably well in their lives and professional careers, that they have for hospitalized patients.

For our creative subjects the higher scores on the clinical dimensions are actually less suggestive of psychopathology than of good intellect, richness and complexity of personality, and a general lack of defensiveness—in other words, of an openness to experience. We must also note, though, that there is in the *Minnesota Multiphasic Personality Inventory* profiles of many of our creative subjects rather clear evidence of psychopathology, but also evidence of adequate control mechanisms, as the success with which they live their productive lives testifies.

The most striking aspect, however, of the scores on the several scales of the *Minnesota Multiphasic Personality Inventory* for all our male creative groups is an extremely high peak on the Mf (femininity) scale.

This tendency for creative men to score unusually high on femininity is also demonstrated on the Fe (femininity) scale of the *California Psychological Inventory* (*CPI*) (Gough, 1957) and on the masculinity-femininity scale of the *Strong Vocational Interest Blank* (Strong, 1959). Scores on the latter scale (where high scores indicate more masculinity) correlate −.48 with rated creativity (MacKinnon, 1962).

The evidence is clear: the more creative a person is the more he reveals an openness to his own feelings and emotions, a sensitive intellect and understanding self-awareness, and wide-ranging interests including many which in the American culture are thought of as feminine. In the realm of sexual indentification and interests, our creative subjects appear to give more expression to the feminine side of their nature than do less creative persons. In the language of the Swiss psychologist, Carl G. Jung (1956), creative persons are not so completely identified with their masculine *persona* roles as to blind themselves to or to deny expression to the more feminine traits of the *anima*. For some the balance between masculine and feminine traits, interests and identifications is a precarious one. Moreover, for several of our subjects, we believe that their presently achieved reconciliation of these opposites of their nature has been barely effected and only after considerable psychic stress and turmoil.

The perceptiveness of the creative person and his openness to richness and complexity of experience are also strikingly revealed on the *Barron-Welsh Art Scale* (Barron and Welsh, 1952) of the *Welsh Figure Preference Test* (Welsh, 1959). This test presents to the subject a set of 62 abstract line drawings which range from simple and symmetrical figures to complex and asymmetrical ones. In the original study which standardized this test some 80 painters from New York, San Francisco, New Orleans, Chicago and Minneapolis showed a marked preference for the complex and asymmetrical or, as they often referred to them, the vital and dynamic figures. A contrasting sample of non-artists revealed a preference for simple and symmetrical drawings.

All creative groups we have studied have shown a clear preference for the complex and asymmetrical, and in general the more creative a person is the stronger is this preference. Similarly, in our several samples, scores on an Institute scale which measures the preference for perceptual complexity are significantly correlated with creativity. In a sample of architects the correlation is +.48. If one considers for a moment the meaning of these preferences, it is clear that creative persons are especially disposed to admit complexity and even disorder into their perceptions without being made anxious by the resulting chaos. It is not so much that they like disorder per se, but that they prefer the richness of the disordered to the stark barrenness of the simple. They appear to be challenged by disordered multiplicity which arouses in them a strong need which in them is serviced by a superior capacity to achieve the most difficult and far-reaching ordering of the richness they are willing to experience.

The traits of the creative person reviewed so far suggest that the creative individual, in controlling his impulses, his images and his ideas, eschews the ego-defensive mechanisms of repression and suppression. Much of experience which other less courageous persons would repress or deny is accepted by the creative person. But in accepting so much of his own experience, which for him as for anyone else is disturbing, he must, one would think, experience more anxiety than his more restricted and constricted peers. Evidence that such is precisely his fate is provided in a comparison of the scores of more and of less creative persons on a measure of felt and experienced anxiety, the *Taylor Manifest Anxiety Scale* (Taylor, 1953).

It is not, however, that the creative person is extremely impulsive and uncontrolled. It is rather that he has consciously to assume responsibility for the control and expression of impulses and images which in the neurotically inhibited person are beyond conscious control and expression because they are not admitted into experience. Being unconscious they are controlled in the more inhibited person, not by the conscious ego, but by the unconscious super-ego working through the mechanisms of repression and denial. Our more creative subjects not only experience more anxiety, they also have stronger egos. They score significantly higher on the ego-strength scale of the *Minnesota Multiphasic Personality Inventory.*

COGNITIVE STYLE OF THE CREATIVE PERSON

We may now inquire into the cognitive style of the creative person. In his openness to experience, is he inclined to focus upon his immediate sensory experience, savoring what is, or does he immediately and instinctively perceive the deeper meanings and possibilities inherent in things and situations and ideas which he experiences? In other words, in his perceptions is he a sense-perceptive, concentrating primarily on the sensory attributes of his experience and centering his attention upon the existing facts as they are given, or is he an intuitive-perceptive ever alert to links and bridges between what is present and that which is not yet thought of? Does he focus habitually upon what is or upon what may be?

On a test designed to measure these two cognitive orientations—a preference for sense-perception or sensation vs. a preference for intuitive-perception or intuition (the *Myers-Briggs Type Indicator*, 1958)—three out of four persons in the United States prefer sense-perception to intuition, that is, 75 percent are sensation types.

In view of this it is especially interesting to discover that 90 percent or more of each of our creative samples show a preference for intuition. The percentages of intuitives are: for creative writers 90 percent, mathematicians 92 percent, research scientists 93 percent, and architects 100 percent.

It is not that this finding is surprising; one would not expect creative persons to be stimulus- and object-bound but instead ever alert to the as-yet-not-realized. It is rather the magnitude of the preference for intuitive perception that is so striking among highly creative persons.

Closely related to the creative person's preference for intuition are his preferred interests and his emphasized values.

All the creative groups we have studied have shown essentially the same characteristic pattern of scores on the *Strong Vocational Interest Blank*. From sample to sample there has been some slight variation, but the general pattern is this: relatively high scores on such scales as psychologist, architect, author-journalist, and specialization level, and relatively low scores on such scales as purchasing agent, office man, banker, farmer, carpenter, veterinarian and, amusingly yet understandably, policeman and mortician.

This typical pattern of scores on the *Strong Vocational Interest Blank* suggests that creative persons are inclined to be less interested in small detail, in facts as such, and more concerned with their meanings and implications, possessed of greater cognitive flexibility, and characterized by verbal skills and interest in as well as accuracy in communicating with others.

The Allport-Vernon-Lindzey *Study of Values* (1951), is a test designed to measure in the individual the relative strength of the six values of men as these values have been conceptualized and described by the German psychologist and educator, Eduard Spranger (1928), namely, the theoretical, economic, aesthetic, social, politicall, and religious values. On this test, all of our creative groups indicate as their highest values the theoretical and the aesthetic.

For creative research scientists the theoretical value is the highest, closely followed by the aesthetic. For creative architects the highest value is the aesthetic, with the theoretical value almost as high. For creative mathematicians the two values are both high and approximately equally strong.

It is of some interest, further to note, that, despite the success with which, as entrepreneurs, creative architects carry out their architectural practice, the economic is their lowest value. Indeed in the total sample of 124 architects, the theoretical value correlates with the rated creativity of the architects $+.18$, the aesthetic value $+.35$, and the economic value $-.48$.

Turning now to the life histories of our subjects, we may inquire into the kinds of experiences that nurtured their creativity, and the conditions that fostered those changes in their personalities which brought their creative potentials to full development and expression. Let us now examine the life histories of architects, since this is the group that the author knows best.

Architects, like all the creative groups we have studied, show a high sense of personal autonomy and a zestful commitment to their profession. Moreover, the protocols of their life histories have revealed a number of factors which in their early years could be expected to provide an opportunity and perhaps the necessity for the development of a secure sense of personal autonomy.[1]

LIFE EXPERIENCES WHICH NURTURE CREATIVITY

First, there is a reported lack of intense closeness or intimacy with one or both parents. It is more frequently seen in the relationship with the father rather than with the mother, but is often characteristic of the relationship with both parents. That is, there are neither strong emotional ties of a positive nor of a negative sort. There is neither the type of relationship that fosters over-dependency nor the type that results in severe rejection. Thus, although there may be a certain coolness and distance in the relationship of the child to his parents, there is at least an absence of the type of psychological

[1] Kenneth H. Craik. *"Analysis of the Life History Protocols of 40 Creative Architects."* Unpublished manuscript, 1962.

exploitation that is frequently seen in the life histories of clinical subjects.

Second, and probably closely related to the foregoing, is the suggestion of certain ambiguities in the identification patterns of the architects. When asked with which parent they tended to identify themselves, fifteen of them reported that they identified with neither or with both parents. Thirteen of them tended to identify with their mother and only twelve of the 40 reported an identification with their father alone.

Before speculating about the possible origin and significance of this factor, we might mention some other characteristics of the family constellations that would also tend to foster its appearance. Rather often, there existed a situation where the father was absent from the home (separated, divorced, and what not) in a literal sense, but was very much present psychologically, either because the mother kept alive the father's image or because of visits from the father and the like.

In addition, the mother was frequently an exceptionally autonomous person herself, either because she was the only parent in the home or because she led an active life with interests of her own, apart from her husband's. Thus, the architects often had both masculine and feminine models for autonomous behavior, and sometimes had only a feminine model for it.

In any case, there are at least two speculative leaps that we might make with regard to these identification patterns. In the first instance, we can go from the artistic abilities and sensitivities to the identification pattern. One might hypothesize that a youngster with such artistic predilections will be influenced in his identification choices by the degree to which the value patterns of his parents are nurturant of an artistic orientation. And, indeed, the evidence provided by this sample tends to support the hypothesis. Thus, there are twenty cases in which the youngster identified with the father alone, the father having artistic interests, or identified with the mother alone, the mother having artistic interests, or identified with both parents, at least one of whom had artistic interests.

In five cases, the architect reported identification with neither parent, and in all five cases, neither parent showed artistic interests. Finally, there are six cases in which neither parent showed artistic interests and in which the architect identified with the mother. If we assume that in our culture, the feminine values of the mother are more nurturant of the artistic orientation, we might consider these cases as support for our hypothesis. In summary, then, we have thirty-one cases in support of and nine cases in contradiction to our hypothesis that the artistic value patterns of the parents are a factor in the identification choices of these artistically inclined youngsters.

We might then make a further speculative leap, going from these diffused and perhaps conflicting, identification patterns to the career choice. Thus, we might say that looking at it from the value system of our culture, architecture is a good compromise career for someone with artistic abilities and identification tensions. It is both artistic, feminine, and pure, as well as businesslike, masculine (engineering), and applied. It is a career that in some ways can replicate the tension between the dominant cultural masculinity values and the femininity values that is seen in the early identification patterns of these men.

There are other factors in the early histories in addition to lack of intense closeness and diffused identification patterns that point toward a development of personal autonomy. There is a marked tendency for complete lack of physical punishment and a complete lack of formal religious training. Thus one may infer that in the area of rights and discipline—that is, in the area of personal conduct—there was a good amount of interpersonal give-and-take. Yet with it, one may assume, went a fairly unstructured atmosphere and with that, a requirement of active exploration and internalization of a framework of personal conduct.

In addition, the architects as youngsters had a definite freedom to roam and explore and there was frequent moving by the family, thus providing an enriched environment for exploration and for, possibly, the enhancement of their visual-artistic sensitivities.

Autonomy and some sense of aloneness might be expected to appear concurrently. Reports of aloneness, shyness, solitariness, are not infrequent, nor is evidence of possible social isolation (no dating as an adolescent), although the latter evidence may be ambiguous. There is also a slight tendency for reports to be made that the parental family was in some sense or other different from those in the neighborhood.

In a number of cases, the visual-artistic ability was recognized to some extent during childhood or adolescence and, in some cases, this ability was a source of self-esteem for the youngster. In a few cases, the youngster was provided, *via* this ability, with a certain special status within the family unit. For example, in one case, the architect reports that his family always "rooted for me" during his training and professional career. However, as a general case, it appears that the visual-artistic abilities and interests were pretty much allowed to develop at their own speed and this pace varied considerably among the architects. Although in a few cases there was definite encouragement of the artistic skills, what is perhaps more significant is the general definite lack of strong career channeling pressures. This is generally the case, both for pressures away from architecture, as well as pressures toward architecture by architect-fathers.

These observations permitted the conceptualizing of 17 factors presumably related to the development of autonomous, secure and creative work in architecture which can be briefly described as follows:[2]

1. Lack of intense closeness between the child and the parents and absence of psychological exploitation of the child by the parents
2. Ambiguities in identification with the parents: identification either with both parents or with neither
3. Father physically absent from home, but psychologically present
4. Mother an exceptionally autonomous person
5. Mother with artistic interests
6. Father with artistic interests
7. Father in engineering, business, etc.; mother with artistic interests
8. Lack of physical punishment
9. Lack of formal religious training
10. Freedom to roam widely and to explore
11. Frequent moving by the family
12. Experiences of aloneness, shyness, isolation, solitariness, etc.
13. No dating during adolescence
14. Family different from those in the neighborhood
15. Visual-artistic abilities and interests allowed to develop at their own pace
16. Visual-artistic abilities and interests encouraged and rewarded
17. Lack of strong career-channeling pressures.

That these factors in the life history are indeed related to the creativeness of our architects is indicated in a further analysis. A credit of one point for the presence of each of these factors in the life history protocols of each of the creative architects was assigned and the total for each person taken as a score. The correlation of

[2] *Ibid.*

these life history scores with the rated creativity of the architects is $+.32$, significant beyond the .025 level of confidence.

It is clear from their reports that certainly not all of the creative architects had the kind of happy homes and favorable life circumstances so generally thought to be conducive to sound psychological development. Some underwent harsh treatment at the hands of sadistic fathers. These, to be sure, constitute the minority, but they appear today no less creative than those whose fathers offered them quite satisfactory male figures with whom easy identification could be made, though there is some evidence that they are not as effective or as successful in the financial and business (masculine) aspects of their profession as the others.

FINDING LIFE CAREERS

Settling upon their life careers came early for some, one of whom already at four had decided he wanted to be an architect. Others were slow in coming to a professional identity, not deciding until several years past college that architecture was what they wanted to practice. In the case of several of these, the choice of a life profession was made the more difficult by virtue of the fact that they possessed so many skills and interests, providing them with the possibility of many quite different careers. Several were painters and others sculptors before they became architects and some of them continue today these artistic pursuits in a professional and not merely avocational fashion along with their architectural practice.

In school and college the creative architects were tolerably good students, but in general not outstanding if one may judge from their academic grades. In college they averaged about a B. But what more clearly appears to have characterized their college careers was the independence with which they worked.

In work and courses which caught their interest they could turn in an A performance, but in courses that failed to strike their imagination, they were quite willing to do little or no work at all. In general, their attitude in college appears to have been one of profound skepticism. They were unwilling to accept anything on the mere say-so of their instructors. Nothing was to be accepted on faith or because it had behind it the voice of authority. Such matters might be accepted, but only after the student on his own had demonstrated to himself their validity. In a sense, they were rebellious, but they did not run counter to the standards out of sheer rebelliousness. Rather, they were spirited in their disagreement and one gets the impression that they learned most from those who were not easy with them. Yet clearly many of them were not easy to take. One of the most rebellious, but as it turned out, one of the most creative, was advised by the Dean of his school to quit because he had no talent; and another, having failed in his design dissertation which attacked the stylism of the faculty, took his degree in the art department.

The self-assertive independence which they showed early and manifested so clearly in school and college still characterizes the creative architect. In the total sample, two Institute scales, one measuring self-assertiveness, the other independence, correlate $+.34$ and $+.43$ with rated creativity.

Not only the architects, but all our creative samples, show this relative rejection of external restraints, freedom from crippling inhibitions, and independence in thought and action. One illustration of the point may be based on an interpretation of the profile of scores earned by more creative as compared with less creative subjects on the *California Psychological Inventory*. In the interest of clarity of presentation, I shall once again present data only for architects.

On the first cluster of scales, which are measures of poise, ascendancy and self-assurance, creative architects reveal themselves as dominant (Do) ; possessed of those qualities and attributes which underlie and lead to the achievement of social status (Cs) ; poised, spontaneous, and self-confident in personal and social interaction (Sp) ; though not of an especially sociable or participative temperament (low Sy) ; intelligent, outspoken, sharp-witted, demanding, aggressive, and self-centered; persuasive and verbally fluent, self-confident and self-assured (Sa) ; and relatively uninhibited in expressing their worries and complaints (low Wb).

But it is on the second cluster of scores, those having to do with responsibility, socialization and self-control that creative architects differ most widely from less creative architects. Their scores reveal the creative architects to be relatively free from conventional restraints and inhibitions (low So and Sc), not preoccupied with the impression which they make on others and thus perhaps capable of greater independence and autonomy (low Gi), and relatively ready to recognize and admit self-views which are unusual and unconventional (low Cm).

As for the next cluster of scales, creative architects, like architects in general, are strongly motivated to achieve in situations in which independence in thought and action are called for (Ai). Yet, unlike their colleagues, they are less inclined to strive for achievement in settings where conforming behavior is expected or required (Ac). In efficiency and steadiness of intellectual effort (Ie), however, they do not differ from their fellow workers.

Their scores on the last three scales reveal the creative architects as definitely more psychologically minded (Py), more flexible (Fx), and as having more femininity of interests (Fe) than architects in general.

IMPLICATIONS OF THE FINDINGS

What, we may now ask, are the implications of these findings for the conditions for effective personality change where the primary concern is for the nurturing of creative potential in school and college?

What to me is most strongly suggested by our findings is that we should seek to develop in our students a capacity for intuitive perception, an immediate concern for implications, and meanings, and significances, and possibilities beyond what is presented to the senses. This is not to suggest a slighting of facts, for there is a great wealth of information which every educated person must possess. Without a richness of experience, which may include a considerable body of fact, intuitions may be original but they are not likely to be very creative. Yet I would urge that in our instruction we never present a fact for its own sake, and that in our testing of our students' knowledge we shun questions which require no more than identification of facts. I am convinced that we can measure information which students have learned more reliably, more validly and more economically by objective tests than by essay examinations. Yet it remains true, I believe, that a student's preparation for and actual writing of an essay examination forces him to exercise his intuitive perception.

On another occasion I said what I am now saying by reminding my colleagues that *"ledge,* the second element in the word *knowl-edge,* means sport. Knowledge is the result of playing with what we know, that is, with our facts. A knowledgeable person in science is not, as we are often wont to think, merely one who has an accumulation of facts, but rather one who has the capacity to have sport with what he knows, giving creative rein to his fancy in changing his world of phenomenal appearances into a world of scientific constructs" (MacKinnon, 1953). And so it is in all fields, not science alone.

Rote-learning, learning of facts for their own sake, repeated drill of material, too much emphasis upon facts unrelated to other facts, and excessive concern with memorizing, can all strengthen and reinforce sense-perception. On the other hand, emphasis upon the transfer of training from one subject to another, the searching for common principles in terms of which facts from quite different domains of knowledge can be related, the stressing of analogies, and similes, and metaphors, a seeking for symbolic equivalents of experience in the widest possible number of sensory and imaginal modalities, exercises in imaginative play, training in retreating from the facts in order to see them in larger perspective and in relation to more aspects of the larger context thus achieved; these and still other emphases in learning would, I believe, strengthen the disposition to intuitive perception as well as intuitive thinking.

While our data suggest that a rich development of intuitive powers facilitates creativity, they do not deny the necessity of accurate sense-perception. It is a matter of which gets emphasized. This is true also with the perceptive and judging attitudes, both of which each of us possesses but to different degrees. One must often enough judge and evaluate one's own experience, but it is important that we not prejudge, thus excluding from perception large areas of experience.

The danger in all academic instruction is that we criticize new ideas too soon and too often. Training in criticism is obviously important and so much emphasized I do not need to plead its case. Rather, I would urge that an equal stress be placed on perceptive open-mindedness, discussing with students at least upon occasion the most fantastic of ideas.

It is our duty as professors to profess what we have judged to be true, but it is no less our duty by example to encourage our students to be open to all ideas and especially to those which most challenge and threaten our own judgments. We give lip service to the university as the testing ground for new ideas, but too often our emphasis is upon testing rather than on new ideas.

I am impressed by the discrepancy between the scores our creative subjects earn on the achievement via independence and the achievement via conformance scales of the *California Psychological Inventory.* I am also struck by the descriptions of their behavior when in college. These data are congruent with all our observations in assessment which suggest that these subjects are now and for a long time have been independent characters. It is an independence which manifests itself not in footless rebellion but in the accomplishment of goals which the individual sets himself and which he achieves in his own unique fashion. I would infer from this that if we are to encourage creativity in college students we must give them a maximum of freedom in achieving their educational objectives.

It is our task as educators to set goals for the college and for our individual courses. The goals, I believe, should be set in only the most general fashion, but they must be set high enough to challenge the student and to involve him in the overcoming of obstacles.

More specifically I would suggest that no course or seminar deserves a place in a college curriculum unless it requires of the student the solution of some problem—a research project, a term paper, etc. The requirement, stated in only the most general fashion, permits the student to determine what specifically his own problem will be. Thus he chooses, he sets the problem, and having done so, he might well be left to solve it in his own way. Thus, we would provide the student with what I believe to be one of the necessary conditions for creative achievement: the undertaking of the solution of a problem where the degree of difficulty and frustration is great and the drive toward accomplishment is persistently strong.

If goals are set high enough, repeated periods of frustration will be experienced. It is at these times which I have called periods of withdrawal from the problem that the college community, if it is a stimulating intellectual environment, can contribute importantly to the nourishment of creativity. For it is often in these periods of renunciation of the frustrating problem that those accidents which induce sudden insight and are thus not accidents at all, since one is set for them, occur.

This, as I see it, is the meaning of serendipity, the finding of valuable or agreeable things not sought for. If, when a student withdraws from a problem which has repeatedly frustrated his attempts at solution, he moves in an environment alive with ideas and stimulating converse, the chances of the insight-inducing accident's occurring are maximized.

Finally, I think our data should remind us that our creative students may not always be to our liking. Almost certainly we will at times find them difficult to get along with. Yet if we recognize that some of their behavior which may be most irritating to us arises out of a struggling attempt to reconcile opposites in their nature and to tolerate large quantities of tension as they strive for a creative solution to difficult problems which they have set themselves, we may be in a better position to support and encourage them in their creative striving.

REFERENCES

G. W. ALLPORT, P. E. VERNON AND G. LINDZEY. *Study of Values (Revised Edition)*: *Manual of Directions.* Boston: Houghton Mifflin Company, 1951.

F. BARRON. "The Creative Writer." *California Monthly* 72(5): 11–14, 38–39; 1962.

F. BARRON and G. S. WELSH. "Artistic Perception as a Possible Factor in Personality Style: Its Measurement by a Figure Preference Test." *Journal of Psychology* 33: 199–203; 1952.

H. G. GOUGH. *California Psychological Inventory Manual.* Palo Alto, California: Consulting Psychologists Press, 1957.

H. G. GOUGH and D. G. WOODWORTH. "Stylistic Variations Among Professional Research Scientists." *Journal of Psychology* 49: 87–98; 1960.

S. R. HATHAWAY and J. C. McKINLEY. *Minnesota Multiphasic Personality Inventory.* New York: The Psychological Corporation, 1945.

C. G. JUNG. *Two Essays on Analytical Psychology.* New York: Meridian Books, 1956.

D. W. MACKINNON. "Fact and Fancy in Personality Research." *American Psychologist* 8: 138–46; 1953.

D. W. MACKINNON. "Fostering Creativity in Students of Engineering." *Journal of Engineering Education* 52: 129–42; 1961.

D. W. MACKINNON. "The Personality Correlates of Creativity: A Study of American Architects." Gerhard S. Nielsen, editor. *Proceedings of the XIV International Congress of Applied Psychology, Copenhagen 1961,* Vol. 2: 11–39. Copenhagen: Munksgaard, 1962.

I. B. MYERS. *Some Findings with Regard to Type and Manual for Myers-Briggs Type Indicator, Form E.* Swarthmore, Pennsylvania: Privately printed, 1958.

E. Spranger. *Types of Men*. Translated by Paul J. W. Pigors. Halle (Saale), Germany: Max Niemeyer, 1928.

E. K. Strong, Jr. *Manual for Strong Vocational Interest Blanks for Men and Women, Revised Blanks (Forms M and W)*. Palo Alto, California: Consulting Psychologists Press, 1959.

J. A. Taylor. "A Personality Scale of Manifest Anxiety." *Journal of Abnormal and Social Psychology* 48: 285–90; 1953.

G. S. Welsh. *Welsh Figure Preference Test: Preliminary Manual*. Palo Alto, California: Consulting Psychologists Press, 1959.

What Do You Mean, "Tired"?

S. HOWARD BARTLEY, Director
Laboratory for the Study of Vision and Related Sensory Processes
Department of Psychology, Michigan State University

Almost everybody becomes tired at times, but the conditions under which this happens are often not easily understood. A common remark is, "I don't see why I get so tired." The one making this remark says he hasn't done anything to make him tired. He has reason to believe he is in good health and that his work load is not too great.

Because no one likes to be tired, formulas for how to avoid it and how to relieve it have always been eagerly sought. The formula needed, in my opinion, involves a form of understanding that is not taught in formal educational systems.

Common observations regarding the feeling of tiredness include the following:

1. Tiredness comes and goes throughout the day, and we do not always feel as tired at night as in the morning.

2. We can wake up in the morning after a full night's sleep and feel more tired than when we went to bed.

3. We become more tired in performing an unpleasant task than in doing one we don't mind.

4. Though tired by one task, we can plunge into some other

From *Today's Education*, 58: 40–41, February, 1969.

activity that requires far more energy and can soon become less tired than before. For example, we can be tired at the end of a sedentary workday and can go to a dance in the evening and not feel tired.

5. We can become tired by merely being faced with a disagreeable task; the mere thought of having to do certain things may make us tired.

6. We are able to go for long periods without rest when having a "wonderful time."

7. We make the most mistakes when we are tired and this, in turn, makes us more tired.

8. When overcome with fatigue, we are very unlikely to be enthusiastic about anything; when we are enthusiastic, we rarely feel fatigued.

9. The experience of feeling quite tired in doing a given job is likely to make us feel tired again the next time we are faced with the same job.

10. We cannot always point to what makes us tired.

The usual notion has long been that the cause of fatigue is the depletion of the body's energy reserves and the accumulation of metabolic waste products from tissue activity. If fatigue is depletion of energy, it is something that happens to the cells of the body, primarily the muscle cells. If depletion of energy resources in these cells occurs, one could not expect energy to be restored until more food is eaten or else some stored supply is released. This involves the lapse of considerable time. Some of the observations just stated show that fatigue can disappear quite quickly. Hence the suppositions that relate fatigue to energy depletion do not hold.

If fatigue arose from the accumulation of waste products of the metabolism involved in muscle activity, one could not expect fatigue to be alleviated until these products were gotten rid of. This, too, involves some lapse of time. If the disappearance of fatigue were based upon the forms of restoration just mentioned, fatigue, once built up, would require hours to disappear. But fatigue doesn't act this way; it often comes and goes quickly. Thus, there is something wrong with the common assumption about what causes fatigue or even about what fatigue is.

A careful look at the list of common observations about fatigue shows that the term *fatigue* describes a personal experience (a kind of self-evaluation) rather than a state of muscle tissue. Take the example of the person who wakes up and lies in bed visualizing the effort of getting up and preparing for the day's work. He believes it is Monday and realizes that he will have to do a number of unpleasant things.

The sum of it all is that he feels tired already, and the feelings in his muscles are taken to be solid evidence of that. Then he realizes it is not Monday, but Sunday—the day he can turn over and take another nap. Immediately, his bodily sensations mean something else to him. He interprets them to be those of relaxation, the absence of the tension he had when he went to bed. Instead of feeling tired, he now feels comfortable and goes back to sleep.

This illustrates how the realization of one's state of muscle tone figures in the overall self-assessment called fatigue. At first, the lack of tone was interpreted as inadequacy for getting up and meeting the demands of the day; subsequently, the same bodily feeling was a perfectly appropriate one for lying in bed or going back to sleep. Fatigue was the result in the one case; good feeling was the result in the other.

A second example consistent with the one just given is the person who feels much more tired after a night of deep sleep than he does after a night of light sleep and some insomnia. Various depths of sleep involve different degrees of relaxation so that passing from sleep to the full-waking state (or vice versa) involves time-consuming transitions in the level of muscle tone.

Just as it requires relaxation from tension to go to sleep, it is also necessary to regain a certain amount of muscular tension to be fit to dash into the day's affairs. Deep sleep could well result in a lower level of muscle tone than a lighter sleep and would therefore require a greater amount of time to build up tone to a fully adequate level.

Exactly the same paradox puzzles people who often experience greater fatigue during the morning than in the afternoon. They think that fatigue ought to increase from hour to hour. Believing that fatigue is strictly a phenomenon of energy depletion, they interpret the sensations associated with lack of muscle tone—which may come and go throughout the day—as a lack of energy.

Neither this example nor the previous one, however, can be accounted for by the notion that fatigue is simply a measure of energy state—an evidence of the lack of energy.

Sometimes, fatigue is chronic, and when so, it reflects the individual's general orientation toward life. Body malfunction and disease may underlie chronic fatigue in some instances, but this is not the case in many other instances, as testified to by the unexpected improvements that often result when new interests are awakened in the individual.

My research and thinking have led me to the conclusion that it is incorrect to consider fatigue as the objective measure of an individual's energy resources. The human organism is continually expressing an orientation to the environment, and, as I see it, fatigue is the name for the highest level of this expression, namely, the conscious individual's self-assessment of his feelings of aversion to and inadequacy for carrying on in a responsible way.

Hangloose Identity or Living Death:
the Agonizing Choice of Growing Up Today

POVL W. TOUSSIENG, M.D.
Youth Counseling and Child Development Center,
University of Oklahoma Medical Center
Oklahoma City

By combining insights from work in psychoanalysis and anthropology, Erik Erikson several decades ago formulated a theory of psychosocial development from birth into senescence which has had a monumental influence on all the behavioral sciences. The unique features of this theory are that psychic development is continuously viewed in interaction with the environment and the cultural setting, and that specific tasks are described for each developmental phase. The task of adolescence, crucial for reaching true adulthood, is the achievement of a firm ego identity.

Erikson (4) defines ego identity as follows: "Ego identity, in its subjective aspect, is the awareness of the fact that there is a selfsameness and continuity to the ego's synthesizing methods and that these methods are effective in safeguarding the sameness and

From *Adolescence*, 3 (No. 11): 307–318, 1968. This paper is a condensed version of a presentation at the weekly Colloquium, Department of Psychiatry, Neurology and Behavioral Sciences, University of Oklahoma School of Medicine, Oklahoma City, Oklahoma, March 29, 1968.

continuity of one's meaning for others." In other words, for a child to be able to develop a sense of having a stable meaning to others he must be able to count on a reasonable selfsameness and continuity in his environment, primarily in important adults around him and in his general culture. Youth growing up in today's atomic and electronic era, however, lives in a world that is changing so rapidly, so abruptly, and in such an unpredictable manner that the continuity and stability of the culture, as well as of the adults in that culture, have been severely affected if not practically destroyed.

Insecurity, bewilderment, and confusion are evident in many contemporary adults, although they desperately try to hide it. They vigorously deny that there is any need to make a change. They glorify the "good old days," and more and more savagely criticize and attack those adults and youngsters who struggle to find ways to help them adapt to the new, rapidly changing world, and to assimilate the many changes which already have occurred. A hundred million American adults regularly try to escape from all pain and all tension by resorting to alcohol or by taking tranquilizing drugs. These same adults are very upset about the two million or so youngsters who are experimenting with drugs and call them "escapists." Yet most, if not all, researchers agree that the true drug experimenters among the young are not trying to escape, but are actively seeking answers, particularly related to the question of how to learn to tolerate and integrate the intense and constant stimulation coming from a kaleidoscopic world. They want to learn to live with the pain rather than get away from it, as the adult majority is trying to do.

Unfortunately the escapist stance of most adults today leaves them caught in a vicious cycle of ever-increasing problems and fears. While denying their fear of change and difference, the adults also have to deny the need for change, and thus they become paralyzed and consequently cannot engage effectively in attempts to solve the crucial problems which face mankind today. As these problems are left unsolved, the emergency grows, causing more adult fears and further action paralysis.

The situation does not get any better when the panic erupts into frantic and desperate actions. These actions are becoming increasingly bizarre because they are dictated by the hope that the world can somehow be kept from changing or even that the calendar can somehow be turned back to the 19th Century. Examples of inappropriate reactions of adults to change can be seen in the intensity of emotion aroused by the U.S. Supreme Court decision regarding prayers in public schools, the exaggerated fear of even minor, but vocal, Civil Rights leaders and of the "hippies," and the increasing sadistic adult violence toward young people who openly express their wish to "change things."

Adult fearfulness and aversion to change keeps American Christian churches from making more than token gestures in moving from orthodoxy and towards the practice of Christian ethics, as demanded by many young people today. Even worse, adult control of the schools and of higher education is used to prevent any changes which might truly update the curriculum. As a result, it is becoming more and more difficult for students to find anything in their studies that is relevant to the world in which they live. Yet the world they are not supposed to know about is constantly kept before their eyes by the news media, particularly television, and by their own daily personal experiences.

In addition, an ever-increasing number of parents are quietly resigning from their parental duties. It is not because they do not care; they simply do not know how to respond to the present world, and feel unable to predict what the world will be like even ten years from now. Thus they do not know what to tell their children or how to prepare them for the future. Some parents hold on until their children have reached puberty, then turn them loose. Again, this does not reflect malice or lack of love on the part of the parents, but simply that they feel they have nothing more to offer. And so they turn their children over to other adults, who are considered "experts" or pose as such. These "experts" are primarily teachers and policemen, who, unfortunately, are as unable as the parents to guess what the future might hold for the children, and who are much more prejudiced and tied to the past than are most parents. The result is that many—if not most—contemporary children are left to find growth support from multiple, haphazard, and often totally inappropriate and irrelevant sources.

These developments are particularly unfortunate because, in recent decades, the onset of puberty is tending to occur earlier and earlier, and therefore hits many children at a psychosocially immature age. This would call for more, rather than for less, support during the years of puberty. The children who enter puberty early face a period of adolescence of up to 8–10 years, wherein they are too young to be adults and yet too old to be children. This long period is made even more difficult because of the intense adult pressure on most American children today to grow up in a hurry. Yet at the same time the adult world withholds all adult privileges from the youngsters until they have reached "legal age."

A further handicap to growing up today is that contemporary youngsters have an increasingly difficult time finding suitable adult models with whom they can identify. In addition, as pointed out by Friedenberg (5), schools place the adolescent under overwhelming pressure to accept and identify with patently outmoded values and techniques of living. If the adolescent is able to resist all these pressures, he has nowhere to turn for support and guidance but to other adolescents. In other words, the teen-agers are left to raise themselves and each other—a task that would be difficult enough even if there weren't so much intereference and sabotage. It is a tribute to our youth that they still manage to grow up under such circumstances.

Nowhere is the pressure on youth greater than in the middle- and upper classes of our society. Keniston's (6) penetrating study gives us a chilling picture of the psychological state of generally bright middle-class college students who have suffered no obvious psychological or social hardships while they were growing up but are unable to commit themselves to a career or to the society in which they have grown up. Keniston studied the influence on these students of their families and was less interested in the effect of society itself on his subjects. Nevertheless, many of his findings can be used to support the hypothesis that the struggle of bright and sensitive students in part, or maybe wholly, have resulted from their inability to usefully bridge the gap between the middle-class techniques of living (which they have been taught) and the techniques actually required in order to live successfully in what Daniel Bell (1) has called the "postindustrial society." The symptom picture which they present, especially their fears of caring for others and of making commitments to anything, corresponds closely to what Erikson (4) described as "identity diffusion," the antithesis of a firm ego identity. These students have not been able to find a workable ego identify; they cannot find any continuity between what they have been taught in their suburbs, and what the world in which they live is actually like and requires. They are too honest and too stubborn to settle for a false compromise, and yet they cannot bridge the gap.

Because these uncommitted students still are fighting valiantly they are less severe casualties of their upbringing than the very large group of middle-class youngsters who never have fought back. They have surrendered to adult pressure and allowed themselves to be fitted with a false identity, complete with well-worn but hopelessly outdated 19th Century values. In return for their surrender and submission, these youngsters are showered with praise, approval, and scholarships by adults who in the existence of these "ideal kids," see hope that the future will bring no changes after all. The sad fact is, however, that these youngsters who go through all the "right" motions in their lives are totally out of touch with the real world. They hardly know that a real world exists. It is for this reason that I call them "the living dead."

Between the uncommitted and the living dead there is a large group of youngsters who engage in vigorously independent behavior. Many of these young people are considered delinquent by adult society because they are caught breaking some law. Although adults do not agree on the causes of delinquent behavior, most of them are convinced that delinquent youngsters have either moral or character defects, or are more or less emotionally disturbed. People who, like myself, have had considerable experience with delinquents do indeed find some of them disturbed or warped in their psychological growth. We also find that a large, ever-growing percentage of delinquents do not show sufficient evidence of disturbance to deserve a psychiatric label.

A closer look at these "bad" youngsters will reveal that their behavior represents a refusal to choose "living death." These youngsters are stubbornly, clumsily, dangerously, and often vainly searching, and what they seek is a workable ego identity that will lead to adult maturity in the style of the second half of the 20th Century.

Most of all, these young people—like a handful of honest contemporary adults—are searching for a new and reliable value system that can serve as a guide for and monitor of their behavior. They know their search behavior tends to get out of hand, and they desperately long for adult support and guidance in their search. Instead they receive punishment or "treatment" from adults who see their behavior as rebellious and destructive to the "established values of our society." This adult view is based on the delusion that there still is a sufficient number of people in modern society who try to live by the Judaeo-Christian values they insist they have. But the many adults who talk one way and act in another are all too apparent to today's youngsters. Because of this hypocrisy no honest teen-ager can possibly identify with these adults. It is even more preposterous to insist that adolescent delinquent behavior is "rebel-lion." How can anyone rebel against such nebulous figures?

There are other youngsters whose search is just as intense but does not express itself in antisocial behavior. Their behavior may even be quite constructive. In this category we have, for example, the youngsters who leave their parent's church in order to be able to practice, through unselfish service to others, what they consider to be the essence of the Judaeo-Christian ethics. These young people are invariably viewed as "rebels" and "revolutionaries" by their elders and are treated accordingly. These youngsters do not view themselves as rebels since they actually pursue their beliefs in a positive way. There is no hostility toward adults, and the adult institutions from which they have disassociated themselves, simply because the adolescents consider them irrelevant.

In discussing the topic of authority, a young college student, Karen Wullenweber (8) recently wrote:

"After all, we grew up on the heels of the Nuremberg Trials where men were condemned to death for following orders rather than their conscience. . . . We perceive in those issues in which we dissent some moral aspect which we insist must be taken into account and which isn't. . . . Why would any young person who is concerned about social justice, Civil Rights, the peace movement, and international relations want to commit himself to a Church which does not overtly prove that these are Her concerns too? . . . It is the authentic service which is in fact rendered that constitutes the actual source of authority. When this authentic service is neglected by the authority figure, the basis for obedience then drops out."

It is regrettable that so many adults view these developments with dismay and disgust or try to belittle the quest of the young people for a new identity and new values. In so doing, the adults force the youngsters to leave their homes, their churches and schools, and to expose themselves to many totally unnecessary and grave dangers. In the past few years, thousands of middle-class youngsters have felt compelled to run away from their smug sub-urban existence and eventually experiment with potentially danger-ous drugs in an attempt to find answers in their lives.

There also are small groups of youngsters who seek and find their identity by rebelling against the older generation. These young people are found in the militant Civil Rights groups, in militant student groups, and in other groups sometimes referred to as the "New Left." John Dippel (3), recently retired editorial chairman of the *Daily Princetonian,* in discussing such "student power" groups states: "Spokesmen for student power have conveyed well an awareness of student identity, but have only slightly been able to mobilize this unity of identity into action." Thus the students do find an identity through their negative stance, but they cannot act because they are rebelling against dead issues. As useful as their identity is to them, it is a sham identity because it is based on rebellion without a cause—or even a target.

Nevertheless, even these young people are trying to fight rather than surrender to living death. Recent events at many major universities in the Western world demonstrate that rebellious students, because they will not surrender to the past, can come to represent as much of a threat to existing society as the youngsters who refuse to choose living death. This shows how little there is left of society's official structure.

Slowly and reluctantly, some adults are beginning to realize that police clubs and tear gas bombs cannot stop the calendar. Business firms are having difficulty recruiting promising college graduates because the graduates do not find that business is interested in society. However, business is quietly beginning to make changes in order to adapt to the wishes of these determined young adults. Large law firms have difficulty recruiting enough top students from the best law schools even though starting salaries have been raised substantially. Graduate schools have fewer applicants to choose from even though vastly greater numbers are graduated from college. College students are critical of professional people because they seem to be interested only in making money, or in immersing themselves in their special professional interests without regard for people or for society. Even universities, those magnificent museums of the past and of contempt for ethics and for humanity, are being forced by their students to face the issues of the day and to pay their respect to the dignity of human beings.

The young of today are not fooled when adults claim they are protecting them from dangers the adults fear. The world of many American adults caved in when the Russians launched their Sputnik long before an American satellite was sent into space. As a result, school curricula were made a lot tougher, and training for the eventual operation and invention of new hardware was stressed heavily in schools and colleges. Only the "living dead" youngsters and a handful of others are following the bugle call.

The cream of American youth is being sent to Viet Nam with the excuse that adults are trying to save them from having to live under communism. It is a magnificent tribute to the many American young men, who are not fooled by the adult flag-wavers, that they remain undaunted and maintain a very high morale overseas. Adults are quick to say that this morale is due to superior indoctrination; but it is hard to detect any signs of brainwashing in communications received from the overwhelming majority of those young men who are or who have been in Viet Nam. A good example is the following poem, written by a young Marine, Stephen Brown (2) from Lindenhurst, Long Island, after he and his company had spent forty-five days at Con Thien under continuous shelling. The rest of the company agreed that this poem expressed their feelings better than anything else. (Incidentally, Con Thien means "Place of Angels.")

Hill of the Angels
—a fitting name;
No bells can be heard,
But they are there just the same.
Lifeless and mud-clad,
A body still warm.
The Hill of the Angels
Takes a mother's firstborn.
Sky above is broken
By shell red with heat
And for what? Freedom?
Our reason is gone,
But for the hill of our angels
Death goes on.

"Our reason is gone" reflects the skepticism of these young men; and yet they fight well, and do not become bitter and cynical. The explanation may lie in the fact that many of the young men going overseas see it as an opportunity to get to know themselves under the extreme circumstances of war. They hope to achieve a firm ego identity while learning to master the ever-changing, unpredictable, mortally dangerous and often totally overwhelming situations to which the war exposes them. It is striking how few Viet Nam veterans come back talking about the war; instead they talk about the way in which their experiences there have helped them grow up more than they could have managed in any other way. Thus the war, *because* of its risks and danger, is seen as an opportunity for growth.

Other young people seek that opportunity through LSD and other drugs which are known to involve grave risks, and still others take the big leap by enlisting in the Peace Corps and in Vista. These youngsters carry out what they feel they must do quietly, relentlessly, and without being impressed with the sacrifices they have to make. It is obvious that young men and women with that much strength cannot help but have a profound influence on what will happen in this country in the next ten to twenty years. They are likely to have the ability to build a bridge leading from the present to the future, and to formulate entirely new goals, values, and ways of life for all of us.

The older generation is keenly aware of this. It is obviously threatened by its lack of leverage to control the younger generation. The clear warning coming from the youngsters, that the present power structure in society will be put out of office *in toto* as sufficient numbers of youngsters reach voting age is an even greater threat to the older politicians. As a result, the older generation is increasingly mobilizing its police powers against the youth of today. The objective is not only to "stick" as many young people as possible with criminal records, but also to make it impossible for the more vocal and militant ones to finish their education. An ever-increasing number of young students are being mauled and mutilated by callous policemen who supposedly were trained to protect them. In the U.S., the right to bear arms via the draft is now being used as punishment—a death sentence without due process of law and allowing no defense. Thousands of American young men have been forced to go into permanent exile in foreign countries without even the prospect of a visit to the U.S. One may well ask how many young men, who are able and willing to think, a modern country can afford to lose just to keep the older generation in the saddle a few years longer.

It is inevitable, however, that youth must win out; and it is fitting that we listen to them as to what type of person they see as being able to live in the modern world. First of all, it is clear that youth believes that man must learn to struggle by himself against his fears and impulses before he can possibly bring out his potentials in a way which has real personal and objective meaning. Thus the growth process in children must allow opportunity for much more personal initiative while it still offers the children the necessary protection and support until they no longer need it.

In the years to come, discontinuity rather than continuity is likely to become the norm. In order to live in his environment, man will need an ego identity built on discontinuity rather than continuity; on change rather than on sameness. He must be able to tolerate his changing roles in and his changing meanings to his environment. A person's feeling of selfsameness and continuity will somehow have to include and base itself on all those changes and discontinuities. Thus ego identity will be built on the flexibility and adaptability of the ego as it changes roles in an ever-changing and flexible environment. Ethics, too, will need to be more flexible and adapted to changing situations. (Simmons and Winograd (7) have proposed the name "hangloose ethics.") The danger will still be identity diffusion, which would mean ego flexibility without adaptation—an ego flexibility which is not meaningfully related to the environment most of the time.

Many young people today are trying to work out just such a new identity. They deserve, need, and want help from the older generation. Though most older people feel like the proverbial fish out of water in the new era they still have a wider perspective on many things. Young people are eager to listen to their elders, so long as they are not being given sermons or commercials. In order to remain human, mankind must achieve a meaningful identity as well as values and beliefs. The generation reaching adulthood now is deeply concerned about this very task, and is making major sacrifices to solve it. The future is thus in good hands, and there is hope for mankind.

REFERENCES

1. BELL, DANIEL. "The Postindustrial Society," In Ginzburg, Eli, Ed.: *Technology and Social Change.* New York: Columbia University Press, 1964.
2. BROWN, STEPHEN. *Daily Oklahoman,* Oklahoma City, Okla., October 9, 1967.
3. DIPPEL, JOHN. "Student Power." *Princeton Alumni Weekly,* 1968, 16, pp. 10–15.
4. ERIKSON, ERIK H. "Ego Development and Historical Change," *Psychoanalytic Study of the Child.* New York: International Universities Press, 1946, 2, pp. 359–396.

5. FRIEDENBERG, EDGAR Z. *The Vanishing Adolescent.* New York: Dell Publishing Co., 1959, pp. 223.
6. KENISTON, KENNETH. *The Uncommitted.* New York: Dell Publishing Co., 1965, pp. 500.
7. SIMMONS, J. L., and WINOGRAD, BARRY. *It's Happening.* Santa Barbara: Marc-Laird Publications, 1966, pp. 174.
8. WULLENWEBER, KAREN. "Authority as Collegians See It." *St. Anthony Messenger*, 1968, 75:9, pp. 13–19.

Tactical Self-Presentation After Success and Failure

DAVID J. SCHNEIDER
Department of Psychology, Amherst College
Amherst, Massachusetts

An experiment was performed to explore the effects of success and failure on self-presentation where another person was either in a position to give the subject an evaluation based on his presentation (feedback) or could not give the subject any information about his self-presentation (no feedback). As predicted the failure subjects were more positive about themselves under the feedback condition than under no feedback ($p < .01$), presumably in an effort to get approval from the other person, and the success subjects were more modest under the feedback than under the no-feedback condition ($p < .10$), presumably in an effort to conserve their tentative high self-evaluations by not appearing too immodest. Subsequent analyses showed that some of the failure subjects responded with positive self-presentations to get approval while others seemed to evidence what Cohen has called defensive self-esteem.

Some men brag; others seem too modest. People vary in how they describe themselves, and it is of considerable interest to determine

From *Journal of Personality and Social Psychology*, 13: 262–268, 1969. This report is based on a dissertation (Schneider, 1966) submitted to the Stanford University Psychology Department in partial fulfillment of the requirement for a doctoral degree. The research was supported by a predoctoral fellowship from the Vocational Rehabilitation Administration. The author would like to thank his graduate advisor, Albert Hastorf, and the other members of his committee, Alex Bavelas and Merrill Carlsmith, for their advice and encouragement.

why. One approach might assume that self-presentations mirror individuals' self-concepts, but this does not account for the variability of a single person's self-descriptions over a number of occasions. Another possibility is that self-presentations can be used tactically to seek approval, to gain power or status, etc. Goffman's (1959) analysis of impression management and Jones' (1964) work on ingratiation have highlighted the tactical use of self-presentation to gain favorable social outcomes. The research reported here was done to investigate the roles of success and failure as motivating forces for tactical self-presentations.

One common model of human behavior suggests that behavior is a joint function of the value of goals and of probabilities that the behavior will be successful in achieving these goals (Escalona, 1940; Jones, 1964; Rotter, 1954). One important goal in social interaction is gaining approval from others. Since the individual's feelings of worth and competence are partially dependent on evaluations from others (Cooley, 1922; Festinger, 1954; Mead, 1934), it follows that one way of raising a low self-evaluation to an acceptable level or maintaining an already high one at that level is to seek approval or avoid disapproval from others. Jones, Gergen, and Davis (1962), Jones, Gergen, and Jones (1963) and Gergen (1965) have all demonstrated that instructions to gain approval do seemingly lead to tactical self-presentations, but as yet there is no evidence that varying subjects' own feelings of competence will affect self-presentations.

We suggest that a person who has just failed on an important task, and therefore who has a temporarily lowered estimate of his abilities, may well want and use approval from others to reestablish a more positive self-evaluation. Failure, then, would motivate approval seeking under certain conditions which we will specify later. A person who has succeeded on an important task, on the other hand, will have a temporarily high self-evaluation, and his primary interpersonal motivation should be to avoid disapproval. Given that he would like to maintain and strengthen this positive estimate of his abilities, criticism from others could well "shake" this tenuous self-evaluation and severely damage the strengthening process.

Our assumption is that after failure experiences subjects are motivated to get approval, while after success experiences subjects are motivated to avoid disapproval. We shall presently discuss the tactical implications of these two motivations.

Before tactical self-presentations are used to gain approval or to avoid disapproval the other must be in a position to provide the desired evaluation, and his evaluation must be meaningful. Following Jones (1964), we are suggesting that the probability of receiving a desired evaluation is an important determinant of the use of tactical presentations. This is not altogether obvious. For example, it might be suggested that self-presentation is used as a self-convincing device, in the sense that the mere act of presenting one's self in an attractive manner makes it easier to accept this self as genuine (cf. Festinger & Carlsmith, 1959, and Bem, 1967, for possible explanations of such a process). Thus it is conceivable that receiving an evaluation from another may not be necessary for change in self-evaluation. In the present experiment a subject either could or could not receive an evaluation based on his self-presentation, and the general hypothesis was that tactical self-presentations would occur to a greater degree under conditions of potential feedback.

In the conditions where the subjects have some objective possibility of receiving the evaluation they desire, we assume that a success subject who wants to avoid disapproval will adopt rather conservative tactics of self-presentation. By presenting a moderate self, one that is normative, he will give an evaluator little reason to give him a negative evaluation, and in this way he can hope to protect his tenuous but positive self-evaluation. A failure subject, on the other hand, wants approval and he can get this most directly by presenting a highly positive self, one that if accepted as genuine will generate a highly positive evaluation from the other. This, of course, entails considerable risk since the presentation may well engender a highly negative evaluation if the presentation is not accepted as honest.

In the actual experiment one-third of the subjects failed on a test of an important ability (failure); one-third succeeded on the same task (success); and one-third took the test but received no score (control). The subjects were then interviewed by a "trained" interviewer who was to assess their social sensitivity from a different perspective. Half of the subjects in each condition understood that the interviewer would reveal his evaluation of their ability to them (feedback), while the other half were told that the interviewer would not reveal his assessment to them (no feedback). Thus, half the subjects were in a position to attempt to get a desired evaluation, and the other half would not be able to gain any meaningful feedback based on their self-presentations.

The general design was 2 (Feedback-No Feedback) × 2 (Success-Failure) with control conditions included to investigate the effects of the feedback-no-feedback manipulation in the absence of experimentally aroused motives. Hypothesis 1 states that in the failure condition feedback subjects are more positive in their self-descriptions than no-feedback subjects, and Hypothesis 2 states that for success subjects the feedback manipulation produces more modest self-descriptions than the no-feedback manipulation. Finally, Hypothesis 3 follows from the first two and states that there is an interaction between the success-failure and feedback-no-feedback conditions with the failure feedback subjects being more positive than the success feedback subjects.

The existence of a control condition allows a test of the predicted differences for the experimental conditions against any effects of the feedback-no-feedback manipulation for control subjects. Thus we expect that differences in the failure and success conditions should differ significantly from similar effects for controls.

The subjects took the Marlowe-Crowne Social Desirability scale (Crowne & Marlowe, 1964), but no specific hypotheses were advanced regarding it.

METHOD

Subjects. One hundred and seventeen Stanford male undergraduates were run individually in the six experimental conditions. One subject was dropped from the final data analysis for suspicion of the experimental procedures, six were excluded for various procedural mistakes, and two were randomly eliminated from analysis to create equal Ns in the conditions. Of the 108 subjects whose data were included in the final analysis, 42 participated as a part of introductory psychology requirements, and 66 were recruited from dormitories and paid $1.50 for their hour's participation.

Procedure. The subject was told that he would be working on various personality and ability tests for about an hour. The experimenter gave him the Marlowe-Crowne Social Desirability scale and Form 1 of the self-presentation test. The experimenter said that he would explain the nature of these tests later.

After the subject had finished with these tests, the experimenter explained that the subject was participating in a project concerned with social sensitivity which was defined as the ability "to perceive accurately the feelings, emotions, beliefs, etc., of other people." The subject was led to believe that although people generally considered themselves fairly sensitive, there were actually wide ranges of abilities in this area so that people could not always tell how socially sensitive they were.

The experimenter explained that his research group had developed a valid and reliable test of social sensitivity, the Feldman-Collier Personality Inference Test (PIT),[1] and that scores on this test not only were highly related to more costly real life measures of social sensitivity but also to such traits as leadership and popularity. This was done to insure that the subjects felt that the test was valid, and that social sensitivity as measured by this test was a desirable trait to possess.

In the so-called PIT the subject is presented with a set of initials followed by supposed answers (true, false, or undecided) to three value statements (actually personality test type items, e.g., "man is basically evil"). The subject is informed that these answers have actually been given by a real person with those initials, and his job is to predict this stimulus person's actual responses to three similar value statements. His score is presumably the number of correct predictions.

After completing this test the subjects in the control conditions were told that the test would not be scored immediately because of time limitations. The subjects in the success and failure conditions were told to remain seated, and the experimenter scored the tests against an official-looking key. In reality answers were arbitrarily marked right and wrong such that subjects in the success condition received scores of 17 (of 24 possible) and subjects in the failure condition received scores of 9 correct. The subject was told that he could be given percentile scores based on his performance. In the success condition his percentile score among Stanford students was 79.8, and for the general population, 90.3. For the failure condition these same percentiles were 32.4 and 40.1. All subjects were told that the Stanford percentile was always somewhat lower than the general population percentile because Stanford students were somewhat more socially sensitive than the average person.

Following the success-failure-control manipulations the subject was given instructions leading into the interview. He was told that

---

[1] The Feldman-Collier Test was originally developed by Stephen Jones.

although the PIT was reasonably valid, the research group had been looking for new approaches to the measurement of social sensitivity because the test "might not give us the entire picture." An interviewing technique had been developed, and initial data suggested measurement of a somewhat different aspect of social sensitivity from the PIT. Specifically, the subject was told that the experimenter was interested in the correlation of the interviewer measure with the true-false test he took earlier (Marlowe-Crowne), and that the interviewers were to write up a brief description of their experiences with the subjects so that some insight might be gained into the dynamics of interviewer ratings of social sensitivity.

The interviewers were described as college students who were interested in social sensitivity and had received some training in the assessment of social sensitivity. The desire here was to insure that the subjects regarded the interviewer's assessments as reasonably valid without thinking that the interviewer was so expert and objective that he could never be fooled.

The subjects were further informed that the interviewer would begin by chatting with them and that later a standard questionnaire would be given. This standard questionnaire was in reality the second measure of self-presentation. The subject was shown a copy of this and told that it did resemble the earlier test he had taken, and that the earlier test had been for practice since the test was a bit unusual. To insure the plausibility of this statement the subject was told to tear up the earlier form if he so desired "since it was only for practice." In the feedback conditions the subject was told that the interviewer would leave after the interview to consider his evaluation of the subject's social sensitivity, and that he would return to deliver this evaluation. The subjects were further told that they were free to discuss the interview and the evaluation with the interviewer at that time. In the no-feedback conditions they were informed that at the conclusion of the interview the interviewer would leave to work on his evaluation and that the subject would never see this: "Until we're very sure what the interviewers are rating, we don't feel it's fair to give you this rating."

Each subject was assured that the interviewer did not know his previous score (in the success and failure conditions), and that the interviewer would never be able to find out what this score was.

The interview. After the experimenter left, the interviewer entered, introduced himself to the subject, and proceeded to engage him in amenities until a pleasant conversational atmosphere had been established. In general the interviewers were completely free to discuss whatever made them and the subjects comfortable, and the general tenor of the conversation was designed to be warm and pleasant.[2]

After about 5 minutes of such conversation the interviewer asked the subject to read aloud his answers to the self-presentation questionnaire, and the interviewer recorded these answers and ratings. Then the interviewer left and the experimenter re-entered the experimental room. He asked the subject to take a pad of paper on his desk and to indicate "somewhere near the top of the sheet what your estimate of your own social sensitivity is at this time. I want you to express this as a percentile so please indicate what percentage of Stanford males you feel are below you in social sensitivity." This was a manipulation check for the success-failure manipulation. After the subject had done this he was asked to make a similar rating for what he thought the interviewer's rating of him would be. Finally the subjects were debriefed and probed for lack of suspicion.

Self-presentation. The two self-presentation forms were identical in format although the items differed.[3] The two forms were not actually parallel, but the median correlation between them was .81 for the six conditions.

In each form there were 12 socially desirable (positive) items (e.g., "well adjusted in general") and 12 socially undesirable (negative) items (e.g., "hard to warm up to"). For each item the subject was asked to make a rating on a 5-point scale as to how descriptive of him the item was. A rating of 5 indicated "highly representative." Under the assumption that a positive self-presentation could be achieved both by giving high ratings to positive items and low ratings to negative items, the negative items were reverse scored, so that for both positive and negative items a high score indicated a positive self-presentation.

RESULTS

Manipulation check. At the end of the experiment subjects indicated how good they felt they were at social sensitivity; these esti-

---

[2] Michael Clausing and Alan Paulson served ably as interviewers. They were blind to the hypotheses and experimental conditions.

[3] Items for the two forms were originally taken from the Triads Test developed by Dickoff (1961). During pretesting new items were constructed and some of the original items changed in wording somewhat.

TABLE 1

Means of Adjusted Final Self-Presentation Scores and of Unadjusted Differences
between First and Second Forms

Group	Positive items		Negative items		Total self-presentation	
	Feedback	No feedback	Feedback	No feedback	Feedback	No feedback
Success	42.16	42.32	42.22	44.49	84.38	86.81
	(−2.61)	(−2.56)	(−1.89)	(.28)	(−4.50)	(−2.28)
Failure	45.06	42.01	43.23	41.33	88.27	83.34
	(.33)	(−2.39)	(−.39)	(−1.28)	(−.06)	(−3.67)
Control	41.87	43.72	43.41	44.05	85.27	87.78
	(−3.22)	(−.78)	(−2.06)	(.28)	(−5.28)	(−.50)

Note.—Differences in parentheses.

mates were expressed as percentiles. An analysis of variance for these data indicates that the only F greater than 1 is $F = 16.38$ for the success-failure-control manipulation. The success subjects had significantly higher self-evaluations than the failure subjects ($t = 5.72$, $p < .001$, $df = 68$); the success subjects were higher than control ($t = 2.62$, $p < .01$, $df = 68$); and the control subjects were higher than failures at $p < .01$ ($t = 3.10$, $df = 68$).[4]

Self-presentation data. The self-presentation data were analyzed through an analysis of covariance technique. The data from all six conditions were used to adjust each subject's positive and negative item scores on the final form for the effects of his initial positive and negative item self-presentation. Then the usual analysis of variance model was used for the adjusted scores with one degree of freedom less for the error term.

Hypothesis 1 predicted that failure-feedback subjects would be more positive than the failure-no-feedback subjects. The data for all conditions are presented in Table 1 and the difference between the two failure conditions is significant at the $p < .01$ level ($t = 3.65$, $df = 34$) in the predicted direction. Hypothesis 2, which predicted more modesty for success-feedback than for success-no-feedback subjects, also received support, although level of significance for this difference is borderline ($t = 1.81$, $p < .10$, $df = 34$).

Hypothesis 3, specifying an interaction between success-failure and feedback–no feedback, was confirmed at the .01 level ($F =$

[4] All t tests are two-tailed.

8.20, $df = 1/67$), and the failure-feedback subjects were significantly more self-enhancing than the success-feedback subjects ($t = 2.90, p < .01, df = 34$).

A comparison of the failure with the control conditions shows a significant interaction ($F = 6.62, p < .05, df = 1/67$), and the failure-feedback subjects were significantly more self-enhancing than the control-feedback subjects ($t = 3.29, p < .01, df = 34$). There is no interaction between the success and control conditions ($F < 1$), and the only effect approaching significance for that analysis is the feedback–no-feedback effect ($F = 3.63, p < .10, df = 1/67$).

While no differences were predicted among several of the individual conditions the differences between the failure–no-feedback, and the success–no-feedback ($t = 2.57, p < .02, df = 34$) and the control–no-feedback conditions ($t = 3.29, p. < .01, df = 34$) were significant. Also the control-feedback was somewhat more modest than the control–no-feedback ($t = 1.85, p < .10, df = 34$). In separate analyses there were no main effects or interactions accountable to the interviewer.

Predictions of the interviewer's rating. At the end of the experiment the subjects were also asked to indicate what rating they felt the interviewer would give them. No specific predictions were made for this measure. As might be expected, this measure correlated fairly highly with the previously administered self-concept measure (the median correlation among the six conditions is .67), and not surprisingly the analysis of variance for this measure shows only a significant success-failure-control effect ($F = 24.23, p < .001, df = 2/101$).

DISCUSSION

The data of the present experiment offer general support for the hypotheses. As predicted, the failure subjects were more self-enhancing in the feedback condition, and the success subjects were inclined to be more modest in the feedback condition.

The major problem with these results is the similarity of the results for the success and the control conditions. It was hypothesized that the modesty effect for the success conditions should be exhibited over and above effects in the control conditions. It is possible that the reasoning about differential modesty in the success conditions is wrong or that the success manipulation was ineffective. One piece of informal evidence for the latter proposition is that during the debriefing session some of the success subjects commented that they had been mildly disappointed by percentile scores of 90 and 80. If this were true for most subjects, it would mean that the success manipulation had been ineffective. On the other hand, there is contrary evidence. The success subjects did report that they thought they were better at social sensitivity than the control subjects $(p < .01)$, and they predicted that they would receive higher evaluations from the interviewer than did the control subjects $(p < .01)$.

Another possibility is that the success subjects felt more successful than control subjects but that this did not affect their basic reactions to the situation; this would indicate that the same processes were going on in the control and in the success conditions. There is, however, some correlational evidence which argues against this view. At the end of the experiment the subjects were asked to predict how positively the interviewer would evaluate them. A reasonable assumption would be that a subject will not attempt a particular tactic unless he feels it will be rewarded by the desired evaluation. Therefore success-feedback subjects who presented moderate selves should have expected higher evaluations than subjects who presented positive selves. This then leads to the prediction of a negative correlation between predicted evaluation and self-presentation for the success-feedback condition. The obtained correlation is $-.28$ $(t = 1.17, df = 16)$, which is in the expected direction although it is not significant. It does, however, differ significantly from the correlation obtained in the control-feedback condition of .51 (the difference is significant at $p < .05$, $t = 2.29$). Although this evidence is not completely convincing, it does tend to support the hypothesis.

It was not anticipated that the control subjects would be more modest in the feedback condition. Since their only chance to gain approval would come from this evaluation based on the interview, we might in fact expect them to be more self-enhancing in the feedback condition. One possible reason for the somewhat greater modesty in the feedback condition is the fact that the instructions had included some emphasis on the fact that the interviewer would be available to talk to the subjects about his evaluation (and presumably his reasons for making a particular evaluation). Under these circumstances the subjects may have been concerned with avoiding a possible public disconfirmation of a too high presentation by a relatively negative evaluation. There is evidence from Haraguchi (1967) that the possibility of revealing consequences leads to a more modest self-presentation. To what extent a similar motivation may have been operating in the success condition cannot be said without further evidence.

Although the results for the failure conditions are strongly consistent with the reasoning about the tactical use of self-presentation after failure, it might be instructive to examine some correlational evidence from the failure-feedback condition. If the reasoning has been correct, subjects who employ highly positive self-presentations in a tactical manner should expect to receive positive evaluations. This leads us to expect a positive correlation between self-presentation and the predicted evaluation, but the obtained correlation is .08. If we examine this correlation separately for those nine subjects with the highest self-evaluations ($M = $ 65th percentile) and those nine subjects with the lowest self-evaluations ($M = $ 39.8th percentile), we find the correlation between self-presentation and predicted evaluation for the high self-evaluation subjects is $-.54$ ($p < .15$, $t = 1.70$, $df = 7$), and for the low self-evaluation subjects, .72 ($p < .05$, $t = 2.75$, $df = 7$). These two correlations differ significantly at the .05 level ($t = 2.60$, $df = 14$). These two groups do not differ in their overall self-presentations (the means are 88.20 and 88.39).

Additional correlational evidence for the failure-feedback subjects is that the Marlowe-Crowne correlated with self-presentation .92 ($p < .001$, $t = 6.21$, $df = 7$) for the high self-evaluation subjects and only .04 for the low self-evaluation subjects.

Seemingly the high self-evaluation subjects do not "buy" the failure manipulation. The best explanation for this pattern is probably Cohen's (1959) notion of defensive self-esteem. He noted: "There is some tendency for the highs (in self-esteem) to repudiate and depersonalize the situation to save face . . . [p. 49]." Here we have subjects who do report high self-evaluations in the face of obvious failure. Perhaps they have convinced themselves that the failure was meaningless and that they need not care about the interviewer's rating (hence the positive self-presentation even though they realize that they will be given a negative evaluation). The higher their need to protect themselves (as measured by the Marlowe-Crowne), the further they seem to insulate their self-concepts and attempt to convince themselves that they are good by presenting a highly positive self.

The low self-evaluation subjects are more in line with our original thinking about the tactical use of self-presentation after failure. They do feel that they have failed and they do expect to receive a positive evaluation for a more positive self-presentation.

One final piece of evidence is an interaction between item type and success-failure-control ($F = 3.01$, $p < .06$, $df = 2/101$). The failure subjects tended to emphasize positive points about themselves (i.e., they said that socially desirable items were characteristic of them), while the control and success subjects de-emphasized negative points (i.e., they said that socially undesirable items were uncharacteristic of them). If we regard an emphasis on positive qualities as the more direct tactic to gain approval, this evidence is consistent with the idea that failure subjects are eager to gain approval while success subjects are trying to avoid disapproval.

In this experiment subjects had a few minutes' conversation with the interviewer before the self-presentation. Although this interview was unstructured, the interviewers did not know the specific hypotheses under investigation and they were blind to the nature of the experimental manipulations. Thus it is unlikely that the interviewers could have systematically affected the results. On the other hand, some of the more interesting and subtle self-presentation tactics may have occurred during the conversation preceding the measurement of self-presentation. No attempt was made to quantify this aspect of the interview, and future investigations might well concentrate on the different ways people attempt to gain approval and avoid disapproval.

REFERENCES

BEM, D. J. Self-perception: An alternative interpretation of cognitive dissonance phenomena. *Psychological Review*, 1967, 74, 183–200.

COHEN, A. R. Situational structure, self-esteem, and threat-oriented reactions to power. In D. Cartwright (Ed.), *Studies in social power*. Ann Arbor, Mich.: Institute for Social Research, 1959.

COOLEY, C. H. *Human nature and the social order*. New York: Scribner, 1922.

CROWNE, D. P., & MARLOWE, D. *The approval motive*. New York: Wiley, 1964.

DICKOFF, H. Reactions to evaluations by another person as a function of self-evaluation and the interaction context. Unpublished doctoral dissertation, Duke University, 1961.

ESCALONA, S. K. The effect of success and failure upon the level of aspiration and behavior in manic-depressive psychoses. *University of Iowa Studies in Child Welfare*, 1940, 16 (3), 199–302.

FESTINGER, L. A theory of social comparison processes. *Human Relations*, 1954, 7, 117–140.

FESTINGER, L., & CARLSMITH, J. M. Cognitive consequences of forced compliance. *Journal of Abnormal and Social Psychology*, 1959, 58, 203–210.

GERGEN, K. The effects of interaction goals and personalistic feedback on presentation of self. *Journal of Personality and Social Psychology*, 1965, 1, 413–425.

GOFFMAN, E. *The presentation of self in everyday life*. Garden City, N.Y.: Doubleday Anchor, 1959.

HARAGUCHI, R. Interpersonal conditions affecting self-presentation. Unpublished doctoral dissertation, State University of New York at Buffalo, 1967.

JONES, E. E. *Ingratiation: A social psychological analysis*. New York: Appleton-Century-Crofts, 1964.

JONES, E. E., GERGEN, K. J., & DAVIS, K. E. Some determinants of reactions to being approved or disapproved as a person. *Psychological Monographs*, 1962, 76(2, Whole No. 521).

JONES, E. E., GERGEN, K. J., & JONES, R. G. Tactics of ingratiation among leaders and subordinates in a status hierarchy. *Psychological Monographs*, 1963, 77(3, Whole No. 566).

MEAD, G. H. *Mind, self, and society*. Chicago: University of Chicago Press, 1934.

ROTTER, J. B. *Social learning and clinical psychology*. New York: Prentice-Hall, 1954.

SCHNEIDER, D. J. Self-presentation as a function of prior success or failure and expectation of feedback of created impression. Unpublished doctoral dissertation, Stanford University, 1966.

The Concept of Self

One aspect of motivation (Section 4) is that of the self concept. To a remarkable extent what one believes about himself provides the lens through which he sees opportunities or barriers. The self concept is basic both in the processes of self-actualization and alienation. The idea of self seems to be increasingly popular in contemporary psychology.

A "new" psychology is emerging which has, as is true with other viewpoints in psychology, a particular emphasis. This new psychology does not yet have a commonly accepted name—some of the terms which refer to similar orientations are: phenomenological, humanistic, and (the term Bonner uses) "proactive" psychology. The emphasis, briefly, is that each person must save himself by visualizing what he may become and moving in that direction. Other psychologies emphasize the processes of biological potentiality, conditioning, and early childhood experiences as the explanations for behavior and personality. Bonner, and many others, say, "Yes, but. . . ." In addition, man can choose, think, dream, and aspire. He not only reacts to environment and the past but he "proacts" by moving forward and choosing his own path for becoming.

Bonner has summarized much of what this book of readings is all about. The editors have been guided in their choices of articles by seeking those which emphasize growth, becoming, choice, responsibility, and self-actualization. Bonner considers all of these and more. He says it is not necessary to carry, throughout life, the burdens of childhood conditioning, impoverished backgrounds, bad habits, inadequate parents, or poor teachers. Also in the life processes are matters of how one responds to deprivation, cruelty, or to educational opportunity. Blaming others may be comforting but it is self-defeating. Assuming responsibility is likely to be more productive—should we say "proactive?"

While emphasis must be placed on choice and responsibility, it is also realistic to acknowledge the pressure of circumstances. Gottlieb presents an article which has many highly pertinent points for the psychology of adjustment. He shows that alienation may have quite different sources for the poor and the middle class individual. But he also shows that the distinctions among socioeconomic class values are not as distinct as some scholars have seemed to indicate. There is, he shows, considerable similarity of values between what he calls the winners and the losers.

The winners and the losers are quite different in the degree of pertinence which they perceive education has to occupation. The losers see no relevancy. The winners are willing to ride with what they perceive to be the inadequacies of formal education. Perhaps we, the editors, are stretching a point when we say that how one perceives educational opportunity is a reflection of the self concept. The confident person says that he is powerful enough to use the system, including its inadequacies, to his advantage. The loser sees the system as a road to failure because he cannot use it—and there is no one to help among his parents, peers, and neighbors. Are we being totally unrealistic to hope that the models which the loser lacks can be supplied by reading, study, and discussion with those *outside* the losers' circle? What are the implications of Gottlieb's assertion that alienation is a product of the inability to come up with the resources for adequately coping with challenge?

The study by Williams and Cole provides at least a partial answer to the above questions. They conclude that the pupil's conception of school is an extension of his conception of himself. They also conclude that school success is certainly not controlled by any one variable—but self concept ranks high.

Much of conventional psychology emphasizes the Stimulus-Response (S-R) relationship. Looked at through this formula, Williams and Cole might be saying: Socio-economic status, emotional adjustment, mental ability, reading achievement, mathematical skill lead to (——→) a healthy self concept. Would it be possible to reverse the formula? Can one find in his in- or out-of-school experiences some reason for patting himself on the back? Are there athletic skills, friendships, good looks, sense of humor, optimism, or whatever which might excuse one for saying, "I'm a good and worthy person and can surmount the academic hurdles"? And with that we might advise jumping the gun and going to the article by Pang on page 323.

A proactive personality is not so much an achievement as a process of becoming. It is more a road to travel than a destination to be reached. A proactive individual is an active agent in actualizing his own self, in becoming all that he can become. He is interested in movement rather than position. He innovates and initiates behavior rather than merely reacting to the behavior of others. We like the word "proactive." It is a good synonym for the process of "self actualization."

The Proactive Personality
HUBERT BONNER
Professor of Psychology
Ohio Wesleyan University

Every psychologist who aims to present a scientific view of the human personality finds himself in a predicament. The more general or nomothetic his description of man is, the more he is impelled to ignore man's uniqueness. This statement holds with special force regarding the problem of psychological types. As a scientist, the psychologist must organize his knowledge of man into more or less stable categories, called *psychological types*. But the moment he classifies man into types, he calls attention to human similarities. Yet, if there is one thing that stands out in the endless research on human behavior, it is that no two human beings are exactly alike.

This difficulty can be reduced if we think of human types not as independent personality categories but as styles of intentional behavior. Every healthy human being approaches life situations in a characteristic manner, which is his unique way of perceiving and controlling himself and the social world which he inhabits. Among such styles of behavior, the best known are introversion and extraversion.

Since my aim in this paper is not to add to the existing typologies but to gain insight into human beings, I shall hypothesize not only that are we all introverted and extraverted in different circumstances but also that we are all proactive—that is, possessed of some degree of forward movement—in different life situations. The degree and extent of proaction will depend on the degree and extent of encouragement or suppression of the natural forward movement of the healthy organism. In this view, I am assuming that, just as we are all born with some degree of intelligence and that this intelligence varies from very high to very low, so we are all endowed with some degree of intentional forward thrust, or proaction. Like intelligence, proaction can be modified by circumstances and by the individual's effort to transform himself in the light of his individual abilities and social conditions.

METHOD AND POINT OF VIEW

The term "method" implies nothing pretentious and no rigorous technique of measurement; for the subject matter of my discussion is not amenable to formulation in measurement terms. It is broadly scientific and accepts information from any source if it expands our field of inquiry, does not go counter to well-established facts, and does not serve as a barrier to the understanding of the living human individual. More affirmatively, it is a way of studying the human being by means of an interrelated descriptive phenomenology, self-anchored perception, and immediate cognition. Each of these will now be amplified.

Descriptive Phenomenology

Phenomenology holds that all human knowledge is based on *lived* experience. It deals with both empirical facts and emerging possibilities. It is the act of immediate absorption in experience as such. As a form of experiential knowledge, phenomenological psychology presupposes consciousness as a basic and central process. This consciousness is an act by means of which objects, persons, and situations present themselves and through which they are apprehended as being what they are. Accordingly, we can know the world of objects and persons only by means of conscious experience. Conscious experience thus gives us access to whatever exists. And since neither life nor consciousness is fixed but always in the making, phenomenological and proactive psychology must always be tentative. It cannot hold anything as permanently established; for psychology, like life itself, has a Rilkean quality in which every ending is but another beginning.

Self-anchored Perception

This form of investigation is based on the conviction, validated by distinguished students of human conduct, that although a plenitude of subjects or cases may in some circumstances be desirable, it is in fact neither necessary nor crucial (Skinner, 1959). The self-anchored mode of research holds that a careful consideration of the single case is often sufficient for the establishment of truth in psychology. More important, this view maintains that a person carefully observing his own subjective experience can add substantial and dependable insight into the nature of human behavior (Bonner, 1965; Stephenson, 1961). The psychologist with the gift of imagination knows that there are occasions when, in order to comprehend the nature of human nature, there is no substitute for his own human nature. Experience has taught him that often he can understand human beings only by means of his own humanity.

Immediate Cognition

Although this is a less threatening and less disparaging term than "introspection," and especially "intuition," it has the quality of being holistic, of seeing things in wholes. It refers to the fact that normally our experience comes to us in the form of immediate understanding of totalities. Except in mental disorders, man's experience comes to him in more or less integrated form, and the more integrated he is as a person, the more dependable are his holistic observations of human behavior. He understands the meaning of other persons' conduct because he is himself a human being.

Methodological Implications. When skillfully integrated by a perceptive psychologist, descriptive phenomenology, self-anchored perception, and immediate cognition are valuable means to the understanding of proactive man. Since proactive man, as we shall see, is a life totality, not a partitioned mechanism, his integrated nature can be disclosed most adequately by means of the "methodology" which I have briefly described.

The general point of view in this study, then, is a broadly scientific humanism. It interprets psychological phenomena "experimentally," that is, as "provisional tries." This point of view is similar to that of John Dewey (1929), who many years ago defined thinking as a form of inner or conceptual experimentation. Such an approach makes room for self-observation as well as the observation of other people's behavior, including all those psychological phenomena, such as love, moral responsibility, creativity, and self-transformation, which, although important characteristics of the proactive personality, are excluded from traditional psychology.

A VIEW OF PROACTIVE MAN

I have said that we are all proactive in some degree. But the extent of the natural forward movement of each individual depends on two important circumstances, namely, the degree of facilitation or suppression provided by the human world in which he lives and his courage to face unstructured situations. Those who live in the past and immediate present feel secure because both temporal dimensions provide them with the safety which comes from knowing what they must do. A repressive socialization will hardly make for an adventurous individual or stimulate in him the freedom to make his own decisions. Proaction is at a low ebb in those persons who, having undergone a restrictive and often arbitrary socialization, have not cultivated the courage to face the consequences of their individual decisions.

To clarify the nature of the proactive style, it is necessary, therefore, to examine the roles of freedom and anxiety in the formation of the proactive personality.

Freedom and Anxiety

I shall not engage in a dispute over the possibility of individual choice, for there are both logical and empirical evidences to substantiate a limited indeterminism in both man and nature. Far more important than quibbling over its possibility is examining its place in the life style of the proactive individual.

Whenever man is faced with the need to reach a decision on vital issues, especially those which relate to his own and other people's destinies, he experiences various degrees of anxiety. Freedom of choice involves the fear of unpredictable consequences. Both the proactive and the less forward-directed individuals experience anxiety in the face of freedom and an unstructured life situation. But the proactive individual, by virtue of his strong desire for new experience and his capacity to assimilate and control anxiety, becomes anxiety's master instead of its slave.

The paradox of intentionality, of forward movement, is that, although anxiety is induced by the unpredictability of human events, the more numerous and far-reaching an individual's choices are, the more satisfaction is in store for him when he gains control over his own conduct. He can say truly of himself that he *lives* instead of *being lived*. He can now view life not as a "useless passion" but as something he can love and enjoy.

Freedom, then, in the sense of making his own choices and reaching his own decisions regarding the person he wants to become, is a powerful psychological incentive of the proactive individual. And, although he is profoundly conscious of life's gratuity and the anxiety which it generates, he prefers the uncertainty of an unpredictable future to the security of a stable existence. This is the record of the "nonadjusted" person, the intense and turbulent individual, the broadly creative human being. It is a style of life that terrifies the less adventurous spirit, and thus its rarity on the continuum of human existence is understandable.

In a sentence, the proactive individual, although facing the same randomness and unpredictability of future events as the rest of us, can mitigate their effects upon himself through bold imagination, moral courage, and a determined effort to see what lies hidden behind his psychological horizon.

Aesthetic View of Life

The proactive individual approaches life with a marked sense of form and symmetry, beauty and harmony. He evaluates experience by his individual standard of fitness rather than by utilitarian categories. Like creative persons generally, he trusts less what he knows and does than he trusts aesthetic experience in the making. In his aesthetic perceptions, as in his loving encounter with the central others in his life, he comes as close as human beings possibly can to blending into a unity the fragments of his existence. By means of his sensitive awareness of all things beautiful, the proactive individual succeeds in transforming the strains and distresses of daily living into a tragic vision of life's possibilities. Living not alone by cold reason but also by aesthetic feeling, the proactive individual can abandon himself to the sensuous and sensual nature of his being, without victimizing himself by conventional and harmful self-accusation.

The intensely aesthetic meaning of his life impels the proactivert to validate truth by affective as well as rational predicates. His style of life confirms what thoughtful men have always known, that healthy human feelings are a necessary basis for understanding and validating truth. For him, facts alone can never be the final ground for truth; they must be allied with aesthetic judgment to make them true and meaningful.

Reference needs to be made to the proactivert's tragic vision of life's possibilities. This is a marked characteristic of his aesthetic style of life. It refers to his seeking of a perfection which is becoming, but never achieved. This tragic sense enables the proactive individual to feel the poignancy and gratuitousness of life, without yielding to cynicism and despair. At such a moment he can succumb to silent grief, and yet give grateful expression to the feeling that life is not wholly destitute of nobility and beauty.

Idealization

My description thus far clearly shows that the proactive individual guides his life by ideals of his own choosing and making. However, it is a matter of great importance to distinguish between healthy and neurotic idealization. Neurotic idealization is a condition of self-deception. The individual in this condition strives to *appear* to be what he is not. It is important for him that others *believe* that he is a certain type of individual, even though he may deviate markedly from the image of himself which he is trying to project. Morally speaking, the neurotic person is hypocritical or insincere—"inauthentic," as the existentialists would say. He is a slave to the image which he compulsively projects, and he wastes his psychological energies in trying to be faultless, a condition which he cannot reach. In him the anxiety which is the lot of all of us is a function not of his awareness of life's imperfectibility or of the awesomeness of human choice but of the fear that others will see through his counterfeit self.

While he is in this state of chronic defense, the neurotic individual is incapable of forward movement. He cannot choose or make decisions, for these entail risk regarding the unpredictable future. His fears are not proofs of his existence, not self-confirmatory, but lead to an intensification of his neurotic condition, of his fear of self-exposure.

The proactive individual, on the other hand, is relatively free of crippling self-deceptions. Although he strives mightily to transform himself in the light of his own ideal of who he wants to be, he finds self-validation only in actualizing what he potentially is.

In short, proactive idealization is the envisioning of ourselves as being different from what we are. Rather than being an act of self-deception and self-falsification, idealization is the process through which the healthy person generally and the proactive individual in particular become authentic persons.

Creativity

In his approach to life, the proactive man is essentially creative. By this word I do not confine myself to artistic and scientific productions or to special skills or uncommon gifts, but I refer to the broader meaning of optimal psychological functioning in the form of self-actualization, constructive imagination, and intuitive perception of new relationships where none were perceived before. But the word has application also in the former sense, for I have found a high incidence of proaction in artists and creative scientists (Bonner, 1965).

The creative aspects of the proactive style reveal themselves in easily recognizable personal characteristics, of which the following seem at the present stage of my concern with the problem to be the most prominent.

First and practically without exception, the proactive man is moved by a strong need for individuation, for being himself as a person. If people are often intimidated by him or find him incomprehensible, it is because they are baffled by his relative unconcern for social adjustment, which they interpret as a form of eccentricity. Were they to look beyond this superficial layer of his being, they would find that his individuation is firmly grounded in the pursuit of excellence. Being moved by this exacting standard, he does not readily adapt himself to the commonplace, and for this reason the less proactive persons cannot fit him into conventional categories.

Second, not finding fulfillment in the existing canons of taste, the proactive man is constantly in pursuit of new values or a fresh reconstruction of the old ones. Transcendence of past accomplishments, both in others and in himself, is therefore another characteristic of the creative, proactive human being. This generates not only tensions in himself but also anxiety in others, which compounds his seeming threat to those who are baffled by his individuality. But instead of being maladjusted in the conventional sense by his transcendence of existing values, he finds increasing personal integration in "adjusting" himself to a world which he himself has largely created.

Finally, the creative individual, almost without exception, has a high degree of intellectual and emotional turbulence. This psychic unrest must never be confused with the emotional agitation and distress of neuroticism for, unlike the unproductiveness of the latter, it is an important source of creative and novel reconstruction.

Self-transformation

Being essentially forward-thrusting, future-oriented, and broadly creative, the proactive individual is constantly engaged in the task of making of himself a "better" human being. In his own eyes this is the most arduous and difficult of all creative acts for, in becoming what he wants to be, he must not only strive unrelentingly toward the ideal of what he wants to become but also transcend the molding power of his past. The degree of his success in achieving these objectives is a measure of his capacity to change himself from what he was yesterday into what he can be tomorrow.

Many a person, born in humble and culturally impoverished circumstances, has outgrown his past and become an individual of exceptional character and achievement. It is not necessary to cite dramatic cases of this transformation, such as Benjamin Franklin and Abraham Lincoln. The world is full of unsung instances. The latest in a long series is Jean Genet, as described by Sartre (1963). Although he had lived a life of crime and sexual perversion and had spent many years in prison, Genet succeeded in overcoming his past and directing his life toward an artistically creative future. He has become deeply aware that in his acts of choice about his own life he has freed himself from the destructive forces of his past. He has "cured" himself in the sense that he has transcended his prior reactive life and directed himself proactively toward a future of superior literary creations.

The proactive person, then, like every healthy and creative individual, resists engulfment by custom and rigid habits, the impairing force of narrow enculturation, and all barriers to a free and active forward movement of his personality. He has both the will and the capacity to resist external pressures toward conformity and to transform himself in the light of his personal goals and values. He is that individual who strives to attain a more free and creative state for himself and his fellow human beings. He exemplifies in his style of living the belief that the future of man is largely of his own making. He validates the view that man is possessed of a creative selfhood.

In fine, proactive man is that being who more than any other human being strives to make of himself a work of art.

CONCLUSION

In this paper I have tried to present as precise a description of the proactive personality as present evidence and discussion permit. It reveals that the proactive person, like all persons, is not an achievement but a process of becoming. It shows him to be what in a general way every superior human being is: an idealist, an innovator, and one who does not fit comfortably into the conventional social scheme.

The proactive man, finally, combines in himself the defiance of a Prometheus and the self-surrender of a Job, in his own unique way. Prometheus was defiant, to be sure; yet his defiance was not willful, but a strong determination to fulfill his proactive being. Job did not meekly resign himself to an arbitrary fate, but expressed trust in his power of endurance. Each had faith in his ability to make himself into a better human being. Together their characters express the Nietzschean view that man is that being who must continually surpass himself.

REFERENCES

BONNER, H. *On being mindful of man.* Boston: Houghton Mifflin, 1965.

DEWEY, J. *The quest for certainty.* New York: Putnam, 1929.

SARTRE, J.-P. *Saint Genet: Actor and martyr.* (Tr. by G. Frechtman). New York: George Braziller, 1963.

SKINNER, B. F. A case history in scientific method. In S. Koch (Ed.), *Psychology: A study of a science.* Vol. 2. *General systematic formulations, learning and special processes.* New York: McGraw-Hill, 1958. Pp. 359–379.

STEPHENSON, W. Scientific creed—1961: The centrality of self. *Psychological Record,* 1961, *11,* 18–25.

Poor Youth: A Study in Forced Alienation
DAVID GOTTLIEB
The Pennsylvania State University

I'm not out to get Whitey . . . I'm just out to get out . . . They talk
about gettin out . . . They carried signs about gettin out . . . Now looks
like you got to burn the place down and shoot your way out . . .

The comments are those of a seventeen year old Black male who
was actively involved in the Newark riots of 1967. He was not part
of an organized movement. He does not believe that he has to
confirm his masculinity through acts of violence. He does not
explain his behavior by stressing the many years that Blacks have
been exploited and discriminated against. He is not seeking ven-
gence. Although he has heard of Carmichel, Brown and King he
knows little of their ideologies nor is he overly concerned with their
intentions. He seeks neither intimate contact with Whites nor
continued existence within a racial ghetto.

His actions and his words make one thing clear . . . he wants
a change of status and he wants it now. He wants out of the slums.
He wants out of unemployment. He wants out of a physical setting
which restricts mobility and maximizes feelings of personal defeat.
He sees himself as standing on the outside and he wants in.

His behavior like that of so many other ghetto youth should
place him in the category marked "Alienated." He is not abiding by
societal expectations. He is not following the established means of
goal attainment. He rejects the laws and folkways which are traditionally employed in the airing of grievances. He is not bothered by
norms which are supposed to govern his behavior and his expressed
attitudes. He not only goes beyond the limits set for adults but he
also violates the special and somewhat more liberal ground rules
which exist for adolescents. He is alienated.

Alienation not only takes many forms but it also touches many
segments of the population. Kenniston's (1965) alienated are significantly different in both background and behavior from Black
urban youth. Being a member of a racial or religious minority may
enhance the probability of withdrawal but it is not a necessary

From *Journal of Social Issues,* 25 (No. 2): 91–120, 1969.

variable. Yet when we talk about alienation the tendency is to include both the Harvard undergraduate who chooses the garb of the Hippie and the Harlem drop out who joins with the Black Muslims. Although both are similar in their overt rejection of traditional means and goals there are important differences.

A major difference is found in the cause of the withdrawal. The middle class adolescent rejects the dominant culture and chooses to remove himself from the established socialization process. No matter whether his assessment be realistic or not—the choice of involvement or estrangement is usually with him.

The middle class Hippy, Teeny Bopper, Beat or adolescent who is not readily identifiable by some group association but adopts a life style which we label as deviant, is not the product of an unjust economic system. He is not the victim of a social order which blocks entry into the dominant culture. The estrangement, for the most part, is the result of a voluntary act. The middle class adolescent has other alternatives. No matter how painful or absurd is the business of growing up in America he can stay within the accepted framework if he chooses to do so. He is not forced to withdraw or to take on the role of the alienated. He most often has sufficient referents who have both the desire and the ability to help him attain the good life.

Kenniston's alienated youth reject the American culture which they see as, "trash, cheap and commercial." It is a rejection of the middle class:

"I have come to experience horror at the good American way of life, namely, the comfortable middle class existence. . . . This seems to be boring me" (1965, 59).

THE POOR ADOLESCENT . . .

The poor adolescent, and this is probably most true of urban Black males, does not reject the middle class style of living. He does not reject the "comfortable middle class life." Given the choice he would gladly exchange his current status with the disenchanted of Harvard, Vassar and Yale. Although he may mock the behavior and fashions of the more affluent he does not see the good life as overly phony, commercial or cheap. His brief encounters with the middle class occur through the mass media and his own forays beyond the ghetto walls. What he sees he likes. He sees well dressed people driving powerful cars. He sees ladies and gentlemen eating in fine restaurants. He sees people who can leave their cars for others to park; he sees these same people being waited upon and catered to by others. The others are frequently Blacks.

Attempting to show him that "all that glitters is not gold" can prove a frustrating business. He is quick to tell you that he recognizes that these people have problems and they are confronted with all kinds of difficulties. He makes clear that he knows that making it is not easy and one has to work. At the same time the hardships that are related to him as being part of upward mobility cannot compare with the misery and pain he has already experienced in his own short life. If the good life means ulcers and mental stress it is a better bargain than rat bites, hunger and a rejecting society.

Certainly sociologists have given considerable attention to the study of social class and variations in attitudes and behavior. In seeking to explain the non-middle class behavior of poor adolescents, sociologists do present a variety of approaches. Although it would be difficult, in any precise fashion, to classify all orientations into neat theoretical categories, there appears to be two prevalent view (Hyman, 1953, 426–442; Hollingshead, 1949; Knupfer, 1963; Svalastoga, 1964; Warner, 1941).

The first would be "They Want in But Get it Knocked Out of Them." This approach is found in the work of Merton as well as in Cohen's analysis of delinquent behavior among poor youth (Cohen, 1954; Merton, 1957, 131–160). In contrast there is the "They Really Do Not Want In" direction proposed by Miller (1958), Warner (1941), Hollingshead (1949), and Friedenberg (1964).

More specifically the "They Want In But Can't Make It" proponents argue that "there is a common American culture which tends to indoctrinate all groups in our society with relatively high status aspirations, and the possession of material goods and high style of living are the sovereign symbols of status and success in American Society" (Cohen, 1961, 106). Ethnic, racial, and class groupings are seen as fairly similar in their aspirations but quite unequal in their abilities to attain the good life. Through everyday experiences, the poor come to learn that the combination of inadequate skills and socially appropriate means minimizes their chances for success. The end result is usually some form of rebellion or apathy.

Counter to the foregoing, the "They Really Do Not Want In"

group views the behavior of lower class youth not so much as a re-action to a social system which prevents entrance into the good life but rather an outcome of a unique and different set of values held by the lower class. Poor youth are seen as having internalized a set of values which happen to be in conflict with the cultural patterns and status criteria assigned to the middle class. Apathy is not the result of failure which comes with admission that "I cannot make it" but rather it is a built in feature of the lower class socialization process. Rebellion occurs not because the system is seen as unfair but because the system demands acceptance of certain values and goals which are incompatible with the values and goals of lower class culture.

WHAT DO THE POOR WANT?

Given the number of studies which have dealt with social class and youth behavior and a national concern with the poor, it does seem odd that we cannot at this stage of the art answer what appear to be fairly simple questions. Namely, what do poor youth want and how do their goals differ from those youth from more affluent back-grounds? Secondly, what are the social factors which appear to facilitate or block attainment of expressed goals? While there are no doubt many factors which could account for our inability to answer these questions, I would propose the following:

In our literature, in our meetings, and in our classrooms we have talked continuously of lower class values, middle class values, and upper class values as if there were a fixed set of criteria for each of these groupings. At the same time research in the field of social stratification makes it abundantly clear that there is much overlap in the values and attitudes of respondents in each of the designated socio-economic categories. The general tendency has been to disre-gard or play down the similarities and to highlight the differences. When explanations are offered to account for the behavior of those in one class who act like those in some other class we resort to the reference group concept. The lower class child who either indicates an interest in higher education or does in fact go to college is viewed as an oddity who is not really a full-fledged member of his own social class but rather a person with a middle class orientation. While this interpretation may be of theoretical comfort, it does little to explain why some middle class youth do not go to college nor why once in college some of these same youth will abandon what we have come to call middle class standards in preference for a life style which we have come to associate with the lower class.

AND WHAT IS "MIDDLE CLASS"?

Where a sociologist is bold enough to define what he means by middle class life the content is often fuzzy and the variables difficult to measure in some precise quantitative form. An example would be in Cohen's attempt to describe the value and behavior of the middle class:

Ambition, a pattern of deferred gratification, an ethic of individual responsibility, the possession of skills especially those of potential academic, economic and occupational value; the rationale cultivation of manners, courtesy and personableness, which involves patience, self-discipline, and the control of emotional expression, physical aggression and violence (1954).

Although we have been quick to speculate on the validity of data obtained through use of standardized tests because we see these instruments as culturally biased, we have, I would propose, built similar biases into our own research methods.

In his discussion of the value systems of different social classes, Hyman utilizes survey data compiled by others (1953). He notes that, in response to a question dealing with college going preferences for their children, poor adults are less likely than other adults to indicate a desire for college. The distribution of responses, by class, is given as evidence of difference in value systems. Because of a failure to consider possible intervening variables this same distribution could be explained in other ways. It could well be that the poor hold lower educational aspirations for their children not because they devalue education but rather that they lack realistic knowledge as to the costs of higher education; that they do not consider it appropriate to make such decisions for their children; or that they fail to see a relationship between higher education and the goals they hold for their children. In any event, I would suggest, that we cannot assume from the marginal distributions that the poor place less value on education than do individuals from other socioeconomic groups.

In the same manner the selection of lower status occupations by poor youth could be explained by lack of sophistication on their part as to the range of occupations which might be available.

Certainly Coleman's study of the Elmtown High School would suggest that when other factors are introduced social class differences tend to have less impact than was reported by Hollingshead in his study of the same school! (1961).

Part of our bias in methodology has stemmed from a failure to differentiate between what we observe in the behavior of a respondent and what the respondent holds as important. The fact that those who live in poverty have kitchens and living rooms which are not as attractive as those found in many suburbs does not mean that the poor necessarily prefer this way of life. Observed life styles at any given time may be as much a result of contemporary social and economic conditions as they are a preference to live in a certain way. There is certainly a need to differentiate between the abilities and the desires of the individual.

BIAS IN RESEARCH SAMPLES . . .

In the selection of research samples we have built in yet another bias which contributes to our inability to be more precise in what we can conclude about youth from different class backgrounds.

Early studies (Lynd and Lynd, 1929; Hollingshead, 1949; Warner, 1941) took place in small communities where most adolescents attended the same high school. In this type of setting the impact of social class would tend to be greater than in a contemporary urban high school where there would be less variation in the socioeconomic status of students. More recently the tendency has been to concentrate on students in suburban high schools and those in college and as a result the research focus is on middle class youth.

Until very recently most research dealing with poor adolescents has focused on the dynamics of delinquency, drug addiction or other forms of deviant behavior. With few exceptions much of what we know about low income adolescents is based on studies of youth in the streets. By comparison there is little empirical data pertaining to a fairly significant portion of the population-lower class youth in urban and rural high schools, at work, in the armed forces or those involved in educational or vocational training programs.

Finally, in looking at the poor we have frequently failed to differentiate between the various ethnic and racial groups. Treating all youth from similar income or occupational backgrounds as if they were cut from a common cloth does not allow for the identification of important differences in values, attitudes and behaviors.

Prior to the presentation and examination of data dealing with what poor youth say they want and what they see as the barriers to goal attainment I would like to make several observations based on recent experiences in working directly with the poor.

"THE GOOD LIFE" . . .

First, in all of my contacts and interviews with urban youth (the personal and detailed interviews number in the hundreds) I have yet to meet one who has expressed a preference for a life of poverty or alienation. I have not heard one who has said that he would want to remain within the ghetto as it now exists. When talking about what they seek their comments bring to mind "the good life" as presented in television shows which deal with the "typical American family." They talk about nice homes and nice cars. They talk about good jobs, jobs with a future. They talk about homes which are large enough to guarantee some privacy from others. They talk about nice neighborhoods and safe places for their children to play. They talk about lawns, trees and summer vacations. They talk about clothes, a proper spouse and educational opportunities for their children. When the urban male, especially the Black, describes the ideal occupation it is a white collar job. There is little interest in dead end jobs or sweaty T shirt employment.

How quickly ghetto youth will take on the chracteristics of the middle class can be noted in observing the changes that occur among these youth when they arrive at a college campus. During the past three summers I have observed inner city Black youth who were part of Upward Bound programs at Yale, Dartmouth and Harvard.

Briefly the purpose of Upward Bound is to identify poor students in need of academic assistance. These same students are assigned to college campuses for varying lengths of time. The students being discussed here were part of a summer program.

Upon arrival the typical pattern is for a quick abandonment of the old life style and the acceptance of the perceived college student culture. Obviously initial changes will be limited to the more visible aspects of the self. Plaid bermuda shorts replace shiny tapered trousers; madras summer caps are substituted for felt hats (an important part of the ghetto peer culture); pipe smoking replaces cigarettes; and there is obvious pride in the wearing of a shirt which carries the name of the college attended. No matter how brief the contact with the college it does appear to have some impact. University staff working with these students are impressed with how quickly new behavior styles are acquired. Changes occur not only in dress but there is an acceptance of the traditional with respect to how college students behave in the classroom, how they study, and how they are responsible for their living quarters. Although there is a tendency for some university officials to look to these same students when there is a theft on campus there is little evidence that they have been guilty of stealing or vandalism. On the contrary there is a general feeling that compared to typical students the Upward Bound enrollees conduct themselves as gentlemen. Other staff note with some surprise the fascination these adolescents have with words and the obvious desire to expand their vocabulary. Desire to become an integral part of the student culture includes involvement in a new set of leisure time activities. These same students will attend and enjoy concerts, foreign films and theater presentations.

Whether they were being naive or whether they were behaving as they felt campus staff would expect them to behave is not the crucial question. Nor is it essential that the observation be made that this is no doubt a selective group hence not an acceptable sample from which to generalize. It is my experience that no matter how poor, how deprived or how disadvantaged, whenever it is suggested that poor youth may in fact hold middle class aspirations there are bound to be cries of sample bias. At the same time critics are unable to indicate precisely what segments of the population might be added or deleted in order for the sample to earn methodological approval.

Nor do I believe it is necessary to speculate on the permanence of these recently acquired behaviors. Obviously without some reinforcement and support the probabilities of continuation are minimized. More important is the fact that these youth by their very presence have indicated some real desire to accept the "establishments" concept of how youth should be socialized.

URBAN POOR WANT MIDDLE CLASS STATUS

It is my position that poor urban youth do in fact seek entrance into a style of life which we have come to identify with middle class status. The observed alienation of the poor is not the result of a voluntary rejection of legitimate means or ends. Poor adolescents do not seek to stand on the side lines. They do not see the middle class culture as either crass or overly commercial. Nor are they inclined to reject a regulated 9 to 5 employment pattern. Their alienation is more a product of an inability to come up with the resources, material, social and psychological requirements for middle class goal attainment than is it a rejection of middle class goals and values. What poor youth lack, are the referents and interventionists who have the ability and desire to help them acquire the skills, both social and educational skills which are essential for upward mobility in our society. Unlike their middle class counterparts poor adolescents do not have access to adults who have the power and desire to assist in the socialization process. Among the poor there is a real shortage of adults who can actually show and tell the adolescent what he should be doing in order to make the grade. There are few referents who can help convince the youngster that there is a meaningful relationship between what he is being asked to do in school and his own goals. There are few who can help explain or prove the real payoff to formal education. Obviously there are few poor parents who have the wherewithal to buy off a son or daughter in order to keep them in school. Finally, there are few adults who will intervene on behalf of the poor adolescent when he is confronted by the demands and pressures of institutional inequity.

WINNERS AND LOSERS

Not all middle class college students embrace the Hippie culture nor do all poor youth fail to gain entrance into the good life. A comparison of two samples of poor youth, one consisting of adolescents who are making it (at least at the time these data were collected) and the second of youth who were not making it (again, at the time these data were obtained), should provide a better understanding of the impact of both values and background factors on adolescent alienation.

In this case those making it will be considered Winners. Winners since at the time of the investigation these youth were following the expected and accepted process—they were enrolled in school when they should have been. The Winners are a sample of 737 low income Black and white male seniors, attending the same high schools, in three different Eastern cities. The sample of Losers consists of 3,602 Black and white urban males, between the ages of 16 and 18. They are losers in that they were neither in school or employed in full time occupations at the time they were studied. The Losers were enrollees in the Job Corps. They do not represent a random sample of Job Corps enrollees since the Job Corps deals with youth between the ages of 16 and 21 from both rural and urban areas. In order to minimize differences between the two samples only urban youth of high school age have been included in the Job Corps sample.[1]

WHO ARE THEY

From the background records of some 100,000 male Job Corps enrollees we get the following profile of the Losers: he is about seventeen and a half years of age; although he has completed nine years of formal education his reading score indicates a 6.7 grade level. While the majority of male enrollees show no previous record of delinquent behavior, twenty-seven per cent (27%) had committed some minor act of delinquency and ten per cent (10%) were convicted of a more serious offense. Less than a fourth had some previous contact with a doctor or a dentist for a ten year period prior to their entrance into the Job Corps. Only ten per cent (10%) held full time jobs at the time they entered the program and of those employed the average hourly salary was less than a $1.00 per hour.

---

[1] These data were not originally collected in order to conduct a comparative analysis. Both sets of data were obtained independently as part of two separate investigations. In both cases paper and pencil questionnaires were the primary source of information. In instances where comparisons are made, similar questions were asked of respondents in both samples. Despite certain methodological shortcomings the data does help pinpoint where variations exist between Winners and Losers.

Comparative data dealing with family structure are presented in the four tables which follow. Each of the tables notes comparisons between Losers and Winners as well as Black and white subjects.

Table I indicates that while Winners are more likely to have

TABLE I

Winners, Losers, Race, and Father's Education
Per Cent—Fathers Who Completed High School

WINNERS		LOSERS	
White %	Black %	White %	Black %
41	46	24	25
N(458)	(269)	(2001)	(1462)

fathers with higher levels of formal education there is little difference between Blacks and Whites within each category. For both racial groups fathers of Winners are almost twice as likely as the fathers of Losers to have completed high school.

The distribution of occupational status for fathers is similar to the table dealing with education with one important exception. While fathers of the Winners are less likely to be laborers than fathers of Losers, Black fathers in both categories hold the lowest occupational positions even though they hold the higher educational

TABLE II

Winners, Losers, Race, and Father's Occupation
Per Cent

Occupational Category	WINNERS		LOSERS	
	White %	Black %	White %	Black %
Professional-Technical	9	6	7	6
White Collar	22	19	21	11
Skilled	46	44	42	39
Labor-Service	14	27	24	35
Other	9	4	6	9
Per Cent	(100)	(100)	(100)	(100)
N	411	256	2074	1453

achievement. This lack of a positive relationship between education and occupational status may, in part at least, explain why Black youth, more so than whites, see other factors in addition to education as being important to upward mobility.

FAMILY STABILITY

A major difference between Black and white youth is found when an examination is made of family stability. Although the Moynihan Report has encountered much in the way of criticism the data obtained from both Winners and Losers would tend to support his observation that there is less family stability in Black homes. Keeping in mind that in both samples we are dealing with fairly homogeneous populations with respect to father's education, occupation and place of residence (again, these are all urban youth) it will be noted that Whites, be they Winners or Losers, are more likely than Blacks to come from homes where they lived with both parents. Less than half the Black Losers and fifty-eight per cent (58%) of the Black Winners come from intact families while more than seventy per cent of the whites in both groups report they lived with both a mother and a father. These differences reflect not only the greater lack of a male role model for Black youth but contributes to the fact that Black youth are less likely than whites to have access to adults who can assist them in the attainment of acceptable goals.

Marked differences are also found when comparisons are made in the current working status of fathers. Again, Winners do better than Losers with Black Losers most likely to report their fathers as being out of work at the time they enrolled in the Job Corps.

TABLE III
Winners, Losers, Race and Family Stability
Per Cent Living With Both Parents

WINNERS		LOSERS	
White %	Black %	White %	Black %
73	58	64	48
N(426)	(252)	(2014)	(1461)

TABLE IV

Winners, Losers, Race, and Father's Current Job Status
Per Cent Fathers Working

WINNERS		LOSERS	
White %	Black %	White %	Black %
88	92	72	51
N(443)	(251)	(2003)	(1362)

It should be anticipated of course that Losers would not fare as well as Winners given the ground rules for entrance into the Job Corps. The Job Corps concentrates on those young men and women who are out of school and out of work. At the same time it is precisely these differences—a deprivation in resources and conditions required for successful mobility—rather than the holding of values which conflict with middle class standards, which play an important part in determining the current status of these youth. Clearly, Black adolescents have to have more going for them in order to make it than do whites. Yet even among the white Losers the impact of family disorganization, father's education and employment history of the father can readily be observed.

As will be noted in the comments and data which follow there appear to be few differences in the expressed goals and desires of both samples of poor youth. There is however variation between Losers and Winners with respect to what they see as the factors which may enhance or prevent them from living the kinds of life they desire. Certainly it would be expected that past encounters and experiences will play some part in how these youth feel about themselves and their chances.

WHAT DO THEY WANT

During the early stages of research with Job Corps enrollees it was found that attempting to identify specific occupational aspirations was a most complex problem. In most cases the youngster would reply that he was not really sure of the job he wanted and that a major reason for his entering the program was to obtain counseling and training so that he could make a realistic decision. In an effort to get some response, the question of occupational preference was rephrased in the following manner:

"Well let's lay aside your previous experiences and the reasons you entered the Job Corps. Now, if you could get any job you wanted, what would it be?"

Not too surprisingly such a question brought about reactions of astonishment. Many enrollees would point out, and rightfully so, that one could not disregard his past, his training and that the future, while still unknown to some extent, had to be considered. Other enrollees would strain themselves to come up with a reply since they assumed it was probably expected that all young people should know at any given time precisely what they wanted to do with their adult lives. Where answers were given, they were in vague terms saying more about the general characteristics of the job and less about a specific occupation. Finally, it became apparent that many of these young men were extremely limited in their scope of the occupation world and the types of employment which could be available to them if they did complete their educational and vocational training. The lack of sophistication as to the range of potential occupational placements reflects once again a lack of referents who could assist the youngster in making realistic career choices. In addition this same uncertainty as to the range of career alternatives may help explain why poor youth are more likely than middle class adolescents to think in terms of less prestigious occupations.

It was primarily because of the reasons mentioned that the data dealing with occupational futures concentrate on the nature of the job as opposed to the identification of a specific career.

DESIRED JOB CHARACTERISTICS

In the tables which follow an attempt will be made, whenever possible, to note comparisons between the Losers and the Winners. Unlike earlier data dealing with background variables the information pertaining to goals were not obtained by asking the same types of questions.

Table V shows a breakdown of certain general job characteristics. It will be noted that matching data from Winners was limited

TABLE V

Winners, Losers, Race and Desired Job Characteristics
Per Cent Selecting Each
(Multiple Choice Item)

CHARACTERISTICS	WINNERS		LOSERS	
	White	Black	White	Black
The pay is good	86	91	89	88
Sure of steady employment	93	89	89	85
If you work hard you can get ahead	93	89	92	89
Opportunity to use own ideas	66	70	70	74
The hours are good	*	*	81	83
The place is clean	*	*	82	87
You can take a break once in a while	*	*	70	73
You don't have to do the same thing all the time	*	*	46	48
Don't have to work hard all the time	*	*	49	62
You can be outdoors a lot	*	*	59	32
You can run big machines	*	*	56	60
You can do complicated things with your hands	*	*	59	69
Use your head a lot	*	*	70	82
N	(443)	(260)	(2097)	(1411)

* Not asked of Winners.

to four items. Where comparisons can be made few differences are noted between the two groups. The greatest variation is in the case of "security in steady employment" where there is a difference of eight per cent (8%) between white Winners and Black Losers.

Among the Losers there are 5 of 13 items in which the difference between Blacks and Whites exceeds five per cent. Each of these might be explained by a general occupational orientation which has been observed among Job Corps enrollees. Reports from staff at the various centers as well as more detailed analysis of existing data indicates that three variables play an important part in determining career orientation: race, age, and residence. The enrollee most likely to show a preference for the more white collar occupations are older, urban, Black youth. However, when comparisons are made between youth of a similar age and residential background it is still the Black who holds the higher level occupational aspirations.

Upon entrance into the Job Corps, Blacks express a greater

desire for training in the white collar areas such as data processing, clerical, sales and general office centered work while Caucasians place a greater initial interest in training related to machinery and construction.

Black youth appear to have an initial indoor-office preference, Caucasians are more likely to seek the out-door shop setting.

In other areas there is general agreement between both racial groups. They do desire a pleasant work setting, job security and an opportunity to use their own ideas. A little less than half note that they are willing to work at tasks where there is little change in routine.

TABLE VI

Winners, Race, and Career Plans
Per Cent Selecting Each Type

Career Category	WINNERS	
	White	Black
Professional-Technical	49	59
Farm-Ranch Owner	1	1
Manager-Official	6	7
Clerical	5	12
Sales	3	1
Skilled Trade-Craft	27	12
Machine Operator	8	4
Service	3	3
Laborer	1	1
Per Cent	(100)	(100)
N	436	228

While direct occupational preferences comparisons between Winners and Losers are not available the expressed choice of Winners does offer some basis for noting general similarities and differences.

Not unlike the racial distribution found among Losers, Black Winners do show a greater preference for the more professional occupations than do Caucasians. Over three-fourths (79%) of the black Winners and less than two-thirds (63%) of the white Winners select an occupation which could be considered as falling within the indoor-white collar job setting (i.e. professional, managerial, sales, and clerical). The greatest differences are found in the "Professional" group with Blacks showing the stronger preference and in the "Skilled Trade or Craft" where Whites indicate a greater interest.

Clearly there are few in the group who anticipate employment at less than the skilled worker level.

LOSERS-WINNERS SAME JOB DESIRES

The occupational choices of the Winners seem to incorporate desired general job characteristics which are very much like those selected by Losers. There is less variation between Winners and Losers, than there is between Blacks and Whites. Both Winners and Losers seek good pay, job security, an opportunity to use their own ideas. Both share a preference for the more complex, prestigious occupations.

Table VII is a further exploration of desired Job characteristics

TABLE VII

Losers, Race and Desired Job Characteristics
Per Cent Selecting Each
(Multiple Choice Item)

		LOSERS	
Characteristics		White	Black
You get along with the people with whom you work		91	89
You get along with the boss		92	89
You can work on your own		67	71
You can tell others what to do		27	35
Others believe your work is important		61	61
You can meet a lot of people		69	77
You are not always being told what to do		64	62
	N	(2111)	(1475)

of Losers with the emphasis on the more interpersonal aspects of the occupation. Differences between Blacks and Caucasians are few with the exception of two items. Black youth are more likely to express a need for telling others what to do and for being in a job setting where they can meet other people. These differences fit in with the already noted observation that Black youth are more inclined than whites to state a preference for jobs that would place them within larger more bureaucratic work settings. The racial differences also reflect a desired shift away from traditional work relationships where Blacks typically played the subordinate role. The majority in both racial groups seek jobs which are perceived as important by others and both recognize the importance of getting along with superiors as well as fellow workers.

Rather than a voluntary posture of alienation the attitudes of Losers toward religion, political involvement, the mass media and leisure time activities suggests a strong acceptance of the middle class life style.

Table VIII deals with how Losers view a variety of different types of involvements.

TABLE VIII

Losers, Race and Personal Preferences and Beliefs
Per Cent Selecting Each
(Multiple Choice Item)

	LOSERS	
Item	White	Black
Like to watch T.V. and listen to radio	79	80
Like new model cars	81	84
Interested in recent elections	69	72
Would vote for president if old enough	88	90
Would like to have children when I marry	87	88
Like to go to church events	77	81
Like athletic events	75	86
Religion is truth	87	86
Like to read newspapers	74	80
N	(2063)	(1392)

The majority—both Black and White certainly enjoy activities common to middle class youth. They watch television and are interested in athletics and new cars. They are probably more accepting of the proposition of religion as "truth" than would be many middle class adolescents and no doubt their involvement with the church would be greater. They say they were interested in the recent election and if old enough they would want to vote. Despite their own experiences with family chaos, few say they would not want children after they marry.

With one exception, a difference of 1% (Religion is "truth") Black Losers were more ready than white Losers to endorse each of the items shown in Table VIII. The greatest variation is found in the area of athletic events where Blacks show the stronger preference.

BLACK ADOLESCENTS WANT MIDDLE CLASS STANDING

Not unlike racial patterns noted throughout the analysis of data dealing with Losers as well as Winners the Black adolescent seems to be more activity orientated and more embracing of middle class styles and ideas. A structural situation could, however, help account for some of the variation between the two racial groups. Among the Losers, who are enrollees in the Job Corps, we have youth who could only enter the program if they met certain criteria of social and economic deprivation. A major factor between the two racial groups is the continuous discrimination which has prevented Black mobility regardless of skill or aspirations. In other words even though Blacks are as likely as Whites to possess higher levels of formal education they have been less likely than whites to obtain employment which correlates with their educational background. As was pointed out earlier Black fathers had more formal education than white fathers and at the same time they were more likely to be unemployed or when employed they were working at lower level occupations. The racial stigma is not an added burden carried by poor whites. Hence even though there is little variation in the socioeconomic and geographical background of both racial groups the whites may well be suffering from a different form of relative deprivation. In this case Blacks can in part, account for their current low status, and rightfully so, in terms of a societal structure which penalizes persons because of their race. In a sense whatever progress they make is more difficult to come by than is the case for the whites. The poor white, I suggest, not having a similar reasonable and more acceptable explanation for his lack of achievement is more likely to question his own abilities and motives. As a result white poor youth, in comparison with Black youth, tend to select occupations where they are dependent upon others for supervision; they select occupations which place a heavier emphasis on physical as opposed to intellectual abilities; they are less desirous of interaction with co-workers; and they are less likely to seek involvement in social, political and leisure time activities.

A similar interpretation may be offered for the Winners. In this case we have whites who have not followed the usual pattern of exodus to other places once change in the racial composition of school and community occur. Rather here are the people who do not possess the resources required for mobility to the more desirable areas. It would seem that at times minority status can be as painful for the white as it is for the Black.

At the same time interaction with Whites in a setting where there is relative equality in institutional status has some impact on the Black adolescent as well. The results, however, appear to be of a more positive nature. The Black may well gain added self confidence and assurance because he believes that even with societal restrictions, unique to the Black, he has at least done as well as whites who have not encountered similar barriers. The reference group coin has two sides: with the racial majority offering the racial minority a basis for comparison which tends to enhance aspirations while the reverse operates in a more negative manner for the racial majority.

TABLE IX

Winners, Race and Self-Concept—Alienation
Per Cent Selecting Each
(Multiple Choice Item)

Items	WINNERS	
	White	Black
Things have become so complicated in the world today that I really don't understand just what is going on	30	24
I feel that I am a person of worth, at least on an equal plane with others	84	96
I often feel lonely	38	38
I enjoy being with people	87	91
I am not interested in school activities that most students seem to like	35	29
I am interested in my schoolwork	71	88
There are a few people who control things in this school, and the rest are out in the cold	41	35
If you want to be part of the leading crowd here, you sometimes have to go against your principles	52	36
I don't enjoy schoolwork, but I feel that I must do it in order to be able to get things I will want later	66	54
Most older people don't really understand me at all	34	36
N	(436)	(251)

Obviously more precise longitudinal and change data would be required in order to test out the validity of such a proposition. In addition there would have to be some control for the racial composition of the setting. No doubt, there would be some added impact, on both racial groups, as each shifts away from traditional status roles: the White to minority, the Black to majority.[2]

At the same time the comparative data available and observations of Job Corps enrollees would tend to add some credence to this type of cross racial reference group interpretation.

Both Tables IX and X deal with aspects of self concept and feelings of alienation as expressed by Winners and Loosers. Since different items were used the results are presented in separate tables.

TABLE X

Losers, Race Self-Concept—Alienation
Per Cent Selecting Each
(Multiple Choice Item)

	LOSERS	
Items	White	Black
Sometimes feel there is no use trying	24	48
Most people are unhappy and can't do anything about it	49	44
I sometimes feel like giving up	47	42
You have to be lucky to get anywhere	23	29
Sometimes I feel I am in a rut with no way out	52	43
Hard to do what I really want	46	57

Variations between the two racial groups goes from no difference, where in both groups over a third (38%) indicate that they often feel lonely; to a difference of seventeen per cent (17%) with Whites being less likely than Blacks to indicate a desire for school work. In each case, regardless of percentage variations the direction of the differences suggests that the Black students are more involved in school activities; are more accepting of the social system of the school; place a greater value on their own worth; and seem less overwhelmed by "their" world.

[2] In an earlier study, "Racial Composition and the Social Systems of Three High Schools" (Gottlieb and Ten Houten, 1965) significant differences in student behavior were found when comparisons were made between students similar in socio-economic status in schools of varying racial compositions.

WHITES SHOW GREATER ALIENATION

The responses of the white students indicates a greater alienation from and dissatisfaction with the school and its activities. Whites, for example, are much less interested in school work and as mentioned earlier, found school work at best a required but not necessarily valued activity.

The greater alienation of the white student is reflected also in their belief that others "control things in the school, and the rest are out in the cold." The greater involvement of the Black student can be seen in the fact that they, more so than the whites, do not feel that membership in the leading crowd demands the abandoning of principles. Aside from the racial differences it is worth pointing out that more than a fourth of all students agree that they do not understand the world in which they find themselves; that they frequently feel lonely; that they are not interested in their schoolwork; that the cost of popularity may be too great; and that the gap between the generations leaves much to be desired.

Whether these sentiments are unique to poor youth alone cannot be determined in this paper. More important is the fact that with the social-economic deprivation is added the more general problem of growing up in a highly contradictory society.

For the Losers a similar pattern is observed with two important exceptions. Table X shows that white Losers are most likely to express sentiments of personal defeat or doubts as to their own abilities to overcome. Black Losers are less inclined to feel there is no use trying or that they are locked into their current status. At the same time Black Losers know from past experience that personal desires and skill alone are not sufficient. The factor of race cannot be isolated from the matter of goal attainment. The Black senses that if he is to succeed the task will be tough and he will need added luck to go along with ability and desire. Finally, as is probably to be expected many of the Losers, regardless of race, see their chances of making it as fairly slim. Almost half in each racial group see a world in which most people are unhappy with their lives and there is little chance for improvement; many of these same youth see themselves as being in a rut with escape being no simple matter.

THE BARRIERS TO THE GOOD LIFE

At the same time these adolescents, Winners and Losers, have not given up. By their presence in school or in the Job Corps they are indicating some real commitment to finding their place within the

TABLE XI

Winners, Losers, Race and Barriers to the Good Life
Per Cent Selecting Each
(Multiple Choice Item)

Barriers	Winners		Losers	
	White	Black	White	Black
Lack of Ability	36	41	50	52
Lack of Education	81	88	69	76
Job Training	*	*	72	72
Lack of Breaks	49	59	43	55
Lack of Clear Goals	31	36	65	67
Family Background	9	16	11	24
Race	9	21	6	28
Unrealistic Goals	27	38	41	54
N	(437)	(255)	(2019)	(1416)

* Not asked of Winners.

social system. From their views of the world, other people, and their own background it is clear that in addition to the usual problems encountered by adolescents these people have a multitude of barriers to overcome if they are to live the good life. Moving away from general observations a clearer picture of what they perceive as their own personal hangups can be noted from the factors which they identify as being the hurdles to goal attainment. Again, there are some sharp contrasts between Winners and Losers as well as Blacks and Whites.

With one exception, the matter of job training, both groups were asked a similar question. Specifically to note the hurdles which they saw as preventing them from living the kind of life they desired.

For all respondents education is perceived as the major variable associated with entrance into the good life. Black Winners, followed by white Winners are more supportive as to the importance of education. The greater support on the part of the Winners would be expected since their remaining in school implies some real acceptance of the importance of formal education. In addition Winners are of course more likely than the Losers to anticipate college entrance and occupations which demand higher education. Still the majority of the Losers, even though many have encountered some disenchantment and conflict with school do not minimize the importance of education.

Losers consider "Job Training" as being important as "Education". In fact few are able to separate the two since they see training for an occupation as being part of an educational process. Although, as was mentioned earlier a similar item was not presented to the Winners. I would suspect that they too would place high value on the need for training that would be related to a specific occupation, and would, as do the Losers, see this as an integral part of their total education.

Losers more so than Winners recognize the discrepancy between the life they desire and the abilities they possess or that are required for goal achievement. This would be expected since, unlike many of the Winners, these young men have already experienced not only job rejection but they have also failed in school. It should also be noted that it is the Black who places the greater emphasis on the ability barrier. This racial difference would also make sense given the earlier observation that Blacks hold the higher aspirations and hence greater skills are required.

BLACKS THINK THEY MUST HAVE "MORE GOING"

Finally the greater stress on ability as well as education on the part of Blacks fits in with the proposition that Blacks, like other minority groups, believe that they must have a little more going for them if they are to compete with others for desirable ends. Variations between the races with respect to the importance of getting the right breaks does support such a proposition. Blacks more than Whites select this item. The Black feeling that race does play an important role in who gets what, will see the breaks and other external factors as essential ingredients. As Table XI indicates over a fifth of the Blacks see race as a potential barrier with Black Losers being most concerned. It would seem that there are also some white youth who believe that race is important to their mobility. Not perhaps unlike some adults here are members of the majority who believe that social changes have gone so far that being white is no longer an advantage and may well be a disadvantage.

Family background is noted by almost a fourth (24%) of Black Losers as yet another barrier.

Only nine per cent (9%) of Winning whites select this item with Black Winners and white Losers falling in the middle. This distribution does reflect earlier differences noted in family organization. For both groups it was shown that Blacks more so than Whites and Losers more so than Winners were most likely to come from broken homes.

The two remaining items deal with the issue of goal identification and goal attainment. In both cases there is a marked contrast between Winners and Losers and among Blacks and Whites. Blacks more so than their white counterparts have doubts as to just how realistic their goals might be. These observed differences could be explained by recalling certain points made earlier: Blacks have the higher goals and perceive the greater interplay of external and nonindividually controllable factors. Losers are more apprehensive about the validity of their goals since they desire goals not too different than Winners even though they have already experienced failure and by their own admission lack the attributes which they feel are essential to goal attainment.

Loosers are almost twice as likely as Winners to point out that a major hurdle to getting what they want is an uncertainty about exactly what it is they do want.

LOSERS CAN'T EXPRESS SPECIFIC CAREER GOALS

Earlier in this paper I attempted to point out that a major characteristic of Losers was their inability to express specific occupational or career goals. In part this inability stems from a lack of awareness as to the variety of career alternatives which might be available. More important here are adolescents who have not had the opportunity, due in large part to an insufficient pool of referents and resources, to make an assessment and selection of future ends. The Losers know there is a better life and they want a part of that better life. They have a general idea as to the material benefits that can be derived from the good life and as already shown, some idea as to what it takes to gain entrance into the good life. What they lack is the ability to focus in on certain future goals and a belief that there is some meaningful relationship between these goals and the advertised means: education, job training, appropriate behavior, and so forth; factors which others have designated as being essential to goal attainment. Early in this paper I expressed the opinion that the poor do not choose alienation. That a major difference between those who make it and those who do not is a difference in the availability of referents who possess the desire and ability to help the adolescent identify and reach desirable goals. This means in addition, referents who can continuously, through one method or another show or convince the adolescent of the payoff relationship between selected goals and prescribed means. These are precisely the kinds of resources, referents, and interventionists that are in comparative abundance among the affluent but in short supply among the poor. Yet as has already been shown even among the poor there is some variation. The Winners while standing in contrast to middle class youth are somewhat better off when compared with Losers. Blacks, and here I can only add to what others have reported elsewhere, be they Winners or Losers fall at the bottom when it comes to having access to resources and referents required for upward mobility.

Examples of this variation in available referents who have both the desire and ability to assist the adolescent can be noted in Table XII.

Table XII shows the distribution of responses of the Winners to

TABLE XII

Winners, Race and Parental Ability and Desire to Assist

		Father		Mother	
		White %	Black %	White %	Black %
Able and willing		74	65	79	82
Able but not willing		7	10	3	2
Willing but not able		13	18	15	12
Neither willing nor able		6	7	3	4
		(100)	(100)	(100)	(100)
	N	(302)	(111)	(327)	(119)

a question which attempts to assess the student's perception of his parents desire and ability to assist in matters of school and career decisions.

The question asked was: "In making decisions about college or a career, students often go to different kinds of people for help. Please rate your mother and father on her or his ability and willingness to help you make the right decision about college or a job".

Only those students who live with parents, step parents or foster parents were asked to answer these questions.

The portion dealing with father's involvement indicates that white Winners can be more dependent on their fathers than can be Black Winners. Almost three fourths (74%) of the Whites see their fathers as having both the desire and ability to help in career and school decisions. This is the case with less than two thirds (65%) of the Blacks. Black Winners are also more likely than Whites to see fathers as lacking the desire to assist even though they possess the ability. These data suggest that even when in the home, Black fathers, are less inclined than white fathers to take an active part in the socialization of their children.

MOTHER-SON RELATIONSHIP

This does not appear to be the case when it comes to the mother-son relationship. Although the difference is small Black mothers, more so than white mothers, are perceived by their sons as being the more helpful. More important is the greater reliance on the mother over the father on the part of the Black adolescent son. Sixty-five per cent (65%) identified the father as being willing and able as compared to eighty-two per cent (82%), a difference of seventeen per cent (17%), who saw the mother in this role. The fact that mothers play the more direct role in the day to day business of child socialization is not surprising. Nor do these data conflict with the observations of others that in the Black family the mother tends to play the more dominant role because of the absence of the father.[3] These data do, however, suggest that even when he is not absent the Black father is less likely than the white father and far less likely than the

---

[3] An excellent summary of research related to the Negro mother and Negro family can be found in: Lee Rainwater and William L. Yance (1967).

Black mother to be involved in the guidance and counseling of his adolescent son.

Why Black fathers are less likely to be involved even though, according to the respondent, they are present in the home is not the concern of this paper. Nor am I proposing, based on these data, that this finding should or could be generalized to other Black families in other places. Rather I have attempted to point out yet another area where the Black adolescent, by comparison with non-Blacks of similar socio-economic background has less of the desirable and important resource. In this case, even though there is control for parental presence in the home, Black youth do not have the same access to potentially helpful referents as do Whites. Nor can Black adolescent sons be as reliant upon their fathers, as can be white sons, when it comes to obtaining assistance about matters of career and school.

TABLE XIII

Losers, Race, and Parental Involvement
Per Cent Selecting Each

		Losers	
		White	Black
Parental Involvement		%	%
Interest and Involvement		31	36
Interest but Little Involvement		46	43
No Interest—No Involvement		19	18
Active Interference		4	3
		(100)	(100)
	N	1989	1164

Table XIII deals with responses to a similar set of questions asked of the Losers. There are however, several important differences. First, the data are limited to parental involvement in general and not mother versus father. Secondly, the responses say less about how the respondent perceives his parents and more about his evaluation of the role actually played by parents in matters of career and school counseling. In other words the respondent was not asked, as was the case with Winners, to rank his parents with regard to their desire and ability to be helpful, but rather to identify the degree of parental involvement.

Variation between the two groups are not great with the possible exception that Black Losers indicate a greater interest and involvement on the part of their parents than do whites. This difference could be explained by the Black mother's greater involvement with her son as reflected in data presented earlier. Clearly for both groups it is evident that these youth do not see their parents as having been actively or deliberately engaged in interfering with the respondent's school career. Rather the data would indicate that here are parents who have a desire to assist their sons but lack ability. If we assume that interest is similar to desire we can make some comparisons between Losers and Winners. The earlier Table (Table XII) showed that most parents were seen as having both a desire and ability to assist the Winners in decisions of school and career. The picture is not quite the same for the Losers. Here only a little more than a third (36%) of the Blacks and a little less than a third of the Whites (31%) indicate that parental interest is matched by involvement.

LOSER AND PARENT

While there is not much difference between Winners and Losers in parental concern it is the Loser who is most likely to see his parent as indifferent or lacking interest. At the same time the majority in both groups see their parents as people who do care. Clearly the lack of involvement or the limited involvement of the Losers cannot be interpreted as indifference, since over three-fourths of the Losers report their parents were in fact interested in the respondents' school career. The lack of involvement on the part of the parents or Losers results, I believe, from a lack of those factors necessary for parental intervention. They lack the ability to assist their children in goal attainment. As pointed out earlier the parents of losers have the lower education; they are more likely to be unemployed; and they have encountered the greater family instability.

Clearly an inability to achieve economic and family stability in one's own life does little to enhance one's role as advisor to others. Here then is a dramatic portrayal of the cycle of poverty in operation between the generations. As if an insufficiency of salient educational, vocational and social skills required for successful competition within our complex society were not enough. The Losing parent is burdened with the day-to-day struggle of economic and family survival. It should not be too surprising then that these parents can do little despite their personal preferences and the preferences of their children to assist their children in the attainment of legitimate and desirable ends.

Unfortunately this deprivation in required resources and referents within the family is not compensated for by what goes on in the schools of the Losers. It is not necessary here to repeat what has already been documented by those who have studied slum schools. We know that most of these places are inadequate particularly in the very areas where the poor need the most in the way of assistance.

One important area, however, in which these schools do tend to fail is worthy of more detailed discussion. As I mentioned earlier a major variable which according to the Losers explains their departure from the school, is the fact that they were unable to see any significant relationship between what they were asked to do in school and their own future expectations. Interestingly enough few of the Losers suggested that their departure from school was due to hostile teachers or nonacceptance of peers. For the most part of both Black and white Losers the "Typical teacher" is pictured as the type of person who is really interested in what happens to the student. Generally the comments of the Losers would suggest that they did not find school to be an unpleasant experience. Nor do the available data indicate that they felt alienated from school activities. More than seventy per cent (70%) in both racial groups say they were interested in these extracurricular events and over two-thirds say they were participants in these activities.

INABILITY TO DEFER IMMEDIATE GRATIFICATION

An inability to defer one's immediate gratifications is yet another explanation offered when accounting for the differential school exodus of youth from various socio-economic backgrounds. Most simply the theory proposes that poor youth are more likely than others to settle for a little less today rather than take their chances on a tomorrow which might bring them more. Again, however, data obtained through questionnaires and interviews would not suggest that this inability to delay was a primary force in leading most of these youth to leave school. As noted earlier the majority were active in school activities of one type or another. Their comments would suggest that financial limitations did not cause them embarrassment with either teachers or peers. In addition few of these youth state that it was a desire for a car, clothes, or freedom which led them to abandon school. Upon leaving school only a small number had immediate plans as to what they would do next and even fewer had a specific job. It may well be that these youth attended schools where a majority of the students came from similar backgrounds and as a result there was little pressure placed on the student to compete with peers for the material possessions which might enhance personal prestige and status. This homogeneity in social and economic background might also explain why respondents did not, for the most part, view their teachers as people indifferent to the needs of the students. Finally, a similarity in social status among students could account for the active involvement of these youth in school functions even though they were of lower class background.

What does seem to be evident and not unlike the conclusions drawn by Stinchcombe in his study of high school alienation—is an important tie in between what the student sees as going on in the classroom, his future expectations, and the school behavior (1965).

Table XIV shows that only a small number of the Losers felt

TABLE XIV

Losers, Race and School-Goal Consensus

		Losers	
		White	Black
Perception		%	%
High Consensus		14	19
Moderate Consensus		35	40
Low Consensus		51	41
		(100)	(100)
	N	2016	1409

there was consensus between what they experienced in school and their future goals. Forty-one per cent (41%) of the Blacks and a little more than half (51%) of the Whites saw little relationship between the requirements of the school and future career orientation. Less than twenty per cent in both groups could be classified as feeling that there was a high level of consensus. Although I have no comparable data for the Winners the findings do allow for some speculation as to the impact on the Losers.

The phenomena appears to operate in two ways among lower class adolescents. As noted earlier, in the discussion of occupational preferences, these youth are far from clear as to the specific occupational goals they seek. This lack of clarity in future roles minimizes the students' chances of making some firm association between that which occurs in the school and some end goals.

In addition, these youth lack knowledge, even though they might have a specific occupation in mind, as to what in the formal educational process is required for success. Although they recognize the importance of education, they do not know how to evaluate the various components of the educational process.

Aside from the importance of the goal consensus factor, there is a lack of adult referents who have the ability to aid the youngster in clarifying goals and assisting in the attainment of these goals. The data on involvement of parents in academic affairs suggest that while most parents desire to assist their children in educational pursuits they lack the necessary skills and sophistication.

IN CONCLUSION . . .

My position in this paper is I hope quite clear. I believe that poor kids do in fact want to be middle class but it is far from easy for them to make the grade. While admittedly the data utilized to support my position have been stretched somewhat, they do support the basic argument. It is not I believe a question of a lower class value system or subculture which contains elements opposed to or in conflict with legitimate means and ends. It is not, as is frequently the case among middle class adolescents, an opposition to that life style which is called middle class. Rather the poor adolescent finds himself alienated because he is without the resources and referents which have become increasingly more important for goal attainment in our society. There is little variation, as was noted in the data, between Winners and Losers with regard to aspirations and goals. The greater difference here was between the Blacks and the Whites in both groups. At the same time there were fairly sharp differences between Winners and Losers in matters of the availability of referents and resources. Both are poor, both are deprived, the Losers much more so. Finding himself without these resources and referents within the structure of his own family the poor adolescent becomes more dependent on others, outside the home. Even here, however, he finds himself deprived. There are few among his relatives or peers who can be of assistance. His alternatives are limited, for the most part, to the resources of the school. Yet here again there is little that will act to compensate for his general deprivation. The slum school, aside from its many other shortcomings, is like many other schools (both high school and college) in that it fails to provide the student with a setting which enables him to see and feel the real pay off. He cannot see meaningful or legitimate consensus between the demands of the formal educational process and the better life he seeks. At the same time, unlike his more affluent counterpart, he does not have the referents who have the power and desire to keep him within the system. There are few poor parents who have the ability to buy him off with promises of material rewards and leisure time activities. He is limited in his contacts with adults who can explain, clarify, and illustrate what the benefits of education will be. There is little that is offered him in the way of guidance and counseling much less more frequently needed intensive therapy. The deprivation is not limited solely to occupational, social, and intellectual resources. He lacks also in those who can provide him with medical and dental care.

It is interesting to note that for many years poor youth have migrated from one community to the next with little attention or assistance from others. Yet along comes the "Hippie movement" and we not only have massive media coverage but the emergence of countless spontaneous service centers to aid the rebellious middle class adolescent. It would seem that despite our expressions to the contrary we do practice the maintaining of the status-quo—the rich must stay rich no matter their preference—while the poor must stay poor no matter their personal desire.

REFERENCES

COHEN, ALBERT K. *Delinquent boys*. Chicago: Free Press, 1954.

COHEN, ALBERT K. and SHORT, JAMES F. Juvenile delinquency. In R. K. Merton and R. A. Nisbet (Eds.), *Contemporary social problems*. New York: Harcourt, Brace, and World, 1961, 106.

COLEMAN, JAMES S. *The adolescent society*. New York: The Free Press of Glencoe, 1961, 61.

FRIEDENBERG, EDGAR Z. An ideology of school withdrawal. *The school dropout*. Washington, D.C.: National Educational Association, 1964, 25–39.

GOTTLIEB, D. and TEN HOUTEN, W. Racial composition and the social systems of three high schools. *Journal of Marriage and the Family*, May 1965, *27*, (2), 204–212.

HOLLINGSHEAD, AUGUST B. *Elmtown's youth*. New York: Wiley, 1949.

HYMAN, HERBERT H. The value systems of different classes: a social psychological contribution to the analysis of stratification. In R. Bendix and S. M. Lipset (Eds.), *Class, status and power*. New York: The Free Press, 1953, 426–442.

KENISTON, KENNETH. *The uncommitted: alienated youth in American society*. New York: Delta Book, 1965.

KNUPFER, GENEVIEVE. Portrait of the underdog. In R. Bendix and S. M. Lipset (Eds.), *Class, status and power*. New York: The Free Press, 1953, 255–263.

LYND, R. S. and LYND, H. M. *Middletown*. New York: Harcourt, Brace, and World, 1929.

MERTON, ROBERT K. Social structure and anomie. *Social theory and social structure,* rev. ed. Chicago: Free Press, 1957, 131–160.

MILLER, W. B. Lower class culture as a generating milieu of gang delinquency. *Journal of Social Issues,* 1958, *14,* (3), 5–19.

RAINWATER, LEE and YANCY, WILLIAM L. *The Moynihan report and the politics of controversy*. Cambridge: M.I.T. Press, 1967.

STINCHCOMBE, ARTHUR I. *Rebellion in a high school*. Chicago: Quadrangle Press, 1965.

SVALASTOGA, KAARE. Social differentiation. In R. E. L. Faris (Ed.), *Handbook of modern sociology*. Chicago: Rand McNally Co., 1964, 530–575.

WARNER, W. LLOYD and LUNT, PAUL S. *The social life of a modern community*. New Haven: Yale University Press, 1941.

Self-Concept and School Adjustment

ROBERT L. WILLIAMS and SPURGEON COLE
Assistant Professors of Psychology
West Georgia College, Carrollton

This study attempted to relate self-concept to several dimensions of the child's experience that are deemed fundamental to effective academic adjustment. It was hypothesized that a child's conception of school would be related to his conception of himself, and thus might be construed as an extension of his self-concept. 80 6th-grade students were used as subjects for all phases of the investigation. Significantly positive correlations were ob-

From *Personnel and Guidance Journal*, 46: 478–481, 1968.

tained between self-concept measures and the following variables: conception of school, social status at school, emotional adjustment, mental ability, reading achievement, and mathematical achievement.

Theorists (Lundholm, 1940; Snygg & Combs, 1949; Rogers, 1951; Sarbin, 1952) have viewed the self-concept as central to man's behavior. The self-concept formulation has been applied with increasing frequency to educational theory and practice. To what extent does a child's conception of himself affect his adjustment to school, or vice versa? Several experimenters (Coopersmith, 1959; Fink, 1962) have obtained positive relationships between the self-concept and academic achievement. Others (Bruck & Bodwin, 1962; Walsh, 1956) have postulated that deficiency in self-esteem may be a significant determinant of underachievement.

A crucial inquiry facing educators is why some students are positively oriented toward academic pursuits while others of ostensibly comparable ability and background are negatively inclined. Differences in academic motivation may partially be attributed to differences in self-concept. Levy (1956) has demonstrated that an individual may view his town, church, school, etc., in much the same light in which he perceives himself. Therefore, a child's conception of school might fundamentally be an extension of his self-concept.

What relationship exists between an individual's self-appraisal and others' evaluation of him? Brookover and his six colleagues (1966), reasoning from the symbolic-interactionist theory of Mead (1934), attempted to relate evaluation of significant others (parents, experts, and counselors) to self-perception of ability and school achievement. They found that positive communication from parents relative to a child's ability led to a significant increment in both self-perception of ability and grade-point average. Communication from experts and counselors did not, however, have a significant effect on either variable. Brookover's group concluded that it is more efficacious to work through established significant others such as parents than to attempt to develop new significant others as bases of influence. One group of significant others not included in the Brookover study is the child's immediate academic peer group. Communication from the peer group may constitute one of the more decisive determinants of both self-evaluation and achievement.

Although research has indicated a positive relationship between self-concept and school achievement, the relationship between self-concept and intellectual ability appears considerably more tenuous.

Wattenberg and Clifford (1964) did not obtain a significant relationship between the self-concept and intellectual ability at the kindergarten level. But what is the effect on self-esteem of several years of negative feedback for the low-ability child in the typical academic situation?

The present study attempted to extend the role of the self-concept in the explication of academic behavior by focusing on the relationship between self-concept indices and a series of variables construed to be fundamental to school adjustment. The series of dependent variables included conception of school, social status at school, emotional adjustment, mental ability, reading achievement, and mathematical achievement.

METHOD

Subjects. The sample included 60 sixth grade students selected from a small urban school and 20 from a rural school.

Instruments and Procedure. The Tennessee Self Concept Scale (Fitts, 1965) provided a measurement of self-esteem. This instrument is a standardized, objective scale that assesses various dimensions of self-evaluation, including physical self, moral-ethical self, personal self, family self, and social self.

The subject's attitude toward school was established by presenting a list of 30 adjectives that might be applied to the school experience, such as "interesting," "confusing," "frustrating," and asking the subject to rate his school experience as he presently perceived it and as he would like it to be along these dimensions. A positive school-concept was one in which there was little discrepancy between the two evaluations, thus the higher the discrepancy score the poorer the school-concept.

An unpublished social esteem scale asked each child to identify other children whom he would like to take home with him, help him with his homework, see chosen class leader, etc. A child's social status was computed from the number of times he was selected for these various roles by the other students.

Emotional adjustment, intellectual ability, reading achievement, and mathematical achievement were measured by the California Test of Personality, the California Short-Form Test of Mental Maturity, and the Reading and Arithmetic sections of the California Achievement Test Battery, respectively. Inasmuch as reading skill is basic to most academic endeavors, it is possible that in numerous instances reading difficulty is the predisposing factor to pervasive academic frustration and negative attitudes toward oneself. Because of the rather common blockage toward mathematics, achievement in this area may likewise be crucial to school adjustment and self-evaluation.

Except for random absences, all students in four self-contained sixth grade classes were administered all instruments. The tests were given at weekly intervals.

RESULTS

The analysis of the results produced few high correlations, but all were statistically significant. A correlation of $-.28$ ($p < .02$) was obtained between scores on the Tennessee Self Concept Scale and the discrepancy scores on the school-concept instrument. A significant relationship ($p < .05$) of $.22$ r was also obtained between the self-concept measures and social esteem indices. That the self-concept is highly related to emotional adjustment was confirmed by the $.62$ r ($p < .001$) between scores on the Tennessee Self Concept Scale and those on the California Test of Personality. In contrast to previous findings (Wattenberg & Clifford, 1964), a significant correlation ($p < .01$) of $.31$ was obtained between self-concept and mental ability. In addition, the analysis revealed a $.31$ r ($p < .01$) between self-concept and reading achievement, and a $.33$ r ($p < .01$) between self-concept and mathematical achievement.

DISCUSSION

The correlational nature of the investigation does not permit dogmatic assertions of cause and effect, but various avenues for facilitating school adjustment and achievement have been suggested. The finding that a student's self-appraisal was significantly related to the group's appraisal of him lends support to Brookover's contention that communication from significant others affects the self-concept and suggests the feasibility of altering the self-concept by changing the conditions of social status. One approach toward enhancing social status might be the structuring of group activities so that the child is permitted to demonstrate a particular skill before his fellow students. The success of this approach would depend on the ingenuity of the teacher in identifying skills even among the lower ability pupils and providing realistic opportunities for the student to manifest these skills before his classmates. Assuming that a positive relationship exists between the teacher and his pupils, the students would tend to identify with the instructor's attitude in their appraisal of a particular child. Therefore, the student who goes unnoticed by the teacher may likewise be overlooked by the other students and the child who is realistically praised by the instructor may concomitantly be commended by his fellow students.

While the present study makes no attempt to identify antecedent factors in the various relationships, this problem must be attacked in future research. Teachers are often held responsible for poor motivation in their classes. In contrast, perhaps the child's conception of school is primarily an extension of his conception of himself, already well established prior to entering school. Levy (1956) has found that self-concept is not an isolated phenomenon but that it spreads out to all phases of life, i.e., the individual may view his town, church, school, etc., in much the same way he construes himself.

Probably the most reasonable position is to infer a reciprocal cause-effect relationship between self-concept and academic adjustment. There is some evidence (Walsh, 1956; Wattenberg & Clifford, 1964) that when intellectual ability is controlled, self-concept is a basic causal factor in determining achievement level in school. However, it cannot be concluded that what happens at school has no effect on attitude toward school or esteem for oneself. Of particular concern are the students of lower ability. Wattenberg and Clifford found no relationship between self-concept and mental ability at the beginning of school experience, but the present experimenter obtained a significant ($p < .01$) relationship between these variables at the sixth grade level. The academic reinforcement consistently received by the brighter student but infrequently by the less bright undoubtedly affects the self-concept. While the slow learner may be adversely affected by existing educational practices, it is assumed that a negative self-concept could be significantly ameliorated by a productive school experience. In the context of the present investigation, a productive school experience may be defined as one in which the learner receives consistent, positive communication from the instructor and his immediate academic peer group concerning his ability and achievement.

A child's academic success is certainly not determined by any one variable. Intellectual ability is one determinant, but self-esteem may prove to be another major determinant. While most school systems ubiquitously administer intelligence and achievement tests, very few attempt to provide valid, reliable measurements of the self-concept. Such may be a function of the lack of reputable, standardized measuring instruments of self-concept for all age levels, or the lack of information on the part of administrators and teachers concerning the possible importance of self-concept to academic adjustment and success. It should be the business of the school to identify children with derogatory self-esteem, to determine the factors that have and are contributing to the low self-appraisal, and to embark on a judicious program of amelioration. Few factors are more fundamental to a child's success and happiness than his evaluation and acceptance of himself.

REFERENCES

BROOKOVER, W. B., ERICKSON, E., HAMACHEK, D., JOINER, L., LePERE, J., PATTERSON, A., & THOMAS, S. Self-concept of ability and school achievement. Paper read at Sixth World Congress of International Sociological Association, Evian, France, September 1966.

BRUCK, M., & BODWIN, R. F. The relationship between self-concept and the presence and absence of scholastic underachievement. *Journal of Clinical Psychology*, 1962, *18*, 181–182.

COOPERSMITH, S. A method for determining types of self-esteem. *Journal of Educational Psychology*, 1959, *59*, 87–94.

FINK, M. B. Self concept as it relates to academic underachievement. *California Journal of Educational Research*, 1962, *13*, 57–62.

FITTS, W. H. *Tennessee Self Concept Scale: manual.* Nashville, Tenn.: Counselor Recordings and Tests, 1965.

LEVY, L. H. The meaning and generality of perceived actual-ideal discrepancies. *Journal of Consulting Psychology*, 1956, *20*, 396–398.

LUNDHOLM, H. Reflections upon the nature of the psychological self. *Psychological Review*, 1940, *47*, 110–127.

MEAD, G. H. *Mind, self, and society.* Chicago: University of Chicago Press, 1934.

ROGERS, C. R. *Client-centered therapy; its current practice, implications, and theory.* Boston: Houghton Mifflin, 1951.

SARBIN, T. R. A preface to a psychological analysis of the self. *Psychological Review*, 1952, *59*, 11–22.

SNYGG, D., & COMBS, A. W. *Individual behavior.* New York: Harper, 1949.

WALSH, A. M. *Self-concepts of bright boys with learning difficulties.* New York: Bureau of Publications, Teachers College, Columbia University, 1956.

WATTENBERG, W. W., & CLIFFORD, C. Relationship of self-concepts to beginning achievement in reading. *Child Development*, 1964, *35*, 461–467.

Section 6
Developing Patterns
of Behavior

It is of value for students of human behavior to remind themselves frequently that people do not act for no reason. Although the behaver may be unaware of the learned reaction patterns and the needs that prompt him to act as he does, these do exist. If a person is to understand and manage his own behavior in the best manner, he must have some knowledge of his needs and his habitual ways of meeting them. Something of this kind must have been in the thoughts of the philosophers who passed on the advice: "Know thyself," and "The unexamined life is not worth living." Man always has acted to manipulate and control his environment, while it, in turn, has furnished reasons for his behavior. In fact, man has done this until more and more of the environment he must deal with is of his own making.

The selections included in this section have something to say about two environmental aspects of man's own making that have come to exert considerable influence upon his behavior. The American college system is one of these. Lipset's article deals with the rebellion that stems from the controls imposed by this system. It is worth noting, in this respect, that such student activism is not confined to this time and this country. Germany, France, China, Russia and other nations have had, or are having, similar experiences. The history of higher education in the United States contains descriptions of student rebellion against authority on college campuses as long ago as three centuries.

Professor Lipset suggests a number of reasons for campus activism and expresses gratification with youth who will organize against perceived injustices and bigotries. But there are limitations even to protest. If protest is to promote change effectively, these facts must be recognized: (1) There is a vast difference between those who oppose because of honest disagreement, those who rebel for "kicks"—for the sake of opposing or to establish a reputation—and those who are out to wreck the system. Those who join protest movements and those who oppose them should be aware of this. (2) Any person or group which projects hostility and which is perceived as attacking seldom fails to be met with hostility and counterattack. Conflict escalates, effective communication is cut off, and it is not until the generated emotions subside that significant issues can be dealt with. (3) Lipset's mention of the indifference, aloofness, and impersonalism, and the poor college instruction which results, should lead to a recognition or re-recognition that schools tend to mirror the supporting culture. This, of course, is explanation rather than excuse. But the problem does extend beyond the campus. Probably one will not be changed without, at the same time, affecting the other.

Many hypotheses are advanced for explaining human behavior, especially the behavior of younger people. Each explanation possesses some creditability and each is logical. Yet no single one of these hypotheses accounts to everyone's satisfaction for the complexity of what people do. Halleck's treatment of student unrest is a case in point. He identifies many of the ills of our times and shows how these may be used as explanations for alienation or activism among students.

In a sense, when one finds a reason or an explanation for behavior, he also provides a justification for acting in that manner. For our actions indeed are environmentally determined to some degree. An excuse or a defense is furnished. As an example, a person might rationalize that the hypocrisy of the older generation, the rigidity of the social system, his family background, or war is responsible for his inability to do anything with his own life. He might be able to blame any or all of these reasons for student unrest, for experimenting with narcotics, for dropping out of school, or anything else which he wishes or does not wish to do. But projecting the blame, as in the case with most of the other defense mechanisms, only makes one feel better for the moment. In the long run this is self-defeating because, like the drug user, the blame projector succeeds mostly in fooling himself and in compounding the problems he must face tomorrow.

Many articles relating to rebellion have been selected for this section on patterns of behavior. Our rationale resides in the fact that presenting different views of rebellion emphasizes the complexity of behavior. In addition, rebellion can be seen as an adjustive as well as a maladjustive behavioral pattern. Carroll's article, for example, lists six factors which contribute to the rebellious pattern and explains each in some detail.

One of the unique features of Carroll's presentation is that the reader becomes less sure that rebellion should be put down. It seems that adults should look upon student protest as a manifestation of idealism, vitality, and commitment to change. It seems that we should examine educational practices, indeed, many of the ways youth are treated (e.g., the voting age, discrimination in employment) as being anachronistic practices which are too rigid to adjust to the inevitability of change. Too, we should all be encouraged because youth has the resiliency, despite many negative features of our culture, to join their efforts and struggle with those of their generation who have not yet yielded to the pressures for conformity.

One of Carroll's six points concerns the impact of mass communication. A different and expanded version of this topic is presented by Hayakawa with his question, "Who's Bringing Up Your Children?" It has been known for a long time that whoever or whatever controls the education of a nation's youth controls the future of that nation. If one is to credit television with the influence that Hayakawa ascribes to it, then neither of the traditional agents of education, schools or parents, any longer is the major determiner of what children learn. One sobering aspect of this situation is that the primary motivation and intent of industry-controlled television is not the welfare of the learner. An attendant concern is that much of what the entertained viewer learns is of an accidental nature. Compared to the formalized education in the schools which is based on certain objectives for learning, the learning gained from television—aside from developing an urge to buy specific products—occurs mostly by chance. The viewer's attitudes, ideas and behavior unavoidably are influenced, but without much thought of direction or outcome. Further, parents and schools must assume responsibility for the teaching and learning which they cause to take place. Television appears relatively far removed from this responsibility.

The article on personality by Dettering may bring the other articles in this section into balance. We believe it does. To begin with, Dettering reminds the reader that responses do not stem just from external events—pressures and environmental stimuli. The transactional model of behavior (the word proactive has been used earlier in this volume) demands acknowledgment of the person himself as an active agent, i.e., a choice maker.

Dettering and Carroll and the editors have mentioned the self-fulfilling prophecy. We suggest that these two authors be read with special attention to the personal significance of the self-fulfilling prophecy. What are the implications of these words for behavior? What are the implications of daydreaming? Of the love and hope of parents? Of the faith and belief of instructors? Of a confident view of one's abilities and potentials? Of contempt for the foregoing questions? What are the implications of Dettering's words: "The other person is not just inside oneself; what is inside oneself *is* the other person"? Is this not closely related to what Buhler (page 126) said about avoiding the despair of loneliness by experiencing the mystical oneness with all men and with the Universe"?

Are you, the reader, intimidated or challenged by the innuendos of so many authors that you are responsible for the people around you? "The trouble with Philadelphia (or Chicago or Denver or Muncie) is us." "He who describes the personality of another describes himself." And now Dettering: "To know what the other person is like comes to depend on what you tell him you are like." It does indeed become a "trifle nightmarish." From this point on the article becomes increasingly mysterious. We are told that every little movement has a meaning all its own. But that meaning varies from person to person because they may not wish to reveal themselves. It seems, in fact, that all we do, say, and wear partakes of the nature of a living projective technique. The study of patterns of behavior may become a lifelong, absorbing, and profitable study—and profitable here means either financially or humanistically.

Rebellion on Campus

SEYMOUR MARTIN LIPSET
Professor of Government and Social Relations
Harvard University

The revival of student activism around the world has resulted in many scholarly efforts to account for the phenomenon. One of these was a conference sponsored by the Office of Education last year at the University of Puerto Rico. It brought together 35 scholars from different countries to present papers and discuss the sources of activism on a comparative scale. (Most of the papers were published in *Daedalus*, Winter 1968.) A number of conclusions about the sources of worldwide student activism with particular reference to the United States may be distilled from the materials presented at San Juan.

Essentially the sources of political activism *among* students must be found in the factors associated with different types of politics. Students are more responsive to political trends, changes in mood, opportunities for action than almost any other group. As a result they have played a major role in stimulating unrest and fostering change in many countries. Their special role has been particularly noted in the Revolution of 1848 in Europe, in the Russian revolutionary movement (largely a student movement until 1905), in the various Chinese movements during the 20th century, and in a host of developing countries: in Latin America from World War I on and in much of Asia and Africa, both during the colonial period and since independence.

Although it may be argued that social unrest causes student unrest, it is important to recognize that once students start expressing their disquiet, they, along with intellectuals, have been the vanguard of social change.

Historically then, a sharp increase in student activism can be expected in a society when accepted political and social values are being questioned, particularly when events are testing the viability of a regime and where policy failures seem to question the legitimacy of social and economic arrangements and institutions. In

From *American Education,* 4 (No. 9): 28–31, October, 1968.

societies where rapid change, instability, or weak legitimacy of political institutions is endemic, there is what looks like almost constant turmoil among students.

General discussion of the political sources, of course, does not explain why students have played such an important role in stimulating protest, reform, and revolution. What are the factors that motivate students to action?

First are the frustrating elements in the student role. Students are by occupation marginal men. They are in transition between dependency on their families for income, status, security, and protection, and taking up their own roles in jobs and families. Studenthood is inherently a tension-creating period. The recent rapid growth in the number of students means that the college population comes increasingly from less-privileged families; at the same time the status placement value of a college degree has declined.

The university has become more meritocratic; it is how well you do, rather than who you are that counts. Hence young people find themselves facing a highly competitive situation. For many middle-class and aspiring working-class youth, pressures to conform to the requirements of the education establishment begin in elementary school and intensify in high school. Hard work and ability at each level only serve to qualify the individual to enter an even more difficult competition at the next rung in the educational ladder. While some succeed many must rank low or show up as mediocre.

Evidence suggests that these tensions affect the emotional stability of many teenagers and university youth. Such tensions find varying outlets: one is rejection of the competitive social system which forced them into the rat race for grades. Although such tensions have always been present in the student role, they have intensified considerably in the last decade and a half.

Youth's idealism is another stimulating factor and is an outgrowth of social expectations. Societies teach youth to adhere to the basic values of the system in absolute terms: equality, honesty, democracy, socialism, and the like. There is a maxim which exists in various forms in many countries: "He who is not a radical at 20 does not have a heart; he who still is one at 40 does not have a head." This is usually interpreted as a conservative view, assuming radicalism is an unintelligent response to politics. But the first part of the maxim may be even more important than the second, for it denotes a social expectation that young people should be radicals, that the older generation believes youthful radicalism is praiseworthy behavior. It is the young conservative, the young "fogy," not the young radical, who is considered out of step.

The emphasis on youthful reformism is even greater in the United States than in many other countries, for American culture generally glorifies youth and depreciates age. Americans dislike admitting their increased age. Hence to look youthful, to behave youthfully; to adopt the dress, the sports, the dances, or the political and social views identified with youth, and to gain acceptance from the youth by such behavior, is a way of holding back age.

Thus many American adults are reluctant to call students or youth to task, even when they consciously disagree with them. Instead they may encourage youth to take independent new positions. This ties in with the part of the American self-image that assumes the United States to be a progressive country, one which accepts reform and change. And the truism that youth will inherit the future is linked with the sense that youth are the bearers of the progressive ideas which will dominate the future, that youth will contribute to the enduring struggle to make the American creed of equality more meaningful.

The real world in fact differs from the ideal, and part of the process of maturing is to learn to operate in a world of conflicting roles, interests, and demands. Such compromises as this requires are viewed by youth as violations of basic morality. Students hang on to such beliefs longer than others. They tend to be committed to ideals rather than institutions. Hence those events which point up the gap between ideals and reality stimulate them to action.

Modern societies, moreover, are characterized by a prolongation of adolescence, usually devoted to educational development. Although physiologically mature and often above the age legally defined as adult, students are expected to refrain from full involvement in the adult world. The very nature of university education is seen as calling for a withdrawal from the mainstream of society. Even though living in a society which stresses that adults should establish their own status based on their individual abilities and achievements, students are expected to remain in limbo, dependent on their family status.

Such a situation can be highly frustrating. Thus the student requires the chance to experiment with adult roles and to exhibit his ability to achieve a position of his own.

Dependency is, of course, built into the university system.

With their stress on frequent examinations and faculty grading, American universities emphasize this dependent relationship even more than those of most other countries. The American system of higher education has remained closer to that of the high school. As a consequence the student who leaves home to attend a university finds that he remains in a highly controlled situation, while many aspects within it urge him to become independent.

Involvement in university life makes politics a particularly critical source of self-expression. Surveys of student attitudes confirm that universities have a liberalizing effect on young people, particularly in areas linked to "universalistic" principles—racial equality, freedom of speech, internationalism, peace. Students have ample opportunity to discuss and study political matters. The university itself, in spite of its emphasis on academic freedom and nonpartisanship, is increasingly involved in politics, as professors fulfill ever growing roles as party activists, commentators on political events, advisers, consultants, and as researchers on policy matters. Many students are thus in centers of considerable political significance, yet have little or no political status themselves.

A variety of circumstances has changed the relationship of the university to the student. With growth of the universities and greater pressures on their staffs to do research, publish, and take part in extramural activities, one should expect to find poorer instruction, more faculty aloofness, and administrative indifference to students. In the United States particularly the research-oriented faculty assigns more and more of the teaching load to graduate students. University administration involves fund raising, lobbying, handling of research contracts, faculty recruiting, and the like. There can be little doubt that today's undergraduate students are of much less concern to the faculty and administration than they were in earlier periods of education.

The university's rising importance as a center of influence and power and as the major accrediting institution of the society has reduced the informal influence of students within the university. Administrators and faculty, however, have sought to maintain their traditional authority and prerogatives, while reducing their own "responsibility" for the quality of the personal and intellectual lives of their students.

Growth of the university is not the whole cause of this development; it reflects even more the extent to which "teaching" has declined as the main identification of the professor's role.

It may be argued that today's students are subject to greater strains and fewer rewards than were those of all but the Depression generation. The fantastic increase in college enrollments has made higher education not only increasingly competitive but more coercive. The demand for "student power"—for increased influence over the decisionmaking process in the university—tends on the whole to be raised by the leftwing activist groups. Yet its receptivity among wider circles of students may reflect an increased sense of grievance. Thus, like workers in bureaucratized industry, students in many countries seem to be seeking to regain, symbolically as a group, the influence which they have lost individually.

Conversely, the often unconscious sense of grievance with their situation (a sense which in many cases is now consciously directed against the university) also may make many students, particularly those from a liberal and leftwing family background, more receptive to political action working against trends in the larger society. The two sources of activism thus reinforce each other; the more directly political uses campus discontent to create a set of issues around which to build a movement, while campus discontent may express itself in wider political issues. These are general aspects of student motivation to activism. It remains to look at why students are more prone to act politically than are other groups.

Young people are more available for new political movements than adults. As new citizens, as people entering the political arena, most are less committed to existing ideologies. They have few or no explicit political commitments. They have no previous personal positions to defend. They are less identified with people and institutions responsible for the status quo. Inherently they know less recent history than adults. For this current generation the key formative events in foreign policy terms have not been fascist or Stalinist expansionism, but the Vietnam war, and in the United States heightened awareness of the oppressed position of the American Negroes.

Students are also more available, because they have less commitment than adults to their "occupational" role. Students have perhaps the most dispensable job requirements of all. They may drop out of school, put off their studies for short or long periods without paying a great price.

Linked with this is the factor of "responsibility." Compared with other groups students simply have fewer responsibilities, fewer commitments to families and jobs. Thus the existence of punitive sanctions against extremist activism is less likely to affect students. Moreover they remain adolescents or juveniles sociologically and are often implicitly treated as such legally, particularly when they violate the law. In many societies a number of student activists are the children of the elite, a fact which serves to reduce the will to punish them. In addition universities are generally run by liberal individuals who are not inclined to invoke severe sanctions against students. Consequently students are under less pressure to conform than are other groups.

The physical situation of the university facilitates student political involvement. The campus is the ideal place to find large numbers of people in a common situation. Many universities have over 30,000 students concentrated in a small area. New ideas which arise as a response to an issue may move readily among the students. A small percentage of the massive student bodies can often make a large demonstration. Thus in 1965–67, although opinion polls indicated that the great majority of American students supported the Vietnam war, the campus opposition was able to have considerable impact because it could be mobilized. The antiwar minority could and did man impressive antiwar demonstrations.

It remains true that the majority of students in all countries are politically quiescent and moderate in their views. The radical activist groups generally have tiny memberships. The Students for a Democratic Society (SDS) reports a total membership of about 30,000 (6,000 pay national dues) out of a student population of seven million. The Harris Poll estimates that there are about 100,000 radical activists nationally. The German Sozializtischen Deutschen Studentbund (also SDS) claims 2,500 and is credited by observers with 10,000 supporters in a German student population that approximates 500,000.

The opinion surveys of the American student population indicate that the large majority are not sympathetic with radical doctrines and tactics. Yet the activist element, both liberals and leftists, has played a major role in influencing American politics in the 1960's.

On the basis of this discussion no society should find it remarkable that a segment of its student population should behave as it has in recent times. It can be strongly argued that the circumstances of students' being a "privileged" group, which gives them the psychic security to support minority causes, are also among the circumstances which make their activism possible. And when these are related by events to a range of major social issues, student activism becomes highly probable. It can even be argued on the same grounds that a politically inactive student population is a cause for greater misgiving and puzzlement than an active one.

What justifies concern, of course, is the existence within the revived student movement of a deeply committed group of activists who are not affiliated with any adult movement and who are contemptuous of democratic procedure. The tactics of civil disobedience, which took hold in the civil rights struggles in the South, have diffused internationally. They are now employed in battles within the university, which cannot deal with them in a manner befitting its educational role. These tactics are also used in efforts to change the policies of democratically elected governments which allow free speech and assembly. There is no question that these are effective tactics, but they also weaken the structure of democratic legitimacy. Such tactics can create an electoral backlash which strengthens rightwingers. More importantly, civil disobedience weakens the respect for the rule of law which guarantees the rights of all minorities, of all whose opinions or traits differ from the majority. Indiscriminate use of such tactics by students and others may result in the undermining of the rule of law and the encouragement to all groups (including the military) to take the law and general power into their own hands whenever they feel frustrated politically. Hence it is important for the future of democracy and of social change that the revived student activism should operate within the processes of democracy.

Hypotheses of Student Unrest

S. L. HALLECK, M.D.
Professor of Psychiatry
University of Wisconsin, Madison

Students can no longer be taken for granted. It does not matter that a great majority of students remain largely content, conservative, and apathetic. A determined minority of restless college students has

From *Phi Delta Kappan,* 50 (No. 1): 2–9, 1968.

forced us to examine and sometimes change institutions, rules, and values which were once considered inviolate.

The most significant aspects of student unrest can be described as follows:

1. Some students reject the political and economic status quo and are making vigorous attempts to change the structure of our society. These are the student activists.

2. Some students reject the values of their society as well as the values of their own past and are developing a style of life which is contradictory to the Western ethics of hard work, self-denial, success, and responsibility. These students sometimes participate in efforts to change the society, but for the most part they are withdrawn and passive. They can be described as alienated.

3. Both activist and alienated students tend to come from affluent middle- or upper-class homes. They are sensitive and perceptive individuals. They are also highly intelligent.

4. Both activist and alienated students have difficulty in relating to the adult generation. They are articulate, irreverent, humorless, and relentless in their contempt for what they view as adult hypocrisy. Such youth are highly peer-oriented. They turn to one another rather than their parents when shaping their belief systems or when seeking emotional support.

5. Alienated students and, to a lesser extent, activist students find it difficult to sustain goal-directed activity. Their capacity to organize for any kind of action is limited. They often fail at work or school. Even their political efforts seem highly disorganized.

6. Alienated students live at the edge of despair. Although they seem at times to be enjoying life, there is always a sense of foreboding about them. Often they become depressed and suicidal. Activist students are more emotionally stable but are also prone to deep feelings of hopelessness and self-pity.

There is no dearth of explanations of the above phenomena. Some explanations seem to be based on opinions which support the prejudices of differing political viewpoints. Others are more scientific and are presented with analytic objectivity. No hypothesis thus far advanced can be considered a sufficient explanation of student unrest. At best, each is only a partial explanation which sheds only a small light upon highly complex phenomena.

Certain propositions often made about students are not hypotheses but are value judgments. The unsupported statement that the behavior of our restless youth represents a healthy and sensible response to the corruptions of our world is exhortative rather than explanatory. Such a position is embraced by those who are discontent with the status quo and wish to emphasize and exploit student restlessness as a phenomenon that justifies their own grievances. Similarly, unsupported statements that students are more emotionally disturbed than they had used to be have no explanatory value. Implying that students act as they do because they are mentally ill serves to demean their behavior by casting doubts upon the validity of the messages which that behavior is designed to communicate.

A more interesting proposition concerning student unrest is that it is neither new nor exceptional. Precedents can be cited which suggest that there were times in our history when students were even more restless than they are now. Periods of unrest do seem to run in cycles, and it is conceivable that we happen to be in an active phase of a predictable cycle. This proposition is reassuring to those who look forward to a quiet future. Its weakness, however, is that it assumes that those forces which make for cyclical behavior will remain relatively constant. My own opinion is that the world is changing so rapidly that using historical precedents to predict future behavior is a risky business. We can deplore student unrest or we can welcome it, but we cannot ignore it or simply wait for it to go away.

THE CRITICAL HYPOTHESIS

Those who are critical of student activism and alienation are most likely to seek its causes in factors which they believe have created a moral weakness in our youth. They believe students are restless because they lack discipline, values, or purpose. These deficiencies are believed to originate within the disturbed family, particularly that family which has been influenced by affluence, liberal thinking, and modern psychological notions of child rearing. While these hypotheses may also appear to those who are sympathetic toward students, they are primarily critical in the sense that they imply that something is wrong with those students who protest or withdraw.

THE PERMISSIVENESS HYPOTHESIS

Perhaps the commonest explanation of student unrest is that it is the result of too much permissiveness in rearing children. The proponents of this view argue that some parents have, through painstaking efforts to avoid creating neuroses in their children, abdicated their responsibility to teach and discipline their children. In so doing they have reared a generation of spoiled, greedy youth who are unable to tolerate the slightest frustration without showing an angry or infantile response.

Although the permissiveness hypothesis has been used in the most crude manner to berate and deplore the behavior of youth, it cannot be lightly dismissed. There is considerable evidence that activist and alienated students are members of well-educated families, deeply committed to liberal doctrines. In such homes children are given unusual freedom to criticize, debate, and question. Restless students also have frequently attended primary and secondary schools dedicated to the ideal of progressive education, schools which in their efforts to maximize freedom and creativity seek to minimize discipline and frustration.

It can, of course, be argued that children raised in permissive homes will be better citizens than those raised in stricter homes. Restless students do seem to be more open to ideas, more involved with social issues, and more flexible than their peers. The critics, however, can point to other characteristics of restless students which seem to be related to their permissive upbringing, and which are not so healthy. The respone of such students to discipline, for example, is in no useful sense adaptive. Arbitrary regulations enrage them. Even rational forms of discipline, such as the need to master basic concepts before moving on to more abstract ideas, bother them. Restless students also react inappropriately when their demands are not immediately accepted. They are prone at such moments to protest violently, to give up and withdraw, or to wrap themselves in a cloak of despair. Much of their abrasiveness and much of their ineffectiveness can be explained by their uncompromising demands for immediate gratification. This inability to tolerate frustration or delay must be considered a weakness or defect.

THE NON-RESPONSIBILITY HYPOTHESIS

Many who are concerned about the dangers of permissiveness also believe that our culture has been "psychologized" to an extent where youth become unwilling to assume responsibility for their own behavior. The expansion of the social and psychological sciences has confronted the public with elaborate deterministic explanations of behavior. When a behavior is totally explained, there is a tendency for people to act as though they are no longer responsible for that behavior. They confuse the theoretical issue of scientific determinism with the society's practical needs to have its citizens remain accountable for their own actions.

When the sociologist documents the impact of poverty and discrimination upon Negro youth, he is conducting a logical and scientific exercise. The subjects of his research, however, are tempted to utilize his findings to support an individual and collective feeling of responsibility. The Negro adolescent who participates in a riot, for example, might say, "How could I do otherwise? I am moved by forces over which I have no control." Psychological explanations are also utilized to avoid accountability. It is becoming more common to hear criminals say, "I should not be held responsible for what I have done because I am neurotic or mentally ill."

Psychiatry, particularly Freudian psychiatry, has been maligned as a critical agent in producing a climate of non-responsibility. While there is nothing in the theoretical doctrines of psychoanalysis which favors abdicating personal responsibility, it does seem that the psychiatrist's ability to expand and legitimize the mental illness role has had an impact on the manner in which people view the question of responsibility. Behavior once considered bad is now considered sick. Sickness implies that one cannot help himself or that one is not responsible for his actions. The proponents of the nonresponsibility hypothesis would argue that by expanding the sick role to include forms of behavior that were once considered in terms of good or bad, the healing professions have helped to create a social climate in which more people manage to avoid accountability for their actions. Youth growing up in such a society are tempted to behave in a pleasure-seeking, antisocial, and irresponsible manner. Many feel that this is exactly what restless students are doing.

The evidence that activist and alienated youth are deeply influenced by a climate of irresponsibility is inconclusive. Some activist students are often impressively willing to hold themselves accountable for their actions. On the other hand, most alienated students are not. They tend to seek medical or psychiatric excuses from their obligations at the first sign of stress. They also have a discouraging tendency to break laws and to insist that their own personal needs and problems are such that they should not be held accountable for these actions. It is almost as if they say, "Because the world is so bad and because it has treated me so badly, I cannot be blamed for my actions. There is no point in holding me accountable for things which I cannot help doing anyway."

THE AFFLUENCE HYPOTHESIS

A third hypothesis which appeals to critics of student unrest is based on the alleged hazards of growing up in an affluent society. It is sometimes argued that affluence which is unearned, and which is unaccompanied by a tradition of service and commitment, creates a sense of restlessness, boredom, and meaninglessness in our youth. The child raised in an affluent society has difficulty finding useful goals. He does not learn to use work or creativity as a means of mastering some aspect of the world. He, therefore, according to this argument, is trapped in a never-ending search for new diversions and new freedoms which sooner or later begin to feel sterile and ungratifying.

It does seem likely that man is less likely to be troubled if he is distracted by some monumental task which dominates his life goals. In a relatively poor society, the very need for survival creates a structured and seemingly purposeful life. In an affluent society, man has the time and freedom to contemplate the meaning of his existence. Many restless students do come from affluent homes and many have decided that their lives are devoid of meaning. Sometimes it seems that their provocative behavior is designed primarily to invent new struggles and even imaginary hardships which will free them from their lethargy and help them atone for their guilt over "having it so good."

The affluence hypothesis has certain undertones of criticism directed towards the parents of restless students. Affluence, after all, does not always produce protest or indolence. Traditionally, many of our most useful public servants have been products of wealthy homes. The critics of student unrest would reserve their harshest barbs for those newly affluent parents who have themselves become so caught up in materialistic, pleasure-seeking life that they have failed to meet their responsibility of teaching children the kinds of values which would lend meaning to a young person's existence.

THE FAMILY-PATHOLOGY HYPOTHESIS

A number of explanations of student unrest focus upon the disturbed family. According to these hypotheses, activist and alienated students behave as they do because they are responding to an unresolved conflict within the family unit. It is usually suggested that the restless student has been subjected to too much pressure by his parents or is "acting out" a need of his parents. A more general approach to the problem focuses upon a family structure in which the father is a weak or shadowy figure. This approach emphasizes the breakdown in authority of the paternal figure, the confusion of sexual roles in our society, and the break with tradition which such confusion produces.

The evidence for the existence of a high degree of pathology in the families of restless students is inconclusive. Sociological studies of students and their families do not support any family-pathology hypothesis. In fact, such studies suggest that activist students, at least, come from rather stable families.

Psychiatrists, on the other hand, find some evidence of serious familial conflict in most of the families of restless students they treat. It must be emphasized, however, that the psychiatrist deals with only a small proportion of such students.

If family disorganization is an important cause of student unrest, the manner in which it exerts its influence must be complex and subtle. Sociological techniques are simply too superficial to get at the complexities of the problem. The findings of psychiatrists are based on depth explorations which may be valid for some families but which cannot be generalized. Neither sociologists nor psychiatrists can provide valid answers. The most we can say is that some aspects of student restlessness may be directly related to family pathology. Certainly, it is conceivable that in today's highly charged social climate, even minimal family disturbances may be translated into highly provocative behavior.

SYMPATHETIC HYPOTHESES

The next group of hypotheses put the student in a favorable light. They view him as a victim of man-made circumstances and maintain that student unrest is a legitimate and rational effort to change these circumstances. The student is viewed as either a helpless victim of a world he never created or as a hero seeking to cleanse the world of the evils of previous generations. To be useful, these hypotheses must not simply define what is wrong with the world but must suggest how various factors have made students more capable of perceiving and acting upon the injustices and irrationalities of our world.

THE TWO-ARMED-CAMPS HYPOTHESIS

This generation of students has grown in an age when the world has been divided into two large camps which compete with each other ideologically, politically, and sometimes militarily. Since the Russians launched their first satellite, the competition has also been educational. Students today are trained in a school system which emphasizes the competitive acquisition of knowledge as a source of power and stability. By the time they leave high school they are better educated than any previous generation of students, but they are also more overworked.

All of this emphasis on education and competition is not easily sustained after the student arrives at the university. By this time he is at least partially "burned out." The personal benefits of intensive studying and searching for a profitable career begin to appear less attractive in an affluent world and particularly in a world which seems to be making it increasingly difficult for a young person to become an integral part of the economic system. As the student comes to view objectively the implications of our competitiveness with communism as a never-ending phenomenon, he also begins to question the social value of his efforts. Even if he maintains enthusiasm for academic work through the undergraduate years, by the time the student reaches graduate school he increasingly asks himself whether the competitive search for knowledge is worth it. At this point he begins to view our competition with the Communist world (and sometimes competitiveness itself) as a form of mass paranoia, and he views the university as an agent of a government which contributes towards the perpetuation of the paranoid system. He reacts by protest or withdrawal.

THE WAR-IN-VIETNAM HYPOTHESIS

Although student unrest began long before the war in Vietnam ever escalated to massive proportions, there can be little doubt that in the past few years this conflict has been the major factor influencing the behavior of students. The war is particularly unpopular on our campuses. A large proportion of students, perhaps the majority, see it as a misguided effort. A significant minority see it as wholly immoral. Much of the restless behavior of students can be directly related to their efforts to do something to stop the war or to their sense of total frustration when they feel powerless to stop it.

The draft and the inequities engendered by the "S" deferment also contribute to unrest. The major issue here is fear. The average male student is plagued with fears that he will fail in school, will be drafted, and will run the risks of being killed in a conflict he may not consider vital to our interests. A second issue is guilt. The university student knows that he is spared from military service only because he is richer or smarter than someone else. While he may believe that the war is immoral, he also knows that his privileged status is immoral. When he accepts the 2S status he suffers guilt. Much of the activism on our campuses is a means of atoning for that guilt. Much of the alienation on our campuses is a means of denying the relevance of the society that created such guilt.

Students also feel some shame in not participating in those aspects of military service that might make them feel more masculine. It is rare for anyone even in peacetime to embrace military service eagerly, and a normal late-adolescent has justifiable concern with interrupting his career to face the harshness of life in the service. The unpopularity of this war gives the student a cogent reason for avoiding military service, but it does not resolve his nagging fears that he is somehow or other being cowardly or less masculine by being treated specially.

It is also true that the anti-war climate on our campuses makes the student progressively more disinclined to serve in this war the longer he remains on campus. Education breeds a dislike of violence. Furthermore, whatever romantic thoughts a young man may have about the war at the age of 18 are somewhat attenuated with a year or two of maturation. Students spend many hours arguing about the war, the draft, and means of avoiding the draft. This preoccupation creates a highly tense situation in which the student feels supported only by his peer groups. He begins to relate to subcultures which become progressively more separated from the rest of the nation and particularly from the adult generation.

THE DETERIORATION-IN-THE-QUALITY-OF-LIFE HYPOTHESIS

There are many who believe that student unrest is an appropriate response to the deterioration of the quality of life in America. Overpopulation which results in crowds, traffic jams, and businesses run on the basis of mass production has taken much of the joy out of life in our towns and cities. Personal care or service is hard to find in any shop, restaurant, or hotel. People begin to feel faceless and insignificant.

Students, it can be argued, are among the first to sense the painful anonymity associated with bigness. This is a particularly serious problem on overcrowded campuses where students are generally isolated from their teachers and other adults. A sense of student-faculty intimacy or a sense of scholarly community are sorely lacking on most of our large campuses. Students find it difficult to develop a sense of identification or loyalty towards a university that they perceive as monolithic and impersonal. In their complaints that they are treated like numbers or IBM cards they strike a poignant note for all of us.

Overcrowding is only a relative thing and would not be so destructive if it were not for the manner in which we have incredibly neglected the planning and development of town and country.

Our cities grow with no respect for the land. Beauty and wilderness are easy prey for the builder and contractor. Clean air and clear streams are almost a thing of the past. An adolescent who grows up in a world in which we must sit back and watch beauty fade and pollution gain comes to despair of the future.

One way of looking at student unrest is as a massive reaction to the destruction of that kind of world and way of life which their forebears enjoyed but which will be denied to them. It is not uncommon to hear a student say to an adult, "In your world life had some hope and meaning, but in the world you have left me these qualities are gone."

THE POLITICAL-HOPELESSNESS HYPOTHESIS

Many individuals see our mass society as immutable. It has been argued that our society is so complex, our systems of checks and balances so intricate, and our interplay of pressure groups so self-equalizing that really effective change is no longer possible. Our business-oriented economy has so indoctrinated us in the role of credit-bound consumers that we are all beholden to a way of life which may not be in our best interests. An increasing number of radical students are convinced that the forces of government, industry, and education are totally interdependent and allied to one another for the purpose of warding off any reasonable attempts to change the society. They believe that a system of life has developed in our country which simply absorbs legal efforts to change our society, even protest, in a manner which ultimately preserves the status quo.*

Guided by the philosophy of Herbert Marcuse, many students are convinced that constructive change within our society is not possible by working through the system. They do not have any sort of vision as to what will replace the old order, but they are convinced that our society is fundamentally irrational and must be destroyed. They do not reject illegal acts or even violence as agents of destruction.

---

* In this regard it is somewhat distressing to note the manner in which hippies and protestors have not only been institutionalized as part of our folklore and humor but have been exploited by the advertising industry, an institution which they initially intended to destroy.

THE CIVIL-RIGHTS HYPOTHESIS

The civil rights movement not only increased youth's awareness of an historical injustice which made it difficult for them to be proud of this country, but also served as a training ground for future radicals. The new campus protest began at Berkeley when students demanded the right to work freely on their own campuses on behalf of oppressed Negroes. Many campus radicals shaped their images of "the Establishment" and of unreasonable authority on the basis of their early work in the civil rights movement. Students throughout the country have developed an amazing empathy and identification with Negroes. Their commitment to the Negro cause has taught them the psychological meaning of oppression and has encouraged them to seek out and attack sources of oppression in their own lives.

NEUTRAL HYPOTHESES

Some explanations of student unrest focus upon impersonal processes. The causes of unrest, according to these hypotheses, are not to be found in the actions or philosophies of other men, but are believed to reside in changes in our highly complex society which seem to create the need for new modes of psychological adaptation.

THE TECHNOLOGY HYPOTHESIS

Man has always lived with hope, particularly with the hope that his efforts in the present will be rewarded with gratification in the future. A certain degree of predictability in the future enables one to make commitments to goals and to other people. To the extent that we live in a society in which past, present, and future lose their interrelatedness, the power of hope to shape man's behavior is diminished. New means of adapting to the world must then be found and the manner in which people relate to one another must be profoundly altered.

Postwar America has been characterized by a massive and continuous growth of technology. Our society is one in which the conditions of everyday life are constantly changing. Moreover, the rate at which technology changes our lives is itself increasing. No one can predict what life will be like in 20 years, 10 years, or even five years. Today's knowledge, today's work skills, and today's values may be totally irrelevant to tomorrow's world. Kenneth Kenniston has described the manner in which some youth, who, when exposed to an ever-increasing rate of technological growth, come to perceive that the values of the past will be totally inappropriate for the world in which they will be adults. Morever, they feel powerless to anticipate or direct the future. In this environment hope no longer sustains. It is adaptive to be cool, and to learn to live in the present.

What are the advantages and disadvantages of living in the present? The advantages are more or less obvious. One is more flexible, and superficially at least more comfortable. It is not necessary to delay gratification, nor need one allow himself to be tortured by the mistakes of the past nor be deluded by unrealistic hopes for the future. The disadvantages of life in the present are more subtle, yet more powerful. To live in the present one must narrow his commitments. He must travel lighly and be ready for anything. More intimate relationships are unlikely, since they cannot be sustained by reference to past experience or to promises of a better future. Passion and romantic longing must be avoided because they may breed pain or impair one's flexibility. In short, if carried to extremes, life in the present is a selfish life which is incompatible with the growth of that intimacy and passion which man has always found to be essential to a fulfilled life.

Distrust of the future and a determination to live in the present seem to be characteristic of both activist and alienated students. The student activist seeks immediate change and has difficulty in developing the patience or optimism for long-term planning. The alienated student adopts the philosophy of the hippie. Believing that the only certainty in life is change, or uncertainty itself, he adapts by "doing his own thing" and behaves as though he is responsible only to himself.

THE MEDIA HYPOTHESES

There are several hypotheses that attempt to relate the growth of new media, particularly television, to the troubling behavior of students. It can be argued, for example, that simply by being available to publicize the activities of protesters and hippies the media exaggerate the importance of these groups. The television camera forces all of us to take seriously forms of behavior that might have been dismissed lightly in earlier decades. Conceivably the medium may be creating a "climate of expectation" in which youth are subtly seduced into dissenting roles which may not represent their actual interests.

It is also true that many television commercials, radio ads, and most modern music are directed towards the youth market. The self-consciousness of youth is thereby heightened. Young people are made more aware of their potentialities and sometimes develop an exaggerated sense of their own power.

Another attempt to relate changing media to student unrest has been implied in the writings of Marshall McLuhan. McLuhan believes that electronic media are bringing us all closer together in a more truly communal and shared society than ever existed. Our youth who have grown up with the new media are ready for such a society. Elders who are committed to sustain the institutions of the past are not. Much of youthful rebellion can then be visualized as an effort to make older people see that the world has changed and that many of the values of the past are now irrelevant.

While McLuhan's hypothesis has some attractiveness, it does not seem as plausible as those which focus upon the psychological impact of the content of various media. Fredric Wertham believes that the massive degree of violence which young people see on television makes them more violent and less responsible. Vance Packard has argued that chronic exposure to the values implied in TV commercials could create a generation of unrealistic, demanding, and present-oriented youth.

I would like to propose my own hypothesis of student unrest based on the manner in which the media influence the character structure of youth by prematurely confronting them with the harsh truths and realities of life, as follows:

As an animal whose growth and development requires him to be dependent upon others for a long period of time, man learns to rely on others for an optimal amount of structure and order in his life. It is obvious that authority is not always benevolent or just, and yet it is true that no man can be at ease if he does not commit a part of himself to some authority, whether it be his church, his family, his government, or an ideology. Nor can one come to develop a firm sense of who he is without making such commitments. It is at least partly through experiencing limitations which are imposed by others, by respecting others, and by emulating those who are respected that one finds his own identity. The process by which one comes to terms with authority is not always deliberate or rational. Sometimes even benevolent authority relies on faith, mystique, or untruth to retain its control.

This is especially relevant to the situation of young people. The most well-meaning parents must on occasion deceive their children because they know that children would find many of the hard and cynical facts of life to be unbearable. Until recently it was possible for young people to begin to experience the world as adults know it only after they had reached adolescence. Most of the time the adolescent absorbed this new knowledge gradually and painlessly. Even when he did feel that his parents had been hypocritical or had deceived him, his awareness of their dishonesty came so gradually that his resentment and rebelliousness were restrained. Today it is different. One of the significant developments in postwar America has been the influence of mass-communication media (particularly television) which are capable of disseminating information to all age groups immediately.

Even before adolescence, television acquaints youth with the cynical facts of life at a time when such truths may be indigestible. Other media communicate knowledge so quickly now that there is little opportunity for anyone to live comfortably with myth or self-delusion. Beliefs which were once casually accepted are vigorously scrutinized. The belief that there is equality for all Americans can hardly be sustained when one has a front-row seat from which he can observe the Negro's unsuccessful struggle to maintain a decent life in this country. Blind faith in the veracity of national leaders is quickly lost when one can watch the proceedings of an organization such as the United Nations in his own living room. I have no doubt that diplomats have always lied to one another, but what is new about this world is that children can now watch them lie in living color.

The hypocrisies of the older generations have always been with us. What is new today is that it is ridiculously easy to expose them. The effect on our youth of premature emergence of truth has been to create a deep skepticism as to the validity of authority. Neither the family, the church, the law, nor any institution demands this decline in respect for authority, but in my opinion it is best understood in terms of the psychological impact of our new media.

THE RELIANCE-ON-SCIENTISM HYPOTHESIS

Today's restless young people have grown up in a world which has not been dominated by religious faith but which has sought many of the answers to the questions of life in science. Many of us believe that science can provide the answers to life. We ask that the speculations and opinions of the social sciences contain the same hard truths as more rigorous findings in the physical and biological sciences. In my work with students, I am often impressed to find how easily they believe or once believed in the perfectability of man. Hostility is not seen as an innate quality of man but rather as a response to frustration. The teachings of the social psychologist that aggression is a learned phenomenon have gained prominence over Freud's more ominous warnings that aggression is innate.

This generation of students seems to have grown up with the belief that original sin in the religious sense of Thanatos in the psychoanalytic sense does not exist. (Much of this belief has been reinforced by the mode of their existence. Many are affluent and have grown up in suburban communities where, except for what they see on television, they are shielded from the tragedies of life. The realities of their own lives convince them that whatever calamities are imposed upon others are not inevitable.) Statements such as, "Life is a vale of tears" or "The masses of men lead lives of quiet desperation" seem absurd to them. In their adherence to scientific rationality they also cannot accept guilt. They are convinced that in a perfectable world man should be joyful and guiltless.

When a person raised with such beliefs encounters the harsh realities of life, he has little to fall back upon. If he perceives his own aggressive tendencies, he is frightened by them and attempts to deny them. He may project his anger upon those whom he feels are frustrating him or he may simply deny that such anger exists. When he perceives the evil of others he is mortified. In his conviction that there are rational solutions to any problem, he cannot help but be intolerant of the irrationalities of those who prevent progress. In his belief that life and especially the sexual aspects of life can be enjoyed without guilt, he becomes highly disturbed when he discovers that he cannot escape his past and that a certain amount of guilt is inevitable. He even becomes plagued with additional guilt over the realization that he is guilty.

The restless student is one who has taken the message of science, rationality, and perfection literally. He is more open to action and change than were earlier generations of students. At the same time, however, he is not equipped to understand or deal with the depth of that irrationality in man which resists change and which leads man to seek his own destruction. Too often such a student finds it necessary to construct "devil" theories of history in which the existence of evil is attributed to only a few who block the progress of the many. He has sacrificed the comfort and patience which comes with the idea of accepting "original" sin.*

Hopefully, this review has been more than an exercise in cataloguing. By emphasizing the diversity of explanations of student unrest, I have attempted to demonstrate the intellectual futility of searching for simple explanations of a highly complex phenomenon. As citizens we may wish either to support or attack the causes which restless students have dramatized. But as scholars concerned with educating and understanding and helping students we need a more objective approach. We must recognize that there is some truth to the most critical as well as the most sympathetic hypotheses.

Some of the hypotheses suggest guidelines for action. The critical hypotheses remind us that youth are not always as wise or powerful as we might suspect. Like adults, their actions are as much determined by personal weaknesses and selfishness as by sensitivity or idealism. While youths certainly do not need more paternalism and coddling, they still need our understanding and guidance. They can still learn much from adults who are committed to the pursuit of ideals in a climate of tolerance, compassion, and responsibility. The critical hypotheses need not be used only to berate students. If their validity is appreciated they can be helpful in freeing adults from that unreasonable guilt which impairs an honest confrontation with the issues which students have raised.

The sympathetic hypotheses emphasize the unusual degree of stress this generation of students has experienced. These hypotheses

---

* Sometimes the student becomes totally overwhelmed with the irrational aspects of the world and reacts by totally abandoning his earlier beliefs. In their disillusionment some alienated students seem to be turning away from the promises of scientism and searching for solace in the most dubious form of mysticism, magic, and astrology.

which invoke the war, overpopulation, and pollution as sources of stress forcefully remind us that student unrest is often an appropriate response to what sometimes seems to be a hopelessly troubled world. Other hypotheses raise many questions for those entrusted with the management of our universities. Does the emphasis on education as a means rather than an end have any meaning in an affluent society? Should youths be encouraged to remain in a passive role as students throughout the first third of their lives? Are there means of bringing young people into important roles in the power structure of our universities and our social system before they reach the age of 25 or 30? Is the 2S classification anything more than a bribe which weakens the moral position of dissenting students and creates havoc upon our campuses? Should it be abolished? To what extent can we continue to depersonalize and enlarge our campuses without creating a generation of alienated youth who feel no sense of identity, no sense that they have a voice in what is done to them, and no sense of commitment to anything but their own interests?

It is my belief that the neutral hypotheses are the most intriguing and the most powerful valid explanations of student unrest. At the same time, they are the most difficult to live with optimistically. If progress itself, in the form of technology, science, or new media, is the most severe stress in the lives of our young people, then we are faced with a seemingly impossible task, namely, how to control progress and change rather than allowing these forces to control us.

Who's Bringing Up Your Children?

S. I. HAYAKAWA, President
San Francisco State College

The semantic environment is the verbally and symbolically created environment in which all human beings live. It is the environment of news, information, beliefs, attitudes, laws, and cultural impera-

Reprinted by permission from *ETC.: A Review of General Semantics,* 25: (No. 3): 299–308; copyright 1968, by the International Society for General Semantics.

tives that constitute your verbal world or mine. A quick way of describing the semantic environment is to say that it is that part of the total environment which your pet dog, lying on the rug at your feet, has no inkling of. It is the world of Shakespeare and Mozart and Bugs Bunny and the Beatles; of Moses and Jesus and Billy Graham; of published batting averages and closing prices on the New York Stock Exchange; of news from Tokyo and Prague and Saigon. The semantic environment is the product of that vast network of communication which we call civilization.

In a way we all share a common semantic environment—one created by the major news services, networks, and the intellectual climate of our times. In another way, each of us inhabits a semantic environment not quite like that of anyone else, since all of us read different magazines and books, listen to different speakers, watch different TV shows, hear different information and rumors at different places of work. Some of us were brought up in Catholic homes, some in Protestant; some read art journals or sports car magazines and others do not.

For most of the history of the human race, the semantic environment of children has been created by their parents and close relatives, who pass on to the young their pictures of the world, their value systems, their standards of behavior. As the children grow older, their semantic environment is expanded by other influences: friends, neighbors, movies, and the big experience of school. Schools continue the process that parents have begun; as a rule parents want their children to "do well" in school, which means to absorb faithfully the messages directed at them by the educational system. The semantic environment of children is never altogether the same as that of their parents, whose minds were formed at another time under other influences. Nevertheless, there is normally some continuity between generations because of a background of shared communications and shared values—and this is true even in immigrant families in which parents speak an Old World mother tongue and the children speak English.

This process of time-binding by which parents play an important role in shaping their children's ideas and values has been going on for perhaps the whole history of the human race. We take the process so much for granted that few of us have awakened to the fact that, for millions and millions of families, especially in the United States, it just isn't taking place any more.

In order to describe what is going on today, let me suggest an analogy. Suppose from the time that your children are old enough to sit up, they are snatched away from you for three or four or more hours a day by a powerful sorcerer. This sorcerer is a story-teller and a spinner of dreams. He plays enchanting music; he is an unfailingly entertaining companion. He makes the children laugh; he teaches them jingles to sing; he is constantly suggesting good things to eat and wonderful toys for their parents to buy them.

Day after day, month after month, year after year, children for a few hours a day live in the wonderful world created by a sorcerer —a world of laughter and music and adventures and incredible goings-on, sometimes frightening, often fun, and always entrancing.

The children grow older, still under the daily spell of the sorcerer. Parents and relatives and teachers may talk to them, but the children find them sometimes censorious, often dull. But the sorcerer is always fascinating so that they sit before him as if drugged, absorbing messages that parents did not originate and often do not even know about. For as much as one-half or more of their waking hours from infancy onward, they live in a semantic environment their parents did not create and make no attempt to control.[1]

The present generation of young people is the first in history to have grown up in the television age. If you were born in 1938, you were ten years old in 1948 and had already lived through your most important formative years, so that in all likelihood you missed the experience of having a television set for a babysitter. But a significant proportion of children born after 1945, brought up in their parents' homes, to be sure, had their imaginative lives, their daydreams, their expectations of the world created by television. Is it any wonder that these children, as they grew to adolescence, often turned out to be complete strangers to their dismayed parents?

The impact of television is due in part to the nature of the medium, in part to the fact that American television is commercially sponsored. This last fact is of tremendous importance, despite

[1] "Children get more verbal impact from radio and television than from parents, teachers, neighbors and church combined. . . . By the time he enters first grade, the average child has spent more hours in front of a television set than he will spend in a college classroom." Nicholas Johnson in the Washington *Post,* June 16, 1968.

"A recent study by the Carnegie Corporation, the Ford Foundation, and the U.S. Office of Education found that preschool youngsters spend 54.1 hours a week watching television." Walker Sandbach, Executive Director of Consumers Union, Inc., in a speech before the Telecommunciations Symposium of the Broadcast Advertising Club of Chicago, March 29, 1968.

Marshall McLuhan's famous dictum. "The medium is the message." I hasten to acknowledge the important point that Professor McLuhan makes about television's influence in shaping our sense of the world through shaping our perceptual habits and our time-sense. But to accept his pronouncement too literally is to say in effect, "Programming doesn't matter. Bad programs have the same effect as good. Programs whose only intent is to sell cigarettes or automobiles are not different in their effect from religious programs, news programs, political education programs. The medium is the message." I do not believe Professor McLuhan's view can be accepted. If the messages of American television were overwhelmingly sponsored, say, by churches and universities instead of by advertisers of consumer goods, would its effects be no different from what they are now?

An important fact about television—regardless of its sponsorship—is that you can have no interaction with it. A child sitting in front of a television set gets no experience in influencing behavior and being influenced in return. Having a puppy is in this sense far more important to a child than having a television set, although of course there is no reason he should not have both. The child who watches television for four hours daily between the ages of three and eighteen spends something like 22,000 hours in passive contemplation of the screen—hours stolen from the time needed to learn to relate to siblings, playmates, parents, grandparents, or strangers. Is there any connection between this fact and the sudden appearance in the past few years of an enormous number of young people from educated and middle-class families who find it difficult or impossible to relate to anybody—and therefore drop out?

I am sure you have met these young people, as I have—boys and girls who are frightened of the ordeal of having to make conversation with their friends' parents or anyone else not of their immediate clique. Many of them communicate, if at all, in monosyllables. Many merely grunt. The task of relating to others is found so threatening and burdensome that some have gone so far as to establish a Sexual Freedom League, in order to justify copulation without communication.

The messages of television are commercials, which are the economic support of the industry. American television is almost completely dominated by advertising.

However, as David Potter says in *People of Plenty*, advertising is only one of several systems of communication that keep a culture functioning. Education is another system of communication; its basic message is, "Be thoughtful, be well-informed, be intelligent." Religion is another system; it says, "Put not your faith in things of this world. Be godly, be spiritual." Industry as a system of communication says, "Work hard; improve your skills; save your money; invest wisely." Government says, "Be a good citizen; strive for a better community, a greater nation."

But advertising is unique among systems of communication, continues Professor Potter, in having no motivation to improve the listener. It encourages impulsive and thoughtless buying; it discourages thrift. It says nothing about the hard work, the years of study, the patient postponement of gratification, that are necessary to get and hold the jobs necessary to pay for the beautiful and expensive way of life advertised in the commercials. It says that material possessions are everything; that this headache remedy, this luxurious carpeting, this new model Camaro, will bring you charm, popularity, sexual fulfillment, domestic tranquility, and the envy and respect of your neighbors. All happiness, all significance, all values that human beings might strive for are translated by advertising into purchasable commodities.

Can anyone doubt the enormous greed for consumer goods that has been revealed in every outbreak of looting and civil disturbance since Watts? The disorders in Detroit in the summer of 1967 were characterized by a lack of racist motivation in many of the looters. Whites helped Negroes and Negroes helped whites to load into their cars and carry off expensive television sets, furniture, and luggage— all in a spirit of interracial brotherhood. We read that a gay, carnival spirit attended the looting. One Detroit newspaper man said the outbreak was simply an explosive response to color television.

Furthermore, in order to attract larger audiences than the next network, all networks have glorified violence to a degree almost impossible to believe for those who are at all selective in their viewing. As Fredric Wertham has said, "Violence on the screen is depicted as a way of life. Few arguments or conflicts on TV are settled without a fight. Never, literally never, is it taught in this School of Violence that violence in itself is something reprehensible. . . . No one can understand the world of today if he does not know what we put and permit on the airwaves. We are hypocritically surprised when young people in the slums fight the police. On the screen. . . . the sport of killing policemen flourishes. . . . Police brutality is also graphically displayed." (*A Sign for Cain,* pp. 199–209)

The militancy of young people, both white and black, eager for social change is often accounted for by saying that they have lost faith in the slow processes of democratic discussion and decision-making. This argument seems to me highly questionable. It is my impression that militant young people, far from being "disillusioned" with democratic processes, are totally unacquainted with them, since they are rarely shown on television. To be sure, national conventions are shown on television every four years, but the arduous, day-to-day debates, fact-finding, and arguments by which social decisions are arrived at by every democratic body from town councils to the Congress of the United States are never shown.

The unfamiliarity of young people with democratic processes is illustrated by the history of the "teach-in." It is a source of both pride and embarrassment to me that the "teach-in" was invented at my home some summers ago by a group of scholars then serving as fellows at the Center for the Advanced Study of Behavioral Sciences at Palo Alto. The original idea was that teachers of every shade of opinion about the war in Vietnam would give their views, so that everyone, especially students, would be better informed about the history of the conflict and the possible solutions. But the original idea was never given a chance. The proposal of the teach-in as debate was scuttled by the youthful organizers (and the middle-aged adolescents who were their faculty advisors) in favor of the teach-in as demonstration. Consequently, from the very first teach-ins at Ann Arbor and Berkeley, speakers defending the American intervention in Vietnam were hooted down. People came to meetings equipped not with lecture-notes on Southeast Asian history, but with guitars.

If young people did not learn of the complexities of the democratic process from their years of viewing television, what did they learn? They learned that social problems are never complicated; they are simply the conflicts between good guys and bad guys. Bad guys can never be reasoned with—you can only shoot it out with them. If the bad guys confront you with superior force, you can lay your body on the line and go down fighting.

Young people also learned from commercials that there is an instant, simple solution to all problems: acid indigestion can be relieved with Alka-Seltzer; unpopularity can be overcome by using

Breck shampoo; feelings of sexual inadequacy can be banished by buying a new Mustang, which will transform you into an instant Casanova.

Television documentaries about the problems of the world offer neat, half-hour wraps-ups of complex events. Highlights are selected, while boring, tedious details are left out. Time is compressed; cause and effect are simplified. In situation dramas, people are presented not in the full complexity of their humanity, like people in real life, but in stereotyped roles. They therefore arrive at their emotional responses quickly and easily, each Pyramus to his Thisbe, each Harlequin to his Columbine. In private as in public affairs, life is not too hard to understand. That's what television says.

But, as the general semanticists are fond of saying, the map is not the territory. All too soon, young people learn that the maps of reality given them by television do not correspond to the actualities. Material possessions and the consumption of all approved national brands do not bring happiness or peace of mind. The world, they discover as they approach adulthood, is far more complicated than they ever suspected. Getting along with other people is not easy; you have to adjust to them as much as they have to adjust to you. The world makes all sorts of demands that the television set never told you about, such as the necessity of study, hard work, patience, a sense of responsibility, a long apprenticeship in a trade or profession, and striving for advancement, before you can enjoy what the world has to offer. Disillusioned young people may at this point rebel against the culture and its "materialism"—not realizing that what they are rejecting is not the culture as such, but merely the culture as depicted by Madison Avenue and the networks.

Even as they reject the culture as they understand it through television, they miss the pleasant fantasies they enjoyed as children when they turned on the set. So they "turn on" in other ways. Having scornfully rejected the notion that they can achieve instant beauty and radiance with Clairol, they espouse the alternative view that they can achieve instant spiritual insight and salvation with LSD. The kinship of the LSD and other drug experiences with television is glaringly obvious: both depend upon "turning on" and passively waiting for something beautiful to happen.

What I have presented may seem like a terrible condemnation of television. It is not intended as such. Television is a wonderful instrument of communication, perhaps more effective than any in the history of the world. As Nicholas Johnson says, it is absurd to try to draw a line between "educational television" and "entertainment." *All* television is educational. All television programs tell us something about the world, shape our expectations and hopes. The messages of television, with words reinforced by music and pictures and action, received in a darkened room in the privacy of one's home, reiterated over and over for those who view it daily, are the most powerful and effective communications ever let loose on the world; they affect millions of families day after day, night after night, every day of the year.

Because television was invented at a particular time, in a particular state of our economy, it was assigned almost entirely to utilization for commercial purposes. This decision was made in ignorance of the possible consequences—an entirely pardonable ignorance, since no one knew at the time what the social impact of this new medium might be. Business and the advertising profession are not to be blamed for making use of this medium as energetically and ingenious as possible. There are no villains in this story; we are all simply victims of the unforeseen consequences of a technological revolution—and a revolution in the technologies of communication always has more far-reaching consequences than anyone can predict.

I am not pleading for more "quality" programing in the manner of many intellectual critics of television. I accept the fact that television is a *mass* medium, that half the people of America (as a brilliant statistician once pointed out) are of less than average intelligence, and that they have as much right to entertainment and instruction by television as the other half. What I am asking is that we give thought to how television might be financed otherwise than by advertising and therefore actuated by motives other than those of salesmanship, direct or indirect. Our national problem is not that we have commercial television, but that we have it almost to the exclusion of all other possible kinds. Is it not possible to get a more balanced choice of alternatives in television fare than we are now getting?

The problems raised here deeply involve students of child development. What kinds of programs are good for children—and at what ages? Does the excessive viewing of television result in fantasy-living, poor study habits, and alienation, as many of us suspect but few of us can prove. These are problems too for students of literature. "Life," said Oscar Wilde, "is an imitation of art." Delmore Schwartz said, "In dreams begin responsibilities." The imaginative representations of life, as depicted by commercial television, are a form of literature, shaping people's daydreams and life-styles, just as surely as *The Song of Roland* or *Huckleberry Finn*. What models of conduct does present-day television programing hold up for the young to emulate? What dreams of future achievement or success does it generate in boys and girls to direct their energies and aspiration?

This paper is speculative. I don't imagine there is a shred of evidence, other than subjective and intuitive, for anything I have said here about television and the state of mind of disaffiliated youth today. The trouble is that what research there is on the effects of television is almost entirely limited to research by advertising agencies on the effectiveness of their campaigns. Inquiries into the over-all effects of television—on politics, on public opinion and decision making, on the life-styles of young people and the psychic lives of young children—are only beginning. This paper is therefore not a presentation of conclusions but a request that we begin making inquiries. What *are* the relations between mass media and family communications? How do we begin answering such questions?

The Syntax of Personality

RICHARD DETTERING
Professor of Education and English
San Francisco State College

The next century, according to Dr. William F. Kiely, "may well be characterized by the conflict of generations."[1] While strife between the young and the old is perennial, it has never before erupted on so intense and planetary a scale. Nowhere in the painful crusades of faith, state against state, class against class, or race against race has

Reprinted from *Etc. A Review of General Semantics,* Vol. 26, No. 2: 139–156, June, 1969, by permission of the International Society for General Semantics.

[1] From an interview reported in the *San Francisco Examiner,* April 4, 1968, p. 47.

a crisis of human misunderstanding played more acutely on raw nerve-ends than in this now-raging civil war. If ever the disciplines of semantics, communication theory, and interpersonal psychology should show what they are worth, that moment is now.

The historic struggles of older peer-groups have been notorious enough for their want of information and feedback—as dramas in which "ignorant armies clash by night." Far more threatening is this impasse between the generations, with its rupture of the time-bound reciprocity which has distinguished man as the only creature whose future enriches his past. Any command of this latest rivalry within our species must try to fathom human nature from new and untried assumptions. There is little time left in which to do this.

Two comments. First, whatever the animal *man* may be, he is not what the connotations of his names and descriptions have led us to surmise. He is not a *thing,* nor is he substance identified with his own body which undergoes changes and disguise while staying fundamentally the same. Nor does the imperishable soul of the theologian or the squirming mass of the behaviorist fit the picture. Personality is an entity unto itself which can be depicted, if at all, only in some enigmatic, metaphorical way by our usual symbolism.

Second, today we have come to suspect and demonstrate how wholly and "magically" personality can change through its internal dynamics, through external agents, or through some combination of the two. Many personality poses come and go in much the way a polyglot may switch his tongues. As we hear a speaker move from English to French to Russian to Swahili, we do not assign his true being to the language he first spoke; nor do we regard one of his languages as more real than the others—at least if he speaks them with equal fluency. Nor do we say his English has transformed itself into French, or his Russian into Swahili.

What we must come to see is that in much the same way personalities are *psychological polyglots.* The system in which the psychological polyglot symbolizes becomes the basis for his personality on any given occasion. Owing to the cultural diversification enhanced by the mass media and rapid transportation, people today can take on more variant personality roles than ever before. We must thus in part study personality as we study comparative linguistics.

FROM THE TRANSACTIONAL PERSPECTIVE

There is at least one relevant framework for discussing personality as a polysymbolic phenomenon. In the classical mode, when we bestowed paternal, pedagogical, or psychotherapeutic attention on a person, we were tempted by centuries of tradition to *deindividualize* him, to "help" him by canceling his uniqueness and by committing or restoring him to some undistinguished norm for citizenship. Yet, at least since Rousseau, there has been mounting criticism of this shake-down and shape-up treatment of pupils, offenders, and patients. In the past decade this protest has reached a new climax in the form of the "third force" psychologies, alternatives to the established forces of behaviorism and psychoanalysis.[2]

These new psychologies have had various characterizations and labels—permissive, nondirective, client (or student) centered, humanistic, phenomenological—but perhaps the most significant name has been *transactional*. The transactional spokesmen have claimed to advance beyond the mere psychology of interaction long used to justify pragmatism and "progressive education." In an *interaction* A and B, although related, keep their identities unaffected; for example, two drivers passing on a highway, two patrons seated in the same theater, two gamblers playing in the same casino. In such cases the presence or behavior of the one person is not important for the other to be or to be doing what he is.

If, however, A and B are in a *transaction* their intimate identities and functions are at stake. One cannot be a husband without a wife, a teacher without a student, a business partner without a business partner. This class of relationships provides a model for countless interpersonal situations. The actual fulfillment is usually short of the ideal, of course; and there is always a danger that the rapport in these dyads will be spoiled by a social distance based on status. The plaintiff "knows" he is right, but his attorney "knows" the law; the patient feels the pain in his elbow even though his physician assures him it is only referred. When there is such a social distance, each partner sees the other as simply a disappointing instrument of his own designs. In a successful transaction, however,

[2] S. I. Hayakawa, Foreword to *Coming into Existence* by Raymond Rogers, New York, 1967.

one must regard the other person not merely as other, but as a special and valued part of his own self. The other person has a meaning apart from his physical presence—something not visible, audible, or smellable.

The transactional perspective is part of a general epistemology in which all external phenomena, including inanimate objects, are to some degree functions of the observer's constructs. The perception of ordinary things reflects "primarily some sort of weighted average of past experience which functions as a prognosis for the future in terms of what the organism is trying to do."[3] So even the most obdurate, lifeless being—the bump on a log—is a kind of "functional probability, a sort of best bet based on the individual's unique past experience as it relates to his purposes."[4]

We are here reminded of John Stuart Mill's definition of matter as "the permanent possibility of sensation." This theory of knowledge and its objects stresses the need for the self to infuse its sensory input with interpretations drawn from past encounters with the environment. Only by such an adjustment do we manage to make sense of the most commonplace experiences.

But the problem of objectivity involves more than the gestalt psychology of perception. There is also a transactional circularity within the systems of human symbolism. Our language often seems to strangle the very events it is used to reveal, though it is the language that we learn to use to make meaningful our nonsymbolic environment.

Take, for example, Ludwig Wittgenstein, who was perhaps the most awesome religious figure of this century. He was convinced that the shadows of symbolism were all that we have to go on. Devoted to a desperate search for some cognitive breakthrough, he pounded the bars of his intellectual cage in self-abasing and often inarticulate anger. His proposal of the concept of the "language game" as the way to "shew the fly the way out of the fly bottle" was his metaphorical caricature of the linguistically created problems of philosophy and life.

Wittgenstein's larger message, perhaps, was for the fly bottle to stop the entry of flies in the first place—for a language policy that would prevent the formulation of pseudomysteries and rhetorical bewitchment. Yet to the end he doubted even his own ability to gain

---

[3] F. P. Kilpatrick, "Perception Theory and General Semantics," *ETC.*, Special Issue on Transactional Psychology, Vol. XII, 1955, p. 259.
[4] *Ibid.*, p. 260.

those crushing prophetic answers in an open universe. He felt he was doomed to research among the shadows, where, unlike the Plato he so admired, he would find philosophic peace in resignation to the absurdity to which language drives us.

If projections from our ecological past and from the displacements of language are needed to confirm and judge impersonal objects, an even greater residue of stored memory and reworked interpretation must be summoned to make sense of people. While the messages we get from others extend from pulsating personal confessions to cold scientific reports, they all send us *some* information about the sender himself: his background, morals, intelligence, veracity, attitudes, emotions, etc. This self-revealing content in even the most objective message generates both our snap opinions and our lasting judgments of the senders. There is even some legerdemain to be suspected in the working out of this most human sort of process.

The most extreme case in which our equipment for symbolic response injects itself into the stimuli provided by another person is what Robert K. Merton called the "self-fulfilling prophecy." Here the receiver of a message can literally *remake* a sender to be what the receiver describes him to be. There are many examples of this insight. There is the paranoid who believes other people are against him and who therefore acts in such a suspicious, provocative, and hostile way that he *turns* others against him, thus vindicating his own illusion. Or there is the blithe good-timer who assumes that others love him and by acting on his assumption, actually gets them to do so. It can even be alleged to work with animals, as witness the old folk belief that if you flee a snarling dog it will be sure to chase and bite you.

In any case, it looks as though social science will come more and more to agree that the self-fulfilling prophecy is profoundly active in many human affairs. A recent article[5] has argued for the possibility that, however false or unsubstantiated, a teacher's expectation about the performance and intelligence of students significantly affects what their performance and intelligence turn out to be. We may well count on many more such studies in the next few years; and the self-fulfilling prophecy, instead of being an intriguing metaphysical speculation, could become a potent instru-

[5] Robert Rosenthal and Lenore F. Jacobson, "Teacher Expectations for the Disadvantaged," *Scientific American,* April 1968, p. 17.

ment of interpersonal and political manipulation, as well as an important reference point in the study of man.

The self-fulfilling prophecy introduces a novel and persisting irritant in the behavioral sciences. Annoying as it is, it would seem more palliated by the transactional treatment than by use of the classical assumption of susceptible subject versus adamant object. Indeed, the person whose behavior is prophesied becomes a function of the prophecy and thus, in his own strange way, like a controllable part of the very body of the prophet.

There is still another unusual, yet mostly unnoticed, peculiarity of the human message-sending venture. Unless there is an almost eccentric effort to understand its devices, the transmissional impetus —for example, the movements of lungs, larynx, lips, and tongue— appears as random, irrelevant, and aimless, while its result (the deciphered and delivered "statement") is systematic, pertinent, and purposeful. What seemingly begins as a set of accidents ends as the surprising execution of a plan, although the plan must have been in command all the way through.

Our hands can artfully play shadows on the wall to amuse children, using intrinsically meaningless contortions of the fingers and knuckles to throw familiar zoological silhouettes. Just so, most of our interpersonal communications seem inappropriate and ludicrous in their initial formulation, although they ultimately yield a clear and identifiable message. Despite the lack of physical correspondence, the inceptive behavior has some powerful correlation with the terminal code.

In our exercise of voice, penmanship, and gestures it takes years—from our infancy—to mesh the gears of our message output formation to create rational and informative input for the receiver. It is most striking that we must think backward from our receipt of a message to make sense of its origin—and not the other way around. Ironically, this reverses the analogy of Plato's cave: The shadows are at once understood, while the "real" figures which cast them are not—at least not until the meaning of the shadows is interpreted back into them. With all human perhaps most organic communication we must acknowledge this retroactivity by which what is sent is cognizable only after the cognition of what is received. This makes the transactional approach even more than we bargained for. The other person is not just inside oneself; what is inside oneself *is* the other person. He is the one we know and talk to, love or hate, help or injure. *Inter*personal relations become *intra*personal, at least in this one respect.

Some unlooked for, even unwanted suggestions now arise. Possibly the significance, coherence, and truth of human communication are always to be found first in some receiver—some listener, viewer, or reader—before they can be detected in the sender: the talker, painter, or writer. In this light the message sender must take heavy responsibility for what his messages *do* to the receivers, however pure and logical their literal form. While a transactional epistemology, as has been mentioned, pertains to both human and inanimate stimuli, it is the human stimuli which are more diagnosable through attention to the human response. With a plain object of nature or some artifact (even with most organisms) we try to go straight to the source, often using instrumental extensions of our senses to discover what's *there* causing our perception. Even if this effort is based on a delusion about the objectivity of nature, it is a delusion far more difficult to maintain when it comes to knowing people. To understand people we must read the telegram they send us; much of the time this is all we need or care to do. Except when there is a communication breakdown we are justified in trusting that the terminal form of the message is a reliable "copy" of the inceptive form.

This notion of copying brings us to one last consideration about the transactional perspective. Parts of the cosmos reflect other parts. Mountain lakes mirror the mountains. Hollow canyons echo sounds. And there are more sophisticated reflections. Terms like bilateral, symmetry, balance, equilibrium, replicate, parity, and mirroring have wandered in and out of the discourse of the physical and life sciences. The most astonishing reflections of all, however, burgeon from our symbol systems; they achieve a literal *copy right*, with a subtlety, flexibility, and freedom unknown in the non-human world. Curiously enough, the scrupulous imitation by a mirror or a lake, a tape or a canyon, limits itself by its very fidelity. In much the same way, traditional representational art is self-restricted in terms of its subject matter compared to abstract art—which, through its flaunted liberty to distort, may in the long run render a more faithful message. The lake of our symbolism suffers no such freezing. As Ludwig von Bertalanffy says, symbols are "freely created." This gives them the power to move beyond mere duplication and to engage in creative diagnosis. George A. Kelly has put it this way:

. . . life, to our way of thinking, is more than mere change. It involves an interesting relationship between parts of our universe wherein one part, the living creature, is able to bring himself around to represent another part, his environment. . . . Our formulation . . . emphasizes *the creative capacity of the living thing to represent the environment, not merely to respond to it.* Because he can represent his environment, he can place alternative constructions upon it.[6]

In this way the lake and the mirror may return some variance in the images of their surroundings, depending on the ripples or the hues of the hour. But this magic falls far short of our symbolism, which can develop reflections that change indefinitely and can mingle chosen facets of the object with an imaginative response.

So much for objects; now, once again, for people. To grasp the self-portraiture of another person calls for this creative, symbolic reflectivity at its peak of power. Audiovisual duplication—the worse for its detail and fidelity—can only hide and disguise the sender's message more completely, as would the hand shadows on the wall were they suddenly to become three-dimensional mirror reflections. The transactional and humanistic perspective on people is sometimes wrongly deemed to imply some absolute capture or immersion of the sender by the receiver—occasionally called "empathy." Not only is such alleged empathy impossible, but even as an unreachable ideal it belies the process of getting to know the other person. We get to know our neighbor as we get to know an artist: by intense critical appreciation of his work. At best, the link is a similarity of structure between the appreciation and the appreciated. If so, this structure is not pictorial or geometrical, but far more unconscious and abstract—shall we say syntactical?

We have been contending that the origin and verification of man's knowledge of man lies in his ability as a receiver to recreate the code of the sender in terms that make sense to the receiver and that this re-creation may reflect the code of the sender only in a most abstract and unrecognizable way. Many questions are yet unanswered. To justify this claim now demands certain assumptions, tacit or expressed, about the creatures who compose the interpersonal relationship. So we must take a look at the ontology of interpersonal psychology. What kind of phenomena are people?

[6] George A. Kelly, *A Theory of Personal Constructs,* New York, 1963, p. 8.

PERSONS AS PERSONAE

In reflecting one another, human beings learn that the messages one sends about himself to another are invariably partial functions of the messages the other is imprinting on him, and vice versa. Thus to know, even to try to say, what the other person is like comes to depend on what you tell him *you* are like. These reflections upon reflections get quite intricate. The typical tangle of interpersonal judgment has been outlined by George A. Kelly:

In interpreting social behavior we are confronted with a spiraliform model. James anticipates what John will do. James also anticipates what John thinks he [James] will do. James further anticipates what John thinks he [James] expects John will do. In addition, James antici- pates what John thinks James expects John to predict that James will do. And so on! We are reminded of the famous illustration of the cat looking in the mirror. In complicated social situations, as in psychotherapy, for example, one may find himself looking at another person through such an infinite series of reflections.[7]

This outside-inside-out relationship, a trifle nightmarish in its over- tones, forces us to search for new criteria in our recognition and judgment of other people.

Despite the idiosyncrasy of each interpersonal settlement, clearly most individuals tend to strike consensus reactions from the totality of people they meet; and they accordingly proceed to implant in the public mind their own unique character type. In commenting on "life styles," Alfred Adler once wrote,

From the beginning of the child's life a training comes about, as a result of which the child permits the growth of a role within himself of which he may be conscious or unconscious. After a while a certain mechanization sets in, so that he finds his way in accordance with his mechanized move- ments and forms of expressions. It is very much like what takes place when a child has memorized a poem. He does not need to find the words; the whole thing has become mechanized and is no longer conscious; the poem runs by itself, as it were. Once acquired, the style of life of a child and his self-evaluation remain constant as long as insight into the self is missing.[8]

[7] *Ibid.*, p. 94.
[8] *The Individual Psychology of Alfred Adler,* ed. Heinz and Rowena Ansbacher, New York, 1956, p. 367.

This sly hardening of an early unconscious role does not emerge in antiseptic autonomy, but presupposes the overt or potential presence and reinforcements of communal audiences.

Here we should recall that the words "person" and "personality" are thought to derive from an Etruscan compound meaning "mask"; the Latin transition means "to sound through," as in speaking through a mask. Throughout their recorded history these words have mixed their meaning with "persona," "actor," "role," and "character," with connotations of performance before company or on a stage. This etymology seems a bit at odds with the way the contemporary idea of personality is now being sanctified in theology, philosophy, and the psychological pursuits. In fact, the humanistic psychologies have taken a lead in promoting the concept of a person to a revered status, along with a touch-me-not caution to meddlers from education, social work, and psychotherapy.

Certainly there is a verbal conflict here, if not a deeper one. Yet once we decide that persons are made and not born, that personality is not a gift or a legacy but an accomplishment, the term "person" can become even more honorific. This is especially so if the accomplishment is learning to play a part, with all the planning, work, and sacrifice that go with it. To become a real person, then, is not a self-unmasking, not a strip job, not a flagrant exposure of the naked self. Rather it is the rough ordeal of trying, through one's total behavior, to convince the rest of the world that one is what he pretends to be. This act of conviction takes as its model the histrionic art forms in which we use speech, countenance, pantomime, dance, and dress to persuade the spectators, not that the medium is the message, but that our medium is the fact which is *messaged*, the fact which the medium expresses. On stage we try to do this professionally, like a magician; but off stage, in our typical daily habits, we do it for real. The more we succeed in these dramatic deeds, the more we seem to depart from what we were before, when we first looked at the plot. To perform is to transform. Though the new monitors of the natural self often fail to see it, the integrity of the performing citizen is found before the footlights and not in the dressing room.

The dramatic arts, then, contain the models for personality. Yet every step in socialization or career cultivation follows the same example, though the staginess is covert and disarming—indeed, it is effective only *because* it is so. From this mass of role-enactments personality arises as a special and inimitable collection of masks.

Unmasking is a will-o'-the-wisp; all we uncover are earlier masks. This may be all that can be meant by the discovery of the real self. On deeper discernment the person always turns out to be interpersonal: he takes roles, he trains people to regard him as such and so, he sends messages about himself, he exhibits a life style. The names of these behaviors become increasingly synonymous as we apply and ponder them.

The lifelong training for a personality seems to have a biological base in the importance of repetition in acquiring a skill. Educators and parents have made a false distinction between physical and mental development. Thus when it comes to mastering a manual task or an athletic feat we go by the maxim that "practice makes perfect" and encourage the child to repeat the tedious steps. In seeking intellectual competence, on the other hand, we became alarmed at learning plateaus and fear that reiteration is a symptom of retardation. This double standard has now come under sharp criticism in a reassessment of the theories of Piaget and Montessori. In the words of David Elkind,

One of the features of cognitive growth which Piaget and Montessori observed, and to which they both attached considerable importance, is the frequently repetitive character of behaviors associated with emerging mental abilities. Piaget and Montessori are almost unique in this regard since within both psychology and education repetitive behavior is often described pejoratively as "rote learning" or "perseveration." Indeed the popular view is that repetition is bad and should be avoided in our dealings with children.[9]

Elkind feels that the two famous educators, on the contrary, saw more clearly the role that small practice and repetition play in mental growth. He concludes by rejecting the popular assumption.

The role of repetitive behavior in intellectual development is not extraordinary when we view mental growth as analogous to physical growth. Repetitive behavior is the bench mark of maturing physical abilities. . . . Mental abilities are realized in the same way.[10]

The final capping analogy, tying in our own main argument, is between these repetitive steps—which seem to occur with the physi-

[9] David Elkind, "Piaget and Montessori," *Harvard Educational Review*, Vol. 37, No. 4, 1967, p. 541.
[10] *Ibid.*, p. 542.

cal maturation of both animals and men—and the rehearsals and endless re-enactments so needed for success on the stage. The little repetitions go into the making of a personality just as they go into the making of a carpenter, a ball player, a mathematician—and the star of stage or screen.

In this histrionic matrix, personality sooner or later becomes the expression of its own creativity. As David Hawkins has put it, "a particular work of art is the product of the artist, but on a longer time scale the artist himself is a product of his work."[11] True of art, which is social *action;* true of personality, which is social *acting.* "How can we know the dancer from the dance?" asked Yeats in one of those epigrammatic insights which psychologists should never put by. True also of morality, which is not a private state but a public deposition, even if God is the only public. "Conscience," wrote H. L. Mencken, "is the inner voice that says someone is looking." Here, again, more truth than cynicism; the "significant other" is essential to the fully human act. The reality of an actor is the rapture, gasps, tears, laughs, and yawns of those who pay to see the show; his morality is their affect about his talent. We cannot know "what is deep down inside." A person cannot be plumbed "inside"; all we can find is another mask, another "outside." The onion theory: layer beneath layer and never a stone.

The tendency of our culture has been to misconstrue the nature of personality by subjecting it to the aristotelian concept of substance. This leads us to seek some immutable reality behind the façades. Then we add to this mistake the illusion that personality is a set of objective qualities instead of a series of dramatic, communicative acts. Once we escape these false expectations about people in general we will cease to be so mystified and dismayed about the particular people we meet and know. We will accept the parade of masks that we call "him" or "her." In so doing we must resign ourselves to an element of permanent uncertainty. This is because, in its persuasive messenger function, personality consists of streams of symbols as much as does a book. Symbols have, among their many intriguing properties, one that closely relates to our belief in the reality and sincerity of another person—the property of ambiguity.

[11] David Hawkins, *The Language of Nature,* New York, 1967, p. 58.

AMBIGUITY IN PERSONALITY

The ambiguity of a symbol is its freedom to play different roles, either through its denotative or connotative reference or through its grammatical or rhetorical position. To mention a symbol's freedom is just a manner of speaking: a symbol can no more have freedom than a teaspoon can. It is rather the human being who has the freedom to employ any symbol ambiguously—that is, in an indefinite number of ways. In the *de facto* usage to which we put them, however, at least our linguistic symbols range from the virtually univocal, like the operating signs in mathematics, to the deliberately equivocal, like many terms in poetry. The amount of manifest ambiguity depends not on what the symbol looks or sounds like, but on the public and private decisions to enslave it in certain ways.

The expression of personality is therefore ambiguity personified. This is one reason why we often agree on what someone is doing yet disagree on why he is doing it. It is also an error to assume that familiarity with the origin and history of such expressions necessarily resolves the debate over their meaning. Many symbols in politics and law as well as in poetry were intended to be read in alternate ways; scholarship simply bares and advertises such multiplicity of meaning.

This fact about language has its parallel in the paradox that often those very people who are well and widely known, who have many "close friends," occasion more dispute over what they "really are" than do individuals of scarce acquaintance. This is further evidence that the more times a symbol is used and exposed and the more people traffic with it, the more malleable it becomes. That concentrated efforts are often made to stabilize the meaning of both linguistic and personality symbols is not surprising, for ambiguity in the wrong situation or at the wrong time can easily lead to communicative chaos.

Still, the intrinsic ambiguity of symbols permits both tyrannical majorities and eccentric deviants to evaluate personalities with impunity. The meanings of human behavior are thrust on the faces and bodies of men by other men; posture and physiognomy are assigned meanings by fiat or convention. But those who judge are judging those who seek to be judged; and, once some arbitrary interpretation of behavior comes to prevail, candidates to popu-

larity or power can easily conform. This is why shrewd diagnosti-
cians look for a less contrived, more unconscious message than tends
to be sent by the obvious symbolism of clothing, facial expression,
and body movement, which at least in our culture provide a person
with his "front." The acting personality is on guard about these
standard forms of self-advertising and finds it easy to deceive
others.

To find and judge those personality symbols that are not
known to be symbols is one way to size up a person more effectively.
Luther counseled those who sought to know a man to watch not his
face but his fist; Lenin peered at his unsuspecting visitors through
the slits between his fingers. Such intuitive leaders realize that,
when a face is known to be observed, its movements are planned for
public effect. But the subconscious responses are far more likely to
send the telltale message of buried emotions and life purpose. Of
course, society at large is quickly tipped off to each new means of
interpersonal espionage. As a case in point, sophisticated people
today are hesitant to reveal their dreams and are very considered in
shaking hands with members of certain minority groups. Thus do
the former victims of such covert observations begin to play their
own countergame.

What, then, if anything, can we rely upon for the truth of
interpersonal communication? Certainly no one symbol or symbol-
unit per se. Rather, each meaningful or cognitive act is a prophecy,
and each relies on its implicit statement as to what will come next.
It is this criterion, not primitive need-fulfillment, that identifies
people as inimitable human beings. Again, George A. Kelly has
stated the point:

. . . nor do we imply that a person seeks "pleasure," that he has special
"needs," or even that there are "satisfactions." In this sense ours is not a
commercial theory. To our way of thinking, there is a consistent movement towards the anticipation of events rather than a series of barters for
temporary satisfactions, and this movement is the essence of human life
itself.[12]

To complete a rhythm, close an unfinished circle, supply the last
word of a sentence—these, more than physical rewards and punish-
ments, typify man's career as a system of symbolic cadences which
can often overcome the normal appetites and passions, or at least

[12] Kelly, *op. cit.,* p. 68.

assimilate them to its own norms. It is here that some of the ambiguities of personality may also be resolved through experimental predictions, although a large number remain scientifically in limbo and are settled only by an arbitrary "court decision."

To understand a person is to be aware of his syntactical anticipations. This presupposes learning the codes in which he sends his messages—verbal and nonverbal, conscious and unconscious. The codes do not rule out ambiguities the way the rules of mathematics are supposed to do, but they do limit the rival meanings which personality symbols acquire. A man whose clothing is a bit loose is wearing an ambiguous symbol which may mean casual folksiness or slovenly insensitivity; the demure young lady may symbolize sweet ingénue or crafty temptress.

Contrary to common belief, to clarify such ambiguities requires not only factual investigation, but also social verdict. Society may *want* to let the ambiguity remain. Factual testimony may incline the social evaluation one way or the other, but an interpretative decision must be made as to its relevance. Thus, if the man with the loose-fitting clothes is occasionally late for appointments, it can still be debated whether this "proves" that he is an insensitive lout or an unconstrained rustic. Such arguments will continue indefinitely if the book is reasonably balanced; and needless to say the self-fulfilling prophecy is the victor. Ambiguity is its usher.

In the exact sciences ambiguity has been unforgivable, though by no means absent. The comparison with the ambiguity of literature has been pointedly made by J. Bronowski:

Neither science nor literature ever gives a complete account of nature or of life. In both of them, the progress from the present account to the next account is made by the exploration of the ambiguities in the language that we use at this moment. In science, these ambiguities are resolved for the time being, and a system without ambiguity is built up provisonally, until it is shown to fall short. . . . But in literature, the ambiguities cannot be resolved even for the time being, and no provisional system of axioms can be set up to describe the human situation as the writer and reader seek to see it together.[13]

Although both physics and poetry contain inevitable ambiguity, progress in physics is an unending process of eliminating it, while

[13] J. Bronowski, "The Logic of the Mind," *American Scientist,* Vol. 54, No. 1, March 1966, p. 13.

the enriching appreciation of poetry requires that we not only tolerate but savor it.

As families of symbolic masks, human beings are more like poems than like theorems. They can rarely be proved or disproved through the rules of some deductive system, nor can they easily be frozen in what they mean. Most of the time they are full of options and unpredictabilities, of ebbs and flows, of undertows and roll-backs.

The ideal of a general science of personality may well be in vain or at least overstated. Whether we can even find *linguistic* universals in man, as Noam Chomski suggests, is unsure; and the discovery of the *dramatic* universals is even more of a dreamy argosy. What we can do is to recognize more fully the individual personalities whose paths we cross. We can do this partly as we divine the author, culture, and century of an unfamiliar work of art. The most apt analogy, however, remains that of the stage; its very banality underscores its universality. By and large, there is no script for the human comedy, and only in its more pathetic and drier scenes is it like the mechanical recitation of a poem. People are more like a set of *improvised* poems fitted into a play. The lines are not memorized and repeated, but spontaneously match the role and the plot. To understand another person's behavior, then, is to fore-cast the scenario he is acting out, hopefully doing credit to his imagination and to his difference from everybody else.

Understanding Student Rebellion

JEROME F. X. CARROLL
Psychology Department
La Salle College, Philadelphia

In his book, *To Seek A Newer World*, the late Senator Robert F. Kennedy (1) cited a quotation from Tennyson which seemed to characterize the mood of the contemporary student activist with remarkable precision:

From *Adolescence*, 4: 163–180, Summer, 1969.

"Ah, what shall I be at fifty,
Should nature keep me alive,
If I find the world so bitter,
When I am but twenty-five?"

Today, students seemingly everywhere are literally besieging their campuses with numerous and sundry acts of rebellion. Their angry shouts of protests, and sometimes destructive actions, bear stark witness to the intensity of their growing sense of frustration and hopelessness.

To the social scientist, these are obvious signs that our educational institutions are seriously falling short in their efforts to take account of and provide for the more important human needs of this "turned on" generation of students. Yet, there are some administrators and faculty who persist either in denying or belittling the significance of these events. They mistakenly interpret the silent, painful endurance of the nonprotesting students to imply satisfaction with things as they are, an implicit endorsement to proceed as usual. They argue that it is, after all, just a handful of "malcontents," "authority-hating anarchists" who are involved. Others feel it is just a fad, like the hulahoop, that will soon pass away.

Other administrators and faculty, while able to see the seriousness of the situation, are unable to examine objectively whether they or the education system they have created is in any way responsible for the student unrest. Sadder yet are those academic decision-makers who would use, advocate, or condone the application of excessive and sometimes brutal force to suppress student protests in order to restore the educational process to its "normal" state.

The basic question which all of us must ask ourselves is, why does anyone rebel against a social system or any particular institution within that system? In a recent address, John W. Gardner (2), former Secretary of Health, Education and Welfare, seemed to provide an answer to this question when he argued that there is an inherent tendency for all institutions to rigidify and decay. Such institutions, he said, "smother individuality, imprison the spirit, thwart the creative impulse, diminish individual adaptability, and limit the possibility of freedom."

He further stated that as ". . . the institutions grow increasingly resistant to criticism, the critics grow increasingly hostile, and the stage is then set for violent collision between angry critics and sluggish institutions." To avoid this destructive mode of confrontation, he maintained that it was essential that a society plan and provide for the periodic, revolutionary, imaginative redesigning of its institutions. Then, and only then, could orderly social changes be effected.

In any meaningful analysis of a worldwide phenomenon such as student rebellion, the causes must be assumed to be multiple, varied, dynamic, and interacting. Further, some of these causes will have originated from events that took place in the distant past, while others will be more a matter of the immediate situation. Still others will have reference to anticipated future occurrences. Some causes will be idiosyncratic, others parochial, and some universal in their nature. While some causes may relate to imagined slights, others will arise from very real difficulties. For one student the urge to rebel may stem from unconscious or hidden motives, while another may be quite conscious of the underlying motives. For any particular student, his motives for rebelling will likely be an admixture of all these elements.

SUGGESTED CAUSES

In attempting to explain the underlying causes of student rebellion I have focused upon six points. The first four have reference to important human needs which I believe are being seriously frustrated by the present system of education. The other two points refer to significant social changes that have taken place, which I believe aggravate the consequences of this frustration. These six points are:

a) The gradual erosion of man's personal sense of significance.
b) The deprivation of man's sense of personal identity.
c) The castration of man's sense of personal potency.
d) Man's alienation from his fellow man.
e) The emergence of adolescence as a distinct and separate state of psychosocial development.
f) The inability of "the establishment" to appreciate the impact of modern communications, especially television, upon youth.

This analysis, I might add, was much influenced by the works of men such as Eric Fromm (3, 4), Rollo May (5), Sidney Jourard (6, 7), John W. Gardner (2), Senator Robert F. Kennedy (1),

Marshall McLuhan (8, 9), and Eldridge Cleaver (10). The time I have spent discussing the causes and consequences of student rebellion with students, faculty, and administrators also has proven to be most instructive and helpful in preparing this work.

MAN'S PERSONAL SIGNIFICANCE

Today, this nation is engaged in a great war in Vietnam which has inflicted more casualties upon us than any other military struggle we have undertaken. It has also severely impeded social reforms and progress at home, while simultaneously damaging the solidarity of our people in a manner unparalleled since the Civil War. Yet, the prime source from which our military forces are drawn remains unrepresented at the polls. Far worse than "taxation without representation" is the sacrifice of life and limbs without representation. Without any legal means of exercising their will on vital matters affecting their very lives, it is hard to imagine how today's youth could derive any sense of personal significance.

For those youths who do possess the power of the ballot, recent events have also seemed to weigh against their sense of significance. Many college students, for example, worked long and hard to promote the candidacies of men such as the late Senator Robert F. Kennedy, Senator Eugene McCarthy, and Governor Nelson Rockefeller. Not only were they unsuccessful in their efforts, but they seemed overnight to have become targets, both literally and figuratively, for a large segment of their elders who charged them with the high crime of having rocked the boat, of having tried to change the traditional procedures for conducting political business.

Students, as do all other human beings, desire and need to be dealt with as unique individuals if they are to maintain a sense of personal significance. Yet many educational institutions are inadequately prepared and equipped to meet the individual needs of their students. Too many colleges and universities are guilty of engaging primarily in the process of providing training rather than education.

This would seem to be nothing more than an extension of the Henry Ford assembly line psychology of mass production, mass consumption—the grinding out of standardized academic products to fill existing slots within the system.

Robert F. Kennedy (1) expressed similar thoughts when he

wrote, ". . . we are more and more ignoring differences, if not trying to obliterate them. We seem headed toward a standardization of the mind, what Goethe called 'The deadly commonplace that fetters us all.' "

It is difficult to envision a student enhancing and/or maintaining his sense of personal worth as he sits in a large lecture room surrounded by several hundred other students who gaze at their lecturer's image on a TV set. The end result is the same for the student in the small classroom in which dialogue between himself and the lecturer is *verboten*. There he must play the role of the sponge, quietly and passively absorbing as ordered!

Then there is that boon to the modern teacher's need to teach within the mass production-oriented education system—the objective exam. How much individuality is there in circling one of four or five fixed, standardized alternatives? Or in the machine scoring which follows?

Other examples of the same issues would include the student's inability to meet individually with his professor, or for that matter, even with the professor's teaching assistant, both of whom often are too busy with more important matters. Not soliciting or ignoring student views and opinions regarding important academic or administrative policies and practices has a similar effect.

The end result of all of the above is frustration—the denial of the individual's ability to experience himself as a worthwhile individual. One reaction to such frustration is that of aggressive rebellion, which is eloquently illustrated by the words of Mario Savio, one of the most articulate of Berkeley's former student activists:

"There is a time when the operation of the machine (of collectivized educational) becomes so odious, makes you so sick at heart that you can't take part . . . You've got to put your bodies upon the gears and upon the levers, upon all the apparatus and you've got to make it stop. . . ." (5, p. 27).

Other less articulate and less courageous students rationalize away their indignation by convincing themselves that "the lemon is really sweet"—that this is the best possible means of obtaining a college education under existing circumstances.

Others react with a quiet, but seething anger while some students wallow in despair and apathy. Still others resign themselves to playing "the game," to the necessity of becoming an educational whore who sells his authentic self for modern man's equivalent of a union card—a diploma.

With his diploma the graduate can aspire to and be considered for society's higher paying jobs. Obtaining such a position guarantees him ready cash and solid credit. Thus, he may enter the great commercial markets, the contemporary materialist's heaven, and consume, consume until he is oblivious to the pain of having sold his soul in order to "get ahead."

THE LOSS OF MAN'S SENSE OF IDENTITY

Fromm (3), in describing the social character best suited for twentieth century capitalism, argued that the system ". . . needs men who cooperate smoothly in large groups; who want to consume more and more, and whose tastes are standardized and can be easily influenced and anticipated . . . men who feel free and independent, not subject to any authority, or principle or conscience—yet willing to be commanded to do what is expected, to fit into the social machine without friction."

This "fitting in without friction," the pressure to conform, to adjust, to "not make waves" is a major principle for "successful" twentieth century living. It is also a major threat to man's sense of identity.

Last summer I worked in a pre-college counseling program for incoming freshmen. The program format afforded me the opportunity to meet with small groups of these freshmen to discuss informally their views on a variety of subjects, including their expectations concerning college.

During these sessions I listened to many of these young men speak of their intentions to "pretend to go along, to play the game." In essence, they were telling me that they had perceived their high school teachers as preferring pretense to authenticity, that to have revealed their true selves would have been too dangerous. They seemed convinced that our educational institutions constituted a corrupt but powerful system which was intolerant and harsh in dealing with anyone who would openly dissent and seek to change it. As far as they could discern, the college experience was not likely to be too different from their previous educational experiences.

This was not the first time I had heard this point of view

expressed on a college campus. What was significant to me was the fact that the men who were expressing this point of view had not even begun their college experience. Anyone who is familiar with the phenomenon of the "self-fulfilling prophecy" can easily foresee the disastrous consequences which would likely follow from this negative expectation.

The experience which I have shared with you is especially depressing if you believe, as I do, that social progress depends to a very large extent upon the idealism, vitality, and commitment of youth. If and when this is jeopardized or destroyed, then society must surely suffer, because it will soon become stagnant, anachronistic and therefore impotent to meet the constant challenge of change.

It is also rather upsetting to contemplate the fact that these students were about to jeopardize their mental health by opting to undertake the game of academic pretense. For as therapists such as Jung (11), Horney (12), Sullivan (13) and Jourard (7) have pointed out, the individual so pretending may soon lose contact with his "real self"—become unable to recognize and distinguish between his persona, or public, phony self and his genuine, authentic, real self. When and if this happens he may begin to manifest signs or symptoms not at all unlike those which the bereaved mourners at a funeral often evidence—depression, apathy, and confusion.

In addition to this pernicious mental set which the students bring to their college campuses, consider the following factors which are also likely to undermine the student's sense of identity.

An individual's name is perhaps one of the most important foundations upon which his sense of identity rests. To be recognized by others by name is a constant reinforcement of a person's sense of identity. Yet in many classes, professors fail to recognize or call upon their students by their names. This might be due to the constantly increasing number of students being assigned to the modern pedagog, or the professor's indifference to the task of teaching, or his disdain for students, or any combination of these factors.

With few exceptions, modern education also fails to provide sufficient opportunities for the individual student to engage in a dialogue with his instructor, to express his unique understanding and grasp of the subject matter. Writing a term paper or an essay exam is insufficient while being restricted to marking true or false, or choosing "a," "b," "c," or "d" is intolerable. Nor is it in the service of identity to allow only the orthodox or approved interpretation to be expressed by the student, i.e., that opinion which agrees with the traditional view, the expert's view, the instructor's view. That is academic brainwashing!

Perhaps the most damaging of all the contemporary forces which serve to undermine the student's personal sense of identity is that which Fromm (3) has called the process of "quantification and abstractification." Fromm attributes this process to the socioeconomic structure which characterizes the twentieth century capitalistic society.

The nature of this structure is such that the twin processes of mass production and mass consumption necessitates an abstract, quantitative evaluation of a "balance sheet" in order that the value of a particular economic operation can be determined. As a result of this mode of evaluation, however, the unique and personal experiences of the countless men and women involved in production and consumption are ignored and/or discounted.

Unfortunately, as Fromm (3) has indicated, this process of quantification and abstractification has spread from the realm of economics to all aspects of modern man's life experiences, including the schools. Today, the quantified, abstract market value of an educational institution—its personnel and "products"—serves to define the identity of that institution to a far greater extent than that of any of the personal, individual experiences of its students, faculty, or administrators.

Colleges and universities thus tend to define their identity in terms of quantitative, abstract criteria such as the number of incoming freshmen with college board scores of 1300 or more, the number of Ph.D's on the faculty, the amount of alumni contributions, the number of books in the library, the number of buildings on the campus, and the size of the state appropriation to the college.

The professor's identity often is defined rather heavily in terms of the number of publications he has, the number of professional organizations with which he is affiliated, and the number and amount of government grants he can secure for the institution.

Students, on the other hand, are defined by such quantitative indices as their college board scores, grade point average, class standing, final examination grade, graduate record examination results, and the going market value of a degree in their academic specialty.

All of the above serves to obscure, distort, and possibly devalue the concrete, personal life experiences which define a healthy individual's sense of identity. These quantitative, abstract criteria represent an extrinsic value system which is being imposed upon the individual by society. Furthermore, these values tend to reward conformity to the status quo, while discouraging innovation and change. Thus, to the degree that they preclude or interfere with the individual's efforts to personally define and affirm his own sense of identity, based on his unique, concrete life experiences, then to that extent the process of quantification and abstractification on college campuses is pathogenic.

THE SENSE OF IMPOTENCY

There was one other repetitive theme heard last summer which was especially disturbing to me, and that was the anguished cry of impotence. It deepened my appreciation of Sullivan's (3) concept of malevolent transformation (the feeling that one lives among enemies) and Horney's (14) basic anxiety (the feeling of being isolated and helpless in a potentially hostile world).

The students seemed to perceive their educational experience as one in which they were being subjected to destructive, dehumanizing, arbitrary, dictatorial forces against which they seemed hopelessly outgunned and outmanned. In other words, they felt they were being "processed" by a system to which they strongly objected but were powerless to challenge or change. This view, by the way, is not unique to incoming college freshmen. It can be heard from students at all levels, both undergraduate and postgraduate.

Today, students feel they should share equally with administrators and faculty, as a tripartite governing body, in deciding upon matters of school policy and practices. Specifically, they believe they should have a significant voice in determining such matters as what will constitute the core curriculum, what courses will be required within a given discipline and for whom, how courses will be conducted, and what materials will be included in these courses.

They are also concerned about participating, along with administrators and faculty, in deciding upon the granting of tenure to professors, the promoting of academicians in rank, the assessment of a professor's teaching effectiveness, the particular grading system to be employed (if one is to be used at all), the setting and raising of tuition and fees, etc.

To the extent that students are being excluded from sharing in the deliberation of such issues—all of which significantly influence their education experiences—then they are made to feel impotent. This, in turn, increases the probability of a violent outburst of student rebellion.

In *To Seek A Newer World* (1), there is a quotation attributed to a University of California student speaking to the Board of Regents which well illustrates the psychological consequences of the sense of impotency.

"We have asked to be heard. You have refused. We have asked for justice. You have called it anarchy. We have asked for freedom. You have called it license. Rather than face the fear and hopelessness you have created, you have called it Communistic. You have accused us of failing to use legitimate channels. But you have closed those channels to us. You, and not us, have built a university based on distrust and dishonesty."

Fromm (3) clearly articulated and illustrated the impotency of modern man in the face of the tremendous forces he has created. I would only add that from my vantage point, it seems that our educational institutions are serving these same forces.

Many students, as I have indicated, have already given up the struggle and resigned themselves to the task of blending in, adjusting, getting by. Others have "dropped out," which may be a more honorable and honest reaction, although more costly in the materialistic sense.

Yet some students have heeded the call of visionary men such as the late Senator Kennedy (1), who argued that personal effort and sacrifice in the service of humanity was not a futile gesture, that each man's personal efforts could have a significant effect when joined with those of countless other similarly disposed individuals. As he often stated

"Some men see things as they are—and say why.
I dream things that never were—and say why not."

Yet to seek to change a powerful system primarily committed to the perpetuation of its status quo nature, takes great moral courage, especially for those who are part of this system. Unfortunately, as Senator Kennedy once remarked, moral courage is ". . . a rarer commodity than bravery in battle or great intellect."

It is far easier to "get by" through simply giving in to the modal or typical life style, although many need an occasional shot of booze, drugs or sex to kill the pain which results from such a choice. Others delude themselves of their impotency by amassing and consuming more and more material goods—false signs of personal power—the new opiate of the masses of impotent people.

MAN'S ALIENATION FROM HIS FELLOW MAN

There are innumerable aspects of twentieth century living which have served to isolate man from man. To name but a few—the expression of a man's worth by the income he earns or the titles he bears, the threat of thermonuclear war, racial prejudice, gross imbalances of wealth and resources among nations and people within nations, the emphasis upon mass production, mass consumption, etc.

As man becomes more and more alienated from his fellowman, and thus more insecure, he will often seek to utilize his fellowman in an exploitative sense for personal aggrandizement or profit. This may be viewed as a form of compensation, a psychic defense against the painful consequences of alienation.

In *Psychology and the Human Dilemma,* May (5) argues that this process ultimately leads to a vicious circle of alienation which takes the following form:

1. Man's sense of being alone and alienated from his fellowman at the time of crisis seems to be precipitated by forces beyond his immediate control and against which he can exercise little personal influence.

2. This gives rise to intense anxiety (May's (5) loss of a sense of personal significance; Tillich's (15) anxiety of meaninglessness; Kierkegaard's (16) fear of nothingness; Fromm's (3) and Jourard's (6) sense of impotence.)

3. Anxiety leads to regression and apathy (resignation, giving up, dropping out).

4. These in turn lead to hostility.

5. Hostility leads to further alienation of man from man.

For the student, the sense of alienation often is experienced as a lack of school spirit, a lack of solidarity, the absence of group identification and indifference. Perhaps professors and administrators contribute to this process through their overemphasis upon competition in grading or their being too busy or insecure to engage in friendly, egalitarian dialogue.

EMERGENCE OF ADOLESCENCE AS A DISTINCT AND SEPARATE STAGE OF PSYCHOSOCIAL DEVELOPMENT

Today's highly specialized, technological-scientific society demands a constant supply of highly trained and educated human replacement parts. This has necessarily lengthened the period of time for the training and educating of our youth, and has, thereby, postponed their assumption of adult responsibilities and privileges. It has also served to separate, more than at any other time in man's history, the child from the adult. As a result, a new breed of human being has evolved—the adolescent—and the overwhelming majority of students are adolescents.

Adolescence, the prolonged interlude between childhood and adulthood, thus has broken the more traditional mode of directly transmitting values from one generation to another. In addition, the scientific orientation of our society often has the effect of calling into question and challenging traditional beliefs and institutions. Today's student, therefore, is inclined to approach problems and issues in a quasi-scientific vein, i.e., with an implicit scientific attitude.

More specifically, he tends to approach a decision on a particular matter by gathering and evaluating the available, empirical evidence before deciding his course of action. It is only under very unusual circumstances that he will look to tradition in order to make his choice.

In part, this disenchantment with tradition and preference for the scientific mode of inquiry stems from his exposure to science throughout his education. Moreover, the society in which he lives surrounds him with scientific news, gadgets, heroes, etc. He is thus conditioned to think and appreciate science. Even the ubiquitous TV ads reflect this scientific bias when they "inform" us, for example, that three out of four physicians prefer Brand A to Brand B.

The contemporary student is, therefore, less tradition-bound than his predecessor. He will then be more inclined to challenge and abandon traditions when, and if, they prove to be invalid, irrelevant, or unnecessary obstacles to his efforts to develop and realize his potentials. Some educators will label this behavior unpatriotic or heretical, but it is neither. It is rather the life style of a new generation with its own unique *Weltanschauugen*.

Further, the adolescent, while waiting in the wings to enter upon the adult stage, has much time to contemplate the significance, relevance and validity of adult values and practices. The discrepancy between what he hears adults preaching and sees them doing is often the occasion for great disillusionment. Thus, when he is invited on stage, he may either decline the offer or enter speaking lines not written in the script.

Perhaps the adult establishment would do better to acknowledge its shortcomings rather than attempt to hide them from the "the children," and to begin a genuine, serious, concerted movement toward the realization of its moral and ethical goals. Then those waiting in the wings might be more eager to go where the adult action is.

THE INABILITY OF "THE ESTABLISHMENT" TO APPRECIATE THE IMPACT OF MODERN COMMUNICATIONS, ESPECIALLY TV, UPON YOUTH

McLuhan (8, 9) argues that due to the achievement of instantaneous, worldwide communications, especially television, we now have become residents in a "global village." Villages, however, are small places where nearly everyone knows what's happening. There are few well-kept secrets in a village, regardless of whether the particular event originates in the Prague or Chicago section of the global village.

Modern methods of communication have also done much to wipe out the man-made and natural barriers which, in the past, have separated nation from nation, man from man. The world has shrunk in size and simultaneously become more intimate and united than ever before in man's history. Today students living in non-Communist nations such as Italy and Japan will stage sympathy protest demonstrations for a Czechoslovakian comrade who sacrificed his life in behalf of his nation's struggle to secure a more humane form of socialism. Students in Germany, Mexico, and France are one with their American counterparts in their opposition to the war in Vietnam.

In addition to bringing everyone into closer contact with one another, modern methods of communication also involve us more intensely in current events, whether we like it or not, than the printed word could ever have achieved. To read about children and adults starving in the U.S. is one thing; to actually watch an infant die "on camera" is another.

Through TV, radio, magazines, etc., our homes have become extensions of the great learning centers. Today, it is possible for most men and women to be exposed to a variety of ideologies, doctrines and theories on countless topics. Each competes for the viewer's attention and allegiance. The days of narrow parochial education are over. Thus, today's youth is much more cosmopolitan in outlook.

In addition, as instantaneous telecommunications enable us to more directly experience events as they actually unfold, they have the potential of deepening our appreciation of cause-and-effect relationships. They also better enable us to integrate feelings and reasoning in a far more complete manner than reading alone could ever accomplish.

As McLuhan (8) has stated, the media is massaging our minds—everyone's, both young and old. But there is this difference to consider. This present generation of youth has grown up with TV as a "given." Yet many of us can remember its introduction into our neighborhoods and homes. Thus, I would agree with those who argue that the present generation is more involved than its predecessors. To a great extent, this is due to the media upon which it has fed.

Today's parents, "the silent generation," remained that way in part because they were often kept in ignorance of significant events and/or experienced them in a less arresting manner. Their encounters with these events were mediated through the printed and spoken word, but without the rich visual imagery that the contemporary youth has known since infancy.

As a result of this communications explosion and its manifold consequences, the college student literally can be described as living in a different psychological world than those who daily plan, administer, and provide for his educational experience. Unless and until these inhabitants from two different psychological worlds are able and willing to seek to understand one another's phenomenological experiences, then conflict must surely ensue, its intensity being directly proportionate to the degree of misunderstanding existing between the two groups—students and educators.

SUMMARY

In this analysis of student rebellion, generally issues and concepts have been emphasized rather than the specific problems of a particular campus. The failure of our educational institutions to provide for planned, periodic, imaginative renewal and its consequent frustration of significant human needs was stressed.

Among those frustrated needs thought to be particularly important were man's need for a personal sense of significance, his need for a self-affirmed sense of personal identity, his need for a sense of personal potency in directing his destiny in life, and his need for a sense of brotherhood and communion with his fellowman.

Also emphasized in this analysis was the impact which modern communications, especially television, has had upon this generation of students. The emergence of adolescence as a distinct and rather discrete period in the socialization process was also emphasized.

Finally, to put this analysis in its proper perspective, it seems important to stress the point that the students' rebellion is not a unique or isolated event. Numerous rebellions are taking place, in nearly every corner of the globe. They involve men and women of all ages, races, political persuasions, religious beliefs or disbeliefs.

Today's classic struggle, of which the student rebellion is but a small part, is one between those who hold to the proposition that human values should be supreme and those who view man merely as a means to an end.

REFERENCES

1. KENNEDY, R. F. *To Seek A Newer World*. N.Y.: Doubleday, 1967.
2. GARDNER, J. W. Continuous renewal: Best route to orderly social change? *Philadelphia Inquirer*. December 15, 1968, Section 7, p. 1.
3. FROMM, E., *The Sane Society*. N.Y.: Holt, Rinehart, & Winston, 1955.
4. FROMM, E. *The Revolution of Hope*. N.Y.: Harper & Row, 1968.

5. MAY, R. *Psychology and the Human Dilemma.* Princeton, N.J.: D. Van Nostrand, 1967.
6. JOURARD, S. M. *Disclosing Man to Himself.* Princeton, N.J.: D. Van Nostrand, 1968.
7. JOURARD, S. M. *Personal Adjustment* (2nd ed.) N.Y.: Macmillan, 1963.
8. MCLUHAN, M., & FIORE, K. *The Medium Is the Message.* N.Y.: Bantam Books, 1967.
9. MCLUHAN, M., & FIORE, K. *War and Peace in the Global Village.* N.Y.: Bantam Books, 1968.
10. CLEAVER, E. *Soul On Ice.* N.Y.: McGraw-Hill, 1968.
11. JUNG, C. G. *Psychological Types.* London: Routledge & Kegan Paul, 1923.
12. HORNEY, K. *Neurosis and Human Growth.* N.Y.: Norton, 1950.
13. SULLIVAN, H. S. *The Interpersonal Theory of Psychiatry.* N.Y.: Norton, 1953.
14. HORNEY, K. *Our Inner Conflicts.* N.Y.: Norton, 1945.
15. TILLICH, P. *The Courage to Be.* New Haven, Conn.: Yale University Press, 1952.
16. KIERKEGAARD, S. *Fear and Trembling and the Sickness unto Death.* Garden City, N.Y.: Doubleday, 1954.

Learning and Ideation

The articles in this section have much relevance for a book dealing with psychological adjustment. They remind us that there are great differences between individuals, that people learn differently, think differently, and develop differently. Life styles and behavior patterns vary so much that it is not safe to label or to judge or classify an individual in terms of the manner in which the majority performs. Yet it is reemphasized that neither should one forget the ties, relationships, and similarities which he shares with mankind in general.

Sociologist Pang indicates that it is not always the joiners, the cooperators, and the conformers who contribute most to society. As a matter of fact, he provides a rationale for the contention that performance in one of the main socializing aspects of the culture, the school, is not all that important. His article could be used as an excuse for waiting until tomorrow to study or for opposing everything that school offers. This is not the intent of the editors. They included this article for altogether different purposes. They wish to point out that: (1) It is not so much what schools offer in terms of information and learning experiences that is faulty, but teachers' perception and evaluation of individuals and pupils' actualization of potential. Educators tend, far too much, to categorize as retarded any person who does not fit the conforming, convergent-thinking mold. Such an evaluation helps to make this true. (2) Pang's listing of distinguished persons labelled as only average or below means simply that school personnel were not simply wrong in their evaluations. The list also suggests that the urge toward self actualization and becoming what one can be may be so strong that it is not always thwarted by unfavorable conditions.

Probably it is true that these distinguished persons did not conform to the system. They opposed—but not to the extent that they renounced the system or were completely excluded by it. What they did do was to learn to use it. Neither opposing or conforming, if consistent and complete, promotes or even permits this. The lesson which the editors wish to emphasize is: The successful person is the individual who can use and exploit (not conform to or oppose) his culture for his own self-development and expression.

The balance between conformity and uniqueness, between independence and dependence, is not an easy one to establish. Identity requires that each person, to some degree, experience himself as separate, distinct, and autonomous. Yet we know that feelings of belonging and being a part of the group also are necessary. Perhaps the key here lies with whether or not the separation is imposed or sought. (See also Heath's article on page 330.) Isolation is of no great concern to the person who has confidence in his ability to join others when he needs to do so. But it can be devastating if it results from rejection. One thinks and learns and develops best in a relationship that provides point and purpose for his behavior.

It may seem strange that an article about young children should be included in a book addressed to college students about their adjustment. Actually, the article by Heath is about youth. And we are especially pleased that he backs his observations about the characteristics of today's youth with some longitudinal research that covers a span of years. Moreover, the article deals with what, how, and under what conditions learning occurs. In addition, it is well paired with Pang's observations —using the system or being defeated by it. Perhaps Heath, as does Pang, is talking about not being too readily "taken in" by the system.

Although we see much merit in Heath's article—especially for parents and teachers—there is some concern about the way readers of this volume may use it. If it becomes a justification or rationalization for disdaining the academic then we have erred in including it. It will do little good for today's college student to blame TV, lack of time with parents, huge school systems, or accelerated learning for his inability to apply himself to the task at hand. If, however, he better understands his motivation, then he will be able to exert more control over his own behaviors. As one example, if the reader's search for meaning and human relatedness impedes learning efficiency, then perhaps he will see merit in dating, dialogue with peers, and discussions with instructors. (We will admit that some instructors may want only to do their own thing but we are equally sure that many are quite willing to deal with students as persons—if the self-fulfilling prophecy phenomenon does not prevent some initial contact.)

The article by Hilliard and Roth carries this theme further. It also possesses the potential for dichotomous interpretation—justification of failure or the alternative of better self-understanding. One can blame mother for the lack of achievement motivation, but blame-placing will not change history. Young people are supposed to outgrow their parents—to become autonomous, self-directed persons. Is it not possible that the young person behaved in such a manner as to make acceptance a difficult matter?

The article by Weiner and Potepan might serve to place the emphasis, relative to formal learning, where it can do the most good. They discuss such things as test anxiety, achievement orientation, and intellectual achievement responsibility, but do not spend time on the historical analysis of Who is to blame. They say, perhaps so subtly that the points might be missed:

Low test anxiety is related to internalized responsibility for success.

Low achievers ascribe (that is something the individual does) their failures to luck, difficulty of the task, and other external sources.

High achievers ascribe their failures to lack of effort and failure to persist.

Fear of examinations is both cause and effect of failure.

Finally, the authors, as good researchers are likely to do, say that their study does not cover all conditions of success or failure. We agree, but insist that the ascribing of responsibility for failure to oneself will often prove to be a profitable starting point for improvement.

Undistinguished School Experiences of Distinguished Persons

HENRY PANG
Department of Sociology
The American University, Washington, D.C.

With the emphasis on early identification of gifted children, over-specialized training and cultural enrichment programs, there is always the danger that we may miss some children who eventually blossom out and rise to great heights. The problem exists because numerous outstanding persons representing various professions were late starters. Some were considered by their parents and teachers to be average in ability, and even below average or retarded. In their childhood or youth these persons often lacked interest and motivation and had considerable difficulties, particularly in the schools. The fact is that with the magnification of mass testing, the emphasis on grades, class rank, letters of reference, and achievement and aptitude scores, we are actually weeding out many potentially creative persons. Of course we must use some criteria for judgment but none is synonymous with creativity.

Perhaps many persons who are outstanding would not be admitted to the schools they attended if they applied for admission today. This is indeed a serious problem for educators and society because the top grade-getters in the schools do not automatically become our top scientists, engineers, artists, businessmen, or writers.

We now have devices to encourage early development of the child, including intellectual stimulation for babies still in their cribs, Operation Headstart for culturally deprived children, and classes for the superior endowed. Despite these programs, there are some children who could not care less and often do [not] respond in the appropriate manner. Fortunately many eminent persons have made great contributions without special treatment, special classes, and extraordinary privileges; still, untold numbers of persons have probably been lost too. The personal characteristics of the majority of eminent persons were often individual initiative, hard work and sacrifice. Some "gifted" persons who demand extra attention, scholarships, and financial aid because of their high IQ scores, percentile

From *Adolescence*, 3: 319–326, Fall, 1968.

rankings, and scores on various standardization tests have a "give me" ethnocentric attitude.

What were the educational backgrounds of some of the distinguished persons in different occupations? Certainly many were not the well-adjusted normal types; they probably would deviate from the norms of individuals administered personality tests. Although they might not score exceptionally high on intelligence and aptitude tests, they undoubtedly would be well above average on most measures. However, it would not be too surprising if they scored average or below average on some tests. Often they were individuals who were not well rounded and were dissatisfied with the school curriculum as well as with their teachers.

The familiar stereotype of the gifted youngster as a bookworm who can recite Shakespeare, work complicated calculus problems, and generally amaze everyone cannot be confirmed by many distinguished persons. Very often it is forgotten or not known that many eminent persons were mediocre or poor by the standards of educational institutions. It is also erroneous to believe that there is always a high and continuous correlation for high ability and achievement which begins with early childhood. Individuals are endowed differently by heredity and provided with dissimilar environments so they do not start out equally. Even persons who are fairly similar may vary in performance. One may descend, and another soar; others rise to the top, and still others take longer, and some never leave the ground.

DISLIKE OF SCHOOL AND MEDIOCRE PERFORMANCE

Eminent persons who disliked and whose performance in school was mediocre or poor include such famed individuals as Sir Humphrey Davy, Isaac Newton, Leo Tolstoy, Winston Churchill, Frédéric François Chopin, Albert Einstein, Theodore Dreiser, Claude Monet, Ivan Turgenev, and Pablo Picasso. Many of these persons, for example, Churchill and Picasso refused to learn if they were not interested. Others were disrespectful or boisterous in school; this was especially true of Monet, who often played hookie from art classes.

Inasmuch as these distinguished persons were only average or below average in school work they were not the teacher's pets or very popular with their classmates. It was said that Picasso brought his pigeon to school daily, was interested only in painting, and had a habit of leaving the classroom when it suited him.

Churchill had so much energy in nonacademic pursuits that teachers would turn him loose on the school grounds so he could work off his excess spirits. Teachers also disliked the spirit of independence of Einstein and believed him to be a dull person. After graduating from college he was unable to obtain a graduate assistantship or a suitable job. And after winning fame, he discovered that many of his teachers did not remember him as a student.

Both Frank Lloyd Wright and Robert Frost disliked school and dropped out because of a lack of interest. Other poor students were famed anthropologist Ralph Linton, and pioneer sociologist Emile Durkheim. The former was on academic probation as an undergraduate, and the latter graduated next to the bottom of his class. Today students in anthropology and sociology may perform better than either of these men, but few will be able to contribute as significantly.

Many eminent persons displayed no particular brilliance even in the fields in which they later won fame. At college writers William Faulkner and John Steinbeck were average in English and literature and both became college dropouts. Psychologist John Watson was considered lazy by his teachers. He made only passing grades, and had a nervous breakdown before he completed his doctorate. Louis Pasteur was fond of art and fishing, and received his degree with no particular brilliancy. His laboratory report was often in error.

Charles Darwin, who liked hunting and collecting beetles, was happy to graduate without honors. Michelangelo was a poor student, and Leonardo da Vinci received no education at all. This might have been an asset for his time and day. General Eisenhower graduated in the bottom third of his class and was unable to obtain a rank higher than Color Sergeant at West Point. Paul Ehrlich was a very poor student; he detested examinations, and usually performed badly. He won the Nobel Prize for his original and creative research in 1908.

OTHER POOR STUDENTS

Philosopher John Hobbes' statement of "I was slow to learn, but I did learn," was true of many eminent persons. Ironically, some individuals did poorly in their fields of specialization. As a student Constantine von Monakow fled from lectures on the nervous system, and yet he became one of the greatest contributors on the structural changes of the brain. Henri Poincaré was a good student of mathematics but could not perform simple arithmetic without making a mistake. Charles Steinmetz also had trouble with arithmetic as a boy. He was so disturbed by his first day of school that he did not return until the next year. Many of his teachers, in his early years of schooling, did not believe he could pass.

Inventor John Fulton could not learn in the formal educational setting because he was constantly coming up with original ideas. In fact many of the great inventors had little formal education and made discoveries or inventions in areas somewhat out of their specialties. Pierre Curie was trained at home, and Michael Faraday received no scientific education at all either at school or at home.

Despite the mediocre records of some of these individuals, their mothers often had extraordinary confidence in their sons' abilities and talents. Both geneticist John Stadler Lewis and President Franklin Roosevelt were poor or average students most of their schooldays, yet their mothers believed that they would make contributions to the world. The mother of Frank Lloyd Wright went so far as to predict that her unborn child would be a boy and would become a great architect. Yet all three men showed no special traits of future greatness as children. As a matter of fact, one of Lewis's teachers said he was "lazy, careless, and would never amount to anything." The father of Sigmund Freud once said that young Sigmund would not amount to anything.

This leads to another point for consideration. Often teachers are not very good at predicting future achievements. In Berkeley psychologist Donald MacKinnon's study of America's outstanding architects, one was told by the Dean of the School of Architecture to quit because of his lack of ability; another one switched to the Art Department because of conflict with the architectural school It seems that, as students, the eminent architects did well in courses they liked but were only average in the courses they disliked. Chemist Justus Von Liebig was told by the rector of the gymnasium that he was "the sorrow of his parents." When a young boy, Enrico Fermi was considered by his mother and teachers as below average in intelligence.

FAILURES OF EXAMINATIONS

Some persons who later became famous had trouble passing entrance examinations or final examinations. The unsuccessful exploits of Einstein and Churchill are better known than others. Because examinations call for a certain amount of conformity-thinking, convergent and memory work, many imaginative and creative thinkers were handicapped. Einstein said he could not think very well until a year after he had taken his final examinations. Anton Chekhov disliked Latin and Greek, and failed his examinations twice.

A student might fail in one school but do well in another. An example of this was Emile Zola, who received a zero in literature at Lycee St. Louis and also failed in German and grammar. He transferred to the Sorbonne, and performed well there.

There are other individuals who failed examinations or failed to meet the standards. Gustave Flaubert was another writer who was a disinterested and poor student with a record of failures in examinations. Artist Paul Cézanne failed to qualify for the École des Beaux-Arts. Composer Giuseppe Verdi was considered to be too old at a school of music, and General Eisenhower was rejected at Annapolis for the same reason. Carl Sandburg planned to enter West Point, but was unable to pass tests in mathematics and English. Mathematician Poincaré had headed his class, but failed the final examination in descriptive geometry; he was unable or unwilling to carry out a mechanical drawing in detail.

Gaining entrance into college was difficult for some eminent persons. Mathematician Évariste Galois was so poor in literature and classics that he was demoted during secondary school, and failed examinations to college twice. Many distinguished persons were not well rounded, and very few fit the Rhodes Scholar mold. Even Cecil Rhodes himself could not meet the standards of the award he created. Louis Pasteur twice took examinations to enter college. The first time he was near the bottom; the second time, a year later, he was third from the top. One question we might ask is, who were all those individuals who scored better than he did and what did they contribute?

Undoubtedly, some potentially creative persons just do not

rank very high in their high-school classes and are not top scorers on College Board Tests. In one study of holders of the Ph.D. degree over half were in the bottom half of their respective high-school graduating classes.

DROPOUTS, FAILURES, AND THE EXPELLED

Many distinguished persons dropped out of their own accord or had to leave because of poor records. Some were expelled or were forced to leave. Eugene O'Neill flunked out at Princeton in his freshman year. Other well-known writers such as Stephen Crane, William Faulkner, F. Scott Fitzgerald and John Steinbeck either dropped out or failed in their college work. Ernest Hemingway never attended college. Obviously, failures for writers, artists, and businessmen are less important than for scientists who need advanced degrees. The dropout rates for persons in graduate schools are surprisingly high even for the more selective universities; the key to the problem will not be better selection but changes in the social organizations of departments.

Many scientists, writers, and businessmen of distinction were failures in school. Copernicus and Charles Steinmetz did not finish college, and Michael Faraday never attended. Robert Frost and Coleridge are distinguished dropouts. In the business world of today, there are Charles Thorton of Litton Inc., and J. Paul Getty of Getty Oil who are both college dropouts, and James Ling of Ling-Temco-Vaught, a high-school dropout. Edwin Land, creator and founder of Polaroid, is another college dropout with outstanding creative abilities.

There were other indifferent students who had problems or disliked school which later led to their expulsion. Augustus Comte, the father of sociology, was expelled. Edgar Allen Poe was expelled from West Point, and John Locke from Oxford. They were not necessarily poor students but they had nonconventional or unpopular views. For others, dismissals came earlier. Chatterton was turned away as a dullard, and Thomas A. Edison was told to leave school because he was "dull" in the first grade. Enrico Fermi was almost expelled for leading a stink-bomb attack when in secondary school. He was not a popular graduate student among his professors. His teachers refused to shake his hand at his orals and they did not have his thesis published, which was the normal procedure for all graduate students. William Randolph Hearst was expelled from Harvard in the middle of his senior year for sending his professors chamber pots marked with their names. Artist Salvador Dali was expelled when he refused to allow teachers whom he considered less skilled than he was to judge his pictures. Certainly none of these individuals mentioned were teacher's pets or the All-American Boy type. Many of their teachers had no particular insight into the future accomplishments of these students who later became renowned.

IMPLICATIONS AND CONCLUSIONS

Although our focus here has been on distinguished persons with mediocre or below-average school records, there are many individuals with brilliant records of scholastic achievement. There is even diversity within occupations. For instance, Robert Oppenheimer was always brilliant from early childhood, yet Albert Einstein appeared to be rather slow and a failure. However, both were outstanding physicists.

Today the slow starter faces greater odds in gaining admission to college. We cannot afford to assume that only the ignorant are kept out, or that only the incapable are flunked out. One of the major purposes of an educational institution is to prepare individuals for creative achievement, yet the standard measures of fitness for college work do not measure potential creativity. It is an extremely difficult task. Our country, and all countries, need creative individuals of all types. Slow and late starters, and poor test takers have contributed significantly, and will continue to do so when given the opportunity. Truly it is sometimes difficult to distinguish between the idiots and the geniuses.

REFERENCES

1. GOERTZEL, V., AND GOERTZEL, G. *Cradles of Eminence*. Boston: Little, Brown and Company, 1962.
2. HUDSON, L. "Academic Sheep and Research Goats." *New Society*, 1964, 22, pp. 9–13.

The Education of Young Children: At the Crossroads?
DOUGLAS H. HEATH

When asked to speak at the NAEYC Conference, I replied I was no expert on early childhood education. I was told not to speak about what you already know but about my research on adolescents that you may not know. So I asked myself if what I was finding was relevant to your interests. I answered yes. So here I am to talk about affluent middle-class white 17-year-olds. Why? Why be so perverse when most of you are more interested in white and black three- and four-year-olds, particularly those from deprived sectors of our society?

For several reasons. I believe our current youth "problem" reflects a characterological change, brought about by the massive societal changes we've undergone, that requires different types of growth experiences than those we needed when young. I also believe that since most of us seldom follow the children we teach into their later childhood and adolescence, we frequently misjudge the effects that our educational programs have upon them. Might we not secure some perspective about what we are and are not doing by stepping back from our three- and four-year-olds to take a wider view of the determinants of healthy development. And finally, I believe the growth process is continuous, not discontinuous, that what we learn about how adolescents grow healthily provides insights about how to help children grow more healthily. So I propose to talk about how our current adolescents are developing and need to develop in this changing society of ours. I will close by asking you some questions about how you are helping your children to become healthier adolescents.

Before we step too impetuously across the threshold of the 1970s into Children's TV Workshop, Head Start and day care programs for two- and three-year-olds, and directed systematic instruction in intellectual skills in nursery schools, let us turn now

Address presented at the 1969 Conference of the National Association for the Education of Young Children, Salt Lake City, Utah, November 12. Reprinted with permission from *Young Children*, Vol. XXV, No. 2, December, 1969. Copyright © 1969, National Association for the Education of Young Children, 1834 Connecticut Ave., N.W., Washington, D.C. 20009.

to examine what has been happening to this first television, accelerated and intellectualized Sputnikian generation.

Since our judgments are biased by the type of information we get, particularly in a mass media, sensationalistic dominated culture, I must tell you that my observations are drawn from a limited but unique collection of data secured from two decades of 17-year-olds that seem to confirm what many others have also noted in most other parts of the country, except perhaps the Deep South, where I have not been. I talk of trends and do not mean to imply my generalizations necessarily apply to a majority of young people—yet.

That some change is occurring in young people seems beyond dispute. The rapid assimilation of drugs like pot into the way of life of increasing numbers of middle-class youth within the past five years represents a dramatic change in the values of youths. The radical rejection of traditional middle-class values by some of our more sensitive and privileged youths who drop out of school to search for more meaningful ways of living through hippiedom, intentional communities and mystical LSD experiences is difficult to understand. The dethronement of traditional academic authorities and the substitution of confrontations and riots for enlightened reason will increasingly occur in the high schools within the next few years. And finally, of all these changes, the one that troubles me the most is the deepening passivity, boredom and disenchantment with their schools that I see in so many adolescents in most of the country.

So what is happening? A graduating senior chosen by his peers to express their feelings and concerns summarized the observations I wish to discuss this way:

And we're distanced from people. Quite often, I think, projects like joining the Peace Corps or working with slum kids are attempts to bridge a gap. Not just a sociological gap, but a gap of the heart. Because these people seem to operate on a more fundamental level than we do. Somehow their actions are more spontaneous and less embalmed by reflection. We worry about relating to people; but, for better or worse, they relate. There is a naturalness—often crude, but a naturalness nonetheless—about them. And too often it is obscured in us. And if this is the burden of the intellectual—if his cross is always to be separated from other men, almost as an observer—then I say he is not an intellectual at all. He is an academician. But nothing more. Because there is something precious in the unenlightened

man; something viable in his ignorance. And that something—hard to define but recognizable, I think, by feeling—is his unsophisticated, unreflected-upon vulnerability to emotion. His ability to forget himself.

This most perceptive, honest, aware, intelligent assessment
illustrates the leading strengths of this generation. But it also tells
us that his generation feels hung up, up tight, in a box about how to
integrate its emotional or irrational life with its rational intellectualism. "Somehow their actions are more spontaneous and less
embalmed by reflection . . . his unsophisticated unreflected-upon
vulnerability to emotion. His ability to forget himself."

We are developing a very self-conscious intellectualized but
inhibited generation that values keeping its cool in order to maintain its self-control so as not to give the appearance of being emotional, sentimental, nostalgic, weak, tender, affectionate, dependent,
enthusiastic, even committed. To be spontaneous is to risk becoming
"vulnerable." To blow one's cool is to lose status among one's peers.
Many of this generation have been called serious, humorless, grim.
Increasingly, pranks are now "for keeps." To destroy a computer
center or burn a library seems today to be a more acceptable playful
option than to put a cow—I guess a VW would be a more appropriate symbol nowadays—in the president's office or to even have a
water fight in the dormitory.

YOUTHS EXPERIENCE INNER VOID

The consequence of the increased separation that many youths
report between their reflective intellectual and emotional lives is an
inner emptiness. Increasing numbers are bored spectators of their
own lives, only "observers." More say they don't feel alive; they
feel "embalmed by reflection." It takes much more intense stimulation nowadays to involve a student—as many teachers have told me
these past years. They must shift their pace more frequently or use
more dramatic, even bizarre, materials to keep the attention of their
students.

But we human beings are not built to be nonemotional and
nonexpressive. We have tear glands with which to cry. We have
facial muscles with which to express feelings. Freud was right. When
these avenues are closed to the expression of tension, tension is re-

leased either through fantasy or diffuse acting out types of behavior. My data do suggest that since the end of World War II, increasing numbers of adolescents say they dream, that they dream repetitively, that they dream more frequently about sex, that they have fantasies about doing something shocking, like destroying property. And when the frustration of blocked emotional needs and of boredom becomes too great, cathartic explosive outbursts into riots and confrontations are more likely to occur. Some of the disturbance on the college campuses is but a displacement to a more permissive setting of the accumulated frustrations of youth who have endured emotionally suppressive, demanding, and frequently, authoritarian elementary and secondary school experiences for 12 years. At last they can get back at the "system."

A second trend that is becoming more prominent in the lives of adolescents is a feeling of being "distanced from people." The graduating senior is right when he says, "We worry about relating to people . . . projects like joining the Peace Corps . . . are attempts to bridge a gap . . . a gap of the heart." My data suggest increasing numbers of 17-year-olds report having fewer close affectional ties with others, do not feel they belong to any group, certainly not to their schools and increasingly not to their own country. I sense a growing privatism, sense of isolation, or what Keniston calls "alienation" from others. This is the day of do your own thing—not our thing. Just to cite some data, note the trend in the percentage of true replies for every fourth year of 17-year-olds since the end of World War II to these questions:

	Entering Classes					
	48–49	52	56	60	64	68
When I was a child I didn't care to be a member of a crowd or gang.	33	35	35	38	49	47
If I were in trouble with several friends who were equally to blame, I would rather take the whole blame than give them away.	63	56	50	57	47	45
My worries seem to disappear when I get into a crowd of lively friends.	71	69	73	68	58	55

The consequence of this sense of estrangement from others is a pervasive feeling of loneliness. Forty per cent of our freshmen say they had always felt lonely even when with other people close to them. The real generation gap is not between the young and old; it is between one young person and another. When you have a close satisfying relationship with a person of your age, you aren't that concerned about communication with persons two decades older than you are. We could have understood one of the many causes of the Free Speech Movement at Berkeley better if we had known that 36 percent of the graduating senior men said at that time they had never made a close friend in college. At Stanford, a strong fraternity college, one-third of the senior men and 25 percent of the senior women said they had never had a date during their four years at the university.

Folk rock speaks for millions of this generation. Some of you may know Simon and Garfunkel's "I am a Rock."

I am a rock
I am an island
I build walls
Their fortress deep and mighty
That none may penetrate
I have no need of friendship
Friendship causes pain
It's laughter and it's loving I disdain
I am a rock
I am an island
Don't talk of love, well
I've heard the word before.
It's sleeping in my memory
I won't disturb the slumber
Of feelings that have died.
If I never loved I never would have cried,
I am a rock, (I am an island)
I have my books
And my poetry to protect me
I am shielded in my armor,
Hiding in my room, safe within
my womb,
I touch no one and no one touches me.
I am a rock, (I am an island)
And a rock feels no pain,
And an island never cries.

Just as we are not built to be cool, so we are not built to be lonely, to be isolated individualists, despite the enshrinement, I would say rationalization, of a nihilistic or anarchistic individualism as a principal value these days. We are built to be touched and hugged and to touch and to hug. But we have developed a touchless society. Have you asked why Esalen and T groups have become so popular these past few years? Why are encounter- and sensitivity-type experiences becoming part of the curriculum of some progressive schools? Simply because this generation needs to be taught how to express its feelings, how to be more at home with its estranged bodily impulses, and how to feel comfortable touching others and being touched by others. Have you asked what is the meaning of the apparent change in sexual morals? Since World War II, so a recent Kinsey Institute study will soon tell us, there has been a 25 percent increase in the number of adolescents who have had premarital relations. But this generation does not explore its sexuality so much for erotic or sensuous pleasure as it does to learn how to become more intimate with another person. The "in" words on the college campuses these days are openness, trust, love and community—all words that describe needs to be intimate, to belong to someone somewhere. The Beatles have said it in their classic "Sgt. Pepper's Lonely Hearts Club Band" that made them famous:

> *We were talking about the space be-*
> *tween us all.*
> *And the people who hide themselves*
> *behind a wall of illusion.*
> *Do you need anybody? I need some-*
> *body to love.*
> *Could it be anybody? I want somebody*
> *to love.*

The values of openness and love become so commanding in college because so many have not experienced them earlier and have not developed the interpersonal skills when younger that are necessary to form close friendships. So when sex becomes imperious, it becomes the route to learn intimacy.

There are other trends I don't have time to discuss in detail. Trends like an increasing sense of imminence, immediacy, "nowness" that stems, in part, from a developing certainty in their own intellectual talents. Increasing numbers of young people believe they know what is best and that their judgments should be acted upon now. My data indicate, for example, an increase since World War II from 25 to 56 percent of 17-year-olds who say they are important persons. Or an increase from 20 to 38 percent who say they know more than experts do.

Or there are the increasing number of adolescents who value the aesthetic rather than the economic or political or even social-altruistic way of life. Psychedelia, hard rock and movies are the media that speak to this generation, as we all know. For increasing numbers of young people, what is true is what is beautiful. Their own subjective reaction, rather than some objective or authoritative standard of right, is the criterion of truth. Increasingly, even the authority that has come from discipline, knowledge and competence is being challenged by youth who are wedded to an existentialist "now" experience and a subjectivist view of truth.

Many questions occur at this point. One is, "If such trends are now in process, what may be causing them?" Another is, "What role has the school had in producing increasing numbers of students who feel estranged from their own emotional lives, other students and the institutions of our country?" And, "If our purpose is to help youngsters grow to become more mature and educable, then what implications does this discussion have for what we do as educators?" Obviously, I must be brief and so very selective in presenting some thoughts about each of these questions.

First, why such trends? Obviously they are the result of many complex social changes. My hunch is that much of the personal and social estrangement is due to a shift in the effective control of the developmental process from the family, neighborhood community and church to the peer culture, mass media and the school. Psychologically, this shift is from thousands of hours of caring, intimacy, interpersonal, spontaneous, cooperative, action-oriented, emotional learning to thousands of hours of passive, observing, conforming, inhibiting and cognitive learning.

Let's examine briefly just the family and mass media effects before examining the school's contribution to the trends I've mentioned.

In contrast to most professionals who would hold that the changes I've suggested must implicate the family primarily, I suggest that the family's influence has been less decisive than that of the mass media and the schools. Why? There are very little data available that suggest there has been any major change in the character of the American middle-class family since World War II that might account for the changes I've described. My evidence indicates that the American middle-class parent has not changed in permissiveness to any appreciable extent since World War II. Only about 15 percent of 17-year-old males have said their parents objected to their friends for the two decades; a constant 55 percent have said they are independent and free of family life. There has been even a slight decline from 65 percent to 55 percent in the number who say they have quarrels with their parents. This and other evidence doesn't suggest that the nature of parental-child relationships and the affective tone of the family have changed markedly. But I do believe there has been a significant change in the typical family that does provide the conditions for other social forces to work their estranging effects. What has changed, I believe, is that the typical family is now much less guarded or protected from other social influences. Families are more mobile now and mobility has been found to be associated with social estrangement. Even more importantly, families have brought into the center of their lives by means of television every conflicting, competing and contradictory example of different ways of life known to man. Given increased parental indecision and confusion about their own values, what happens is that children have become more open at earlier ages to societal pressures and conflicts. They have a less stable centered model of value by which to learn how to meet such conflicts.

TV IS POWERFUL INFLUENCE

I believe all of us underestimate the effects of television on the lives of this generation. Take just one statistic. The average child supposedly looks at television about a thousand hours a year. I can't even estimate the number of additional hours that the longer bus rides to the consolidated schools and the increased homework assignments of the 1960s have required since Sputnik. So I ask you: From what kinds of activities do a thousand hours of TV and schoolwork come each year? They come from being read to by one's parents, from family games and shared activities, and, more importantly, from playing with other children. I don't believe we educators have the remotest idea how many thousands of hours it takes to learn basic human skills like playfulness, the ability to entertain ourselves, empathy, consideration, sympathy and cooperative accommodation to another's needs to achieve some mutual goal. Our children have much less opportunity and time these days than we did to learn these skills.

But television may have other types of effects, though they have never been studied. Certainly, it may expand the informational background of children, even to the point of creating an informational overload or satiation for new information. Certainly, thousands of hours of TV viewing encourage receiving information passively and impressionistically, a mode of relating to the environment that many of our schools also reinforce.

One intriguing possible effect that thousands of hours of TV emotional conditioning may have is to teach inhibition or the suppression of feeling, that is, how to cool one's impulses. To sustain interest, TV must induce some tension, usually through novelty. Human experience is not infinite. A space flight soon becomes very tedious. To stay in with us, television must go way out—into the bizarre, the fantastic, the perverse, the extreme. Now as every pornographer knows and as current studies on the effects of violence in film demonstrate, the portrayal of some emotion induces analagous but a less intense feeling in the viewer. What happens at this point? My hunch is that in most middle-class homes, to express, say, aggression against Susie is punished. Very soon, a child learns to contain the induced anger, particularly when we provide no means for it to be expressed. He learns to inhibit its expression. After thousands of hours of this inhibitory conditioning experience, he automatically and unconsciously learns to "cool" it, "turn off," words, by the way, coined by this generation. Eventually, he can unfeelingly watch a Vietcong peasant being killed or a riot in a city. Our youth do not need to expand their awareness further, as so many believe. They need to learn how to recover their suppressed emotions and integrate them with their awareness through action.

I now turn to my second question, "What has been the effect of recent changes in our schools?" I will confine my few comments to the effects of the size of schools and of the Sputnikian initiated change in our national educational goals. The point I want to emphasize is that if we do not look at the quality of the lives of our students after they have left our schools, we may misjudge the effectiveness of our methods. The current student drug involvement, rebelliousness, disenchantment and boredom may well be the most important measures of the effectiveness of our schools these past 10 years.

ARE LARGE SCHOOLS BETTER?

Conant proposed that we consolidate our small schools into large schools of three and four thousand students in order to provide better academic preparation in the sciences, languages, and to meet the more specialized needs of youngsters. But what do the research data say about the effects of small and large schools?

First, there is no evidence whatsoever that the variety of courses, the number of advanced placement courses, the availability of laboratory facilities, really contribute to the educability of students. Second, considerable evidence now indicates that students in large schools participate in fewer extracurricular activities, hold fewer positions of responsibility in the school, cheat more frequently, are more dissatisfied, feel less responsible for their school. They participate fewer hours with their friends in common activities; they have fewer contact hours with any of the adults in their schools, except their teachers. Students in large schools take more specialized courses and encounter less breadth in their academic work. Since self-esteem and personal competence come from testing one's self in a range of activities, it is understandable why students in large schools feel less competent than those in small schools. Finally, the bureaucratic structure that goes with increased size complicates all relationships and requires more impersonal means of regulating conduct. Students begin to think of themselves as part of an impersonal "system" in which they do not feel needed. What students are demanding nowadays is what they never got in their earlier education: a sense of community, of belongingness, meaningful participation and sense of competence and value. The lesson to be learned is that too narrow a definition of our educational goals—namely, build big schools to develop academic excellence—may produce more important negative effects that only become apparent many years later. I cite this one aspect of our schools in detail because we do have fairly convincing evidence about its effects on the maturing of youngsters.

STUDENTS—BETTER EDUCATED BUT LESS EDUCABLE

What have been the effects of our post-Sputnikian constriction of our national educational goals to the development of only academic excellence? The irony of the past decade is that we may have succeeded in making more students better educated, but we have made increasing numbers of them less educable, that is, less open to further growth, at least in response to our traditional academic expectations. Why? A youth estranged from his own feelings, emotionally isolated from other human beings, narrowly committed to his own intellectual specialty arrives at college. He quickly finds the college demands even greater isolation of his feelings from his intellectual development. He must inhibit his feelings to concentrate on the heavier reading assignments. Many of the demands of a college force social isolation. He is taught in large courses, frequently by means of television; he studies in his individual library carrel and retreats to his single room. He encounters even greater intellectual competition, particularly to get the grades he needs for graduate school. What happens? Increasingly, we see a decline in the quality of his work, a devaluation of the intellectual way of life, and a flight into drugs, SDS or apathy.

Why? My studies do give validity to the Jungian developmental principle that too extended development in one sector of the personality induces resistance to further development in that sector until compensatory development has occurred in the neglected areas of the personality. Too forced intellectual prematuring, as has been happening in our schools, is inducing resistance to further academic work, is leading to the devaluation of rational, logical, enlightened reason, and is encouraging compensatory pursuits of other types of experiences by which to grow more wholly. Much of the drug activity in the adolescent can be understood as an attempt to learn what it means to feel, to feel intensely, to feel alive again, to discover that life can be "beautiful." Our laws against drugs also provide the occasion for small conspiratorial communal groups to develop to which you can belong and transcend your sense of social isolation. And drugs do encourage the development of nonintellectual, noncompetitive values, thus making it possible for some to develop a more humane set of values than what they find mirrored in the intellectualistic, college board, college preparatory marathon in our schools.

Our excessive preoccupation since Sputnik with accelerating intellectual development to achieve academic excellence instead of human excellence, the historic goal of every educational philosopher since Socrates, will continue to generate counter pressures by students for radical educational reform that humanizes their schools.

THE NEEDS OF THIS GENERATION

Our dilemma is how does this generation need to grow to become more mature and educable. It needs to learn how to relive its suppressed childhood and adolescence again, to integrate into its more rational and logically ordered mind its irrational and disorderly impulses and feelings. It needs more social cooperative and intimacy growth experiences in which it learns how to develop more open, trusting relationships with others. It needs to test itself in other than just specialized verbal abstract ways. It needs the opportunity to act responsibly, for it will be through actual encounters with meaningful problems that it will learn what it means to be a whole person. This is what I learn from the drug devotees, the hippies and the activists. I do not believe our youth needs to grow as much in awareness, even knowledge and intellectual skill, as much as it needs to learn how to abandon playfully itself to its own emotional and social needs. If it does not learn this, its prematured intellectualism will sour it to the beauty of life itself and to the human needs of its society.

My third question concerns the implications of these comments and of my other work on maturing which I would like to present in the form of some questions for ourselves.

1. Do we not violate the holistic, systemic nature of the growth process if we emotionally reject the efforts of those who seek ways to develop intellectual skills earlier, even under intense pressure conditions, or, if, on the other hand, we disdainfully dismiss those who claim children need to grow socially in very secure nonthreatening learning environments? Does not each view represent but a partial view of the developmental process? Should we not ask instead, "Are we providing the most favorable environment of which we know to help each child grow in his way as a full person?" Personally, I am

not that keen on trying to accelerate intellectual development, particularly of middle-class youth, because I have seen too many stretched out of shape, turned off, soured intellectuals whose academicism was compensatory for deeply inadequate personal and social relationships. But I hope I am open to evidence that may indicate such acceleration does not eventually make a child less educable for later intellectual experiences, which I do believe is happening now in increasing numbers of academically prematured youth.

2. But surely all of us would agree that our goal is to help a child become in his way a more mature person. Is not one source of our mutual conflict and argument that we do not agree about the criteria that define healthy growth or maturing? Certainly, some manifest signs of health are joy, enthusiasm, surplus energy for expressive activities, as well as an inner freedom to abandon one's self in some transcendent activity, like a close relationship with another or an ideal or cause. I do not have time at this point to describe a model of healthy growth that has emerged from some 15 years of research with adolescents and young adults, but I would suggest that there is some convergence occurring in research in mental health indicating that there are invariant genotypic, culture-free dimensions along which all persons develop as they become more mature that may provide us with the criteria that we need.

3. Is not the maturity or healthiness of a child's behavioral change only determinable over a period of time? Those of you who recall Lois Murphy's Colin remember his aggressive, almost sadistic, outbursts. Yet, such uncontrolled expressions of impulse were only exaggerated and transient signs of a growing assertive mastery of life, another important attitude associated with healthy growth. Too frequently, we misjudge the seeming disorganization, confusion, tension and anxiety of a child and act to moderate it when that disorganization is the herald of a new opening to growth. Again, studies of adolescents suggest we must learn to distinguish between what I call educable and noneducable types of disorganization when we seek to evaluate the maturing effects of the educational methods we introduce. Should we not be skeptical of all evaluational research that does not seek to identify the persistence over time of the particular effects we believe a specific educational technique has?

4. To assess the effects of a talking typewriter or a Head Start or a Montessori-type program, should we not cast a very wide net to determine the breadth of possible psychological effects such methods

may have. I recall watching a film of O. K. Moore's talking type-writer. I was most impressed to watch very young children learning to read. But I was also very disturbed by the almost compulsive tension under which one of the little girls worked. I've often won-dered how educable she is today? Who knows what the most important effects of some Head Start programs are? It may be that some are not as effective as we would hope in preparing some chil-dren for academic work, but some may have induced changes in the attitudes of some of the participating mothers about their other children and the school, the effects of which may not show up until later. And certainly one would want to ask what happens to the social skills of children who are given several years of a traditional Montessori program? So I would urge we evaluate the effects of what we do within a holistic context, within the context of the intellectual-personal-social-familial life of the child.

5. As we move to use new educational technologies, like the Children's Workshop television programs or develop new learning settings, like educational parks for 15,000 children, including nur-sery and kindergarten children, should we not examine their likely effects within the context of the effects of other nonschool influences in the lives of our children? As helpful as television may be in imparting more information or accelerating the perceptual discrimi-nation of letters, might its use in the school not only aggravate the passivity, the social isolation and inhibitory effects it may be having in the home? I do not intend to condemn television. I only want to point out we need to be sensitive to its full effects on the maturing of our children. Will the new wall-less grade schools and increasing specialization of teachers in elementary schools only accentuate a sense of anomie and social isolation? Already some evidence indicates children who have team teachers are not as tied to their teachers nor know as many of their peers in the classroom. Will these effects be compounded by other estrangement experiences so that in the process of giving children allegedly more "expert" mathematics instruction, we prevent them from having the experi-ence of being known all the way around by at least one person in the school? As educational technology and specialization move to provide ways to individualize the formal academic instruction of each child, do we risk isolating him further from those social experi-ences he may need by which to learn how to take another person's viewpoint, how to argue, how to communicate clearly, how to think consistently, how to listen, how to share with and care for another?

Perhaps these are more important developmental experiences to have than to learn one's numbers four months earlier than one might otherwise.

6. Finally, do not we educators, particularly those swayed too much by academic professors, frequently misjudge the crucial determinants of a youth's growth, including his intellectual development? Did not Piaget himself say in 1928 that it was the quality of a child's personal relationships that was the decisive factor that transformed egocentric into socialized thought? Did not Coleman's report on the correlates of academic growth in our schools make essentially the same point? Carl Rogers' recent research on why a person develops healthily, almost all of the studies on the determinants of growth in college, and my own studies on the determinants of educability and maturity consistently confirm Piaget's insight. Now, if it is so that enduring personal, again including intellectual, growth is so intimately tied to a person's openness to learning from others, to social attitudes and communicative skills, then are contemporary youth becoming more educable and mature if they are becoming increasingly estranged and separated from not just those over 30 but from those of their own age? Do we not need to put much more sustained effort and funds into high quality research that identifies how to help a child grow healthily in his relationships with others? As Maslow and other leaders of the sensitivity movement insist, should we not put as much effort into learning how to educate for affective and social development as we are in learning how to educate for cognitive development? I do not mean we should learn how better to adjust our children to this society. I mean we need to help them learn those affective, social, and intellectual attitudes and skills that will help them create for themselves the optimal relation between the expectations of society and their own needs and demands. Should we not be learning how to educate our children to become healthily maladjusted to this society in order to help them create the society that should be?

Spurred by the work of Piaget, Hunt, Bruner and others, compelled by the tragic educational deprivation of our black children, entranced by the promise of our new educational technologies to individualize more efficiently our means to promote intellectual growth, it is clear the leading edge of current educational research and change today is the cultivation and acceleration of cognitive growth. These developments have brought us to a crossroad. But the crossroad is *not* the choice between stimulating the intellectual as opposed to nurturing the social and emotional—as if one could separate any child into such categories anyway. We must choose both if we are to prepare our children for their world of tomorrow. Our real choice is a different one. Will we choose between educating only part of our children, whether it be emphasizing primarily intellectual or primarily social development, or will we choose to educate for maturity and educability? Will the National Association for the Education of Young Children choose to remain faithful to the implications of its name? Will it insist that it stand for wholeness in an increasingly fragmented, divided and estranged world?

Maternal Attitudes and the Non-Achievement Syndrome

THOMAS HILLIARD
Assistant Professor of Psychology
Chicago City College
ROBERT M. ROTH
Associate Professor of Psychology
Illinois Institute of Technology

This study investigated the relationship between the mother-child relationship and academic achievement. The population consisted of 45 male achievers and underachievers from a local suburban high school and their mothers. The nature of the mother-child relationship was measured by the Mother-Child Relationship Evaluation. Generally it was found that mothers of achievers were more accepting of their children than were mothers of underachievers. Further, achievers and underachievers differed in the ability to perceive accurately the maternal attitudes. These findings were interpreted in terms of the etiology of underachievement as described by Roth and Meyersburg in the Non-Achievement Syndrome. These dynamics involve material rejection and the attempts of the underachiever to maintain a dependent relationship with the parents, and the avoidance of adolescent independence via underachievement.

Presently, there is a voluminous body of literature supporting the relationship of academic underachievement to personality function-

From *Personnel and Guidance Journal,* 47: 424–434, 1969.

ing. Taylor's review (1964) of the literature indicates level of achievement to be related to such variables as anxiety, self-concept, independence, interpersonal relations, etc. Roth and Meyersburg (1963) report that academic underachievement is related to a consistent syndrome of interdependent personality traits, having a uniform etiology and psychodynamic organization.

Since most present attempts at understanding behavioral disorders acknowledge the developmental significance of experiences in the home, it seems reasonable that the relationship between academic underachievement and the parent-child relationships should be investigated. More specifically, there is a need for research directed to the mother-child relationship, since the most intensive parent-child interaction during crucial developmental stages occurs with the mother. One way of assessing the mother-child relationship is by measuring the mother's attitudes toward child-rearing practices. There has been little research, however, designed to measure quantitatively maternal attitudes and their relationship to academic underachievement. Drews and Teahan (1957) have reported an attempt to explore maternal attitudes of the mothers of achievers and underachievers. They found that mothers of achievers were more authoritarian and restrictive than mothers of underachievers. However, a weakness of this research was that it failed to take into account the student's perception of the attitudes. A phenomenological approach is justified, since behavior is conceived of as a function of reality, as perceived by the individual. Thus, a person behaves not in terms of reality but in terms of his perception of that reality, which is related to his needs, values, etc. Serot and Teevan (1961) even found the parent-child relationship to be unrelated to the adjustment of high school students, while the student's perceptions of the parent-child relationship was predictive of the student's adjustment.

More recently, Davids and Hainsworth (1967) using the Parental Attitude Research Inventory, investigated the relationship between maternal attitudes and the academic achievement of bright teenage boys. They also measured the boys' perceptions of the avowed maternal attitude and the relationship between the perceived and avowed maternal attitudes. There were no significant differences between the maternal attitudes of the mothers of achievers and mothers of underachievers. While the two groups of boys did not differ in their perceptions of maternal hostility, the underachievers did perceive their mothers as significantly more controlling. Finally, there was a significant correlation between the perceptions held by mothers of achievers and their sons' perceptions of the control factor, although there were no significant correlations between the avowed maternal attitudes and their sons' perceptions on the hostility variables. Their study was quite similar to the present investigation, though there were several differences. First, the two studies used different measuring instruments, and, therefore, tapped slightly different attitude universes. Also, the subjects in the current study were not aware of the relationship of the study to their child's achievement, while those in the former did know the purposes of the study.

The purpose of this study, then, was to test the following hypotheses:

1. Mothers of achievers will be more accepting than mothers of underachievers.

2. Achievers will perceive their mothers as more accepting than will underachievers.

3. There will be a significant correlation between the measured maternal attitudes and their sons' perceptions of these attitudes.

METHOD

Subjects

A total of 90 subjects was used. They consisted of 45 high school males and their mothers. The students, all juniors and seniors, were categorized into achiever and underachiever groups on the basis of their high school records. The achievers were defined as those students who scored at or above the 75th percentile of their class on the California Test of Mental Maturity (CTMMA) and whose cumulative grade point averages (GPA's) were above the 50th percentile of their present class. Underachievers were defined as those students scoring at or above the 75th percentile of the CTMMA, but whose cumulative GPA's were below the 50th percentile of their class. Twenty-four achievers and 21 underachievers were identified.

In the selection of subjects, only those subjects with consistently high or low grades were used to ensure that the level of achievement was chronic rather than due to transient factors.

One interesting finding of this study was that academic under-achievement was primarily a male phenomenon. Initially, no attempt was made to control for sex differences. However, a search of the records indicated that girls who fit the criteria for underachievement were so limited in number that it was decided to limit the study to males. Brickman (1965), using an almost identical population, had reported similar findings.

Research Instrument

The instrument used to provide an objective estimate of the mother's attitudes toward child rearing was the Mother-Child Relationship Evaluation (M-CRE) (Roth, 1960). This measure is a Likert-type self-report inventory with which the subjects respond to 48 statements about attitudes toward child rearing. The subjects are asked to rate each statement along a five-point scale from Strongly Agree to Strongly Disagree, providing a quantitative measure of the intensity of the attitudes.

Scores on the M-CRE may be evaluated along several attitudinal dimensions. One dimension is along a continuum of Acceptance, measuring the degree or amount of acceptance. A second class of attitudes measured is the nonacceptance attitude which includes Rejection, Overprotection, and Overindulgence.

Procedure

The perceived maternal attitudes of the students were obtained through a group administration of the M-CRE. The children and their mothers were informed that this investigation was to measure current attitudes toward child-rearing practices. None of the subjects were aware that the study was related to underachievement. The students were given specific instructions to "respond to the statements as you think your mother would." The tests were administered by the principal investigator.

The actual maternal attitudes were obtained by requesting the students to take the M-CRE to their mothers, have them respond to the inventory, and return them the following day. Of the original 50 students tested, 45 returned with completed forms.

RESULTS

The data in Table 1 indicate significant differences between the mean scores of mothers of achievers and mothers of underachievers

TABLE 1

Means and t-Ratios Among M-CRE Scores of Mothers of Achievers and Mothers of Underachievers

Attitudes	Mothers of Achievers	Mothers of Underachievers	t-Ratios
Acceptance	41.83	38.00	2.961*
Overprotection	28.25	29.28	.799
Overindulgence	27.04	28.57	1.210
Rejection	31.37	33.71	1.900*

* Significant at .05 level.

on the Acceptance and Rejection Scales. The differences on the Acceptance Scale were significant at the .01 level and on the Rejection Scale at the .05 level and were in the direction of greater acceptance by the mothers of achievers.

The second hypothesis which predicted that achievers in comparison to underachievers will perceive their mothers as significantly more accepting was partially supported. Table 2 indicates that there was a significant difference between the mean scores of achievers and underachievers on the Rejection Scale only. This difference was in the predicted direction and significant at the .01 level.

TABLE 2

Means and t-Ratios Among the Perceived M-CRE Scores of Archievers and Underachievers

Attitudes	Achievers	Underachievers	t-Ratios
Acceptance	39.08	37.90	1.0333
Overprotection	30.12	29.05	.6490
Overindulgence	28.41	29.28	.6500
Rejection	31.70	35.38	—2.5000*

* Significant at .01 level.

The data in Table 3 indicate that there was a difference in the maternal attitude—perceived maternal attitude congruence between achievers and underachievers. Underachievers tended to be more accurate in their perceptions of the maternal attitudes as is

TABLE 3

Correlation Coefficients Between Maternal Attitudes and Perceived Maternal Attitudes

Attitudes	Underachievers	Achievers
Rejection	0.356*	0.136
Overprotection	—0.191	0.302
Overindulgence	0.561†	0.130
Acceptance	0.467*	0.249

* Significant at .05 level.
† Significant at .01 level.

indicated by the correlations between the maternal attitudes and the perceived maternal attitudes. Underachievers indicated significant positive correlations between the measured maternal attitudes and the measured perceived maternal attitudes on the Acceptance, Rejection, and Overindulgence Scales, but there was no significant correlation on the Overprotection Scale. A trend in the opposite direction was indicated with the achievers. The correlation between the maternal attitudes and the perceived maternal attitudes did not reach significance on any of the scales. These findings would suggest that achievers tended to be insensitive to the maternal attitudes.

DISCUSSION

The findings in this study indicated support for the hypothesis that *achievement and underachievement are related to maternal attitudes; however, this relationship was demonstrated in only the Acceptance and the Rejection Scales.* Mothers of achievers were more accepting and less rejecting. The second hypothesis that achievement and underachievement would be related to the students' perceived maternal attitudes found even less support. The only significant relationship was found on the Rejection Scale in which the underachievers saw their mothers as significantly more rejecting than did the achievers. This was consistent with the actual maternal attitude. However, the achievers did *not* see their mothers as significantly more accepting, which the actual attitude indicated.

Perhaps the most interesting results involve the third hypothesis which predicted that there would be significant relationships between the maternal attitudes and the perceived maternal attitudes. This was supported in three of the four attitudes for the underachiever and in *none* of the attitudes of the achievers.

Thus the results of this study indicated that for the underachievers, their mothers were more rejecting and less accepting. The underachievers saw their mothers as more rejecting and were quite sensitive to their mothers' attitudes toward them. On the other hand, the achievers whose mothers were more accepting and less rejecting did not view their mothers' attitudes in that way nor were they aware of any of their mothers' attitudes toward them. Thus, the results indicate real qualitative differences in the achievers' and underachievers' perceptual orientation about their mothers' attitudes toward them.

In terms of the actual rejection by the underachievers' mothers, attention is called to the etiology of underachievement as described by Roth and Meyersburg (1963).

The psychogenesis involves a series of very subtle devaluations of the child, stemming from the parent-child relationship. In our experience, the most frequent pattern is that of the parent who pays no attention at all to the accomplishments or failures of the child. (These students frequently exclaim, "What's the use, nobody gives a damn," in reference to their current college failure.) The life space of the child and the life space of the parent are in different realms, a state of affairs which constitutes a parental rejection. The only way a child can bring the life spaces together, albeit momentarily, is through the production of a crisis, occasionally necessitating outsiders such as police, teacher, principal, or a counselor.

Next in frequency is the parent who attends only to the child's failures and rarely to his successes. The latter are taken for granted, but the failures are punished. Thus, the contact between parent and child is through failure. If the child succeeds, he is alone, but if he fails, he is part of the concern of his parents.

Both of these early experiences lead to three devasting, incipient pathological processes:

The first of these is a process of self-denigration. In order for the child to maintain some kind of identity with the parent he must learn to see himself as a failure. He must hold back his productivity and blame himself for his lacks. Hostility, he is taught, is received by him and never expressed toward others. When he does experience resentments he directs them against himself and thus supports his own constructs about himself as being worth little [Roth, 1963, p. 531–538].

Thus the underachievers' mothers attitudes or rejection is consistent with this etiology and with the findings of Roth and Puri (1967) that underachievers are significantly more intrapunitive than are achievers.

On the other side of this coin are the findings regarding the achievers whose mothers are more accepting but who are relatively insensitive to their mothers' attitudinal system toward them. Christopher (1967) concludes from his study that:

. . . males in this study no longer employ the family group as a referent for their achievement behavior. Such a finding seems consistent with the view that adolescence brings a severing of familial ties. There is, however, clear evidence of a relationship between perceived parental valuing of achievement and the fact of achievement. This finding suggests that family values persist through the adolescent period, are internalized by the male studies, and bear a functional relationship to achievement [Christopher, 1967, p. 924].

Thus, the underachiever presents a picture of dependence which is organized around attempts at maintaining relationships with the parents as a primary motivation. Their immaturity is well documented. Therefore, this underachievement can be viewed as instrumental not only in maintaining parental relationships on a dependent level but also as a way of warding off adolescence with its demands for independence strivings. The achievers can be viewed as having had the appropriate acceptance at home and thus are able to deal effectively with the required severing of family ties in which their awareness of maternal attitude is reduced but their effectiveness as independent people is supported by their achievement.

REFERENCES

BRICKMAN, M. The underachievement pattern: selected characteristics. Unpublished paper, Illinois Institute of Technology, 1965.

CHRISTOPHER, S. A. Parental relationship and value orientation as factors in academic achievement. *Personnel and Guidance Journal,* 1967, *45,* 921–925.

DAVIDS, A., & HAINSWORTH, P. K. Maternal attitudes about family life and child rearing as avowed by mothers and perceived by their under-achieving and high achieving sons. *Journal of Consulting Psychology,* 1967, 31(1), 29–37.

DREWS, E., & TEAHAN, J. E. Parental attitudes and academic achievement. *Journal of Clinical Psychology,* 1961, *8,* 318–321.

ROTH, R. M. *The Mother-Child Relationship Evaluation.* Los Angeles: Psychological Services, 1960.

ROTH, R. M., & MEYERSBURG, H. The non-achievement syndrome. *Personnel and Guidance Journal,* 1963, *41,* 535–540.

ROTH, R. M., & PURI, P. The direction of aggression and the non-achievement syndrome. *Journal of Counseling Psychology,* 1967, *14*(3), 277–281.

SEROT, N., & TEEVAN, R. Perception of the parent-child relationship and its relations to child's adjustment. *Child Development,* 1961, *32,* 373–378.

TAYLOR, R. G. Personality traits and discrepant achievement: a review. *Journal of Counseling Psychology,* 1964, *11,* 76–82.

Personality Characteristics and Affective Reactions Toward Exams of Superior and Failing College Students

BERNARD WEINER and PENELOPE A. POTEPAN
University of California, Los Angeles

Test anxiety, achievement orientation, and intellectual achievement responsibility (internal versus external locus of control) were assessed among 107 college students who had either failed or performed excellently on a

From *Journal of Educational Psychology,* 61: 144–151, 1970. The authors wish to thank Judith Goldman, Andy Kukla, and Phyllis Labbee for their aid and many suggestions. Computing assistance was obtained from the Health Sciences Computing Facility, University of California at Los Angeles, sponsored by National Institute of Health Grant No. FR–3.

midterm exam. In addition, the affect which they associated with the final exam was reported at various times following the midterm feedback. The data revealed that the measured personality dimensions discriminated succeeding from failing males, but did not differentiate between corresponding female groups. Correlational analysis also yielded systematic relationships between the individual difference variables. Finally, self-report ratings revealed that the change in level of fear as the exam date approached was related to the level of achievement needs. These data were interpreted using Miller's model of conflict.

In this study a partial description of the personality characteristics of excelling and failing college students, as well as a record of their affective reactions toward exams, is provided. Three personality characteristics of successful and unsuccessful students were assessed: test anxiety (Mandler & Sarason, 1952), achievement orientation (Atkinson, 1964), and intellectual achievement responsibility (Crandall, Katkovsky, & Crandall, 1965). Test anxiety refers to the tendency to respond with fear in achievement-related contexts, and the disposition to engage in activities which are instrumental to the avoidance of achievement tasks. It has been demonstrated that test anxiety interferes with intellectual development (Sarason, Hill, & Zimbardo, 1964) as well as with achievement performance (Kestenbaum & Weiner, 1970). The second personality dimension investigated, achievement orientation, is defined here as the difference between the motive to approach success (need for achievement) and the motive to avoid the threat of failure. Individuals believed to be high in this motivational disposition voluntarily approach achievement-related tasks, persist in situations of failure, and choose realistic risks (see Weiner, 1970). Finally, intellectual achievement responsibility, the third trait under consideration, refers to the readiness to attribute successful or failed actions to oneself (ability and/or effort expenditure), rather than to external sources such as luck, task difficulty, etc. In a grade-school population self-attribution among males has been found to correlate with the amount of time spent in achievement activities, as well as with achievement performance (Crandall, Katkovsky, & Preston, 1962). In sum, the three traits measured in this research intuitively are pertinent to classroom performance, and have been shown empirically to relate to achievement behaviors.

The interrelationships between the three variables under discussion have been subject to some study. The components of the achievement tendency, that is, need for achievement and anxiety about failure, are uncorrelated (see Atkinson, 1964). Recently there has been a relatively successful attempt to assess the resultant of the approach and avoidance tendencies with a single instrument (Mehrabian, 1968). Because this motivational measure (which is employed in the present research) theoretically includes anxiety as a subpart, it is expected that achievement orientation will be inversely related to test anxiety. It is anticipated that achievement motivation also will be related to causal ascriptions, although the association between these variables has been found to be dependent upon the outcome of achivement-related actions. Weiner and Kukla (1970) demonstrated that subjects high in resultant achievement motivation attribute success internally to their ability and effort more than individuals low in resultant achievement motivation. However, in situations of failure the total internal versus external attributions for the two motive groups did not differ. Yet there was evidence that the groups did exhibit important attributional differences in situations of failure: the high-achievement-oriented group ascribed their failures to a lack of effort, whereas the low-achievement-oriented group perceived themselves as deficient in ability. Weiner and Kukla contend that ascription of failure to a lack of ability intimates that the individual will then abandon the activity. Conversely, attribution of failure to a lack of effort suggests that the individual attempting the task will persist, for effort expenditure subjectively can be controlled and augmented. It was argued by Weiner and Kukla that the pattern of causal ascription for failure may give rise to the differential persistence in the face of failure which is displayed by the contrasting achievement motive groups.

The discussion thus far leads to the following summary statements concerning the initial hypotheses in this study:

1. Successful students will be higher in achievement orientation, lower in test anxiety, higher in internal responsibility for success (greater perceived ability and effort), lower in ascribing failure to a lack of ability, and higher in attributing failure to a lack of effort, than failing students.

2. Achievement orientation will relate negatively to test anxiety, positively to internal responsibility for success (both ability and effort), positively with perception of failure as caused by a lack of effort, and inversely with the perception of failure as caused by a lack of ability. The inverse relationships with perceived responsibil-

ities should hold for test anxiety. Finally, internal ability ascriptions for success and failure should correlate negatively, while attributions of success and failure to effort should correlate positively. Thus, "locus of control" (Rotter, 1966) is dependent upon both the outcome of an achievement related event and the particular internal causal factor (ability or effort).

It has already been indicated that affective reactions toward exams also are examined in this research. The analysis of these emotional responses was guided by Miller's (1959) model of conflict. Miller's model specifies that there may be both an approach and an avoidance tendency toward a goal, and these tendencies differentially increase or decrease as a function of the organism's distance from the goal. The steepness of the gradients of approach and avoidance, or their responsiveness to distance from the goal, is determined, in part, by the source of the drive stimuli which theoretically generate the behavior. When the source of the drive stimuli is internal, such as those produced by water and food deprivation, then the gradient is relatively little influenced by distance from the goal object. However, when the drive stimuli are elicited by external cues, such as those which are contiguously presented with the onset of an aversive stimulus, then the gradient is comparatively greatly affected by distance from the goal.

The subjects selected for the present study performed exceptionally well or poorly on a midterm examination in introductory psychology. At various times prior to the final exam the successful students were questioned concerning their positive hopes about success, while the failing students were asked to reveal their negative anticipations concerning failure. Following Miller, the relative change in affect as a function of distance (time) from the final exam should be determined, in part, by the extent to which the produced affect is dependent upon internal versus external stimuli (see Brown, 1957). This, in turn, may be a function of the personality characteristics which have already been discussed. If individuals high in achievement orientation, or low in test anxiety, believe that a prior success was caused by their high ability (which is an internalized, stable causal attribute), then their positive anticipations concerning success should be less influenced by time from the examination than individuals low in achievement orientation, or high in anxiety. In a similar manner, if students low in achievement orientation, or high in anxiety, attribute failure to a perceived low level of ability, then their fears about the final exam should be less influenced by the passage of time than those of the high-achievement, low-anxiety groups.

Hypotheses 3 and 4 follow from the prior discussion and from a consideration of the individual difference variables:

3. Individuals high in anxiety, low in achievement orientation, or high in self-attribution of failure to low ability, are expected to have greater fears concerning the final exam, given an initial failure experience, than individuals low in test anxiety, high in achievement orientation, or low in attribution of failure to a lack of ability. Conversely, students high in achievement orientation or in internal responsibility for success should display greater future hopes, given a prior success, than students low in these personality dimensions.

4. The steepness of the approach and avoidance gradients, or the affective lability of emotions as a function of time from the final exam, will be influenced by individual difference variables. The low-achievement group, which internalizes failure to the stable attribute of ability, is hypothesized to have a flatter avoidance gradient than the high-achievement group. On the other hand, the approach gradient of individuals high in achievement motivation, who are believed to internalize success, should be less influenced by time from the final exam than the approach gradient of the low-achievement-oriented individuals, who are believed relatively to attribute success to external sources.

METHOD

Subjects

Following the midterm examination in three different introductory psychology classes, all students receiving the grades of A, D, or F ($N = 173$) were invited to participate in a "research project concerning student attitudes towards . . . certain course procedures." For participating, the subjects were offered either $3.00 or credit toward a course experimental requirement. One hundred and thirty-six of the students contacted (79%) arrived for the initial testing session. Of these, 19 were either Negro, Mexican-American, or Oriental. Inasmuch as 15 of these 19 (79%) were among the failures, all were eliminated from the data analysis to increase the homogeneity of the to-be-compared groups. (One unexpected finding of this study was the manifest poor performance of the minority students, in spite of the stringent admission requirements at the University of California at Los Angeles. There was a sufficient number of failing females ($n = 10$) to report some of their data, although statistical comparisons which included this group were not performed). Eliminating these 19 students from the analysis left an initial N of 117. Finally, 10 subjects did not complete the entire experiment, leaving a final N of 107. Thus, 67% of those originally selected were included in the completed data analysis.

Procedure

During the initial experimental session, test anxiety, achievement orientation, and intellectual achievement responsibility were assessed. Test anxiety was measured with the Test Anxiety Questionnaire (Mandler & Sarason, 1952), a self-report inventory of situationally aroused anxiety. Responses on this inventory are recorded on a Likert-type scale anchored at the extremes (e.g., perspire a great deal during exams versus do not perspire), and the final score was determined by subdividing each scale into five equal units and summing the scores of the individual items. A self-rating scale developed by Mehrabian (1968) was employed to assess achievement orientation. The items on this scale tap, in part, the kind of affect (hope or fear), the direction of behavior (approach or avoidance), and the preference for risk (intermediate versus easy or difficult) elicited in achievement contexts. These factors have been found to differentiate between individuals high or low in achievement motivation. Responses to the items range from strong agreement ($+3$) to strong disagreement (-3). Typical items are:

1. I more often attempt difficult tasks that I am not sure I can do than easier tasks I believe I can do.
2. Getting turned down after a job interview can be more painful to me than the pleasure of getting hired.

The final individual difference measure was a correspondent form of the Intellectual Achievement Responsibility scale developed by Crandall et al. (1965). The revised scale used in this study was more appropriate for a college population than the Crandall et al. measure, which was devised for children. The modified scale consists of 28 two-choice items: one of the choices represents an internal ascription, while the other is an external attribution.[2] Half of the items involve successful acts, while the remaining half represent unsuccessful outcomes. Sample items are:

1. If you correctly answer a true-false item that few other people get right, is it usually because:
   You were lucky; or
   You thought about the answer very carefully.
2. Suppose that you had studied for a certain profession and were not successful. Do you think that this would probably happen because:
   You did not get the breaks at crucial times; or
   You did not work hard enough.

The internal stems on this scale also can be subdivided into ability ascriptions (Because: "You're not a very skillful player"; "You're good at the subject"), and motivational attributions ("You studied especially hard"; "You did not try your best").

Following the individual difference assessment, the students reported their positive or negative anticipations concerning the final exam. Prior research (Epstein & Fenz, 1965) has shown that it is not feasible to obtain independent self-reports on both approach and avoidance tendencies from the same subjects. Therefore, in this investigation successful students reported only positive feelings, and failing students only their fears. Affective concerns were assessed with eight items, answered on a Likert-type scale anchored at the extremes. Questions for the success group included:

1. In general, would you characterize your feeling toward the final exam as one of positive anticipation?
2. How much are you looking forward to the consequences of the final exam?
3. Do you consider the final exam a challenge from which you may derive satisfaction?

Parallel items were constructed for the failure group (e.g., in the above items substitute the word "negative" for "positive," "dread" for "looking forward to," etc.). Scores were determined by subdividing each item scale into 28 equal units, and adding the scores across individual items to reach a total affect score.

The first testing session occurred approximately 3 weeks after

[2] Four of the 28 items pair internal motivation with internal ability choices within the success and failure conditions.

the midterm exam was given (2 weeks after the results were distributed). This was approximately 4 weeks from the date of the final exam. Two weeks, 1 week, and 3 days from the final, the subjects were mailed the identical eight questions, and sent back their completed answers. Thus, the time prior to the final exam was halved at each testing. (A fifth testing also was attempted immediately prior to the final exam by providing two of the self-report inventories at the fourth mailing, and including instructions as to when the fifth report should be completed. Unfortunately (but not unexpectedly) few of the respondents complied with this latter request).

RESULTS

Table 1 gives the mean individual difference scores for the male and female subjects in the two extreme performance groups. Looking first at the male data, it can be seen that all the differences are in the predicted direction, with all but one (attribution of failure to a lack of effort, or M−) approaching or attaining significance. That is, successful male students are lower in test anxiety, higher in achievement orientation, more likely to attribute success to their

TABLE 1

Mean Scores on the Personality Indexes according to Sex and
Midterm Exam Performance

| Sex condition | n | Anxiety | Achieve-ment | Resultant Z score (ach-anx) | Achievement responsibility | | | | | |
					A+	M+	I+	A−	M−	I−
Males										
Success	29	41.13	11.62	.44	6.14	4.86	11.00	3.86	4.28	8.14
Failure	22	46.00	4.00	−.58	5.23	3.96	9.18	5.00	4.23	9.23
t difference		1.95	1.77	2.43*	1.90	2.14*	2.94†	2.28*	<1	2.06*
Females										
Success	32	41.53	5.94	.08	5.91	3.97	9.88	4.47	4.34	8.81
Failure	24	44.83	8.50	−.09	5.17	4.38	9.54	4.67	4.46	9.13
t difference		1.22	<1	<1	1.68	1.03	<1	<1	<1	<1
Minority failure	10	49.30	2.60		4.10	3.20	7.30	5.40	4.40	9.80

Note.—Abbreviated: A+ = success attributed to ability, A− = failure attributed to ability, M+ = success attributed to motivation, M− = failure attributed to motivation, I+ =internalized success [(A+) + (M+)], I− = internalized failure [(A−) + (M−)].
*p < .05.
† p < .01.

own ability (A+) and effort (M+), and less likely to attribute failure to a lack of ability (A—) than the failing male students. A resultant achievement index (Z score of achievement orientation minus Z score) of test anxiety (see Atkinson, 1964) also was derived because of the failure to find a significant relationship between achievement orientation and test anxiety (see discussion which follows). As would be foreseen from the analyses already presented, successful male students score higher on this index then failing students. Inspection of Table 1 also reveals that within the female population none of the predicted differences reach significance. Indeed, only one of the mean differences even approaches an acceptable significance level.

The correlations between the individual difference measures are presented in Table 2. Table 2 reveals that, as predicted, test anxiety correlates negatively with achievement orientation (ns), negatively with A ($p < .01$), and positively with A— ($p < .01$). Further, achievement orientation correlates positively with A+ ($p < .05$), M+ ($p < .01$), and M— (ns), and negatively with A— ($p < .01$).

TABLE 2

Intercorrelations of Personality Variables

Variable	Variable number							
	1	2	3	4	5	6	7	8
1. Test Anxiety								
2. Achievement Orientation	—.13							
3. Resultant Achievement[a]	—.75	.75						
4. Internal Ability Success (A+)	—.31†	.21*	.35†					
5. Internal Motivation Success (M+)	.11	.29†	.12	—.10				
6. Total Internal Success (I+)[b]	—.17	.37†	.36†	.72	.62			
7. Internal Ability Failure (A—)	.25†	—.25†	—.33†	—.37†	—.14	—.37†		
8. Internal Motivation Failure (M—)	.02	.14	.08	.16	.30†	.16	—.40†	
9. Total Internal Failure (I—)[c]	.26†	—.13	—.26†	—.24*	.11	—.24*	.67	.42

Note.—N = 107. The reader should note that correlations between the composite indexes and their components (see footnotes a, b, and c) will result in spuriously high figures. Therefore, the significance levels of these correlations are omitted. Further, the subject population is composed of extreme groups, and therefor the correlations may be somewhat inflated.

[a] Achievement orientation—test anxiety.
[b] Total internal success = (A+) + (M+).
[c] Total internal failure = (A—) + (M—).
* $p < .05$.
† $p < .01$.

The relationships between causal ascriptions and achievement needs generally are enhanced when the resultant achievement index is used to determine the strength of achievement concerns. Finally, the tendency to attribute both success and failure internally to ability, that is, the correlation between A+ and A−, is negative ($p < .01$), while the tendency to attribute success and failure internally to motivation, that is, the correlation between M+ and M−, is positive ($p < .01$). The general pattern of correlations was very similar for both males and females, and for superior and failing students.

Turning next to the reported affect, the results indicate that the positive affect ratings are unrelated to any of the individual difference measures. However, given a failure experience, subjects high in test anxiety (above the median), low in achievement orientation (below the median), or low in resultant achievement motivation have greater fears about the final exam than subjects classified into the alternative motive groups; respectively, $t = 2.36$ ($df = 44, p < .05$); $t = 1.49$ ($df = 44, p < .20$); $t = 2.29$ ($df = 44, p < .05$). The negative affect ratings are not related to self-responsibility for failure ($t < 1$).

The change in affect ratings as a function of time from the final exam and level of resultant achievement motivation are portrayed in Figure 1. The figure shows the significant overall differences previously reported between the high- and low-motive groups in the failure condition and the virtual identity of the affect level for the motive groups in the success condition. Figure 1 also indicates that, although the low resultant achievement group has greater fears in the failure condition, only the high resultant achievement group displays increments in fear as the exam date is approached. (This is not merely a ceiling effect, for the highest obtained mean score was only 70% of the total possible score.) That is, the high-motive group, which empirically has been shown to be less likely to attribute failure to an internalized stable factor, has a steeper avoidance gradient than the group which is comparatively internal about attribution of failure to low ability. While this interaction did not reach statistical significance with analysis of variance procedures, $F = 1.79$, $df = 1/132$, $p > .10$, a nonparametric analysis revealed that more subjects in the high group (65%) exhibit increments in introspective fear judgments from the first to the fourth testing than low subjects (35%; $p < .05$, Fisher Exact Test). Results for the groups differing in test anxiety are in the same direction, but do not reach significance ($p < .20$). However, the direct measure of

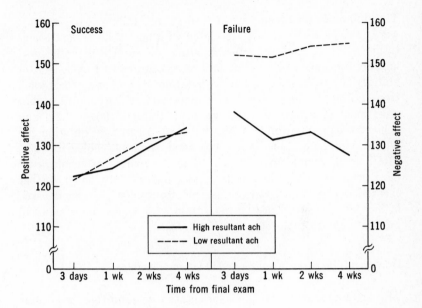

Fig. 1. Reported affect as a function of time from the final exam for groups classified according to level of resultant achievement motivation and midterm exam performance.

ascription of failure to low ability (A−) is unrelated to change in negative affect as the exam time draws near.

Figure 1 also shows, contrary to expectation, that the positive affect associated with success decreases as the exam is approached ($F < 1$). The minor variation in affect is unrelated to any of the individual difference measures.

DISCUSSION

The discussion can be logically grouped into three topics: differences between excelling and failing students, analysis of the individual difference measures and underlying personality dimensions, and the magnitude and change of affect related to exams.

Excelling and Failing Students

The differentiations between succeeding and failing male students were quite clear. Success is associated with high achievement orientation, low test anxiety, self-attribution for success to both effort and ability, and a belief that failure was not caused by a lack of ability. These dimensions, however, did not discriminate succeeding from failing females. There is a literature which indicates that assessment of achievement motivation (Atkinson, 1964, p. 226) and achievement responsibility (Crandall et al., 1962) is of questionable validity for females. On the other hand, some psychologists (e.g., McClelland, 1966) have argued that a separate psychology of motivation is needed for males and females. Only much further theoretical and empirical work can help to resolve the difficult issue of lack of correspondence between results for males and females in motivational research.

Individual Differences: Assessment and Interrelationships

The success of the achievement-orientation scale in this study adds to the validity of the Mehrabian instrument. This measure of achievement strivings could be an important contribution, for, like other objective instruments, it is relatively easy to administer and score. Further, it has reliability properties which the traditional Thematic Apperception Test (TAT) procedure lacks. The low correlation found in this study between test anxiety and achievement orientation suggests that the Mehrabian measure is primarily one of approach motivation, as is the TAT index, rather than a resultant (approach minus avoidance) index.

Similarly, the promising results using the modified version of the Crandall et al. (1962) measure indicate that transformation of some of the items so they are appropriate for adults does not destroy the validity of the index. Two findings of considerable theoretical significance which pertain to the scale were the negative correlation between internal responsibility for success $(I+)$ and failure $(I-)$, and the complex interactions with achievement orientation. If locus of control is, in part, determined by the outcome (success or failure) of an event, then it cannot be considered a unidimensional structure. In addition, the results in this investigation bearing upon the ability and effort attributions indicate that internal control must be further subdivided into more basic elements. Finally, the systematic relationships between achievement-related needs and causal ascription strongly suggest that achievement motive systems can be considered complex cognitive networks in which attributions for success and failure play an essential role (see Weiner and Kukla, 1970, for further elaboration of this point).

Affect and Affective Change

The decrease in approach motivation as the exam date drew near strongly suggests that a "pure" approach assessment is not possible, given the unpleasant affect associated with exams. The inclusions of "fears" in the ratings of the successful students may account for the lack of significant findings related to positive affect.

The change in affect predictions were the most "unusual" hypotheses in this study. Therefore, the partial support of the predictions in the failure condition is most encouraging. It appears that the Miller (1959) model can be extended to situations in which a rather remote analogy is made to internal and external stimuli. These writers, however, can offer no explanation for the failure of the A+ and A— scores directly to predict affective change. Indeed, perhaps the reported affect was not mediated by the degree of internality-externality, although this dimension did give rise to the original hypotheses and guided the experimental procedure. Clearly, further research is needed to clarify these findings.

REFERENCES

ATKINSON, J. W. *An introduction to motivation.* Princeton: Van Nostrand, 1964.

BROWN, J. S. Principles of intrapersonal conflict. *Conflict Resolution*, 1957, *1*, 135–154.

CRANDALL, V. C., KATKOVSKY, W., & CRANDALL, V. J. Children's belief in their own control of reinforcements in intellectual-academic achievement situations. *Child Development*, 1965, *36*, 91–109.

CRANDALL, V. C., KATKOVSKY, W., & PRESTON, A. Motivational and ability determinants of young children's intellectual achievement behaviors. *Child Development*, 1962, *33*, 643–661.

EPSTEIN, S., & FENZ, W. D. Steepness of approach and avoidance gradients in humans as a function of experience: Theory and experiment. *Journal of Experimental Psychology*, 1965, *70*, 1–12.

KESTENBAUM, J., & WEINER, B. Achievement performance related to achievement motivation and test anxiety. *Journal of Consulting and Clinical Psychology*, 1970, in press.

MANDLER, G., & SARASON, S. B. A study of anxiety and learning. *Journal of Abnormal and Social Psychology*, 1952, *47*, 166–173.

MCCLELLAND, D. Longitudinal trends in the relation of thought to action. *Journal of Consulting Psychology*, 1966, *30*, 479–483.

MEHRABIAN, A. Male and female scales of the tendency to achieve. *Educational and Psychological Measurement*, 1968, *28*, 493–502.

MILLER, N. E. Liberalization of basic S-R concepts: Extensions to conflict behavior, motivation, and social learning. In S. Koch (Ed.), *Psychology: A study of a science*. Vol. 2. New York: McGraw-Hill, 1959.

ROTTER, J. B. Generalized expectancies for internal versus external control of reinforcement. *Psychological Monographs*, 1966, *80* (1, Whole No. 609).

SARASON, S., HILL, K., & ZIMBARDO, P. A longitudinal study of the relation of test anxiety to performance on intelligence and achievement tests. *Monographs of the Society for Research in Child Development*, 1964, *29* (7, Serial No. 98).

WEINER, B. New conceptions in the study of achievement motivation. In B. Maher (Ed.), *Progress in experimental personality research*. Vol. 5. New York: Academic Press, 1970, in press.

WEINER, B., & KUKLA, A. An attributional analysis of achievement motivation. *Journal of Personality and Social Psychology*, 1970, in press.

Stress, Pressure, and Defensive Behavior

Some people react to pressure by putting on more steam. Others lament their fate but keep plugging away. Keniston reports on those who try to run away. He proposes that alienation or refusal to join or conform to the academic community may actually be a valuable behavior, especially when the system itself happens to be inadequate. Even so there is a definite difference between the person who rejects the system and the person who merely refuses to conform to certain aspects of it. For most of mankind is identified with some sort of system or establishment and, in a sense, one cannot be rejected without the other. We know that a person without ties or a feeling of being a part of something is denied psychologically important sources of self-validation and actualization. Despite the feeling of the students studied by Keniston that conformity means the destruction of individuality, a person cannot be an individual apart from the group, the social context of the system.

There is much difference between the individual who rejects selectively and the one who exercises no choice but to oppose everything that represents the system. There is much difference between the person who rejects because of a conviction and one who is against all authority as a matter of principle.

Whether or not the dropout may be transferring his rebellious tendencies from an authoritarian family to the campus, as the author suggests, and whether or not his college is antiquated, unfeeling, and impersonal, his dropping out does not typically brighten his prospects for the future. There may be much to be said for the student who protests selectively and who participates in effecting needed reforms as part of the system.

Keniston asks whether or not colleges can deal with differences in students, especially if the differences are large enough to merit calling the student by another name —alienated, rebellious, disenchanted. Kubany indicates that a name itself is an important factor in adjustment. A would-be political servant of the 1920's and 1930's was Norman Thomas, a man who tried repeatedly to become a candidate for the presidency of the United States. Occasionally he ran for election. He was, however, a *Socialist* and received little serious consideration. The very name "Socialist" set in motion preconceived ideas that here was a real danger to the democratic way of life. Oddly enough, the reforms and programs promulgated by Socialist Thomas have become law and practices in our nation since that time—medicare, social security, unemployment insurance, aid to dependents, and, in some instances, aid to college students. But these reforms were sponsored by Democrats and Republicans. The message to students is what Kubany is emphasizing in a different context. Words are not just symbols. Words are forces that shape our reactions, our way of life, and our vision of that which might be.

The editors have found that Kubany is quite right in his assertion that applying a classificatory system does not help much. We found, in the counseling center, that we could work quite well with people in need of help without calling the person or the difficulty neurotic, psychotic, compulsive, manic-depressive, or schizophrenic. The behavior was discussed and plans were made to remove or mitigate the source of misery, or defenses were planned with the upset person to meet and deal with the causes.

It is, as Kubany asserts, more helpful to speak of an individual who does not get along with others in just those words rather than to call him sociopathic. The reader may find it advantageous in describing his own behavior as well as that of others to avoid the names which do injury, and to try to describe, in behavioral terms, what gets in the way of better adjustment. It is a distinctly erroneous cliché which says "Sticks and stones will break my bones, but names will not hurt me."

"Pot," alcohol, amphetamines, barbiturates, and other drugs affecting mental functioning would have the same sequalae regardless of the names given to them. Rationalization, projection, blame-placing, defensive posturing could be designated by other words without changing the implications for adjustment. Drugs or psychological defense mechanisms may have the effect of allaying or reducing tension, but, chronically used, they tend to become "non-adjustive adjustive mechanisms." The names or categories of the adjustive approach are of little practical consequence. One performs a certain act to reduce pressure, anxiety, or pain only to find that problems are added and compounded. Singer's selection suggests the futility of trying to resolve complex problems—anxiety, fear, self-depreciation—by means of simple solutions. In this way various authors emphasize one of the principles which the editors used in selecting articles; the really simple solution to problems of adjustment is the strenuous one of accepting responsibility for one's choice of behavior.

Although there are several drugs of an hallucinogenic nature which are not considered in the article one must also think about them. Especially this may apply to the kinds of individuals who are prone to experiment, to risk, and to suffer addiction. Whether this happens because of the urge to be turned on, tuned in, or escape from, drugs probably are most appealing to those who question their own ability and who are looking for an easy way to become, or at least to feel, adequate in the face of stress.

Anything which offers the easy way always is tempting. Americans, and particularly younger Americans, always have been impatient. They want immediate results. Any gadget which promises to provide need satisfaction quickly and without effort, no matter how high the risk, will get some takers. Inadequate people who wish, in one fell swoop, to be adequate are the prime drug targets. Perhaps the answers lie not so much in attempting to outlaw the drugs as in examining and dealing with those aspects of the culture which create anxious, purposeless, and hostile people.

There are so many controversies, so many misconceptions, and so many expert opinions regarding marijuana that it seems useless to add another verdict. Singer's article is included in the section on Stress and Pressure more to assure that it receives some consideration by the reader than to provide some incontrovertible conclusions. It will be noted by many readers that alcohol is used by the adult generation—and yet they criticize marijuana. (It may be noted by all generations that recent studies indicate that alcohol inevitably and inexorably kills some brain cells each time it is consumed.)

College Students and Children in Developmental Institutions

KENNETH KENISTON
Associate Professor of Psychology
Department of Psychiatry
Yale University School of Medicine

At first glance, few groups seem more dissimilar than the talented, privileged students who attend residential liberal arts colleges and the unwanted or neglected children who live in group residential centers. Yet behind the real differences in age and social privilege that separate these two groups, there are profound similarities in their situations. Essentially the same issues arise in planning for what one college dean calls "the care and feeding of college students" as in planning for the group residential care of children.

As Erving Goffman has pointed out, there are a few institutions in modern society that may encompass practically all aspects of a person's life. He calls these "total institutions,"[1] for in them residential life, social life, and work life are combined—often within the same walls, certainly within the same institutional framework. As examples he cites merchant ships, military services, mental hospitals, prisons, monasteries, and residential treatment institutions. He might also have cited institutions for neglected and dependent children.

This concept of "total institution" becomes more useful if we distinguish between different kinds of total institutions. There are three types: (1) those institutions that could be called *instrumental* because they are trying to get a job done in the outside world—for instance, a merchant ship carrying a cargo across the sea; (2) those institutions whose purpose is at least nominally *therapeutic*, preventative, or corrective, such as a prison or mental hospital; and (3) a small group of institutions whose explicit purpose is *developmental*, such as a residential college, a boarding school, or a residential center for neglected and dependent children.

From *Children*, 14 (No. 1) : 3–7, January-February, 1967.

[1] Goffman, Erving: On the characteristics of total institutions. *In* Asylums: essays on the social situation of mental patients and other inmates. Anchor Publishing Co., Garden City, N.Y. 1961.

A residential college, of course, is less "total" than an army or a prison: Students are on the whole free to enter and leave at will. But for most college students, during the academic year at least, their lives are embodied and to some extent regulated within a single framework and a set of walls. And obviously group residential centers for children are total institutions in the full sense of the word.

Developmental institutions, whether colleges or children's "homes," have a number of common characteristics. For one, they at least nominally accept as their primary objective the promotion of the "normal" or optimal development of their charges, the residents. They therefore usually try to ally themselves with what they take to be the natural forces for growth and development in the individual. They see their task as somehow stimulating, supporting, and confirming the development of each resident. In this respect they differ sharply from an instrumental institution like an army or a merchant ship, which may ignore or even impede the individual's overall development. And they also differ from therapeutic institutions like good mental hospitals, which have as a primary task to intervene and correct faulty development. This does not mean that developmental institutions like colleges or institutions for children do not have ways of correcting faulty development. But, on the whole, their goals are not so much to correct failures as to promote normal, healthy growth.

A second characteristic of developmental institutions is that they exercise quasi-familial functions. Ordinarily, such institutions arise in situations where families cannot or are thought not to be able to do an adequate job. A children's institution, for example, usually enters the picture when there is no family that can take care of the child, or when the child's actual family is exerting a destructive influence on his development. Boarding schools and residential colleges generally arise because individual families cannot provide the kind of "character-building," intellectual stimulation, or environmental enrichment provided by a residential school. This does not mean that developmental institutions should think of themselves as families, for they can never perform all the functions of a family.

Many of the same kinds of practical and theoretical problems arise in all developmental institutions, whether they are dealing with adolescents and young adults or with infants and young children. Some of these problems were underscored in two studies with which I have recently been involved. One of these was a study of "alienated" college students—a small group of students who were extreme in their rejection of what they took to be the dominant values and roles of institutions in American society. The second is an ongoing study of gifted students who drop out of college.

THE PSYCHOLOGY OF ALIENATION

For about 6 years, I was involved in the study of alienated undergraduates at Harvard University. The initial research consisted chiefly of objective tests—the systematic comparison of alienated and nonalienated students through the use of questionnaires. Almost 2,000 students were involved, but although these statistical studies yielded useful information, they did not take me very far toward the question I was trying to answer: Why is it that some students are alienated whereas others are not?

To try to answer this question I turned to a more intensive study of 12 students who had been selected because of the extreme degree of their alienation as measured by questionnaires. This group was contrasted with another group of the same size at the opposite pole—"extremely unalienated"—and with a third control group that was not extreme in either way. All three groups were studied over the last 3 years of their college careers.

Each student spent altogether about 200 hours participating in the research. Each was interviewed about his views of the world, his current behavior, and his life history, and each took part in a large number of psychological experiments.

A comparison of the data from the alienated group with that from the other two groups revealed a number of distinctive patterns of ideology, behavior, life history, and fantasy among the alienated students. In addition to being alienated from American culture, they were on the whole pessimistic, distrustful, resentful, and cynical about human nature. They saw themselves as outsiders whose isolation and aloneness was part of the human condition, not their own personal problem. To them, the universe seemed a formless and unstructured chaos lacking in meaning and purpose. And they rejected all cooperative group endeavors on the grounds that conformity means the destruction of individuality.

Most of these students came from a similar family constellation. Characteristically, they described their mothers as magnetic, emotional, passionate, and attractive women to whom they, the sons, were extremely, often excessively, close. At the same time they described their mothers as possessive, confining, restrictive, nagging, and intrusive.

About their fathers, these alienated students volunteered very little information. When pressed to discuss their fathers, they described them as disappointed, frustrated, detached, outwardly cold men. However, the alienated students usually imagined that their fathers had, at one point in their own youth, possessed considerable imagination, idealism, and fire, which had been lost in adulthood. So the father, as the son saw him, was a man deeply disappointed by his own failure to realize his youthful dreams.

Such a family constellation, we felt, had obvious relationships to the development of alienation. Seeing their fathers as men who had been broken by life or by their marriages and thus defeated by "the American way of life," these students were determined not to let what happened to their fathers happen to them. In rejecting their fathers, they also felt it necessary to reject the society that, as they saw it, had ruined their fathers. In other words, from their fathers these students had derived an image of conventional masculine adulthood that was repugnant to them, so they spurned conventional adulthood in American society.[2]

In further explaining the alienation of these students, I should point out that Harvard undergraduates tend to be somewhat more alienated as seniors than as freshmen, although rarely to the extreme that these students reached. In addition, these students were on the whole an unusually imaginative, artistically oriented, and talented group of young men who argued that American society was in general not particularly hospitable to talented, creative persons. They were clearly reacting to the wider society as well as to their parents and family experiences.

FOUR MAJOR ISSUES

When I discuss this material, I am often asked a number of related questions: Is alienation a kind of psychopathology? Why did the

[2] Keniston, Kenneth: The uncommitted. Harcourt, Brace & World, Inc., New York. 1965.

researchers not do more to cure these students of their alienation? Is it not a dreadful commentary on a college that its students become more alienated? Should the institution be doing something to change such students? Is alienation a good thing or a bad thing?

None of these questions can be answered simply. I mention them only because they point to two crucial issues that arise whenever we begin thinking about the development of a person in an institution:

1. What is "normal" development?

This first issue could be called the normative question—that is, the question of what kind of development the institution is trying to promote. Is the goal of a college, for example, to produce well-trained adults who will be able to fit smoothly into their positions in society? Or is it to promote critical intelligence and detachment from the immediate pressures and values of society? If we think that a smooth fit with society is the objective, then obviously any college that "alienates" its students from the prevailing society is a bad college. But if we think that critical intelligence and capacity for detachment from society is a good thing, then we may very well applaud a college that to some extent increases alienation in its students.

The normative question almost inevitably arises when one begins thinking about or planning an institutional framework that will encourage the "normal development" of the individual. Indeed, the terms "normal development" and "the optimal development of each individual" can be dangerous phrases since they may obscure the underlying value questions involved. We know that individuals can be stimulated to develop in a great variety of very different ways. But certain pathways to development may be mutually exclusive. For example, if a college tries to promote what some alumni groups call "loyalty and guts," it may be difficult for it also to promote such a quality as the critical use of intellect. Or in the case of small children, major emphasis on the group, as in the Israeli kibbutzim, may make it very difficult for a child to develop the intense attachment to a single mothering person that is characteristic of good family life in most Western societies.

It is not enough, then, to talk merely about "normal development" as the goal of a developmental institution. We know that parents have unconscious, preconscious, and conscious objectives in child rearing. They try to prevent Johnny from becoming like his alcoholic Uncle Harry; or to encourage Gertrude to become like her mother; or to develop orderliness, neatness, and parsimony in one child, or grace, freedom, agility, and imagination in another. The enormous variation in personalities produced by ordinary "healthy" families suggests that it is almost impossible not to stimulate certain developmental potentials and to inhibit or retard others.

But in a developmental institution, in contrast to a family, the normative question—what is "normal" development?—has to be made far more explicit and conscious in planning, programing, and evaluation. In these processes ethical questions cannot be avoided, they can only be evaded; and when they are evaded—when they are not openly faced and rationally considered—the results may be disastrous. For example, one way of characterizing those hygienic institutions whose toll on children's development has been so well documented[3-5] is to note that they have answered the normative question with an unconscious decision to produce children who will be as little trouble as possible, a goal that can be reached only by sacrificing the child's individuality.

Some American colleges operate with a comparable unconscious goal—to keep their students out of trouble until they are old enough to enter the labor market. Fortunately, adolescents are more resilient and rebellious than infants and can sometimes overcome this kind of pressure. But the long-run consequences of having this goal may be only slightly less deplorable than the consequences of having the goal of keeping children out of trouble in an antiseptic nursery. In children's institutions and in colleges alike, it is crucial to examine, reflect upon, and make explicit the specific developmental and educational objectives of the institution.

2. For what kind of society?

The second crucial issue raised by the study of alienated students is closely related to the first. It has to do with the nature of the society

---

[3] Provence, Sally; Lipton, Rose C.: Infants in institutions. International Universities Press, NewYork. 1962.

[4] Spitz, René A.: Hospitalism—an inquiry into the genesis of psychiatric condition in early childhood. *In* The psychoanalytic study of the child, vol. 1, 1945. International Universities Press, New York.

[5] Bowlby, John: Maternal care and mental health. World Health Organization Technical Monograph Series No. 2. Geneva. 1951.

into which the developing individual will eventually move, and the demands, characteristics, and needs of that wider society. If, for example, it were clear that we lived in the best of all possible worlds, then alienation from our present society would definitely be an irrational and deplorable response. We would prescribe therapy for the alienated students and abolition or reform for "alienating" institutions. Or if we felt that criticism of society was always destructive, we should similarly deplore any degree of alienation.

In other words, any judgment as to the kind of human development we should ideally promote must be closely related to our picture of the nature of the wider society, of the demands it makes, and of its long-range needs. A developmental institution is preparing individuals for a particular society with special characteristics, pressures, and opportunities. It may be, for example, that certain kinds of child rearing will produce the kind of character structure and personality organization that is well suited to a Polynesian village but profoundly unsuited to American society. Or again, the kibbutz system of child rearing may produce the kind of adult who contributes a great deal to a kibbutz but one who would be unhappy and unproductive in American society.

Thus, in planning for the program or staffing of a developmental institution, we must consider the kind of society in which the "products" of the institution will live and their capacity for fulfillment and productivity in such a society. This does not mean that our goals should be to develop people who will unreflectively "adjust" to society. Obviously society needs social critics, independent thinkers, and even alienated men and women. But social critics also have to function within society.

Another study I have been involved in raises two more questions that are relevant to program planning in a developmental institution. This is an exploratory study of talented college dropouts. Every year hundreds of thousands of talented well-prepared young Americans drop out of colleges before graduating. We are trying to find out why. What does this mean in relation to the student's development? For whom is dropping out a progressive step, and for whom is it a regressive step?

This research at Yale University is in midstream. We are not even sure of all the questions we will ask, much less of the answers. But we are beginning to believe with Anna Freud that dropouts are people for whom the 4 years of college come at the worst possible time from a developmental point of view.[6] They feel, consciously and unconsciously, that further psychological development is impossible as long as they remain within a collegiate setting; and in many or most cases, they are probably right. At least those who return (the majority) believe that their years away have enabled them to grow and mature, and the judgments of their friends and teachers usually confirm this belief.

In our exploratory clinical studies, we have found that dropouts often have difficult problems of identification with their parents, problems that seem to prevent that slow and gradual development of commitments and the consolidation of identity that usually take place in students of their age. And one reason why dropouts find these problems (which are, after all, universal) so difficult to resolve within a collegiate context has to do with their perceptions of the college environment.

Thus we find an almost universal but often unconscious tendency among these college dropouts to perceive the college as a whole as if it were a large-scale edition of their families. We have been repeatedly impressed with the striking parallel between dropouts' descriptions of the college and their descriptions of their parents. One sophomore, for example, was struggling with great problems of identification with a father who was overtly sadistic and brutal but who at the same time manifested through alcoholism an underlying passivity and dependency. This student describes the college as being authoritarian, harsh, and repressive, yet lacking in any real strength, decisiveness, or moral purpose. Another student, in the throes of attempting to reconcile conflicting identifications with warring parents, perceived the college as containing two conflicting sets of pressures, clearly identifiable with his parents.

This kind of "institutional transference"—equating the institution with the family—seems to be particularly widespread among students who drop out of college. Students who persist in college seem considerably less prone to identify college with their parents. To be sure, they, too, tend to relate to the institution globally, almost as if it were a family. But for them the college is like a *new* family, a facilitating, liberating environment in which they can escape earlier family pressures and move forward in their development.

[6] Group for the Advancement of Psychiatry: Sex and the college student. Atheneum Publishers, New York. 1966. P. 33.

Another incidental finding of this study is how few colleges recognize the existence of dropouts. Of every 100 freshmen entering 4-year colleges in America, only 40 graduate from the same college 4 years later. Transfers and temporary or permanent interruptions of college are the rule rather than the exception. But most colleges keep few figures about "dropouts," ignore their existence, or with little factual basis treat them all as psychological "misfits" or academic "failures."

This study of dropouts underscores two further issues that arise in all developmental institutions:

3. What are the effects of the institution as a whole, of its climate, culture, or morale, on the individual?

In the end, we can no doubt analyze a student's perception of a college into a thousand component interpersonal relationships and experiences. But the student himself experiences the institution globally *as an entity;* and he tends to relate himself to it almost as if it were a single, crucial person in his life. This fact may help explain one of the puzzling results of many studies of college students. It has been shown again and again that probably the most potent factor in determining how colleges affect students' development is that intangible quality called "institution morale," "college climate" or "campus culture." The effectiveness of an institution in promoting development seems more closely related to the characteristics of the institution as a whole than to any of its constitutent parts—students, faculty, facilities, programs, residential arrangements, or curriculum.

In many discussions of the relationship of the college to students' development, this quality of "climate" is neglected, perhaps because it is so difficult to define and measure precisely. We hear endless discussions of curriculum reform, promotion policies, admissions procedures, and residential facilities, but very few discussions of how to create or facilitate the right kind of "climate" or "morale." Yet even an unmotivated and unpromising student, if he is fortunate enough to enter a first-class college with very high institutional morale, may find himself caught up in a general tide of enthusiasm that pushes him to a height of personal and intellectual development that he never before dreamed of. On the other hand, even a highly motivated freshman, if he enters an institution with low morale, may stagnate or regress.

In young children the ability to relate to an institution as a whole is, of course, more limited than it is in adolescents. Nevertheless, in developmental institutions for young children, the climate of the institution as a whole may similarly be more important than any specific programs, staffing policies, or residential arrangements. It is conceivable, for example, that there may be institutions for children where the physical facilities are poor, where the staff philosophy is reactionary, and yet where—for reasons that we do not quite understand—children manage to flourish and grow. And it is also possible that there are institutions with advanced facilities and modern ideas about child development where for lack of a good "climate" somehow everything seems to go wrong, including the children's development.

In thinking about how to create institutions that encourage human growth, we must recognize that individuals experience and respond to institutions as a whole, not only to their parts. We therefore need to plan not merely for programs, schedules, living arrangements, and so on, but also for how all of these variables might interact to produce the kind of staff morale, institutional climate, and intangible culture that nourishes healthy development.

4. Can the institution deal realistically and supportively with individuals who are "deviant" or "atypical" in terms of its ideals and norms?

All institutions, and especially developmental institutions, tend to have an implicit or explicit image of the "average expectable individual," the "typical Yale man," or the "normal child." Procedures, programs, publicity, and even perceptions are organized around this image. At times in a college the image of "the typical student" is so powerful that it blinds administration and faculty to the fact that a majority of students in no way conform to this image.

Other developmental institutions also tend to develop systematic blind spots and irrational ways of responding to members who do not fit their definition of the "average expectable individual." Sometimes the existence of persons who do not fit the expected pattern of development is simply denied by a refusal to notice that they exist. Sometimes those whose development deviates from the expected are treated as misfits, failures, or malcontents. In either case, their lives are dominated by fear, shame, and a sense of their own inadequacy.

One of the marks of a superior developmental institution, whether a college or a residence for children, is its capacity both to recognize explicitly and support persons whose developmental needs and schedules deviate from the mythical or actual norm—without needing to relegate them to a limbo of abnormality, psychopathology, failure, or nonexistence. Those American colleges that clearly facilitate genuine intellectual and personal growth are noted for their emphasis on encouraging individuality and recognizing the special qualities of each student.

Such colleges tend to have flexible institutional programs, to apply their rules according to the individual's needs and his development, and to be highly tolerant of dissent and deviance, both on campus and off. These colleges, and I suspect those children's institutions that facilitate healthy personality growth, explicitly recognize that individual human beings have differing needs at different stages of development, that the rates and phases of normal human growth are highly variable, and that, in a sense, exceptional development is not the exception at all but the rule in human life.

IN SUMMARY

Thus, despite the real differences between children in institutions and students in college, similar issues arise with regard to both groups. Both groups live in "developmental institutions" and the effectiveness of the institutions in promoting their growth depends in good part on how well these questions are answered: What is "normal" development? For what kind of society? What is the right "climate"? Can deviance be accepted? Planning, maintaining, or improving developmental institutions, therefore, demands not only attention to sound programing, staffing, and financing, but also a rational and informed examination of the underlying goals for its residents in the context of what is known about human development.

Anxiety—Yes; Mental Illness—No

ALBERT J. KUBANY
General Motors Institute
Flint, Michigan

A large amount of professional attention has been expressed about the mental illness concept and the medical model it connotes. In a recent article Ellis concludes that the term mental illness is "likely to be around for some time," and the question of whether or not to label individuals mentally ill may well become academic. Szasz and Mowrer have argued for the elimination of the mental illness concept; however, like the weather, everybody talks about it but nobody does anything about it. The problem seems serious; definitive action to change the situation *must* take place if we are to experience a significant breakthrough in the handling of these increasingly critical human problems confronting these individuals and society.

To review briefly, the concept of mental illness does carry with it a large number of associations from which none of us, professional or layman, can divorce ourselves. Depending upon our previous experience, we see mental pictures that range from a catatonic schizophrenic huddled like a ball in a corner to a raving, uncontrolled maniac in a barred room. The label mental illness is applied to the alcoholic and the senile. It is an all-or-nothing label which covers up the fact that each of us experiences various degrees of correctable problems.

There is no doubt that the individuals who experience these problems are mentally ill if, by that, we mean that their thought processes and associations are mentally based and are causing derangement to occur which has proved handicapping in adapting to their environment. It is possible to regard these conditions as mental illness if one chooses to define them that way. The fact remains, however, that the words "mentally ill" do little to help the involved individual and do a great deal to perpetuate the condition.

There are those, including some professionals, who seem too eager to use the label mental illness in describing individual be-

Reprinted from *Etc. A Review of General Semantics,* Vol. 26, No. 4: 475–480, 1969, by permission of the International Society for General Semantics.

havior. Some of this appears related to a professional insecurity and a need to enhance one's professional expertise. It is less helpful to say "John is suffering from a severe mental illness" than to say "John has many clashes with associates at work."

Whatever advantages may exist in having a unified concept called mental illness, the disadvantages would seem to far outweigh them. There is a social and legal discrimination which continues to exist; there is the demoralizing self-denigration that occurs with individuals so labeled; the label has a pervasive connotation implying that all facets of a person's mental functioning are impaired; some individuals are inclined to accept the condition as a crutch for evading moral responsibilities; the label itself creates a fear which causes individuals who might normally seek help to avoid doing so; it connotes a medical model implying that, if the right pills are taken or prescribed treatment is followed, a cure will take place.

Is it possible that the words "mental illness" are innocent enough and name changing is ridiculous? One might suggest that all that needs to be done to remove the unfavorable connotations is to properly define the term. Yet to expect that the general population, or for that matter even professionals, could change these associations is semantically comparable to a leopard's changing its spots. Such a change can exist only on the theoretical level. We cannot arbitrarily delete from our minds old connotations as if wiping the slate clean to start again. This is because we, and humanity in general, suffer from a semantic "illness" that allows our language to largely dictate how we think. We are word bound; that is, we are prisoners of our word associations. This has been documented many times.

Man, even modern man, is not basically logical. One need only note such examples as the change that takes place in the acceptability level when poor people are successively called the underprivileged, the disadvantaged, the deprived, etc., or the many names that are derived by the military to modify the preconceived connotations of older names. For example, the satellite labeled "Spy in the Sky" was quickly relabeled to give it a more positive weather mission.

We see as humorous many revealing examples of semantic juggling. You are snobbish, I am discriminating; changing your mind shows unreliability, changing my mind shows flexibility. We speak of governmental interference when the object is undesirable, but governmental regulation when it is advantageous; Department of War during hostilities, but Department of Defense during peacetime. A civil rights orator is a rabble-rouser in one view, or a champion of the underdog in another: you are displaying a violent temper, but I show righteous indignation, etc., etc. We are all victims of our associations, and the words we use to label a condition truly become all-important in our perceptions of that condition.

The mental illness label itself attaches such a strong stigma to the individual that treatment of these emotionally based conditions may be facilitated by a label or name change. There simply are too many fixed connotations associated with the words "mental illness" even though some may be true at one time with one person while some others are true at another time with a different person. For example, some may have a mental illness in the sense of a biological-chemical problem; or some may be "evilly" or "sinfully" oriented; or some may be dangerous to themselves or others; etc., etc. No one is all of these at any one time.

The concept mental illness, apart from the fact that the medical illness model is likely improper, is on the surface a negatively loaded, threatening stigma. The only realistic way to wipe the slate clean, semantically and therapeutically, and to put the entire field in a new perspective is to change the labels. A term is needed that has new referents that are positive, or at least neutral, or that connotes the temporary and hopeful aspects of the condition. The label should promote an open-mindedness that is not created by the mental illness label. Without further evidence, it is the intent here to assume that the label mental illness has sufficient negative connotations to seriously jeopardize its usefulness in mental health applications and justify a new concept and a new context.

A movement attempt should thus be made to bring about this concept change and create an entirely new context for laymen and workers in this area. It is therefore suggested that the concept mental illness be dropped from the thinking and speaking of everyone associated with this field. Accepting the illogic of it, the term mental health should be retained. No one possesses complete mental health. This concept should not exist except as a theoretical ideal toward which we might all strive, yet expect to fall short.

A variety of words and expressions may be used instead of mental illness. It would not seem necessary to focus on a single concept; rather, a variety of nonthreatening, positively oriented terms would be appropriate. For example, adaptation in some form is almost invariably involved in these conditions. It would be desirable to refer to *adaptation problems* since this referent is purposely not sufficiently explicit. Since some indication of seriousness might be desired by the client, it would be possible to refer to different levels of adaptation problems. It seems important to avoid diagnostic categories since these tend to create an explicit atmosphere involving a variety of assumptions which probably are not true. Definitions of the various adaptation problem levels might be as follows:

First level: Refers to practically every individual in our social structure who has some unreasoned anxieties or problems adapting to their work or personal situation.

Second level: Those individuals with sufficiently serious adaptation problems to seek some help. Usually resolved by a series of visits or group help experience.

Third level: Those adaptation problems of sufficient seriousness that vocational and personal lives are seriously hampered or interrupted.

Fourth level: Adaptation problems where institutionalization is required.

The adaptation concept makes no presumption about how one should adapt and does nothing to structure the adaptation. It allows the individual the freedom to adapt and relate to his environment in whatever ways he may choose, but adaptation in some form is necessary for all individuals. It has the connotations of being realistic, practical, effective, pragmatic, etc. It basically relates to the individual's choice of changing himself to adapt to the environment or changing his environment to adapt to himself. Acknowledging that all of us operating in society are relatively normal and are at a first level of maladaptation will encourage more individuals to seek the help that is needed.

Rather than label adaptation problems as psychoneurosis, manic-depressive, schizophrenia psychosis, mental illness, etc., for which the treatment is not essentially different, it would seem helpful to the person experiencing the problems to feel part of a broad class of individuals who are similarly affected. This labeling system simply acknowledges that all of us have adaptation problems, but some have more serious ones than others.

Since this simple classification scheme will not be readily acceptable to many because of the strength of past classificatory systems, other labels may be needed. The mental health worker should not, however, be trapped into reverting to the old classificatory schemes but should rather use other names similar to the adaptation syndrome. Suggested here are such concepts as anxiety, anxiety crisis or state, emotional imbalance, sociopsychological stress, interpersonal or social-developmental problems, hypertension or extreme hypertension, stress, adjustment, neurosis, etc., or other nonthreatening, nonexplicit labels.

What's in a name? Shakespeare was insufficiently cognizant of the power of a name when he suggested that a rose by any other name would smell as sweet. The intense feelings of the Capulets toward the Montagues should have given him a hint.

What's in a name? Our whole existence is tied to the labels we use to describe ourselves and others. A name change may thus enable the mental health worker to work more positively with persons needing help and avoid the many assumptions that occur once a "frightening" label is uttered.

It is hoped that a new concept and changed words will bring about a change in the associations of everyone working in this field as well as everyone seriously affected by these problems; and, as trite as this semantic juggling may sound, we all can experience the dawn of a new approach to the study and treatment of psychological disturbances.

REFERENCES

ADAMS, HENRY, B., "Mental Illness or Interpersonal Behavior," Symposium, American Psychiatric Association Annual Meeting, St. Louis, August 30, 1962.

ALBEE, GEORGE W., "Emerging Conceptions of Mental Illness and Models of Treatment," American Psychiatric Association Annual Meeting, Boston, May 13, 1968.

AUSUBEL, D., "Personality Disorder Is Disease," *American Psychologist*, 1961, Vol. 16, pp. 69–74.

BOIS, J. SAMUEL, *Explorations in Awareness*, New York: Harper, 1957, p. 219.

CHASE, STUART, *The Power of Words*, New York: Harcourt Brace, 1954, p. 308.

ELLIS, ALBERT, "Should Some People Be Labeled Mentally Ill?" *Journal of Counseling Psychology*, 1967, Vol. 31, pp. 435–446.

JOHNSON, WENDELL, *Verbal Man: The Enchantment of Words*, New York: Collier Books, 1965, p. 159.

Mower, O. H., " 'Sin' The Lesser of Two Evils," *American Psychologist,* 1960, Vol. 15, pp. 301–304.

Szasz, T. S., "Naming and the Myth of Mental Illness," *American Psychologist,* 1961, Vol. 16, pp. 59–65.

———, "The Myth of Mental Illness," *American Psychologist,* 1960, Vol. 15, pp. 113–116.

Primer on Pot

HARVEY SINGER
Dean of Students
New York City Schools

Two years ago the news spread like wildfire on a large college campus. "There's going to be a 'grass' sale," was the big story, whispered in hallways between classes and on the lawn. Today, "grass," marijuana, does not create so much excitement on campus. According to a student estimate quoted by *The New York Times,* "Up to eighty-five per cent of the students at various colleges and universities have tried marijuana at least once," and estimates of the number who use it regularly range from six to twenty-five per cent.

Marijuana use is popular off the college campus, too. Considerable numbers, from high school students to doctors, "turn on" regularly, in spite of the strict Federal and local laws prohibiting its possession and use. The United Nations estimated in 1951 that 200,000,000 people in the world then used marijuana regularly. The figure is undoubtedly much higher today.

In spite of this widespread use, many people, especially the majority of the "over-thirties," know little if anything about marijuana, and the little they think they know is often more fiction than fact. But they should know the truth, for the younger generation is growing up in its midst.

Marijuana and hashish come from the flowering tops of the

Reprinted by permission from the November, 1969, issue of *The Progressive* magazine, copyright © 1969 by The Progressive, Inc.

hemp plant, the female *cannabis sativa*. This plant grows, often to a height of six to eight feet, generally in warm climates. In its best form it comes from particularly hot areas, such as Mexico (Acapulco Gold is a favorite), but it has been grown, quite easily in fact, in many areas of the United States.

Marijuana, or "pot," is the weaker of the two. It is made by drying the plant, and then finely chopping the leaves, twigs, and seeds. The finished product is greenish-brown in color and looks much like ordinary tea. Hashish does not contain the twigs and seeds, but only the pure resin of the plant. It is usually prepared as small black or brown cakes which are purer than marijuana, and are, consequently, much more potent.

In the United States, pot is usually sold in "nickel bags." These are small manila envelopes, about two inches by three inches in size, which sell for five (hence the name) dollars, and contain enough marijuana to be rolled into as many as twenty cigarettes. The cigarettes, which are called "joints," look much like ordinary hand rolled cigarettes, but have twisted or tucked in ends, to prevent loose grains of their expensive contents from spilling out.

A joint is not smoked like an ordinary cigarette, and the experienced pot smoker has had to learn a special way to smoke. He purses his lips, but keeps them slightly open as he inhales. As the acrid smoke enters his mouth it mixes with air, making a hissing sound as he inhales deeply. The smoker then holds the smoke in his lungs as long as he can to get the maximum effect of the drug before exhaling.

The butt is called a "roach." It is often held with a tweezers or hair pin, a "roach holder," so it can be smoked down as far as possible. The small amount of marijuana remaining is then remixed back into the bag to be smoked at some later time.

The effects of marijuana on the smoker are as difficult to describe or predict as are the effects of most other highly subjective experiences. They vary from person to person, and even for the same person at different times. This variation occurs because the effects of all drugs depend on three interrelated factors. Scientists call these factors the drug itself, the "set," and the "setting." The effect of the first factor, the drug, is fairly obvious. Simply stated, each drug has its own special effects. Not quite so obvious are the effects of the set and the setting.

The term "set" refers to a person's expectations. When a person expects something will happen, he becomes ready, or psychologically set, for that thing to happen, and his psychological set actually helps to cause the very effect which he expects. Doctors have long known that a patient's psychological set is an important factor in determining the effects of a drug on that patient. When a patient expects that a certain drug will make him tired, for example, or happy, or hungry, it will probably make him feel much the way he expects it to.

Thus, a physician who does not want to prescribe sleeping pills needlessly may prescribe placebos to some of his patients. These are pills which have no chemical effect on the body whatsoever. However, the fact that patients *believe* them to be sleeping pills usually makes placebos effective as such for many of them.

The term "setting" refers to the environment or social setting in which a person finds himself. This, too, is a significant factor in determining how a drug will affect a person. A drug may be taken while alone, in a friendly atmosphere, or in a hostile or unpleasant atmosphere. Even a powerful drug will produce considerably different effects when taken under these different settings.

Although these three factors, the drug, the set, and the setting, are each important in determining the effects of a drug, the importance of each factor often varies considerably. One of the major causes of this variation is the particular drug in question. The weaker the drug, the less dramatic will be its pharmacological effects on the body, and consequently, the greater will be the effects of set and setting.

Because marijuana is a relatively mild drug, the effects of set and setting are especially important in determining its effects. The person who expects to be greatly affected by marijuana will, in all probability, be greatly affected by it, while the skeptic may notice little or no effect at all. Similarly, the person who uses it in a comfortable social setting will be much more likely to find its effects pleasant than the one who uses it under less than optimal conditions.

Herein lies the greatest shortcoming of some of the laboratory experiments which have attempted to evaluate the effects of marijuana on humans. For set and setting in a laboratory cannot possibly be anything like what they are at a pot party or in one's home, the places where pot is most often smoked.

The best way, then, and perhaps the only way to understand the effects of marijuana is to smoke some at a pot party. Or, if this is too radical a proposal, talk to pot smokers. Although your conclusions may not be considered valid by some scientists, this is the only way, short of smoking it yourself, to achieve any genuine understanding of what pot does to the people who smoke it.

Asking a veteran pot smoker what it is like to be high will usually elicit the same answer he gives to the novice who asks, "How will I know when I'm high?" The usual answer is, "You'll just know." And the new user does, at some point, "just know" that he is high. If pressed further, the veteran will probably explain that he just feels good. His head feels funny—a tight, full, buzzing feeling which comes in waves, alternately building to a peak and receding.

It is a happy, friendly feeling, much like the high many people experience with alcohol. Like the drinker, the smoker often giggles and talks a great deal, and he also has somewhat dulled attention and a distorted sense of time.

Drs. Norman E. Zinberg and Andrew T. Weil of the Boston University School of Medicine, who have conducted recent research projects on marijuana, reported in *The New York Times* May 11, 1969, that unlike an alcohol high, pot users "appear to be able to compensate 100 per cent for the nonspecific adverse effects of ordinary doses on ordinary psychological performance." Even driving ability appears to be unaffected by marijuana use, according to a soon to be published study by the Washington State Department of Motor Vehicles and the University of Washington.

But best of all, the pot smokers brag, there is no marijuana hangover. Most smokers claim they even feel better the morning after than they did the morning before.

A question which is often raised by non-smokers is whether or not marijuana is an aphrodisiac. Medically, it is not. Marijuana generally produces one effect—euphoria. To the extent that a feeling of euphoria may increase some people's sexual excitation, it might be considered, for them, an aphrodisiac. But it is no more so than, say, a few martinis.

On the other hand, Dr. Hardin Jones, of the Donner Laboratory at the University of California at Berkeley, claims marijuana is a mild aphrodisiac because "it enhances sensitivity and makes a person more receptive to sensual stimuli . . ." But this condition, says Dr. Jones, "lasts only a short period of time, and chronic marijuana users find that sex activities without the drug are difficult and confusing."

Another question which is often raised concerns the mixing of marijuana and alcohol. Although there does not appear to be any experimental evidence available, it is known that few smokers drink whiskey while smoking. Whiskey, most claim, makes it much harder to become high on marijuana. Some smokers enjoy drinking sweet wine while smoking, however, insisting that wine makes for a better high. But this contention is widely debated among devotees, all trying to achieve the best high.

Real objects often appear slightly distorted to marijuana smokers, but extremely large doses are necessary to produce any true hallucinations. Even frequent pot smokers, "pot heads" as they are called, will probabley never experience any hallucinations, as it is highly unlikely that they will ever consume the large doses necessary to produce them. A smoker knows when he has smoked enough, and unlike many drinkers, he simply does not want more. Once high, he rarely continues smoking, even if there is pressure from others to do so.

As for bad effects, most smokers claim there are none, and medical experts generally tend to agree, although some do not. A notable opponent is the American Medical Association, which contends that frequent users are often lethargic and neglect their personal appearance, and, because the smoke is irritating, may suffer from respiratory disorders. Some other authorities claim even more serious disorders. The Massachusetts Medical Society, for one, lists among the dangers of marijuana use, acute intoxication, personality deterioration, and even possible psychosis in predisposed individuals.

Dr. Jones claims marijuana 1) is habit forming; 2) is addictive "with continued use;" 3) promotes a curiosity about harder drugs; 4) produces cumulative efforts; 5) interferes with normal perceptions; 6) disturbs the reference memory; 7) may bring on wholesale abandonment of goals and ambitions.

Most researchers, on the other hand, feel that marijuana is harmless, or at least relatively so. And their research findings seem to confirm their feelings. A monumental scientific study on marijuana was conducted at the behest of the late Mayor of New York, Fiorello LaGuardia. In 1938, Mayor LaGuardia and the New York Academy of Medicine appointed a Committee on Marijuana, consisting of twenty-eight leading physicians, psychiatrists, chemists, pharmacologists, and sociologists. The Committee concluded decisively in 1944, following its six years of research, that marijuana use:

Does not cause aggressiveness.
Is not at all related to crimes of violence.
Is not addictive.
Does not alter the individual's personality structure.
Does not cause mental or physical deterioration.
Has possibilities for considerable medical applications.

Although this study was completed twenty-five years ago, it is still the most comprehensive work in its field. The President's Crime Commission, in its report issued some two and a half years ago, came to the same general conclusions. A British Advisory Committee on Drug Dependence only a year ago found no evidence that pot smoking led either to violence or serious dependence.

After extensive experimentation, Drs. Zinberg and Weil concluded, as reported in their article in *The New York Times*, that "marijuana is a relatively harmless intoxicant." Other researchers, such as Dr. Max Fink of the New York Medical College, go even further. Dr. Fink was reported by the *Times* on February 2, 1969, to have contended that there are "no facts about marijuana being dangerous."

Why, then, was the Marijuana Tax Act of 1937 and much subsequent Federal and state legislation enacted, making marijuana illegal for individuals, and research into its medical uses virtually impossible? The primary reason appears to be a basic ignorance of the truth about marijuana. Although the LaGuardia Committee Report is well known scientifically, few people, legislators and law enforcement officials included, have ever read it, or even heard of it.

But what of the charge that easily ninety per cent of today's heroin addicts began by smoking marijuana? This charge is completely true. However, the conclusion which one is tempted to draw—that marijuana use leads to heroin use—cannot be substantiated. For although most heroin users began by smoking marijuana, the consensus of surveys of the number of pot smokers as compared with the number of heroin users leads to the common sense conclusion that the vast majority of marijuana users will never even try heroin. Dr. Roger O. Egeberg, the new health chief of the Department of Health, Education and Welfare, stated recently, "I don't personally think marijuana leads to heroin." It is extremely difficult to find a dealer who handles both drugs. Furthermore, although most heroin addicts were former pot heads, they also used alcohol, and for that matter, as children, milk. No one would contend that milk drinking leads to heroin addiction, yet to blame marijuana requires much the same logic.

It must be admitted, in fairness, that marijuana smokers are more likely than non-users to experiment with other drugs. But perhaps more significant is *why* this is likely to be the case. To a large extent, it appears to be attributable to the fact that most of what young people have heard about marijuana from adults is untrue. When they smoke marijuana they quickly find that they do not hallucinate, or steal cars, or become psychotic, or turn into "dope fiends." Why then, they feel, if adults are not to be believed about marijuana, should they know the score about other drugs?

About the worst that can honestly be said about marijuana at the present time is that its sale and possession are illegal. Mere possession is, in many places, a felony, which means that a conviction can have far reaching consequences. This is especially true for young people, whose entire lives may be affected by a single conviction.

So stringent are these laws that many authorities, including a considerable number of those who are critical of marijuana, are currently urging a relaxation of anti-marijuana laws, or at the least, a lessening of the criminal penalties which are being imposed. Among them are Dr. James L. Goddard, former director of the Food and Drug Administration, Dr. Roger Egeberg, and Dr. Stanley F. Yolles, director of the National Institute of Mental Health, who have stated that current criminal laws relating to marijuana are not only unrealistic, but also unenforceable. Representative Claude Pepper of Florida, and Senator Harold E. Hughes of Iowa are only two of a number of members of Congress who have assailed the severe legal penalties imposed on marijuana users. It is encouraging that many localities will probably soon follow the lead of Illinois, which recently reduced the charge for possession of marijuana from a felony to a misdemeanor; yet, even as this was happening, President Nixon was urging that current laws be made even tougher.

The anti-marijuana laws might logically seem to be a considerable deterrent to its use, but obviously this is not the case. Prohibition did not stop the sale and consumption of alcohol, and anti-marijuana laws are proving even less effective where pot is concerned. Rather, these laws are making marijuana considerably more attractive to today's youth, rebellious as many of them are. They are also putting much of the profits derived from its importation and sale directly into the hands of organized crime.

On the basis of these facts, what might be a rational approach to the marijuana problem?

The first step certainly appears to be a recognition that marijuana is not in itself a serious problem, or at least that it is a problem only insofar as contemporary American society makes it one.

But this problem, the one which society has created, is significant. And it is far more serious than the arrest records of the relatively few unlucky young marijuana smokers who are caught. For youngsters know that marijuana is not addictive, as are alcohol (pharmacologically, a drug) and barbiturates (which are more dangerously addictive than heroin). They know, too, that marijuana is considerably less habit forming than tobacco, another dangerous drug. Yet alcohol, barbiturates, and tobacco, as well as many other drugs, are legal, usually not even requiring medical supervision, because "the establishment" likes to use them. Only because the establishment does not use marijuana is it illegal.

The damage done by these attitudes on the part of many adults has had far-reaching effects on today's youth. For they see them as hypocrisy and as ignorance—two of the major causes of the phenomenon which is popularly called the "generation gap."

Legalizing marijuana, understanding what it is and treating it more realistically and more honestly, may not seem a large step toward bridging this gap. But it may be a large step toward a better understanding of the younger generation. And this, in turn, may be the first real step toward bridging the generation gap.

Section 9
Vocational Orientation and Adjustment

Whether we like it or not, members of our culture are evaluated and, to a large extent, develop their own feelings of personal worth in terms of employment and production. To be considered as worth something, a man must do something. Furthermore, the tangible evidence of success influences how one is perceived by others and how he comes to see himself. Automobiles, houses, clothes —all speak loudly concerning status. Although they certainly are not synonymous with personal worth they often are confused with it. Materialism is a fact of our existence, and a job is a necessity. Not only does it provide for sustenance, it provides an avenue for self-expression. One joins the culture with a job. He often is rejected, or at least feels himself to be so, without one.

This point of view is so thoroughly engrained in most of us that we may be unaware that we hold it as strongly as we do until someone challenges the beliefs on which it is based. Childs' article does this. It questions attitudes which have been fundamental to the American way of life for hundreds of years. These comprise the so-called work or production ethic that assesses an individual's worth and status in terms of his job and the type of goods or services which result.

Such a point of view was both necessary and effective in an economy of scarcity. Each man's effort was needed and the products it represented were essential. In an economy of abundance, however, the producer is less important than the consumer for the operation of the system. When the agents of production can more than meet the demand for goods, the operation of the economic system is facilitated by increasing demand rather than by increasing an already too large supply. Hence, we have programs designed not to produce any needed commodity but to keep people busy because it is good for them; because they would lead dissatisfied, aimless lives without work and because we are convinced that to receive money without working for it would create a nation of indolent, immoral, and degenerate people. Although it may be that this is true, it also may be that humans need, not work, but creative and stimulating activity and that the two are not necessarily synonymous. Perhaps one day we will be able to entrust the non-challenging, boring and tiring aspects of production to machines and free ourselves to enjoy more fully art, recreation, literature, and the like. Certainly we cannot pit men in production competition against machines. They were invented to serve rather than to defeat us.

In this respect, it is well for the person looking for employment to consider the personal service fields—details about which are excerpted from the *Manpower Report of the President*. Patterns of employment and job forecasts for the next decade indicate that automation is not apt to replace workers in the services and professional areas and that the demand can be expected to increase with the population. A change of emphasis from effectiveness in handling and working with material objects to expertise in dealing with people will be necessary. This is recognized by the last selection for this section. Interpersonal skills are not appreciably different whether one is dealing with others in the office, on the job, at home, or at the club.

The excerpt from the *Manpower Report of the President* is presented in hope that some students will be tempted, or encouraged if already tempted, to prepare for occupations in the fields where employment is most plentiful. However choice is more than a matter of job availability—it relates also to what one thinks of himself, as emphatically concluded by Korman. A person who has high self-esteem (HSE) can say, "I have the ability. I can become a member of the profession or occupation I choose." Facts of life in the employment world are not only objective statistics of employment and employment shortages but also subjective feelings of self-esteem.

It is not always easy to recognize the behaviors that get in the way of occupation, or other kinds of, adjustment. In the first place, the behaviors have been with us for a long time. In many instances we act habitually without really being aware of our actions and of their impact on others. In the second place self-defeating behaviors often function to protect the image a person has of himself. Hence they are not easy either to recognize or to change. For example, a person may project the blame for his own actions upon others; he may displace to a subordinate the feelings triggered by a superior, or he may make excuses and refuse to accept responsibility.

Almost always an individual's ways of defeating himself are more obvious to others. If he is to see the effect of his own actions with any objectivity at all, he must do so through the eyes of someone else. And for this, communication is essential. Listening to the feedback which others provide is a highly significant factor in behavioral improvement.

The student is likely to ask, "Where does self-esteem come from? Is it something we are born with?" The answer to the latter question is "No." Self-esteem, as suggested by earlier articles rather than those in this section, comes from parental treatment and school experiences. But that is about as unproductive an explanation as it would be to say that self-esteem is hereditary. Self-esteem comes also, as shown in the articles on pages 244, 302, 353, and others, from vigorous attack on today's challenges. Self-esteem is a gradual accretion of the day-after-day use of one's own talents.

Is the Work Ethic Realistic in an Age of Automation?

G. B. CHILDS

Professor of Secondary Education
and Associate Director of the Extension Division
University of Nebraska

American education is faced with a problem the very existence of which is recognized by but relatively few educators. Those who are aware of it do not agree on its true dimensions. However, awareness of the problem is growing and with increased awareness there is coming to be an increase in understanding.

The problem is how to deal with the impact of automation on our society.

That awareness of the problem exists is indicated by the considerable number of books, bulletins, and articles now being written about it and the increased attention the topic is receiving at educational meetings.

For example, the introductory paragraph in Grant Venn's book, *Man, Education, and Work*, reads as follows:

Technological change has, rather suddenly, thrown up a dramatic challenge to this nation's political, economic, social, and educational institutions. Though the full scope of this challenge may not be comprehended for years to come, its dimensions are now clear enough to call for a massive response on the part of American education. All levels of education, *and particularly post-secondary* education, must quickly move to assume greater responsibilities for preparing men and women for entry into the changed and changing world of technological work.

A second example comes from an address by Ralph Burhoe, executive officer of the American Academy of Arts and Sciences, at the 1964 Annual Conference of the Association for Higher Education. He said:

The revolutionary impact of science and its technologies on human culture in the past century is trivial compared with what it could be in the next century. New knowledge in the sciences is doubling every decade or two, and one has only to know a little about the potentialities of the technology

From *Phi Delta Kappan*, 46: 370–375, 1965.

of automation and computers to realize that equally as plausible as a successful trip to the moon is a society of men whose material needs are largely supplied by artificial brawn and artificial brains to carry on much of the labor and thinking that we now do.

These examples point up the seriousness of the problem that we face, a problem that can be resolved only by fundamental changes in some of our most deeply rooted convictions.

Until recently, no society has been able seriously to consider the possibility that it could reasonably expect to provide the members of that society with all the goods and services they need and want. The resultant philosophy of scarcity has had a profound effect upon the way people think.

Since the total amount of goods produced, even under optimum conditions, would be less than the amount needed, it was imperative that everyone contribute his effort to the end that total production would be as great as possible. Work, being necessary, came to have a very central significance in our social and economic thinking. Work is necessary, work is desirable, work is good.

It is through work that one receives economic rewards. This is the basis for our system of distributing economic goods. One works, he gets paid for working, and with the money he receives he buys goods and services.

The central nature of work in our society is manifest in other ways. It is through work that one achieves identity. One of the first questions we ask of a stranger is, "What do you do?" On the basis of the reply we assign him to some mental category. Work is one of the principal means by which the individual gains stature in the group.

Work provides the principal means of social interaction in our society and for large numbers of people offers the only means of establishing social contacts.

Work for some is pleasurable as a release from boredom; for others it provides an opportunity to do something constructive. Work can be therapeutic in providing relief from tension in familiar routines.

Work is so central to our lives that we take it for granted and our ideas about work are so deeply ingrained that we rarely examine them. Of course everyone should work and of course he should be paid for working. Work is good. Non-work is bad. He who works is good. He is industrious, provident, a contributor to society, a wage earner. He who does not work is improvident, shiftless, indolent, and a hindrance rather than an asset to society. While in our benevolence we cannot let him starve, neither should he receive more than a bare subsistence lest we encourage him in his slothful ways.

This is the way we tend, as a society, to think. And we think this way because to do so is compatible with a system which, with temporary dislocations, has operated successfully throughout economic history.

But the system will continue to work only if there is a reasonable likelihood that there are enough jobs to go around, that everyone who wants a job can find one, and that the incomes received from these jobs will allow the job holders to maintain a relatively high standard of living.

There are strong indications that the accepted concepts, under the increasing impact of automation, must be reviewed.

We are decreasingly successful in balancing the number of jobs with the number of job seekers. This is in part due to the increasing population. The 1963 Manpower Report of the President states, "The net growth of the labor force in the Sixties is expected to be about 13 million, more than 50 per cent greater than in the Fifties. Unless the growth of the new job opportunities is also accelerated, unemployment totals will rise."

Unfortunately, while the number of job seekers is increasing, there is an actual decline in the ability of the economy to provide job opportunities. Quoting again from the 1963 Manpower Report: "The annual rate of increase [of employment] in the last five years (0.9 per cent) was only about half the rate for the previous ten years. And the average number of new jobs added to nonfarm employment each year dropped from 900,000 during the first post-war decade to 485,000 in the more recent period."

The result of the operation of these two factors, an increase in the number of job seekers and a relative decline in the number of job opportunities, is of course unemployment.

According to the 1964 Manpower Report of the President, "About 4,200,000 persons were unemployed, on the average, during each month of 1963, 5.7 per cent of the civilian labor force as compared with 5.6 per cent in 1962. This was the sixth consecutive year that unemployment in the United States averaged over 5.5 per cent—far too high for far too long."

It is necessary, also, to note that while the unemployment

figures reported by the government serve as a useful index, they by no means tell the full story. In the first place, they take into account only the people actually seeking work at any given time. They do not count the people who have lost one job but have not yet begun to seek another.

Also, they do not take into account those who have become discouraged in the search for work and have given the cause up as hopeless. As the 1964 Manpower Report says, "Where opportunities are chronically limited, some persons give up a fruitless search for work and rely on charity or in other ways subsist without recourse to work—and no longer are included in the statistical measure of the unemployed." The report further states that by age 55, eight out of every 100 men are no longer seeking work. By age 60, the number has increased to 15 out of every 100.

But this condition of hopelessness is not confined to older workers. In 1964 Manpower Report says, "Nearly 350,000 young men under the age of 25 are neither in school nor in the labor force; they are not trying to find jobs and so are not counted as part of the labor force or included in the unemployment figures." These are young men who have reached the age where entry into the labor force is ordinarily an all-important purpose and who are part of a group that we have traditionally looked upon as one of our country's most important resources.

In addition to excluding people not actively seeking work, the unemployment figures exclude those who have failed to secure full-time jobs and are subsisting on part-time employment. In 1963, according to the 1964 Manpower Report, "another 2.6 million workers who wanted full-time employment could find only part-time work." When this number is added to the 4.2 million completely unemployed, the total constitutes 9 per cent of those seeking employment.

Even these figures do not point up the total dimensions of the problem. The 1964 Manpower Report says, "The pervasiveness of unemployment is only partially indicated by the average figures cited above. Although 4.2 million persons were unemployed on the average each month during 1963, an estimated total of 15 million persons were unemployed at some time during the year."

There is one more factor which must be considered in regard to the extent to which workers are no longer needed in our economy and that is in connection with those who hold jobs which are no longer necessary, a phenomenon popularly known as featherbedding. The Fund for the Republic states that "the under-employed (including those no longer needed and those on part-time jobs), according to some authorities, total as high as 25 per cent of the labor force."

The 1963 Manpower Report summarizes the point: "The economy not only has been unsuccessful in recent years in approaching full utilization of manpower resources but, in fact, has moved farther away from this objective."

The very heart of the present socio-economic system lies in the ability to balance the number of jobs with the number of job seekers. Not only are we failing to do it; there is strong evidence to suggest that we may be even less successful in the future.

Unfortunately, there are no clear-cut estimates of the rate at which automation is presently eliminating jobs or will eliminate them in the future. There is, however, some evidence which points to the extent of the problem.

J. Snyder, chairman and president of United States Industries, is frequently quoted as saying that automation is a major factor in eliminating more than 40,000 jobs a week. In addition, automation is displacing people indirectly, through "silent firings" of workers who would have been hired for jobs rendered unnecessary by automation.

The *Saturday Evening Post* for June 27–July 4, 1964, carried an article by David R. Jones entitled "Steel: The Giant Under Fire." It says in part, "With . . . improvements lopping· off the man-hours needed for steelmaking, the industry has already stopped the spiral of labor costs and actually reduced these costs by 7 per cent since 1961.

"Steelmakers say this is only the beginning. Only a couple of rolling mills so far are fully automated with computer controls, but as this spreads the savings will be fantastic. 'They're going to be able to run one of our mills with five guys and a computer instead of the 230 working there now,' confides one official."

Grant Venn has this to say about the displacement of workers from their jobs:

The impact of these devices [automated machines and computers] on the labor market has been profound. Automatic elevators have recently displaced 40,000 elevator operators in New York City alone. New equipment in the Census Bureau enabled 50 statisticians to do the work in 1960 that required 4,000 such people in 1950. The check-writing staff in the Treasury

Department has been reduced from 400 people to four. The airline flight engineer and the railroad fireman may soon disappear completely. . . . Mechanical cotton pickers have reduced farm jobs in lush Tulare County, California, from 25,000 to 17,000. Thirty thousand packing-house workers have been 'automated out' of their jobs in the past few years. Enormous machines have helped reduce employment in the coal fields from 415,000 in 1950 to 136,000 in 1962. While construction work has leaped 32 per cent since 1956, construction jobs have shown a 24 per cent decline.

Directing himself also to the employment problem created by the increase of automation, W. H. Ferry, vice-president of the Fund for the Republic, says,

The unemployed and under-employed are no longer almost exclusively the unskilled, the recent immigrants, the colored, the groups at the end of the economic scale, who have customarily borne the heaviest weight of economic slides. White-collar workers are joining this group as automation reaches the office. There is some reason for thinking that white-collar workers will after a few years comprise most of the growing category of technologically displaced. Herbert Simon has observed that by 1985 machines can do away with all of middle management, "if Americans want it that way."

Robert Theobald, in a bulletin published by the Center for the Study of Liberal Education for Adults quotes Ralph Bellman, a computer expert for the Rand Corporation, as follows:

Industrial automation has reached the point of no return: the pace will increase astronomically in the next decade. The scientific know-how to automate American industry almost completely is already available and is certain to be used.

Banks could cut their staffs in half easily by further automation; the steel and automotive industries could increase their use of automation a hundredfold.

Lower and middle management as well as production workers will be displaced for there will no longer be a need for decision making at that level.

Unemployment resulting from automation would be greater right now except that many industries are holding back—at a sacrifice to their profits . . . to avoid increasing the severity of the problem. Self-restraint on the part of industries cannot continue indefinitely.

Automation itself will produce few jobs.

Two per cent of the population—by implication the 2 per cent at the upper administrative and executive levels—will in the discernible future be able to produce all the goods and services needed to feed, clothe, and run our society with the aid of machines.

There is, of course, no way at present of knowing if Mr. Bellman is right or, if so, how rapidly his predictions will be realized. They lend support, however, to other of Mr. Ferry's conclusions. In a report titled "Caught on the Horn of Plenty" he said:

The United States is advancing rapidly into a national economy in which there will not be enough jobs of the conventional kind to go around. The acceleration of technology is responsible. A social and political crisis will be the result. Substitutes for such presently accepted goals as full employment will have to be found. Fresh definitions of the conceptions of work, leisure, abundance, and scarcity are needed. Economic theories adequate to an *industrial* revolution are not good enough for the conditions of the *scientific* revolution.

Suppose, however, that we ignore the predictions and consider only what we know. We know that the number of people in the age brackets into which most workers fall will increase greatly in the next few years. We know that there will be increasing advances in the areas of technology and of automation, with machines taking over more and more the tasks which people previously performed. We know also that for a number of years in a period of generally high prosperity the economy has been unable to provide full employment and that the rate of unemployment is on the increase. The 1963 Manpower Report says, "if in the next five years we provide new employment at the rate of the last five, by 1967 unemployment will come to over 5.5 million, or more than 7 per cent of the 1967 labor force."

On the basis of what we know, it is unreasonable to suppose that, in the years ahead, there will not be large numbers of people who will be unable to find jobs in the marketplace no matter how assiduously they seek them. We face the likelihood, indeed almost the certainty, that there will be increasing numbers of people who in their entire lives will not hold a market-supported job. Yet our society is based on the belief that those who are willing to work will be provided with an opportunity to work and thus achieve a decent standard of living.

This creates a problem unprecedented in history. There have been times when economic setbacks or economic adjustments have resulted in large-scale unemployment, but there was always in the background the generally held certainty that when the period of adjustment was over nearly full employment would again be realized. The scientific revolution now taking place does not permit us to look to the future with this same degree of certainty.

The problem for education created by this situation is one of great dimensions. While the work ethic is deeply rooted in our society, it is also true that people hold with great conviction the belief that "all men are created equal, that they are endowed by their Creator with certain unalienable rights, that among these are life, liberty, and the pursuit of happiness." As a society we do believe in the worth of the individual and the right of all men to live in such a way that they can retain their dignity and self-respect.

It is inconceivable that large numbers of people, nurtured on these beliefs, will be content to be regarded as worthless and to accept an economic existence at the subsistence level because the rules say that you must work to be important even when there are no jobs to be obtained no matter how hard you try. Even the least perceptive of men will recognize an inconsistency in this situation.

The problem facing us is one which only education can resolve. It cannot be resolved by those in political life. The person seeking political office, knowing how deep-seated the work ethic is, must seek election on promises to bend his every effort toward the achievement of full employment even should it become clear that full employment is no longer a realistic goal. The labor leader must necessarily work within the framework of concepts that labor, as a group, understands.

Neither is it the responsibility of the leader in business or industry to resolve the problem. While he might be concerned, or sympathetic, and quite willing to work toward the alleviation of the impact of automation, his primary concern must be in furthering the efficient operation of the business for which he is responsible.

Adlai Stevenson, in an address before the graduate faculty of the New School of Social Research on April 20, 1964, recognized the central role of education in a world of automation when he said:

The American standard of living for generations to come will be largely determined by how well the country walks the narrow and nervous border between automation's promise of either plenty or misery. . . . It is the educator, not the engineer, not the businessman, not the union official, not the bureaucrat, who must tell us how to keep our youngsters in school to prepare them for a productive life.

The task faced by education is a formidable one. Some authorities question whether Americans can accomodate themselves either to the idea or to the use of abundant leisure.

The first approach for educators is to acquaint themselves with the nature and dimensions of the problem created by automation. Much more study is required before we can know what the full impact of automation will be. This will require the best efforts of our economists, our social scientists, and our business researchers.

In the meantime, and increasingly as knowledge becomes available, we can acquaint people with what we do know. There can be little hope for smooth social adjustment to great economic change unless the general public is well informed of the nature of the situation which exists.

The second thing which education can do is to readjust its vocational sights. There is little purpose in preparing people for jobs which will no longer exist because of technological change. Jobs which require little skill or which are physically or mentally repetitive in nature will all but disappear.

Certainly vocational educators are aware of this problem and programs offered by schools do undergo change. It is true, however, that while many people are without employment, a considerable number of jobs requiring a high level of skill or highly specialized training remain unfilled. The rate of change in our vocational education programs must be accelerated to correct this imbalance. A general upgrading of vocational skills across the entire spectrum of the occupational world must be realized.

Help will be available from the federal government with this phase of the problem. The Manpower Development and Training Act of 1962, the Vocational Education Act of 1963, and the Economic Opportunities Act (the "anti-poverty bill") of 1964 are undoubtedly but forerunners of other attempts by the government to attack this problem.

Third, and undoubtedly most important if the indicated trends turn out to be realities, our educational system must prepare people to live in a world in which work will not hold the central position it has held in the past. It will be off to one side, contributing to society, but not dominating it. Concern will have to shift more to the development of people as decent human beings and less to preparing them to become cogs in an economic machine.

Preparation for freedom from toil in an economy of abundance where job opportunities are limited is just as reasonable an educational goal as preparation for toil in an economy of scarcity where the need exists for everyone to work. It's just that the idea takes some getting used to.

One problem is that our educational enterprise is not geared to the attainment of this new objective. Educators have not thought in these terms because up until recently there has been no occasion for them to do so. To devise an educational program which will prepare people for wise use of non-work time will require the best thought of all educators and social philosophers.

Also, there are few precedents to follow. Greece and Rome did produce high levels of civilization by releasing a small group from the necessity for work by creating a broad base of slave labor. Today we have the possibility of releasing a much larger group by using machines to do the "slave labor." It is this group, which Mr. Ferry refers to as the "liberated margin," about which we must be concerned. We must be concerned that society accept the new leisure as a good in itself. But we must also be concerned that our educational system prepare people to make wise use of this leisure; that they will lead useful lives, useful to themselves and also to society.

It will be argued that our economic system cannot support large numbers of people who do not contribute to the production of goods and services. But this is not the problem. Machines can produce much more efficiently than people. The output per man-hour has been rising rapidly as machines are increasingly used to aid production. There is reason to believe that productivity will increase even more rapidly in the future.

The problem is not one of production. We can produce the economic goods to give every person in our society the opportunity to live with dignity. The problem is one of distribution. It will do no good to increase the country's productive capacity through automation if in the process the ability of increasingly large numbers of people to have access to these goods is reduced because their incomes are related to work and there is no work.

This, together with the need to develop in people the capacity to live rich and full lives in a society characterized by leisure, is the problem that we face. It presents us with a tremendous challenge and a great opportunity. If we succeed, the world could truly be a wonderful place in which to live. If we fail, the results could be disastrous.

This is a challenge which educators should eagerly accept. Never before have we had the same opportunity to concentrate our efforts on the development in people of those characteristics which make them human. Gerard Piel, president and publisher of *The Scientific American,* in an address before the 1964 Conference of the Association for Higher Education, states this well:

No rate of expansion in the output (Gross National Product) of our economy can overtake the rate at which human beings are being displaced from the *productive* process. There are signs that people can be and are being displaced even faster from such *nonproductive* . . . functions as clerking and selling. Work that can be done by machines is either too dull, repetitive, demanding, dangerous, or degrading for human beings; it is better done by machines. The liberation of people from such servitude should set them free for the exercise of their more recognizably human capacities. Among these are learning, teaching, research, social and public service, the crafts, arts, and letters. Characteristically, these activities engage people in interaction with people rather than with things. Admittedly nonproductive, such activities are highly rewarding to the individuals so engaged and redound richly to the wealth of the nation.

Here, then, in the long and short perspective of this survey are the signs that history in America has entered on a new phase. In the America of the not so distant future we may expect to see wiser use of our capacity to generate abundance: the deployment of that capacity to the cherishing of our natural resources, to the building of more spacious cities, to attaining a happier accommodation of Americans to their bountiful environment, and so to the evocation and fulfillment of individual human endowment.

Inevitably, the transition to this latest phase of human evolution . . . must bring our values and our institutions into disarry and even into crisis. The acceleration of history has brought the old regime of scarcity to a sudden end in our time. . . . We are learning that, in our day, the well-being of each man can increase only with increases in the well-being of all men. The ancient habit of truth-seeking has disclosed the noblest and most generous aims to human life and placed in our hands the means to accomplish those ends here on earth.

Sir Julian Huxley states it more simply. He said, "Machines are going to do the jobs now. Man has got to learn to *live.*"

Manpower Demand and Supply in Professional Occupations
UNITED STATES DEPARTMENT OF LABOR

The manpower demand-and-supply situation in the professions has entered a period of rapid change. Employment requirements will continue to rise faster in professional and technical occupations than in any other major occupational group during the foreseeable future, as they have in recent decades. But the supply of college-educated personnel—the chief source of professional manpower—is mounting to unprecedented levels.

The great numbers of young people born in the years of extremely high birth rates after World War II are now attaining college graduation age. The proportions of young people completing college and going on to postgraduate study continue to rise. Largely for these reasons, the supply of new entrants into the professions is expected to catch up with the growing demand on an overall basis in the coming decade. Already, personnel shortages are much abated in some fields.

This does not mean, however, that manpower needs have been or will be met in all professions. On the contrary, personnel shortages are expected to persist in many specialties and local areas, unless training can be radically increased in shortage fields and better personnel utilization effected. In addition, there is need for more effective approaches to a most difficult problem—achieving an occupational and geographic allocation of personnel in line with economic and social needs, within a system which has as a basic tenet freedom of occupational and job choice for the individual.

This problem will assume major proportions in coming years in connection with women's choice of career fields. Teaching, the largest field of professional employment for women, is expected to grow much more slowly over the next decade than most other professions and to provide jobs for a far smaller proportion of women college graduates than in the past. Thus, the question arises whether, and by what means, women can be attracted in greater

From *Manpower Report of the President,* A Report on Manpower Requirements, Resources, Utilization, and Training, Washington, D.C.: U.S. Government Printing Office, 1970, pp. 161–189.

numbers to shortage fields, such as nursing and library science, where many women already work, and also afforded broader opportunity in professions now staffed predominantly by men.

In the scientific and engineering professions, challenges of a different kind but of even greater urgency lie ahead. Domestic problems whose speedy solution is essential to the national well-being—particularly those of environmental pollution and urban blight—will impose great new demands for scientific and engineering leadership and skills. They will require new interdisciplinary approaches, perhaps the evolution of new professions, and a new emphasis in scientific education on relevance to urgent national problems.

This chapter begins with an overview of the changing manpower supply-and-demand situation in prospect in professional and technical occupations as a whole, as indicated by the Department of Labor's projections. It then considers in greater detail the contrasting manpower development in teaching and the two other largest professional and technical fields—the natural sciences and engineering and the health occupations. The need to widen professional opportunities for women and Negroes and the persistent lag in higher education of youth—both white and black—from lower socioeconomic groups, are also discussed.

No short-cut solutions are or can be suggested to any of these problems. It will not be easy, for example, to achieve the greatly expanded training and improved utilization of health manpower urgently needed; nor to shift the focus of scientific education and research to domestic needs; nor to help the increasing numbers of women college graduates who will have to seek jobs outside teaching to elect and enter other career fields; nor to overcome the barriers which impede the professional preparation of Negroes and disadvantaged youth. Progress in solving these problems will require the combined efforts of many groups—not merely employers, professional educators, and agencies concerned with the support of graduate education but also, among others, the counselors and teachers who influence young people's educational aspirations and choice of career fields.

The changing manpower situation in the professions offers both a challenge and an opportunity. With foresighted planning, it should now be possible to move ahead much more rapidly in meeting immediate personnel shortages and long-range manpower needs in both established and emerging professional fields and, in so doing, to open career opportunities on a more equal basis to all able young people.

OVERALL TRENDS IN DEMAND AND SUPPLY

Manpower requirements in professional and technical occupations will be about half again as high in 1980 as in 1968, according to the Department of Labor's projections.[1] This expected increase in demand will involve an expansion in professional and technical employment greater in absolute numbers than has yet been achieved over any series of years—an average yearly gain of well over 400,000 in the work force in these occupations from 1968 to 1980, compared with an increase of about 335,000 per year from 1958 to 1968 and much lower figures in preceding decades. In percentage terms the growth rate is expected to slacken, however, to an annual average rate of slightly more than 4 percent, compared with nearly 5 percent from 1958 to 1968. And the differential in employment growth rates between professional and technical workers and the total work force will be much below the sixfold difference since World War II, though still quite large—probably at least 100 percent.

The Growing Demand for Professional Personnel

Employment requirements are expected to increase in nearly every professional and technical field, although at widely different rates. (See chart 21.) Among the most rapidly growing occupations will be those directly related to work with computers—for example, systems analyst and computer programer, in which employment may double or triple by 1980. Among the slowest growing will be elementary and secondary school teaching, where the rate of employment growth will be much below the average rate (25 percent) projected for all occupations. Personnel needs are leveling off in school teaching as a whole (for demographic reasons discussed later in this chapter), despite the continuing shortages of qualified

[1] The Department of Labor's projections referred to in this chapter were developed by the Bureau of Labor Statistics and are part of that Bureau's overall model of industrial and occupational projections to 1980.

teachers in some specialties and "difficult" areas, notably urban ghettos and rural poverty pockets.

These projections of the employment future are, of course, heavily influenced by the economic, political, and demographic assumptions which underlie them. First of all, the Department of Labor's manpower projections assume full employment, with the unemployment rate down to 3 percent in 1980. They also assume that the size of the Armed Forces and the pattern of defense expenditures in 1980 will reflect a "cold war," not a "hot war," situation; that scientific and technological advances will continue at about the same rapid rate as in the recent past; and that expenditures for research and development will go on increasing, although at a slower rate than in the late 1950's and early 1960's.

Employment requirements will rise much faster in some professions than in others

Percent growth in selected occupations, 1968–80

	0–25	25–50	50–75	75–100	100 or more
All occupations	→				
All professional and technical occupations		→			
Systems analysts					→
Programers					→
Psychologists				→	
Medical laboratory workers[1]				→	
Physicians			→		
Registered nurses			→		
Social workers			→		
Engineers		→			
Natural scientists		→			
College and university teachers[2]		→			
Engineering and science technicians		→			
Elementary school teachers	→				
Secondary school teachers	→				

[1] Includes technologists, technicians, and aides.
[2] Full-time, holding rank of instructor or above.
Source: Department of Labor.

The projected large increases in requirements for professional and technical manpower represent the growth in effective demand judged to be most probable under the indicated assumptions. They would provide enough highly trained workers for moderate continued advances in education, health care, housing, and other aspects of living standards for the growing population. An even more rapid growth in the professional work force would be essential, however, to achieve the kinds of overall improvement in the conditions of American life called for by a recent illustrative study of national "aspiration goals."[2] If the necessary priorities could be set and large resources committed to progress in the social and economic areas covered by these goals, the demand for professional manpower would mount much higher than is indicated by the requirements projections.

Another large source of manpower needs, not reflected in either the projections of employment requirements or the analysis of national goals, is the inevitable loss of personnel through deaths, retirements, and transfers to jobs outside the professional and technical category. In some of the slower growing professions (for example, elementary and secondary school teaching), replacement needs will be a greater source of job openings than new positions. In professional and technical occupations as a group, replacement needs are expected to create well over 4 million job openings during the 1968–80 period. Altogether, approximately 9.4 million new professional and technical workers will be needed in these 12 years to offset these personnel losses and meet the indicated employment growth requirements.

The Mounting Supply of College Graduates

The expansion in professional employment was built in the past, and will be conditioned in the future, on a sharp rise in the number of college graduates. Between 1958 and 1968, the number of bachelor's and first professional degrees increased by over 80 percent—from 363,000 to 667,000. These soaring graduation figures stemmed mainly from growth in the proportion of young people going to

[2] Initiated in 1960 by President Eisenhower's Commission on National Goals, the project was carried forward by the National Planning Association, which made a special study for the Department of Labor of the manpower implications of the various goals. See Leonard A. Lecht, *Manpower Needs for National Goals in the 1970's* (New York: Frederick A. Praeger, 1969).

college, because of far-reaching economic and social pressures and motivations. The college-age population rose only moderately. In the decade ahead, the mounting demand for a college education will be coupled with sharp increases in the numbers of college-age youth, and graduations will continue to rise rapidly.

According to projections by the U.S. Office of Education, the number of bachelor's and first professional degrees awarded by the Nation's colleges and universities will probably rise from 667,000 in 1968 to about 1.1 million in 1980, or by roughly 60 percent. Besides allowing for expected increases in the college-age population, these projections assume a continuance of recent upward trends in college enrollment and graduation rates.

An even more rapid increase in graduate than in baccalaureate degrees is shown by the Office of Education projections, on the assumption that the proportion of college graduates obtaining higher degrees will continue to rise in line with recent trends. The growth in the number of master's degrees awarded is projected at well over 100 percent between 1968 and 1980; in Ph.D.'s, at more than 150 percent. (See table 1.)

TABLE 1

Actual and Projected Earned Degrees, 1948 to 1980

Academic year ending June 30	Bachelor's and first professional degrees	Master's degrees	Ph.D.'s
1948	271,000	42,000	4,200
1958	363,000	65,000	8,900
1968	667,000	177,000	23,100
1969	755,000	189,000	26,100
1970	772,000	211,000	29,000
1975	928,000	302,000	45,600
1980	1,074,000	382,000	59,600

Source: Department of Health, Education, and Welfare, Office of Education.

These increases in graduate degrees will be contingent, however, on greatly expanded support of higher education and also on a continued rise in the proportion of college graduates electing to pursue postgraduate studies. Areas of Federal Government policy which will be particularly influential are Selective Service and the magnitude of financial aid to graduate education through guaranteed loans and other means.

Impact of Selective Service. With respect to Selective Service, the projections assume that the long-range effect on graduate education will be quite limited—that students who have to interrupt or postpone their graduate education for military service will generally resume it after completing their tours of duty.

The change in Selective Service regulations in February 1968, sharply restricting deferments for postbaccalaureate study, was not followed by the sharp decline in graduate enrollments in the 1968–69 school year which many educators had feared. But neither did enrollments increase to the levels projected before the change in draft regulations. In some fields—including law, history, and psychology—the number of men students dropped significantly. The decline was concentrated among first-year graduate students, who, for a variety of reasons, were the most likely to be eligible for the draft and refused deferments.

Draft calls continued to have some impact on enrollments in the first term of the 1969–70 academic year (for which fall enrollment data were not yet available when this report was prepared). However, an Executive order issued by the President as of October 1, 1969, permitted graduate students ordered for induction to complete the full academic year (not merely one semester as under previous regulations) before reporting for duty. In addition, enactment in November 1969 of legislation requested by the President permitting the selection of draft-eligible men for callup on a random basis, instead of on the oldest-first basis, ended any disproportionate concentration of callups among present and potential graduate students. The new random selection system became effective in January 1970.

The impact of military service on graduate enrollments should diminish still more from 1970–71 onward, as the students who were drafted complete the required 2 years of service and begin to return to the universities. However, the full effect of the return flow will probably not be felt until the following year.

From a long-run point of view, a much more important question is how many veterans decide to enter or reenter postgraduate study. Veterans' educational benefits will be available to help them do this, but under present legislation these benefits are not large enough to cover more than a fraction of total tuition and living costs.[3] The number of veterans who find it economically desirable

[3] See the discussion of Services to Returning Veterans in the chapter on New Developments in Manpower Programs.

and practicable to pursue graduate education will therefore depend heavily on the availability of guaranteed loans and other types of assistance. Thus, the problem of graduate education of veterans is part of the broader issue of the level of graduate student support—which is likely to be much more important than Selective Service callups in determining the future supply of highly educated manpower.

Graduate Student Support. Greatly increased Federal support for graduate students during the 1960's has been an important element in converting the large potential demand for such education into mounting graduate enrollments and degree completions. In 1968–69 the number of predoctoral fellowships and traineeships awarded by the Federal agencies with the largest graduate student support programs reached a peak of about 54,000. (See table 2.) In addition, many research assistantships were made possible by federally supported research programs, and other awards and traineeships were

TABLE 2
Students with Federally Supported
Predoctoral Fellowships and Traineeships, 1961–70

Academic year ending June 30	Number of students aided (thousands)	Percent of all full-time graduate enrollments
1961	9.4	7.5
1962	13.3	10.0
1963	15.6	10.5
1964	17.7	10.8
1965	22.3	11.3
1966	28.3	12.3
1967	41.7	16.1
1968	53.6	17.8
1969	53.7	16.9
1970	45.1	(²)

[1] Preliminary.
[2] Not available.

Note: Includes data on predoctoral fellowships and traineeships awarded by the Atomic Energy Commission, National Aeronautics and Space Administration, National Science Foundation, Department of Housing and Urban Development, Department of Interior, and Department of Health, Education, and Welfare's Office of Education, Public Health Service, and Social and Rehabilitation Service. Data for National Institutes of Health and National Institute of Mental Health training grants are not available.

Source: Unpublished data from Federal Interagency Committee on Education.

offered. Altogether, the number of graduate students aided that year was probably close to 100,000.

During the past 2 years, however, the upward trend in graduate student support has halted, as table 2 indicates. After rising from slightly under 10,000 in 1960–61 to about 54,000 in 1967–68, the number of students supported first leveled off and then fell sharply —to about 45,000 in the current academic year. The growth in Federal funds for research in colleges and universities recently leveled off also; in view of the sharply rising costs, this has undoubtedly meant a reduction in new research assistantships. Furthermore, opportunities for college teaching assistantships are now becoming scarce, both because of the greater availability of fully qualified Ph.D.'s and because colleges are reevaluating the use of graduate students for undergraduate teaching assignments.

Prospective Supply-and-Demand Relationships

A rough appraisal of the overall supply-and-demand situation ahead for college-educated personnel is possible on the basis of the Department of Labor's projections. In this appraisal, allowance has been made not only for the expected supply of college graduates and the projected requirements for professional and technical manpower but also for two other key factors—what proportion of new college graduates will enter professional and kindred occupations and, conversely, what proportion of the job openings in these fields will be filled by these graduates.

Only about two-thirds of all employed college graduates were in professional and kindred occupations in 1968. This proportion has not changed significantly in recent years—because the rising demand for college-trained personnel in the professions has been offset by equivalent increases in requirements in other fields of work, especially administrative and managerial occupations. The projections assume that this situation will persist—that the proportion of college graduates going into professional and technical work will still be about 2 out of 3 in 1980. On the other hand, the proportion of professional and technical jobs filled by people with a college education is expected to increase slightly (from three-fifths in 1968 to two-thirds in 1980), reflecting both the growing numbers of college graduates available and the rising educational demands of many jobs.

With allowance for all these factors, it appears that a rough overall balance between the supply of college-educated personnel and the requirements for them in professional and other fields is possible and likely—that demand and supply will each total somewhat more than 10 million over the 1968–80 period as a whole.[4] But emphatically, this does not mean that supply and demand will be in balance in all professional fields or all areas of the country. A more adequate overall supply of professional manpower is in sight than has been available in most years since World War II. Yet qualified personnel will continue to be scarce in some specialties and local areas, unless more effective efforts, including better occupational guidance, can be made to increase the numbers of new entrants and reentrants in these fields and to improve personnel utilization.

Furthermore, large commitments of national resources to meeting the country's domestic needs, such as are suggested by the National Goals project, could mean intensified and more widespread personnel shortages. Though the aspiration goals developed through this project are only one illustration of possible social objectives for the Nation, it is significant that the anticipated supply of college graduates would fall short of that required for full attainment of all the goals. Choices would have to be made and priorities set—for example, among the goals in education, health care, housing, urban renewal, and research and development. The priorities decided upon could have a tremendous impact on the types and numbers of professional and technical workers needed, as well as on employment requirements in other occupations.

Because of the crucial relation of Government policy decisions to both the prospective supply of Ph.D.'s and the demand for them in different specialties, future supply-and-demand relationships in this segment of the professional work force have peculiar uncertainty. Another imponderable factor is the capacity of these highly trained personnel to themselves generate new and added demands for their services, through their own scientific breakthroughs.

The country's urgent domestic problems should evoke creative

[4] Most of the supply of college-educated workers will be new college graduates. However, the supply projections also include an allowance for entrance into the labor force of persons who graduated from college before 1968 but who were neither working nor looking for work in that year. Some will be reentrants (that is, persons employed in some previous year); others will be delayed entrants without work experience. Immigrants are still another source of college-trained manpower and the major source of men entrants other than new degree recipients.

efforts from specialists in both established and emerging fields and lead to demands for top-trained personnel which cannot yet be assessed in specific terms. Some shifts in the patterns of specialization of Ph.D.'s, as of workers with lower levels of training, are very likely, however.

An effective attack on problems such as urban blight and environmental pollution will require knowledge and techniques from many fields, including the natural and social sciences and the health professions. This implies the use of interdisciplinary teams working on the problems, or the development of interdisciplinary specialties, or—most probably—both. The National Science Board has urged the establishment of social problem research institutes that will enable engineers and natural, social, and behavioral scientists and other professional workers to pool their insights and techniques for effective social engineering.

Another innovative approach—recommended by the Behavioral and Social Sciences Survey Committee, set up jointly by the National Academy of Sciences and the Social Science Research Council—is the establishment of postgraduate schools of applied behavioral science. These schools would give their students both a broad background of social science knowledge and techniques for applying this knowledge to immediate, critical problems.

Developments of this kind will surely change professional functions and the content of professional education. Taken together, they are also likely to add to the total demand for highly educated personnel.

NATURAL SCIENTISTS AND ENGINEERS

Past Trends and Short-Run Shifts in Manpower Requirements

The rapid growth in scientific and technical employment since World War II has been at once the source and the outcome of this country's advancing civilian and defense technology. Employment of natural scientists and engineers reached 1½ million in 1968, about double the number (740,000) in 1953. (See chart 22.) This was an even more rapid gain than in professional and technical employment as a whole (which rose by about 90 percent during the same period).

Great increases in Federal expenditures for research and development—primarily for the defense, atomic energy, space, and health programs—were a major factor in this expansion in scientific and engineering employment. Government R&D expenditures rose from a little over $3 billion in 1953 to $17 billion in 1968. But employment of scientists and engineers also rose in R&D projects financed by private industry, and in production, teaching, and other activities financed only in small part by the Government. The proportion of scientists and engineers in R&D work is still no more than 36 percent (as compared with 30 percent in 1953).

In the last several years, however, growth in scientific and engineering employment has been restricted. The Federal budgetary situation has led to a leveling off in Government expenditures for research and development. And in view of rising costs in research and development, as in other sectors of the economy, a leveling off in funds can mean a reduction in R&D staffs.

As early as 1968, there was evidence of a loosening supply-and-demand situation among R&D scientists and engineers. A survey of Ph.D.'s in private industry, conducted by the Department of Labor for the National Science Foundation,[5] found no general shortage of personnel with this top level of education, although qualified workers could not be recruited in some developing specialties. According to the company officials interviewed, supply-and-demand conditions for Ph.D.'s in science and engineering were more in balance in 1968 than they had been in the preceding few years. The respondents generally attributed this change to the reduced growth in Federal Government support for R&D projects in colleges and universities.[6]

Since that time, there has been further restriction of Federal R&D funds—with an impact on manpower requirements not measured as yet. In addition, it is anticipated that the ending or sharp reduction of the Vietnam war would bring cutbacks in defense research and production and lead to layoffs of scientists and engineers in some localities.

[5] "Ph.D. Scientists and Engineers in Private Industry, 1968–80" (Washington: Department of Labor, Bureau of Labor Statistics, in press).

[6] Federal support for research and development in colleges and universities (excluding federally funded research centers) increased by 20 percent a year from 1959 through 1966 but by only 3 percent a year during the following 3-year period (in current dollars). In constant dollars (adjusted for cost increases), Federal support for research and development in these institutions actually declined over the past 3 years.

Employment of scientists and engineers has grown steadily in research and development and other activities

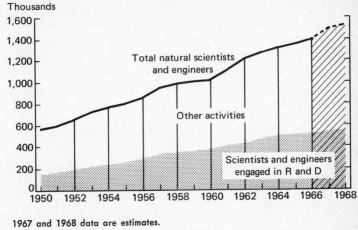

1967 and 1968 data are estimates.
Source: Department of Labor.

Short-term fluctuations in employment opportunities are almost inevitable in science and engineering, in view of these professions' heavy involvement in "mission-oriented" Government work. In 1963 and 1964, for example, defense contract changes and cutbacks led to some layoffs of engineers and other technical personnel, particularly by aerospace companies.

Following these layoffs, many of the displaced scientists and engineers, especially the older ones, had prolonged periods of unemployment. The engineers without college degrees, who presumably had achieved professional status through experience in a particular kind of defense work, were often unable to qualify for other professional engineering jobs.[7]

The serious adjustment problems which engineers and scientists

[7] See papers submitted at a National Symposium on Stabilization of Engineering and Scientific Employment in Industry at San Jose State College, San Jose, Calif., sponsored by the Manpower Research Group, Center for Interdisciplinary Studies, in November 1966: (1) Dr. R. P. Loomba, "Results of the San Francisco Bay Area Layoff Study"; (2) Dr. Joseph D. Mooney, "Results of the Boston Layoff Study"; (3) Mr. Robert Brandwein, "Results of the Boeing Layoff Study with Special Reference to Engineers/Scientists"; (4) Dr. Walter E. Langway, "Results of the Long Island Defense Layoff Study with Special Reference to Engineers and Scientists"; (5) Dr. Leslie Fishman, "Results of the Martin (Denver, Colo.) Layoff Study with Special Reference to Professionals."

—particularly those who are highly specialized and narrowly trained or in the older age groups—could face following defense cutbacks are thus underlined by past experience. They raise an issue which must be faced in planning for such cutbacks—namely, what are and should be the responsibilities of the Government and the employers involved for helping the displaced workers to obtain—and, if necessary, train for and move to—new positions commensurate with their education and previous experience.

The Long-Term Outlook

In the longer view, however, the outlook is for strong growth in requirements for scientists and engineers. New dimensions of demand for scientific and engineering talents in solving urgent national problems are clearly discernible. These relate to the cumulative impact on the environment of population growth; increasingly rapid depletion of natural resources; and the effect of chemical, biological, and nuclear contaminants. New techniques will be needed not merely to prevent environmental pollution but also to reverse destroying processes (such as those occurring in Lake Erie). In addition, a range of innovative techniques will be required to uncover additional resources in terrestrial depths and in the sea and to develop new substitute materials and new ways of processing ores and other raw materials not now economically usable.

These present and emerging needs will pose great demands for new specialties as well as old. At the same time, the more traditional demands upon the scientific and engineering professions will show further growth. Breakthroughs in science continue, each opening new opportunities and leading to new ventures in exploration and exploitation of natural resources. These discoveries are proceeding not only in the physical sciences but even more notably in the biological sciences and in the hybrid fields interpenetrating both. In engineering, added demands will be imposed for the development of increasingly complex products and processes and increasing automation in all sectors of the economy.

How large the future requirements for engineers and scientists could be is suggested by two sets of projections already drawn upon in this chapter. One is the National Goals project, which developed "aspiration goals" aimed at overall improvement in the quality of American life. To fully achieve the goals in all 16 specified areas by

1975 would require over 2 million engineers,[8] nearly twice the number employed in 1968. This figure can be regarded as an upper limit on requirements, unrealistically high in terms of the country's resources though not in terms of social and economic aspirations.

The Department of Labor's projections of manpower requirements also indicate rapid long-term growth in demand for engineers and scientists, though not at the pace called for by the National Goals study.

The increase in effective demand for engineers is projected at about 40 percent between 1968 and 1980. This would be a somewhat slower growth than occurred in the profession between 1958 and 1968, when the number of engineers rose from about 725,000 to 1.1 million. In the natural sciences, the projected growth in requirements would be slightly higher than that in engineering—about 50 percent. Here again, however, the growth rate is expected to be slower from 1968 to 1980 than during the preceding decade, when employment of scientists rose from 270,000 to 465,000.

On the average, about 74,000 new engineers would be needed annually during the 1968–80 period to make possible the projected employment growth and replace those who die, retire, or transfer to other fields of work. Not all of these new recruits will come from the engineering schools, however. In the past, many workers other than new engineering graduates have entered the profession (including technicians upgraded to engineering jobs, immigrants, and graduates of college departments other than engineering). On the other hand, many engineering graduates have gone into other occupations. If these partly offsetting factors continue in line with past trends, an average of approximately 45,000 engineering graduates would be needed annually to meet projected requirements.

In comparison, projections of earned degrees by the U.S. Office of Education indicate an annual average of about 43,000 new engineering graduates with bachelor's degrees over the 1968–80 period—implying that over the period as a whole, the supply of engineers will fall slightly short of demand.

This shortfall could be intensified if, as seems possible, more workers without engineering degrees find it increasingly difficult to enter professional engineering positions (because of the increasing knowledge requirements). The supply of new engineers could also be significantly reduced by sharp declines (not reflected in the gradua-

8 Lecht, op. cit., p. 147.

tion projections) in the proportion of college students entering and completing engineering curriculums. Although starting salaries for engineering graduates have been and are substantially above the average for all men college graduates, the proportion obtaining degrees in engineering has decreased substantially (from about 15 percent in 1958 to 10 percent in 1968).

The Commission on Human Resources and Advanced Education analyzed this problem, in the context of its finding that the supply of new engineering graduates would probably fall short of the demand over the next decade—and to a greater degree than is suggested by the Department of Labor's projections. The Commission emphasized the high dropout rates from engineering schools and concluded that:

The [shortage] problem is not so much one of initially attracting more students to a career in engineering; at the beginning of high school, there are more than enough potential aspirants to fill all the demands projected a decade hence. . . . Rather, the problem is one of retaining a larger portion of the highly qualified students who enter the program. Whatever the causes of attrition—an overly rigorous curriculum, ineffective teaching practices, failure to hold the student's interest in an engineering career— engineering schools would do well to follow the example of medical schools, which have recently made intensive studies of factors affecting retention of students in their programs.[9]

In the natural sciences as a whole, personnel supply and demand is expected to be in better balance than in engineering over the 1968–80 period, according to the Department of Labor's projections. The number of new scientists needed annually to staff additional positions and meet replacement needs is likely to average somewhat under 45,000. This would include an average of over 20,000 openings per year for physical scientists, over 15,000 for biological scientists, and close to 8,000 for mathematicians. Recent enrollment trends suggest that the numbers of new graduates should be adequate to meet these demands on an overall basis.

Undoubtedly, labor shortages will occur in some specialties and subfields as new programs are developed, e.g., in marine sciences and in the control of environmental pollution. But the general shortage of trained scientific manpower should be at an end—offer-

[9] John K. Folger, Helen S. Astin, and Alan E. Bayer, "Human Resources and Higher Education: Staff Report of the Commission on Human Resources and Advanced Education" (New York: Russell Sage Foundation, in press).

ing the opportunity to focus less on the numbers of students and more on the evolution of new fields of study directed toward urgent national problems.

TEACHERS

Elementary and Secondary School Teachers

The shortage of elementary and secondary school teachers, a source of wide concern in communities throughout the country as recently as 1966–1967, was much reduced in 1969. However, the need for teachers has not been fully met as yet in rural schools or in city slums, nor in specialized teaching assignments of many kinds.

According to a survey by the National Education Association in midsummer 1969, only two of the 49 participating States reported substantial shortages of teacher applicants. Three years before, 20 States had such shortages. In 1969, for the first time in many years, two States reported an excess of applicants over requirements. Nevertheless, about a fourth of the States had a moderate overall shortage of applicants, and nearly all of them reported difficulty in filling vacancies in rural schools. A considerable number of school systems in small communities and in the central cities of large metropolitan areas also reported some difficulties in obtaining needed teachers, mainly for elementary school and specialized teaching assignments. Shortages of mathematics teachers and of qualified teachers for special and remedial education, work with the disadvantaged, industrial arts, and vocational education were emphasized particularly. Teachers of physical and natural sciences and women teachers of health and physical education were also in short supply.

By far the most important reason for the sudden improvement in the teacher supply-and-demand situation was the sharp increase in the number of new college graduates at the end of the 1960's, when college graduations began to reflect the upsurge in births after World War II. At the same time, the demand for new school teachers, which had climbed persistently over most of the postwar period, turned downward (as is shown in table 3). Here again, the cause was demographic—a marked slowing of the growth in the school-age population, leading to an actual decrease in the numbers of additional teaching positions required annually.

TABLE 3

Actual and Projected Demand for New Elementary and Secondary School
Teachers Compared With Number of College Graduates, 1963 to 1978

[Numbers in thousands]

Year	Total teachers employed	Number required for growth and replacement	New teachers required[1]	Total number of college graduates[2]	New teachers required as percent of graduates
1963	1,806	209	157	444	35
1965	1,951	208	156	530	29
1967	2,097	222	166	591	28
1968	2,178	239	179	667	27
1969	2,225	209	157	755	21
1970	2,245	190	142–190	772	18–25
1973	2,286	189	142–189	859	17–22
1975	2,304	183	137–183	928	15–20
1978	2,334	187	140–187	1,029	14–18

Figures for 1963–1969 represent 75 percent of the total number required for growth and replacement, with a conservative allowance for the numbers of teachers who returned to the profession. Since the return flow of experienced teachers may possibly decline during the 1970's, the ranges shown indicate the numbers and percents of new teachers that would be required with a return flow ranging from 0 to 25 percent.

[2] Includes bachelor's and first professional degrees awarded.

Source: Based on data from the Department of Health, Education, and Welfare, Office of Education.

During the 1970's, school enrollments will level off even more. In the elementary schools, an actual decline in enrollments is anticipated up to 1976 (reflecting the recent decline in births). After that, elementary enrollments will probably begin to climb slowly again, but in 1980 they are expected to be still slightly below their 1968 level. Secondary school enrollments will continue to rise, but much less rapidly than in recent years—probably by only about 14 percent over the 1968–1980 period, or only about one-fifth as fast as during the preceding 12 years.

This leveling off in enrollments implies only a small demand for new teachers to staff added positions. But there is a second large source of demand for new teachers—namely, replacement requirements. During the 1970's, as in the recent past, many more new teachers will be required to replace those who retire, die, or leave the profession for other reasons than will be needed to handle increased enrollments. Altogether, requirements for new teachers to staff new positions and fill vacancies are expected to total about 2.3 million over the 1968–1980 period—roughly 1.1 million in elementary and 1.2 million in secondary schools. Compared with the numbers of college graduates expected in coming years, this will be a relatively limited demand.

Projections have been made of the potential supply-and-demand situation, based on the demand figures just presented, Office of Education projections of college graduations, and two other key assumptions—first, that the reentry of former teachers (mostly married women) into the professions will continue in line with past trends and, second and most critical, that the proportion of young people entering teaching will also be much the same as in the recent past.

On this basis, the number of new college graduates seeking to enter elementary school teaching during the 1968–1980 period as a whole could be nearly double the projected demand, and the number seeking secondary school positions could be nearly 75 percent above requirements. Whether any such oversupply of teacher candidates actually develops will depend in large measure on how well young people are apprised of the employment outlook in teaching and the extent to which they act as "economic men" (and women) in their choice of profession.

Another way of looking at the situation is to estimate year by year what proportion of the new college graduates could be readily absorbed in teaching. As table 3 shows, this proportion is steadily declining. In 1963, the demand for new college graduates for teaching positions amounted to about 35 percent of the total number awarded bachelor's and first professional degrees. By 1969, this proportion had fallen to little more than 20 percent. It will go on decreasing rapidly—unless, as is most unlikely, the schools stop hiring experienced teachers wishing to return to the profession and take on only new graduates. Thus the outlook is for an increasing overall supply of personnel in the profession as the 1970's proceed.

Nevertheless, some teacher shortages will persist indefinitely unless stronger remedial action is taken. As the National Education Association's 1969 survey indicated, recruitment difficulties continue in schools in urban ghettos and depressed rural areas, where both working and living conditions are hard. Yet progress can be made in recruiting adequate teaching staffs for such areas if these conditions are improved and if sufficient incentives are offered. New York City, for example, has achieved a sudden shift from a shortage to a surplus of teacher candidates, despite the recent upheavals in the city school system. One important reason for the city's unusual success in meeting teacher requirements in the fall of 1969 was undoubtedly its adoption of "a salary scale unsurpassed in any major city."[10]

Shortages of teachers with training in mathematics, science, and other specialties in demand in private industry may continue also, unless teacher salaries become more competitive with those offered outside education. In addition, in rapidly growing specialties, such as preschool education and the education of handicapped children, there may be continued difficulty in finding qualified staff, unless student teachers are given special incentives to train in these fields.

The generally increasing supply of teachers offers school systems the opportunity to concentrate on meeting special needs of these kinds, and also to staff broader programs in elementary and secondary education which have been postponed or curtailed during the long period of teacher shortages. For example, many more teachers are needed—and could be available within a very few years—for enlarged vocational education programs, so that all high school students not bound for college could get occupational training. Additional teachers are also needed for large-scale expansion of remedial education programs, beginning in the elementary grades; this could help greatly to remedy educational deficiencies, raise reading levels, and cut school dropout rates.

The shocking amount of illiteracy still prevalent in the population was recently emphasized by the Comissioner of Education. The Office of Education is now planning a campaign to promote the "Right to Read" for everyone—which will, of course, increase the demand for teachers skilled in literacy training.[11]

Specialized education for handicapped children is still another area of need for expanded services and additional teachers. In 1968, only two-fifths of the Nation's school-age children with visual, hearing, speech, emotional, mental, or other handicaps requiring special educational services were being provided with such services.[12] In kindergarten and preschool education, the need for program and staff expansion is probably even greater—and under-

---

[10] "Year of School Opportunity," *New York Times,* Sept. 8, 1969.

[11] "The Right to Read—Target for the 70's," an address by James E. Allen, Jr., Assistant Secretary for Education and U.S. Commissioner of Education, before the 1969 Annual Convention of the National Association of State Boards of Education, Century Plaza Hotel, Los Angeles, Calif., Sept. 23, 1969.

[12] "1968 Commissioner's Assessment Report on the State of the Education Profession" (Washington: U.S. Office of Education, in press).

lined by findings as to the critical importance of very early schooling for disadvantaged children.

It must be emphasized that all these areas of teaching require special training. Prospective teachers must receive the kinds of preparation essential for employment in these and other areas of unmet need, if the abundant teacher supply in prospect is to be used effectively in attacking the country's critical educational problems.

College and University Teachers

In higher education, the outlook is for an early easing of the acute shortages of faculty that characterized most of the 1960's. Continued improvement in teacher supply is expected, relative to demand, as the numbers of graduate-degree recipients (the major source of college faculty) grow more rapidly than enrollments (the key demand factor).

Both past and prospective trends in college enrollments broadly reflect several years later the same patterns of change as have occurred in secondary and, before that, elementary school enrollments. In the mid-1960's, the great numbers of young people born after World War II began to move out of the high schools and to inundate the colleges—in numbers increased not only by strictly demographic factors but also by the steadily rising demand for a college education. In contrast, college faculties of the 1960's were drawn mainly from age groups born before World War II, when birth rates were low.

In the 1970's, this situation will tend to reverse itself. College enrollments will go on increasing, but more slowly, while the numbers of graduates earning master's and doctoral degrees—the main source of candidates for college teaching posts—will mount sharply.

According to projections by the U.S. Office of Education, the total number of full-time college teachers for degree programs will be about 415,000 in 1980, compared to 298,000 in 1968.[13] This would represent an average annual increase of only 3 percent during the 12-year period, about one-third the annual rate of increase in college teachers from 1960 to 1968. The slow increase in college enrollments will be the main factor restricting faculty growth.

---

[13] These estimates exclude part-time and junior teaching staff; Ph.D.'s engaged part time in college teaching usually have primary positions of other types and so are counted as employed in other occupations.

Nearly as many new recruits to college teaching (close to 100,000 between 1968 and 1980) will be needed to replace teachers who die or retire as will be required for the projected slow expansion in teaching staffs in degree-credit programs. Altogether, requirements for new college teachers from these two sources are likely to total about 200,000 during the 12-year period.

To meet this demand for new teachers, colleges and universities will be able to draw on record numbers of new graduates with advanced degrees. The Office of Education projections of such degrees (shown in table 1 earlier in this chapter) indicate a rise of more than 150 percent in Ph.D.'s between 1968 and 1980, and a doubling in master's degrees—on the assumption that the proportions of college graduates obtaining these degrees will continue to rise as in the recent past. However, as already indicated, an increase in doctoral degrees of the magnitude projected will be contingent on many uncertain factors, including large increases in both public and private support of graduate education. In addition, the proportion of college graduates going on to postgraduate study could be influenced by economic factors not operative before the last couple of years—notably, the shifting supply-and-demand situation in college teaching and the recent leveling off in R&D programs.

These caveats, however, relate only to the magnitude of the impending increases in advanced degrees in the arts and sciences, not to the near certainty that such increases will occur. A growing supply of new Ph.D. recipients can be expected during the 1970's, and with it a strengthening of the faculties in many institutions which have recently been unable to recruit the desired numbers of faculty members with Ph.D.'s.

Though progress in remedying this situation should start immediately, it will take a considerable number of years to really satisfy the demand for Ph.D.'s in college faculties. According to projections by the National Science Foundation covering the 1970's:

The requirements for science doctorates will greately exceed the probable supply available to the colleges and universities throughout most of the period. By the end of the decade the growing numbers of doctorates will begin to approximate the academic requirements, and after 1975 the situation should be greatly improved.

The point at which the demand for Ph.D.'s for college teaching will be fully met in each major discipline (in the sense that 90 percent or more of the faculty members in the field in 4-year institutions will have Ph.D.'s) has been estimated by the Commission on Human Resources and Advanced Education. Their projections suggest that this point may be reached in the mid-1970's in the physical sciences and mathematics but not until the 1980's in other fields (probably even later in the humanities).[14]

The greater availability of Ph.D.'s should be helpful in improving the quality of education at institutions that fall significantly below the national average in the proportion of faculty members holding this degree. Among these are many of the predominantly Negro colleges and universities, which face shortages of Ph.D.'s of crisis proportions because of the recruitment of their faculty by predominantly white institutions. They will need substantial aid in improving their salaries and facilities in order to benefit from the expected greater supply of such highly trained teachers.

For teachers without Ph.D. degrees, demand is expected to drop sharply in college degree-credit programs.[15] However, such teachers should find many opportunities in the expanding nondegree programs and in special fields, including extension, mail, and TV teaching. Furthermore, in junior and community colleges, an aptitude for teaching and work-related experience may be valued more highly for many positions, even in degree-credit courses, than the research-oriented doctorate. Special teacher-preparation programs to meet the needs of these colleges are increasing in number, and the generally favorable supply situation in college teaching should aid their further development.

HEALTH MANPOWER

The demand for medical care has outstripped the Nation's health manpower resources throughout the 1960's. Shortages of physicians and nurses, the subject of wide public concern, have led to rapidly increased utilization of auxiliary health workers and thus to intensified labor shortages in the supporting health occupations. Personnel shortages are acute in virtually all segments of the "health services

---

14 Folger, Astin, and Bayer, op. cit.

15 The master's degree is, to an increasing extent, the desired level of preparation for teaching in elementary and secondary schools. This accounts in part for both increased demand for persons with the degree and the greater numbers earning it.

industry"—hospitals, nursing homes, offices of medical practitioners, and medical laboratories.

What these shortages mean in terms of inadequate health care was well described by the National Advisory Commission on Health Manpower. In discussing the "health crisis" in the country, the Commission said in part:

. . . The indicators of such a crisis are evident to us as Commission members and private citizens: long delays to see a physician for routine care; lengthy periods spent in the well-named "waiting room," and then hurried and sometimes impersonal attention in a limited appointment time; difficulty in obtaining care on nights and weekends, except through hospital emergency rooms; . . . reduction of hospital services because of a lack of nurses; . . . uneven distribution of care, as indicated by the health statistics of the rural poor, urban ghetto dwellers, migrant workers, and other minority groups, which occasionally resemble the health statistics of a developing country. . . .[16]

Yet employment has increased rapidly in the health services industry—by 50 percent between 1960 and 1968, to a total of about 4.3 million in the latter year.[17] The rate of employment growth in the industry was more than three times the average rate for the economy as a whole in the same period, and it will probably continue to outpace the employment rise in most other industries in the decade ahead.

The growth in demand for health services is impelled by forces which generate unremitting pressure to expand these services to the limit of available manpower or beyond. Large population growth and increasing public awareness of the value of health care are basic factors underlying the steadily rising demand for health services. The expansion of health insurance coverage has helped to finance this care; a large majority of Americans now have some coverage under health insurance plans. Government subsidies for hospital construction have also raised manpower requirements, as did the past increases in Government support of medical research, which has recently leveled off. The Medicare program and the expansion of health services for low-income groups under the amended Social

[16] *Report of the National Advisory Commission on Health Manpower* (Washington: U.S. Government Printing Office, 1967), p. 1.

[17] Includes private wage and salary, government, self-employed, and unpaid family workers. Another 400,000 workers in health occupations are employed outside the health service industry—many in the health units of manufacturing and trade establishments, in pharmacies, and in research.

Security Act (Medicaid) have been added sources of demand. Rapid development of biomedical science and technology, by enlarging the scope of medical services, has further increased the demand for these services.

Efforts are already underway to ease the shortages of professional and supporting personnel through special training programs and better utilization of the existing supply of qualified health manpower. But much further progress in these and other directions (discussed below) will be essential to meet health manpower requirements.

Physicians

The shortage of physicians to meet the Nation's urgent needs for medical services is probably as high as 50,000, according to estimates by the U.S. Public Health Service. Compared to the 295,000 physicians professionally active in the United States in 1968,[18] this represents a shortage rate of about 15 percent.

The scarcity of physicians would be more serious were it not for the contributions of physicians who are graduates of foreign medical schools. In 1967, about 40,000 physicians, comprising 14 percent of all those active in the country, were graduates of such schools.

Aided by the influx of foreign-trained physicians, the ratio of physicians to population has inched upward recently, after remaining the same for many years (about 150 per 100,000 people). The ratio is much higher in some geographic areas than others, however. There were nearly 60 percent more physicians per 100,000 people in the Northeastern States than in the Southern States in 1967. In all regions, shortages of doctors are worse in small communities than in metropolitan areas. Even within a city or metropolitan area, the ratio of physicians to population may be much lower in poor ghetto neighborhoods than in adjoining, more affluent ones.

Because of the sharply increased numbers of physicians in specialized practice and in teaching, research, and administration, the number providing family health services has dropped. In 1950, there were 76 general practitioners, internists, and pediatricians per 100,000 population. By 1967, this ratio had fallen to 49 per 100,000.

A very rapid continued growth in requirements for physicians is projected. The total number of physicians required for patient

[18] Includes M.D.'s only.

care, medical research, and teaching is expected to be about 50 percent above the 1968 employment level by 1980.[19]

This needed growth in the profession—added to the demand for doctors to replace those who die, retire, or stop practicing for other reasons—implies a need for about 20,000 new physicians a year between 1968 and 1980. Yet if medical schools were to continue operating at their current capacity, and if about the same number of immigrant physicians were licensed as in recent years (about 1,800 a year between 1964 and 1968),[20] only about 10,000 doctors would join the work force each year—half the projected requirement.

To meet the implied deficit in supply is far beyond the capacity of the country's medical schools, which had a 1968–69 graduating class of only about 8,200. Some expansion in medical school enrollments is anticipated, with assistance under the Health Professions Educational Assistance Act of 1963; projects already funded or approved should raise their enrollments from about 36,000 to 46,000 between 1968 and 1980. On the other hand, the leveling off in Federal funds for medical research may hamper expansion in medical schools and could even lead to reductions in graduations in some cases, though the chief impact will be on the levels of research and postgraduate training.

Further expansion of the medical schools is an important objective. But in medicine, the lead time required to set up a training institution and for this institution's first entering class to qualify for practice may extend for 8 to 12 years. The best hope of quick, substantial improvement in the availability of medical services lies in large-scale efforts to achieve better utilization and allocation of the present supply of physicians and of those who will shortly enter practice.

Registered Nurses

The shortage of registered nurses has probably received even more attention than that of physicians. Although the number of regis-

---

[19] The projections of requirements (by the Bureau of Labor Statistics) represent estimates of the effective demand for workers in 1980, developed under a specific set of assumptions, rather than estimates of manpower needs to provide specific standards or goals of medical care. For an illustration of this latter concept and the expanded personnel requirements it could imply, see Lecht, op. cit., pp. 74–76.

[20] *Journal of the American Medical Association,* State Board issue, June 16, 1969.

tered nurses has been increasing at a faster rate than the population—rising from 282 per 100,000 population in 1960 to 338 per 100,000 in 1969—it has not kept pace with the increasing demand for health care services. A joint American Hospital Association–Public Health Service study in 1966 indicated an urgent need for 57,000 additional nurses to serve hospital patients. The overall shortage of nurses is considerably more severe.

In nursing as in medicine, personnel shortages tend to be much more acute in small cities and rural areas than in large metropolitan areas and in some localities within the same city than in others. They are also worse in some regions than others. For example, the ratio of nurses to population is about half as large in the South as in the Northeast.

Requirements for registered nurses in 1980 are likely to be about 1½ times the 660,000 employed in 1968, according to the Department of Labor's projections. In addition, replacement needs will be heavy (an estimated 260,000 between 1968 and 1980), since nursing, like other fields staffed predominantly by women, loses large numbers each year because of family responsibilities.[21]

Altogether, the number of new nurses required to fill additional positions and to meet replacement needs will probably average more than 50,000 a year. In comparison, about 42,000 nurses graduated from nursing schools during 1968, and not all of them entered nursing. Thus, to meet projected requirements, the annual number of graduates must be increased by at least 8,000 a year between 1968 and 1980.

This increase should be within reach, in view of the projected rapid growth in college enrollments. However, most of the increase will be in graduates of 2-year (associate degree) college nursing programs, with the balance coming from 4-year programs. The proportion of new nurses trained in 3-year diploma programs in hospitals, the traditional form of nursing education, is likely to decline slowly.

Nursing schools should be aided in attracting more students by the changing labor market situation in the largest "women's profession"—school teaching (as discussed in the section on Women

---

[21] This replacement figure is a net one—the difference between the total number of nurses expected to leave the work force because of death or retirement or for other reasons between 1968 and 1980 (roughly 450,000) and the number of inactive nurses expected to return to the profession (estimated at 190,000).

Professional Workers). How many more young women actually enter nurse training will depend heavily, however, on the extent of improvement in salaries and working conditions in the profession. Nursing has been at a disadvantage in the past because pay standards and conditions of employment have lagged behind those in many other fields of work with less demanding educational and training requirements. But nursing salaries have been upgraded significantly in many areas during the last few years. If this trend continues and other sources of dissatisfaction among nurses are reduced, these developments should help not only to bring more young people into the profession but also to reduce turnover and encourage former nurses to return to duty.

Other Health Occupations

As employment demand has increased in the established health professions, many new occupations have emerged. There is a strong trend toward increased diversification and specialization of health care services, impelled by both shortages of top professional personnel and advances in medicine and technology.

Many of the allied and supporting occupations now have personnel shortages also. According to surveys of hospitals and nursing homes in 1966, provision of optimum care services would require at least a third more workers than were then employed in the following specialties: Occupational, physical, and recreational therapy; clinical social work; speech pathology; and audiology. There was similar need for additional inhalation therapists in hospitals and medical record librarians in nursing homes.

In some of the allied health occupations, the personnel shortages can be traced to limited training facilities. Many have high turnover rates, in part because of the large numbers of young women employed. But low pay and poor working conditions are also prevalent. Workers in the lower level occupations such as nurse aide, orderly, and hospital attendants have only recently been brought under the Fair Labor Standards Act; their minimum hourly wage, increased from $1.30 to $1.45 as of February 1, 1970, will not catch up with the $1.60 minimum for workers previously covered by the law until 1971. Most employees of hospitals and nursing homes lack collective bargaining rights. Most hospital workers also lack unemployment insurance protection, though UI coverage would be extended to them by the amendments to the UI law recommended by the Administration and passed by the House of Representatives during 1969.[22] Many are not covered by State workmen's compensation laws. The rate of improvement in their employment conditions will largely determine the rate of progress possible in attracting more workers into supporting health occupations.

Action to Relieve Personnel Shortages

In seeking solutions to the health manpower crisis, experts place increasing emphasis on improving the utilization of health workers. Some have even suggested that there would be no shortage of health manpower if the existing work force were properly utilized. Others believe that the development of additional manpower should be given primary emphasis. There is little doubt that progress must be made in both directions to meet health manpower needs.

Developing Health Manpower. The education and training required for the approximately 200 health occupations range from a few weeks of on-the-job training for a nurse aide to 10 or more years of post-high school education and training for a physician.

The education and training of health manpower at all levels have been aided by a number of Federal programs, including those authorized by the Health Professions Educational Assistance Act of 1963, Nurse Training Act of 1964, Allied Health Professions Personnel Training Act of 1966, Health Manpower Act of 1968, Vocational Education Act of 1963, Manpower Development and Training Act of 1962, and the Economic Opportunity Act of 1964.

Much study and innovation are also taking place with respect to the education of health workers. Medical schools are working with colleges to shorten the total period of education for some of their students. They are also examining postdoctoral (internship and residency) training in search of ways to shorten the training period. Progress is also being made in increasing the size of medical school classes.

Nursing education is being studied by the National Commission for the Study of Nursing and Nursing Education. The trend is toward less dependence on diploma schools of nursing based in

[22] For a discussion of this proposed legislation, see the chapter on Income Maintenance and Work Incentives.

hospitals and more on academic programs in universities, colleges, and junior colleges. There is considerable debate, however, concerning the effects of these education changes on both the quantity and quality of professional nursing personnel.

New schools of allied health professions are being developed, with core curriculums common to occupations with related skills. Health service institutions are experimenting with career ladder and upgrading programs. The problem, however, with many of these innovations is that they are isolated from the mainstream of medical practice and are not seriously evaluated by concerned professional and employer groups.

Despite the efforts to expand educational and training opportunities for health workers, the number of such opportunities is still inadequate to meet the demand. But this is only one of several reasons for the insufficient supply of health workers. Except for the medical professions, health occupations have generally lower status and levels of pay than many other career fields requiring no more education and training. In addition, opportunities for promotion and career mobility are often restricted by licensing laws, accrediting standards, problems associated with professional liability and negligence, professional societies, and tradition. To move from one occupational level to the next higher, an individual often has to leave his job and complete a prescribed amount of classroom training, regardless of what he may have learned on the job. By contrast, in many other fields of work, individuals can move up a career ladder through on-the-job training and experience.

To develop the required manpower and compete with other industries for badly needed workers, the health industry must be able to offer rewarding careers, particularly for young people entering the labor force. In addition, the industry needs to make much greater efforts to develop jobs for poor people with relatively little formal education, thus utilizing their abilities to supplement scarce manpower resources. Neighborhood Health Centers, established by the Office of Economic Opportunity to train and employ the disadvantaged in supporting health occupations and in new kinds of positions such as family health worker, have demonstrated the value of this approach.

The Department of Labor has several training programs aimed at developing better promotional opportunities for health workers. The Nurse Aid to LPN (Licensed Practical Nurse) Upgrading Program is sponsored by the New York City Department of Hospitals and the American Federation of State, County, and Municipal Employees. This program enables a nurse aide to become an LPN through a combination of on-the-job and classroom training without leaving her job to attend an LPN school. It shows that personnel needs can be met by upgrading workers already in the health industry, rather than by the more common practice of recruiting inexperienced workers for formal training programs.

Another effort to build on existing skills is being made by the Santa Clara County Medical Society in California. Under a contract with the Department of Labor, this physicians' association is developing training, education, and employment opportunities for 50 former medical corpsmen released from military service. The objective is to show how their military health training and experience can be utilized to meet civilian ends.

Utilization of Health Manpower. Interest in improving the utilization and efficiency of the work force is growing in the health industry for two reasons—recognition that not enough health workers will be trained in the near future to meet the population's health service needs, and concern over the rising cost of health services.

The National Advisory Commission on Health Manpower stated the need to improve utilization in the following terms:

There is a crisis in American health care. The intuition of the average citizen has foundation in fact. He senses the contradiction of increasing employment of health manpower and decreasing personal attention to patients. The crisis, however, is not simply one of numbers. It is true that substantially increased numbers of health manpower will be needed over time. But if additional personnel are employed in the present manner and within the present patterns and "systems" of care, they will not avert, or even perhaps alleviate, the crisis. Unless we improve the system through which health care is provided, care will continue to become less satisfactory, even though there are massive increases in cost and in numbers of health personnel.[23]

The pressing need to improve physicians' productivity has led a number of medical societies to explore medical practices and to identify functions that might be handled by properly trained, though less highly educated, health workers. The American Pediatric Society, for example, has found that a good many tasks per-

[23] National Advisory Commission on Health Manpower, op. cit., p. 2.

formed by pediatricians could be handled by pediatric assistants. Another experiment underway is the Duke University physician's assistant program designed to develop "an intermediate level professional with sophisticated and extensive technical capabilities" to perform many tasks that are now the sole province of the physician and thus free the physician for more demanding services.

In hospitals, where manpower utilization has been of special concern, the Department of Labor has sponsored several studies. One of these, by Northeastern University, involved analysis of hiring standards and tasks performed in 22 paramedical occupations in Boston hospitals. The researchers are to recommend changes in hiring standards and work assignments designed to improve personnel utilization and the quantity and quality of patient care.[24]

The Health Services Mobility Study, being conducted by the Research Foundation of the City University of New York, will cover all occupational categories in New York City hospitals and include the development of new methods for examining hospital tasks. This study is funded jointly by the Office of Economic Opportunity and the Departments of Labor and Health, Education, and Welfare.

Another approach to improving the efficiency of health workers is through the use of new, labor-saving technology. The many technological advances made so far in the health field have been aimed chiefly at new and improved services and have usually increased, rather than decreased, manpower requirements. Technology could, however, be used to a much greater extent than at present for the purpose of increasing the productivity of health workers.[25]

Suggested Areas of Action. Following are some areas in which action is already underway and should be pursued further by the health services industry in an effort to alleviate its critical manpower shortages.

The *attractiveness of health careers* must be improved. Sufficient numbers of workers will be attracted to health occupations only if the pay scales and fringe benefits are improved and made more competitive with those in other fields; if new opportunities for

[24] "Restructuring Paramedical Occupations" (Boston: Northeastern University, under contract with the Department of Labor, Manpower Administration, in process).

[25] For a discussion of this subject, see *Technology and Manpower in the Health Service Industry, 1965–75* (Washington: Department of Labor, Manpower Administration, 1967), Manpower Research Bulletin No. 14.

promotion and career advancement are opened; and if artificial standards for hiring and promotion are removed.

The health industry should take more aggressive action to *improve the utilization* of the health work force. Task analysis techniques can be used to arrive at a more rational organization of work tasks and to assist in the development of new kinds of positions as assistants to professional workers in short supply. More extensive use can be made of in-service training programs to develop maximum competence in the health work force. New technology, improved building design, and better layout of work areas should be used to increase worker efficiency.

There is a great need for *effective planning and coordination* of health manpower activities at all levels—local, State, and national. The health industry is fragmented into a large number of independent health care institutions, private practitioners, and group practices. This structure results in an unusual diversity of occupations and training methods and makes it very difficult for the industry to develop systematic plans for meeting its manpower needs. The major organizations and institutions in the health industry should work closely together in planning an industrywide approach to manpower development and utilization.

Efforts are already underway to develop comprehensive health services. A great variety of local, State, and regional organizations have been established, with assistance from the Department of Health, Education, and Welfare, to develop systematic plans and improve the delivery of health care. These organizations are becoming increasingly aware of manpower problems. They should work closely with the local and State committees of the Cooperative Area Manpower Planning System (CAMPS) in identifying health manpower needs and in developing education and training programs.[26]

WIDENING ACCESS TO PROFESSIONAL EDUCATION AND EMPLOYMENT

So far in this chapter, attention has centered on questions of manpower demand and supply, and on the measures needed to strengthen the resources of professional personnel and to improve

[26] See the chapter on New Developments in Manpower Programs for a discussion of CAMPS.

their utilization, especially in the health fields. These are matters of national concern, in view of the critical role of the professions in dealing with the full spectrum of domestic and international problems.

The professions can be looked at from quite a different point of view, however—as a field of employment opportunity near the top of the economic and social ladder. Similarly, higher education can and should be viewed not merely as a source of highly trained manpower but as a key to personal development and rewarding employment, which should be open on an equal basis to all groups in American society.

Accordingly, the remainder of this chapter is concerned with three groups which face special obstacles in preparing for and achieving professional employment—people of low socioeconomic status, Negroes, and women workers. The brief discussions of these overlapping groups point to quite different problems but suggest a common need—for intensified efforts to insure that people of potential ability are not barred from opportunity for professional development.

Higher Education for Youth in Low-Income Groups

The second Commission on Human Resources and Advanced Education recently concluded, after an extensive study, that there has been, since the 1954 report of the first Commission of Human Resources, "a gratifying decrease in the percentage of able young people who fail to enter college."[27] But the Commission also found that:

To a substantial fraction of young people, access to higher education and to the professional and specialized fields becomes gradually but firmly closed by a complex set of barriers associated with low socioeconomic status. . . .

One of the analyses shows that of 100 male high school graduates who stood high in scholastic ability and who came from homes of high socioeconomic level, 66 graduated from college and 26 continued immediately in graduate or professional schools. In contrast, of 100 male high school graduates of comparable scholastic ability, but from homes of low socioeconomic status, only 37 graduates from college and only 15 continued immediately in graduate or professional schools.[28]

[27] Folger, Astin, and Bayer, op. cit.
[28] Ibid.

The wide variation in enrollment rates among States also suggests that a great many capable young people still do not enter college. In 1965, according to U.S. Office of Education data, a little over half the high school graduates in the country went to college; the percentage ranged from as high as two-thirds of the graduates in States with a well-developed system of free or inexpensive higher education to as low as one-third in States with less adequate facilities for higher education. For poor and even for middle-class young people in States without readily accessible and inexpensive opportunities for higher education, lack of funds was obviously a major deterrent to college attendance.

Junior and Community Colleges. The accelerated development of community and junior colleges is one of the most important avenues to higher education of young people from low-income families.

The growth of 2-year institutions has been phenomenal during the past decade. By 1969, 1,000 of these institutions enrolled 2 million students, triple the 1960 figures. As the Carnegie Commission on Higher Education reported:

The advance of the junior college movement over the last decade has greatly increased the accessibility of higher education to hundreds of thousands of American youth. A further extension of the growing junior college movement will continue this trend.

Colleges to serve inner-city youth are urgently required in many of our major metropolitan areas. To meet this need, it is estimated that 500 community colleges and 50 urban four-year colleges should be established by 1976.[29]

Two-year institutions are perhaps more responsive to the needs of poor and disadvantaged youth than are other institutions of higher education. They enroll more than a third of all black college students, for example, and facilitate attendance for students from low-income backgrounds in three basic ways: They are academically accessible; tuition fees are low and in some cases nonexistent; and admission policies are relatively "open." In California, for example, admission to the ninety-two 2-year-public institutions is granted to anyone who can benefit from the instruction.

The impact that junior colleges can have on enrollment rates is

[29] Carnegie Commission on Higher Education, *Quality and Equality: New Levels of Federal Responsibility for Higher Education,* A Special Report and Recommendations by the Commission, December 1968 (Hightstown, N.J.: McGraw-Hill Book Co., 1968), pp. 36–37.

shown by a study which compared college attendance rates in cities with and without community colleges but with similar demographic and industrial characteristics. In cities without colleges, only 22 percent of the able students from families in the lower socioeconomic group managed to go on to higher education. By contrast, the college attendance rate of such young people was more than twice as high in cities with a community college. In all cities, however, the proportion going to college was still far lower among such young people than among those in the same ability group but from high socioeconomic backgrounds. About 80 percent of the latter went to college, regardless of the availability of local college opportunities.[30]

It must be recognized that the chances of graduating from college are much less for students who start out in a junior college than for those able to enroll in a 4-year institution. Nearly three-fourths of all junior and community college students are in academic programs, from which those with satisfactory records may transfer to the third year in a 4-year institution, but only about 1 out of every 3 actually makes such a transfer. However, 1 or 2 years in occupationally oriented junior college programs can have great economic value for young people from low-income families—by preparing them for technical and other occupations, many of which have personnel shortages and offer the possibility of later promotions up the occupational ladder. Strengthening of such occupational programs should be greatly aided as progress is made in implementing the 1968 amendments to the Vocational Education Act.

Besides equipping youth for entry positions, community colleges are facilitating this upgrading process. Many of them are establishing career education programs, offering advanced training in such fields as the allied health occupations, education, and engineering technology. By helping these institutions expand career education opportunities, the Nation can help to develop and utilize the potential of many disadvantaged young people who would otherwise lack access to higher level jobs.[31]

[30] L. L. Medsker and J. W. Trent, *The Influence of Different Types of Public Higher Institutions on College Attendance from Varying Socioeconomic and Ability Levels* (Berkeley: Center for Research and Development in Higher Education, University of California, 1965), U.S. Office of Education Project No. 438.

[31] Special help is being given to disadvantaged people in preparing for subprofessional careers through the Department of Labor's New Careers program. For a discussion of the program see the chapter on New Developments in Manpower Programs.

Financial Aid to Undergraduate Students. Great progress in over-coming financial barriers to college attendance has also been made through Federal student aid programs.

The College Work-Study Program initiated under the Economic Opportunity Act of 1964 provides aid in the form of on-campus and off-campus jobs. The Educational Opportunity Grant Program established under the Higher Education Act of 1965 provides outright grants to exceptionally needy students. In addition, there are two loan programs—first, the loan program established by the pioneering National Defense Education Act of 1958 and, second, the Guaranteed Loan Program set up under the Higher Education Act of 1965. The NDEA program provides direct Government loans to needy college students and offers partial forgiveness of the loans to those who enter the teaching profession. The Guaranteed Loan Program, which aids many young people from middle-income families, helps students obtain loans from participating financial institutions; the Federal Government guarantees the loans and contributes part of the interest payment.

Roughly 1 out of 4 undergraduates were aided by one or more of these Federal programs in 1968–69. The largest number of beneficiaries obtained guaranteed loans. Students benefiting from the other programs total more than 770,000—including nearly 280,000 from low-income families who received Educational Opportunity Grants. (See table 4.)

TABLE 4

College Undergraduates Receiving Support Under Federal Student Aid Programs, Academic Years 1967–70[1]

[Thousands]

Program	Actual, 1967–68	Estimated	
		1968–69	1969–70
Total[2]	1,173	1,559	1,657
Guaranteed Loan Program[3]	515	787	924
National Defense student loans[3]	429	442	398
Educational Opportunity Grant Program	202	271	281
College Work-Study Program[3]	314	395	375

[1] Does not include programs under the Veterans Administration.

[2] Items do not add to totals because some students received support under more than one program.

[3] Graduate students are eligible to participate in these programs. The number in the Guaranteed Loan Program is believed to be substantial; the number in work-study and National Defense student loan programs, small.

Source: Department of Health, Education, and Welfare, Office of Education.

The magnitude of these aid programs may suggest that virtually all young people who need help in going to college can get it. This is by no means true, however. Relatively few students in junior colleges—only about 6 percent of the total in 1968–69—receive Federal aid. For this reason, a large proportion of them must combine work and study—a necessity which may well contribute to their high college dropout rates. If real progress is to be made in the higher education and professional preparation of poor young people —many of them members of minority groups—continued and enlarged financial aid programs will certainly be needed.

Professional Education and Employment of Negroes

For Negroes who obtain a college education, employment opportunities have widened dramatically since the mid-1960's in both professional and managerial occupations. The proportion of men college graduates holding professional jobs is now substantially higher for Negroes than for whites. In managerial occupations the proportion of Negro male graduates has more than doubled in just 4 years (1964–68). College-educated Negro women have also made professional progress. (See table 5.)

With this opening of doors in professional and managerial employment has come a sharp increase in college attendance by

TABLE 5

Employed College Graduates in Professional and Managerial Occupations, by Sex and Color, 1964 and 1968

[Numbers in thousands]

| | Men | | | | Women | |
| | | Percent in professional and managerial occupations | | | | Percent in professional and managerial occuptions |
Year and color	Number	Total	Profes- sional	Mana- gerial	Number	
1964						
White	5,158	81.8	60.0	21.8	2,107	82.7
Negro and other races	266	69.2	63.9	5.3	166	72.9
1968						
White	6,076	83.5	60.2	23.3	2,599	85.5
Negro and other races	279	80.3	68.8	11.5	280	82.1

Negro youth. This rise in enrollments has been stimulated by recognition of the increased economic and social value of college education for Negroes. It has been made possible by the development of community colleges and the financial aid to poor students (just discussed), coupled with the admission of many more Negroes to predominantly white institutions and a variety of other efforts to assist their college education. The proportion of Negro youth graduating from college is far below that of white youth, however, and the number receiving graduate degrees continues to be unsatisfactorily small.

There are, of course, many reasons for this—beginning with the deprived cultural background and inadequate primary and secondary education of large numbers of Negro youth. But encouraging progress has already been made in helping young people to overcome these obstacles. It is of national importance that this progress continue—that whatever needs to be done is done to insure greater expansion in the undergraduate and postgraduate education of Negro youth. As the recent employment record indicates, one of the most certain routes to satisfactory occupational and economic gains by Negroes lies in this direction.

Recent Employment Gains. Four out of every five Negro college graduates were in professional and managerial occupations in 1969. The proportion was much the same for men and women (80 and 82 percent) and was much higher for both than in 1964. The movement of Negro graduates into professional and administrative jobs was so rapid during this period that it nearly closed the gap between the proportion of Negro and white graduates in these fields of work.

These figures, of course, apply only to college graduates—who still represent a much smaller proportion of Negro than of white workers (7 percent compared with 13 percent in 1968). They are also overall figures, giving no indication of the grades of the positions held by Negro and white professional workers of the same age and educational level. Nevertheless, the sharply rising proportion of college-educated Negroes in these high-status, relatively high-paid fields of work has great significance. It testifies to the effective change in industry and Government hiring policies in the years since the 1964 Civil Rights Act.

Prior to 1964, few recruiters visited predominantly Negro colleges in search of talent, but that year marked the turning point. The number of recruiters who made their first trips to these institutions in the spring of 1964 are a small fraction of the number who visit them today. Placement officials at Howard University, in Washington, D.C., for example, reported that about 600 companies sent representatives in 1967–68 to recruit from a class of about 1,000 seniors, and in 1969 recruitment efforts at the university were even greater. Florida A&M University in Tallahassee reported visits by recruiters from 500 companies in 1969, seeking "graduates who can fill jobs right across the board in business and industry." According to scattered information available, black students completing college last year often had their choice of several job offers. In addition, the Federal Government has made systematic efforts to recruit and upgrade Negroes in professional and other positions.[32]

Although quantitative data are not available on the kinds of jobs offered to Negro graduates, recent company recruitment efforts have certainly opened up positions outside the four professions traditionally chosen by Negro college students—teaching, medicine, the ministry, and law. The particularly sharp rise in managerial jobs between 1964 and 1968 provides additional evidence of their widening opportunities (table 5).

It must be recognized, however, that unfavorable changes have also occurred in the employment situation of Negro professionals, particularly in teaching and educational administration in Southern and border States. According to a study by the Maryland State Department of Education, there were 237 Negro school principals in that State in 1954, when the Supreme Court declared that segregated schools are unconstitutional. By September 1969, the number had decreased to 169, a decline of close to 30 percent, even though the number of schools in the State increased by 25 percent during the same period. Reports from a number of Southern States indicate that Negro principals and teachers were displaced as school desegregation progressed, even when the school systems were growing. In other parts of the country, however, demand for Negro teachers has increased enough to offset, at least in numerical terms, the reduction in opportunities in the South. The total number of school teachers who were Negro (or of other races except white) rose by about 25,000 in the country as a whole between 1964 and 1968 (from about 190,000 to 215,000).

---

[32] For a discussion of Government action in this area, see the chapter on Toward Equal Employment Opportunity.

Widening Opportunities for Professional Training. Preparation of Negro students for the wide range of professional and administrative positions now open to them is being aided by two major developments in Negro higher education—the broadening of curriculum offerings now in process in the predominantly Negro colleges and the rapidly rising enrollment of Negroes in the chiefly white institutions.

Teaching was still by far the largest field of training in predominantly Negro colleges in the 1963–64 school year. Almost half the bachelor's degrees and 80 percent of the master's degrees awarded by these institutions that year were in education. Very few of their graduates had majored in accounting or engineering, the two largest professional fields for men. But recently, 34 public Negro colleges, joined together in an effort to obtain financial and professional assistance in strengthening their curriculums, reported an increase in degree programs in fields with a strong demand for new graduates. Of these 34 colleges, the number offering degree programs in business had risen in a decade from 19 to 28; in accounting from 3 to 13; in economics from 6 to 14; and in nursing from 1 to 9.

As these new academic opportunities have opened, the proportion of students preparing for teaching, the ministry, law, and medicine has declined sharply, according to reports from several institutions. At North Carolina Central University in Durham, for example, where the great majority of students used to prepare for these fields, there has been a major shift into other fields offering favorable opportunities for graduates. Similarly, at Morehouse College in Atlanta, where most students used to prepare for teaching or the ministry, only nine out of the 131 students in the 1969 graduating class had majored in these fields.

A still more significant factor in widening the fields of specialization of Negro students is, however, their rising enrollment in colleges and universities with a much wider range of offerings than most predominantly black institutions have yet been able to provide. In the fall of 1964, there were about 234,000 Negro college students, roughly half in predominantly Negro colleges. By 1968 the number had risen to 434,000, with a majority in predominantly white institutions.

What these figures imply with regard to students' fields of specialization is suggested by a 1966 survey of the characteristics of college students conducted by the Bureau of Census. In all types of institutions taken together, only 23 percent of the Negro students were education majors—perhaps half the percentage majoring in education at predominantly Negro institutions.

Furthermore, most opportunities for Ph.D. studies by Negro, as well as white, students are at the major universities offering doctoral programs in many disciplines. Both the wide range of fields in which Negroes are earning Ph.D.'s and the unfortunately small numbers yet involved are indicated by a Ford Foundation survey of Negro Ph.D. recipients in 1967 and 1968. In a representative group of predominantly white graduate schools, 83 Negroes obtained doctorates in 22 different fields (with the largest numbers in education, biology, and chemistry).

Needed Expansion in College Education of Negroes. The major barrier to further growth in employment of Negroes in professional and managerial occupations is the limited number with sufficient education. In 1968, fewer than half a million Negroes had 4 or more years of college education; in 1969, the figure was probably a little higher. The gap between Negroes and whites in the proportion with at least 4 years of college was actually wider in 1968 than in 1960.

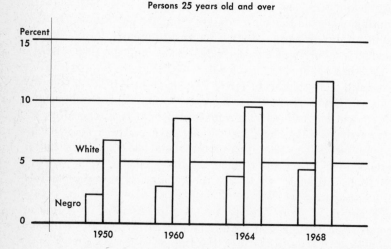

Proportion of Negroes who are college graduates is increasing but remains much lower than for whites

Persons 25 years old and over

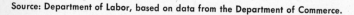

Source: Department of Labor, based on data from the Department of Commerce.

Though gains in college education were substantial among Negroes during this period, they were larger among whites. (See chart 23.)

The extremely small proportion of Negroes who have completed 5 or more years of college is of great significance from the viewpoint of their professional preparation. In 1968, only about 1 out of every 100 Negroes aged 25 or over had as much education as this, compared with 4 out of every 100 whites. Moreover, of the relatively few Negroes with postgraduate training, a high proportion probably are teachers with master's degrees in education.

It is apparent that action to expand Negro college education—and thereby enable increasing numbers to qualify for professional and other high-level jobs—should proceed in two major directions. It should be aimed, on the one hand, at enabling and motivating more Negro youth to enter and complete college and, on the other, at rapid enlargement in the numbers of Negroes obtaining doctoral degrees or other specifically professional training in a wide range of high-demand fields.

Assistance to all Negro youth in preparing for medicine and dentistry is a particularly urgent need. One reason why Negroes suffer so severely from the lack of medical care is the very small number of Negro physicians and dentists. Recent reports indicate that only 2 percent of all physicians and only 2.4 percent of all medical school students are Negroes. Furthermore, fewer than 2 percent of all dental students are Negroes, and the number of Negro dentists has actually been declining over the past 30 years. The situation is likely to deteriorate further unless positive remedial action is taken, since students may be less willing to make the sacrifices involved in preparing for these professions when alternative professional opportunities are available.

Programs aimed at raising the educational sights of able youth from poor families have had demonstrated success. For example, the Upward Bound Program, established and supported under the Economic Opportunity Act, aided 24,000 poor high school students during fiscal 1969, of whom half were Negroes. A high proportion of Upward Bound students have entered and stayed in college. However, the number of young people whom it has been possible to help through this program, with the limited budgetary resources available, has been very small relative to the total need. It has been estimated that perhaps 600,000 youth, the majority Negroes, would qualify for aid under the program.

The establishment of community colleges in more local areas

will also be an important means of increasing college enrollments of poor Negro youth, as will the availability of financial assistance to students. In addition, strong support should be given both to the efforts of white institutions to enroll more Negroes and to those of the predominantly Negro institutions to improve the quality and range of their educational offerings. The latter institutions will certainly be called on to play a continuing major role in higher education of Negroes. They need more funds for faculty salaries, libraries, laboratories, and other facilities and equipment if they are to make hoped-for progress in equipping Negro youth for the opportunities now open to them.

Women Professional Workers

The growing numbers of college-educated women seeking to enter professional employment face the probability of a major shift in their pattern of employment. The need for them to seek broadened opportunity in career fields outside the traditional "women's professions" is likely to have much more urgency in the 1970's than in any previous period.

This prospect stems from the changing supply-and-demand situation in school teaching—the Nation's largest profession, which now employs about 2 out of every 5 women in professional and related jobs. With the expected sharp decline in the proportion of new college graduates needed in teaching (discussed earlier in this chapter), the number of professionally oriented young women available to prepare for nursing, social work, and other "women's professions" should increase—thus helping to overcome the personnel shortages in these fields (also discussed in preceding sections). But the arithmetic of demand-and-supply indicates that these fields will not offer enough opportunities for the mounting numbers of women college graduates. The slow, long-term trend toward wider opportunities for women in other professional and technical fields and in business administration will have to accelerate if the rising career expectations of women are to be met and their potential contribution to the economy realized.

Fields of Professional Employment. There were 3.9 million women professional workers in 1968, more than 1½ times the number 10 years before. This increase reflected the expanding employment requirements in teaching, nursing, and other professions staffed largely by women. The even more rapidly rising personnel demand in many other professional fields, especially science and engineering, benefited women only slightly. The number of women preparing for and entering these fields continued to be small.

Two professions—school teaching and nursing—employ a sizable majority of all women professional workers; the proportion was about 2 out of every 3 in both 1950 and 1960 and is undoubtedly much the same today. Common characteristics of these professions and of others staffed predominantly by women—such as library science, social and welfare work, and dietetics—include their service orientation and heavy concentration in the nonprofit sectors of the economy. Another is their relatively low salary levels, which have been one of the major reasons why so few men have been attracted to these occupations.

Personnel shortages have been still another problem shared by these professions. For a complex of reasons—including the low pay scales, sometimes poor working conditions, lack of child-care facilities, and rapidly mounting employment requirements the "women's professions" have been plagued by a scarcity of qualified workers over the past two decades. Most of them still have a widespread need for additional personnel, though this is no longer true of teaching.

The shortages of trained personnel have stimulated efforts to attract more men into these fields. In teaching, these efforts have been spurred by educators' belief that boys would be helped by having more men teachers whom they could look up to as models. As a result, the proportion of men teachers has risen—from 25 to 30 percent between 1958 and 1968—with, of course, a corresponding drop in the proportion of women teachers. In social work also, men have been recruited actively, and their representation in the profession, while still well below 50 percent, is probably higher than in school teaching. On the other hand, in nursing—the second largest profession for women—efforts to recruit men to help meet widespread personnel shortages have yielded insignificant results; women continue to constitute almost 100 percent of all professional nurses. Women also continue to represent most of the work force in the shortage-plagued occupation of librarian, as in that of dietitian. (See chart 24.) Yet in libraries, as well as in schools and social agencies, a great many of the administrative and other top-level positions are filled by men.

Efforts in the reverse direction, to improve women's representation in professions staffed largely by men, have had somewhat varied but generally limited results. Fields in which women have made some progress in employment include the social sciences, psychology, health technology, physical and occupational therapy, recreation work, editing and reporting, personnel work, accounting, mathematics, and statistics. As employment requirements have grown in these professions, women with the appropriate training and work experience have shared modestly in the employment gains.

In the other major professions—including medicine, dentistry, law, engineering, natural sciences, architecture, and college teaching—the proportion of women remains very small. The few women who have entered these fields have generally been talented and highly motivated, and often conspicuously successful. But their example has not opened the door to wider participation of women in their professions. There were, for example, only 17,000 women physicians in 1965, out of a total of 278,000 physicians in the country. Women's entrance into law has been even slower than into medicine; in 1966, the 8,000 women lawyers represented only about 3 percent of the profession, the same percentage as for the past 15 years.

Factors Affecting Women's Choice of Professions. Why has the concentration of women professional workers in a few occupational fields remained so persistently high—so resistant to efforts aimed at broadening their career choices and opportunities?

The first, and probably the most important, reason that women gravitate into these professions is the culturally inculcated view—shared by employers, the community, and the majority of women—that these are the appropriate fields for members of their sex. Most of the "women's professions" are people oriented, and all focus on service. Women and men tend to have different career values, which influence their choice of a field of professional training. For example, according to a recent analysis of professional workers' ratings of various occupational values, the men most often gave first importance to "creative work," women to "helping others."[33]

This orientation of interests and values is reflected not only in the nature of women's traditional professions but also in the selec-

[33] Deborah David, "Career Patterns and Values; A Study of Men and Women in Scientific, Professional, and Technical Occupations" (New York: Columbia University, under grant from the Department of Labor, Manpower Administration, in process).

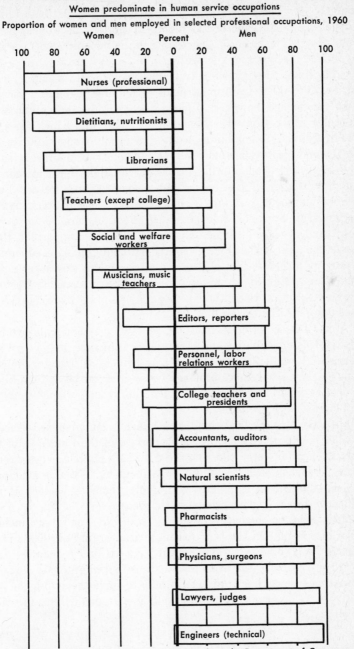

Women predominate in human service occupations

Proportion of women and men employed in selected professional occupations, 1960

Source: Department of Labor, based on data from the Department of Commerce.

tion of career fields by women who have gone outside these professions. It helps to explain the higher proportion of women in the social than in the natural sciences and in the biological sciences than in chemistry, physics, or engineering.

The influx of professionally trained women into teaching, nursing, and the other traditional fields is not due merely to occupational preference, however. Under present circumstances, these are the fields which women can enter most easily and which raise the fewest obstacles to combining work with family responsibilities. All the women's professions offer jobs throughout the country, in small as well as large communities—a matter of importance to married women who want to go wherever their husband's job is located. Part-time employment is often feasible in these occupations, and in teaching the work schedule and long vacation periods fit in well with married women's home obligations. Still more important, these occupations can generally be entered without graduate education. Though a master's degree is essential for many positions, it can usually be obtained after entrance into the profession. Doctoral degrees are not required, though they may be preferred for top-level positions—the kind generally filled by men.

In contrast, professions such as law, medicine, and college teaching customarily demand a commitment of time and energy and a continuity of employment which may be very difficult for married women. They also require prolonged post-graduate education, likely to involve much more serious problems for young women than for young men.

Women still lag far behind men in achieving advanced degrees. In March 1968, nearly as large a proportion of the women as of the men in the labor force had completed 4 years of college (between 7 and 8 percent in each case). But only about half as large a proportion of women had completed 5 or more years (3 percent of the women, compared with 6 percent of the men).

Obstacles on the path to graduate education for women include home responsibilities, custom, public attitudes, limited career aspirations, and women's special difficulty in obtaining financial support. Since many of the women who are potential graduate students are married, part-time study might help to solve their problem. Yet most fellowships, both private and public, are open only to full-time students.

Even with proper educational credentials, women often meet

employer resistance in seeking professional employment outside their traditional fields. Employers' frequent reluctance to hire women stems, at least in part, from the belief that they may stop work after only a few months or years because of family responsibilities and that business clients and the public prefer to deal with men. In addition, there is often outright preference for men in positions of prestige and responsibility. Despite recent Federal and State legislation forbidding discrimination in employment on the basis of sex, many women still hesitate to prepare for professions now dominated by men, where they envisage possible rejection or great difficulty in entering and advancing in their professions.

Need for Broader Professional Opportunities. It is evident that the obstacles to change in the pattern of women's professional employment are complex and deep-rooted. But it is essential to promote broader utilization of college-educated women for two reasons—the prospective supply-and-demand situation, referred to earlier, and the need to come closer, in both letter and spirit, to equal employment opportunity for women.

The magnitude of employment demand for women in their traditional professions will be much restricted during the next 10 years by the leveling off of employment requirements in school teaching. It may be affected also, though certainly to a lesser extent, by the movement of men into teaching and social work, major women's professions.

Yet the number of women seeking a college education is rising rapidly—faster than the comparable figure for men. Women enrolled in college for the first time constituted 43 percent of all first-time enrollees of both sexes in 1968, compared with 40 percent in 1958. The total number of women college students rose to 2.8 million in the fall of 1968, about 2½ times the number 10 years before.

In addition, a slow but steady rise is occurring in the number of women pursuing graduate studies. Between the 1957–58 and 1967–68 academic years, the proportion of women among graduate degree recipients rose from 33 to 36 percent of those earning master's degrees, and from 11 to 13 percent of those earning doctorates.

The interest of college women in utilizing their education in paid employment has recently been noticeably intensified among women 25 to 34 years of age. The proportion of this group in the work force jumped from 45 to 55 percent between 1959 and 1968.

Education continues to be the leading undergraduate major of women . . .

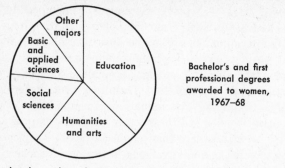

Bachelor's and first professional degrees awarded to women, 1967–68

but the numbers of women earning degrees in other fields are rising rapidly.

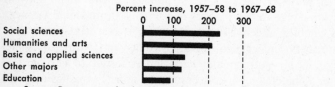

Percent increase, 1957–58 to 1967–68

Source: Department of Labor, based on data from the Department of Health, Education, and Welfare.

This increase probably relates as much to lower birth rates and women's higher job aspirations as to the availability of jobs for which they qualify.

The recent broadening of young women's fields of academic preparation is one development favoring wider professional opportunities for them. The largest group (over a third of all those earning bachelor's and first professional degrees in 1967–68) still major in education. But the numbers majoring in the social sciences and humanities and even the basic and applied sciences have risen much faster than the number of education majors over the past 10 years (as shown in chart above). Coupled with the increase in postgraduate education of women, this shift in fields of study should mean that increasing numbers of young women will be prepared for and seeking positions in fields such as computer programing, journalism, biological science research, and college teaching.

Pressure on employers to accept women on an equal basis in these and other professional occupations has, of course, been increased by the equal employment opportunity legislation. Women's organizations and agencies have long supported such legislation and are working for its extension into areas not yet covered. They also support efforts which could lead to greater breadth of occupational choice among women, including wider dissemination of occupational outlook information, more positive counseling of girls about areas of employment other than the traditional women's fields, and increased financial aid to women and girls for educational purposes. Another direction of action has been taken by groups of women sociologists, psychologists, and political scientists, who are working through their professional societies to persuade colleges and universities to improve opportunities for women as faculty members and students in their respective disciplines.

There are indications also that women are moving slowly but steadily into professional and management jobs in private industry. Some major companies report, for example, that they are employing more women in positions such as accountant, systems analyst, marketing representative, chemist, and management trainee, and in other "judgment-level" jobs. Some have recently begun to send recruiters to women's colleges to interview seniors for these jobs.

These beginnings are a development of top importance to the employment prospects for college-educated women and should be encouraged and extended as much as possible. Managerial work is a very large and growing field of employment for men college graduates, but one which only a few women have entered as yet. A major expansion in employment of women in management jobs, as well as in a broad range of professions, will be essential over the next decade to utilize commensurately the rapidly growing force of women college graduates who will seek jobs.

Self-Esteem as a Moderator in Vocational Choice: Replications and Extensions

ABRAHAM K. KORMAN

Department of Psychology

New York University

The purpose of the research reported in this paper was to test in different types of vocational choice situations the hypothesis that self-esteem operates as a moderator on the vocational choice process in that high self-esteem (HSE) individuals are more likely to seek self-fulfillment than are low self-esteem (LSE) individuals. Four separate studies were all supportive of the proposition.

There are now several studies in research literature which support the hypothesis that the extent to which individuals choose careers which are need-fulfilling and those in which they believe they will be adequate is a positive function of the self-esteem of the individual (Korman, 1966, 1967a). Such differential choice patterns have been hypothesized to result from tendencies toward "balance" where individuals who perceive themselves as need-fulfilling and adequate (i.e., have HSE) choose vocational roles where they will have their needs fulfilled and will be adequate. On the other hand, situations of self-perceived need-fulfillment and adequacy are not "balanced" situations for those who have LSE; hence they do not serve as incentives for them.

Since the implications of this hypothesis, should it continue to be supported, have considerable importance for counseling processes as well as theoretical significance, it was felt that further testing of the proposition was desirable. A number of further studies were undertaken in order both to replicate these previous findings using different instruments and to extend them to different dimensions of the vocational choice process. It is the purpose of this paper to report these studies.

Study 1 consisted of testing the hypothesis that HSE individuals who enter a given occupation are more likely to describe themselves according to generally given stereotypes of that occupa-

From *Journal of Applied Psychology*, 53: 188–192, 1969. Studies 2, 3, and 4 in this paper were presented at the meeting of the American Psychological Association, Washington, D.C., 1967.

tion than both LSE people who enter that occupation and a random sample of those who enter different occupations. A second prediction was that there would be no difference between the latter two groups. In addition, it was felt that this hypothesis would hold for either specifically defined occupational choices (e.g., sales and accounting, as in our previous research) or grosser defined choice (e.g., business management in general). This latter aspect constitutes an attempt to extend previous findings.

The specific predictions which were made (in line with the above) were as follows: (a) HSE individuals in sales were most likely to describe themselves as being "sociable," "talkative," "aggressive," and having "initiative"; (b) HSE individuals in accounting were most likely to describe themselves as being "precise," "self-controlled," "organized," and "thorough"; (c) HSE individuals in general business were most likely to describe themselves as being "practical," "rational," and "responsible."

Study 2 also attempted to generalize the previous research to those whose occupational choice was more generalized in nature in that the interest here was in those whose occupational choice was "the world of business" rather than the more specific roles of sales, accounting, personnel, etc. The prediction was that HSE individuals who had chosen business as a career would be different from HSE individuals who had chosen something other than business as a career in the direction of having greater need for material security and less need for social service. On the other hand, there should be no difference on these dependent variables between LSE individuals who had chosen business and LSE people who had not chosen business.

Study 3 consisted of a replication of Studies 1 and 2 in the area of "numerical abilities." It was predicted that individuals of HSE who had chosen numerically-oriented occupations (accounting and/or statistics) would see themselves as having higher numerical abilities than HSE individuals who had not chosen numerically-oriented occupations. On the other hand, such differences should not exist for those of LSE.

Study 4 proceeded from the assumption that the desire to engage in what is perceived to be ethical behavior is relatively widespread in nature, at least on a conscious self-descriptive basis. Hence, it was hypothesized that for individuals of HSE, the perceived ethicality of the behavior to be engaged in would be predictive of job choice, whereas such predictions would break down for those of LSE. More specifically, it was predicted that HSE individuals who had chosen business occupations would rate various business behaviors as being more ethical than HSE individuals who had not chosen business occupations. On the other hand, for LSE individuals, there would be no relationship between the judged ethicality of business behaviors and occupational choice.

METHOD

Sample

(a) The Ss for Study 1 consisted of male students at a far western state university. Of these, 22 had made career commitments to marketing and sales, 35 to accounting, 36 to general business, and 42 to some area unrelated to business. (b) The "business career" sample for Study 2 consisted of 65 male upper division business school majors at a different far western state university who indicated a specific commitment to enter the world of business, but who had not chosen a specific career such as sales, accounting, etc. The "nonbusiness career" sample consisted of 58 upper and lower division male students in a number of different major areas at two eastern universities. Most prominent of the major areas were education, the social and biological sciences, and social work. (c) The sample for Study 3 consisted of 67 lower division students at a private eastern university who had made a definite occupational choice. (d) The sample for Study 4 consisted of 53 males and 29 females. Since previous work by the author has shown a sex difference in the ethical judgments used in this study, sexes were analyzed separately.

Measuring Instruments

(a) Self-esteem in all studies was measured by the Self-Assurance Scale of the Ghiselli Self-Description Inventory, with the cutoff in all cases for "high" and "low" self-esteem the 50th percentile on the nationwide norms. (b) The tendency to describe oneself according to certain adjectives in Study 1 was measured by Gough Adjective Checklist (Gough, 1952). (c) The need for "material security" and "social service" in Study 2 were measured by the scales of the same name of the Crites Vocation Reaction Survey (Korman, 1966). (*d*) Self-perceived "numerical abilities" were measured by the Ability Assessment Questionnaire. This is an instrument of self-perceived abilities described by Korman (1967a). (*e*) "Occupational choice" was measured by questionnaire procedures found in previous research to have high reliability and concurrent validity (Korman, 1966). (*f*) Judgments of the "Ethicality of Business Behavior" in Study 4 were measured by having *S*s rate, on a 4-point scale, the ethicality of 25 incidents which have actually occurred in the business world in recent years.

Procedures

The general procedure in all cases was to administer the questionnaires in regular class meetings or as part of introductory psychology research participation requirements. No systematic difference has been found between any of these procedures.

RESULTS

Study 1

Table 1 presents the results from this study, showing in all cases strong support for the hypothesis. The HSE individual does, in all cases, describe himself more as meeting the occupational image in the specific occupation than does the LSE individual in the occupation or a random sample of individuals who have made different occupational choices. Furthermore, this occurs no matter which occupation is referred to.

There was one possibly contaminating factor to these results, that, perhaps, the higher the self-esteem, the higher the frequency of words used to describe oneself. In other words, in a free response situation, such as the Gough Adjective Check List, where the person is asked to describe himself according to a set of adjectives with sheer number of adjectives chosen uncontrolled for, perhaps the only difference between HSE and LSE people is in the total number of words chosen. A check for this, using frequency of choosing a

TABLE 1

Adjective Self-Descriptions According to Occupational Choice and Self-Esteem

Item	High self-esteem	Low self-esteem	Random sample
Frequency of choosing "Practical," "Rational," and "Responsible"			
	1. Business majors	2. Business majors	3. Nonbus majors
M	2.73	1.90	2.12
SD	.60	.84	.94
N	15	21	42
	$t_{1\ \&\ 3} = 2.35**$		
	$t_{2\ \&\ 3} = .92$		
Frequency of choosing "Precise," "Self-Controlled," "Organized," and "Thorough"			
	1. Acct. majors	2. Acct. majors	3. Nonacct. majors
M	2.35	1.33	1.60
SD	1.21	1.53	1.43
N	14	21	42
	$t_{1\ \&\ 3} = 1.79*$		
	$t_{2\ \&\ 3} = .69$		
Frequency of choosing "Initiative," "Aggressive," "Sociable," and "Talkative"			
	1. Sales majors	2. Sales majors	3. Nonsales majors
M	2.43	1.77	1.78
SD	1.34	1.29	1.13
N	9	13	42
	$t_{1\ \&\ 3} = 3.61**$		
	$t_{2\ \&\ 3} = .03$		

Note.—All tests in this table are one-tailed tests.
* $p < .05$.
** $p < .01$.

random sample of 30 adjectives, indicated that this was not the case. The mean frequency of choice was exactly the same for the two self-esteem groups, carried out to one decimal place. Hence, this cannot explain the results.

Study 2

Table 2 presents the results of this investigation, with strong support once again being indicated for both hypotheses. The HSE business group is significantly higher than the HSE nonbusiness group

TABLE 2

Needs for Material Security and Social Service According to
Self-Esteem and Vocational Choice

Item	High self-esteem	Low self-esteem	High self-esteem	Low self-esteem
		Material security		
	1. Business	2. Business	3. Non-business	4. Non-business
M	7.59	6.08	6.07	6.61
SD	3.2	3.6	3.3	3.2
N	29	36	27	31
		t_1 & $_3 = 1.77*$		
		t_2 & $_4 = .65$		
		Social service		
	1. Business	2. Businesss	3. Non-business	4. Non-business
M	4.13	5.53	6.89	6.55
SD	2.9	3.6	4.4	4.2
N	29	36	27	31
		t_1 & $_3 = 2.65**$		
		t_2 & $_4 = 1.09$		

Note.—All tests in this table are one-tailed tests.
 * $p < .05$.
** $p < .01$.

on "material security" and significantly lower on "social service." For the LSE groups neither result occurs, with the means actually reversed for "material security."

Study 3

Table 3 presents the results for this study with strong support once again. HSE "quantitative occupation" individuals see themselves as having greater numerical abilities than HSE "nonquantitative occupations," whereas the differences are not significant for the LSE groups.

Study 4

The data for this study were analyzed by computing the mean judged ethicality of each of the 24 incidents for each of the four

TABLE 3

Self-Perceived Numerical Abilities according to Self-Esteem and Vocational Choice

Item	1. High self-esteem quantitative	2. Low self-esteem quantitative	3. High self-esteem non-quantitative	4. Low self-esteem non-quantitative
M	13.00	10.56	8.69	9.52
SD	1.1	2.53	2.9	3.1
N	7	16	23	21
		$t_{1 \& 3} = 3.99*$		
		$t_{2 \& 4} = 1.11$		

Note.—All tests in this table are one-tailed tests.
* $p < .01$.

groups. All hypotheses were supported. Male HSE business ($n = 13$) rated the incidents as more ethical than male HSE nonbusiness ($n = 10$) (sign test, $p < .01$), whereas there was no difference between the male LSE business ($n = 17$) and nonbusiness ($n = 13$) groups (sign test, $p = .27$). Similarly, female HSE business ($n = 5$) were higher than nonbusiness ($n = 8$) (sign test, $p < .02$), whereas there were no differences for the female business ($n = 7$) and nonbusiness ($n = 9$) (sign test, $p = .50$).

DISCUSSION

Taking in context the results of the four studies reported here and the results reported in previous research, (Korman, 1966, 1967a), there is a highly consistent trend of evidence which argues that people differing in self-esteem choose occupations differently. Basically, the high self-esteem person seems to look at himself and say "I like what I see and I am going to give it its desires and needs," whereas the low self-esteem person seems to say, when looking at himself "I do not like what I see and I am not going to give it its desires and needs." While this may be a slight oversimplification, it seems to summarize, in essence, the kinds of results found over a wide variety of different instruments, different samples, and differing levels of choice specificity. It is further strengthened by our related finding that even when the LSE individual is provided with fulfillment of his desires, it does not lead to satisfaction on his part (Korman, 1967b). (However, continued fulfillment of his needs *might* lead to a reevaluation of self, and thus change his determinants of satisfaction. There is little research on this.)

At least two further questions of interest occur here. The first is why this behavior occurs. A second is on what basis LSE people make vocational choices, if not on the basis of need-fulfillment. In terms of the first question, there are, of course, a variety of explanations ranging from childhood training patterns not to be contradictory in behavior to conceptions of a need for "social reality" comparable to that of physical reality. For both of these cases, situations of inconsistency would then be anxiety-provoking and, hence, to be avoided.

Turning to the second question, perhaps the LSE individual attempts to implement the value of an "ideal self" rather than an "actual self," a possibility which would generally be consistent with the notion of the LSE person as an individual who dislikes himself.[3] In addition, it may be that such "ideal self" fulfillment is more determinate of his job satisfaction than his "actual self" fulfillment. A second possibility is that his behavior may be, at least partially, a function of social norms, that is, he may choose and be satisfied according to perceived social norms as to what is desirable and what is undesirable. However, since these possible explanations are not inconsistent with one another, since the relationship between self-esteem and persuasibility may be more complex than this (cf. Cox & Bauer, 1964), and since little research is available on either of them, such conjectures at this time are speculative only.

REFERENCES

Cox, O., & Bauer, R. Self-confidence and persuasibility in women. *Public Opinion Quarterly,* 1964, 28, 453–456.

Gough, H. *The Adjective Checklist.* Palo Alto, Calif.: Consulting Psychologists Press, 1954.

Korman, A. K. The self-esteem variable in vocational choice. *Journal of Applied Psychology,* 1966, 50, 479–486.

Korman, A. K. Self-esteem as a moderator of the relationship between self-perceived abilities and vocational choice. *Journal of Applied Psychology,* 1967, 51, 65–67. (a)

Korman, A. K. Relevance of personal need satisfaction for overall satisfaction as a function of self-esteem. *Journal of Applied Psychology,* 1967, 51, 533–538. (b)

[3] I am indebted to Mr. Jeffrey Greenhaus for this suggestion.

Section 10
Interpersonal Relationships and Communication

A distinguished American, John Gardner, makes some penetrating comments in the first article in this section. He points out that with present rates of social change there is no tranquility to disrupt, that instant antiquity is built into every institution, and that this problem requires an imaginative redesign rather than an attempt to repair.

Probably it is true that all institutions function to perpetuate themselves. Even after the problems they were established to deal with are gone, the institutions remain. They make work and create problems rather than solve them. They become ends in themselves rather than serving as means to an end. The human being must be eternally vigilant lest the institutions which he creates to serve him do not come to demand so much that he becomes the servant.

Here is a whole new concept. We have viewed with concern the tendency of man to become directed by the machines, computers, and technology that he has created to serve him. We need to expand this concern to include the social institutions he also has created.

Gardner's point that "Our society must be a good problem-solving mechanism" is especially well taken. The importance of the individual in the process of living, becoming, and problem solving, and the fact that we create new problems as fast as we solve the old ones, are really basic considerations. Further, he draws an important distinction between "drowning in a torrent of communication" and really communicating. This needs both emphasis and reiteration. As he says, "Communication in a creative society must be more than a flow of messages; it must be a means of conflict resolution. . . ." This is true of most of the contacts we maintain. There is indeed much similarity between the functioning of persons and the manner in which groups of persons operate. In a sense, nations, states, communities, and even bridge clubs possess characteristic patterns of acting and also may be said to have personalities. Up to this time, we have not been very successful in teaching individuals to communicate in order to resolve interpersonal conflicts. Perhaps we need to begin here before we attempt to transform communication patterns for institutions. Perhaps if we only could do this, other communication hang-ups would tend to right themselves.

Before we redesign, however, we need to be sure we do not perpetuate antiquity. As the author emphasizes, "Man has a notable gift for making the same mistake over and over." Is communication which is relevant and which is used as a means of conflict resolution the answer? Should we start learning this? We, the editors, think so.

One of the most basic of human associations, the marriage relationship, is one of those which can be made more rewarding through communication. Anyone who will be or is married can find in Professor Hayakawa's remarks advice which, if applied, will make their own marital experience more rewarding. A number of his statements profitably may be read, thought about, and read again. Such as the assertion that "Good communication is . . . at the heart of good sexuality." And the elaboration that ". . . what makes for good adult sexuality is not essentially different from what makes for emotional stability and maturity."

One indeed is left out when he is not communicated with. And as we have said, a relationship demands communication just as communication demands a relationship. Without either, or both, marriage may offer little more than a roommate and a bed partner and sex may be only slightly more meaningful than masturbation.

If we did not know it already, and if the articles by Gardner and Hayakawa did not make it clear, the article by Samover, Brooks, and Porter does show that communication is a pervasive activity. This message is not as important as its implications. The person seeking better adjustment and greater self-actualization would be wise to stop taking communication for granted. Many do and the results are poor, inadequate, and even misleading attempts at interpersonal relationships.

The inadequacy of a considerable number of our attempts is called to attention by Gibb's discussion of "Defensive Communication." There are so many lessons to be learned from the article that we hesitate to cite those we feel to be particularly noteworthy. Although Gibb does not use the word, we will indicate the need for *honesty*. Listeners immediately become suspicious, begin to seek meaning disguised under words, begin making private interpretations when they feel that the speaker is not being candid or that he is hiding behind a facade. Moreover, others are quick to detect the existence of these facades. Another barrier to communication is the speaker's belief that he cannot treat another honestly—as he would a peer. Of course, defensive communication is also dependent upon the receiver.

As an example of one of the "defense mechanisms" at work in speech, it is recommended that the reader study his very next class—lecture or discussion—to see how many of the phenomena of which Gibb speaks can be seen in action. We think an outcome might be the generation of a desire to learn more about the important dynamics of communication. We return again to this subject in the articles in Sections 12 and 13—especially those articles on pages 576, 619, 631, and 638.

Communication is a basic aspect of interpersonal relationships, and Wald cites a specific and almost overwhelming communications problem. Just a few days ago a mother of twelve in Oregon wrote an indignant letter to the newspaper which carried editorials about abortion, birth control, and overpopulation. *She* had raised twelve fine sons and daughters and no one, but no one, should interfere with anyone's "God-given" right to have children. Except, of course, birth control would be justifiable if it were used on criminals and dependents—but not when used on good citizens and loyal taxpayers! Did she pay sufficient taxes to send twelve children through public school? Do her children pollute the atmosphere less than a car thief serving time in prison? Is the area her children claim from the hills and valleys of Oregon (for roofs, driveways, and highways) still available so that water might soak into the ground and generate constantly flowing rivers? Does the water they (and others of the expanding population) dam to provide for drinking, washing, power and irrigation still remain open to fish spawning? Or provide for wild life to drink? These questions are going to merit serious consideration NOW. It may be, many people besides Wald have warned, that the quality of interpersonal relationships is more important than the quantity of people. The problem is open for communication between the "God-given reproductive right" people and those who are concerned with the quality of life. We propose that there is no problem of adjustment which transcends in importance the one which Wald outlines.

We, the People
JOHN W. GARDNER

In order to think clearly about social change, we must first dispose of the notion that it is a process that alters a tranquil status quo. Today there is no tranquility left to alter. The disruption has occurred, and one of the purposes of social change is to find new solutions that will preserve old values. When the spring dries up the farmer seeks a new source of water, not for love of novelty but to bring himself back into balance with his environment.

Our status quo has been knocked head over heels by the revolutions in science and technology, in transportation, in communication and the processing of information, in industry, agriculture and education, in demography and biomedical affairs.

The swift pace of these revolutions makes it desperately necessary that our institutions be adaptable. When they are not, the sweep of events isolates them and dramatizes their anachronistic character. Even institutions that are fairly young (as history goes) find themselves woefully out of date. The rush of change brings a kind of instant antiquity.

And it isn't enough just to change institutions. Some of today's college-age critics have a feeling that if they could tear down existing institutions better ones would surely rise. But all too often in history we have seen the tearing down, or collapse, of institutions and their replacement by institutions essentially no better. As an institution builder man has a notable gift for making the same mistake over and over.

One source of such repeated mistakes is to ignore the flaws in human nature that survive all social transformations. Man's inclination to tyrannize over his fellow man, his impulse to prejudice, his greed, his lust for power—all must be held in check by culture and by social institutions. Some of our young critics imagine that somehow those traits will disappear when their bright new world dawns. But they will not disappear. If we jettison procedures developed over centuries to protect us from the ferocity of our fellow man, we shall regret it bitterly.

An address delivered on November 21, 1968 on the occasion of his receiving the first Robert Andrews Millikan Award from the California Institute of Technology. Used by permission of the California Institute of Technology.

A second reason men make the same mistake over and over is that they fail to recognize certain tendencies intrinsic to human institutions. *All* social institutions tend sooner or later to rigidify and to smother individuality. This is particularly true of modern, highly organized societies, capitalist or communist. Many of the attributes most galling to the critics of our own system are equally characteristic of every large-scale modern society. If we are to alter those attributes for the better, we shall have to be very knowing indeed about the design of human institutions.

A first step toward a sound philosophy of institutional redesign would be to break our habit of concentrating exclusively on routine repair activities. The mechanic faced with a defective carburetor can put it back in working order and stop there. Or, if he is a very gifted mechanic, he may sit down and design an improved unit, less subject to breakdown. If he is still more imaginative, he may think of a whole new means, simpler and more efficient, for mixing air and fuel in the proper proportions for combustion.

At this critical time in our history, we can less and less afford to limit ourselves to routine repair of breakdowns in our institutions. More and more, we must undertake the imaginative redesign of institutions. In our history as a nation, we have done quite a lot of social inventing and innovating. Among the consequences: the Bill of Rights, the Land-Grant college, the County Agent, the Federal Reserve System.

If we are serious about redesign, then we must address ourselves to one of the central and universally neglected aspects of the problem: the decay of human institutions. As they decay they imprison the spirit, they thwart the creative impulse, they diminish individual adaptability and limit the possibility of freedom. As the institutions grow increasingly resistant to criticism, the critics grow increasingly hostile. And the stage is set for one of the most familiar dramas of contemporary life—the violent collision between angry critics and sluggish institutions.

That human institutions require periodic redesign (if only because of their tendency to decay) is not a minor fact about them nor easily overlooked. Taking the whole span of history, there is no more obvious lesson to be learned.

How curious, then, that in all of history, with all the immensely varied principles on which societies have been designed and operated, no people has seriously attempted to take into account the aging of institutions and to provide for their continuous renewal. Why shouldn't we be the first to do so?

One of the reasons people interested in improving the society never examine the requirements of continuous renewal is that they are preoccupied with specific evils that need to be corrected. I don't blame them. So am I. That's what I work on every day of my life, and I would not seek to divert anyone from the attacks on poverty, discrimination, inadequate housing, unemployment, faulty education, and all the other matters that urgently need our attention.

But somehow, someone must dig deeper. Each reformer comes to his task with a little bundle of desired changes. The society is intolerable, he asserts, because it has these specifiable defects: a, b, c . . . and so on. The implication is that, if appropriate reforms are carried through and the defects corrected, the society will be wholly satisfactory and the work of the reformer done.

That is a primitive way of viewing social change. The true task is to design a society, and institutions, capable of continuous change, continuous renewal, continuous responsiveness. We are creating new problems as fast as we solve the old ones. Our society must be a good problem-solving mechanism. It is not so today.

In addition, our ideas of what a good society is evolve and change over the years. If our institutions are capable of continuous renewal, we can move by successive approximations toward the kind of society we want.

The individual is the ultimate source of social renewal. It follows that the self-renewing society will be one that fosters creative, free, and self-renewing individuals. But, the end toward which all modern societies, *whatever their ideology*, seem to be moving is the beehive model of society—a society in which the total system perfects itself as the individual is steadily dwarfed. All modern technological societies, whatever their ideology, are moving toward ever larger and more embracing systems of organization, toward ever greater specialization of function on the part of individuals, toward ever greater dominance of the system's purposes over individual purposes. Social critics tend to believe that the smothering of individuality is a consequence of intentional decisions by the people at the top. Right-wingers blame government leaders, left-wingers blame corporate leaders. But people in power are in some measure victims of the same trends. The hostility of the critics (right-wing or left) to the people at the top (federal or corporate) is strengthened by a nostalgic conception of power. They see the people at the top as almost completely free to shape events to their will. But that is a wholly unreal notion of how a modern, intricately organized system works. The modern leader is always in some measure caught in the system. To a considerable degree, the system determines how and when he will exercise power. And if present trends continue, this will become more rather than less so. The queen bee is as much a prisoner of the system as is any other in the hive.

Now I am going to try to list for you the attributes of a society capable of resisting this trend, capable of fostering creative individuals, capable of renewing itself.

1. *Pluralism.* The creative society will be characterized by variety, alternatives, choices, and multiple foci of power and initiative. We have had in this society a high degree of just such pluralism. But the logic of modern, large-scale organization, governmental or corporate, tends to squeeze out pluralism and to move toward one comprehensively articulated system of power. We must work against that trend. In our own society, this means, in practical terms, a concern for the vitality of local leadership, for the strength and autonomy of State and local government, for the vigor and creativity of the private sector, and for various kinds of decentralization.

2. *Release of individual potential.* The society capable of continuous renewal will be one that develops to the fullest its human resources, that removes obstacles to individual fulfillment, that emphasizes education, lifelong learning, and self-discovery. In these matters our record is uneven—brilliant in some respects, shameful in others. We have worked hard and accomplished much toward combatting the conditions that stunt human growth and thwart individual promise. But we have allowed our black citizens and some other minorities to live in conditions that make a mockery of our ideals. And we are still far from having created, for either black or white, an educational system that produces self-discoverers and lifelong learners.

Removal of the barriers to individual fulfillment involves far more than education, of course. We must be certain that no individual suffers a lifelong physical handicap because his family could not afford early medical attention. We must enable blind, deaf, and crippled children to live useful lives. We must combat all the other destroyers of human promise—alcoholism, mental illness, and so on.

3. *Internal communication.* A society that is capable of continuous renewal will have excellent internal communications among its diverse constituent elements. In my judgment we do not have that today. We are drowning in a torrent of communication, but most of it is irrelevant to this particular need. Serious gaps in communication still exist between the businessman and the working man, between white and black, between young and old, between conservative and liberal, between public and private sectors.

They are not wholly out of touch. But they do not engage in the kind of open and constructive dialogue that would permit each to understand the other's values and assumptions. Communication in a creative society must be more than a flow of messages; it must be a means of conflict resolution, a means of cutting through the rigidities that divide and paralyze a community.

4. *Dissent.* The creative society must provide for dissent, for the emergence of alternatives to official doctrine or widely accepted assumptions. It must provide for honest appraisal of the disparity between existing conditions and widely professed ideals. Despite assertions to the contrary by social critics, our society rates very high in sheer volume of expressed dissent. But we are still short of technically expert, knowing dissent on many of the highly complex matters that affect our lives. And we have still not discovered how to counteract the process by which every organization filters the feedback on performance in order to screen out the things it doesn't want to face up to.

5. *Participation.* In order to have a vital society we must have as high a degree of participation by the individual as we can manage. Personally, I do *not* believe that the urge to participate actively in the shaping of one's social institutions is a powerful human motive. On the contrary, it appears to me to be a notably weak and undependable impulse. But we must fan that uncertain flame! Why? I shall suggest one reason that has to do with the perils of this moment in history and one reason that is timeless.

This is a moment when men, here and around the world, have in some measure withdrawn faith in their institutions. They are questioning, reexamining. At such a time, there can be nothing more healthy, nothing more healing, than for men to participate directly in the reshaping of the institutions that no longer enjoy their confidence. It is the only way that confidence will be reestablished. And there is among many people today a healthy impulse toward such participation. People want to have their say, they want to be heard, feel that they count, feel that they're "connected."

The timeless reason is that participation preserves the vitality of institutions and nurtures a healthy relationship between the individual and society. When people, for whatever reason (oppression, laziness, complacency), take no part in their institutions, the institutions themselves decay at an accelerating rate.

But if we are to make participation possible, we must restore the sense of community and the vitality of local leadership. It is only at the local level that the average citizen will ever have the opportunity to participate.

And we need to develop further the service idea inherent in the Peace Corps and VISTA. People who are serving a meaningful cause no longer feel "unconnected." Life gains significance.

6. *Leadership.* A society capable of renewal will have a plentiful supply of relevant leadership. On this score we are in poor shape. The specialization of modern society channels executive and analytical talent into professional and specialist areas and away from leadership.

A free society does not need leaders to tell it what to do; it has grown beyond paternalistic leadership. But it does urgently need leaders to symbolize its values, to clarify choices, to help sift priorities, and most of all perhaps to keep hope alive, hope that we can find our way through the troubles of the day, despite confusion and cross-purposes, despite our own folly, despite the bitterness of conflict.

7. *Conflict resolution.* The society capable of renewal will have developed effective means of conflict resolution to deal with the fierce antagonisms that divide and immobilize a community or a nation. I do not regard this as an impossible goal. It is really only in the past 15 or 20 years that anyone has worked systematically and analytically on the problem of resolving human conflicts. And we have learned a great deal—far more than we have ever applied. It is not the fact of conflict itself that threatens a society. Conflict is a

part of life. What endangers a society are the consequences of violent, prolonged, and savage conflict—deeply embedded hatreds, devastating breakdowns in communication, and the rigidity of entrenched defensive positions.

8. *Values.* A society capable of renewal must have deeply rooted values. If it believes in nothing, it cannot generate the high level of motivation essential to renewal. The values must be worthy of a great civilization, and they must be compatible with the process of renewal. We are fortunate in that respect. Freedom, justice, equality of opportunity, the worth and dignity of the individual—these are values that are supremely compatible with social renewal. Our problem is not to find better values but to be faithful to those we profess.

9. *Morale.* A society capable of continuous renewal will have morale, conviction, confidence. We have in some measure lost confidence. It is not easy to say how we shall regain it, since morale and confidence are emergent characteristics, not to be ordered up like lamb chops at the corner restaurant. It is my belief that our loss of confidence is traceable to a variety of factors: the severity of internal conflict, the failure of leadership, the incapacity of society to solve obvious and grave problems, a visible disparity between the values we profess and the practices we tolerate. If this is true, then the restoral of confidence may take some time. The one hopeful possibility is that if we *begin* to make some progress in rolling back our troubles, our confidence may surge back. The return of confidence does not depend on achieving our goals at once. It does depend on seeing light at the end of the tunnel.

The light at the end of the tunnel is there. But it is going to require great courage and commitment and steadiness of purpose to move us toward it. It is going to require a great burst of national energy. A considerable part of that burst of energy will have to go toward tackling the tough substantive problems, such as poverty and discrimination. But, while we're tackling them, we're also going to have to think about how we can design this society to be a better problem-solving mechanism.

It can be done. We can create the first society in history that is capable of continuous renewal. But not by just letting events take their course. We have to build into the system the characteristics we want. The logic of large-scale organization tends to squeeze out pluralism and participation. We must preserve them. The self-affirming characteristics of all human organizations tend to suppress dissent. We must foster it. All human institutions tend to decay. We must design ours for continuous renewal.

We still have a choice. If we want a society on the beehive model, all we need do is relax and we'll drift into it. If we want a society built around the creative possibilities of the self-directing individual, then we have tasks to perform.

Each of you has tasks to perform. You are that self-directing individual. Start where you are. Make yourself a better person. Make yours a better community. Make this a better nation. This free society begins with you. It mustn't end with you.

I am not proposing new duties; I am calling you back to old duties. Remember the Preamble to the Constitution? "We, the people of the United States, in order to form a more perfect union, establish justice, insure domestic tranquility, provide for the common defense, promote the general welfare, and secure the blessings of liberty to ourselves and our posterity . . ." Great phrases, and the greatest of all is, "We, the people of the United States." Not we the public officials of the United States. Not we the certified experts in public administration. Not we who have time to think about these things when we're not busy running our businesses or practicing our professions. Just we, the people.

We have elected a new President. No matter how gifted he may prove to be, he cannot save us from ourselves. He cannot function effectively unless we are actively and intelligently at work on our own problems. No matter how accomplished our public servants are, the inner mystery of democracy will always involve that old and good idea: "We, the people."

You and I and others like us, acting in our own communities across the nation, can pull this fragmented society together again. We can recreate an America in which men speak to one another in trust and mutual respect, sharing common objectives, working toward common goals. We can return this nation to a path of confidence and well-being. We can design a society capable of continuous renewal.

You and I can do these things. No one can do them for us.

Semantics and Sexuality
S. I. HAYAKAWA
President, San Francisco State College

The reproductive system of many forms of life is extraordinarily wasteful, involving an infant mortality rate of just a shade under 100 per cent. The American brine shrimp, ways Susan Michelmore, in a book called *Sexual Reproduction,* lay so many eggs that they form a thick encrustation around the edges of the salt ponds in which they live. She says, "The female cod may lay six million eggs in one breeding season, a salmon thirty million." I have been told, too, that certain species of oysters lay so many eggs that if by some miracle they were all to grow up to adult size the world would be knee deep in oysters.

There is an important relationship between the wastefulness of the system of reproduction and the level of development of an animal. Leon Adams, in his book, *Striped Bass Fishing on the Pacific Coast,* says that "one female bass may have from 11,000 to more than 4,000,000 babies; that is by actual sample count of the eggs from her ovaries." When the eggs are released, the males release milt over them. Some eggs get fertilized; many do not. The fertilized eggs are preyed upon by many creatures of the sea. They are eaten as eggs, as larvae, as fry, as fingerlings. Every legally catchable striped bass—which by California law must be sixteen inches long and is therefore about five years old—is the sole survivor out of millions of his siblings.

Despite the enormous rate of reproduction among fish, their sexual life would appear, from the human point of view, to leave much to be desired. In the case of the trout, for example, the female selects a clear, gravelly, sheltered stream in which to lay her eggs. The gentleman trout then comes along and fertilizes them somewhat later—a most unsociable procedure.

A psychiatrist once told me that he had a patient who had heard about the trout's mating habits and sighed, "Ah, that's the way it should be!" Perhaps that's why he was a patient.

A much more advanced stage in sexual reproduction is repre-

Reprinted by permission from *ETC. A Review of General Semantics,* Vol. 25, No. 2; June, 1968; copyright 1968 by the International Society for General Semantics.

sented by those creatures which give their offspring their start in life inside the body of the female, as is true of, for example, the viviparous perch of San Francisco Bay, birds and reptiles that lay hard-shelled eggs, and all mammals.

For fertilization to take place, certain interindividual processes must take place: male and female must get each other's attention, stimulate each other, secure each other's cooperation or compliance, until the female finally assumes the appropriate position for receiving the sperm. This process of interindividual interaction, whether brief or protracted, and whether occurring among fish, lobsters, reptiles, birds, elephants, or human beings, is known as courtship.

Perhaps I have said enough to indicate already that communication is a necessary part of sexual behavior of all but the most elementary forms of life.

But human beings are the creatures who have specialized in communication as their specific means of survival. No other creature is able, as human beings are, to build languages involving vocabularies of hundreds of thousands of words if necessary in order to communicate the complexities of his experience. No other creature is able to send messages to his fellow creatures at great distances—indeed, to all parts of the world. No other creature can encode his thoughts in permanent marks on paper in order to pass on messages from the dead to the living, from the living to those yet unborn. No other creature governs his life and social relations so completely by patterned networks of communication: religions, schools, governments, and laws. No other creature so freely utilizes the materials of his environment not only to increase his safety and comfort but also to send messages: by means of food or flowers, by dress and personal adornment, by dance and ceremony, by architecture and music.

So if communication is necessary to the love life of the sparrow, the crocodile, or the Canadian elk, how much richer and more complex are the problems of communication in the love life of human beings! And general semantics, which is the study of communication and sign behavior and symbolic action in all their forms, must surely have something to contribute to the study of human sexuality.

There are many puzzles about human sexuality. I have already spoken of the wastefulness of the reproductive process in the lower forms of life. As one goes up the scale of biological complexity, the infant mortality rate goes steadily downward. In contrast to the millions that fish give birth to in order to ensure the continuance of their species, amphibians such as frogs reproduce in the thousands, reptiles in the hundreds, mammals and birds in the dozens.

The increasing complexity of organisms as they move up the evolutionary scale is accompanied by the increasing length of dependency of the young. The striped bass is on his own in the hostile waters of the San Joaquin river from the moment he is a fertilized egg. For him there is no period of maturation within a shelled egg, or inside the warmth of a maternal womb, before being thrown on his own resources.

But infants of higher forms of life are fed and nurtured in their nests in infancy. A puppy is well on his way to being a well-formed dog when he is born, but he is still suckled and cared for for many months after birth before he is on his own. During infancy, all mammals experience a period of dependency during which they undergo some kind of education from their elders.

The period of dependency has an enormously important function. The longer the period of infant dependency in any creature, the greater is his reliance in later life on information-gathering and processing as his survival mechanism and the less his reliance upon built-in reflexes, usually called instincts.

As we go up the scale of biological complexity, it is fascinating to observe to what degree this complexity is essentially a matter of the ability of an organism to take in and utilize for purposes of survival more and more information about the environment. The octopus and the oyster are both of the order Mollusca. They provide a fascinating contrast. Oysters, in the interests of survival, gave up locomotion; they attached themselves to rocks and covered themselves with hard shells, which, along with their fantastic birth rate, are their basic survival mechanisms. But oysters sacrificed a lot in order to achieve security. They have few adventures, and, as everyone realizes, if you stay in one place all your life, you don't get to know very much. That is the lesson of the oyster.

In contrast, the octopus remained without armor plating. With no shell to protect him, he had to keep moving. He went places and did things, developing techniques of rapid locomotion, concealment, and food entrapment in order to survive. The octopus, as the British biologist J. Z. Young has shown, is by far the smartest of the mollusca, being capable of learning and even of certain elementary kinds of problem-solving. In other words, mobility brings you in contact with many aspects of the environment and therefore inevitably develops intelligence.

Or take the matter of the warm-bloodedness of mammals. The cold-blooded animal is the prisoner of the temperature he happens to be in. In cold weather, he slows down to a complete halt—like the alligators that lie motionless at the bottom of the pool in the Sacramento zoo in January. The warm-blooded animals, including the birds, maintain their body heat regardless of outside temperature.

Able to stay cool in hot climates and to stay warm in cold climates, mammals have great mobility, and are able to live in and wander around in far more places than the reptiles.

Warm-bloodedness is inextricably connected with mobility, therefore expanded opportunities for information-gathering, and therefore intelligence. The anatomical and nervous structures necessary to take in and utilize a great abundance of information and the habits of sociability to ensure the sharing of that information—these are the dominant characteristics of the higher mammals.

These characteristics achieve their highest development in man, whom Weston La Barre calls *The Human Animal* in a book of that title and whom Desmond Morris in the title of a more recent book calls *The Naked Ape*. The sexuality of human beings is profoundly a part of, and an extension of, their mammalian and primate nature.

It is of enormous human consequence that our remote ancestors lived in trees. In the trees they were safe from prowling quadrupeds, such as tigers and jaguars. Anatomical adaptation made life in the trees possible: the grasping hands and feet to enable locomotion in the treetops; the ability to rotate the arms in their sockets; the eyes side by side at the front of the face and not at the sides of the head as in quadrupeds, so that there would be binocular vision essential to the accurate judging of distances when swinging from branch to branch.

Think for a moment about the hand. A horse cannot scratch its own back; monkeys and people can. With the hand at the end of a brachiating, jointed arm, monkeys and human beings grasp things, bring them close to inspect them with their binocular eyes, put things in their mouths to taste or bite. These are all primate ways of taking in detailed information about the world.

If you have a small baby who is always putting things in his mouth, don't slap him as stupid mothers do. The baby is merely being true to his basic nature. Simply don't leave things around that are unsafe—and make sure to leave a number of things around that he may bite and taste and chew and spit out. It's all part of his education.

The big problem of tree-dwelling creatures is the danger of falling out. The grasping hands and feet are, of course, insurance against this danger. But their babies too are in danger of falling out. Therefore the species of tree-dwelling primates that survived developed out of necessity the principle of having one baby at a time and taking extremely good care of it—which is the reason that ape and human mothers have one pair of teats high up on the chest, rather than a long row of them along the whole under side, like sows.

Also, the baby of the tree-dwelling primate was born with an instinct, which human babies are also born with, for grasping with its hands the fur of its mother and sustaining its own weight. An extremely close interindividual process develops between baby and mother. Babies hold their mothers and are held; they are cuddled and rocked and played with and carried from place to place. The mammalian process of suckling gives gratification to both baby and mother, making them necessary to each other. Some larger quadrupeds, for example the elephant, are like the higher primates in having one baby at a time, and therefore developing an intense mother-child relationship.

The cherishing of each individual life is not simply a moral demand peculiar to highly developed civilizations. It is a basic demand of uniparous mammals, including elephants, who, as many readers will remember from the accounts of the explorer Carl Akeley, attempt furiously to save each other's lives and mourn deeply the death of one of their group.

For the purposes of taking in information, human beings have great visual acuity, excellent hearing, an extraordinarily delicate sense of touch (especially at the lips and tongue and fingertips), a nervous system that transmits data with great rapidity, but a very limited sense of smell—not one-tenth as acute as that of the dog and even less acute than that of the elephant, who holds up the wet tip of his proboscis and turns it from side to side like radar to detect the faint odors from any direction.

Weston La Barre says that the sense of smell is subordinated in the tree-dwelling primates because of the greater importance of vision to creatures living high above the ground. But he further suggests that the sense of smell may well have been repressed. Baby primates clinging to their mothers would keep her fur soiled. Nests would frequently be fouled. Perhaps the repression of smell was necessary among higher primates so that they could endure each other at close quarters.

Whatever the evolutionary facts may be, Professor La Barre's suggestion certainly fits in with an observation we have all made at one time or another, namely, that people usually prefer smelly company to no company at all—and as soon as they are absorbed in socializing they don't notice the smells any more. Any crowded dance hall or night club gives evidence of the ease with which human beings adjust to strong odors—to say nothing of the smell of New York City, even without a garbage men's strike.

But the most important fact about human beings is their nonseasonal sexuality. Almost all other creatures have a mating season, an estrous cycle—periods of being in heat interspersed with long periods of sexual quiescence or apathy. The female of many mammals is sexually receptive only during ovulation, which, as in the porcupine, according to Sally Carrighar in *Wild Heritage,* is only once a year.

Male sea lions attend their females during the mating season, but as soon as the mating is over, they take off, leaving the care of the young to the females. They go hunting, or go to the club to shoot pool, or whatever it is that menfolk do when they're by themselves, and the ladies don't see them again until next mating season.

But human beings are different. The adult male is capable of being sexually aroused with or without provocation at practically any time. Female receptivity is interrupted by childbirth, but not by pregnancy. Shortly after the pregnancy is over, the female is back in business again. Human beings are just about always interested in sex. "Never on Sunday" is not a biological rule—merely a professional one.

At first it seems quite illogical that human beings, with the great reproductive economy that enables them to continue the race and multiply while bearing only a few young, should be so permanently and obsessively interested in sex. The reason for this is that sexual activity in human beings, as Weston La Barre says, serves two purposes—not merely reproduction, but the ensuring of social cohesion. Not merely procreation, but recreation. With his nonseasonal sexual interest, the male does not leave the female to bring up the young by herself. Baby and mother are tied to each other by suckling and by the prolonged dependency of the human infant. The male is tied to the mother by sexual interest—and has to learn to get along with the children. The advantage to the species is that the young of an information-gathering class of life have much to learn from the father as well as the mother.

Thus the life-long patterns of human communication and inter-action are learned in the family. Sons and daughters learn to relate to mothers and fathers and to each other. This basic training in communication will serve them all their lives. And Freudians are quite right in attributing many of the difficulties of adult life to unresolved problems of communication and interrelationship left over from childhood experience.

Desmond Morris has an ingenious argument about the relation of man's sexuality to his way of life. "The naked ape," he writes, "is the sexiest primate alive." Because men were hunters, and because they had to cooperate in the hunt, and because sexual rivalries among weapon-using men would jeopardize cooperation, and be-cause men had to take some share in the education of children, the pairing of one man with one woman made a lot of biological sense, says Morris. Such stable pairing would reduce jealousies among men, establish peace and cooperation in the group, and give the children the well-protected childhood necessary for them to develop their brain capacity.

"Given this situation as a starting point," Morris writes, "we can see how often things grew from it. The naked ape had to de-velop the capacity for falling in love, for becoming sexually im-printed on a single partner, for evolving a pair-bond."

What prepares the human being for the pair-bond is his own long childhood, involving deep attachment to his mother. As the child grows up he needs another relationship as stable and as strong.

Because in mature pairing a deep and lasting relationship is sought, human courtship is more protracted, more elaborate, than that of any other creature. There is a vast amount of small talk in courtship—the exchange of words not for the sake of transmitting information so much as for the sake of assessing the nature of the interpersonal relationship or evoking emotional states. If each hears in the voice of the other the affection and reassurance evocative of the sounds they heard as babies from their own parents, they feel more and more at ease with each other.

Courtship for human beings is an immense communicative process. Dancing together, picnicking, going to ball games or movies, talking and teasing and testing each other, the couple finds occasion after occasion for comparing each other's reactions to the world, adjusting to each other, trying to decide if there is enough depth to the relationship to make it a durable one.

All the senses are brought into play. Assessments of the partner's sincerity or insincerity, gentleness or callousness, thoughtfulness or selfishness are made by reading subverbal as well as verbal cues: the way your partner holds your hand, takes your arm, or returns your gaze. The long courtship is certainly an essential part of what Morris calls sexual imprinting. As the song-writers say, it is the touch of *your* hand, it is *your* smile, *your* hair, that mean so much to me—and not someone else's hand or smile or hair.

And when it comes to mating, this too, like courtship, is richer for human beings than for other animals. "In baboons," says Morris, "the time taken from mounting to ejaculation is no more than seven to eight seconds . . . the female does not appear to experience any kind of climax." For human beings, sex is infinitely sexier than for the baboon; "the hunting life that gave us naked skins and more sensitive hands has given us much greater scope for sexually stimulating body-to-body contacts. . . . Stroking, rubbing, pressing and caressing occur in abundance and far exceed anything found in other primate species. Also, specialized organs such as lips, ear-lobes, nipples, breasts and genitals are richly endowed with nerve-endings and have become highly sensitized to erotic tactile stimulation."

But just as important as the tactile signals are the visual signals—the responsive facial expression of the partner—and the auditory signals—the voice husky with sexual excitement.

Sexual union then is a profound person-to-person communication, the culmination of all the communications antecedent to it. The sexually attractive and the sexually sensitive areas of the body are largely in front. It is therefore by no means accidental that a vast majority of the human race unite sexually in face-to-face position. "The frontal approach means that the in-coming sexual signals and rewards are kept tightly linked with the identity signals from the partner," writes Morris. "Face-to-face sex is 'personalized sex.' "

In other words we are so constructed as to derive additional sexual pleasure from knowing who we're sleeping with. The sexual act derives richness from all the prior imprintings of the valued partner. And sexual pleasure is cumulative, each imprinting reinforcing the effect of past imprintings.

Sexual anarchists and advocates of sexual freedom proclaim that the general attitudes and legislation in favor of durable monogamous relationships are merely cultural prejudices, and that monogamy is contrary to human nature. Although Morris uses the term "pair-bond" in place of "monogamy" and "imprinting" in place of "love," those who read his book will find new grounds for questioning the easy dogmatism of sexual freedom advocates about the nature of human nature.

For human beings sexual imprintings necessarily involve communicative imprintings. Reinforcing the sensual pair-bond for a couple who have lived together for many years are all the communications they have exchanged, the understandings they have established, the feelings they have shared. They have talked to each other about themselves, their friends, the adventures they have had, their home, their financial problems, their children, their political decisions, and their philosophies.

For the talkative class of life, a pair-bond is never solely the result of conditioning to mutually pleasurable erotic sensations. In the human pair-bond the erotic is inextricably bound up with the semantic.

Nature has so distributed our nerve-endings and constructed our bodies and brains that the profoundest joy we can experience comes from an erotic-semantic attachment reinforced by repeated imprintings over a long period of time.

Like a work of art, a durable pair-bond is not instinctually given. It is an achievement, and like all other worth-while human achievements, it is the product of patience, thought, and self-discipline.

Good communication is therefore at the heart of good sexuality. How can it be nurtured?

Certainly training in communication and responsiveness begins in infancy. Babies need to be cuddled and held and patted and talked to—all through their babyhood. To deprive babies of this kind of stimulation is to leave them deprived of a necessary ingredient in their education. Even the understanding of language in later life may be impaired by lack of contact with the experiences language stands for. As Lawrence K. Frank has written: "Without tactile communication, interpersonal relations would be bare and largely meaningless, with a minimum of affective coloring or emotional provocation, since linguistic and much of kinetic communication are signs and symbols which become operative only by evoking some of the responses which were initially stimulated by the tactile stimuli for which these signs and symbols are surrogates."

Elementary lessons in interaction are begun from the first moment the mother tries to coax a smile from the baby and the baby learns to smile in response. A somewhat more advanced lesson is the game of pattycake (variants of which are found in all cultures) in which the mother elicits the baby's response and the baby, by responding, elicits the mother's response in a continuing interaction.

Certainly there is not space here to go into all the ingredients of child-rearing that bear upon the development of the child's communicative abilities, but one general rule can be stated: just as we learn to swim by swimming, so we learn to communicate by communicating. Children throughout their childhood must have ample opportunity to interact with other children and adults of both sexes and, if possible, of many different ages. Our present culture segregates the old into retirement communities, the young married with their small children into tract homes, and the more prosperous middle-aged into fashionable suburbs. I think we are all deprived by this segregation—and small children most of all.

Television is a wonderful invention, bringing the whole amazing world into our living rooms. But valuable as television is, it must be used wisely. Too often, mothers use the television set as a pacifier, and millions of young children all over America are placed in front of television sets to be out of mother's way.

But the terrible thing about a television set is that you can have no interaction with it. No matter what the child says or does, the TV set continues to do what it was going to do anyway—so that the child gets no experience in influencing behavior and being influenced in return.

Having a puppy is in this sense far more important to a child than having a television set, although of course there is no reason he should not have both. The great American tragedy is the family of parents and children sitting with their TV dinners in their laps, watching the program, *and not talking to one another!*

The child who watches TV for four hours daily between the ages of three and eighteen spends something like 22,000 hours in passive contemplation of the screen—hours stolen from the time needed to learn to relate to siblings, playmates, parents, grandparents, and neighbors. Is there any connection between this fact and the sudden appearance in the past few years of an enormous number of young people who don't know how to relate to anybody—and drop out?

The mother who thinks she is saving herself time and trouble by setting her child for hours and hours daily in front of the television set instead of telling him stories or reading him books is certainly deceiving herself. The time and trouble she saves now may be only a fraction of what she will lose in worries later on.

Fathers have their own way of evading their parental responsibilities—and one of them is to get terribly wrapped up in their business or career. They often justify their neglect by saying that it is not neglect at all—they are merely trying to provide for their children as well as possible. But children need emotional just as much as financial support; they need father's companionship even more than they need the private swimming pool paid for by father's absence.

And father, staying late at the office to plan a new strategy for the sale of automatic garage doors, doesn't know what he is missing: communication with his children, watching the growth of their bodies, the expansion of their minds, and the emergence of their unique and individual personalities.

I am afraid it must be clear from what I am saying that what makes for good adult sexuality is not essentially different from what makes for emotional stability and maturity. So let me expand on some aspects of the problem of maturity as they affect sexual relations.

One of the fascinating things that Dr. Eric Berne says in his famous book, *Games People Play,* is that we all have three ego states—states of mind—which he calls Parent, Adult, and Child. The Parent in you is protective, admonitory, often scolding or censorious, as your own parents were to you when you were a child. The Adult in you is busy taking in information about the environment and solving problems in the light of that information. The Child is playful, imaginative, mischievous, irresponsible, exasperating, and lovable. Dr. Berne's theory is most quickly illustrated by his own example. He bought an expensive car when his book became successful. He explained that his Child—that is, the Child in him—bought it; his Adult paid for it; his Parent tells him not to drive too fast.

Now, in any love relationship, all people have their emotional ups and downs. Couples who get along supremely well are those profoundly attuned to each other's moods. Most of the time the man and woman relate to each other as Adults, discussing realistically their finances, their children's education, their social obligations, or whatever.

Sometimes, however, the woman is ill or nervous or anxious or afraid and needs protection, in which case the man can be a Parent to her Child. She is "baby" who can depend on "Big Daddy" to protect her.

But sometimes it's the other way. The man has had reverses in business or career. He is anxious or discouraged. At this point, the woman is Parent, the wonderful, protective mother whose love protects and strengthens her little boy.

Sometimes, as they worry about their children—and especially about their children's friends—they talk as Parent to Parent; and the favorite remark of communication at this level is, "What *is* the younger generation coming to?"

Then when the man and woman make love, they may become teasing, giggly, playful, spontaneous, emotionally expressive—a Child-to-Child relationship.

A complete love relationship over a long period of time necessarily means, then, sensitivity to the moods of the other and the ability to respond to them. If the woman cannot be the big strong mother when her big strong husband is for the time being a frightened little boy, or if the man cannot be the protective father when his wife is a scared little girl, then there's something lacking in the relationship.

Even more seriously, if either one remains persistently the child when adult thinking and adult decisions are called for, there is something very much wrong in the relationship.

In courtship, one can easily be misled by a pleasant Child-to-Child relationship; the couple go to parties and dances and the girl can say, "But he's such *fun* to be with!" After marriage, however, it is sometimes discovered, too late, that the boy who was such fun to be with is incurably a boy, incapable of assuming adult responsibilities.

So to young people going steady but not yet married, perhaps it would be good advice to say, "It's nice that you have such good times together. But don't marry until you've faced some kind of big troublesome problem together—not interpersonal problems between you, but problems given by the world around you. If you can gain strength from each other by confronting this problem, if your respect for each other increases as you discover each other's emotional resources, maybe you *are* meant for each other."

Let me quote from a letter received by Mrs. Alice Kermeen, director of the San Francisco State College Faculty Program Series, from a lady in Oakland after a recent weekend seminar.

The lady is intellectually inclined. She goes to seminars and is excited by the ideas and wants to be friends on an intellectual basis with some of the fine lecturers she has heard. Invariably, she gets the door politely slammed in her face. The men seem terribly afraid of getting involved. "I am forced to the conclusion," she writes, "that if a man *doesn't* want 'to get involved,' then he sees no point in talking to a woman *at all*. A thinking woman is to most men some sort of contradiction in terms."

"I really don't think," the lady from Oakland continues, "that men decide deliberately to exclude women from intellectual discussions. It's more that it doesn't occur to them to include a woman among their circle of friends on the basis of the ideas she is able to contribute. Ideas are not what women are for."

At the end of her letter the lady adds, "My husband has just read this and he has a reply which may shed light on the male viewpoint. He said, 'You're too pretty to be friends with.' (He's prejudiced.) I pursued this with, 'Why can't women be people to men?' His reply is that it is the male nature to be interested in the femaleness of the female rather than any other aspect of her. . . .

"Go fight *that!* I quit."

So my final question for discussion here is that raised by the lady from Oakland. Is it the male nature to be interested in the femaleness of the female to the exclusion of interest in her ideas?

I don't think so. We have in the United States long established the principle that women are as much entitled to a college education as men. But we don't in actual practice believe in the principle. On the whole, girls are not encouraged to pursue their intellectual interests—or even their interest in sports, mechanics, or anything else not specifically defined as a legitimate female interest by *Good Housekeeping Magazine*. If a young girl gets excited about mathematics or philosophy or sports car racing, her elders smile among themselves and say, "She'll soon get over all this nonsense when she has her own babies to take care of."

But today with child-spacing an almost universal practice and all sorts of electrical appliances in the home, babies and housework need not be full-time occupations, especially as the children grow to school age. Thousands of women take jobs today not because the family needs the extra money, but because they cannot endure the boredom of underemployed hands and minds.

Perhaps these working women in teaching, in office jobs, in industry, in public office, have part of the answer to the lady from Oakland. As men become more accustomed to dealing with women executives, women colleagues, women members of congress, women competitors in business, they will listen to them for their ideas as well as look over their charms.

If the highest levels of sexuality are achieved only through fullness of communication, it is clear that the more things a man and wife have to communicate about—not only children and food and neighbors, but also current events, the stock market, automobiles, politics, religion, philosophy, natural history, or science—the more enriched will be the relationship between them.

The real frustration of women, so well expressed by the lady from Oakland, is their exclusion from the mainstream. It is a frustration that women experience in common with Negroes. The solution to these frustrations lies partly in the re-education of menfolk on the one hand and white folk on the other to enable them to adjust gracefully to the inevitable changes that lie ahead. It also lies in the determination of courageous women and courageous Negroes to fight their way into the mainstream despite all attempts to keep them in their places.

REFERENCES

Leon Adams, *Striped Bass Fishing on the Pacific Coast.* Palo Alto: Pacific Books, 1958.

Sally Carrighar, *Wild Heritage.* Boston: Houghton Mifflin, 1965.

Lawrence K. Frank, "Tactile Communication." *ETC.*, XVI (1958), 31–79.

Weston La Barre, *The Human Animal.* Chicago: University of Chicago Press, 1954.

Susan Michelmore, *Sexual Reproduction.* New York: American Museum Science Books, 1964.

Desmond Morris, *The Naked Ape.* New York: McGraw-Hill, 1967.

J. Z. Young, *Doubt and Certainty in Science.* New York: Oxford University Press, 1951.

A Survey of Adult Communication Activities

LARRY A. SAMOVAR
Professor of Speech, San Diego State College
ROBERT D. BROOKS
Communication and Public Address Dept.
University of Wisconsin
RICHARD E. PORTER
San Diego State College

The present survey investigated the communication activities of a general adult population. Particular attention was given to speaking and listening activities. The study includes a broad spectrum of occupations.

Questionnaires containing a communication log were mailed to four hundred randomly selected adults in the San Diego area. (One hundred and seventy-three logs were returned.) The logs, divided into fifteen minute segments, contained the following categories: sleep, no communication, conversation, television, reading, listening, speaking. Brief definitions for each of these categories were contained in a cover letter.

Results, in general, indicated: 1) that administrators, salesmen, students, teachers and professionals rank as high communicators; 2) approximately three-fourths (72.8%) of our waking time is given over to communication activities.

In 1928 and again in 1930, Rankin reported the results of his surveys of adult communication habits [6]. His primary question has permanent relevance to the field of communication: How many of our waking hours are devoted to communication activities? While Rankin's work was indeed pioneering, an argument can be made that his findings can not be generalized to an adult population of today. The *n* for the studies was quite small (21 and 47 respectively); more than half of the data were based on the responses of school teachers—whose communication activities may be far from typical; and the data were gathered in an era that predates the electronic revolution. The frequency with which Rankin's work is cited today is perhaps best explained by the absence of contemporary data [1]. To our knowledge, no survey of the speaking and listening habits of a general adult population has appeared since Rankin's.

From *The Journal of Communication*, 19: 301–307, 1969.

Recent investigations have tended to focus upon a particular occupational segment or upon a particular occupational group. Roethlisberger's 1941 study of business executives showed that their environment consisted largely of verbal communication [7]; Bird reported the communication patterns of dieticians in 1956 [2]; Breiter investigated the communication habits of housewives in 1957 [3]; Goetzinger and Valentine reported the communication patterns of an academic community in 1962 [4]; the same authors reported their study of top-level personnel in the Air Defense Command in 1963 [5]. Additionally, numerous studies have been conducted on limited topics, such as "upward" and "downward" communication patterns within a specific institution or industry.

The present study is an investigation of the communication activities of a general adult population. Particular attention was given to speaking and listening activities. The study includes a broad spectrum of occupations.

METHODOLOGY

Questionnaires containing a communication log were mailed to four hundred randomly selected adults in the metropolitan San Diego area. The log, quite similar to the one employed by Rankin, covered a normal weekday from awakening until 12:00 A.M. in fifteen-minute segments. Respondents filled in the log at personally convenient intervals throughout the day. The subjects were instructed to use code letters to designate the major communication activities in which they had engaged during each fifteen-minute segment. Communication categories for which code letters were assigned were: sleep—S; no communication—N; conversation—C; television—T; reading—R; listening—L; speaking—S. We were not concerned with writing activities.

Certain additional measures were based on the general procedure employed by Rankin. Thus two scores were calculated for speaking activities: S (one-way speaking) and S_t (S plus one-half the time logged in conversation). Three scores were calculated for listening activities: L (one-way listening), L_t (L plus one-half of the time logged in conversation), and LT_t (L_t plus the time logged in television).

Returned questionnaires were sorted according to fourteen occupational classes, most of which are commonly included in U.S. Census Bureau reports. Two measurements were tabulated for each occupation group: the average total time each group devoted to communication and the mean time each group logged in the specific types of communication activities.

RESULTS

One hundred and seventy-three communication logs were returned, forty-three percent of the total sample. While in some categories the response is quite limited (farmers and retired people particularly), the total response percentage is considerably above the norm for surveys of this kind. Thus within the general limitations inherent in mail survey techniques, and within the specific limitations of the sample studied here, we present the results below as indicative of contemporary adult communication habits.

Three questions guided the tabulation of the results for this survey.

1. *Which occupations logged the highest total time in communication activity and which the lowest?*

"Total time" was measured by two methods: as a percentage of the waking hours and as a percentage of the 24-hour day. The relevant data, including rank orderings, are presented in Table 1. The general pattern reflected in both measures is not surprising.

> 1-a. Administrators, salesmen, students, teachers, and professionals rank as high communicators.
>
> 1-b. Farmers, housewives, clerical workers, skilled craftsmen, and retired people rank as low communicators.

As one would expect, occupations which require contact with other people are generally associated with greater communication activity.

2. *Which occupations logged the highest time in specific types of communication activity?*

TABLE 1

Mean percent of time devoted to communication activity by occupation

Communication Category	Waking Hours	Waking Hour Rank	24-Hour Day	24-Hour Rank
Administrative	97.0	1	60.2	1
Agricultural	58.5	14	37.6	14
Civil Service	79.4	4	47.1	9
Clerical	65.5	12	43.4	11
Engineer	61.9	13	47.4	8
Housewife	66.5	10	42.1	13
Professional	76.4	6	50.0	5
Retired	65.6	11	42.8	12
Sales	86.3	2	55.2	2
Skilled	72.0	9	45.6	10
Student	82.7	3	53.0	3
Teacher	77.2	5	50.2	4
Technical	73.4	8	47.5	7
Unskilled	73.9	7	47.6	6
'Means for returned sample ($n = 173$)	72.8		47.2	

The findings relevant to this question are presented in Table 2. They can be summarized as follows:

2-a. Salesmen, teachers, and administrators—in that order—logged the highest speaking time by both the S and S_t measures.

2-b. Administrators and students logged the highest time in each of the listening measures (L, L_t, and LT_t).

2-c. While the n for agriculture is too small to permit sound generalization, the data indicate that farmers engage in conversation more than any other occupational group surveyed here. However, perhaps an equally reasonable interpretation of the data is this: farmers are more likely than other people to use "conversation" as a label for their speaking and listening behavior.

2-d. Salesmen logged the highest television time. However, when the salesmen's television time is compared to their other activity scores, television appears to be a tertiary activity. Farmers, clerical workers, retired people, and skilled craftsmen all logged television as their second highest communication activity.

TABLE 2

Percent of waking hours devoted to communication activities

Occupation Category	Communication Activity Means								
	n	S	L	C	T	R	L$_t$	LT$_t$	S$_t$
Administrative	22	23	20	29	12	13	35	48	37
Agricultural	3	0*	0*	40	18	0*	20	39	20
Civil Service	10	15	12	27	10	15	26	36	28
Clerical	28	15	13	18	16	5	21	38	24
Engineer	9	9	11	16	5	20	19	25	17
Housewife	20	9	13	27	7	12	26	33	23
Professional	8	19	14	27	9	8	28	36	32
Retired	3	7	9	12	17	21	15	31	13
Sales	17	27	9	24	19	8	21	40	39
Skilled	14	13	9	26	16	9	22	38	25
Student	15	5	20	25	13	20	33	46	17
Teacher	9	26	7	23	10	11	19	28	38
Technical	7	15	16	24	10	9	28	38	27
Unskilled	8	13	10	31	11	9	25	36	29
Means for returned sample (n = 173)		15.2	13.1	24.1	12.2	11.1	25.1	37.4	27.3

C = Conversation
T = Television
L = Listening
S = Speaking
R = Reading
L$_t$ = Listening, plus one-half of conversation
LT$_t$ = Total listening, L$_t$ plus one-half of television
S$_t$ = Total speaking, S plus one-half of conversation
C + T + L + S + R ≠ 100%
* = Less than 1%

2-e. Retired people, students, and engineers logged the highest reading time.

A third method of analysis is addressed to this question:

3. *With respect to the total returned sample, what ordering of communication activities emerges?*

Data relevant to this question are also included in Table 2. The findings are summarized below.

3-a. Based on percentages of waking hours, the rank order of activity means was found to be conversation (24.1%), speaking (15.2%), listening (13.1%), television (12.2%), and reading (11.1%).

3-b. Total listening time (LT$_t$) is greater than total speaking time (S$_t$) for all groups except teachers.

3-c. No group logged listening (L) as its highest communication activity.

3-d. No group logged television as its highest communication activity.

3-e. Without adjustment for ties, 50% of the groups logged reading as their lowest activity; only engineers logged reading as their highest communication activity.

CONCLUSION

Beyond the particular results detailed above, we believe that two general conclusions merit emphasis: (1) We live in a verbal environment indeed. Approximately three-fourths (72.8%) of our waking time is given to communication activities. All the occupational groups surveyed here reported spending more than half their waking hours in communication activities. And these are conservative data since they do not reflect the additional time given to such communication activities as writing, listening to the radio, or attending the movies. (2) Speaking and listening skills should receive considerable attention in education curricula. Approximately two-thirds (64.6%) of our subjects' waking hours is given to communication activities which require speaking or listening abilities. This too is a conservative estimate since the data do not include radio or movie activities. McLuhan's argument that we are returning to an oral-aural tribal society appears to be an understatement. Our data indicate we are there today.

REFERENCES

1. Among the many current publications which apparently rely upon the Rankin data are the following: BERLO, DAVID K. *The Process of Communciation*. New York: Holt, Rinehart, and Winston, 1960; HENNING, JAMES H. *Improving Oral Communication*. New York: McGraw-Hill, 1966; NICHOLS, RALPH G. AND LEONARD A. STEVENS, *Are You Listening?* New York: McGraw-Hill, 1957; OLIVER, ROBERT T. AND RUPERT L. CORTRIGHT, *Effective Speech*. New York: Holt, Rinehart and Winston, 1961; RAHSKOPF, HORACE G. *Basic Speech Improvement*. New York: Harper and Row, 1965; ROBINSON, KARL F. AND E. J. KERIKAS, *Teaching Speech: Methods and Materials*. New York: David McKay Co., 1963; ROSS, RAYMOND, *Speech Communication: Fundamentals and*

Practice. Englewood Cliffs, New Jersey: Prentice-Hall, 1965; WILSON, JOHN F. AND CARROLL C. ARNOLD, *Public Speaking as a Liberal Art*. Boston: Allyn and Bacon, 1968.

2. BIRD, DONALD E. "This is Your Listening Life." *Journal of the American Dietetic Association* 32: 534–36, 1956.

3. BREITER, LILA R. "Research in Listening and its Importance to Literature." Unpublished Master's thesis, Brooklyn College, 1957.

4. GOETZINGER, C. S. AND M. A. VALENTINE, "Communication Channels, Media, Directional Flow and Attitudes in an Academic Community." *Journal of Communication* 12: 23–26, 1962.

5. ———. "Communication Patterns, Interaction and Attitudes of Top-Level Personnel in the Air Defense Command." *Journal of Communication* 13: 54–57, 1963.

6. RANKIN, PAUL T. "The Importance of Listening Ability." *English Journal* 17: 623–30, 1928. PAUL T. RANKIN "Listening Ability: Its Importance, Measurement, and Development." *Chicago Schools Journal* 12: 177–79, 1930.

7. ROETHLISBERGER, F. J. *Management and Morale*. Cambridge, Mass., 1941.

Defensive Communication

JACK R. GIBB

One way to understand communication is to view it as a people process rather than as a language process. If one is to make fundamental improvement in communication, he must make changes in interpersonal relationships. One possible type of alteration—and the one with which this paper is concerned—is that of reducing the degree of defensiveness.

DEFINITION AND SIGNIFICANCE

Defensive behavior is defined as that behavior which occurs when an individual perceives threat or anticipates threat in the group. The person who behaves defensively, even though he also gives some

From *The Journal of Communication*, 11:141–148, September, 1961.

attention to the common task, devotes an appreciable portion of his energy to defending himself. Besides talking about the topic, he thinks about how he appears to others, how he may be seen more favorably, how he may win, dominate, impress, or escape punishment, and/or how he may avoid or mitigate a perceived or an anticipated attack.

Such inner feelings and outward acts tend to create similarly defensive postures in others; and, if unchecked, the ensuing circular response becomes increasingly destructive. Defensive behavior, in short, engenders defensive listening, and this in turn produces postural, facial, and verbal cues which raise the defense level of the original communicator.

Defense arousal prevents the listener from concentrating upon the message. Not only do defensive communicators send off multiple value, motive, and affect cues, but also defensive recipients distort what they receive. As a person becomes more and more defensive, he becomes less and less able to perceive accurately the motives, the values, and the emotions of the sender. The writer's analyses of tape recorded discussions revealed that increases in defensive behavior were correlated positively with losses in efficiency in communication.[1] Specifically, distortions became greater when defensive states existed in the groups.

The converse, moreover, also is true. The more "supportive" or defense reductive the climate the less the receiver reads into the communication distorted loadings which arise from projections of his own anxieties, motives, and concerns. As defenses are reduced, the receivers become better able to concentrate upon the structure, the content, and the cognitive meanings of the message.

CATEGORIES OF DEFENSIVE AND SUPPORTIVE COMMUNICATION

In working over an eight-year period with recordings of discussions occurring in varied settings, the writer developed the six pairs of defensive and supportive categories presented in Table 1. Behavior which a listener perceives as possessing any of the characteristics listed in the left-hand column arouses defensiveness, whereas that

[1] J. R. Gibb, "Defense Level and Influence Potential in Small Groups," in L. Petrullo and B. M. Bass (eds.), *Leadership and Interpersonal Behavior* (New York: Holt, Rinehart and Winston, Inc., 1961), pp. 63–81.

TABLE 1

Categories of Behavior Characteristic of Supportive and
Defensive Climates in Small Groups

Defensive Climates	Supportive Climates
1. Evaluation	1. Description
2. Control	2. Problem orientation
3. Strategy	3. Spontaneity
4. Neutrality	4. Empathy
5. Superiority	5. Equality
6. Certainty	6. Provisionalism

which he interprets as having any of the qualities designated as supportive reduces defensive feelings. The degree to which these reactions occur depends upon the personal level of defensiveness and upon the general climate in the group at the time.[2]

Evaluation and Description

Speech or other behavior which appears evaluative increases defensiveness. If by expression, manner of speech, tone of voice, or verbal content the sender seems to be evaluating or judging the listener, then the receiver goes on guard. Of course, other factors may inhibit the reaction. If the listener thought that the speaker regarded him as an equal and was being open and spontaneous, for example, the evaluativeness in a message would be neutralized and perhaps not even perceived. This same principle applies equally to the other five categories of potentially defense-producing climates. The six sets are interactive.

Because our attitudes toward other persons are frequently, and often necessarily, evaluative, expressions which the defensive person will regard as nonjudgmental are hard to frame. Even the simplest question usually conveys the answer that the sender wishes or implies the response that would fit into his value system. A mother, for example, immediately following an earth tremor that shook the house, sought for her small son with the question: "Bobby, where are you?" The timid and plaintive "Mommy, I didn't do it" indicated how Bobby's chronic mild defensiveness predisposed him to

[2] J. R. Gibb, "Sociopsychological Processes of Group Instruction," in N. B. Henry (ed.), *The Dynamics of Instructional Groups* (Fifty-ninth Yearbook of the National Society for the Study of Education, Part II, 1960), pp. 115–135.

react with a projection of his own guilt and in the context of his chronic assumption that questions are full of accusation.

Anyone who has attempted to train professionals to use information-seeking speech with neutral affect appreciates how difficult it is to teach a person to say even the simple "who did that?" without being seen as accusing. Speech is so frequently judgmental that there is a reality base for the defensive interpretations which are so common.

When insecure, group members are particularly likely to place blame, to see others as fitting into categories of good or bad, to make moral judgments of their colleagues, and to question the value, motive, and affect loadings of the speech which they hear. Since value loadings imply a judgment of others, a belief that the standards of the speaker differ from his own causes the listener to become defensive.

Descriptive speech, in contrast to that which is evaluative, tends to arouse a minimum of uneasiness. Speech acts which the listener perceives as genuine requests for information or as material with neutral loadings is descriptive. Specifically, presentations of feelings, events, perceptions, or processes which do not ask or imply that the receiver change behavior or attitude are minimally defense producing. The difficulty in avoiding overtone is illustrated by the problems of news reporters in writing stories about unions, communists, Negroes, and religious activities without tipping off the "party" line of the newspaper. One can often tell from the opening words in a news article which side the newspaper's editorial policy favors.

Control and Problem Orientation

Speech which is used to control the listener evokes resistance. In most of our social intercourse someone is trying to do something to someone else—to change an attitude, to influence behavior, or to restrict the field of activity. The degree to which attempts to control produce defensiveness depends upon the openness of the effort, for a suspicion that hidden motives exist heightens resistance. For this reason attempts of nondirective therapists and progressive educators to refrain from imposing a set of values, a point of view, or a problem solution upon the receivers meet with many barriers. Since the norm is control, noncontrollers must earn the perceptions that their efforts have no hidden motives. A bombardment of persuasive "messages" in the fields of politics, education, special causes, advertising, religion, medicine, industrial relations, and guidance has bred cynical and paranoidal responses in listeners.

Implicit in all attempts to alter another person is the assumption by the change agent that the person to be altered is inadequate. That the speaker secretly views the listener as ignorant, unable to make his own decisions, uninformed, immature, unwise, or possessed of wrong or inadequate attitudes is a subconscious perception which gives the latter a valid base for defensive reactions.

Methods of control are many and varied. Legalistic insistence on detail, restrictive regulations and policies, conformity norms, and all laws are among the methods. Gestures, facial expressions, other forms of nonverbal communication, and even such simple acts as holding a door open in a particular manner are means of imposing one's will upon another and hence are potential sources of resistance.

Problem orientation, on the other hand, is the antithesis of persuasion. When the sender communicates a desire to collaborate in defining a mutual problem and in seeking its solution, he tends to create the same problem orientation in the listener; and, of greater importance, he implies that he has no predetermined solution, attitude, or method to impose. Such behavior is permissive in that it allows the receiver to set his own goals, make his own decisions, and evaluate his own progress—or to share with the sender in doing so. The exact methods of attaining permissiveness are not known, but they must involve a constellation of cues and they certainly go beyond mere verbal assurances that the communicator has no hidden desires to exercise control.

Strategy and Spontaneity

When the sender is perceived as engaged in a stratagem involving ambiguous and multiple motivations, the receiver becomes defensive. No one wishes to be a guinea pig, a role player, or an impressed actor, and no one likes to be the victim of some hidden motivation. That which is concealed, also, may appear larger than it really is with the degree of defensiveness of the listener determining the perceived size of the suppressed element. The intense reaction of the reading audience to the material in the *Hidden Persuaders* indicates the prevalence of defensive reactions to multiple motivations behind strategy. Group members who are seen as "taking a role," as feigning emotion, as toying with their colleagues, as withholding information, or as having special sources of data are especially resented. One participant once complained that another was "using a listening technique" on him!

A large part of the adverse reaction to much of the so-called human relations training is a feeling against what are perceived as gimmicks and tricks to fool or to "involve" people, to make a person think he is making his own decision, or to make the listener feel that the sender is genuinely interested in him as a person. Particularly violent reactions occur when it appears that someone is trying to make a stratagem appear spontaneous. One person has reported a boss who incurred resentment by habitually using the gimmick of "spontaneously" looking at his watch and saying, "My gosh, look at the time—I must run to an appointment." The belief was that the boss would create less irritation by honestly asking to be excused.

Similarly, the deliberate assumption of guilelessness and natural simplicity is especially resented. Monitoring the tapes of feedback and evaluation sessions in training groups indicates the surprising extent to which members perceive the strategies of their colleagues. This perceptual clarity may be quite shocking to the strategist, who usually feels that he has cleverly hidden the motivational aura around the "gimmick."

This aversion to deceit may account for one's resistance to politicians who are suspected of behind-the-scenes planning to get his vote, to psychologists whose listening apparently is motivated by more than the manifest or content-level interest in his behavior, or to the sophisticated, smooth, or clever person whose "one-up-manship" is marked with guile. In training groups the role-flexible person frequently is resented because his changes in behavior are perceived as strategic maneuvers.

In contrast, behavior which appears to be spontaneous and free of deception is defense reductive. If the communicator is seen as having a clean id, as having uncomplicated motivations, as being straightforward and honest, and as behaving spontaneously in response to the situation, he is likely to arouse minimal defense.

Neutrality and Empathy

When neutrality in speech appears to the listener to indicate a lack of concern for his welfare, he becomes defensive. Group members usually desire to be perceived as valued persons, as individuals of special worth, and as objects of concern and affection. The clinical, detached, person-is-an-object-of-study attitude on the part of many psychologist-trainers is resented by group members. Speech with low affect that communicates little warmth or caring is in such contrast with the affect-laden speech in social situations that it sometimes communicates rejection.

Communication that conveys empathy for the feelings and respect for the worth of the listener, however, is particularly supportive and defense reductive. Reassurance results when a message indicates that the speaker identifies himself with the listener's problems, shares his feelings, and accepts his emotional reactions at face value. Abortive efforts to deny the legitimacy of the receiver's emotions by assuring the receiver that he need not feel bad, that he should not feel rejected, or that he is overly anxious, though often intended as support giving, may impress the listener as lack of acceptance. The combination of understanding and empathizing with the other person's emotions with no accompanying effort to change him apparently is supportive at a high level.

The importance of gestural behavioral cues in communicating empathy should be mentioned. Apparently spontaneous facial and bodily evidences of concern are often interpreted as especially valid evidence of deep-level acceptance.

Superiority and Equality

When a person communicates to another that he feels superior in position, power, wealth, intellectual ability, physical characteristics, or other ways, he arouses defensiveness. Here, as with the other sources of disturbance, whatever arouses feelings of inadequacy causes the listener to center upon the affect loading of the statement rather than upon the cognitive elements. The receiver then reacts by not hearing the message, by forgetting it, by competing with the sender, or by becoming jealous of him.

The person who is perceived as feeling superior communicates that he is not willing to enter into a shared problem-solving relationship, that he probably does not desire feedback, that he does not require help, and/or that he will be likely to try to reduce the power, the status, or the worth of the receiver.

Many ways exist for creating the atmosphere that the sender

feels himself equal to the listener. Defenses are reduced when one perceives the sender as being willing to enter into participative planning with mutual trust and respect. Differences in talent, ability, worth, appearance, status, and power often exist, but the low defense communicator seems to attach little importance to these distinctions.

Certainty and Provisionalism

The effects of dogmatism in producing defensiveness are well known. Those who seem to know the answers, to require no additional data, and to regard themselves as teachers rather than as co-workers tend to put others on guard. Moreover, in the writer's experiment, listeners often perceived manifest expressions of certainty as connoting inward feelings of inferiority. They saw the dogmatic individual as needing to be right, as wanting to win an argument rather than solve a problem, and as seeing his ideas as truths to be defended. This kind of behavior often was associated with acts which others regarded as attempts to exercise control. People who were right seemed to have low tolerance for members who were "wrong"—i.e., who did not agree with the sender.

One reduces the defensiveness of the listener when he communicates that he is willing to experiment with his own behavior, attitudes, and ideas. The person who appears to be taking provisional attitudes, to be investigating issues rather than taking sides on them, to be problem solving rather than debating, and to be willing to experiment and explore tends to communicate that the listener may have some control over the shared quest or the investigation of the ideas. If a person is genuinely searching for information and data, he does not resent help or company along the way.

CONCLUSION

The implications of the above material for the parent, the teacher, the manager, the administrator, or the therapist are fairly obvious. Arousing defensiveness interferes with communication and thus makes it difficult—and sometimes impossible—for anyone to convey ideas clearly and to move effectively toward the solution of therapeutic, educational, or managerial problems.

A Better World for Fewer Children

GEORGE WALD
Higgins Professor of Biology
Harvard University

None of the things that now most need to be done for our country and for the world have much chance of working unless coupled with the control of population. By present indications our present population of 3.5 billions will have doubled by the end of this century. Long before that, we can expect famine on an unprecedented scale in many parts of the world.

Yet this in itself is not the heart of the problem. If it were, one would have some small reason for optimism; for in the last decade the world's food supplies have increased more rapidly than its population.

The concept that food is the primary problem is a prevalent and dangerous misunderstanding. It implies that the main point of the human enterprise from now on will be to see how many persons can be kept alive on the surface of the earth. A distinguished demographer recently estimated that with what he calls "proper management" we could support a world population of forty billions.

Of course, under those conditions people would not eat meat; there would be no place for cows, sheep, or pigs in such a world. This would be an altogether bankrupt view of the human enterprise. Humanity still has a chance at creating an ever wider, richer, and more meaningful culture. This would degrade it to simple production—a meaningless venture in simple multiplication. Even that, however well managed, must come to an end, as the potential resources of the planet become insufficient to feed further numbers of people.

The point then is not how many people one can feed on this planet, but what population can best fulfill human potentialities. One is interested not in the quantity but in the quality of human life. From that point of view the world is probably already overpopulated. China and India were once great cultures, enormously creative in the sciences, the visual arts, and literature; but those

Reprinted by permission from the April, 1970 issue of *The Progressive* magazine, copyright © 1970 by the Progressive, Inc.

aspects of Indian and Chinese culture declined centuries ago for reasons associated, I think, with overpopulation.

The Western world also is becoming crowded; I do not think it irrelevant that the quality of our production in the arts has declined greatly in the last century or two. Western science is flourishing, but the productivity of the individual scientist is nothing like what it was up to a century ago. It would take four to six top scientists of the present generation to approach in productivity, scope, and quality the contributions of Charles Darwin, Hermann von Helmholtz, or James Clerk Maxwell. Those men had no labor-saving devices, so far as I know not even secretaries—no dictaphones, microfilm, computerized information, retrieval services, and the like. They did, however, have peace and quiet, the chance to walk through green fields, along quiet rivers, and to find relief from all the crowding, noise, filth, and endless distractions of modern urban life.

A second profound misunderstanding has plagued many earlier discussions of the population problem. This is the widely prevalent view that the poor are over-reproducing, the well-to-do are under-reproducing, and the quality of the human race is hence going downhill. Quite apart from the naive assumption that the economically poor are necessarily also genetically inferior, there are other, almost as serious troubles with this view of the problem.

We are beginning to realize now that it is precisely the well-to-do and their children who make the most trouble—who are at once the biggest consumers and the biggest polluters. That is true individually, and has its national aspects. It is claimed by reliable sources that an American child uses fifty times as much of the world's resources as an Indian child. Our country, which contains only about six per cent of the world's population, uses about forty per cent of the world's resources, and accounts for about fifty per cent of the world's industrial pollution.

So it is essential that we bring world population under control, not only to keep it from increasing further, but if possible cut it down from its present level. That won't be easy or altogether pleasant. Indeed, it will be so difficult that we would be well advised to choose any viable alternative. But there is none. It is that or disaster. We are not being *asked*, but *told* to control world population. That is now our only chance of a meaningful survival. And whatever is done now must be done quickly, not only because the population is increasing so explosively, but because as one consequence the quality of human life has already been eroded. We must be aware of the danger that persons of future generations, even more out of contact than we with the potentialities of a less crowded world, will have lost a wider human view, and will have become unable to help themselves. In that sense we may be the last generation that can save humanity.

So what to do? First, as rapidly as possible make convenient, safe, and cheap—I would rather say free—means of birth control universally available. That, however, will certainly not be enough. I think we must as rapidly as possible make convenient, safe, altogether legal, and cheap—again I would rather say free—means of abortion universally available.

I hope for the early advent of a safe and efficient abortion pill. There are recent reports of encouraging work in this direction, from England and Sweden, with one of the prostaglandins. I think the condition we must try to achieve everywhere and as rapidly as possible is to see to it that nowhere in the world need a woman have an unwanted child. Having got there, we can take stock and see whether that is yet enough. Very likely not; and then we shall have to go on with a variety of other reasonable procedures. We might begin some of those procedures much sooner: for example, legislate tax discouragements rather than incentives for bearing children, particularly beyond the first two.

Many people still have trouble with the thought of legalized abortion. Of course the Roman Catholic Church is deeply opposed to it. Lately it has at least considered accepting contraception, before officially deciding against it. It seems to me likely that having once opened the question of contraception, it will now prove very difficult to close.

Abortion, however, is not only rejected by the Catholic hierarchy, but apparently also by large numbers of Catholic laymen. They regard abortion as highly immoral, indeed a form of murder.

It is difficult for me to appreciate the morality of that position in view of the present condition of the world's children. If we were in fact taking proper care of children all over the world, raising them with enough food and shelter and clothing so that they had the chance to fulfill their genetic potentialities, then we might have the privilege of feeling that every embryo should be born. As it is, however, the world's population is now mainly held down through infant mortality. What is killing those children is war, famine, disease, and poverty. That is our present condition, one in which we turn the Four Horsemen of the Apocalypse loose upon the children of the earth. Surely we can and must do better than that.

It is not as though we were asked to introduce abortion into a world that is not already practicing it. It is in fact practiced very widely, not only in those few nations where it is legal, but in others where it is illegal, and frowned upon by tradition and religion. Indeed, some recent statistics seem to show that it is particularly prevalent in a number of Roman Catholic countries, in which other means of birth control are not available.

Data on the extent of illegal abortion are difficult to obtain and not altogether reliable. However, a recent study estimates that in France there is one abortion for each live birth; that in Latin America as a whole there is one abortion for every two live births; and that in Uruguay, there are three abortions to each live birth. (Alice S. Rossi, U.S. Public Health Service, writing in *Dissent*, July–August, 1969).

In numbers of underdeveloped countries, through ignorance, poverty, and the low state of technology, abortion is the principal method of birth control. A lot of this happens under brutal circumstances. The women do it to themselves, or to one another, or at best with the help of some self-taught midwife. All of them suffer, and many of them die. It is one of the penalties of poverty. What goes as morality, in this as in so many other things, sits more lightly on the well-to-do. The poor must bear it in suffering and terror, and at times must pay for it with their lives.

It is precisely a high concern for human life, and most of all for children and what becomes of them, that makes me believe that we must achieve as rapidly as possible universally available, and preferably free, birth control and abortion. Being born unwanted is no favor to any child. Being born to hunger, want, disease, and the ravages of total war is no favor to any child. We need to make a world in which fewer children are born, and in which we take better care of all of them.

So that is my program: *a better world for fewer children.*

Section 11
Heterosexual Relationships and Marriage

The establishment and maintenance of heterosexual relationships is an aspect of adjustment in which most of us spend a major part of our lives. And the interaction which we have with significant others as children, dates, marriage partners, and parents exerts a definite influence upon how we see ourselves, the masculinity or femininity of the roles we adopt, and the kind of people we are.

One has only to pick up a magazine or newspaper or to turn on a television set to become aware that sex is a major preoccupation in our culture. Like many of the parts of our living, the ways in which we manage our sexual affairs and the cultural points of view upon which these are based are changing. Whether this change is rapid—in the nature of a revolution—or slow and evolutionary is a matter upon which there is considerable difference of opinion. Reiss, for example, views the change to more permissive sexual standards as normal and evolutionary. Others appear disposed to see the change as so abrupt that marriage relationships lack dependable guides for behavior. The reader, no doubt, has some convictions of his own about such questions as sex roles, sexual permissiveness, and whether or not The Pill has effected the double standard. The basic question from the standpoint of the psychology of adjustment must deal with the management of one's own heterosexual relationships.

Discussions of sex behavior standards are likely to be attended with more heat than light. Many believe that there has been a revolution in standards of behaviors and others, such as Reiss, think that young people believe and act much as their parents do. There are some who argue that there is a marked change accompanied by the advantage of greater openness and freedom. Others, agreeing that there is a marked change, point to the increased rate of illegitimate birth, hasty marriages of pregnant girls, and the increased incidence of venereal disease—despite the wonder drugs.

The reader, no doubt, has some current convictions about sex behavior. The editors advise that whatever these are, they should be analyzed and evaluated and then changed only slowly and deliberately. The Reiss article seems to suggest a sort of other-directed orientation, i.e., a "what do the masses do" viewpoint. As a result of our counseling experiences, the editors suggest that statistics do not create a conscience or feelings of guilt. Permissive behavior by a girl who does not have a permissive attitude may give rise to a neurosis. The real question is not, "How are America's sex standards changing?" The vital question for the psychology of adjustment is, "What is salutary sexual behavior for me and those whom I influence?"

Dr. Harlow has, for a number of years, been making productive hypotheses for the psychology of adjustment by the questions he raises about humans which are inferred from his observation of monkeys. He tells how the heterosexual affectional system develops in guinea pigs and in monkeys, and how important affection and contact are for satisfactory functioning as mature individuals.

Burchinal provides both statistics and postulations regarding causes and results of early marriages. But perhaps age is implied as making too much difference. That is, the equation of psychological maturity with physical maturity does not hold. Difficulties in marital adjustment which more properly should be attributed to inadequate learning of processes of interacting appear to be ascribed to the age *per se*. Actually, some individuals at age sixteen well may maintain more effective marital relationships than others of two or three times that age.

The following points occur to the editors as a result of their consideration of the article.

1. Learned interpersonal-transaction behaviors may affect marriage success to a much greater degree than do the ages of participants.

2. Individuals learn certain patterns of family-interaction behavior in their families of origin. Whether effective or ineffective, these patterns are passed from generation to generation through parent-child interaction.

3. If behaviors are learned they can be interrupted and modified, i.e., more effective behaviors can be substituted. Interaction patterns which operate to defeat participants fall in this category.

4. Marriage is the most crucial interpersonal relationship which most individuals maintain in terms of their own personal psychological welfare; the psychological effectiveness of their children; the general effectiveness of society in terms of its individual numbers.

5. The importance and the possibilities for learning suggest education for marriage, either as provided and required by society or sought by individuals. Marriages make too much difference to everyone to let them fail, especially when enough is known so that improvement is possible.

The advantages of the direct and purposeful study of marriage as an institution and of one's own marriage in particular is shown in the article by Otto. He suggests that even in those marriages that are currently deemed to be successful there are dimensions worth exploring for further enhancement. His belief that something very much like the family structure we have known will persist for some time. This he says is due to imprinting and the models which have been provided. We would like to suggest that the family in its present structure will survive because that form has, through the centuries, proven its viability.

How and Why America's Sex Standards are Changing
IRA L. REISS
Professor of Sociology
University of Iowa, Iowa City

The popular notion that America is undergoing a sexual "revolution" is a myth. The belief that our more permissive sexual code is a sign of a general breakdown of morality is also a myth. These two myths have arisen in part because we have so little reliable information about American sexual behavior. The enormous public interest in sex seems to have been matched by moralizing and reticence in scholarly research—a situation that has only recently begun to be corrected.

What *has* been happening recently is that our young people have been assuming more responsibility for their own sexual standards and behavior. The influence of their parents has been progressively declining. The greater independence given to the young has long been evident in other fields—employment, spending, and prestige, to name three. The parallel change in sexual-behavior patterns would have been evident if similar research had been made in this area. One also could have foreseen that those groups least subject to the demands of old orthodoxies, like religion, would emerge as the most sexually permissive of all—men in general, liberals, non-churchgoers, Negroes, the highly educated.

In short, today's more permissive sexual standards represent not revolution but evolution, not anomie but normality.

My own research into current sexual behavior was directed primarily to the question, Why are some groups of people more sexually permissive than other groups? My study involved a representative sample of about 1500 people, 21 and older, from all over the country; and about 1200 high-school and college students, 16 to 22 years old, from three different states. On the pages that follow, I will first discuss some of the more important of my findings; then suggest seven general propositions that can be induced from these findings; and, finally, present a comprehensive theory about modern American sexual behavior.

From *Trans*-action, 5 (No. 4) 26–32, March, 1968. Copyright © 1968 by *Trans*-action magazine, St. Louis, Missouri.

ARE RACE DIFFERENCES ROOTED IN CLASS?

A good many sociologists believe that most of the real differences between Negroes and whites are class differences—that if Negroes and whites from the same class were compared, any apparent differences would vanish. Thus, some critics of the Moynihan Report accused Daniel P. Moynihan of ignoring how much lower-class whites may resemble lower-class Negroes.

But my findings show that there are large variations in the way whites and Negroes *of precisely the same class* view premarital sexual permissiveness. Among the poor, for instance, only 32 percent of white males approve of intercourse before marriage under some circumstances—compared with 70 percent of Negro males. The variation is even more dramatic among lower-class females: 5 percent of whites compared with 33 percent of Negroes. Generally, high-school and college students of all classes were found to be more permissive than those in the adult sample. But even among students there were variations associated with race. (See Table 1.)

TABLE 1

Percent Accepting Premarital Sex

	Lower-class adults*	Lower-class students**
White men	32% of 202	56% of 96
Negro men	70% of 49	86% of 88
White women	5% of 221	17% of 109
Negro women	33% of 63	42% of 90

* From National Adult Sample
** From Five-School Student Sample

The difference between Negro and white acceptance of premarital intercourse is not due to any racial superiority or inferiority. All that this finding suggests is that we should be much more subtle in studying Negro-white differences, and not assume that variations in education, income, or occupation are enough to account for all these differences. The history of slavery, the depressing effects of discrimination and low status—all indicate that the Negro's entire cultural base may be different from the white's.

Another response to this finding on sexual attitudes can, of course, be disbelief. Do people really tell the truth about their sex lives? National studies have revealed that they do—women will actually talk more freely about their sex lives than about their husbands' incomes. And various validity checks indicate that they did in this case.

But people are not always consistent: They may not practice what they preach. So I decided to compare people's sexual attitudes with their actual sexual behavior. Table 2 indicates the degree of correspondence between attitudes and behavior in a sample of 248 unmarried, white, junior and senior college-students.

TABLE 2

Sexual Standards and Actual Behavior

Current Standard	Most Extreme Current Behavior			Number of Respondents
	Kissing	Petting	Coitus	
Kissing	64%	32%	4%	25
Petting	15%	78%	7%	139
Coitus	5%	31%	64%	84

Obviously, the students do not *always* act as they believe. But in the great majority of cases belief and action do coincide. For example, 64 percent of those who consider coitus acceptable are actually having coitus; only 7 percent of those who accept nothing beyond petting, and 4 percent of those who accept nothing beyond kissing, are having coitus. So it is fairly safe to conclude that, in this case, attitudes are good clues to behavior.

GUILT IS NO INHIBITOR

What about guilt feelings? Don't they block any transition toward more permissive sexual attitudes and behavior? Here the findings are quite unexpected. *Guilt feelings do not generally inhibit sexual behavior.* Eighty-seven percent of the women and 58 percent of the men said they had eventually come to accept sexual activities that had once made them feel guilty. (Some—largely males—had never felt guilty.) Seventy-eight percent had *never* desisted from any sexual activity that had made them feel guilty. Typically, a person will feel some guilt about his sexual behavior, but will continue his conduct until the guilt diminishes. Then he will move on to more advanced behavior—and new guilt feelings—until over that; and so on. People differed, mainly, in the sexual behavior they were willing to start, and in how quickly they moved on to more advanced forms.

The factor that most decisively motivated women to engage in coitus and to approve of coitus was the belief that they were in love. Of those who accepted coitus, 78 percent said they had been in love—compared with 60 percent of those who accepted only petting, and 40 percent of those who accepted only kissing. (Thus, parents who don't want their children to have sexual experiences but do want them to have "love" experiences are indirectly encouraging what they are trying to prevent.)

How do parents' beliefs influence their children's sexual attitudes and conduct?

Curiously enough, almost two-thirds of the students felt that their sexual standards were at least similar to those of their parents. This was as true for Negro males as for white females—although about 80 percent of the former accept premarital intercourse as against only about 20 percent of the latter. Perhaps these students are deluded, but perhaps they see through the "chastity" facade of their parents to the underlying similarities in attitude. It may be that the parents' views on independence, love, pleasure, responsibility, deferred gratification, conformity, and adventurousness are linked with the sexual attitudes of their children; that a similarity in these values implies a similarity in sexual beliefs. Probably these parental values, like religiousness, help determine which youngsters move quickly and with relatively little guilt through the various stages of sexual behavior. Religiousness, for the group of white students, is a particularly good index: Youngsters who rank high on church attendance rank low on premarital coitus, and are generally conservative.

Despite the fact that 63 to 68 percent of the students felt that their sexual standards were close to their parents' standards, a larger percentage felt that their standards were even closer to those of peers (77 percent) and to those of very close friends (89 percent). Thus, the conflict in views between peers and parents is not so sharp as might be expected. Then too, perhaps parents' values have a greater influence on their children's choice of friends than we usually acknowledge.

THE IMPORTANCE OF RESPONSIBILITY

This brings us to another key question. Are differences in sexual standards between parents and children due to changing cultural standards? Or are they due to their different roles in life—that is, to the difference between being young, and being parents responsible for the young? Were the parents of today that different when they courted?

My findings do show that older people tend to be less permissive about sex—but this difference is not very marked. What is significant is that childless couples—similar to couples with children of courtship age in every other respect, including age—are much more willing to accept premarital intercourse as standard (23 to 13 percent). Furthermore, parents tend to be *less* sexually permissive the *more* responsibility they have for young people. Now, if the primary cause of parent-child divergences in sexual standards is that cultural standards in general have been changing, then older people should, by and large, be strikingly more conservative about sex. They aren't. But since parents are more conservative about sex than nonparents of the same age, it would seem that the primary cause of parent-child divergences over sex is role and responsibility—the parents of today were *not* that different when courting.

Being responsible for others, incidentally, inhibits permissiveness even when the dependents are siblings. The first-born are far less likely to approve of premarital intercourse (39 percent) than are the youngest children (58 percent).

Another intriguing question is, How do parents feel about the sexual activities of their boy children—as opposed to their girl children? The answer depends upon the sex of the parent. The more daughters a white father has, the more strongly he feels about his standards—although his standards are no stricter than average. The more sons he has, the less strongly he feels about his beliefs. White mothers showed the reverse tendency, but much more weakly—the more sons, the stronger the mothers' insistence upon whatever standards they believed in. Perhaps white parents feel this way because of their unfamiliarity with the special sexual problems of a child of the opposite sex—combined with an increasing awareness of these problems.

What explains these differences in attitude between groups—

differences between men and women as well as between Negroes and whites? Women are more committed to marriage than men, so girls become more committed to marriage too, and to low-permissive parental values. The economic pressures on Negroes work to break up their families, and weaken commitment to marital values, so Negroes tend to be more permissive. Then too, whites have a greater stake in the orthodox institution of marriage: More white married people than unmarried people reported that they were happy. Among Negroes, the pattern was reversed. But in discussing weak commitments to marriage we are dealing with one of the "older" sources of sexual permissiveness.

The sources of the new American permissiveness are somewhat different. They include access to contraception; ways to combat venereal infection; and—quite as important—an intellectualized philosophy about the desirability of sex accompanying affection. "Respectable," college-educated people have integrated this new philosophy with their generally liberal attitudes about the family, politics, and religion. And this represents a new and more lasting support for sexual permissiveness, since it is based on a positive philosophy rather than hedonism, despair, or desperation.

In my own study, I found that among the more permissive groups were those in which the fathers were professional men. This finding is important: It shows that the upper segments of our society, like the lower, have a highly permissive group in their midst—despite the neat picture described by some people of permissiveness steadily declining as one raises one's gaze toward the upper classes.

PATTERNS OF PERMISSIVENESS

All these findings, though seemingly diverse, actually fall into definite patterns, or clusters of relationships. These patterns can be expressed in seven basic propositions:

1. The *less* sexually permissive a group is, traditionally, the *greater* the likelihood that new social forces will cause its members to become more permissive.

Traditionally high-permissive groups, such as Negro men, were the least likely to have their sexual standards changed by social forces like church-attendance, love affairs, and romantic love. Traditionally low-permissive groups, such as white females, showed the greatest sensitivity to these social forces. In addition, the lower social classes are reported to have a tradition of greater sexual permissiveness, so the finding that their permissiveness is less sensitive to certain social forces also fits this proposition.

2. The more liberal the group, the more likely that social forces will help maintain high sexual permissiveness.

There was diverse support for this proposition. Students, upper-class females in liberal settings, and urban dwellers have by and large accepted more permissiveness than those in more conservative settings.

Indeed, liberalism in general seems to be yet another cause of the new permissiveness in America. Thus, a group that was traditionally low-permissive regarding sex (the upper class), but that is liberal in such fields as religion and politics, would be very likely to shift toward greater premarital permissiveness.

3. According to their ties to marital and family institutions, people will differ in their sensitivity to social forces that affect permissiveness.

This proposition emphasizes, mainly, male-female differences in courting. Women have a stronger attachment to and investment in marriage, childbearing, and family ties. This affects their courtship roles. There are fundamental male-female differences in acceptance of permissiveness, therefore, in line with differences in courtship role.

Romantic love led more women than men to become permissive (this finding was particularly true if the woman was a faithful churchgoer). Having a steady date affected women predominantly, and exclusiveness was linked with permissiveness. Early dating, and its link with permissiveness, varied by race, but was far more commonly linked with permissiveness in men than in women. The number of steadies, and the number of times in love, was associated with permissiveness for females, but was curvilinear for males—that is, a man with no steadies, or a number of steadies, tended to be more permissive than a man who had gone steady only once.

Such male-female differences, however, are significant only for whites. Among Negroes, male-female patterns in these areas are quite similar.

4. The higher the overall level of permissiveness in a group, the greater the extent of equalitarianism within abstinence and double-standard subgroups.

Permissiveness is a measure not only of what a person will accept for himself and his own sex, but of what behavior he is willing to allow the opposite sex. Permissiveness, I found, tends to be associated with sexual equalitarianism in one particular fashion: I found, strangely enough, that a good way to measure the *general* permissiveness of a group is to measure the equalitarianism of two subgroups—the abstinent, and believers in the double-standard. (Nonequalitarianism in abstinence means, usually, petting is acceptable for men, but only kissing for women. Equalitarianism within the double-standard means that intercourse is acceptable for women when in love, for men anytime. The nonequalitarian double-standard considers all unmarried women's coitus wrong.) In a generally high-permissive group (such as men), those adherents who do accept abstinence or the double-standard will be more equalitarian than will their counterparts in low-permissive groups (such as women). The implication is that the ethos of a high-permissive group encourages female sexuality and thereby also encourages equalitarianism throughout the group.

5. The potential for permissiveness derived from parents' values is a key determinant as to how rapidly, how much, and in what direction a person's premarital sexual standards and behavior change.

What distinguishes an individual's sexual behavior is not its starting point—white college-educated females, for instance, almost always start only with kissing—but how far, how fast, and in what direction the individual is willing to go. The fact is that almost all sexual behavior is eventually repeated, and comes to be accepted. And a person's basic values encourage or discourage his willingness to try something new and possibly guilt-producing. Therefore, these basic values—derived, in large part, from parental teaching, direct or implicit—are keys to permissiveness.

Since the young often feel that their sex standards are similar to their parents', we can conclude that, consciously or not, high-permissive parents intellectually and emotionally breed high-permissive children.

6. A youth tends to see permissiveness as a continuous scale with his parents' standards at the low point, his peers' at the high point, and himself between but closer to his peers—and closest to those he considers his most intimate friends.

The findings indicate that those who consider their standards closer to parents' than to peers' are less permissive than the others.

The most permissive within one group generally reported the greatest distance from parents, and greatest similarity to peers and friends. This does not contradict the previous proposition, since parents are on the continuum and exert enough influence so that their children don't go all the way to the opposite end. But it does indicate, and the data bear out, that parents are associated with relatively low permissiveness; that the courtship group is associated with relatively high permissiveness; and that the respondents felt closer to the latter. Older, more permissive students were less likely to give "parental guidance" as a reason for their standards.

7. Greater responsibility for other members of the family, and lesser participation in courtship, are both associated with low-permissiveness.

The only child, it was found, had the most permissive attitude. Older children, generally, were less permissive than their younger brothers and sisters. The older children usually have greater responsibility for the young siblings; children without siblings have no such responsibilities at all.

The findings also showed that as the number of children, and their ages, increased, the parents' permissiveness decreased. Here again, apparently, parental responsibility grew, and the decline in permissiveness supports the proposition above.

On the other hand, as a young person gets more and more caught up in courtship, he is progressively freed from parental domination. He has less responsibility for others, and he becomes more permissive. The fact that students are more sexually liberal than many other groups must be due partly to their involvement in courtship, and to their distance from the family.

Thus a generational clash of some sort is almost inevitable. When children reach their late teens or early 20s, they also reach the peak of their permissiveness; their parents, at the same time, reach the nadir of theirs.

These findings show that both the family and courtship institutions are key determinants of whether a person accepts or rejects premarital sexuality. Even when young people have almost full independence in courtship, as they do in our system, they do not copulate at random. They display parental and family values by the association of sex with affection, by choice of partners, by equalitarianism, and so on.

However, parental influence must inevitably, to some extent, conflict with the pressures of courting, and the standards of the courting group. Young people are tempted by close association with attractive members of the opposite sex, usually without having any regular heterosexual outlet. Also, youth is a time for taking risks and having adventures. Therefore, the greater the freedom to react autonomously within the courtship group, the greater the tendency toward liberalized sexual behavior.

This autonomy has always been strong in America. Visitors in the 19th century were amazed at freedom of mate choice here, and the equalitarianism between sexes, at least as compared with Europe. The trend has grown.

Now, families are oriented toward the bearing and rearing of children—and for this, premarital sex is largely irrelevant. It becomes relevant only if it encourages marriages the parents want— but relevant negatively if it encourages births out of wedlock, or the "wrong," or no, marriages. Most societies tolerate intercourse between an engaged couple, for this doesn't seriously threaten the marital institution; and even prostitution gains some acceptance because it does not promote unacceptable marital unions. The conflict between the family and courtship systems depends on the extent to which each perceives the other as threatening its interests. My own findings indicate that this conflict is present, but not always as sharply as the popular press would have us believe.

Courtship pressures tend toward high-permissiveness; family pressures toward low-permissiveness. It follows that whatever promotes the child's independence from the family promotes high-permissiveness. For example, independence is an important element in the liberal position; a liberal setting, therefore, generally encourages sexual as well as other independence.

A COMPREHENSIVE THEORY

To summarize all these findings into one comprehensive theory runs the risk of oversimplifying—if the findings and thought that went into the theory are not kept clearly in mind. With this *caveat*, I think a fair theoretical summary of the meaning of the foregoing material would be: How much premarital sexual permissiveness is considered acceptable in a courtship group varies directly with the independence of that group, and with the general permissiveness in the adult cultural environment.

In other words, when the social and cultural forces working on two groups are approximately the same, the differences in permissiveness are caused by differences in independence. But when independence is equal, differences come from differences in the sociocultural setting.

There is, therefore, to repeat, no sexual revolution today. Increased premarital sexuality is not usually a result of breakdown of standards, but a particular, and different, type of organized system. To parents, more firmly identified with tradition—that is, with older systems—and with greater responsibilities toward the young, toward the family, and toward marriage, greater premarital sexuality seems deviant. But it is, nevertheless, an integral part of society—their sociey.

In short, there has been a gradually increasing acceptance of and overtness about sexuality. The basic change is toward greater equalitarianism, greater female acceptance of permissiveness, and more open discussion. In the next decade, we can expect a step-up in the pace of this change.

The greater change, actually, is in sexual attitude, rather than in behavior. If behavior has not altered in the last century as much as we might think, attitudes *have*—and attitudes and behavior seem closer today than for many generations. Judging by my findings, and the statements of my respondents, we can expect them to become closer still, and to proceed in tandem into a period of greater permissiveness, and even greater frankness. I do not, however, foresee extreme change in the years to come—such as full male-female equality. This is not possible unless male and female roles in the family are also equal, and men and women share equal responsibility for child-rearing and family support.

FURTHER READINGS SUGGESTED BY THE AUTHOR:

The Encyclopedia of Sexual Behavior edited by ALBERT ELLIS AND ALBERT ALBARBANEL (New York City: Hawthorn Books, 1961). The most complete and authoritative source of its kind available. Contains articles by approximately 100 authorities in the field.

Journal of Social Issues—"The Sexual Renaissance in America"—April 1966. Many of the key figures in this area have contributed to this special journal issue: ROBERT BELL, JESSIE BERNARD, CARLFRED BRODERICK, HAROLD CHRISTENSEN, PAUL GEBHARD, LESTER KIRKENDALL,

Roger Libby, Lee Rainwater, Ira L. Reiss, Robert Sherwin, and Clark Vincent.

The Sexual Behavior of Young People by Michael Schofield (Boston: Little, Brown and Co., 1965). A recent, carefully executed study of English teenagers with much fascinating information that can be compared with American studies.

The Heterosexual Affectional System in Monkeys
HARRY F. HARLOW
Director, Primate Laboratory
University of Wisconsin, Madison

The inspiration for this address came from observational data obtained from seven guinea pigs—two males and three females in a colony and two females brought in temporarily. Observations were provided by my ten-year-old daughter Pamela. These observations were made with love and endearment, and the behavior observed was endearment and love. Furthermore, these observations were made at a level of objectivity difficult for an adult to attain in this field.

Male and female guinea pigs are very fond of each other. They stare blissfully into the limpid pink or ruby or midnight-blue pools of each other's eyes. They nuzzle and they cuddle and the end production is not characterized by rush or rape. After all, one does not have to hurry if there is no hurry to be had. This, Pamela has witnessed several times. A caged, virgin adult female was brought by a friend for mating. Twirp, Pamela's large, black, gentle male, was put into the cage with the new female. He purred, nuzzled her, brushed up against her, smelled and licked her, and gradually conquered the frightened animal. A half-hour later they were snuggled up next to each other, peaceful and content, and they lived in bliss for several weeks until another friend brought in her female and Twirp repeated his patient, gentle approach. Twirp has con-

From *American Psychologist*, 17: 1–9, January, 1962. This research was supported by funds received from the Graduate School of the University of Wisconsin, from the Ford Foundation, and from Grant M-4528, National Institutes of Health.

vinced me that some male guinea pigs, at least, are endowed with an innate sense of decency, and I am happy to say that this is the way most male monkeys behave. I presume that there are some men who have as deep a depth of dignity as guinea pigs.

The guest stands, unfortunately, ended peaceful coexistence in the colony. For many months the five adult guinea pigs had lived amiably in one large cage, with Twirp in command and the second male playing second fiddle. While Twirp was host to the visiting females, White Patch commanded the permanent harem. When Twirp was reintroduced to the colony cage, it took but ten seconds to discover that he would not be tolerated. White Patch bared his teeth and lunged at Twirp, and to save the males, a new cage was acquired.

This led to various divisions of the females and led Pamela to discover particular male guinea pigs like particular female guinea pigs, and they squeal piteously when separated, even when the female is so bulging with babies that she can offer the male nothing in terms of drive reduction. Particular female guinea pigs like particular male guinea pigs. Tastes seem fairly stable, for even after weeks of peaceful residence with the unfavored male, the female will still attempt to get to her favorite male, and after weeks of quiet residence with unfavored females, the male will still try to get to his favorite female.

The females, like the males, defend their rights. In the happy one-cage days two females were separated from the group to care for their litters. White Thrush, in an advanced stage of pregnancy, lived alone with the males. When Chirp was returned to the colony cage after three weeks of maternal chores, both males approached enthusiastically, making friendly gestures. But Hell hath no fury like a female guinea pig spurned, and White Thrush would not tolerate infidelity. She hissed at Chirp, and lunged, and as Chirp fled from the cage, White Thrush pursued, teeth bared. The males also pursued, clucking and purring in anticipation. The males won, and White Thrush sulked the rest of the day. Guinea pigs apparently have a well-developed heterosexual affectional system.

Sex behavior in the guinea pig has been intensively investigated, and there are exhaustive studies on what has been called the sex drive, but I know of no previous mention of or allusion to the guinea pig's heterosexual affectional system. No doubt this stems from the paradigm which has been established for research in this area.

In a typical experiment a male guinea pig and a female guinea pig in estrus are taken from their individual cages, dropped into a barren chamber, and observed for 15 minutes. In such a situation there is a high probability that something is going to happen and that it will happen rapidly and repeatedly. The thing that happens will be reliable and valid, and all that one needs to do to score it is to count. It is my suggestion that from this time onward it be known as the "flesh count." Sometimes I wonder how men and women would behave if they were dropped naked into a barren chamber with full realization that they had only fifteen minutes to take advantage of the opportunities offered them. No doubt there would be individual differences, but we would obtain little information on the human heterosexual affectional system from such an experiment.

Sex is not an adventitious act. It is not here today and gone tomorrow. It starts with the cradle, and as a part of the human tragedy it wanes before the grave. We have traced and are tracing the development of the heterosexual affectional system in monkeys.

We believe that the heterosexual affectional system in the rhesus monkey, like all the other affectional systems, goes through a series of developmental stages—an infantile heterosexual stage, a preadolescent stage, and an adolescent and mature heterosexual stage. Although these stages are in considerable part overlapping and cannot be sharply differentiated in time, we would think of the infantile stage as lasting throughout the first year and being characterized by inadequate and often inappropriate sexual play and posturing. The preadolescent stage, beginning in the second year and ending in the third year in the female and the fourth year in the male, is characterized by adequate and appropriate sexual play and posturing, but incompleteness. The adolescent and adult stage is characterized by behaviors which are similar in form but give rise to productive outcomes which are also reproductive.

Since in this paper sex is an unavoidable issue, we present illustrations of normal adult macaque monkey sex behavior. Sexual invitation may be initiated by the female by a present pattern with buttocks oriented toward the male, tail elevated, and the female looking backward with a fear-grimace (not threat) pattern involving flattened ears and lip smacking. As you can see, this pattern need not involve rape nor even rush on the part of the male. The male may also solicit, by assuming a posture of soliciting either grooming or more intimate favors. These patterns seldom elicit violent, uncontrolled, reflex behaviors. Normal male and female overt sex behavior is shown by the male having assumed the complex sex posture in-

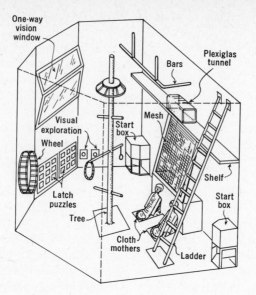

Fig. 1. *Playroom test situation.*

volving ankle clasp, dorsoventral mounting, and clasp of the female's buttocks. The partner demonstrates the complete female sexual pattern of elevating the buttocks, lowering the head, and looking backward. There have been millions of rhesus monkeys for millions of years, and there will be more in the future.

We have traced the development of the infantile heterosexual stage during the first year of life in two test situations using observational techniques. One is our playroom, illustrated in Figure 1, which consists of a room 8 ft. high with 36 feet of floor space. In this room are a platform, ladder, revolving wheel, and flying rings to encourage the infants' adaptation to a three-dimensional world, and there is an assortment of puzzles and toys for quieter activities. Two groups of four infants each, half of each group male and half female, have been observed in the playroom daily over many months. The second apparatus is shown in Figure 2. This is the playpen situation, and it consists of four large living cages and adjoining pens. Each living cage houses a mother and infant, and a three-inch by five-inch opening in the wall between cage and playpen units enables the infants to leave the home cage at any time but restrains the mothers. The playpen units are separated by wire-

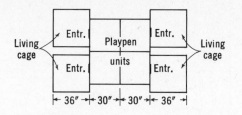

F<small>IG</small>. 2. *Playpen test situation.*

mesh panels which are removed one or two hours a day to allow the
infants to interact in pairs during the first 180 days and both in
pairs and in groups of four during the next half-year of life. Again,
we are referring to data gathered from two playpen setups, each
housing four infants and their real or surrogate mothers. Insofar as
the infantile heterosexual stage is concerned, it makes little or no
difference from which situation we take our data.

The outstanding finding in both the playroom and playpen is
that male and female infants show differences in sex behavior from
the second month of life onward. The males show earlier and more
frequent sex behavior than do females, and there are differences in
the patterns displayed by the sexes. The males almost never assume
the female sex-posture patterns, even in the earliest months. The
females, on the other hand, sometimes display the male pattern of
sex posturing, but this is infrequent after ten months of age. Predominantly, females show the female pattern and exceptional instance are to other females, not males. Frequency of sex behavior for
both males and females increases progressively with age. There is no
latency period—except when the monkeys are very tired.

The early infantile sexual behaviors are fragmentary, transient,
and involve little more than passivity by the female and disoriented
grasping and thrusting by the male. Thus, the male may thrust at
the companion's head in a completely disoriented manner or laterally across the midline of the body. However, it is our opinion that
these behaviors are more polymorphous than perverse.

Thus, as soon as the sexual responses can be observed and
measured, male and female sexual behaviors differ in form. Furthermore, there are many other behaviors which differ between males
and females as soon as they can be observed and measured. Figure 3
shows the development of threat responses by males and females in

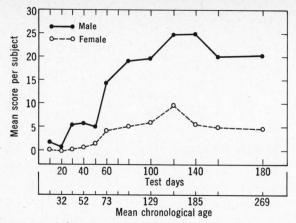

Fɪɢ. 3. *Frequency of threat responses by males and females in the playroom.*

the playroom, and these differences are not only statistically significant, but they also have face validity. Analysis of this behavior shows that males threaten other males and females but that females are innately blessed with better manners; in particular, little girl monkeys do not threaten little boy monkeys.

The withdrawal pattern—retreat when confronted by another monkey—is graphed for the playroom in Figure 4, and the significance is obvious. Females evince a much higher incidence of passive responses, which are characterized by immobility with buttocks oriented toward the male and head averted, and a similar pattern, rigidity, in which the body is stiffened and fixed.

In all probability the withdrawal and passivity behavior of the female and the forceful behavior of the male gradually lead to the

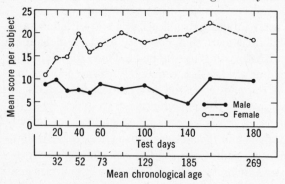

Fɪɢ. 4. *Frequency of withdrawal responses by males and females in the playroom.*

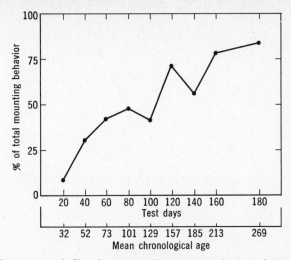

FIG. 5. *Percentage of all male mounts (immature and mature) in the playroom that shows dorsal orientation (mature pattern).*

development of normal sex behaviors. The tendency for the female to orient away from the male and for the male to clasp and tussle at the female's buttocks predisposes the consorts to assume the proper positions. The development of the dorsally oriented male sex-behavior pattern as observed in the playroom situation is shown in Figure 5 and may be described as a composite yearning and learning curve.

Infant male and female monkeys show clear-cut differences in behavior of far greater social significance than neonatal and infantile sex responses. Grooming patterns, which are basic to macaque socialization, show late maturation, but as is seen in Figure 6, when they appear, they sharply differentiate the two sexes. Caressing is both a property and prerogative of the females. Basic to normal macaque socialization is the infant-infant or peer-peer affectional system, and this arises out of and is dependent upon the play patterns which we have described elsewhere and only mention here. As is shown in the solid lines of Figure 7, play behavior in the playroom is typically initiated by males, seldom by females. However, let us not belittle the female, for they also serve who only stand and wait. Contact play is far more frequent among the males than the females and is almost invariably initiated by the males. Playpen data graphed in Figure 8 show that real rough-and-tumble play is strictly for the boys.

I am convinced that these data have almost total generality to

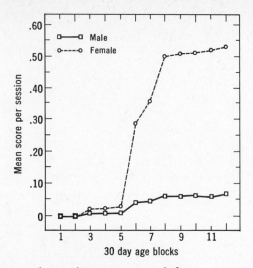

Fig. 6. *Frequency of grooming responses made by males and females in the playroom.*

man. Several months ago I was present at a school picnic attended by 25 second-graders and their parents. While the parents sat and the girls stood around or skipped about hand in hand, 13 boys tackled and wrestled, chased and retreated. No little girl chased any little boy, but some little boys chased some little girls. Human beings have been here for two million years, and they'll probably be here two million more.

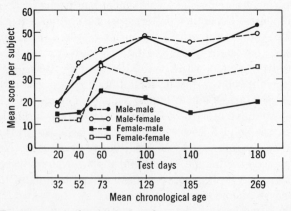

Fig. 7. *Frequency of play-initiations by males and females to monkeys of the same (male-male, female-female) and other sex (male-female, female-male). Observations are from the playroom.*

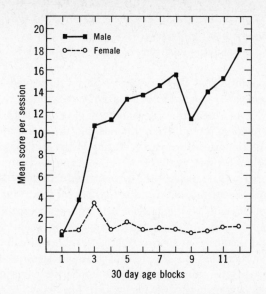

FIG. 8. *Frequency of occurrence of "rough-and-tumble" play for two males and two females in the playroom through the first year of life.*

These secondary sex-behavior differences probably exist throughout the primate order, and, moreover, they are innately determined biological differences regardless of any cultural overlap. Because of their nature they tend automatically to produce sexual segregation during middle and later childhood, but fortunately this separation is neither complete nor permanent. Behavioral differences may very well make it easy through cultural means to impose a sexual latency period in the human being from childhood to puberty. We emphasize the fact that the latency period is not a biological stage in which primary sex behavior is suppressed, but a cultural stage built upon secondary behavioral differences.

We believe that our data offer convincing evidence that sex behaviors differ in large part because of genetic factors. However, we claim no originality for the discovery of intersex behavioral differences. In 1759 Laurence Sterne in his book *Tristram Shandy* described male and female differences at the most critical period in Tristram Shandy's development; indeed, it would not be possible to conceive of a more critical period.

"*Pray, my dear,* quoth my mother, *have you not forgot to wind up the clock?*—— *Good G*——! cried my father, making an exclamation, but taking care to moderate his voice at the same time———*Did ever woman, since the creation of the world, interrupt a man with such a silly question?*"[1]

Men and women have differed in the past and they will differ in the future.

It is possible that the listener has been dismayed by the frequent reference to sex and the relatively infrequent reference to affection. Out of these infantile behavior patterns, both sexual and nonsexual, develop the affectional bonds and the social ordering that appear to be important or even essential to the full development of the heterosexual affectional system of macaques. Traumatic affectional errors, both transient and prolonged, may have devastating effects upon subsequent social and sexual behaviors.

For some years we have been attempting to establish experimental neuroses in infant monkeys by having them live on unfriendly and inconsistent mother surrogates. One preparation was a rejecting mother that on schedule or demand separated her baby when a wire frame embedded in her spun-nylon covering was displaced violently upward and backward. The baby was disturbed, but as soon as the frame was returned to its resting position, the baby returned to cling to its surrogate mother as tightly as ever. Next we developed an air-blast mother with a series of nozzles down the entire center of her body which released compressed air under high pressure—an extremely noxious stimulus to monkeys. The blasted baby never even left the mother, but in its moments of agony and duress, clung more and more tightly to the unworthy mother. Where else can a baby get protection? Apparently our infant had never read Neal Miller's theory that avoidance gradients are precipitous and approach gradients gradual and tenuous, for love conquered all.

We next devised a shaking mother, which on schedule or demand shook her infant with unconscionable violence until its teeth chattered. The infant endured its tribulations by clinging more and more tightly. At the present time we believe we may be on the threshold of success through Jay Mowbray's creation of the porcupine mother, which extrudes brass spikes all over its central surface. Preliminary studies on two infants suggest that they are emotionally disturbed. Whether or not we eventually succeed, the fact remains that babies are reluctant to develop experimental neuroses, and at one time we even wondered if this were possible.

---

[1] Sterne, Laurence. *The life and opinions of Tristram Shandy, Gentleman.* J. A. Work (Ed.), New York: The Odyssey Press, 1940, p. 5.

During the time that we were producing these evil mothers, we observed the monkeys which we had separated from their mothers at birth and raised under various mothered and nonmothered conditions. The first 47 baby monkeys were raised during the first year of life in wire cages so arranged that the infants could see and hear and call to other infants but not contact them. Now they are five to seven years old and sexually mature. As month after month and year after year have passed, these monkeys have appeared to be less and less normal. We have seen them sitting in their cages strangely mute, staring fixedly into space, relatively indifferent to people and other monkeys. Some clutch their heads in both hands and rock back and forth—the autistic behavior pattern that we have seen in babies raised on wire surrogates. Others, when approached or even left alone, go into violent frenzies of rage, grasping and tearing at their legs with such fury that they sometimes require medical care.

Eventually we realized that we had a laboratory full of neurotic monkeys. We had failed to produce neurotic monkeys by thoughtful planning and creative research, but we had succeeded in producing neurotic monkeys through misadventure. To err is human.

Because of housing pressures some of these monkeys and many of our surrogate-raised monkeys lived in pairs for several years while growing to sexual maturity, but we have seldom seen normal sex behavior, and we certainly have not had the validating criterion of newborn baby monkeys. Instead, these monkeys treat each other like brother and sister, proving that two can live in complete propinquity with perfect propriety as long as no one cares.

Their reason for being, as we saw it, was to produce babies for our researches, and so at this point we deliberately initiated a breeding program which was frighteningly unsuccessful. When the older, wire-cage-raised males were paired with the females at the peak of estrus, the introduction led only to fighting, so violent and vicious that separation was essential to survival. In no case was there any indication of normal sex behavior. Frequently the females were the aggressors; even the normal praying mantis waits until the sex act is completed.

Pairing such cloth-surrogate-raised monkeys as were sexually mature gave little better end results. Violent aggression was not the rule, and there was attempted sex behavior, but it was unreproductive since both the male and female behaviors were of the infantile type we have already described.

At this point we took the 17 oldest of our cage-raised animals, females showing consistent estrous cycles and males obviously mature, and engaged in an intensive re-education program, pairing the females with our most experienced, patient, and gentle males, and the males with our most eager, amiable, and successful breeding females. When the laboratory-bred females were smaller than the sophisticated males, the girls would back away and sit down facing the males, looking appealingly at these would-be consorts. Their hearts were in the right place, but nothing else was. When the females were larger than the males, we can only hope that they misunderstood the males' intentions, for after a brief period of courtship, they would attack and maul the ill-fated male. Females show no respect for a male they can dominate.

The training program for the males was equally unsatisfactory. They approached the females with a blind enthusiasm, but it was a misdirected enthusiasm. Frequently the males would grasp the females by the side of the body and thrust laterally, leaving them working at cross purposes with reality. Even the most persistent attempts by these females to set the boys straight came to naught. Finally, these females either stared at the males with complete contempt or attacked them in utter frustration. It became obvious that they, like their human counterpart, prefer maturer men. We realized then that we had established, not a program of breeding, but a program of brooding.

We had in fact been warned. Our first seven laboratory-born babies were raised in individual cages while being trained on a learning test battery. William Mason planned to test their social behaviors subsequently, and great care had been taken to keep the babies socially isolated and to prevent any physical contacts. Neonatal baby monkeys require 24-hour-a-day care, and infant monkeys need ministrations beyond a 40-hour week. We had assigned the evening care to Kathy, a maternal bit of fluff who had worked for several years as a monkey tester while studying to become an elementary school teacher.

Checking on his wards one night near 10 P.M., Mason found Kathy sitting on the floor surrounded by seven baby monkeys, all eight of the primates playing happily together. Before the horrified scientist could express his outrage, Kathy had risen to her full height of five feet two. Already anticipating the carping criticism which he was formulating, she shook her finger in his face and spoke with conviction: "Dr. Mason, I'm an education student and I know that it is improper and immoral to blight the social development of little children. I am right and you are wrong!"

Although we were angry with Kathy, we did think there was a certain humor in the situation and we did not worry about our monkeys. We simply transferred Kathy to an office job. Alas, she could not have been more right and we could not have been more wrong! We have already described the social-sexual life of these 7 monkeys and the next 40 to come.

Two years later we had more than theoretical reasons to be disturbed because Mason tested a group of these isolation-raised monkeys, then between 2.5 and 3.5 years of age, and found evidence of severe social abnormalities, which might be described as a sociopathic syndrome. He matched the laboratory-raised monkeys on the basis of weight and dentition patterns with monkeys that had been born and raised in the wild for the first 12 to 18 months, then captured and subjected to various kinds of housing and caging treatments for the next year or two. In the best situations the laboratory-raised monkeys, as compared with feral monkeys, showed infantile sexual behavior, absence of grooming, exaggerated aggression, and absence of affectional interaction as measured by cooperation.

We are now quite certain that this sociopathic syndrome does not stem from the fact that the baby monkeys were raised in the laboratory but from *how* they were raised in the laboratory. Our infants raised in the laboratory by real monkey mothers and permitted opportunity for the development of normal infant-infant affection demonstrate normal male and female sexual behavior when they enter the second year of life. Furthermore, our playroom and playpen studies show that infant monkeys raised on cloth mothers but given the opportunity to form normal infant-infant affectional patterns, also develop normal sexual responses.

In a desperate attempt to assist a group of 18 three- to four-year-old cloth-surrogate-raised monkeys, half of them males and half females, we engaged in a group-psychotherapy program, placing these animals for two months on the monkey island in the Madison Zoo. Their summer vacation on the enchanted island was not without avail, and social grooming responses rapidly developed and were frequent in occurrence. After a few days of misunderstanding, patterns of social ordering developed, and a number of males and females developed friendship patterns. Unfortunately, sexual behavior was infrequent, and the behavior that was observed was completely inadequate—at least from our point of view. In desperation we finally introduced our most experienced, most patient, and most kindly breeding male, Smiley, and he rapidly established himself as king of the island and prepared to take full advantage of the wealth of opportunity which surrounded him. Fortunately, the traumatic experiences he encountered with unreceptive females have left no apparent permanent emotional scars, and now that he has been returned to our laboratory breeding colony, he is again making an important contribution to our research program. If normal sexual behavior occurred, no member of our observational team ever saw it, and had a female become pregnant, we would have believed in parthenogenesis.

But let us return to the monkeys that we left on the island and the older ones that we left in their cages. A year has passed, and the frustrations that both we and our monkeys experienced are in some small part nothing but a memory. We constructed larger and more comfortable breeding cages, and we designed a very large experimental breeding room 8 feet by 8 feet by 8 feet in size with appropriate platforms and a six-foot tree. Apparently we designed successful seraglios for I can report that not all love's labors have been lost. It does appear that the males are completely expendable unless they can be used in a program of artificial insemination. Certainly we can find no evidence that there is a destiny that shapes their ends unless some Skinnerite can help us with the shaping process. We have, however, had better success with some of the females, particularly the females raised on cloth surrogates.

Even so, one of the wire-caged-raised females is a mother and another is pregnant. Three cloth-surrogate females are mothers and four or five are expectant. We give all the credit to three breeding males. One, Smiley, does not take "no" for an answer. Smiley has a way with females. Patient, gentle, and persuasive, he has overcome more than one planned program of passive resistance. One female did not become pregnant until the fifth successive month of training. Month after month she has changed, and now she is mad about the boy. Male No. 342 behaves very much like Smiley. Even when females threaten him, he does not harm them. Given time, he has been able to overcome more than one reluctant dragon, and he is a master of the power of positive suggestion.

Breeding male No. 496 has helped us greatly, particularly with the younger, cloth-surrogate-raised females. His approach differs from that of Smiley and No. 342. His technique transcends seduction, and in contract bridge terms it may be described as an approach-forcing system.

Combining our human and male-monkey talents, we are winning the good fight and imparting to naive and even resistant female monkeys the priceless gift of motherhood. Possibly it is a Pyrrhic victory. As every scientist knows, the solution of one scientific problem inevitably leads to another, and this is our fate. Month after month female monkeys that never knew a real mother, themselves become mothers—helpless, hopeless, heartless mothers devoid, or almost devoid, of any maternal feeling.

Trends and Prospects for Young Marriages in the United States

LEE G. BURCHINAL
Deputy Director, Division of Educational Research
U.S. Office of Education

Married adolescents represent a small but conspicuous segment of the adolescent population. How small, of course, depends upon the age definitions used; how conspicuous, in large part, depends upon the criteria used to evaluate youthful marriages. Considerable variation for both definitions and assessment of young marriages exists in the literature.[1] Lack of precise agreement in defining young marriage is not too serious, however, because nearly all of the studies on the subject pertain to marriages involving females who are 18 years of age or less. In this discussion, therefore, young marriages are defined as those involving at least one partner, typically a female, who is not yet 19 years of age. Specifically excluded

From *Journal of Marriage and the Family*, Vol. 27, No. 2: 243–254, 1965.
[1] Lee G. Burchinal, "Research on Young Marriage: Implications for Family Life Education," *Family Life Coordinator*, 9 (September–December 1960), pp. 6–24; reprinted in *Sourcebook in Marriage and the Family*, ed. by Marvin B. Sussman, Boston: Houghton Mifflin, 2nd Ed., 1963, pp. 508–529. This report contains an annotated bibliography of 39 popular and technical publications related to youthful marriages.

are studies of married college students. Aside from the fact that only a small proportion of college marriages are entered into before the age of 19, the two populations probably differ greatly in many respects, including their economic resources, interests, and experiences, and the capacities of couples for solving problems and relating to others.[2]

In the following discussion, data on young marriage are organized around a historical review of rates; consideration of factors affecting young marriage decisions; review of characteristics of such marriages; an assessment of their outcomes; and, finally, discussion of some implications, based on present research.

YOUNG MARRIAGE RATES

From the marriage rates listed in Table 1 by single years of age from 15–18 for the decennial censuses from 1910 through 1960, it is clear that:

1. Young marriage rates increased consistently for males and females, white and nonwhite alike, from 1910 through 1950.

2. For the most part, young marriage rates remained substantially unchanged between 1950 and 1960.

3. Among nonwhite females, the largest increases in young marriage rates occurred between 1910 and 1930, with little further change after 1930; whereas among white females, rates remained relatively constant from 1910 to 1940, with the big increases coming between 1940 and 1950, and with virtually no changes occurring between 1950 and 1960.

4. With few exceptions, young marriage rates among nonwhites were higher than and sometimes almost double those among whites.

5. A possibly important exception to difference in marriage rates between whites and nonwhites occurred among 18-year-old females in 1960. In 1950, 23.2 percent of white females as compared with 29.3 percent of nonwhite females aged 18 were married. In

[2] Clyde Foreman, "Levels of Aspiration and Marital Status on the College Campus," unpublished dissertation, Seattle: University of Washington Library, Doctoral Dissertation Series, Publication #22, 1957; also, Chilman's study of marriages among students at Syracuse University found that students married late in their college careers: Catherine S. Chilman, "Undergraduate Marriages and Higher Education," unpublished manuscript.

contrast, by 1960 a smaller percentage of 18-year-old nonwhite females (23.6) than white females (24.5) were married.

6. Young marriages predominantly involve females. In 1960, for instance, percentages for marriage among males 17 and 18 years of age ranged from about two to slightly over five percent. Corresponding rates for females ranged from 12 to 24 percent.

Not shown in Table 1 are the absolute numbers of young marriages. Much confusion exists between the absolute numbers and

TABLE 1

Percent of Any Age Level Among the 15–18-Year-Old Population Who Were of the Married Status During the Given Year by Sex and Color*

	Female											
	White						Nonwhite					
Age	1910	1920	1930	1940	1950	1960	1910	1920	1930	1940	1950	1960
15	1.1	1.3	1.1	1.0	1.0	2.3	2.1	2.7	2.9	2.6	2.8	2.9
16	3.4	3.8	3.9	3.4	5.6	5.6	6.6	7.8	8.8	7.6	8.1	6.8
17	8.1	9.1	9.1	8.0	12.7	12.0	13.0	17.9	18.7	16.4	17.3	13.6
18	15.9	17.9	17.7	16.2	23.2	24.5	24.4	32.2	32.7	28.9	29.3	23.6
	Males											
15	0.1	0.2	0.1	0.1	0.6	0.6	0.1	0.3	0.2	0.3	0.4	0.7
16	0.1	0.3	0.2	0.3	0.6	0.9	0.2	0.6	0.4	0.6	0.4	1.1
17	0.3	0.8	0.6	0.6	1.2	1.9	0.9	1.6	1.4	1.4	1.8	2.1
18	1.2	2.4	1.9	1.9	3.4	5.4	3.0	5.3	4.2	4.2	4.8	5.3

* Adapted from Bureau of Census, Population Characteristics, for the respective years.

rates of young marriages. In 1910, for example, 296,293 females aged 15 through 18 were married; in 1960, 589,508 females in this age group were married, but the rate of marriages among these females rose only slightly, from eight to almost 11 percent. Although only one percent of males aged 15 to 18 were married in 1910, and only two percent were married in 1960, the number of married men in this age group increased ten-fold, from 19,026 to 119,223 in 1960.

Further increases in the frequencies of young marriage will occur, largely because the population base of youth aged 15 to 18 is expanding each year. In 1964, one million more adolescents will become 17 years old than in 1963. In this year's crop of 3,700,000 17-year-olds, approximately 258,000 will be married, based on the 1960 rate of 12 percent for girls and two percent for boys.[3]

[3] Based on data reported in "Rising Tide of the 17-Year-Olds Presents Major Social Problems," *Population Profile* (September 7, 1964).

Current population survey data provide the only estimates for young marriage rates since 1960. Unpublished data from the Bureau of Census indicate that for the two youngest age groups for which data are reported, 14 to 17 and 18 and 19, marriage rates for both males and females in 1963 are slightly less than comparable rates for 1960.[4]

In summary, young marriage rates, contrary to widely circulated assertions, are not going up, up, and up. Young marriage rates have remained stable or have declined slightly since 1950, and only a small proportion of high-school-age students are married.[5]

FACTORS AFFECTING YOUNG MARRIAGE RATES

The attention of sociologists generally has been focused on "explaining" the long-term trend toward younger ages at marriage in the United States. With this trend now apparently arrested, consideration must be given to why young marriage rates have remained relatively stable despite rapid social changes that have included acceleration of the psycho-social development of youth, earlier adoption of adult roles, and greater emancipation of young people.

Consider, for instance, the vast difference in the sociological conditions that influenced the socialization processes for youths who became 16 to 18 years of age in 1950 as compared with 1964. The former cohort was born in 1932–1934, felt the pinch of the depression, and entered adolescence during World War II. The latter cohort was born between 1946 and 1948 and grew up during the postwar boom. The two groups of youths grew up in much different social worlds, yet marriage was about as attractive at ages 16 through 18 for members of the one group as for those of the other.

Obviously, available data are not adequate for "explaining" the recent stability in young marriage rates. Information is needed on changes or stability in young marriage rates for various status, regional, residential, color, and ethnic groupings of youth, because

---

[4] *Current Population Reports,* p. 20.

[5] For details, see Burchinal, *op. cit.,* p. 10; Vladimir de Lissovoy and Mary Ellen Hitchcock, "High School Marriages in Pennsylvania: Problems and School Board Policies," *Pennsylvania School Boards Association Bulletin,* 28 (June 1964), pp. 31–35; and Vladimir de Lissovoy and Mary Ellen Hitchcock, "Student Marriage Rates Remain Low in Pennsylvania," *Pennsylvania School Journal,* 112 (April 1964), pp. 374–375.

the general pattern of stability may hide marked increases for some subgroups and equally marked decreases for others.

Especially needed is research in various subgroupings on the relative saliency of factors that promote or restrain movement toward young marriages. For now, however, available information is used to assess the impact of selected factors upon young marriage rates; and beyond the limits of these data, suggestions are made regarding the probable influences of broad societal developments upon young marriage decisions.

In a previous overview of research on young marriage, the author examined the support for ten factors believed to contribute to young marriage decisions.[6] The first four factors, previously dismissed as spurious, remain questionable in light of the recent stability in youthful marriage rates. These are:

1. The insecurity of our times, which has created needs among young people to find someone with whom they can have unquestionable loyalty and love.

2. The cult of personal happiness and the rejection of intellectualism and achievement.

3. The bandwagon effect: one marriage contributes to another, and soon "everybody is doing it."

4. The impact of World War II, the Korean War, and the continuation of the draft.

The following two "explanations" are stressed by popular writers; however, the research data bearing on these conditions is inconclusive and contradictory.[7]

5. An escape from an unhappy home, school, or community situation.

6. An attempt to resolve personal or social adjustment problems.

Another factor that is widely acclaimed as a "cause" of young marriages is:

7. The reduction of economic risks in marriage as a result of current prosperity.

As an instrumental factor in most marriage decisions, reduction of economic risks no doubt contributes to young marriage decisions as well, but this factor has limited value in accounting for youthful marriage decisions. Historically, marriage rates in general, including young marriage rates, have risen with prosperity and have declined

---

[6] Burchinal, *op. cit.*

[7] *Ibid.;* see also Robert J. Havighurst *et al., Growing Up in River City,* New York: John Wiley, 1962, p. 185.

in periods of depression or recession (see Table 1). Assurance of employment, often recently obtained, was a commonly cited factor in marriage decisions reported by young brides interviewed in Iowa and Nebraska.[8] Although it is hard to say to what degree the general affluence of American society serves to promote young marriages, without question, high rates of unemployment among young men are not conducive to young marriages. Unemployment rates of young people between the ages of 16 and 24 are more than twice the average for workers of all ages. School dropouts and nonwhites are particularly disadvantaged.[9] Thus, even in the midst of general affluence, widespread employment among young workers may serve as an impediment to young marriages.

Factors That May Favor Young Marriage

Very likely, the most probable explanation for the maintenance of present levels of young marriages lies in the balance of influences stemming from the American dating and courtship process and images of married life which in some cases favor but which in other cases discourage young marriages. Among important conditions that promote young marriage decisions are:

8. Encouragement from romantic and glamorous images of marriage and the corresponding unrealistic overevaluation of marriage.

9. Acceleration of adult status as reflected in advanced levels of heterosexual interaction at younger ages.

10. Stimulation of sexual drives by sex appeals and intense physical expressions of affection in mass media, with the result that premarital pregnancy becomes a precipitating factor in many if not most youthful marriage decisions.

Idealized images of marriage, though perhaps intensified and more unrealistic among adolescents, are held by many young adults as well. The higher rates of disillusionment, unhappiness, separation,

[8] Lee G. Burchinal, "Comparisons of Factors Related to Adjustment in Pregnancy-Provoked and Non-Pregnancy-Provoked Youthful Marriages," *Midwest Sociologist,* 21 (July 1959), pp. 92–96; J. Joel Moss and Ruby Gingles, "The Relationship of Personality to the Incidence of Early Marriage," *Marriage and Family Living,* 21 (November 1959), pp. 373–377.

[9] "Younger Workers," *Manpower Report of the President and a Report on Manpower Requirements, Resources, Utilization, and Training,* Washington, D.C.: U.S. Government Printing Office, March 1964, pp. 123–132.

and divorce among young than among other marriages (described later), however, probably reflect the greater degree of prevalence of glamorized and naïve views of marriage among adolescents who marry at younger ages. Other indications of the impulsiveness of many young marriages include the brief period of acquaintance-ship or engagement preceding most young marriages,[10] their meager economic bases (also described later), the fact that such marriages often occur despite parental opposition,[11] and their greater degree of departure from religiously endogamous norms.[12]

Acceleration of adult relationships, especially through younger ages of dating, appears to be linked with younger marriage. In contrast with those who had not married by the time they would have graduated from high school, an Iowa study found that girls who were married had started dating younger, begun going steady earlier, gone steady more often, been "in love" more frequently, dated more frequently at younger ages, had a larger number of close friends who also married young, and more frequently dated men older than themselves.[13] Results of studies in Nebraska and in Columbus, Ohio, confirmed the Iowa findings.[14]

Early and serious dating generally promotes movement toward increased physical involvement, with the result that premarital pregnancy often becomes the precipitating factor in marriage deci-sions. Estimates of premarital pregnancy rates among young mar-riages range from over 30 percent to nearly 90 percent when both spouses are of high school age in comparison with approximately 20 percent of all brides.[15]

Idealization of marriage, earlier and more serious dating, and increased intimacy among youths, however, have not led to an in-crease in young marriage rates. Operating against these and related

10 Burchinal, "Comparison of Factors . . .," *op. cit.*

11 Lee G. Burchinal, "How Successful Are School-Age Marriages?" *Iowa Farm Science,* 13 (June 1962), pp. 3–9.

12 Lee G. Burchinal and Loren E. Chancellor, *Factors Related to Inter-religious Marriages in Iowa, 1953–1957,* Ames, Iowa: Iowa Agricultural and Home Economics Experiment Station, Research Bulletin 510, November 1962; Lee G. Burchinal and Loren E. Chancellor, "Ages at Marriage, Occupations of Grooms and Interreligious Marriages," *Social Forces,* 40 (May 1962), pp. 348–354.

13 Lee G. Burchinal, "Adolescent Role Deprivation and High School Age Marriage," *Marriage and Family Living,* 21 (November 1959), pp. 380–382.

14 Moss and Gingles, *op. cit.;* and Rachel M. Inselberg, "Social and Psy-chological Factors Associated with High School Marriages," *Journal of Home Economics,* 53 (November 1961), pp. 766–772.

15 Burchinal, "Research on Young Marriage . . .," *op. cit.*

factors that should increase young marriage rates are other factors that should discourage young marriages.

Factors That May Operate Against Young Marriages

Within middle-class society, dating and courtship norms generally have the effect of discouraging rather than encouraging movement toward young marriage. Evidence from a number of studies provides little support for the "Hollywood" notion of dating and courtship for most youths. Student preferences for dates and mates are more consistent with mature and realistic conceptions of marriage than with the frivolous trivia assumed to go with dating today.[16] These norms, however, apply much less to lower-status youths, particularly those who drop out of school and to whom young marriage is most attractive. Yet diffusion of middle-class norms to lower-class youths and increased saliency of these norms among middle-class youths, especially as these norms are reinforced by increased educational requirements and the upward drift in job requirements, should serve to lengthen the dating period and forestall some impulsive youthful marriages.

There also are countervailing influences against young marriages resulting from earlier ages at dating and other indications of acceleration of heterosexual behavior. Most youths who begin dating early, at ages 13 or 14, for example, do not marry by age 17 or 18; and it is unlikely that ages for initial dating will decline much below their present levels. Furthermore, it seems clear that dating among adolescents becomes an enjoyable end in itself rather than only a means to the end of marriage. Research is needed to specify the conditions under which early dating leads to early marriage, as seems to be typical for the small proportion of youths who marry young; and, on the other hand, to specify what other conditions and processes accompany early dating which does not lead to early marriage, as seems to be the case for the majority of adolescents.

Although premarital pregnancy probably is the single most compelling factor affecting the timing of a young marriage, it is probable that movement toward marriage generated by heavy petting, intercourse, and pregnancy may be offset by further develop-

---

[16] For a review of dating and courtship norms and values, see Lee G. Burchinal, "The Premarital Dyad and Love Involvement," in *Handbook on Marriage and Family,* ed. by Harold T. Christensen, Chicago: Rand-McNally, 1964, pp. 626–641.

ment and diffusion of those dating patterns described by Lowry, Blood, Hill, and others,[17] and by changes in values and norms for degrees of sexual behavior appropriate to differing levels of affection. Greater permissiveness, with the assurance of affection, reflects the emerging equalitarian and personal-centered dating, courtship, and marriage system in the United States. For middle-class youth particularly, emerging sexual norms allow for varying degrees of physical expression of affection as part of the dating relationship itself, quite separate from expectations of moving toward engagement or marriage.[18] Widespread availability and increased use of contraceptives also permit intercourse without pregnancy among those who wish to move their affectional relationship to that level, and when pregnancies occur, alternatives to marriage are more readily available and accepted by the girl, the couple, and their parents.

Increased school and post-high-school attendance should be associated with a reduction in young marriage rates. Among 17-year-olds, school dropout rates declined from 32 percent in 1950 to 24 percent in 1960. Post-high-school attendance rates continue to climb. As the value of education diffuses further through lower-class subcultures, marriage rates among 16- and 17-year-olds may decline. Changes in marriage rates among 18-year-olds due to increased school enrollment are more difficult to forecast, because 18 is the modal age at first marriage among females and, for most, represents the year of high school graduation. Marriage rates for 18-year-olds may also decline due to post-high-school education plans; however, it is possible that marriage rates among 18-year-old females will edge upward as lower-status youth defer marriage until after high school but, following subcultural norms for earlier marriage, marry soon after graduation. Also, with increased post-high-school education among lower-status youths, part of whose subcultural expectation is for earlier marriage, college marriage rates may be expected to climb. Again, more precise research, based on large samples with longitudinal designs, is needed.

Increased employment among women, including the mothers and older sisters of today's adolescent girls, has undoubtedly contributed to the enhanced status of women and to expectations among adolescent females of enjoying a period of young adult inde-

[17] *Ibid.*
[18] Ira L. Reiss, *Premarital Sex Standards in America,* Glencoe, Ill.: Free Press, 1960.

pendence before marriage. Many young females want to work a few years after high school, enjoy independent living, travel, and other aspects of young adulthood before "settling down" to marriage. In short, their norms are increasingly similar to those of young men. In this pattern, young marriage would appear less attractive and marriage plans would be moved into the early twenties.

Rising levels of expectation for marriage, in the interpersonal sense as well as materially, are hardly conducive to young marriages. The female's increased status, her potential financial contribution to the family, the personal qualities expected in a spouse by both parties, the need for assurance of a steady income, mainly based on the husband's education, work history, and initiative, all point to caution in movement toward marriage during high school years or immediately thereafter.

One additional development should be noted: the influence of counseling and guidance programs and family life parental education and related education programs conducted by high schools, community organizations, and churches. Although the influence of these programs is largely limited to upwardly mobile lower-class and middle-class youths and their parents, such programs probably have contributed to more serious consideration of marriage at younger ages, and, consequently, to the decreased likelihood of impulsive young marriages.

In summary, factors believed to encourage young marriages are offset by others that prompt youths to postpone marriages until their early twenties.[19] Taken together, however, it is suggested that the balance of these countervailing developments may be toward support of conditions that encourage later instead of earlier marriage for some groups of youths.

CHARACTERISTICS OF YOUNG MARRIAGES

In addition to information about factors believed to influence young marriage decisions, some information is available for selected characteristics for the small minority of youths who marry young.

---

[19] In discussing the influence of selected trends upon young marriage rates, there has been no attempt to develop cross-national comparisons. For such a discussion, see J. Joel Moss, "Teenage Marriage: Cross-National Trends and Sociological Factors in the Decision of When To Marry,"*Acta Sociologica*, 8 (Fasc. 1–2, 1964), pp. 98–117.

Among the generalizations concerning characteristics of young marriage and young spouses are the following:

1. As shown in Table 1, youthful marriages predominantly involve young females and their slightly older husbands. Not shown in Table 1, however, is the fact that the age difference between spouses is inversely related to the age of the bride. For 15-year-old brides, the average groom is 5.5 years older; for 18-year-old brides, he is 3.6 years older; the difference is 2.3 years at age 21, and falls to 1.6 years at age 28.[20]

2. Approximately one-third to over one-half of all young marriages involve premarital pregnancies. Premarital pregnancies are highest among couples in which both spouses are still of school age, and such pregnancies are lower among couples represented by older husbands. Data already have been presented on this point.

3. Young marriages are not elopments: instead, they reflect the characteristics of conventional weddings. In Iowa in 1956, Burchinal and Chancellor found that about 73 percent of all marriages involving brides who were under 19 years of age occurred in the county in which the bride lived, and 92 percent of the weddings were performed by clergymen.[21]

4. Educational levels of young husbands and wives are lower than those for single persons of comparable ages. As shown in Table 2, school dropout rates are particularly high among 16- and 17-year-old married persons and remain higher among 18- and 19-year-old married persons. Estimates of school dropout rates for married girls range from about half to over 90 percent and from about 35 to 45 percent for married boys. Few married students who drop out ever re-enter school.[22]

5. Students who marry before they have graduated from high school generally have lower measured intelligence scores and have lower grades than unmarried students.[23]

6. Young marriages disproportionately involve persons from lower- or working-clas backgrounds (see Table 3).[24] The occupational status of grooms entering first marriages in Iowa from 1953 to 1957 is shown by

[20] Paul H. Jacobson, *American Marriage and Divorce*, New York: Rinehart, 1959, p. 63.

[21] Lee G. Burchinal and Loren Chancellor, "What About School-Age Marriage?" *Iowa Farm Science*, 12 (June 1958), pp. 12–14.

[22] Lee G. Burchinal, "School Policies and School Age Marriages," *Family Life Coordinator*, 8 (March 1960), pp. 45–46; Havighurst *et al., op. cit.*, p. 119; de Lissovoy and Hitchcock, *op. cit.*

[23] Havighurst *et al., op. cit.*, pp. 120–121.

[24] Exceptions to this family established generalization may occur among marriages involving youths from small town and rural areas: see Moss and Gingles, *op. cit.*; and de Lissovoy and Hitchcock, "High School Marriages in Pennsylvania," paper presented at the National Council on Family Relations annual meeting, Miami, Fla., October 1964.

TABLE 2

Martial Status and Educational Levels Among Males and Females,
Aged 14–19, 1950*

		14 and 15		16 and 17		18 and 19	
		Single	Married	Single	Married	Single	Married
				Males			
No school years completed		1.1	2.1	0.9	1.7	0.8	0.7
Elementary	1–4 years	5.8	4.2	4.1	9.5	3.5	6.2
	5–7 years	38.1	16.6	13.3	18.3	9.5	16.8
	8 years	30.4	17.5	13.2	14.5	9.5	15.1
High School	1–3 years	22.6	15.3	63.1	37.4	33.5	33.8
	4 years	0.1	1.7	3.5	4.6	32.7	22.5
College	1–3 years			0.2	0.6	8.4	2.5
	4 or more					0.1	0.2
Not reported		1.9	42.6	1.7	13.4	2.0	2.2
				Females			
No school years completed		0.9	1.7	0.7	0.6	0.6	0.6
Elementary	1–4 years	3.4	8.4	2.2	4.8	1.8	3.2
	5–7 years	30.1	35.3	7.7	19.2	4.7	11.8
	8 years	34.3	26.3	9.1	18.8	5.5	12.7
High School	1–3 years	29.5	20.8	73.0	49.7	28.1	39.1
	4 years	0.2	0.7	5.5	4.7	45.2	28.7
College	1–3 years			0.4	0.2	12.2	2.2
	4 or more					0.2	0.1
Not reported		1.6	6.8	1.4	2.0	1.7	1.6

* Adopted from the United States Census of Population: 1950, Report P.E. No. 5B, Volume IV, Part 5, Chapter B, Table 8, p. 5B-63. Data for 1960 are not yet available.

ages of brides and grooms. As the ages of the brides or grooms increased, the proportion of marriages involving high-status grooms increased, and the proportion of marriages involving lowest-status grooms decreased[25].

7. With lower levels of education and with employment largely limited to unskilled and semiskilled jobs, young marriages generally are established and maintained on a meager economic basis. In two studies, mean annual incomes of young couples were approximately $3,000 to $3,800.[26]

8. Parental financial assistance represents an important contribution to the economic livelihood of the young couples.

[25] Burchinal and Chancellor, "Factors Related to Interreligious Marriages in Iowa," *op. cit.*, and "Ages at Marriage, Occupations of Grooms and Interreligious Marriages," *op. cit.*
[26] Burchinal, "Research on Young Marriages . . .," *op. cit.*; Rachel M. Inselberg, "Marital Problems and Satisfactions in High School Marriages," *Marriage and Family Living*, 24 (February 1962), pp. 74–77.

Table 3

First Occupational Status Distributions of Grooms by Ages of Brides
and Grooms, Iowa, White Marriages, 1953–1957

Occupational Status of Grooms*	Ages of Brides				
	17 or Under	18	19–22	23–29	30 or over
N	11,088	15,736	37,019	10,394	2,198
High	26.1	28.8	43.9	51.1	46.1
Middle	19.3	21.5	20.9	24.4	29.2
Low	42.8	36.4	23.9	18.6	22.6
Armed Forces	11.8	13.3	11.3	5.9	2.1
	Ages of Grooms				
N	2,580	4,404	35,951	28,771	4,727
High	34.4	27.7	34.4	45.8	49.2
Middle	16.3	19.6	19.4	24.1	26.6
Low	40.2	38.7	30.2	24.6	22.3
Armed Forces	9.1	14.0	16.0	5.5	1.9

* High occupational status occupations include professionals, managers, farm operators and owners, officials, and proprietors; middle-status occupations include clerks, sales, and operatives; and low status occupations include domestics, farm laborers, and other laborers.

A minority of young couples always maintain their own residences; most must double-up with relatives; and most report receiving other forms of family assistance as well, including payment for rent if they are not living with relatives, cash for food, furniture, car payments, and other bills.[27]

OUTCOMES OF YOUNG MARRIAGES

Two sets of data can be used to examine the outcomes of young marriages. One set consists of objective standards such as divorce and separation rates; the other includes subjective ratings or evaluations of marriage. Both point to greater stresses encountered in young marriages.

Divorce rates are between two and four times greater among young marriages than among marriages begun by persons in their twenties.[28]

[27] Burchinal, "Comparisons of Factors . . .," *op. cit.*, pp. 94–95.
[28] See Thomas P. Monohan, "Does Age at Marriage Matter in Divorce?" *Social Forces*, 32 (October 1963), pp. 81–87.

TABLE 4

Percentages for Divorce, Legal Separation, and Separation Due to Marital Discord by Sex, Color, and Age, 1950 and 1960*

	Male						Female					
	White		Nonwhite		Total		White		Nonwhite		Total	
Age	N	%	N	%	N	%	N	%	N	%	N	%
						1960							
15	7,845	8.5	1,246	22.4	9,091	10.4	26,607	6.8	4,927	14.2	31,534	7.9
16	11,621	7.3	1,834	17.6	13,455	8.7	68,465	5.6	11,380	12.0	79,845	6.6
17	24,338	7.0	3,544	14.6	27,882	8.0	148,698	5.6	22,701	11.2	171,399	6.3
18	59,726	4.9	7,815	11.0	67,541	5.6	268,037	4.9	35,628	11.6	303,665	5.7
						1950							
15	7,330	28.0	655	19.1	7,985	27.1	16,805	5.8	4,160	14.5	20,965	7.5
16	7,810	19.8	925	11.4	8,735	18.9	50,920	5.5	12,305	15.0	63,225	7.4
17	12,965	8.9	3,005	12.6	15,970	9.6	112,655	5.1	23,980	13.6	136,635	6.6
18	34,890	5.6	7,380	11.8	42,270	6.6	226,920	4.8	42,175	14.3	269,095	6.3

* From "Detailed Characteristics," United States Census of Population, 1960, Series PC (1), 1D, Table 176, pp. 1–424 to 1–427; and 1950 United States Census of Population, U.S. Summary, "Detailed Characteristics," Table 104, pp. 182–183.

Additional data for combined divorce and separation rates are reported for 1950 and 1960 in Table 4 for white and nonwhite marriages by the ages of males and females involved. (Separation represents legal separation or living apart due to marital discord, and not separations imposed because of military service, illness, or employment.) The combined rates were highest for youngest spouses and declined consistently for all groups from age 15 through 18. For both sexes, nonwhite rates generally exceeded those for whites, often being twice as large. In general, rates for given age-sex-color groupings were approximately the same in 1960 as in 1950.

Even when some of the effects associated with status are controlled, marriages begun at younger ages in contrast to those begun by persons in their twenties still have higher divorce rates. For instance, survival rates for Iowa marriages from 1953 to 1957 varied among the three status levels used, but survival rates were always lower in each status level for the marriages involving the brides 19 or younger in comparison with brides who were 20 or older.[29]

Various self-assessments of marriages point to more difficulties associated with younger ages of marriage. Persons who married in their teens generally rated their marriages as being less satisfactory than persons who married later in life. Most of these differences hold for early- and later-married couples who have been married for ten to 15 years.[30]

At least two studies have focused on self-assessment of satisfaction among young couples. According to these two investigations in different localities, from approximately one-third to over one-half of young husbands and wives reported they regretted that they married when they did.[31] Regret was reported by a greater proportion of premaritally pregnant wives than by those who did not marry under such circumstances.[32]

The preceding uniform negative assessments of the outcomes of

[29] Lee G. Burchinal and Loren E. Chancellor, *Survival Rates Among Religiously Homogamous and Interreligious Marriages,* Ames, Iowa: Iowa Agricultural and Home Economics Experiment Station, Research Bulletin 512, December 1962; and Lee G. Burchinal and Loren E. Chancellor, "Survival Rates Among Religiously Homogamous and Interreligious Marriages," *Social Forces,* 41 (May 1963), pp. 353–362.

[30] For a review of relevant studies, see Burchinal, "Research on Young Marriage . . .," *op. cit.*

[31] Burchinal, "How Successful Are School-Age Marriages?" and "Comparisons of Factors . . .," *op. cit.;* and Inselberg, "Marital Problems and Satisfactions in High School Marriages," *op. cit.,* p. 77.

[32] Burchinal, "Comparisons of Factors . . .," *op. cit.*

TABLE 5

Hypothesied Relationships Between Selected Characteristics and Outcomes of Young Marriages

Forecast of Marital Competence and Satisfaction

Characteristic	Poorest	Intermediate	Best
Ages at Marriage	Both 17 or younger	Female 17, male 20 or older	Female at least 18, male 20 or older
Educational attainment	Both school dropouts	Female dropout, male high school graduate	Both high school graduates, male, at least, with some post-high school education
Pregnancy	Premarital pregnancy	No premarital pregnancy, pregnancy immediately following marriage	Pregnancy delayed until at least one year following marriage
Acquaintance before marriage	Less than six months, no engagement period, formal or informal	One year, at least, with at least six months engagement or understanding to marry	Several years, with at least six months engagement or understanding to marry
Previous dating patterns	Limited number of dating partners, went steady immediately, or short period between first date and first date with fiancé	Some dating experience before first dating fiancé	Numerous different dates, played the field, some previous experience with going steady
Personality dynamics	Generally poor interpersonal skills, lacking maturity, limited interests, poor personal and social adjustment	Mixed	Generally competent in interpersonal relations, flexible, mature, maintaining healthy and pleasurable relations with others

Motivation for marrying	Drift into marriage, because of pregnancy, seemed like the thing to do, just wanted to, or other impulsive reasons with no strong emphasis on marital and parental roles	Mixed, marriage as preferred to career, though had previous post-high-school educational aspirations and for females perhaps tentative plans to work, etc.	No post-high-school educational aspirations and, for females: marriage, family, and homemaking preferred as career over working, living independently; positive emphasis upon role as wife and mother
Status of families of orientation	Both lower	Mixed, lower, and middle or high	Both middle or high
Parental attitudes before marriage	Strongly opposed	Mildly opposed or resigned acceptance	Supportive once the decision was clear
Wedding	Elopement and civil ceremony		Conventional, hometown, and church-sanctioned
Economic basis	Virtually completely dependent upon relatives	Low dependence upon relatives, mostly independent income, even if near hardship level	At least assured income above self-perceived hardship level
Residence	Always lived with in-laws or other relatives	Doubled up with relatives some of the time, independent other periods of time	Always maintained own independent place of residence
Post-marriage parental views	Rejecting or punitive, assistance provided as a method of controlling the marriage	Cool	Psychologically supportive, sincerely want to help the young couple, assistance provided with no strings attached

young marriage apply to the youthful married population as a whole. It is important not to overgeneralize findings of comparatively greater disillusionment, discord, and divorce among many youthful marriages to all young couples. Not all young marriages are doomed to failure or unhappiness. There are many successful and competent youthful marriages. In addition to describing the greater probability of discord among young marriages it is equally important to identify correlates of success in young marriages. Yet this important research problem goes virtually untouched.

In the absence of adequate data, however, some hypotheses can be advanced for forecasting the probable success of young marriages with different kinds of premarital and postmarital characteristics. In Table 5, 14 conditions are related to the general outcomes of young marriages. Some factors are directly based upon research results; others are based upon inferences from general knowledge of correlates of marital competency. All are presented tentatively, as suggestions for discussion or hypotheses for further research.

The forecast is gloomiest for marriages with the characteristics listed in the left-hand column of Table 5 and is most optimistic for those having characteristics listed in the right-hand column. Of course, both the positive and negative factors are interrelated and combine into clusters. With the presence of an increasing number of negative factors, forecasts for competent or satisfying marital relations would become more doubtful; whereas with the presence of an increasing number of positive factors, more competent or successful marital and parental interaction could be expected. Factors listed in Table 5 are also useful for assessing possible outcomes of young marriages that reflect a mixture of conditions, some of which are positively related to socially desired marital outcomes and others of which are not. Consider, for instance, the common mixed type which occurs when a school-aged girl who had not planned for any post-high-school education becomes pregnant and marries before graduation, with only mild parental support, and whose husband is in his early twenties and is employed with a steady, modest income. In such cases, problems typically associated with pregnancy-provoked young marriages would be less serious.[33]

Forecasts of marital outcomes for various other types are not necessary. Research is needed to determine what mixtures of conditions produce what kinds of marital outcomes. Until these data are

[33] *Ibid.*

available, we are left with documentation for somewhat greater risks of young marriage in general and with hypotheses for how risks vary by characteristics of young married couples.

IMPLICATIONS

It is not necessary to reiterate various implications of young marriages for family life education, marriage counseling, and related programs that have been discussed in a previous review of young marriages.[34] Instead, several general observations are offered:

1. Age per se is not an adequate criterion for predicting the degree of marital competence of couples. Numerous factors related to readiness for marriage are correlated with age, but these relationships are not immutable; for some categories of youths, marriage may not entail any greater risk than for the population as a whole, but for other categories of youths, marital forecasts are extremely pessimistic. One of the goals of family life education and counseling should be to decrease the relationship between age and competency for marriage, given at least a minimum age of 18 or 19.

2. Behind age at marriage are numerous confounding influences which increase the risks for achieving marital success at age 16 or 17 and possibly even at age 18. A general index of many conditions that are negatively related to competency in marriage is the lower-status background of a predominant number of youths who marry before the age of 18. Competency in marriage and family relationships today requires a set of values, personality characteristics, and interpersonal skills associated with middle-class society. At the risk of overgeneralizing, data from numerous studies indicate that child-rearing and family relationship patterns of lower-status families are in direct contrast to those that research shows are associated with emotional health, school achievement, goal setting and attainment, social success, and reasonably competent interpersonal relations— all required for competent marital relationships.[35] Under these conditions, attempts to alter high risks associated with young marriages require educational, counseling, social services, and related programs, including attempts to change values, role expecta-

[34] Burchinal, "Research on Young Marriages . . . ," *op. cit.*
[35] Catherine Chilman, "Child-Rearing and Family Relationship Patterns of the Very Poor," *Welfare in Review,* 3 (January 1965), pp. 9–19.

tions, and behavioral patterns among lower-class families toward middle-class values and goals. To contribute even modestly to better preparation for marriage and adult living, programs will have to exceed anything that is currently envisioned.

3. Another factor standing behind young marriages, both in promoting decisions to marry and in eroding the basis for marriage, is premarital pregnancy. Also disruptive to young marriages are unexpected pregnancies during the first year of the marriage. Greater and more vigorous educational efforts are needed to prevent both circumstances. For newly married youths, requested instruction in birth control and family planning may be an important contribution to the satisfaction of the couple and to their level of living. Efforts to help pregnant girls, whether single or married, to continue their education, acquire homemaking skills, and become more competent mothers and wives also will greatly assist these marriages.[36]

4. There are justifiable grounds for discouraging young marriages, but a young marriage, no matter what the circumstances are and no matter how injudicious it may seem, is not a crime and, if used as grounds for punitive reactions, probably will only promote the completion of the self-fulfilling prophecy of greater risks of young marriages. Inadequate understanding of the causes of these marriages, however, leads many well-meaning persons to take actions which only serve to increase the obstacles confronting youthful couples and which put additional burdens on these couples. For instance, some school boards require the withdrawal or suspension of married students. This restrictive policy is intended to prevent additional marriages among high school students, but the few studies that have been attempted show that restrictive policies have little effect on high school marriage rates.[37] Instead, such policies

[36] Examples of programs for pregnant girls include demonstration or experimental programs such as "School Centered Rehabilitation Program for Pregnant School-Age Girls in Washington, D.C.," being conducted by the Washington, D.C. Public Schools and directed by Mrs. Elizabeth M. Goodman, with support from the Children's Bureau, U.S. Welfare Administration; and the "Interagency Program for Pregnant Girls," being conducted by the Oakland Interagency Project, Oakland, California, with support from the Ford Foundation.

[37] Burchinal, "School Policies and School Age Marriages," *op. cit.*, pp. 43–48; and Lee G. Burchinal, "Do Restrictive Policies Curb Teen Marriages?" *Overview*, 1 (March 1960), pp. 72–73. For a recent report describing lack of constructive school policies regarding student marriages, see: John G. Willmarth and Leroy G. Olsen, "Practices and Attitudes of 253 High School

only guarantee that married youths will be prevented from acquiring a basic education necessary for employment today. Also, parents are warned against the "hidden dangers" of subsidizing the marriages of their children.[38]

According to the preceding admonition, youths who marry are to be left to flounder if they encounter economic or other difficulties. Actually, the causes leading to young marriages are extremely complex. Attempts to alter young marriage rates must deal with these causes and not with spurious ones. Threats or actual failure to support young marriages which occur probably have little influence on the marriage plans of other youths. Marriage plans grow out of a complex of factors involving previous dating histories, family relationships, personality characteristics, and life goals.[39]

5. Aside from the fact that restrictive school policies, curfews, and other "tough-minded" solutions probably will have little influence on the processes that lead to young marriages, stringent policies such as these cannot be justified in relation to the relatively low and stable or possible declining rates of marriage among 15-17-year-olds.

6. It may be that long-term trends toward younger age at marriage have selected from the young population about as large a proportion of adolescents as possible who, for various reasons, are disposed to marriage; and that now, with countertrends becoming more obvious, continuation of early dating, emancipation of youth, and varying degrees of physical involvement will not result in higher young marriage rates. More likely, it could be argued, a greater proportion of youths are being better prepared and helped to prolong dating experiences, without moving quickly into courtship

---

Principals Regarding Teen-age Marriages and Unwed Pregnant Girls," *Clearing House*, 39 (November 1964), pp. 171–175. The Willmarth and Olsen report contains eight references to similar studies of high school policies regarding married students.

[38] Rosalind Russell, as told to Lester David, "I'm Glad I Didn't Marry Young," *Reader's Digest*, 74 (February 1959), pp. 75–77. See also, David R. Mace, "The Hidden Danger in 'Subsidized' Marriage," *McCall's*, 88 (September 1961), pp. 36, 157; reprinted in *Reader's Digest*, 80 (January 1962), pp. 37–39.

[39] In addition to the previous discussion of factors affecting young marriage rates, see Lee G. Burchinal, "Young Marriages," in *Foundations for Christian Family Policy*, ed. by Elizabeth S. Genne and William H. Genne, New York: National Council of Churches of Christ in the U.S.A., 1960. Contained in this paper is a diagram relating knowledge, inferences, and value judgments to development of programs to prepare youths for dating, courtship, and marriage decisions.

and marriage. Continued stability in or possible slight declines in young marriage rates may be expected, although the absolute number of such marriages will continue to increase. Also, it well could be that increases in young marriage rates may occur among certain subgroups and that declines in similar rates will occur among other subgroups.

Another result of continuing trends in dating and courtship patterns may be the development of a pronounced modal age for first marriage at 19 or 20 for females and at 21 or 22 for men, with a considerably smaller range in ages at first marriage than has been true. Data from the 1970 census of population will provide a test of the push toward marriage at age 19 or in the early twenties, which is beyond the limits of young marriage as used in this discussion.

Programs to help youths avoid injudicious marriage decisions may well serve best by not focusing on the risks of youthful marriage per se, but, instead, by assisting youths to develop their personalities, interests, and potentials as fully as possible. Socialization experiences in the home and community programs in schools, churches, and other organizations can play a part in this process. Research and demonstration projects are needed to determine in what ways socialization, schools, and community processes influence dating, affectional, sexual, and marriage decisions of youths; and how dating, courtship, and marriage outcomes vary according to types of programs and experiences youths had before marriage. Programs of planned social change may also influence young marriage decisions.

8. Aside from their immediate intended effects, programs to provide for expanded opportunities for youths may operate against young marriages by giving lower-class youths reason for aspiring to middle-class norms and values, one of which is to defer marriage until the twenties. Programs that might have this added consequence include the various methods now being developed to make education more meaningful to lower-class youths, to prevent school dropouts, to expand educational and job opportunities, to reduce the effects of racial discrimination, and, in general, to provide challenge to youths and to increase their sense of significance. For all youths, the Peace Corps, community development projects, and the developing VISTA program as part of the war on poverty, offer opportunities for service, enriched growth and development, and exciting participation in the larger society. By providing attractive alternate

roles to marriage, these national service programs also might encourage postponement of marriage during or immediately following
high school.

Has Monogamy Failed?
HERBERT A. OTTO
Fellow, American Association of Marriage Counselors

Never before in the history of Western civilization has the institution of marriage been under the searching scrutiny it is today.
Never before have so many people questioned the cultural and
theological heritage of monogamy—and set out in search of alternatives. The American family of the 1970s is entering an unprecedented era of change and transition, with a massive reappraisal of
the family and its functioning in the offing.

The U.S. statistic of one divorce per every four marriages is all
too familiar. Other figures are even more disquieting. For example,
a recent government study revealed that one-third of all first-born
children in the United States from 1964 through 1966 were conceived out of wedlock, thereby forcing many hasty marriages that
might not have occurred otherwise. Some marriage specialists estimate that anywhere from 40 to 60 per cent of all marriages are at
any given time "subclinical." The couples involved could materially
benefit from the help of a marriage counselor, but they never reach
a clinic. Divorce is still the most widely accepted means of coping
with a marriage beset by problems. Relatively few couples having
marital difficulties are aware of available marriage counseling services or utilize them. Divorce today is very much a part of the
social fabric, and some sociologists refer to a "divorce culture." It is
safe to say that most men, women, and children in this country have
been touched by the divorce experience—either in their own families, or among friends and close acquaintances.

The other day a good friend, senior executive of a large com-

From *Saturday Review*, 53 (No. 17): 23–25+, April 25, 1970. Copyright
1970 Saturday Review, Inc.

pany and in his early forties, dropped by for a visit. He told me he had been thinking of divorce after sixteen years of marriage. The couple have a boy, twelve, and two girls, one of whom is ten, the other eight. "We've grown apart over the years, and we have nothing in common left anymore other than the children. There are at least twenty years of enjoying life still ahead of me. I was worried about the children until we discussed it with them. So many of their schoolmates have had divorced parents or parents who had remarried, they are accustomed to the idea. It's part of life. Of course, if the older ones need help, I want them to see a good psychiatrist while we go through with this. My wife is still a good-looking woman, younger than I, and probably will remarry. I'm not thinking of it now, but I'll probably remarry someday." This situation illustrates an attitude and the climate of the times. Divorce has become as much an institution as marriage.

Paradoxically, the high divorce rate can be viewed as both a symptom of the failure of monogamy and an indication of its success. A large majority of men and women remarry within four years after their divorce. As Dr. Bernard Steinzor points out in his latest book, *When Parents Divorce*, "divorce has become an expression of the increasing personal freedom afforded the average citizen." It is a fact that the average citizen continues to pursue personal freedom within the framework of marriage. Serial monogamy or progressive monogamy is today so widespread that it has arrived as an alternative structure. According to one analyst, we are close to the day when 85 per cent of all men and women reaching the age of sixty-five will have been remarried at least once. I am reminded of a cartoon that appeared in *The New Yorker* some time ago: A young couple is shown leaving what is identified by a sign as the home of a justice of the peace. The bride, dressed in the latest mod fashion, turns brightly to her young man and says, "Darling! Our first marriage!"

The full-scale emergence of serial monogamy has been accompanied by an explosive upswing of experimentation with other alternative structures. Begun by the under-thirty generation and hippie tribal families, the 1960s have seen the growth of a new commune movement. This movement has started to attract significant segments of the older, established population. For example, I recently conducted a weekend marathon in Chicago—under the auspices of the Oasis Center—that was open to the public. Seven out of thirty-six participants were members of communes. Three of the seven were successful professional men in their mid-forties. Another participant, a college professor in his early thirties, mentioned that he had been a member of a commune composed of several psychiatrists, an engineer, a teacher, and a chemist. When I visited New York following the Chicago weekend, a senior editor of a large publishing house casually mentioned that he and some friends were in the process of organizing a commune. They were looking for a large brownstone close to their offices.

The commune movement even has its own journal, *Modern Utopian*. Issued by the Alternatives Foundation of Berkeley, California, it is in its fourth year of publication. In 1969, this journal published the first comprehensive directory of intentional or utopian communes in the United States and the world. The addresses of close to two hundred intentional communities in this country are given. (It has been estimated that there are four to six times this number of communes in the United States.) California leads the *Modern Utopian* directory with more than thirty listed. New York has twenty-eight and Pennsylvania thirteen, with communes listed from thirty-five other states. Half a dozen books that I know of are currently in preparation on the commune movement.

Communes of various types exist, varying from agricultural subsistence to religious. To provide a base for economic survival, many of the communes furnish services or construct marketable products such as hammocks or wooden toys for preschoolers. Others operate printing presses or schools. Most communes not located in cities raise some of their own food. Relatively rare is the commune that is self-supporting solely on the basis of its agricultural operation. Sizes vary with anywhere from twelve persons or fewer to a hundred persons or more as members of an intentional community. The educational and vocational backgrounds of members also vary widely. The young people and school dropouts are currently being joined by a growing number of "Establishment dropouts." Many of these are people who have made successful contributions in their chosen vocations or professions and have grown disillusioned, or who are seeking to explore new life-styles.

Communes often have their beginnings when several persons who know each other well, like each other, and have similar values decide to live together. Sometimes a commune is formed around a common interest, craft, or unifying creative goal. Political views or convictions may also play a role in the formation of a commune. There are a number of peace-movement and radical communes;

sometimes these are composed of political activists, and sometimes of people who see the commune movement as a "radical approach to revolution." Members of one such group, the Twin Oaks community in Virginia, think of themselves as a post-revolutionary society. As detailed in *Modern Utopian*, this "radical commune" was organized as the result of a university conference:

Twin Oaks was started by a group of people who met while attending an "academic" conference during 1966 at Ann Arbor, Michigan, on the formation of a Walden II community. One of the Twin Oakers related how this conference resulted in a very elaborate, academic type plan on how to get a Walden II community going. But when the conference was over, the professors all returned to their teaching posts, and nobody had any idea where they could get the several million dollars that the plan called for to start the thing. So eight people decided to start right away with whatever resources they could get together. . . .

For while Twin Oaks was designed to be a living experiment in community, it also aims to stimulate others to do the same. As one member said, "We generally hold to the opinion that people who *don't* start communities (or join them) are slightly immoral." It's all part of the revolution being over—they define revolution as a "radical restructuring" of society, both economic and, more important, cultural. (But maybe you can't really separate the two.) One member summed up a desirable post-revolutionary society as: "A society that creates people who are committed to non-aggression; a society of people concerned for one another; a society where one man's gain is not another man's loss; a society where disagreeable work is minimized and leisure is valued; a society in which people come first; an economic system of equality; a society which is constantly trying to improve in its ability to create happy, productive, creative people."

The personal property a member brings to a commune remains his, although he may be expected to share it when needed. Some purists object that, since members do not donate personal property for the benefit of the group, the current social experiments should not be referred to as "communes." Obviously, the term has acquired a new meaning and definition. The emphasis today is on the exploration of alternate models for togetherness, the shaping of growing dynamic environments, the exploration of new life-styles, and the enjoyment of living together.

A number of communes are deliberately organized for the purpose of group marriage. The concept of group marriage, however, differs widely. Some communes exclusively composed of couples have a living arrangement similar to the "big family" or group family that originated in Sweden in 1967. These married couples share the same home, expenses, household chores, and the upbringing of the children. Infidelity is not encouraged. Other group-marriage communes tolerate or encourage the sharing of husbands and wives. On the other end of the group-marriage continuum are communes such as The Family near Taos, New Mexico. This group of more than fifty members discourages pairing—"Everyone is married to everyone. The children are everyone's."

The life-span of many communes is relatively short due to four major disintegrative pressures that fragment intentional communities. Disagreement over household chores or work to be performed is a major source of disruption. When members fail to fulfill their obligations, disillusionment and demoralization often set in. Closely related are interpersonal conflicts, frequently fueled by the exchange of sex partners and resultant jealousy. Drugs do not seem to create a major problem in most communes, as there is either a permissive attitude or drug use is discouraged or forbidden. A small number of religious/mystical communes use drugs for sacramental purposes and as a means of communion.

The problems associated with economic survival generate considerable pressure. A final strong force that contributes to the collapse of communes stems from the hostility of surrounding communities. There are innumerable instances of harassment by neighbors, strangers, civil authorities, and police. The persistent and violent nature of this persecution is probably traceable to deep-seated feelings of threat and outrage when the neighboring communities discover a group in their midst suspected of having unorthodox living arrangements. These pervasive feelings of resistance and anger (which may be partially subconscious) are conceivably engendered in many persons by what they perceive to be a threat to the existing family structure.

The weight of tradition and the strong imprinting of parental and familial models assure that for some time to come the overwhelming bulk of the population will opt for something close to the family structures they have known. In view of this strong thrust, it is all the more surprising that preventive programs (other than didactic approaches) that center on the strengthening of the family are almost unknown. Also sadly lacking is massive federal support for programs designed to help marriages and families beset by problems. A network of federally supported marriage-counseling clinics making marital and premarital counseling services available throughout every state in the Union could accomplish a great deal toward reducing marital unhappiness and divorce.

Present-day medical science widely recommends that we have an annual physical check-up as a means of prevention. In a similar manner, annual assessment and evaluation should be available to couples interested in developing and improving their marriages. The goal would be to identify, strengthen, and develop family potential *before* crises arise, with the main focus on helping a family achieve an even more loving, enjoyable, creative, and satisfying marriage relationship. The plan of a marriage and family potential center was developed in 1967 and 1968 by a colleague, Dr. Lacey Hall, and myself during my stay in Chicago. The project was supported by the Stone Foundation, but, owing to a number of complex reasons, the program was never fully implemented. As a part of the work in Chicago, and also under the auspices of the National Center for the Exploration of Human Potential, a number of "More Joy in Your Marriage" groups and classes have been conducted and have shown considerable promise as a preventive approach.

Another highly promising field of inquiry is the area of family strengths. Little or no research and conceptualization had been done in relation to this area until the work of the Human Potentialities Research Project at the University of Utah, from 1960 through 1967. Paradoxically, family counseling and treatment programs have been offered for decades without a clearly developed framework of what was meant by family strengths, or what constitutes a "healthy family." In spite of extensive efforts to obtain foundation or government support for this research, no financial support was forthcoming. Ours remains a pathology-oriented culture saddled with the bias that the study of disorganization, illness, and dysfunction is the surest road to understanding the forces that go into the making of health and optimum functioning.

The emergence of alternative structures and the experimentation with new modes of married and family togetherness expresses a strong need to bring greater health and optimum functioning to a framework of interpersonal relationships formerly regarded as "frozen" and not amenable to change. There is no question that sex-role and parental-role rigidities are in the process of diminishing, and new dimensions of flexibility are making their appearance in marriage and the family. It is also evident that we are a pluralistic society with pluralistic needs. In this time of change and accelerated social evolution, we should encourage innovation and experimentation in the development of new forms of social and communal living. It is possible to invent and try out many models without hurting or destroying another person. Perhaps we need to recognize clearly that the objective of any model is to provide an atmosphere of sustenance, loving, caring, and adventuring. This makes growth and unfoldment possible.

It is in this light that the attention of an increasing number of well-known humanistic psychologists has been drawn to the institution of marriage. A new recognition of the many dimensions and possibilities of monogamy is beginning to emerge. For example, Dr. Jack Gibb and Dr. Everett Shostrom have each been conducting a series of couples groups at Growth Centers designed to revitalize and deepen love in the marital relationship.

Another eminent psychologist and author, Dr. Sidney Jourard, suggests that we "re-invent marriage" by engaging in "serial polygamy to the same person." He points out that many marriages pass through a cycle of gratifying the needs of both partners, and are experienced as fulfilling until an impasse is reached. One partner or the other finds continuation in that form intolerable, and the marriage is usually legally dissolved at that point. He believes it is possible for the couple at this juncture to struggle with the impasse and to evolve a new marriage with each other, one that includes change, yet preserves some of the old pattern that remains viable. This is the second marriage that, whatever form it takes, will also reach its end. There may then again be a time of estrangement, a period of experimentation, and a remarriage in a new way—and so on for as long as continued association with the same spouse remains meaningful for both partners.

One of the originators of the group marathon technique, Dr. Frederick Stoller, has another interesting proposal to add new dimensions to marriage and family relationships. He suggests an "intimate network of families." His intimate network consists of a circle of three or four families who meet together regularly and frequently, share in reciprocal fashion any of their intimate secrets, and offer one another a variety of services. The families do not hesitate to influence one another in terms of values and attitudes. Such an intimate family network would be neither stagnant nor polite, but would involve an extension of the boundaries of the immediate family.

Another possibility to introduce new elements of growth and creativity to monogamy is contained in my own concept of the "new marriage," i.e., marriage as a framework for developing personal potential. This concept is based on the hypothesis that we are all functioning at a small fraction of our capacity to live fully in its total meaning of loving, caring, creating, and adventuring. Consequently, the actualizing of our potential can become the most exciting adventure of our lifetime. From this perspective, any marriage can be envisioned as a framework for actualizing personal potential. Thus, marriage offers us an opportunity to grow, and an opportunity to develop and deepen the capacity for loving and caring. Only in a continuing relationship is there a possibility for love to become deeper and fuller so that it envelops all of our life and extends into the community. However, growth, by its very nature, is not smooth and easy, for growth involves change and the emergence of the new. But growth and the actualization of personal potential are also a joyous and deeply satisfying process that can bring to marriage a *joie de vivre*, an excitement, and a new quality of zest for living.

There are a number of characteristics that form a unique Gestalt and distinguish the new marriage from contemporary marriage patterns:

There is a clear acknowledgment by both partners concerning the *personal relevance* of the human potentialities hypothesis: that the healthy individual is functioning at a fraction of his potential.

Love and understanding become dynamic elements in the actualization of the marital partners' personal potential.

Partners in the new marriage conceive of their union as an evolving, developing, flexible, loving relationship.

In the new marriage there is planned action and commitment to achieve realization of marriage potential.

The new marriage is here-and-now oriented and not bound to the past.

There is clear awareness by husband and wife that their interpersonal or relationship environment, as well as their physical environment, directly affects the actualization of individual potential.

There is clear recognition by spouses that personality and the actualization of human potential have much to do with the social institutions and structures within which man functions. The need for institutional and environmental regeneration is acknowledged by both partners as being personally relevant, leading to involvement in social action.

Husband and wife have an interest in exploring the spiritual dimensions of the new marriage.

Since it is often difficult for two people to actualize more of their marriage potential by themselves, participants in the new marriage will seek out group experiences designed to deepen their relationship and functioning as a couple. Such experiences are now being offered at Growth Centers that have sprung up in many parts of the United States. Extension divisions of institutions of higher learning and church organizations are also increasingly offering such group experiences. Based on my many years of practice as marriage counselor, it has long been my conclusion that every marriage needs periodic rejuvenation and revitalization. This is best accomplished in a couples group that focuses on the development of greater intimacy, freedom, joy, and affection.

The challenge of marriage is the adventure of uncovering the depth of our love, the height of our humanity. It means risking ourselves physically and emotionally; leaving old habit patterns, and developing new ones; being able to express our desires fully, while sensitive to the needs of the other; being aware that each changes at his own rate, and unafraid to ask for help when needed.

Has monogamy failed? My answer is "no." Monogamy is no longer a rigid institution, but instead an evolving one. There is a multiplicity of models and dimensions that we have not even begun to explore. It takes a certain amount of openness to beome aware on not only an intellectual level but a feeling level that these possibilities face us with a choice. Then it takes courage to recognize that this choice in a measure represents our faith in monogamy. Finally, there is the fact that every marriage has a potential for greater commitment, enjoyment, and communication, for more love, understanding, and warmth. Actualizing this potential can offer new dimensions in living and new opportunities for personal growth, and can add new strength and affirmation to a marriage.

Finding and Using Psychological Help

Asking for and making optimum use of help of any nature in this culture is complicated by the common belief that people of value and status are strong and self-sufficient. The helper is looked up to and the person who needs help is considered to be weak and of inferior status. Despite the fact that each and every one of us is dependent upon others for our physical, economic, and psychological well being, we tend to feel that self-sufficiency and individualism are personality traits which should be cultivated. When this attitude is carried too far (as we—the editors—believe that it is), people tend to postpone or avoid asking for help with personal problems. Hence, problems that could have been dealt with easily in their earlier stages are postponed until situations become so complicated that they require much effort and entail much inconvenience.

This is especially true of psychological or mental health problems and particularly true of males. Although much has been done to remove the stigma previously attached to mental illness, some resistance to admitting problems of this nature continues. Furthermore, the masculine stereotype leads us to feel that a male should be strong, stoical, reasonable, and unemotional if he, in terms of the frequently heard injunction, is to "be a man." To ask for and to benefit from help, one must admit to some inadequacy, and to some irrrationality. He must own up to having feelings and to some lack of control. As we have said, women can do this more easily than men. Possibly, as a result, they live longer and have fewer ailments indicative of psychological stress. Although women seek psychological help much more frequently, more men wind up in mental institutions.

Mental health, however, is not a clear-cut matter of being sick or being well. There are few, if any, among us who are as effective, as well-adjusted, and as healthy as we could be. Even the most stable personality has its breaking point. Also, it usually is not possible for any of us to view his own condition or behavior with sufficient clarity and objectivity to become maximally effective by himself. Psychological help is not a need of the sick alone. Moreover, none of us is so effective or so well-adjusted that he cannot benefit from individual or group counseling. For it is seldom enough to say, "Be better," or to enjoin, "Be more effective in this way or that way." A do-it-yourself psychology which is gained from reading is apt to lack the preciseness to specify and to personalize those behaviors which need changing and to be unable to furnish objective feedback concerning progress in those directions.

Roger's article is of great significance in this respect. He describes a number of the ways in which participation in therapy groups can aid in learning more effective interpersonal, transaction skills. He believes, as do we, that such groups can be of assistance to everyone. A person cannot be himself or even establish what sort of self to be without lengthy and meaningful association with others. They furnish the standards by which he sees and evaluates himself. In an intensive group experience, one has this needed human contact and he has it under conditions where the feedback concerning the effectiveness of his behavior can be made explicit and understandable. It seems entirely plausible that the next generation or two will be much more candid and casual about emotional feelings, and that discussion of them will become a recognized part of school curricula.

Farnsworth offers some good practical suggestions for facilitating mental health or actualizing self to people of all ages. We do not see these terms as different (See the article on page 382.) For one does not occur in the absence of the other. Both are positive in nature and both require the active and purposeful participation of the individual if he is to be a positive individual in what happens to him.

The tendency to disclose oneself is an inseparable aspect of the task of seeking aid. If a therapist, or counselor, or a friend is to provide help he must know the point at which the pressure should be lifted. These helpers must know, through feedback, if they are being effective. This knowledge is purchased at the cost of self-disclosure on the part of the counselee. Some of the above remarks about the tendency to avoid seeking help seem to be confirmed by the Pederson and Higbee study. Women apparently are more willing to seek help from others than are tough, self-sufficient men. This seems to be true even when women have not had the initiation in self-disclosure which would have been brought about by a warm, trustful, and empathic mother.

Pederson and Higbee devote attention to the nature of the relationship between discloser and target person. This may lead the reader to view this relationship as something that simply does or does not exist. Again, as has been done so many times in the earlier parts of this book, it is worth emphasizing that the discloser is an active agent in the situation. Are there choices he can make about how much he can disclose? What are the advantages and hazards of self-disclosure? And here we feel the responsibility to advise that self-disclosure is probably less hazardous when it occurs with a specialist—therapist or counselor —than with such target persons as are mentioned in the article. The specialist knows, for instance, the normality of many feelings which persons are typically loath to disclose. Furthermore, the competent counselor can control the pace of self-disclosure so that unwarranted anxiety can be minimized.

Interpersonal Relationships: U.S.A. 2000

CARL R. ROGERS
Resident Fellow
Western Behavioral Sciences Institute
La Jolla, California

I want to make it very clear at the outset that I am not making predictions about the year 2000. I am going to sketch possibilities, alternative routes which we may travel.

One important reason for refusing to make predictions is that for the first time in history man is not only taking his future seriously, but he also has adequate technology and power to shape and form that future. He is endeavoring to *choose* his future rather than simply living out some inevitable trend. And we do not know what he will choose. So we do not know what man's relation to man will be in this country 32 years from now. But we can see certain possibilities.

MAN'S GREATEST PROBLEM

Before I try to sketch some of those possibilities I should like to point to the greatest problem which man faces in the years to come. It is not the hydrogen bomb, fearful as that may be. It is not the population explosion, though the consequences of that are awful to contemplate. It is instead a problem which is rarely mentioned or discussed. It is the question of how much change the human being can accept, absorb, and assimilate, and the rate at which he can take it. Can he keep up with the ever-increasing rate of technological change, or is there some point at which the human organism goes to pieces? Can he leave the static ways and static guidelines which have dominated all of his history and adopt the process ways, the continual changingness which must be his if he is to survive? There is much to make us pessimistic about this. If we consider the incredible difficulties in bringing about change in our great bureaucracies of government, education, and religion, we become

From *Journal of Applied Behavioral Sciences,* Vol. 4, No. 3: 265–280, 1968.

hopeless. When we see how frequently the people take action which is clearly against their long-range welfare—such as the resolute refusal to face up to the problem of the urban ghettos—we become discouraged.

But I see two elements on the other side of the balance. The first is the ability of the Western democratic cultures to respond appropriately—at the very last cliff-hanging moment—to those trends which challenge their survival.

The second element I have observed in individuals in therapy, in intensive encounter groups, and in organizations. It is the magnetic attraction of the experience of change, growth, fulfillment. Even though growth may involve intense pain and suffering, once the individual or group has tasted the excitement of this changingness, persons are drawn to it as to a magnet. Once a degree of actualization has been savored, the individual or the group is willing to take the frightening risk of launching out into a world of process, with few fixed landmarks, where the direction is guided from within. So, in this field of interpersonal relations, though there is much reason for despair, I believe that if our citizens experience something of the pain and risk of a growth toward personal enrichment they will grasp for more.

With this context of uncertainty about our ability or willingness to assimilate change, let us look at some specific areas of interpersonal relationships as they may be.

URBAN CROWDING AND ITS POSSIBLE EFFECTS

The world population will more than double in the next 32 years, a ghastly trend which will affect us in unknown ways. The population of the United States, which was comfortably remembered in my grammar school days in 1915 as 100 million, 52 years later reached 200 million, 22 years from now is predicted to reach 300 million, and in the year 2000 will be between 320 and 340 million, though hopefully it will be starting to stabilize itself at about that time. The great bulk of these millions will reside in a great megalopolis, of which there will probably be three. One trend which we may follow is to crowd more and more closely together, as we are now crowded in our ghettos. I understand that Philip Hauser, the noted demographer, has stated that if all of us were crowded together as closely as the residents of Harlem all of the people in the entire United States could be contained in the five boroughs of New York City. The future may resemble this, if we choose to push in more and more closely together.

Such crowding has consequences. Even in rats, as Calhoun[1] has so vividly shown, overcrowding results in poor mothering, poor nest building, bizarre sexual behavior, cannibalism, and complete alienation, with some rats behaving like zombies, paying no attention to others, coming out of their solitary burrows only for food. The resemblance to human behavior in crowded rooming house areas, the complete lack of involvement which permits people to watch a long-drawn-out murder without so much as calling the police, the poor family relationships—this could be a trend which will be carried even further by the year 2000.

On the other hand, we could learn to decentralize our great urban areas, to make them manageable, to provide not only for more efficiency but for warmer and more human interpersonal relationships. We could use more space, build smaller cities with great park and garden areas, devise plans for neighborhood building which would promote *humanization,* not dehumanization. What will the choice be?

CLOSENESS AND INTIMACY IN THE YEAR 2000

In my estimation, one of the most rapidly growing social phenomena in the United States is the spread of the intensive group experience—sensitivity training, basic encounter groups, T groups (the labels are unimportant). The growth of this phenomenon is rendered more striking when one realizes that it is a "grass roots" movement. There is not a university nor a foundation nor a government agency which has given it any significant approval or support until the last five or six years. Yet it has permeated industry, is coming into education, is reaching families, professionals in the helping fields, and many other individuals. Why? I believe it is because people—ordinary people—have discovered that it alleviates their loneliness and permits them to grow, to risk, to change. It brings persons into real relationships with persons.

[1] Calhoun, J. B. Population density and social pathology. *Sci. American,* 1962, *206* (2), 139–150.

In our affluent society the individual's survival needs are satisfied. For the first time, he is freed to become aware of his isolation, aware of his alienation, aware of the fact that he is, during most of his life, a role interacting with other roles, a mask meeting other masks. And for the first time he is aware that this is not a *necessary* tragedy of life, that he does not have to live out his days in this fashion. So he is seeking, with great determination and inventiveness, ways of modifying this existential loneliness. The intensive group experience, perhaps the most significant social invention of this century, is an important one of these ways.

What will grow out of the current use of basic encounter groups, marathons, "labs," and the like? I have no idea what *forms* will proliferate out of these roots during the coming decades, but I believe men will discover new bases of intimacy which will be highly fulfilling. I believe there will be possibilities for the *rapid* development of closeness between and among persons, a closeness which is not artificial, but is real and deep, and which will be well suited to our increasing mobility of living. Temporary relationships will be able to achieve the richness and meaning which heretofore have been associated only with lifelong attachments.

There will be more awareness of what is going on within the person, an openness to all of one's experience—the sensory input of sound and taste and hearing and sight and smell, the richness of kaleidoscopically changing ideas and concepts, the wealth of feelings—positive, negative, and ambivalent, intense and moderate—toward oneself and toward others.

There will be the development of a whole new style of communication in which the person can, in effect, say, "I'm telling you the way it *is*, in me—my ideas, my desires, my feelings, my hopes, my angers, my fears, my despairs," and where the response will be equally open. We shall be experimenting with ways in which a whole person can communicate himself to another whole person. We shall discover that security resides not in hiding oneself but in being more fully known, and consequently in coming to know the other more fully. Aloneness will be something one chooses out of a desire for privacy, not an isolation into which one is forced.

In all of this I believe we shall be experimenting with a new ideal of what man may become, a model very *sharply* different from the historical view of man as a creature playing various appropriate roles. We seem to be aiming for a new *reality* in relationships, a new openness in communication, a love for one another which grows not out of a romantic blindness but out of the profound respect which is nearly always engendered by reality in relationships.

I recognize that many individuals in our culture are frightened in the depths of their being by this new picture of man—this flowing, changing, open, expressive, creative person. They may be able to stop the trend or even to reverse it. It is conceivable that we shall go in for the manufactured "image," as on TV, or may insist more strongly than ever that teachers are *teachers*, parents are *parents*, bosses are *manipulators*—that we may rigidify every role and stereo-type in new and more armor-plated ways. We may insist with new force that the only significant aspect of man is his rational and intellectual being and that nothing else matters. We may assert that he is a machine and no more. Yet I do not believe this will happen. The magnetism of the new man, toward which we are groping, is too great. Much of what I say in the remainder of this paper is based on the conviction that we are, for better or for worse, in labor pains and growth pains—turning toward this new view of man as becom-ing and being—a continuing, growing *process*.

MAN-WOMAN RELATIONSHIPS

What do the coming decades hold for us in the realm of intimacy between boy and girl, man and woman? Here too enormous forces are at work, and choices are being made which will not, I believe, be reversed by the year 2000.

In the first place the trend toward greater freedom in sexual relationships, in adolescents and adults, is likely to continue, whether this direction frightens us or not. Many elements have conspired together to bring about a change in such behavior, and the advent of "the Pill" is only one of these. It seems probable that sexual intimacy will be a part of "going steady" or of any continuing special interest in a member of the opposite sex. The attitude of prurience is fast dying out, and sexual activity is seen as a poten-tially joyful and enriching part of a relationship. The attitude of possessiveness—of owning another person, which historically has dominated sexual unions—is likely to be greatly diminished. It is certain that there will be enormous variations in the quality of these sexual relationships—from those where sex is a purely physical con-tact which has almost the same solitary quality as masturbation to those in which the sexual aspect is an expression of an increasing sharing of feelings, of experiences, of interests, of each other.

By the year 2000 it will be quite feasible to ensure that there will be no children in a union. By one of the several means currently under study, each individual will be assured of lasting infertility in early adolescence. It will take positive action, permissible only after a thoughtful decision, to reestablish fertility. This will reverse the present situation where only by positive action can one *prevent* conception. Also, by that time, computerized matching of prospective partners will be far more sophisticated than it is today and will be of great help to an individual in finding a congenial companion of the opposite sex.

Some of the temporary unions thus formed may be legalized as a type of marriage—with no permanent commitment, with no children (by mutual agreement), and, if the union breaks up, no legal accusations, no necessity for showing legal cause, and no alimony.

It is becoming increasingly clear that a man-woman relationship will have *permanence* only in the degree in which it satisfies the emotional, psychological, intellectual, and physical needs of the partners. This means that the *permanent* marriage of the future will be even better than marriage in the present, because the ideals and goals for that marriage will be of a higher order. The partners will be demanding more of the relationship than they do today.

If a couple feel deeply committed to each other and mutually wish to remain together to raise a family, then this will be a new and more binding type of marriage. Each will accept the obligations involved in having and rearing children. There may be a mutual agreement as to whether or not the marriage includes sexual faithfulness to one's mate. Perhaps by the year 2000 we shall have reached the point where, through education and social pressure, a couple will decide to have children only when they have shown evidence of a mature commitment to each other, of a sort which is likely to have permanence.

What I am describing is a whole continuum of man-woman relationships, from the most casual dating and casual sex relationship to a rich and fulfilling partnership in which communication is open and real, where each is concerned with promoting the personal growth of the partner, and where there is a long-range commitment to each other which will form a sound basis for having and rearing children in an environment of love. Some parts of this continuum will exist within a legal framework; some will not.

One may say, with a large measure of truth, that much of this continuum already exists. But an awareness of, and an open acceptance of, this continuum by society will change its whole quality. Suppose it were openly accepted that some "marriages" are no more than ill-mated and transitory unions and that they will be broken. If children are not permitted in such marriages, then one divorce in every two marriages (the current rate in California) is no longer seen as a tragedy. The dissolving of the union may be painful, but it is not a *social* catastrophe, and the experience may be a necessary step in the personal growth of the two individuals toward greater maturity.

PARENTS AND CHILDREN

What of the relationships between parents and their children? Here it is terribly difficult to foresee the future. If parents in general hold to the static views which have served reasonably well through the centuries of little change—"I know the values that are important in life," "I am wiser than my child in knowing the direction his life should take"—then the generation gap will grow so large that our culture will literally be split wide open. This may be the course of future events.

But there are straws in the wind which point in another way. Some parents wish to be *persons*—growing, changing persons—living in person-to-person relationships with the youngsters in their families. So we see the development of family encounter groups (still in their infancy) in which parents learn about themselves from their own and others' children, and children learn about themselves from their own and others' parents. Here the self-insights, the awareness of how one comes across to the other generation, bring changes in behavior and new ways of relating based on an open respect for oneself, out of which can grow a genuine respect for the other.

A new type of parent education is also developing in which there is respect for the parent as a person with feelings and rights as well as for the child and his feelings and rights. We find family groups where parent and child each *listen* to the other, where honest, open expression is also mutual. Parental authority and childhood submission give way before a realness which confronts realness. Such family relationships are not necessarily smooth, and the problems of process living are as perplexing as the problems brought on by static views; but there is communication and there is respect, and the generation gap becomes simply the communication gap which in some degree separates all individuals.

It may be hard for us to realize that some help for this new type of family relationship may come from industry. Some corporations, realizing that to start to educate a child at six is much too late, are beginning to dream up learning activities, learning "packages," which will not only be fun for the children but which will involve the whole family in mutually pleasurable and communicative activities. Everyone will have a good time learning—together.

Let me turn to quite a different facet of the relations of parents and children. What will the future hold for children from broken homes—who will continue to exist even if my most optimistic speculations come true? I trust there will be widespread experimentation in dealing with these youngsters. Perhaps we should take a lesson from the *kibbutzim*, where the child is cared for and gains his security from workers who love children and are trained to care for them, and where the contacts with parents, though relatively brief, tend to be full of love and fun. Perhaps some of the "hippie" groups are showing the way in their small, close communities where the child is, ideally at least, cared for by all. We are in desperate need of creative approaches to this problem. Almost anything would be better than the present situation. Now the child is often fought over in court. He learns that one parent is bad, the other good. He is often exposed to the attempts of each parent to win him away, emotionally, from the other. He is often experienced as a burden by the mother, who is attempting to reestablish herself in a job and a new life. Or he is the sole focus of the mother's affections, which may be even worse. *He* is the one who suffers from divorce, and we have been most unimaginative in trying to promote his welfare. Hence my hope is that there will be many types of experimentation three decades from now, in helping the child of divorced parents to grow in the most favorable possible environment.

LEARNING IN INTERPERSONAL RELATIONSHIPS

What of education in the year 2000, especially as it involves interpersonal relationships?

It is possible that education will continue much as it is—concerned only with words, symbols, rational concepts based on the authoritative role of the teacher, further dehumanized by teaching machines, computerized knowledge, and increased use of tests and examinations. This is possible, because educators are showing greater resistance to change than any other institutional group. Yet I regard it as unlikely, because a revolution in education is long overdue, and the unrest of students is only one sign of this. So that I am going to speculate on some of the other possibilities.

It seems likely that schools will be greatly deemphasized in favor of a much broader, thoughtfully devised *environment for learning,* where the experiences of the student will be challenging, rewarding, affirmative, and pleasurable.

The teacher or professor will have largely disappeared. His place will be taken by a facilitator of learning, chosen for his facilitative attitudes as much as for his knowledge. He will be skilled in stimulating individual and group initiative in learning, skilled in facilitating discussions-in-depth of the *meaning* to the student of what is being learned, skilled in fostering creativity, skilled in providing the resources for learning. Among these resources will be much in the way of programmed learning, to be used as the student finds these learnings appropriate; much in the way of audio-visual aids such as filmed lectures and demonstrations by experts in each field; much in the way of computerized knowledge on which the student can draw. But these "hardware" possibilities are not my main concern.

We shall, I believe, see the facilitator focusing his major attention on the prime period for learning—from infancy to age six or eight. Among the most important learnings will be the personal and interpersonal. Every child will develop confidence in his own ability to learn, since he will be rewarded for learning at his own pace. Each child will learn that he is a person of worth, because he has unique and worthwhile capacities. He will learn how to be himself in a group—to listen, but also to speak, to learn about himself, but also to confront and give feedback to others. He will learn to be an individual, not a faceless conformist. He will learn, through simulations and computerized games, to meet many of the life problems he will face. He will find it permissible to engage in fantasy and daydreams, to think creative thoughts, to capture these in words or paints or constructions. He will find that learning, even difficult learning, is fun, both as an individual activity and in cooperation with others. His discipline will be self-discipline.

His learning will not be confined to the ancient intellectual concepts and specializations. It will not be a *preparation* for living. It will be, in itself, an *experience* in living. Feelings of inadequacy, hatred, a desire for power, feelings of love and awe and respect, feelings of fear and dread, unhappiness with parents or with other children—all these will be an open part of his curriculum, as worthy of exploration as history or mathematics. In fact this openness to feelings will enable him to learn content material more readily. His will be an education in becoming a whole human being, and the learnings will involve him deeply, openly, exploringly, in an awareness of his relationship to himself, an awareness of his relationships to the world of others, as well as in an awareness of the world of abstract knowledge.

Because learning has been exciting, because he has participated heavily and responsibly in choosing the directions of his learning, because he has discovered the world to be a fantastically changing place, he will wish to continue his learning into adult life. Thus communities will set up centers which are rich environments for learning, and the student will *never be graduated*. He will always be a part of a "commencement."

PERSONS IN INDUSTRY

In view of my past prejudices I find it somewhat difficult but necessary to say that of all of the institutions of present-day American life, industry is perhaps best prepared to meet the year 2000. I am not speaking of its technical ability. I am speaking of the vision it is acquiring in regard to the importance of persons, of interpersonal relationships, and of open communication. That vision, to be sure, is often unrealized but it does exist.

Let me speculate briefly on the interpersonal aspect of industrial functioning. It is becoming increasingly clear to the leaders of any complex modern industry that the old hierarchical system of boss and employees is obsolete. If a factory is turning out one simple product, such a system may still work. But if it is in the business of producing vehicles for space or elaborate electronic devices, it is definitely inadequate. What takes its place? The only road to true efficiency seems to be that of persons communicating freely with persons—from below to above, from peer to peer, from above to below, from a member of one division to a member of another division. It is only through this elaborate, individually initiated network of open human communication that the essential information and know-how can pervade the organization. No one individual can possibly "direct" such complexity.

Thus if I were to hazard a guess in regard to industry in the year 2000 it would be something different from the predictions about increasing technical skill, increasing automation, increasing management by computers, and the like. All of those predictions will doubtless come true but the interpersonal aspect is less often discussed. I see many industries, by the year 2000, giving as much attention to the quality of interpersonal relationships and the quality of communication as they currently do to the technological aspects of their business. They will come to value persons as persons, and to recognize that only out of the *communicated* knowledge of all members of the organization can innovation and progress come. They will pay more attention to breakdowns in personal communication than to breakdowns of the circuitry in their computers. They will be forced to recognize that only as they are promoting the growth and fulfillment of the individuals on the payroll will they be promoting the growth and development of the organization.

What I have said will apply, I believe, not only to persons in management but to persons classed as "labor." The distinction grows less with every technological advance. It also applies, obviously, to the increasingly direct and personal communication between persons in management and persons in the labor force, if an industry is to become and remain healthily productive.

RELIGION AS INTERPERSONAL LIVING

Historically, much of man's life has revolved around his relationship to his God or gods and around his relationship to others who share his religious views. What will be the situation three decades from now?

It is definitely conceivable that out of a deep fear of the rapidly changing world he is creating, man may seek refuge in a sure dogma, a simplistic answer to life's complexities, a religion which will serve him as a security blanket. This seems unlikely, but I can imagine the circumstances under which it might occur.

The more likely possibility—or so it appears to me—is that by the year 2000, *institutionalized* religion, already on the wane as a significant factor in everyday life, will have faded to a point where it is of only slight importance in the community. Theology may still exist as a scholastic exercise, but in reality the God of authoritative answers will be not only dead but buried.

This does not mean at all that the concerns which have been the basis of religion will have vanished. The mysterious process of life, the mystery of the universe and how it came to be, the tragedy of man's alienation from himself and from others, the puzzle of the meaning of individual life—these mysteries will all be very much present. There may, indeed, be a *greater appreciation* of mystery as our knowledge increases (just as theoretical physicists now marvel at the true *mystery* of what they have discovered).

But religion, to the extent that the term is used, will consist of tentatively held hypotheses which are lived out and corrected in the interpersonal world. Groups, probably much smaller than present-day congregations, will wrestle with the ethical and moral and philosophical questions which are posed by the rapidly changing world. The individual will forge, with the support of the group, the stance he will take in the universe—a stance which he cannot regard as final because more data will continually be coming in.

In the open questioning and honest struggle to face reality which exist in such a group, it is likely that a sense of true community will develop—a community based not on a common creed nor an unchanging ritual but on the personal ties of individuals who have become deeply related to one another as they attempt to comprehend and to face, as living men, the mysteries of existence. The religion of the future will be man's existential choice of his way of living in an unknown tomorrow, a choice made more bearable because formed in a community of individuals who are like-minded, but like-minded only in their searching.

In line with the thread which runs through all of my remarks, it may well be that out of these many searching groups there may emerge a more unitary view of man, a view which might bind us together. Man as a creature with ability to remember the past and foresee the future, a creature with the capacity for choosing among alternatives, a creature whose deepest urges are for harmonious and loving relationships with his fellows, a creature with the capacity to understand the reasons for his destructive behaviors, man as a person who has at least limited powers to form himself and to shape his future in the way he desires—this might be a crude sketch of the unifying view which could give us hope in a universe we cannot understand.

THE RELATIONSHIP WITH THE SLUM DWELLER

I have left until the last the most difficult area: the relationship between the persons in the urban ghettos (Negroes and other minority groups) and the persons outside the ghetto.

Our inability to accept the changing nature of this anguished struggle is one of the deepest reasons for pessimism regarding the future. The more favored community seems, thus far, unwilling and unable to understand the effects upon individuals of a lifetime of defeat, frustration, and rejection. It seems, thus far, unable to comprehend that rebellion is *most* likely, not least likely, to occur in the very cities and situations in which there is, at last, some hope. We seem reluctant to give the ghetto dweller responsibility, the one thing which might restore his human dignity—because he will make mistakes. We seem to have no recognition that learning from mistakes is the only true way to independence. And, most tragically of all, we appear—on both sides—to have lost the belief that communication is possible. Thus I cannot deny the possibility that the next decades will see a growing rebellion, a bloody guerrilla warfare in our cities, with concentration camps, with military government, with fear and hatred in the heart of every citizen. It took a century for the hatreds between the North and the South to diminish to manageable proportions. How many centuries will it take for the hatreds of this new war to die down, a war which it may be too late to prevent?

What makes it, from my point of view, incredibly tragic is that the deepest, most basic issues revolve around communication. Distrust, suspicion, disillusionment have grown to such mammoth proportions on both sides—though perhaps especially on the part of the ghetto dweller—that it is taken for granted that communication is no longer possible. Yet funds, however great, and vocational retraining and housing projects and all the rest can do little without free, direct, honest communication between persons.

Is it impossible? It is my contention that if we mounted a massive effort to reestablish communication, in groups ranging from militant blacks through liberals of both colors to conservative whites; if we drew into this effort dedicated individuals; from the ghetto and outside, who were desirous of improving relationships; if we drew on the expert knowledge available in the social and behavioral sciences; if we backed this effort with a sum at least equivalent to the cost of all our B-52 bombers—then there might be a chance of preventing the bloody tragedy which faces us.

I should not want to be understood as saying that improved communication, improved interpersonal relationships, would *resolve* the situation. What I am saying is that if, in small groups or large, the hatreds and the disillusionments could be accepted and *understood;* if suspicion and despair could be fully voiced and met with respect; then out of such groups might slowly grow a mutual respect in which responsible decisions could be taken and realistic solutions worked out. In these decisions the ghetto dweller would be a fully involved participant, as would the person from outside. Leadership in the ghetto would meet on a fully equal basis with leadership in the "establishment." Both would bear responsibility, through black power and white power, for seeing that the decisions were *carried out*. Idealistic, you say? But we have the knowledge and the wealth which would make such a massive effort possible. And if we choose to follow the present trend, we have in South Vietnam a full color picture of how guerrilla warfare not only sacrifices lives but brutalizes the minds and hearts of the living. Shall we permit it to happen here? Or shall we choose to make a great and concerted effort to behave as persons with persons? On this issue I dare not even speculate.

CONCLUSION

Perhaps it is just as well that I conclude on this somberly precarious note. I hope I have made it clear that the potentialities for change and enrichment in the interpersonal world of the year 2000 most assuredly exist. There can be more of intimacy, less of loneliness, an infusion of emotional and intellectual learning in our relationships, better ways of resolving conflicts openly, man-woman relationships which are enriching, family relationships which are real, a sense of community which enables us to face the unknown. All of this is possible if as a people we choose to move into the new mode of living openly as a continually changing process.

Lifetime Mental Health Plan: 1. The Adult Years, 2. Adolescence, 3. Childhood

DANA L. FARNSWORTH, Psychiatrist
Professor-Director, University Health Services
Harvard University
(As told to and reported by Lester David)

THE ADULT YEARS

I know of no greater need confronting Americans today than the maintenance of good mental health. For mental and emotional illness is the No. 1 health problem in the country, potentially affecting every family.

Let me make it clear that mental health means a good deal more than the absence of mental illness. It means being able:

To live happily, fully and satisfyingly with ourselves and others.

To perform at our highest capacity and find satisfaction in the things we do.

To use leisure time enjoyably and profitably.

To deal capably with the stresses of life, to tolerate the anxieties that inevitably will come our way, to endure the frustrations that will assail us, to exhibit sincerity, compassion and humanity toward other human beings.

We all wish these things for ourselves and those we love, but few of us know how to go about achieving them. Nor, indeed, I must hasten to say, can medical science supply all the answers. However, research in mental illness and health has been moving forward rapidly. *These investigations have shown that there are certain positive steps we can take in important stages of our lives that can help put us and our children on the road to good mental health.*

Here, then, is a "lifetime" mental health guide—suggestions that can help you and your child become emotionally balanced, effective individuals, capable of handling life's demands ably and maturely.

This article, dealing with adulthood and old age, will be followed, during the next two weeks, by articles on how parents can raise young children and teen-agers in the proper emotional atmosphere and how young adults can deal with some of their own often-bewildering problems.

These rules, put into practice, can go a long way toward keeping you in good mental health:

Become actively and genuinely interested in the people with whom you live and work

When you have an investment in the human race, you help keep yourself on a level emotional keel. Directing your thoughts and emotions outward, toward others, prevents them from being channeled inward, toward yourself. Self-centeredness causes misery and keeps one from using his abilities with satisfactions. A man or woman sincerely interested in neighbors, in community problems affecting children, in the welfare of others and the like, is less apt to fret or stew about himself and, therefore, less likely to go into an emotional tailspin.

Learn to recognize all the disguises hostility can adopt

A key to good mental health is the ability to handle feelings of anger toward the world and its people. Now this hostility can take many forms—excessive griping against the boss or the job; nagging or ridiculing your mate; using money as a weapon against him or her; being too busy outside to be a loving wife or husband; excessive gossiping, criticizing, jealousy. When you recognize these or similar patterns of behavior, make an effort to correct them. Don't let them continue because they tend to grow worse. If necessary, seek professional counsel.

Ride that hobby horse you got started on when you were younger

If you haven't acquired a hobby, it still isn't too late to get started. Pick one as different as possible from your work. If you work outdoors, select an indoor one. If you are sedentary, choose an active one.

Learn to laugh at yourself

Practice if you must, but do learn! President Kennedy once said he took his job very seriously, but not himself. The individual who takes himself too seriously feels put upon, even persecuted. He can get more and more wound up, and then emotional problems are around the corner. A publication of the American Medical Association points out that "you just can't stay tense when you're smiling or laughing, inwardly or outwardly. People with a built-in sense of humor don't crack up."

Rewrite your life script every so often

"How are things going?" a woman once asked a friend. The question was ordinary but the reply was a classic. "Dull," the friend sighed. "Life is so *daily*." I've yet to hear a more apt description. Life is indeed too "daily" for many of us. Routine followed endlessly begets boredom, which in turn causes fatigue; and then emotional problems may not be far off.

Once a mother was surprised to see her seven-year-old son coming home from school from the opposite direction. "I got tired walking the same blocks and seeing the same things," he explained, "so I walked different."

Naturally, routine is essential for proper functioning but—like that little boy—try to "walk different" occasionally. Take a completely different kind of vacation than you did last year, plan surprise Sunday trips for the family, scramble your workday once in a while. Take a "wild" adult education course at your local high school, like weaving or gourmet cooking.

Accept the hard fact that you will never be worry-free as long as you live

Constant happiness and the absence of stress and anxiety are not reasonable goals for anybody. Conflict is an inescapable part of modern living—and the resolution of those conflicts you face day to day produces real satisfaction.

Many persons actually create crippling problems for themselves by worrying about worry. While science still doesn't have the complete answers, studies are showing that stress may not be the dread killer everyone fears. For example, a new survey by Dr. Lawrence E. Hinkle of Cornell University Medical School discloses that the aggressive, hard-driving executive—commonly thought to be "coronary-prone"—is no more apt to suffer heart disease than clerks, machinists or night watchmen.

Sensibly, avoid excess tension and seek help if it's prolonged, but don't grimly seek relaxation via alcohol or tranquilizers at each spasm of worry. Some worry is good for you, and you'll never escape it in this life.

Wives and husbands—take a daily talk break

Rosalind Russell, the stage and motion picture star, once told an interviewer that she and her husband have a kind of "parents' hour" every afternoon before dinner. They chat quietly about the day's events, each listening to the other, renewing their friendship, planning for the next day or month or year. When children are young, parents' hour may be held after they have gone to sleep; when they are older, they can be told that Mom and Dad aren't to be interrupted. It's a wonderful way to prevent the sad but all-too-frequent drifting apart of couples.

Attention, husbands!
Include the world in your personal goals

What kind of goals should you set? Too many men set materialistic objectives for themselves, such as the accumulation of money, attainment of power or achievement of security. Each of these is self-limiting and, in the end, self-defeating. Once they are attained, there is nothing else but questing after more of the same. And if money, power and security should be lost, so may be the man himself.

Rather, include improvement of the human race in your personal goal. Seek money, if you wish, not for its own sake but ultimately to invest in something that can benefit mankind. Feel you want to become the best lawyer, accountant, machinist or whatever, not for what you can take from these occupations, but for what you can contribute to them in terms of helping people. The feeling that you are part of the world and giving to it makes your life more meaningful and adds immeasurably to mental health.

Special to wives—avoid the martyr trap in those first hectic years of marriage

When the children are young, you work an endless day. You are harried, frazzled and tired—and, come evening, you are expected to be a bright, cheerful, attractive mate. It's so easy to feel sorry for yourself.

Don't. I may sound harsh; but a wife who feels exploited doesn't need escape from her burden so much as an overhaul of her attitudes. Granted it's a hard lot, but complaining does no good and is bound to increase as time goes on. By middle years, such a wife is apt to be a whining, griping, unhappy person who gives little joy to anyone and gets little for herself out of life. The older you are, the more like yourself you become.

Accept the situation and do the best you can to make things easier. Work to your capacity and don't try the impossible. If some things don't get done, it won't be a tragedy. Experiment with different schedules of work. Re-arrange your kitchen so things are easier to reach. Take an occasional rest. Enlist your husband's help. And make it your business to go out, anywhere, regularly. Bear in mind that, at best, the rough period will be over soon.

CHILDHOOD

Your prime goal as a parent is to help your child grow up with the good inner feeling that he or she is a perfectly capable, worthwhile human being, able to stand on his or her own feet. Six rules can go a long way toward accomplishing this objective.

Give them emotional support when they need it most— right at the start of their life

A baby comes into the world utterly dependent upon other human beings. If the help he needs is forthcoming promptly and consistently, accompanied by love, he learns very early one of the most important lessons of his entire life—that he can rely upon people. The baby whose first basic needs are met begins to develop a positive, confident outlook essential for later emotional health. Chances are that through life, he will have the feeling that things are going to work out well for him.

If parents are not warmly responsive to an infant, he is apt to develop a suspicion and a mistrust of people. He may later withdraw from them, refusing to be their friend, in order to protect himself from hurt. Such a person cannot become a warm and loving wife or husband.

Of course, when I suggest parents respond to their infants' needs, I certainly do not mean that babies must be hovered over and entertained every minute. Strike a happy medium.

Start them early on the road to independence

Once I watched a very small child trying to button his coat. His mother, suddenly aware he was having difficulties, quickly said: "Here, let Mommy fix it." And she did. But she also did nothing to help her son feel capable.

Most parents don't realize that even very young boys and girls strive to be independent, and so they miss important chances that can help encourage emotional growth. Shortly after a child passes his first birthday, he begins to show that he has a mind and a will of his own and insists on trying to do things himself. As Dr. Fred V. Hein and I wrote in a college text: "This is the time for him to establish a balance between love and hate, cooperation and individuality, freedom and restraint. If the child masters the tasks of this period successfully, he develops self-control and retains his self-esteem. If he does not, he may have a lasting sense of doubt and shame about both himself and others; he will be afraid of 'self' government."

You can help him achieve this balance by permitting him to try his own wings, while at the same time protecting him from real dangers. Let him stand, walk, climb, do as much as possible for himself, and praise him for his accomplishments. Have you seen the smile of triumph that lights up a toddler's face when he's done something all by himself—fixed a toy, carried a package or even just stood up? He glows inside, too, with a wonderful feeling of "I can."

As he grows, the child becomes more and more concerned with doing useful things. *The things he achieves himself become crucially important to him.* He gains confidence by trying and succeeding. So let him try out his basic knowledge and skills. Let your son try to climb that fence, build a tree house, manage his affairs. Let your daughter arrange her own social activities, even plan her own party.

Be sure, of course, that you do not expect too much of your child, criticize him with undue harshness or permit activities that are unsafe at his age.

Give them time to digest new experiences

Periods of stimulation should be followed by time for relaxation or contemplation. Play should not be so tightly organized that children cannot indulge in some fantasy or let their poetic and romantic aspects develop. Social changes come rapidly in a child's life; he should be given time to assimilate them. I look with considerable uneasiness on the efforts of many of our "efficiency experts" who would like to keep children in school the year-round to make them learn more and mature faster.

Teach children to make up their minds

A 12-year-old boy came home from school one day and told his mother he wanted to run for class president, but wasn't quite sure. That evening at dinner, while the boy sat quietly, his parents debated whether he ought to make the race, discussing the pros and cons and, finally, deciding that he should not because his schedule for the next year would be too heavy.

Too many parents do all or most of the problem-solving for their children. As a result, the child never learns how to make up his mind about things, crucial for good mental health. Every human being must make decisions all through life, and those who never learn how are seriously handicapped.

A child can be taught to make decisions by allowing him to do so as often as possible and to profit by his mistakes. In all of his day-to-day problems, let him understand you have faith in his ability to unravel them. Listen to and discuss the facts with him. Suggest approaches and give the child the benefit of your wisdom and experience. But avoid taking over his independent right to decide upon the clothes he should wear, school problems and the like.

Common sense should dictate the kind of problems best left to a child's judgment. Those with potentially serious consequences, of course, must still be decided by Mother and Father.

Keep the lines of understanding open

Whenever I talk to parent groups about their adolescent youngsters, one complaint invariably occupies much, if not most, of the discussion: "Our children never tell us anything!" When communication lines break down between parents and children, unhappiness and even tragedy may result. For their part, parents may think and do all the wrong things and thus build a wall between themselves and their children that may never be removed. As for teen-agers, they may develop antagonism toward their parents that can trigger all sorts of things, such as a rush into too-early marriage to escape unhappiness at home. When they grow into adulthood, youngsters may always regard all persons in authority, such as bosses, with fear or mistrust.

In every case of broken communications, the trouble started many years before the child's adolescence. Unwittingly, parents themselves had begun snipping the wires when the children were young. You can keep the lines intact, so that messages (and understanding) can move freely between the generations, in these ways:

• By realizing that each of your children is an individual, with his own abilities, personalities and needs. Don't expect one to match another's accomplishments; rather, help him take pride and pleasure in what *he* does well.

• By curbing your temper. Frequent displays of great anger can so terrify a child that he withdraws emotionally from you. Justified irritation at something he does wrong is acceptable, and even beneficial, but uncontrollable rage is something else.

• By refusing to make sex a taboo subject in the house. You cannot expect an adolescent suddenly to talk freely to you about sexual matters if nobody has mentioned it in 16 years. Frank and open discussion about the physical and emotional aspects of sex relationships can help instill a healthy positive attitude in children.

• By being courteous to your child, listening when he speaks, respecting his rights and feelings.

• By presenting logical arguments for your decisions. "Because I say so" is a poor reply when a child asks why he is required to do something. Giving sensible reasons makes you a fair and reasonable person in your child's eyes. He may not acquiesce gracefully, but inwardly, in most cases, he will probably see your point.

• By disciplining him properly and fairly when necessary. I know of no better way of showing a child he is truly loved than by firm discipline. And a child who knows he is loved is not likely to draw too far away from his family.

Commend them for what they do well instead of condemning them for what they don't

It's natural for parents to want their children to succeed. In their anxiety to be helpful, however, many unwittingly chip away a child's self-confidence by over-stressing shortcomings and trouble can arise.

A 21-year-old college co-ed, under treatment for a severe neurosis, told her therapist: "If I came home from kindergarten with two stars, Mother wanted to know how come I didn't get three like the day before. If I got four marks over 90, she wondered how come the fifth was only 80."

Psychiatrists know that many persons with personality problems report they too seldom received praise at home for their accomplishments. Rather, their areas of weakness were constantly being pointed out. Over and over, they say: "I grew up feeling I couldn't do anything right."

A child's confidence in himself—and hence his ability to withstand the emotional buffeting that life can deal out—is built up layer by layer as he grows. Pounding away at weaknesses creates feelings of inadequacy and unworthiness—but stressing his good qualities builds up his inner strength.

Many parents feel guilty when their children do not turn out as well as they think they should. This is not justified unless they really haven't tried to train their children or haven't loved and respected them. Even then it is of no help unless it motivates efforts to try to learn how to develop better relations with them. Being a parent is not easy and mistakes are always made; they will not be too harmful if love and respect prevail.

These suggestions, if carried out, can help a boy or girl develop a healthy personality, free from feelings of inferiority and inadequacy, with a big head start toward a lifetime of mental health.

ADOLESCENCE: THE DEPENDENT INDEPENDENTS

Starting about age 12 and extending into early adulthood comes a time of bewilderingly rapid change, confusion and paradox—those thoroughly misunderstood teen years.

It is during this period that a boy or girl must acquire a "sense of identity"—as important for good mental health as the proper development of any major body organ is for good physical health.

The adolescent must discover what kind of a person he is, what is important to him, what goals are worth pursuing. He must, moreover, feel that he belongs somewhere in the world, that he is accepted there, that what he does and plans to do has meaning and importance for others.

If his early personal and family relationships have been good, the adolescent in search of himself will make his discoveries with a minimum of trouble for all concerned. Others will have difficulty. Still others, sadly enough, will never find the answers—and our newspapers and magazines are full of what can happen when they don't.

The youngster with no clear idea of where he fits into society is apt to develop a contempt for all the values other people hold important. Therefore he will find a kind of comfort in all sorts of destructive acts such as gang fights, stealing, vandalism, the unrestricted use of drugs, uninhibited sexual activity and the like. He is the chronic truant. He runs away from home. He is the high-school dropout; he may get to college, but is not likely to stay there long.

How can you help your son or daughter in this crucial quest for identity? In these ways:

By listening to your child

The countless young people I've talked with in the past 30 years feel the failure or inability to listen to or examine their point of view is just about the most exasperating of all parental traits.

One boy said that he started to discuss a matter of importance to him but, at the start, made an obvious factual mistake. At once his father pounced on the error, corrected him and offered a free lecture on the subject. By the time the father got around to asking him to continue, the boy had lost heart and "clammed up." Result:

the son felt aggrieved and misunderstood, the father felt unappreci-ated and rejected, and something that might have helped the boy toward self-understanding never got aired.

As they search for identity, youngsters will express in very ob-vious ways their utter scorn for the customs and habits older persons consider proper. They will dress outlandishly, wear their hair in absurd styles, voice frank contempt for ideas their parents hold dear and act in all sorts of rebellious ways.

Adolescents often take their cue for this kind of behavior from the "gang" or the "crowd," whose members all feel the same way. Oddly enough, this allegiance to the group is a bridge toward inde-pendence and should be recognized as such. The crowd helps the individual member break away from his parents, gives him a feeling he can do things, a feeling of belonging again. And what else is this but a groping toward that all-important identity we have been stressing?

Unfortunately (for parents) the group also encourages bravado, shamelessness, even a contempt for the older folks. Make no mistake—the kids feel guilty about this, but the guilt is absorbed by the group as a whole. Of course, this attitude is difficult for parents to tolerate. Defiance is bad enough, but contempt is even worse. Nonetheless, such behavior on your youngster's part must be understood as a temporary defense to help him break away from his parents with a minumum of suffering.

When your child says or implies that "you're square, a fossil, and you just don't understand kids," he's saying in effect: "Look, Mom and Dad, the more decent you are to me, the sooner I can come back to you." Listen, not to the words, but to the unspoken thoughts. It takes stability and courage, of course, but try to accept the attacks that come your way without lashing back or becoming worried and upset about the situation.

The parent who truly loves his child and can remember some-thing of his own stormy adolescence will take a wait-and-watch attitude.

It will pay off.

By recognizing signs of impending emotional trouble

Only an expert can tell for certain if an adolescent's conflicts in his search for identity are becoming too much for him to manage. Some indications to seek professional advice include: An unexplained and prolonged decline in school achievement; the appearance of extreme phobias or fears that persist; imaginary companions; frequent, violent outbursts of temper; withdrawal from his usual forms of activity; outright anti-social behavior such as any form of delinquency.

These are difficult times for parents, I know. You are troubled by changing moral codes, youthful experimentation with drugs, teen-age drinking, auto accidents. I can understand why parents can become fearful and suspicious of their growing children. Exercise proper supervision, of course, but at the same time trust them and let them know you do. They will become responsible persons sooner, if they know their parents have faith in them, than if they are constantly watched or suspected of some sort of mischief. Extremely revealing was one student's explanation of why nobody cheats in a certain professor's class. "He doesn't expect us to," the boy said.

By remembering your own feelings in adolescence

I would prescribe for every parent of a teen-ager a few minutes of solitary memory-searching every so often. Try to recall those years not so long ago when you were seeking to find your way in a strange, confusing world. Most of us have deliberately pushed into the backs of our minds memories of feelings we had in adolescence, especially the painful ones and those we were a little ashamed we had.

But dredging up some of them will help you in your job of parenthood. By being able to feel what your child is going through, you can't help becoming more understanding.

YOUNG ADULTS

In the first part of this article, my remarks were addressed to parents. Now we reach the age where you are responsible for yourself. It is harder for persons your age to maintain emotional equilibrium than it was in years gone by. That's because the world is no longer simple as it once was.

For one thing, you face an uncertain future. For the first time in history, man can destroy himself and others by a force he himself has loosed. If you are to achieve security, it must come from inside yourself, because certainly there is no security outside.

For another, life has become fantastically complex. Opportunities, good or bad, are almost limitless. There are so many facets in the world up ahead for you, so many specialties, and specialties within specialties, that you find it extremely hard to pinpoint a place in it for yourself. An old Dutch proverb says it best: "He who has a choice has a problem."

Furthermore, you realize that to make your way successfully, wherever you land, you must learn more and keep on learning for the rest of your life. The education earlier generations received in school was enough to last a lifetime, but this is no longer true. Technology advances so fast that much of what you learn in most areas becomes obsolete in a few years.

Finally, you are aware that, in a few more years, a very small percentage of skilled people will be able to produce in abundance a high percentage of the material goods we need. The great majority of others, and that may include you, will have to find new ways to occupy their time, new forms of service to one another, new significance for their lives.

How do you cope with these pressures? There is no simple formula, nor any prescription a doctor can hand out that can guarantee a conquest of these and other tensions. We can, however, offer some guidelines that can help you find your place in life with the least incapacitating conflict. Following are suggestions for this stage of your life that can help keep you in good mental health in years to come.

Don't feel pressured to pick a lifework at the end of high school or beginning of college

Remember that college is the place to test new ideas. Never again will you have such freedom to examine and perhaps to try new modes of thinking and behavior, to discard what is unsatisfactory and to adopt a way of life which promises to be rewarding.

Don't try to solve any of your personal problems with drugs.

Increasing numbers of young people, especially college students, are hoping to find a prompt solution to their inner conflicts in a pill or injection. Many are now experimenting with hallucinogenic agents such as LSD-25, the so-called "consciousness-expanding" drug. Neither LSD, marijuana, pep pills or any other drug can, by itself, solve anything. They can, however, produce great harm.

Self-Disclosure and Relationship to the Target Person

DARHL M. PEDERSON and KENNETH L. HIGBEE
Department of Psychology
Brigham Young University

The amount that a person is willing to disclose about himself to another person is related to characteristics of himself (i.e., the discloser), to attributes of the person to whom he is disclosing (i.e., the target person), and to the nature of the relationship between them. Early studies have found that people differ in the amount and type of disclosure according to the target person involved in their disclosure (Jourard, 1959; Jourard and Lasakow, 1958). Four target persons—mother, father, best male friend, and best female friend—were used in these studies.

Jourard (1959) tested a group of female nursing faculty members and found that the amount of their disclosure to their colleagues was related to both perceived closeness of relationship with and amount of liking for the particular colleague.

Fitzgerald (1963) attempted to use self-disclosure as an index of social distance. Measures of self-disclosure to three target persons and measures of liking for these persons were administered to college women. The results indicated that self-disclosure reflected social distance in that more was revealed to the girl liked best than to the "average" girl, and more was revealed to the "average" girl than to the girl liked least. Thus, this study also suggests that self-disclosure is related to the degree of liking that the disclosure has for the target person.

Jourard and Landsman (1960) found, however, that liking was only slightly correlated with disclosure in a sample of male graduate students. The amount of self-disclosure was more highly correlated with the degree to which they knew the others and with the amount

From *Merrill-Palmer Quarterly,* 15: 213–220, 1969.

the others had disclosed to them than it was to their degree of liking for the target person. This suggests that there may be other variables besides liking which are descriptive of the relationship between the discloser and the target person and which are important determinants of the amount and nature of self-disclosure to the target person. Also, the type of relationship that may foster a great amount of self-disclosure is likely to vary from one target person to another. An analysis is required of the correlation of self-disclosure with the nature of the relationship the discloser has with each particular target person rather than with target persons in general. Finally, since Jourard and Landsman (1960) used males whereas other investigators have used females, some of the differences in the findings may be attributable to sex differences. Several investigations have indicated that important sex differences exist in the process of self-disclosure (Himelstein and Lubin, 1966; Jourard, 1958; Jourard and Landsman, 1960; Jourard and Lasakow, 1958; Jourard and Richman, 1963; Pedersen and Higbee, 1967).

The purpose of this study is to investigate various descriptions of the relationship between the discloser and the target person which may be important correlates of the amount of self-disclosure to the target person. The analysis was completed for the two sexes separately.

METHOD

Procedure

Three measuring instruments were administered during two one-hour class periods to 107 Brigham Young University students enrolled in two introductory psychology classes. There were 56 males and 51 females. The subjects recorded their answers on IBM answer sheets so they could be machine-scored and automatically punched into IBM cards. Scores on the measuring instruments and their intercorrelations were then obtained from their answers using an IBM 7040 computer.

Measuring Instruments

Jourard Self-Disclosure Inventory (SD-60)—The SD-60 was used by Jourard in early studies (cf. Jourard and Lasakow, 1958). It contains ten statements in each of six topic areas: attitudes and opinions, tastes and interests, work (or studies), money, personality, and body. The subjects were asked to indicate the extent they have discussed each of the 60 statements with each of four target persons—mother, father, best male friend, and best female friend—according to the following scale:

1. Have told the other person nothing about this aspect of me.
2. Have talked in general terms about this item. The other person has only a general idea about this aspect of me.
3. Have talked in full and complete detail about this item to the other person. He knows me fully in this respect and could describe me accurately.

An X category which was used by Jourard and Lasakow (1958) was not included in the present study because it was not considered to be on a continuum with the other three. The X category is as follows: Have lied or misrepresented myself to the other person so that he has a false picture of me.

Social Accessibility Scale (SA)—The SA was developed by Rickers-Ovsiankina and Kusmin (1958). It measures social accessibility, a characteristic similar to self-disclosure. Social accessibility refers to the readiness of the subjects to express and communicate matters of personal significance. The SA consists of 50 questions to which each subject was asked to indicate what his reaction would be if he were asked by: (a) a stranger whom he would never see again, (b) an acquaintance, and (c) his best friend. The following scale was used to indicate to whom the subject would give a true answer: (1) No one, (2) A stranger, (3) An acquaintance, and (4) Your best friend.

The SA differs from the SD-60 in at least two important aspects. First, the SA asks the subjects to indicate what they *would* disclose, rather than what they *have* disclosed. Second, the SA involves different target persons from those used in the SD-60.

Target Person Rating Scale (TPRS)—The TPRS consists of 11 pairs of adjectives which are opposite in meaning and which are separated by an 8-point scale. For each of the 11 adjective pairs, the subjects were instructed to describe four target persons—mother, father, best male friend, and best female friend—as that target person has related to them. They were not to be concerned with the person in general. They were to describe only his or her relationship to them. The adjective pairs in the order in which they were used in the TPRS are as follows: Close-Distant, Warm-Cold, Rejecting-Accepting, Disliking-Liking, Trustful-Distrustful, Interested-Disinterested, Moral-Immoral, Friendly-Unfriendly, Fair-Unfair, Unselfish-Selfish, and Bad-Good. For all adjective pairs except the third, fourth, and eleventh, the more positive adjective was assigned to the left side of the 8-point scale, and for the other pairs the positive adjective was assigned to the right side of the scale. This was done to reduce the possibility that the subjects would use a response set to mark a particular location on the scale.

RESULTS AND DISCUSSION

The significant correlations between self-disclosure and the ratings of the discloser-target person relationships for the various target persons are presented in Table 1 for both males and females. To provide for more consistent reading and interpretation of the correlations in Table 1 the signs of all correlations involving adjective pairs other than 3, 4, and 11 have been reversed. Therefore, in all cases a positive correlation represents high self-disclosure going with a more favorable rating of the target-person's relationship with the discloser.

For both males and females disclosure to a given target person generally yields more correlations with ratings of that particular target person than with ratings of any other target person. This provides some construct validity for the TPRS, since it would be expected that the disclosure of one person to another would correlate more with his relationship with the person to whom he is disclosing than with his relationship to anyone else.

Except for disclosure to the mother for females, the subject's disclosure to one parent seems to be related to several important aspects of his rating of his relationship with his other parent. A likely explanation of this result is that a person's description of his relationship to one parent is correlated with his description of his relationship to the other parent. That is, a person tends to describe his relationship to one parent as being similar to his relationship to the other parent. However, even though disclosure to one parent is related to ratings of both parents, disclosure to either parent does not relate to any ratings of relationships with target persons other than parents. Also, disclosure to the best male friend and to the best female friend for both sexes involved only scattered correlations with ratings of relationships with other target persons.

TABLE 1

Significant Correlations of Self-Disclosure (SD-60) with Ratings of Relationships with Various Target Persons (TPRS) for Males and Females

		Males						Females			
TPRS Target Person	TPRS Adjectives[a]	SD–60				TPRS Target Person	TPRS Adjectives	SD–60			
		M	F	BMF	BFF			M	F	BMF	BFF
M	Close	.52	.62			M	Close	.40			
	Warm	.30	.31				Accepting	.35			
	Friendly		.27				Interested	.32			
							Friendly	.32			
							Good	.43			
F	Close	.32	.48			F	Warm	.38	.38		
	Warm		.33				Accepting		.43		
	Accepting	.29					Liking	.30	.37		
	Liking	.32	.38				Trustful	.29			
	Interested		.36				Interested	.45	.36		
	Friendly	.37	.44				Friendly	.35	.40		
	Fair	.28	.35				Fair	.30			
	Unselfish	.34	.35				Good		.34		
	Good	.37	.48								
BMF	Close			.41		BMF	Close			.63	
	Warm			.27			Warm			.41	
	Accepting			.35			Liking			.31	.37
	Moral	.29	.27				Interested				.32
							Fair	.35			
BFF	Close				.59	BFF	Liking		—.30		
	Warm			.30	.60						
	Accepting			.34	.52						
	Liking			.33	.47						
	Trustful				.41						
	Interested				.57						
	Friendly				.48						
	Fair				.34						
	Unselfish				.33						

NOTE—Correlations equal to or greater than .27 for males and .28 for females are significant at the .05 level, and correlations equal to or greater than .35 for males and .36 for females are significant at the .01 level.

[a] To conserve space only the more favorable adjective in each pair is presented.

Some interesting relationships appear when the correlational patterns are examined in great detail. For males, the only TPRS adjectives which correlated significantly with disclosure to mother were Closeness and Warmth. Other descriptions of their relationship to their mothers are independent of self-disclosure. Those descriptions which were related to greater self-disclosure of females to their mothers were Close, Accepting, Interested, Friendly, and Good. For both males and females, closeness appears to be a critical quality of the relationship with mother in eliciting self-disclosure. Whereas warmth of the relationship is relevant for males, it is not for females. However, females are more discriminating than males in that more qualities of the relationship relate to self-disclosure. Daughters disclose more to mothers who demonstrate unconditional maternal love for them. Self-disclosure to mothers is apparently independent of her character traits—Trustful, Moral, Fair, and Unselfish. The others—Warmth and Liking—while not character traits are also not necessarily involved in maternal love. A mother can love her child without necessarily being warm, and liking a child may be quite different from loving it.

Disclosure to the father for both males and females relates to a number of ratings of their relationships with both the mother and the father, and also more adjectives are involved than with disclosure to the mother. This suggests that the disclosure of children to their mothers is more independent of how their mothers relate to them than disclosure to their fathers is of how their fathers relate to them. This corroborates the finding by Jourard and Richman (1963) that both males and females disclose more to their mothers than to their fathers. The disclosure of males to their fathers is related to the traits of Close, Warm, Liking, Interested, Friendly, Fair, Unselfish, and Good. Only the traits of Accepting, Trustful, and Moral were not involved. The disclosure of females to their fathers is a little less discriminating than the disclosure of males to their fathers. The descriptions of the father in his relationship to the daughter which are correlated with self-disclosure are Warm, Accepting, Liking, Interested, Friendly and Good. These are the same descriptions that were involved in female's disclosure to mother with the addition of Warm and Liking and the deletion of Close.

The disclosure of females to their best male friend is related to Close, Warm, and Liking. It is likely that for females the BMF is a boyfriend, fiance, or husband—someone with whom the female is emotionally close. The fact that Good, Trustful, Moral, Fair, and Unselfish were not significantly correlated indicates that for women affection in the relationship with their best male friend has more to do with disclosure than the characteristics of the male involved in the relationship. Males are more discriminating than females in their disclosure to the opposite-sex friend. All of the TPRS traits except Moral and Good are significantly correlated with the disclosure of males to the BFF. Females disclose more freely to their opposite-sex friends. Fewer characteristics of the relationship between the two relate to amount of self-disclosure. This interpretation may account in part for the general finding that females disclose more than males.

The disclosure of females to their best female friend is not related to any ratings of their relationship with that friend. Females appear not to be too discriminating as to what the relationship is like with their best female friend in disclosing to her. They disclose to the BFF regardless of the nature of their relationship. For males the same general trend is true. They are not as discriminating in disclosure to the same-sex friend as they are in disclosure to the opposite-sex friend. Only three of the TPRS scales—Close, Warm, and Accepting—correlated with disclosure of males to the BMF, whereas nine scales were related to disclosure to the BFF. The descriptions of the relationship with BMF which correlate with self-disclosure are approximately the same for males and females.

The significant correlations between social accessibility and the ratings of the discloser-target person relationships for the various target persons are presented in Table 2. There were no significant correlations between SA and TPRS for males, nor between SA and TPRS, F and BFF scales for females. As was the case in Table 1, the signs of the correlations in Table 2 have been adjusted so that a positive correlation represents high social accessibility going with a more positive rating of the discloser-target person relationship.

Table 2 shows that the female who rates her mother's relationship to her as Cold, Distrustful, and Selfish tends to score high on

TABLE 2

Significant Correlations of Social Accessibility (SA) with Ratings of Relationships with Various Target Persons (TPRS) for Females

TPRS Target Person	TPRS Adjectives[a]	SA
M	Warm	—.33
	Trustful	—.29
	Unselfish	—.42
BMF	Close	.34
	Warm	.31

[a] To conserve space only the more favorable adjective in each pair is presented.

the SA. An interpretation of this finding is that females who see their mothers as not being interested in them are more willing to talk about personal matters to acquaintances, friends, and/or strangers. The correlations between SA and TPRS BMF in Table 2 are consistent with this interpretation. Females who rate their relationship with their best male friend as Close and Warm tend to say they will disclose more to strangers, acquaintances, and friends —which includes the BMF. One interpretation of the results presented in Table 2 is that females who do not feel they can disclose to their mothers are more willing to disclose to others, even people they do not know well, and that perhaps the self-disclosure that would normally be directed toward such mothers is displaced to others, including the best male friend.

SUMMARY

The Jourard Self-Disclosure Inventory (SD-60) and the Social Accessibility Scale (SA) were administered to 107 students—56 males and 51 females—in introductory psychology classes at Brigham Young University. Ss also completed a Target Person Rating Scale (TPRS) which asked them to rate four target persons— mother, father, best male friend, and best female friend—as to how the target persons related to them, on 11 pairs of adjectives. Correlations of TPRS ratings for each sex with the SD-60 and SA scores indicated that: (a) there are differences both with respect to sex of subject and type of target person in those traits describing the relationship between the discloser and the target-person that are related to amount of disclosure; (b) the disclosure of both sexes to a particular parent was related to their rating of the other parent's relationship to them; (c) both sexes seemed to be less discriminating in disclosure to their same-sex friend than in disclosure to the opposite-sex friend; and (d) the female who rated her mother's relationship to her as cold, distrustful, and selfish tended to be willing to disclose to strangers, acquaintances, and/or best friends.

REFERENCES

FITZGERALD, M. P. Self-disclosure and expressed self-esteem, social distance, and areas of the self revealed. *J. Psychol.*, 1963, 56(2), 405–412.

HIMELSTEIN, P. & LUBIN, B. Relationships of the MMPI K scale and a measure of self-disclosure in a normal population. *Psychol. Rep.*, 1966, 19, 166.

JOURARD, S. M. Self-disclosure and other-cathexis. *J. Abnorm. Soc. Psychol.*, 1959, 59, 428–431.

JOURARD, S. M. & LANDSMAN, M. J. Cognition, cathexis, and the dyadic effect in men's self-disclosing behavior. *Merrill-Palmer Quart.*, 1960, 6, 178–185

JOURARD, S. M. & LASAKOW, P. Some factors in self-disclosure. *J. Abnorm. Soc. Psychol.*, 1958, 56, 91–98.

JOURARD, S. M. & RICHMAN, P. Factors in the self-disclosure inputs of college students. *Merrill-Palmer Quart.*, 1963, 9, 141–148.

PEDERSEN, D. M. & HIGBEE, K. L. Personality correlates of self-disclosure. Paper presented at the meeting of the Rocky Mountain Psychol. Ass., Salt Lake City, May 1967.

RICKERS-OVSIANKINA, M. A. & KUSMIN, A. A. Individual differences in social accessibility. *Psychol. Rep.*, 1958, 4, 391–406.

Section 13
Self-Actualized Living

In the previous section, the subject of needing and using psychological help was discussed. Although it may seem logical on the face of it to see dependence upon others as antithetical to such activities as self-actualization and self-management, this is not the case. A person cannot be helped very much unless he wants it to happen. Help must be solicited or self-managed rather than imposed. And there is only one person who can put the plans into action successfully. In counseling we are somewhat disappointed when someone conveys the message, "Here I am. Do something for me."

In this section Felt emphasizes that mental health means a good deal more than the mere absence of mental illness. He emphasizes the importance of an active and purposeful seeking for positive experience. One does not wait for something to happen and then behave and feel accordingly. He takes action and establishes conditions which will make it possible for him to behave effectively and to feel good about himself. As much as he can, he stacks the deck in his own favor. Contrary to certain aspects of a competitive culture and the point of view of some individuals, this does not mean the exploitation of others. To exploit others results in rejection and negative feedback. It is ineffective because one really does not get what he needs from his associates.

The phenomenological approach described by Landsman illustrates the fact that development demands active and serious participation of the individual. Psychologists who hold this point of view believe that events can be studied only as they exist for the experiencer. That is, the individual ascribes his own meaning to what happens and his interpretations furnish the basis for his behavior. I do not eat an apple because you are hungry anymore than you run because I am frightened. Each of us attributes meaning and acts on the basis of his own perceptions.

Professor Landsman's article carries a threefold message. (1) It describes the variety of experiences that may enrich living. (2) It emphasizes the key role of human interaction and communication. And (3) it suggests that a richness of experience lies all about us if we can broaden and sharpen our ability to tune it in. When one limits his involvement and experience in order to avoid discomfort, he also restricts his opportunity for enjoyment. There is no excitement and little challenge in a sure thing. To paraphrase a comment of Landsman's, a person who carefully puts to death any excitement in his life, just as carefully contributes to his own psychological destruction. For one is really alive only in proportion to his capacity to allow himself to experience.

Kelley states that different people see the same situation at the same time in quite different ways. If this be so, his article will be sermonizing to some readers, it will be viewed with cynicism by others, and perhaps some—hopefully *most*—will see it as outlining some steps for becoming better human beings. Those young people who have viewed the older generation as being thing- and profit-oriented rather than people-oriented will find that at least one of the older generation is very much human-oriented.

Kelley's article seems to be addressed to teachers; we hope many teachers and teachers-to-be will read his message and take the "needs" to heart. However, the article is every bit as pertinent to the student of adjustment as it is to teachers. After all teachers are humans who need to possess respect (the article defines the word) for people—and so do we all. Wholeness is unity of mind and body and unity of the individual with others.

Maslow expresses the thought we had for the purpose of this volume. It is not primarily a book on maladjustment and how to avoid or cure it. The major theme is how to be a better, more effective person whatever work we might do or whatever independent and unique role we might play. Maslow makes this theme specific in focusing on self-actualization and peak experiences. Becoming the best of whatever we might be—son or daughter, wife or husband, mother or father, laborer or manager, entrepreneur or author, chemist or salesman, senator or citizen, etc.—is an emphasis which the serious student of adjustment must consider.

Maslow concerns himself with matters that are usually ignored. For example, there is a tendency to shy away from the admission of peak experiences. Note that peak experiences are more spontaneous in childhood. Note that they can be encouraged by appreciating them and reflecting upon them. Note that they are often the result of work and striving. Note that art and music are only examples of *many* ways of achieving peak experiences—but our conviction is that none of these avenues should be allowed to become obstructed.

Maslow's article is a positive and optimistic one concerning human potential. The author speaks of "peak experiences" and "ecstasies of living" as possibilities for all persons. He whets the appetite. One is tempted to reach out; to try to find out how he can get some for himself. Then he is told that this is a process which can be taught and learned; something accessible. The avenues of music, sex, dancing are mentioned. And it occurs to us that none of these call for the coldly objective intellectual approach. Rather there is a feeling; a necessity for affective involvement, for movement in unison, for the sharing of experience, for a being in tune with. It appears that actualization of self is a process which depends upon experiencing with or joining with someone or something outside of self. This may be one of the conditions in which the needs of the individual become "synergic with and not opposed to the needs of society."

Achieving identity and actualizing self appears to be a two-pronged process: becoming a part of, as well as becoming apart from, the group. Perhaps one does not occur without the other. Perhaps a realization and an implementation of this will help to gain a place with "the growing tip of mankind" and render more possible "the ecstasy of living."

How to Be Yourself

JAMES W. FELT, S.J.
Chairman, Department of Philosophy
University of Santa Clara

"Be yourself!" Psychologists urge this upon us. Philosophers stress it. We increasingly recognize that it is profoundly necessary. But just what does it *mean* to "be yourself"?

In a sense this is a large question, and so I want to focus on just one sense in which I think "Be yourself" is often *mis*understood. I attack such a misinterpretation, of course, on the basis of what I believe to be an essential ingredient in what it does mean to "be yourself."

If there is anything we do with relish and at every available opportunity it is make *things* out of *events*. When there is flashing we make a thing out of it and call it "lightning." When we get a shock we say there is "electricity" in the wire. When everything has been shaking we say, "That was an earthquake," just as we might, in another context, say, "That was an elephant." And this is natural for us, because things are not only easier to deal with than events, they are also easier to talk about. Both the language and the logic we inherit from the Greeks put a premium on the fixed, on the changeless, on *things*.

And so both psychotherapists and their patients spontaneously talk of "discarding masks," of "peeling off layers," of "uncovering the real self," as one would uncover the body by disrobing it. The question is, what can this "real self" signify?

When I "discard a false self" I am obviously not throwing away some *thing* as I would a gum wrapper: I am ceasing to live my life in an unauthentic way. What right, then, do I have to suppose that there is a "true self" waiting to be found under these "masks," as I would expect to find my foot if I took off my sock? But suppose that there is such a "myself" which I am to "be." Suppose, in other words, to "be yourself" means to "live up to your true self (which is already latent within you)." Then what is the nature of that self? The unspoken assumption seems to be that this "true self" was

From *America*, 705, May 25, 1968. © *America*, National Catholic Weekly, New York, N.Y.

given from eternity or at least from conception, that it has a definite character, that it is just waiting to be filled out, as the acorn is waiting to turn into the oak. My problem in this case is simply to discover, to uncover, my "true self" so that I can live up to it.

Such a view is not far from the Greek idea of fate. We find something like this, I think, in Hermann Hesse's famous novel *Demian*. Its appeal to youth surely lies in its "Be yourself" theme. Hesse himself places on the title page of his work the following lines from its text: "I wanted only to live in accord with the promptings which came from my true self. Why was that so very difficult?"

But at the same time this true self of Hesse's is the self of fate:

"At this point a sharp realization burned within me: each man has his 'function' but none which he can choose himself, define, or perform as he pleases. . . . An enlightened man had but one duty— to seek the way to himself. . . . He might end up as poet or madman, as prophet or criminal—that was not his affair, ultimately it was of no concern. His task was to discover his own destiny—not an arbitrary one—and live it out wholly and resolutely within himself" (Bantam edition, pp. 107-8).

The ideal that Hesse holds up for us is the man who "seeks nothing but his own fate," the man who "only seeks his destiny."

But if, on the contrary, "Be yourself" means simply "Live authentically," then what sort of self is the object of this exhortation? There is just plain old me, the product of all my past experiences, my physical and mental limitations, above all of my past decisions. But this me is never settled nor is it prefabricated. It is always on the way, always in the process of self-creation. At every moment I am creating the me that I choose to be: there is nothing fated here. Whatever my limitations, whatever my past, I hold this me in my hands at every moment, to fashion as I will. Bergson claims we have an immediate experience, if we would only recognize it, "of being creators of our intentions, of our decisions, of our acts, and by that, of our habits, our characters, ourselves." To be myself, then, does not amount to uncovering the sort of me that I was born or fated to be. It means discovering my own true freedom to fashion myself as I can and as I will.

In that sense psychotherapy may often leave off where it should begin. To discover *how* I am the product of my past only fills in the details of the obvious generalization that of course I *am* the product of my past. What I need at this point is to realize that, notwithstanding these limitations of the past, to learn to be myself means precisely to discover that I am in fact free to create my ever-emerging self on my own and in my own way.

If, then, I understand "Be yourself" to mean, "Uncover and live up to that destined self latent in you," I either chain myself to whatever image I evoke of this self, or else I abandon all responsibility for my actions on the grounds that what I do spontaneously lives up automatically to the demands of this hidden true self. But if I am skeptical of the existence of such a prefabricated self, if I take "Be yourself" to mean, "Live authentically, according to values as you yourself grasp them," then I am thrown onto my own responsibility about my life. My fate then consists precisely in the formation of that self which I myself create with every new decision of my freedom. It is I who at every moment decide what sort of man I shall be, and this is my human dignity. To be myself is to be free.

Human Experience and Human Relationship

TED LANDSMAN

Professor of Education
University of Florida, Gainesville

The distinctive elements of experience, values, perceptions and feelings have assumed new significance for a number of "humanistic" psychologists in recent years. Yet, all about us in the psychological sciences the study of behavior seems comfortably ensconced as the focus of the discipline. There is also no doubt but that the behavioristic psychologists, and there are few of any other kind, have successfully though in a limited fashion established both the scientific nature of a behavioral science and its pertinence, in a critically limited scope, to the affairs of men and their institutions such as nations.

A chapter in *Personality Theory and Counseling Practice,* Department of Personnel Services, College of Education (Gainesville: University of Florida, 1961), pp. 42–52.

Phenomenology and/or phenomenological psychology defines itself as the science or study of experience, on the other hand, but has done painfully little to justify the claim. Only recently has phenomenology been given serious notice by psychology and this perhaps is only because of the professional security now earned by the behavioral scientist.

In this paper, I should like to move us forward, perhaps by inches, in the systematic study of human experience. This focus upon experience is not chosen to replace behavior as the central subject matter of psychology; Combs and Snygg (2) have already pointed out that the study of perception or experience in and of itself contributes to the prediction of behavior. However, I would not hide a prophetic premonition that the study of human experience, in and of itself, holds values of itself either as a central focus for psychology, or as the central focus of a discipline of its own whether it be called phenomenology or existentialism.

One must ask one's self: Is experience important in the affairs of men? Are joy and exhilaration, depression or blinding hostility of consequence in reality or are such matters for poets and philosophers alone?

Those psychologists, mostly clinicians and counselors, who chose to deal with experience, found themselves mostly ruminating about the naughty, the noxious and the nefarious, in short, the negative. Because of our sudden and immensely rich experience with the emotionally and psychologically dissatisfied, and hurt in clinical and counseling experience, our theories and our research in the experience of humans centered largely about the unhappy half or the adjustment continuum. Now recently, with the emphasis upon counseling in the schools, with the growth of a concept of the "helping relationship" in general, for all humans regardless of their high or low state of adjustment, we have opened the hidden half of the adjustment continuum, the realm of positive experience.

As in the case of the relationship of experience to behavior; I expect our study of positive human relationship will enlighten our understanding of maladjustment. It will also, in and of itself, contribute to our understanding of the manner in which man manifests his destiny, how he improves the natural world with the expression of the drive towards self-realization, growth, enhancement or what have you.

I should like in this paper to make some preliminary systematic organizations for a theory of human experience. This theory would recognize a particular experience, that of the human relationship, as of critical consequence. And this paper will limit itself to the positive aspects of human experience; not because it is in my nature to do so but because such is our largest gap in phenomenology, existentialism, and psychology itself. As pointed out to us by Bollnow (1), we have dealt only with the dark valleys and with the dismal abyss in human experience; now the meaning of the happiness experience, the reaching, seeking, striving for the heights of human hearts and minds lies before us for study. Hopefully such a discipline or study may lead us to the increase of such experience amongst men.

THE DERIVATION OF THE OBSERVATIONS

While our observations for previous theory came largely from clinical work, the observations of positive human experience must be drawn from a wider source. Still included are those rare, exciting and growth signalling events described in counseling. In addition, the sources are personal friendships and loves, teaching student relationships of unusual maturity and richness, the world of literature, and—with no apologies—that discipline which was the first to deal with human experience of the heights—albeit in most nonsystematic, sometimes dogmatic fashion—the world of religion and religious experience. Some systematic, well-planned research approaches to these kinds of experiences are drawn upon but I confess to the utilization of a careful collection of personal experiences of friends and students. As I illustrate principles with examples, I caution you, however, against assuming that all these are my own experiences. Like, Grace Metalious, author of *Peyton Place,* were they all my own experiences, I would not have had the time to write this paper.

THE EPISTEMOLOGICAL PROBLEM

The continuously haunting issue which has frightened many phenomenologists is the unknowability or unverifiability of another's experience. Though you and I may both call the color of a flag "red" we may hold in the recesses of our minds meanings which are quite different. Though we may say we understand each other, we really may not; every teacher who has asked a class if they understood a concept and noted all thirty heads nodding in assent knows this principle.

Without attempting an elaborate attack upon the issue, I suggest you reason from the Cartesian, "I think, therefore I am." You might say, "I am, therefore I experience." And as I describe these experiences you might each individually check your own understanding of your own experience and make a personal judgment of its validity—do you recognize the experience as it is described?

Now, then, the aforegoing should have told you that this paper really concerns and should be so titled: "Empirical observations leading to a theory of human experience and human relationship with specific emphasis upon the positive experiences."

THE KINDS AND DIMENSIONS OF POSITIVE EXPERIENCE

Experience may be defined as the organized awareness of internal modification in the organism. It is composed of perceptions and sensations but these are described and exist not in external dimension but in received or perceived dimension. It is a category of organization of the third level; that is it is composed of perceptions which in turn are composed of sensations. A child may receive the sensation of the reflection of light from the blackboard, perceive therefore the number "4" upon it, and experience the discovery of number relationships.

I. Experiences involve any of three relationships, either with the external world in general (such as the experience of a sunset), or with another person (as in being loved), or with self (as in the discovery of one's ability to solve problems).

II. Experiences possess the dimensions of time and intensity (the terms "profundity," "height" or "depth" seem also synonymous with "intensity"). The sunset may last for forty-five minutes, the love for ten years, and discovery of self for a fraction of a second. The intensity may be small in that the sunset may modify the organism only minutely—the experience of its beauty has meaning and effect only for that moment or only many, many such sunsets or such brief perceptions of beauty would be required to contribute to the organism's reaching of the heights of existence. The love both long and intense may and should be deeply felt and both its intensity and duration would make significant growth in the individual. The self-discovery of a fraction of time, may be of such self-shaking intensity as to affect the person's life, living, accomplishment for the remainder of his existence. There is such a thing as phenomenological time; the sunset may seem to have lasted for days, but I refer here to a wholly external measure of time—the ticking of the clock. The factor of intensity, however, I believe gives the phenomenological significance to the experience. Its existence, the intensity, can only be dealt with phenomenologically, that is, insofar as it affects the human being inwardly.

CATEGORIES OF INTENSE, POSITIVE EXPERIENCE

The operation of the dimensions of intensity and each of the three major groups of experiences (with self, others and the external world) may be seen within some significant categories of experiences. I should like to distinguish at least five such major categories of positive experience. These are those events in one's lifetime which seem to hold the potential for high excitement and personal joy:

I. Conquest of a problem or skill. The first time the child rolls on a new buggy speedily down hill, now balanced on two wheels; the discovery that you can teach so that children like you; Karen (7), the CP child who discovers she can write a letter to Emmett Kelley; (vicariously, the "Rain in Spain" song of *My Fair Lady*. "She's got it!"). These are "I've got it!" or "I can do it" or "I've done it!" experiences—a kind of self-experience—a self-discovery.

II. The Excitement Experience. Closely related to the "I've done it" experience is the excitement experience. While I do not propose it as a solution to all juvenile delinquency, it follows from these theoretical constructions that children's lives and adult's lives, to be enriching, must have within them the factor of excitement. Three families are out together on a picnic. A large log extends across a swift creek. One child starts across and his father smiles and watches. A second starts across. His father says: "Gee, John, it's fun but you might fall in, get all wet and besides there might be snakes around that water." Both parents are right but only one of these two children will likely have an intense positive experience that afternoon.

Two adults who carefully put to death any excitement in their marriage just as carefully contribute to each other's psychological destruction.

III. The Direct Experience of Beauty. I have already mentioned a sunset. One of Florida's great natural resources—the sea—gives unlimited solace and joy. A Japanese poem tells us, "The Sea—something to look at when we are angry." Look out upon eternally rolling breakers. Alone is a line of dipping pelicans and a traveler is far off in the distance. Similarly there is the pearly nautilus, the Grecian urn, the beauty of one's own handiwork, the beauty of a gentle child. To me, there is a welling within as I see an aged patriarch, with long beard, longer suffering wrinkles on a father-like face, swaying in prayer in a synagogue, his whole body draped with the old prayer shawl. And perhaps the beauty which exceeds that of any sunset, sea, mountain, moon or even music—the overwhelming beauty of a lovely woman.

IV. The Cloture or Completion Experience. The completion of a long, perhaps even tedious job, the moment you put the last page in the doctoral dissertation, the last note of a musical composition, the completion of the last question on an examination, the last coat of paint on the cabinet you have been building, are some instances. In *The Chinese Room* (3), a harried bank executive, anxiety ridden because of a plot to drive him to suicide, rides to a country club lunch with his chauffeur. He sees a farmer building a ditch to drain a field before sunset. He sends the farmer on with his chauffeur to his lunch, takes the pick in hand and labors through the afternoon. Aching and now in "peak experience," he struggles with the last stroke and stands by in *exhausted joy* as the water rushes by in the completed ditch. While camping out at a state park, my son and I watched an old man struggle to split a gigantic oak log, for perhaps two hours. Later, rather than sooner, he heard the crackle of surrender to his wedge and he saw the last inch part and the single log was in two pieces. Both the man and my son will long remember that seemingly simple experience.

V. The Earned Success or Praise Experiences. The use of praise has been so long a part of even our limited experience theories that I will not develop it here. But I will point out the adjective, "earned." The use of a small lie of praise to encourage a child is not derogated here, but rather I point out that such "pump priming" or false praise is of use only when there is further water to be drawn. It will bring out ability and skill but will not make a well out of a dry hole.

THE HUMAN RELATIONSHIP EXPERIENCE

A category of experience which must have honor by itself is the human relationship experience. It is one perhaps to be counted with the five mentioned above. Shoben (10) has pointed out how alienation seems to destroy the human being. Shoben summarizes the experiences of Arctic explorers in loneliness, the experience of the chronically sick and others. The loneliness and alienation seems to result in psychosis or psychotic-like symptoms. The extreme negative of human relationship is apparently not hate but indifference to or from others or alienation, or loneliness.

The "Caring For." The need for others has been both philosophically and psychologically explored (and perhaps reached its silly season in McCall's motto—"the Magazine of Togetherness." McCall's now has dropped that particular call to greatness). We seek now a realistic contemplation of man's need for another. How shall it be described and what is its essence? And what is its order in the scheme of man's needs?

Human relationship may perhaps best be described as "one person *caring for* another." The "caring for" is the essence, it seems to me, the stuff which binds men invisibly together, makes seemingly separate subjects act in concert. It is found in the phenomenon of one person "caring for" another. I have heard some friends with great feeling describe the "caring for" as the basic reason for their meaningful existence. "This is the only reason to live."

As in the instance of the catalogue of other experiences, the "caring for" exists in the dimension of time, and has varying qualities, and can be earned or false as in earned or false praise.

I. Over the dimension of time, a fleeting smile of a stranger may be contrasted with a life-long friendship of twin brothers. Early this fall, in between two talks at Middle Tennessee State College, I wandered over the campus. A number of students, none of whom I shall probably ever see again, each smiled and said "hello" as I passed. This warmed me then and still does now. From the first day of my life to this one, I have known my older brother with increasing warmth. Both of these experiences are positive—they differ in time of duration and, of course, in ultimate effect. Relationships may be fleeting or may be durable.

II. The intensity dimension is nowhere better seen than in human relationship. Though either brief or enduring, any relationship may be superficial or achieve heights. A relatively brief meeting though usually also short, can also be of considerable depth. I have fallen into deep interaction for perhaps only a few hours or days with new friends and have left considerably enriched. There are acquaintances whose relationships are quite durable but of little consequence. And then of course, there is that penultimate, an enduring relationship over time. As I look back upon one such relationship I have a similar recollection sensation to the time when I stood upon the rim of the Grand Canyon—timeless beauty, almost frightening height. Of course, there are those who fear heights, who will not fly, and those who revel in it and seek the stratospheres of human relationship with no less striving than does the physical engineer who seeks to circle the sun.

It is also apparent that relationships which are *durable may vary during their existence in experienced intensity.* Excluding any present loves, how do you feel now about the woman with whom you were last in love? I am reminded of Mew's "Sea Love":

> Tide be runnin' the great world over;
>   'Twas only last June month I mind that we
> Was thinkin' the toss and the call in the breast of the lover
>   So everlastin' as the sea.
> Heer's the same little fishes that sputter and swim,
>   Wi' the moon's old glim on the grey, wet sand;
> An him no more to me, nor me to him,
> Than the wind goin' over my hand.

The variation does not necessarily move to the lesser level although there seems to be some evidence of a kind of regression phenomenon—relationships eventually returning to some sort of mean.

The last problem, that of building relationship experiences or perhaps one human relationship experience alone which is lasting and durable as well as achieving ever exceeded heights, may perhaps be the personal problem of our age.

III. The false vs. the earned "caring for." The "caring for," the relationship of intensity, is easily and often pseudo or apparently false in its immediate experienced form. And it is not only the adolescent or puppy love which confuses. In adult forms the press of immediate need may make the press of the handshake oh, so firm. The politician in search of votes can appear to be a life-long friend. Often the need-press is no more apparent to the seeker than it is to the sought. The student in need of a grade can develop a seeming deep relationship with the instructor. The fräulein goes to bed willingly with the captor who provides food and scarce feminine luxuries. The teenager marries in seeming peak happiness for financial security, social status or to escape from an alcoholic father.

Perhaps no other single factor exceeds the sex needs themselves in contributing to the confusion between a pseudo and an earned "caring for." In like manner, however, it would be a serious mistake to exclude the operation of sex needs and physical satisfaction from the exploration of human relationship experiences. As with the sex-experience itself, I would rather not deal with it at all than deal with it in a superficial or casual manner in this paper and so will leave it for later discussions.

The "earning" involved in the successful, intense, and durable human relationship comes from the ability of the self of the "caring for" person to bring active fulfillment to the basic need of the "cared for" person. There is no caring for without a consequent need to be cared for. This basic need is described quite accurately by Combs and Snygg (2) as the need for the maintenance and enhancement of self. To the extent that the caring for person provides self-enhancement, self-regard for the loved one, he will be loved in return. The nature of the earning must vary tremendously in that it is quite phenomenological. The things which provide the basic need for one may be quite different from that needed by another. An acquaintance asks only good food and sex from his cared-for wife. Another asks beauty, grace and tenderness. Another asks continuous verbal response—"talk to me." The meeting of each other's basic need is the true earning. And the meeting of a secondary need or a momentary need too easily masks for a moment a misjudged relationship.

IV. The dimension of "Openness." A new dimension to experience. Two people who care for one another and feel cared for by each other vary in the degree of *openness* to each other. The experience of wanting to be known by another and wanting to know another must undoubtedly affect the durability and intensity of a relationship. The willingness to be open, to reveal or disclose self, so effectively described by Rogers (9) and Jourard (6), has consistently in Jourard's data correlated with positive adjustment. Others may describe this as being "honest" with one another.

Now for a moment I wish to tie together earned love with being known or open to others. A simple statement made by some of us in our thinking in this area is something like this: "A person wishes to be loved as he is, accepted as he is." One might argue further then that caring for should not have to be earned but should be a free gift. The earning which I have discussed previously is not an earning by a specific attempt to earn love but rather an earning through the kind of self or person the cared for person happens to be—that is, a self which provides the basic need of another person as seen by the needing person. The openness in the relationship, therefore, would follow directly from the feeling that "the self I am is what this other person needs; therefore, I can be what I am without pretense or without walls and this will satisfy." Here is a statement from a friend who describes her need to be known both for the good and the bad: "I want love and loving, closeness, contact, sharing, being with, being known, being valued. Right now, I want so much to be close to someone who knows me as I am—the good which is there and the good which I want to be there, and the bad which is there even though I might wish it weren't, but which is at this moment as truly me as the good, and wants to be known and understood—and values me anyway."

The fact that openness or being known is not necessarily a function of time nor of formal relationship is shown in the research of Fitts (4) and Wittreich (11). Fitts found that wives and husbands did not seem to predict each other's self concept much better than did teachers and students. And Wittreich using the distorted room of the Ames demonstrations found that people married less than one year seemed to be constant in avoiding distortion of their mates in contrast to couples married two to three years.

V. The Magnification Capacity of Human Relationship Experience. Probably none of the positive experiences of humans approaches the potential of the human relationship experiences. No sunset is greater than human love, nor can it substitute for human love. I wonder even if experiences of self-discovery are generally of greater intensity than those of the caring-for experience. And of the human relationship experiences perhaps none compares with the one where you reach out, tentatively, hardly hopefully, terribly needfully for a particular person—to discover by a few words or a touch of fingers that the same person was reaching out tentatively, hardly hopefully and terribly needfully for you.

Beyond the power of human relationship itself is its potential for the magnification of any experience. There is such a thing as the walking alone in sand by the sea shore. But it is another thing to be walking hand in hand by that same sea shore with the cared for person. There is such a thing as sitting upon a small cliff overlooking a clear lagoon. Above rise tall pines and oaks to a flawless sky, before you is the foliage of early fall, below in green, clear water, unruffled, small groups of fish swim and play. You might think such beauty to be unsurpassed—until you might sit upon that same cliff beside the cared-for person. I am reminded of Aiken's poem "Music I heard with you was more than music . . ." This will surely provide an intriguing measurement problem for, unlike the sharing of bread, the sharing of experience does not diminish each person's share, but increases it.

Remaining Issues. While I do not want to pretend to cover all aspects of a theory of human experience, there are some significant gaps that require at least mention and later development. These include such issues as: the conditions which create that individual who is unafraid of the heights in human experience; ways of providing these positive experiences in child rearing; the effect of such seeking for intensity upon counseling practices; the variety of kinds of caring for relationships; the relevancy of formal human relationships such as marriage partners, siblings, to intensity of relationship; the limits of the caring for relationship in intensity and in number of cared for people; and the role of the self concept and of religious experience.

A second area in which at present I feel a sense of lack of completion is in the re-working of the above general statements into operationally testable hypotheses. It seems to be that such must be our objective, but I submit them as they are without apology.

THE RESULTS OF POSITIVE HUMAN EXPERIENCE

The final question concerns the results of positive human experience and positive human relationship. It would seem that the maximization of positive human experience is perhaps the key to the maximization of self-actualization. There is a significant differentiation between self-actualization and so-called "normal adjustment." We know that a basic feeling of security and of being wanted is the stuff out of which relative normalcy or good adjustment is made. I am considering the provision of these profound, intense, experiences as something on top of the basic feeling of security which might be created in a normally good home.

Should then we be able to provide for our children and for adults such profound, intense, "peak," experiences, experiences of excitement and challenge, of beauty and self-discovery, of the heights of human relationship, of caring for and being cared for, what might the results be. I would anticipate that such persons would seek for creativity and for personal productivity. I would hypothesize a significant change in human inter-relationship at all levels. (I hope you will notice with admiration that I am resisting the temptation to predict that such will solve the problems of world peace and downtown parking.) I do see within such a personal condition for humans a reaching for healthy heights in life and living, the giving of the most of meaning out of personal existence. It suggests that a psychology or phenomenology so oriented would seek to transmute the visions of poets and theologians into the reality of man's relationship with man. Such a discipline would search for human relationships which are profound and enduring, the creation of relationships, if you wish, which are no less than noble. I would hope for no less for my counselees, want no less for myself, my family, my students, wish no less for you.

REFERENCES

1. BOLLNOW, O. F. Der begriff des beilen. *Situation,* 1, 1954, pp. 15–25.
2. COMBS, A. W. AND SNYGG, D. *Individual Behavior* (rev. ed.), N.Y.: Harper and Bros., 1959.

3. CONNELL, VIVIAN. *The Chinese Room*. New York: Bantam, 1960.
4. FITTS, W. H. *The Role of the Self Concept in Social Perception*. Doctoral Dissertation: Vanderbilt University, 1954.
5. JOURARD, S. M. *Personal Adjustment*. N.Y.: Macmillan, 1959.
6. JOURARD, S. M. "Self-disclosure and healthy personality," *Mental Hygiene*, 43, 1959, pp. 499–507.
7. KILLILEA, MARGARET. *Marie Karen*. New York: Prentice-Hall, 1952.
8. MASLOW, A. H. *Motivation and Personality*. New York: Harper, 1954.
9. ROGERS, C. R. "Characteristics of a helping relationship," *Pers. & Guid. J*. 37, 1958, pp. 26–31.
10. SHOBEN, E. J. "Love, loneliness and logic," *J. Individ. Psychol*. 16, 1960, pp. 11–24.
11. WITTREICH, W. J. "The Hour Phenomenon: a case of selectives perceptual distortion," *J. Abn. Soc. Psychol*. 47, 1925, pp. 705–712.

The Meaning of Wholeness

EARL C. KELLEY

Distinguished Professor Emeritus
Wayne State University

Recently there has been more and more attention given to the psychosomatic nature of the human organism. Even some of those who make their living by ministering to our health have taken it up, at least in some degree. It is now fairly common to have an M.D. make indirect allusions to this fact.

The human organism has two selves, living together in the same body structure. There is the physical self and the psychological self. This is not intended to be a denial of the unity of man, but we have to admit that there are two of them because they feed on different stuffs. The physical self feeds on such things as meat and vegetables; the psychological self feeds on the perceptive stuff of growth, such as what people say, music, sunsets, or, according to one's lot, squalor, degradation. The perceptive stuff of growth cannot be seen,

From *Etc., A Review of General Semantics,* Vol. 26, No. 1: 7–15, March, 1969, by permission of the International Society for General Semantics.

as the physical stuff can. If we could see it, it is possible that we might come to have a whole new set of attitudes toward those less fortunate than we. I say it is just possible, realizing that our attitudes are built on a whole set of circumstances that have nothing to do with compassion or any other of the more human emotions.

At any rate, we have paid far more attention to the physical self than we have to the psychological self. It is hard to say which is the more important because both are essential. The psychological self cannot even exist without a body. I suppose one could cite examples of the physical self existing without much psychological self, but such people are hardly even human, although they are entitled to our compassion, our love, and our best efforts.

The point here is that we have paid too little attention to the psychological self in the past, and while every person must have a body to inhabit, what a person feels is far more important than what he knows. What he knows is important, of course, because that is what he uses to behave with. And the eventual pay-off is in behavior—what a person does. The task of the educator is to pay much attention to the perceptive stuff of growth. This he can do without fear of the neglect of the physical self. The various athletic coaches will see to that.

One of the most important facts about the perceptive stuff of growth is that it is selective, so that the individual sees what he has had experience to see and what is in line with his purposes. The purposive nature of the human individual is described more fully in Chapter 6 of *Education and the Nature of Man.*[1] I will not go into it again in this paper. At any rate, experience alone is not enough to account for what happens. The fact that no two people see the same thing at the same spot in the same way is truly significant. The fact that no two people perceive alike is particularly true in the case of our dealings with other people. It seems to me that other people are the most complex things that we have to view. And this accounts for much of what has seemed to us to be strange indeed. In the first psychology course I ever took the instructor had an "incident" occur and then asked each of us to write what we thought we had seen. When it came about that none of us had seen the same thing we all laughed merrily and then the teacher proceeded as though it were not so—as though people *do* see the same thing in the same way.

[1] Kelley and Rasey (New York: Harper, 1952).

The psychological self has boundaries. These are invisible, as all of the psychological self is. But without boundaries there would be no entity. This self has two overwhelming needs. One is to defend itself; the other is to "keep" other people—to maintain and strengthen its social relationships. How to defend one's self and to do it without alienating other people must surely be the biggest adjustment that the human organism faces. It is simple to defend one's self if that is the only consideration. But everybody has to have other people in order to be provided with the perceptive stuff of growth. Without other people we would become like plants; in fact, there is some evidence that even plants are quite dependent on each other. We are therefore built by the people with whom we come in contact, and we build them. This is an answer to the age-old question, "Am I my brother's keeper?" We had better be; he is the stuff of which we are built, and the quality of life we enjoy depends on him.

It helps me to think of this boundary as a screen. Of course there is no screen, but there seems to be a flow in and out, as there would be if there were a screen. Those things which are perceived to be enhancing are admitted, and those that are seen to be endangering are kept out.

It seems that the outward flow is sometimes kept more open than the inward flow. Fearful people build thick screens. We once had a friend, quite a frequent visitor in our home, who was almost all output and very little intake. She would come in and say, "How are you?" If I were to say I just murdered my wife and her body lay in the next room, this woman would say, "You must hear what has just happened to me!" She never really comprehended that my retirement was approaching and that we would move away, though it was often mentioned in her presence.

If intake and defense were all there was to life, we would not have needed to evolve beyond the oyster. It has a good thick covering and lies at the bottom of the sea, opening up as long as there is food to be had, and closing when it feels endangered. But there is more to life than the oyster knows; and we are not oysters.

Sometimes the flow of the perceptive stuff of growth is cut off altogether in both directions. The people who do this we call catatonic. They just exist. There are infants who just exist too—infants who never cry or smile or babble. We call these autistic, and every large city has a ward in its hospital for them. So far as I know, nobody knows what causes a baby to be autistic, although there has been recent research on them. The research leads to a certain amount of speculation, however; it seems likely that these infants have looked out upon a hostile world and have decided to have none of it. These infants seldom live beyond eighteen months.

Whether infant or adult, and whether complete or incomplete, such people shut off the stuff out of which they are built and become prisoners in their own fortresses.

We need to develop people with open selves, or as nearly open as can be achieved. Thus they will learn more readily. I have found in my teaching that if I could achieve this, learning would be greatly increased. And so, particularly in the later years, I worked more on this than on anything else. If I could bring about confidence and reduce or abolish fear, the learner would become more and more able to take in what there was to take from his environment. In the main, this is where all of today's large classes and impersonal relationships break down; this is one of the causes of the present rebellion. I once knew a professor of history who proclaimed that he did not *want* to know his students because he might become fond of them and this would cause a loss of interest in his subject matter. Such attitudes destroy what I hold to be the primary function of the teacher—that of relating to and building people. Of course we have to have something for them to learn, and they will not all learn the same things anyway.

Too often teachers teach in such a way as to make their learners value themselves less and less. This is the wrong way to teach. We need to develop people who will think well of themselves. People who think well of themselves are in turn able to think well of others. This is essential to the complete human being.

We need to develop people who will think well of their teachers. This can be achieved only by having teachers who deserve to be held in confidence and respect. This cannot be achieved by the double-cross, by the surprise test, by asking questions whose answers are to be found only in the footnotes of some textbook, or by any other of the multitudinous methods that have been developed by many teachers. It is not possible for learners to respect a person who is waiting to trick them.

We need people who will see their stake in others, since that is the stuff of which we are built. It is difficult for us to be much better than the stuff of which we are built. This again may be the answer to the age-old question, "Am I my brother's keeper?"

We need people who will see themselves as part of a becoming world, rather than a static world. Thus will not only change be expected, but it will be welcomed. The fact that we do not know what tomorrow will bring should be an exciting thing, a thing that adds interest to life, not something to be dreaded and viewed with apprehension. This view of the universe will add much to the way in which life is held.

We need people who are naturally optimistic. There is no point in being purposive unless we think that the next spot we are in will be better than the one we now occupy. This is essentially what optimism means.

We need people who possess moral courage. I do not mean to limit this to the old set of morals, but to include much more than that. It is a call for people who are nonconformist in the ways that really matter. Thus the moralist can be thwarted in ways that will disturb him most. It is not the little things so many do that are the mark of the real nonconformist. I do not think I need spell these things out in any more detail; let the reader supply the specifics.

We need people who value what a human being is above the outside values so common in our society. This is my concept of what materialism is. What do we care most about? Do we care most about how another human being feels—what is happening to him—or do we care more about a raise in pay, a better automobile, a finer home, a better standing with our neighbors?

It would be easy to say that open selves are produced by having a chance to live the life that is good to live. But this calls for some explanation. The life that is good to live is primarily one in which the individual is loved and is able to feel it. By love I do not mean the sort of love that is accompanied by soft music and moonlight. That is all right too, but the love of an adult for a child is quite another matter. It is more a matter of caring, of concern for the feelings of the child. Nobody can be without this kind of love and grow into anything that is truly human.

The unloved grow into a different kind of people altogether. They do not have the usual capacity for relating to other people. Their handshake is quite noticeably withdrawn. These and many other symptoms reveal the fact that in their infancy and during their childhood they have lacked this most important ingredient.

We have known for a long time that rich environments produce increased intelligence and that poor environments reduce it. By this it is meant that the environment has to be rich not in the material things of life, but rather in the human things. Some of the richest homes from the material point of view are actually the poorest places for children to inhabit, and some of the poorest places materially are filled with love and companionship, the very best places for children to be. We have been slow to recognize this, probably because it has contradicted the precepts so many of us hold dear. The general public has assumed that a wealthy home is a good home, and it has been difficult to persuade people that the opposite may be true.

Each person in our world is different from any other person who has been or will be. This uniqueness is a fact of life which we need to come to value, rather than trying to decry it and counteract it. This fact of life has been provided for by the action of the chromosomes in the cells from which the individual is conceived, and it cannot be altered. There is one partial exception in the case of identical twins, but even here it is impossible to give identical experiences. Even when both are paddled, it makes a great deal of difference which one is paddled first. I have dealt at some length with this in "The Significance of Being Unique," published first in *ETC*. I will not, therefore, devote much space to it now, except to say that if teachers took this into account it would reduce or eliminate the despair that so many teachers feel when, at the end of a course, not everybody knows the same things exactly as the teacher thinks he taught them. Actually, it is because of the very nature of people that they cannot come up with identical answers. Each has to interpret what he sees and hears in the light of his own experience and purpose. Thus differences should be expected and welcomed, rather than decried.

Students need to be involved in what they are doing. This involvement has to be planned for by the teacher or by the students themselves. It will not come about by itself. Of course the student does not have to have his own way about everything, but even if his involvement is actually planned by his fellows, he needs to have a feeling that he had a say in the planning. It makes a great deal of difference whether or not one has been consulted. Few people, and certainly not the ones we can have the most confidence in for the future, do anything with much verve or enthusiasm just because they are told to do it by someone in authority. This is the old teacher-pupil planning about which so much has been said and written, and so little has been done.

In order to live the life that is good to live, one needs to be respected as a person. One can hardly be a whole person unless he is respected by others. The word "respect" is a most interesting one. *Spect* comes from the word which means "to look" and *re* means to repeat, to do again. Thus to be respected means to be looked at again. In order to be looked at again one has to be worth more than a passing glance.

All these factors help to build courage, which is essential to all humanness. For without courage one becomes a mere shadow of a human being. Courage makes it possible to attack many of the problems of life in a truly human and functional way. It makes all the difference between the craven and the bold.

But what do we teachers see as we look out upon the world which we have had a large hand in creating? We see threats taking the place of positive action. We see that we still believe in the theory that "getting tough" will solve problems instead of making them worse and perhaps driving them underground. Or we see students acting as though they were forced to strike and to make demands which, at least to us, seem unreasonable and impossible to comply with. We have left them no choice but to rebel, and, in their frenzy, they make demands which cannot be met. This is the only outlet left to them.

We see fear actually being used as a teaching technique. Fear is an emotion that has no place in the student-teacher relationship. It provokes all kinds of adverse behaviors. It is the cause of many of the evil happenings in our social structure. And to think that we knowingly and deliberately use it!

We see whole people taught piecemeal. Somehow the learner is supposed to put all the pieces together, but he seldom does. The old system of teaching subjects separately, which might have had some validity when schools started centuries ago, still holds us in its grip. The thought of approaching our environment as a whole seems never to have occurred to most educators.

We see many forms of rejection in teaching practice. There are so many ways which even well-meaning teachers have of rejecting people that it is almost impossible to count them. I once had a doctoral student who proposed to do a two-semester-hour study of rejection by visiting schools. In about two weeks he came back and said this was no two-hour study; it was so vast that it would make a doctoral dissertation.

I do not think that we have the right to reject anybody. This does not mean that I would admit anybody to any class regardless of his preparation to do what the class was set up to do. I am thinking mostly of our captive audiences in our elementary and secondary schools. If we are going to require that they be there, it is then also essential that we have something to do which has meaning to them—and that we have the freedom to do it. Rejection leads to alienation from self and others, and it is indeed a poor reason for requiring people to be there.

We will have to give up our faith in violence as a method. Violence never has made anyone better or more educable. Our faith in violence has come full circle now, and we are suffering the consequences.

What we need in this land of ours is better people; and if we are to have better people, the teachers of the nation will have to produce them. The parents and other adults who have influence over our young are products of the old system and have no way of knowing any better. What we need is a revolution among teachers, not in salaries and working conditions, but in attitude and emotion. This would bring about conditions in which our young would have no need for revolt.

Music Education and Peak Experience
ABRAHAM H. MASLOW
Professor of Psychology
Brandeis University, Waltham, Massachusetts

Something big is happening. It's happening to everything that concerns human beings. Everything the human being generates is involved, and certainly education is involved. A new *Weltanschauung* is in the process of being developed, a new *Zeitgeist*, a new set of values and a new way of finding them—certainly a new image of man. There is a new kind of psychology, presently called the humanistic, existential, third-force psychology, which at this transitional moment is certainly different in many important ways from

From *Music Educators Journal*, 54 (No. 6): 72–75, 163–171, February, 1968. Copyright © *Music Educators Journal*, February, 1968. Reprinted with permission.

the Freudian and behavioristic psychologies, the two great comprehensive, dominating psychologies.

To sketch this briefly and to indicate that I am talking about a life philosophy, the beginning of a new century, it is evident that there are new conceptions of interpersonal relationships. There is a new image of society. There is a new conception of the goals of society, of all the social institutions, and of all the social sciences, which are a part of society. There is a new economics, for instance, a new conception of politics. I have written in the past several years of revolutions and have tried to apply these revolutions to religion, to science, and to work. There is a newer conception of education popping along that I will mention briefly, because it will be the background for my iconoclastic ideas about music, music education, and creativeness.

First, I would mention psychologies of learning. If one took a course or picked up a book in the psychology of learning, most of it, in my opinion, would, be beside the point—that is, beside the "humanistic" point. Most of it would present learning as the acquisition of associations, of skills and capacities that are *external* and not *intrinsic* to the human character, to the human personality, to the person himself. It is a matter of picking up coins or keys or possessions or something of the sort in order to pick up reinforcements and conditioned reflexes that are, in a certain, very profound sense, expendable. It does not really matter if one has a conditioned reflex; if I salivate to the sound of a buzzer and then this extinguishes, nothing has happened to me; I have lost nothing of any consequence whatever. We might almost say that these extensive books on the psychology of learning are of no consequence, at least to the human center, to the human soul, to the human essence.

Generated by this new humanistic philosophy is also a new conception of learning, of teaching, and of education. Stated simply, such a concept holds that the function of education, the goal of education—the human goal, the humanistic goal, the goal so far as human beings are concerned—is ultimately the "self-actualization" of a person, the becoming fully human, the development of the fullest height that the human species can stand up to or that the particular individual can come to. In a less technical way, it is helping the person to become the best that he is able to become.

Such a goal involves very serious shifts in what we would teach in a course in the psychology of learning. It is not going to be a matter of associative learning. Associative learning in general is certainly useful, extremely useful for learning things that are of no real consequence. And many of the things we must learn are like that. If one needs to memorize the vocabulary of some other language, he would learn it by sheer rote memory. Here, the laws of association can be a help. Or if one wants to learn all sorts of automatic habits in driving, responding to a red signal light or something of the sort, then conditioning is of consequence. It is important and useful, especially in a technological society. But in terms of becoming a better person, in terms of self-development and self-fulfillment, or in terms of "becoming fully human," the great learning experiences are very different.

In my life, such experiences have been far more important than classes, listening to lectures, memorizing the branches of the twelve cranial nerves and dissecting a human brain, or memorizing the insertions of the muscles, or the kinds of things that one does in medical schools, in biology courses, or other such courses.

Far more important for me have been such experiences as having a child. Our first baby changed me as a psychologist. It made the behaviorism I had been brought up in look so foolish that I could not stomach it any more. It was impossible. Having a second baby, and learning how profoundly different people are even before birth, made it impossible for me to think in terms of the kind of learning psychology in which one can teach anybody anything. Or the John B. Watson theory of, "Give me two babies and I will make one into this and one into the other." It is as if he never had any children. We know only too well that a parent cannot make his children into anything. Children make themselves into something. The best we can do and frequently the most effect we can have is by serving as something to react against if the child presses too hard.

Another profound learning experience that I value far more highly than any particular course or any degree that I have ever had was my personal psychoanalysis: discovering my own identity, my own self. Another basic experience—far more important—was getting married. This was certainly far more important than my Ph.D. by way of instructiveness. If one thinks in terms of the developing of the kinds of wisdom, the kinds of understanding, the kinds of life skills that we would want, then he must think in terms of what I would like to call *intrinsic* education—*instrinsic* learning; that is, learning to be a human being in general, and second, learning to be this particular human being. I am now very busily occupied in trying to catch up with all the epiphenomena of this notion of intrinsic education. Certainly one thing I can tell you. Our conventional education looks mighty sick. Once you start thinking in this framework, that is, in terms of making a good human being, and if then you ask the question about the courses that you took in high school, "How did my trigonometry course help me to become a better human being?" an echo answers, "By gosh, it didn't!" In a certain sense, trigonometry was a waste of time. My early music education was also not very successful, because it taught a child who had a very profound feeling for music and a great love for the piano *not* to learn it. I had a piano teacher who taught me that music is something to stay away from. And I had to relearn music as an adult, all by myself.

Observe that I have been talking about ends. This is a revolution that is a repudiation of nineteenth-century science and of contemporary professional philosophy, which is essentially a technology and not a philosophy of ends. I have rejected thereby, as theories of human nature, positivism, behaviorism, and objectivism. I have rejected thereby, the whole model of science and all its works that have been derived from the historical accident that science began with the study of nonpersonal, nonhuman things, which in fact had no ends. The development of physics, astronomy, mechanics, chemistry, and biology was in fact impossible until it had become value-free, value-neutral, so that pure descriptiveness was now possible. The great mistake that we are now learning about is that this model, which developed from the study of objects and of things, has been illegitimately used for the study of human beings. It is a terrible technique. It has not worked.

Most of the psychology on this positivistic model, on this objectivistic, associationistic, value-free, value-neutral model of science, as it piles up like a coral reef or like mountains and mountains of small facts about this and that, was certainly not false, but merely trivial. I would like to point out here that in order not to sell my own science short, I think we do know a great deal about things that *do* matter to the human being, but I would maintain that what has mattered to the human being that we have learned has been learned by nonphysicalistic techniques, by the humanistic science techniques of which we have become more conscious.

In speaking of the world situation at the opening ceremonies of a recent Lincoln Center Festival, Archibald MacLeish said in part:

. . . What is wrong is not the great discoveries of science—information is always better than ignorance, no matter what informtion or what ignorance. What is wrong is the belief behind the information, the belief that information will change the world. It won't. Information without human understanding is like an answer without its question—meaningless. And human understanding is only possible through the arts. It is the work of art that creates the human perspective in which information turns to truth. . . .

In a certain sense I disagree with MacLeish, although I can understand why he said this. What he is talking about is information *short of this new revolution,* short of the humanistic psychologies, short of the conceptions of the sciences that not only repudiate the notion of being value-free and value-neutral, but actually assume as an obligation, as a duty, the necessity for discovery of values—the empirical discovery, demonstration, and verification of the values that are inherent in human nature itself. This work is now busily going on.

What Mr. MacLeish said was appropriate for the era from 1920 to 1930. It is appropriate today if one doesn't know about the new psychologies. "And human understanding is only possible through the arts." That *was* true. Fortunately, it is no longer true. It now is possible to gather information that can contribute to human understanding, that carries imbedded within it value hints, vectorial and directional information, information that goes someplace instead of just inertly lying there like flapjacks.

"It is the work of art that creates the human perspective in which information turns to truth." I deny that, and we had better argue about that. We must have some criteria for distinguishing good art from bad art. They do not yet exist in the realms of art so far as I know. They are beginning to exist, and I would like to leave one hint, an empirical hint. A possibility is beginning to emerge that we would have some criteria for discriminating good art from bad art.

If your situation is like mine, you know that we are in a complete and total confusion of values in the arts. In music, you try to prove something about the virtues of John Cage as against Beethoven—or Elvis Presley. In painting and architecture similar confusion is present. We have no shared values anymore. I don't bother to read music criticism. It is useless to me. So is art criticism, which I have also given up reading. Book reviews I find useless frequently. There is a complete chaos and anarchy of standards. For instance, the *Saturday Review* recently carried a favorable review of one of Jean Genet's crummy books. Written by a professor of theology, it was total confusion. It was the approach that Evil now has become Good because there is some kind of paradox while playing with words: if evil becomes totally evil, then it somehow becomes good, and there were rhapsodies to the beauties of sodomy and drug addiction which, for a poor psychologist who spends most of his time trying to rescue people from the anguish of these kinds of things, were incomprehensible. How can a grown man recommend this book as a chapter in ethics and a guide to the young?

If Archibald MacLeish says that works of art lead to the truth, Archibald MacLeish is thinking about particular works of art that Archibald MacLeish has picked out, but ones his son might not agree with. And *then*, MacLeish really has nothing much to say. There is no way of convincing anybody about this point. I think this could be some symbol of the way in which I feel that we are at a turning point. We are moving around the corner. Something new is happening. There are discernible differences—and these are not differences in taste or arbitrary values. These are empirical discoveries. They are new things that have been found out, and from these are generated all sorts of propositions about values and education.

One is the discovery that the human being *has higher needs,* that he has instincts—like needs, which are a part of his biological equipment—the need to be dignified, for instance, and to be respected, and the need to be free for self-development. The discovery of higher needs carries with it all sorts of revolutionary implications.

Secondly, the point I have already made about the social sciences: many people are beginning to discover that the physicalistic, mechanistic model was a mistake and that it has led us . . . where? To atom bombs. To a beautiful technology of killing, as in the concentration camps. To Eichmann. An Eichmann cannot be refuted with a positivistic philosophy or science. He just cannot; and he never got it until the moment he died. He didn't know what was wrong. As far as he was concerned, nothing was wrong; he had done a good job. He *did* do a good job, if you forget about the ends and the values. I point out that professional science and professional philosophy are dedicated to the proposition of forgetting about the values, excluding them. This, therefore must lead to Eichmanns, to atom bombs, and to who knows what!

The great discoveries Freud made, we can now add to. His one big mistake, which we are correcting now, is that he thought of the unconscious merely as undesirable evil. But unconsciousness carries in it also the roots of creativeness, of joy, of happiness, of goodness, of its own human ethics and values. We know that there is such a thing as a healthy unconscious as well as an unhealthy one. And the new psychologies are studying this at full tilt. The existential psychiatrists and psychotherapists are actually putting it into practice. New kinds of therapies are being practiced.

So we have a good conscious and a bad conscious—and a good unconscious and a bad unconscious. Furthermore, the good is real, in a non-Freudian sense. Freud was committed by his own positivism. Remember, Freud came out of a physicalistic, chemicalistic science. He was a neurologist. And a sworn oath that is in print called for a project to develop a psychology that could be entirely reduced to physical and chemical statements. This is what he dedicated himself to. He himself disproved his point. And about this higher nature that I claim we have discovered and that, of course, exists, the question is, how do we explain it? The Freudian explanation has been reductive. Explain it away. If I am a kind man, this is a reaction formation against my rage to kill. Somehow, the killing is more basic than the kindness. And the kindness is a way of trying to cover up, repress, and defend myself against realizing the fact that I am truly a murderer. If I am generous, this is a reaction formation against stinginess. I am really stingy inside. This is a very peculiar thing. Somehow there is the begging of the question that is so obvious now. Why did he not say, for instance, that maybe killing people was a reaction formation against loving them? It is just as legitimate a conclusion and, as a matter of fact, more true for many people.

But to return to the principal idea, this exciting new development in science, this new moment in history. I have a very strong sense of being in the middle of a historical wave. One hundred and fifty years from now, what will the historians say about this age? What was really important? What was going? What was finished? My belief is that much of what makes the headlines is finished, and the growing tip of mankind is what is now growing and will flourish in a hundred or two hundred years, if we manage to endure. Historians will be talking about this movement as the sweep of history, that here, as Whitehead pointed out, when you get a new model, a new paradigm, a new way of perceiving, new definitions of the old words, words which now mean something else, suddenly, you have an illumination, an insight. You can see things in a different way. That, for instance, as one of the consequences generated by what I have been talking about, is flat denial. Empirical, mind you. I am not being pious, or arbitrary, or *a priori,* or wishful. This is an empirical denial of the Freudian contention of a necessary, intrinsic, built-in opposition between the needs of the individual and the needs of society and civilization. It just is not so. We now know something about how to set up the conditions in which the needs of the individual become synergic with, not opposed to, the needs of society, and in which they both work to the same ends. This is an empirical statement, I claim.

Another empirical statement is about the peak experiences. This is the most dramatic and probably the most relevant for this particular audience. We have made studies of peak experiences by asking groups of people and individuals such questions as, What was the most ecstatic moment of your life? Or as one investigator asked, Have you experienced transcendent ecstasy? One might think that in a general population, such questions might get only blank stares, but there were many answers. Apparently, the transcendent ecstasies had all been kept private, because there is no way of speaking about them in public. They are sort of embarrassing, shameful, not scientific—which, for many people, is the ultimate sin.

In our investigations of peak experiences, we found many, many triggers, many kinds of experiences that would set them off. Apparently all people, or almost all people, have peak experiences, or ecstasies. The question might be asked in terms of the single, most joyous, happiest, most blissful moment of your whole life. You might ask questions of the kind I asked. How did you feel different about yourself at that time? How did the world look different? What did you feel like? What were your impulses? How did you change if you did? I want to report that the two easiest ways of getting peak experiences (in terms of simple statistics in empirical reports) are through music and through sex. I will push aside sex education, as such discussions are premature—although I am certain that one day we will not giggle over it, but will take it quite seriously and teach children that like music, like love, like insight, like a beautiful meadow, like a cute baby, or whatever, that there are many paths to heaven, and sex is one of them, and music is one of them. These happen to be the easiest ones, the most widespread, and the ones that are easiest to understand.

For our purposes in identifying and studying peak experiences, we can say it is justified to make a list of these kinds of triggers. The list gets so long that it becomes necessary to make generalizations. It looks as if any experience of real excellence, of real perfection, of any moving toward the perfect justice or toward perfect values tends to produce a peak experience. Not always. But this is the generalization I would make for the many kinds of things that we have concentrated on. Remember, I am talking here as a scientist. This doesn't sound like scientific talk, but this is a new kind of science. A dissertation will soon be published which will show that out of this humanistic science has come, I would say, one of the real childbearing improvements since Adam and Eve. It is a dissertation on peak experiences in natural childbirth. And this can be a potent source of peak experiences. We know just how to encourage peak experiences; we know the best way for women to have children in such a fashion that the childbearing mother is apt to have a great and mystical experience, a religious experience if you wish—an illumination, a revelation, an insight. That is what they call it, by the way, in the interviews—to simply become a different kind of person because, in a fair number of peak experiences, there ensues what I have called "the cognition of being."

We must make a new vocabulary for all these untilled, these unworked problems. This "cognition of being" means really the cognition that Plato and Socrates were talking about; almost, you could say, a technology of happiness, of pure excellence, pure truth, pure goodness, and so on. Well, why *not* a technology of joy, of happiness? I must add that this is the only known technique for inducing peak experiences in fathers. It had occurred to us, as my wife and I had first gotten to these surveys in college students, that many triggers were discovered. One of them was that while women talked about peak experiences from having children, men didn't. Now we have a way to teach men also to have peak experiences from childbirth. This means, in a certain condensed sense, being changed, seeing things differently, living in a different world, having different cognitions, in a certain sense some move toward living happily ever after. Now these are data, various paths to mystical experiences. I think that I had better pass them by as they are so numerous.

For our purposes, let's proceed to music in this relation. So far, I have found that these peak experiences are reported from what we might call "classical music." I have not found a peak experience from John Cage or from an Andy Warhol movie, from abstract expressionistic kind of painting, or the like. I just haven't. The peak experience that has reported the great joy, the ecstacy, the visions of another world, or another level of living, have come from classical music—the great classics. Also I must report to you that this melts over, fuses over, into dancing or rhythm. So far as this realm of research is concerned, there really isn't much difference; they melt into each other. I may add even, that when I was talking about music as a path to peak experiences, I included dancing. For me they have already melted together. The rhythmic experience, even the very simple rhythmic experience—the good dancing of a rumba, or the kinds of things that the kids can do with drums: I don't know whether you want to call that music, dancing, rhythm, athletics, or something else. The love for the body, awareness of the body, and a reverence of the body—that kind of thing that gets mixed in there—these are clearly good paths to peak experiences. These in turn are good paths (not guaranteed, but statistically likely to be good paths) to the "cognition of being," to the perceiving of the Platonic essences, the intrinsic values, the ultimate values of being, which in turn is a therapeutic-like help toward both the curing-of-sicknesses kind of therapy and also the growth toward self-actualization, the growth toward full humanness. In other words, peak experiences often have consequences. They can have very, very important consequences. Music and art in a certain sense can do the same; there is a certain overlap. They can do the same there as psychotherapy, if one keeps his goals right, and if one knows just what he is about, and if one is conscious of what he is going toward. We can certainly talk, on the one hand, of the breaking up of symptoms, like the breaking up of clichés, of anxieties, or the like, or on the other hand, we can talk about the development of spontaneity, and of courage, and of Olympian or God-like humor and suchness, sensory awareness, body awareness, and the like.

Far from least, it happens that music and rhythm and dancing are excellent ways of moving toward the discovering of identity. We are built in such a fashion that this kind of trigger, this kind of stimulation, tends to do all kinds of things to our autonomic nervous systems, endocrine glands, to our feelings, and to our emotions. It just does. We just do not know enough about physiology to understand why it does. But it does, and these are unmistakable experiences. It is a little like pain, which is also an unmistakable experience. In experientially empty people, which includes a tragically large proportion of the population, people who do not know what is going on inside themselves and who live by clocks, schedules, rules, laws, hints from the neighbors—other-directed people— this is a way of discovering what the self is like. There are signals from inside, there are voices that yell out, "By gosh this is good, don't ever doubt it!" This is a path, one of the ways that we try to teach self-actualization and the discovery of self. The discovery of identity comes via the impulse voices, via the ability to listen to your own guts, and to their reactions and to what is going on inside of you. This is also an experimental kind of education that, if we had the time to talk about it, would lead us into another parallel educational establishment, another *kind* of school.

Mathematics can be just as beautiful, just as peak-producing as music; of course, there are mathematics teachers who have devoted themselves to preventing this. I had no glimpse of mathematics as a study in aesthetics until I was thirty years old, until I read some books on the subject. So can history, or anthropology (in the sense of learning another culture), social anthropology, or palaeontology, or the study of science. Here again I want to talk data. If one works with great creators, great scientists, the creative scientists, *that* is the way they talk. The picture of the scientist must change. The image of the scientist, which most high school kids have, as one who never smiles, who bleeds embalming fluid rather than blood, and whom the high school girls are horrified by and wouldn't want to marry. "Marry one of those monsters who will do experiments on my babies?" they might think. This conception of scientists is giving way to an understanding of the creative scientist, and the creative scientist lives by peak experiences. He lives for the moments of glory when a problem solves itself, when suddenly through a microscope he sees things in a very different way, the moments of revelation, of illumination, insight, understanding, ecstacy. These are vital for them. Scientists are very, very shy and embarrassed about this. They refuse to talk about this in public. It takes a very, very delicate kind of a midwife to get these things out, but I have gotten them out. They are there, and if one can manage to convince a creative scientist that he is not going to be laughed at for these things, then he will blushingly admit the fact of having a high emotional experience from, for example, the moment in which the crucial correlation turns out right. They just don't talk about it, and as for the usual textbook on how you do science, it is total nonsense.

My point here is that it is possible; that if we are conscious enough of what we are doing, that is if we are philosophical enough in the insightful sense too, we may be able to use those experiences that most easily produce ecstacies, that most easily produce revelations, experiences, illumination, bliss, and rapture experiences. We may be able to use them as a model by which to reevaluate history teaching or any other kind of teaching.

Finally, the impression that I want to try to work out—and I would certainly suggest that this is a problem for everyone involved in arts education—is that effective education in music, education in art, education in dancing and rhythm, is intrinsically far closer than the core curriculum to intrinsic education of the kind that I am talking about, of learning one's identity as an essential part of education. If education doesn't do that, it is useless. Education is learning to grow, learning what to grow toward, learning what is good and bad, learning what is desirable and undesirable, learning what to choose and what not to choose. In this realm of intrinsic learning, intrinsic teaching, and intrinsic education I think that the arts, and especially the ones that I have mentioned, are so close to our psychological and biological core, so close to this identity, this biological identity, that rather than think of these courses as a sort of whipped or luxury cream, they must become basic experiences in education. I mean that this kind of education can be a glimpse into the infinite, into ultimate values. This intrinsic education may very well have art education, music education, and dancing education at its core. (I think dancing is the one I would choose first for children. It is the easiest for the two-, three-, or four-year-old children—just plain rhythm.) Such experiences could very well serve as the model, the means by which perhaps we could rescue the rest of the school curriculum from the value-free, value-neutral, goal-less meaninglessness into which it has fallen.

Name Index

Subject Index